ORGANIZATIONS IN DEPTH

ORGANIZATIONS IN DEPTH

The Psychoanalysis of Organizations

YIANNIS GABRIEL

with
Larry Hirschhorn, Marion McCollom Hampton,
Howard S. Schwartz and Glenn Swogger Jr

contributions from
Seth Allcorn, Ben Askew-Renaut, Herman Bingham,
Adrian Carr, Robert French, Susan Long, Sharon Mason,
Paul Moxnes, Lawrence Rosenthal and Peter Simpson

SAGE Publications
London • Thousand Oaks • New Delhi

Editorial matter and Chapters 1, 2, 4, 7, 8, 9, 11, 12 © Yiannis Gabriel 1999
Introduction and Chapter 3 © Yiannis Gabriel and Howard S. Schwartz 1999
Chapter 5 © Yiannis Gabriel and Marion McCollom Hampton 1999
Chapter 6 © Yiannis Gabriel and Larry Hirschhorn 1999
Chapter 10 © Glenn Swogger Jr 1999

First published 1999

All rights reserved. No part of this publication may be reproduced, stored in a retrieval system, transmitted or utilized in any form or by any means, electronic, mechanical, photocopying, recording or otherwise, without permission in writing from the Publishers.

SAGE Publications Ltd
6 Bonhill Street
London EC2A 4PU

SAGE Publications Inc
2455 Teller Road
Thousand Oaks, California 91320

SAGE Publications India Pvt Ltd
32, M-Block Market
Greater Kailash – I
New Delhi 110 048

British Library Cataloguing in Publication data

A catalogue record for this book is available from the British Library

ISBN 0 7619 5260 8
ISBN 0 7619 5261 6 (pbk)

Library of Congress catalog card number 99-072771

Typeset by Keystroke, Jacaranda Lodge, Wolverhampton
Printed in Great Britain by The Alden Press, Oxford

CONTENTS

	Preface	vii
	Introduction: Psychoanalysis and Organization *with Howard S. Schwartz*	1
1	Core Psychoanalytic Ideas and Theories	13
2	Psychoanalysis, Clinical Practice and the Human Sciences	35
3	Individual and Organization *with Howard S. Schwartz*	58
4	Organization and Individual	81
5	Work Groups *with Marion McCollom Hampton*	112
6	Leaders and Followers *with Larry Hirschhorn*	139
7	Psychoanalysis and Culture	166
8	Organizational Culture	191
9	The Emotional Life of Organizations	211
10	Psychoanalysis and Ethics in Organizations *by Glenn Swogger Jr*	232
11	Psychoanalytic Research into Organizations	251
12	Concluding Thoughts: Towards a New Conception of Management	280
	Glossary	289
	References	312
	Index	327

CONTRIBUTORS

Seth Allcorn, *Berkana Consulting Group, North Carolina, USA* — 160
Ben Askew-Renaut, *University of Bath, England* — 157
Herman Bingham, *Counsellor/investigator for the US Postal Service* — 120
Adrian Carr, *University of Western Sydney, Australia* — 93, 254
Robert French, *University of the West of England* — 99
Susan Long, *Swinburne University, Melbourne, Australia* — 262
Sharon Mason, *Brock University, Ontario, Canada* — 93
Paul Moxnes, *Norwegian School of Management, Oslo* — 131
Lawrence Rosenthal, *University of California, Berkeley* — 182
Peter Simpson, *University of the West of England* — 99

PREFACE

This book is the result of a deeply held conviction that psychoanalysis can make a great contribution to the study of organizational phenomena. The book stands at the intersection of two academic traditions which have grown relatively independently of each other. Organization theory has examined the behaviour of people in the large public spaces of organizations, while psychoanalysis has explored the intimate and private spaces of their personal lives. In recent years, however, as public and private lives have become increasingly difficult to disentangle, the two traditions have been moving closer together. Organization theory has turned to the study of non-rational phenomena in organizations: emotions, symbolism, aesthetics, sexuality, rhetoric. Psychoanalysis, for its part, has been rediscovering some of the wider horizons of its early years, stretching beyond the consultation room to address cultural, political and social phenomena. At the same time, our view of organizations has also undergone a change. To be sure, we still view them as dominant features of the macrocosm, the social and political landscape we inhabit. But we also recognize them as an inevitable presence in the microcosm, our intimate, personal lives. They are part of us, at least from that very first day at school when we leave our parental embrace to become one of many, a face among unknowns, a name on a register.

The time now seems right to examine systematically the insights that psychoanalysis can offer to the study of organizations. The psychoanalytic study of organizations is not a new area, even if many of its contributions have gone unnoticed by mainstream organization theory. Past contributions range from the pioneering work of the Tavistock Institute to the leadership scholarship of Levinson and Zaleznik; from the studies of organizational pathologies by Kets de Vries and Hirschhorn to the exploration of narcissistic phenomena by Schwartz and Sievers; from the studies of group processes by Bion to the enquiries into bureaucracy of Baum and Diamond. This book brings together the insights offered by this scholarship and presents them to a wider audience, one which is not necessarily familiar with psychoanalytic ideas and may initially react to them with apprehension. I hope to show that psychoanalytic insights can complement and deepen current theorizing on organizations undertaken from other perspectives.

The book is addressed to a multiple readership: to novice and expert alike, to those with and those without systematic knowledge of psychoanalytic theories and concepts, to those with primarily theoretical and to those with primarily practical interests. The book is also addressed to those organizational scholars who are interested in the psychoanalytic approach but are unwilling to read the voluminous original bibliography. The book's structure and content reflect the diversity of its audience. Practitioners will find a number of practical cases and illustrative materials displayed in boxes; readers new to psychoanalysis will find a presentation of its core theories in the early chapters of the book and synoptic treatments of key terms in the Glossary; organizational scholars will find in-depth treatments of the psychoanalytic contributions to the study of organizational phenomena, such as groups, leadership and culture, in the later chapters of the book. Doctoral students will find a chapter on research strategies and tactics (Chapter 11). Each chapter is self-contained and does not rely on a reading of the preceding chapters.

Many scholars have made valuable contributions to this book. Several have contributed case studies, essays and illustrations which are included as boxed materials in the text. Larry Hirschhorn, Marion McCollom Hampton, Howard Schwartz and Glenn Swogger participated in lengthy and stimulating discussions in the early planning of the book and have authored or co-authored chapters of this book. The International Society for the Psychoanalytic Study of Organizations, both in its annual symposium and its lively and constructive Internet discussion list, has been a great source of inspiration and a valuable sounding board for some of the ideas presented here. Numerous colleagues have provided me with suggestions, feedback and criticism during the writing of the book. My thanks to all of them, and in particular to Seth Allcorn, Howell Baum, Ana Magnolia Bezerra Mendes, Adrian Carr, Michael Diamond, Steve Fineman, Larry Gould, Leo Gruenfeld, Rose Mersky, Burkard Sievers and Andrew Sturdy. I also wish to thank my students at the University of Bath: their lasting interest in the subject and their remarkable ability to use psychoanalytic insights to understand their own experiences of organizations have been sources of inspiration for this book. One piece included in this book, by Ben Askew-Renaut, began as an essay submitted for one of my courses. Several more could have been included had space permitted. My thanks, too, to Rosemary Nixon and all the people at Sage, who as always have shown the highest levels of competence in bringing this book to the public.

INTRODUCTION: PSYCHOANALYSIS AND ORGANIZATION

with Howard S. Schwartz

At first glance, psychoanalysis and organization do not go well together. When we think of psychoanalysis we think of individuals, their worries and problems. We think of irrationality, of instability, of mental illness. But organizations are not individuals, obviously. And while most of us would be ready to admit that irrational and even crazy things occasionally go on within organizations, it is hard to say that this is what organizations are about. On the contrary, organizations usually appear to be quite ordinary, stable, even mundane; the way in which they go about their business seems to make perfectly good sense. What can psychoanalysis possibly tell us about organizations? Can it tell us only about unusual, pathological individuals or exceptional events within organizations? Or only about the occasional organization characterized by so much irrationality that it may be said to have gone crazy? In this book, we shall argue that the psychoanalytic conception of organizations goes far beyond the examination of the pathological and the unusual. Psychoanalysis can provide a deep understanding of many features of organizations, even those that appear perfectly straightforward and ordinary. It does this by examining not so much the behaviour of individuals in organizations, but rather the *meaning* of their behaviour and the deeper *motives* for their actions.

When we address ourselves to the meaning of events and the motives of actions, we find that the mundane disappears, and that even apparently ordinary events arise for reasons that are not evident. The distinctions between the rational and the irrational may become a bit blurred. Actions which appear on the surface to make perfectly good sense can turn out to serve ends which have little to do with organizational efficiency and rationality. Such actions may in the end turn out to be better understood by reference to motives which some organizational members may not openly acknowledge or may prefer not to understand. The idea of stability fares no better, for we find that underneath the appearance of stability and order, an appearance often cultivated with great care by organizational leaders, lie tension, conflict and flux, always threatening to change the order of things.

The idea that what goes on at the surface of an organization is not all that there is, and that understanding organizations often means comprehending matters that lie beneath the surface, matters that some organizational participants may prefer not to know about, is not an idea that is likely to gain easy acceptance; nor should it. It is one for which a strong case must be made in terms of the gain in understanding that it achieves. This is the case made in this book. This book does not seek to disparage traditional concepts and theories of organizational studies. Instead, it seeks to qualify, extend and complement some of the insights of mainstream organizational theory by coupling it with a psychological tradition which does justice to the full complexities, ambiguities and conflicts of human beings. The time for a closer rapprochement between organizational theory and the psychoanalytic tradition seems right. In recent years, some of mainstream organizational theory has moved to explore irrational, symbolic and emotional forces in accounting for the behaviours of individuals and groups in organizations. This has brought it closer to the themes which have always preoccupied psychoanalysis. At the same time, increasing numbers of psychoanalytic scholars, consultants and clinicians have turned their attention to the world of organizations, its discontents and dysfunctions.

MR COOK'S NASA

Some scholars may object to the idea that there are hidden depths in organizations. Instead, they may prefer to focus on what is actually said, on what can be observed and established beyond all doubt. We believe that such an approach forecloses many interesting lines of enquiry. The example that follows offers an illustration of something underneath the surface of organizations, a depth whose exploration can enable us to make better sense of phenomena at the surface.

Following the Challenger space shuttle disaster, the United States government created a commission, headed by former Secretary of State William P. Rogers, to investigate the causes. At first, the commission was in the dark about the causes of the disaster and tended to view it as a freak accident, something entirely at odds with the image of technological sophistication, competence and responsibility presented by NASA at the time. So, when a NASA budget analyst named Richard C. Cook came before them with a story that was at variance with this image of NASA, they tended to be dismissive.

Cook's job had been to keep track of the development of the space shuttle's solid rocket boosters (SRBs), the element whose failure was ultimately found to have caused the explosion, and to assess the budgetary impacts of any problems that occurred. In a memorandum written on 23 July 1985, six months before the disaster, Cook warned that flight safety was being compromised by erosion of the boosters' O-ring seals, and that failure of these parts could be catastrophic. Following the explosion, he wrote another memo referring to the earlier one, which someone leaked to the Rogers Commission. He was then called to testify on 12 February 1986. In his testimony, Cook claimed that his information was solely based on what engineers on the SRB project had told him, something that turned out to be entirely accurate. Yet, when NASA officials were invited to comment on his charges, they categorically refuted them:

> ROGERS: Ah, it's fair to say that after or at about the same time Mr Cook's memorandum was written in July, 85, that you and your team were, had been and were at that time conducting a lot of investigations, doing a lot of work about the O-rings.
> [DAVID] WINTERHALTER [acting director of NASA's shuttle propulsion division]: That's correct, sir.
> ROGERS: But in the final analysis, the qualified people, the engineers and others who were assigned responsibility of their decisions have to make the decisions.
> WINTERHALTER: That's true. And I pride, I prided myself on our division to be particularly

good team workers. We gave our differences, we work 'em out . . . At no time . . . during that period did any of my people come to me, give any indication that they felt there was any, any safety of flight problems in their area.

Q: Was it the view of your division, the propulsion group, that the seal design, as it was installed and operating in the shuttle system was ah, safe and adequate?

WINTERHALTER: It was.

(*The New York Times*, 13 February 1986: B11)

The *Times* reported further that a 'parade' of NASA officials testified that Mr Cook's concerns were out of proportion and that the issue of seal erosion had been dealt with carefully by NASA engineering experts and managers. They said, quite erroneously as it turned out,[1] that seal problems had diminished in 1985. While they did not deny Cook's claim that the seals had eroded, they did claim that more competent professionals than he had concluded they were safe.[2]

The next day, the *Times* gave Cook a chance to respond. What is important to note, at this point, is not only that Cook's version of events was at odds with that of the officials, but also that his general image of NASA was substantially different.

In his first major interview since publication of his internal memorandum . . . Richard C. Cook, said that propulsion engineers at the National Aeronautics and Space Administration 'whispered' in his ear since he arrived last July that the seals were unsafe and even 'held their breath' when earlier shuttles were launched . . .

Mr Cook said he based his warning memorandum last July on conversations with engineers in the agency's propulsion division who were concerned about erosion of the rocket's safety seals. 'They began to tell me that some of these were being eaten away,' he said, 'and rather innocently I asked what does that mean?'

'They said to me, almost in a whisper in my ear, that the thing could blow up,' he continued. 'I was shocked.' In his July memorandum, Mr Cook explained, 'I was simply paraphrasing what this engineering group was telling me. I was not making it up that flight safety was being compromised and the results could be catastrophic. I didn't put it in my memorandum, but one of them said to me, 'When this thing goes up, we hold our breath.' (*The New York Times*, 14 February 1986: B4)

Compare this image of NASA with that held by one of its senior officials:

Today, L. Michael Weeks, deputy associate Administrator for space flight, the space agency's second-ranking shuttle official, said that the climate at the agency actually encouraged individuals two or three levels below him to speak their minds on safety concerns. He said that working-level engineers 'don't hesitate to tell Mike Weeks anything' and 'quite often will argue right on the spot at a significant meeting with me or Jesse,' a reference to Jesse W. Moore, the top shuttle official. (*The New York Times*, 14 February 1986: B4)

Now the picture of NASA presented by Cook was evidently far from the idea of NASA that was in the minds of its officials. Cook's NASA was a place in which engineers agonized over the flaws in their equipment and feared for the lives of astronauts, but did not feel that they could voice their concerns. The NASA of its management, on the other hand, was a place in which communication between ranks was open and free, in which concerns about safety were addressed directly and competently, and in which, on that basis, safety very simply was not a matter that needed to be worried about. It does not appear that NASA officials were lying or being disingenuous. Rather, they appeared to maintain their representations with perfect conviction.

Nor was it simply that certain elements of organizational functioning were not within their purview, for in fact they had a very elaborate idea of how those elements functioned; it is just that their idea was contrary to the reality as experienced by Mr Cook and the engineers who had talked to him. Seen from the perspective of the senior officials, the Challenger disaster was a one-off, unpredictable abnormality. Seen from the perspective of Mr Cook and his informants, it is surprising that the accident did not happen earlier. In fact, the accident was the natural culmination of a situation in which people were afraid to speak their minds.

> [Cook] said such concerns [as those about the O-rings] got submerged because 'the whole culture of the place' calls for a 'can-do attitude that NASA can do what ever it tries to do, can solve any problem that comes up . . . Cook said that, in meetings called by the shuttle program managers, a middle-level engineer with safety concerns is 'just a little guy.'
>
> 'You aren't going to find an engineer with 20 years' experience and a livelihood to protect stand up and say, 'Excuse me, but we might have an explosion on the next shuttle flight because the O-rings might break.' It's just not going to happen.'
>
> 'If some did get up, he would quickly be branded a nay-sayer,' Mr Cook said. (*The New York Times*, 14 February 1986: B4)

Along the same lines, NASA veteran John Naugle, commenting on the way NASA changed during the Nixon administration:

> Up until that era there, I never worried about saying what I felt. I always felt my bosses, while they might not agree with me, they might slap me down, they might quarrel with me, but they were not going to throw me out just because I brought them bad news. And somewhere between the time [Nixon appointee] Fletcher came on board and the time he left, I no longer felt that way. (Trento, 1987: 121)

What we have here is a sharp contrast between two images of NASA, each of which leads to very different conclusions about the causes of the disaster, as well as its meaning. One, held by management, is an image of an organization that is open to communication, in which everyone can say openly what they think. This image is positive and desirable. It makes perfectly good sense in terms of our beliefs about the way in which organizations should function and perhaps in terms of what we perceive to be NASA's earlier successes. The other image, which emerges from Cook's account, supported by the testimonies of many engineers, is one of an organization dominated by enforced silence and conformity, which muffles its employees and is impervious to criticism. This image is disturbing and may be at variance with what some insiders and some outsiders like to believe. In the former image, the employees emerge as independent professionals, doing a job which contributes to the organization's formidable technical achievements. In the latter image, the employees are individuals merely earning a living, frightened to do anything that may jeopardize their livelihoods.

This raises several questions. Which one of the two images is 'right' and which one is 'wrong'? Which corresponds to the real organization? How can two images at such variance co-exist within the same organization? How can different people working together maintain such different perceptions? Furthermore, is it possible that the same individual may hold both images at the same time? ('Somewhere between the time Fletcher came on board and the time he left'.) What are the implications for the organization of the fact that such inconsistent images were held simultaneously?

INTRODUCTION

The Challenger disaster has been the subject of several books and articles which enable us to address some of these questions (McConnell, 1987; Trento, 1987; McCurdy, 1993; Vaughan, 1996; Allcorn and Diamond, 1997; Adams and Balfour, 1998). While their authors differ in the many points of interpretation and explanation, they generally agree that the agency's senior officials failed to recognize numerous warning signals, both in terms of technical failures and in terms of the ways in which technical failures were identified and discussed. They seemed to be blind to the failures themselves, and they were blind to the fact that the agency was preventing its staff from expressing legitimate concerns. Their blindness was not the result of ignorance, stupidity or *naïveté*. Rather, it is as if they kept themselves from knowing, as if it were too painful for them to acknowledge that an organization they loved and cared for was fallible or that it was experienced by some of its members as tyrannical and oppressive.

This is where psychoanalysis can make a contribution. Non-psychoanalytic approaches may content themselves by arguing that, to defend their interests, individuals lie, distort and disregard inconvenient facts. A psychoanalytic approach, on the other hand, envisages a possibility where individuals deceive themselves, without actually lying or being disingenuous. Our perceptions and ideas about the social reality of which we are part are not neutral. They are shaped by feelings, such as pride, anxiety and pain, as well as by earlier experiences in our lives which, unknown to us, have left deep marks on our mental personality. If we sometimes deceive ourselves, it is because reality is too painful or too complex and our desires too precious to forsake. Seen from this perspective, the blindness of the NASA officials to technical flaws with catastrophic potential, as well as to their organization's unwillingness to tolerate 'bad news', was not accidental – it was the product of *repression*, a process whereby dangerous or unpleasant ideas are prevented from reaching consciousness and restricted to an unconscious part of the mind. Managers worried about potential disasters may disregard signs of danger and discard warnings as defeatist talk of nay-sayers; in this way, troubling parts of reality are avoided by being replaced with desirable but unrealistic fictions. This process may be reinforced if managers are surrounded by others who are likewise inclined to re-shape their view of reality according to their desires, or if current worries trigger off memories of earlier painful events in their personal histories which threaten to overwhelm them.

PSYCHOANALYSIS, DEPTH PSYCHOLOGY AND THE UNCONSCIOUS

The concept of the *unconscious* lies at the very centre of psychoanalysis, the field of psychology established by Sigmund Freud. In spite of many changes and developments which psychoanalysis has undergone since its early beginnings, the unconscious has remained at the heart of its arguments. It is also the defining characteristic of that branch of psychology referred to before Freud as 'depth psychology' which includes other, non-Freudian traditions. Although Freud did not invent the concept of the unconscious, he sought to make its study the object of serious, empirically testable investigations. Psychoanalysis, he argued, 'as a specialist science, a branch of psychology – a depth-psychology or psychology of the unconscious – is quite unfit to construct a Weltanschauung of its own: it must accept the scientific one' (Freud, 1933: 193).

Unlike some other depth psychologists, Freud's emphasis on the scientific method never faltered. Yet, in postulating that a part of our mental lives is unconscious, he challenged some of the assumptions of his time, arguing that the psychology of consciousness is unable to explain a wide variety of mental phenomena, such as dreams, neurotic symptoms and hypnotic states. It was initially to account for such phenomena that he postulated the idea that some mental processes and some ideas and desires exist outside our consciousness, in the unconscious part of our mind. Freud rejected the view of the unconscious as a spiritual or mystical entity, viewing it as something normal, ordered and subject to normal scientific scrutiny. He rejected intuition, divination and revelation as sources of knowledge of the unconscious, proposing instead a system of analytic interpretations and constructions for accessing and exploring the unconscious. Freud's concept must not be confused with the common misconception of the unconscious (or the 'subconscious' as it is sometimes referred to) as a messy jumble of ideas and impulses arising out of the depths of the human soul. Nor does Freud's unconscious bear much resemblance to the virgin and unpolluted personality core (the 'noble savage' in all of us) which has become the trademark of some humanistic schools of psychology. Instead, the unconscious is, in the first place, the state of ideas and desires which have undergone repression. Repression and unconscious are linked in Freudian theory like Siamese twins. 'We obtain the proof of the unconscious from the theory of repression. The repressed is the prototype of the unconscious for us' (Freud, 1923: 362).

Unconscious ideas and desires do not behave like conscious ones. They cannot be accessed through introspection (i.e. by asking questions of oneself and looking inward); they cannot be corrected or changed by appeal to logic or material evidence; they do not lead to action geared to achieving desired results. Above all, unconscious ideas and desires cannot be discussed freely because powerful psychic forces keep them repressed. We all spend much mental energy defending ourselves against disturbing or embarrassing ideas and desires, by keeping them unconscious. In this way, much as the NASA officials did, we censor our thoughts, our desires and even our feelings. If political censors seek to eliminate ideas and images which threaten the regime, mental censors seek to suppress those ideas and desires which they envisage as threatening our psychological well-being or even survival. *The idea that repression is a form of mental defence against threatening psychic phenomena lies at the heart of Freudian psychology and much of depth psychology* (key idea 1).

INTERPRETATION

If the unconscious is by definition inaccessible to consciousness, how can we be sure of its existence, how can we ever hope to know its contents? To answer these questions, Freud relied on his view that unconscious material (ideas, desires, thoughts and feelings) is the result of a process of repression in the service of psychological defence. But he also used a key corollary of this idea, which he initially formulated through his study of neurotic symptoms (such as a compulsive cough or an irrational fear of horses) and dreams. *Repressed ideas do not disappear without trace from a person's life, but they seek expression in various subterfuges* (key idea 2). During sleep, for instance, when the censors are less vigilant, repressed ideas may be expressed through dreams. In waking life, a repressed feeling may be manifested by changing into its opposite or by being *displaced* on to a different object. Interpretation is a process whereby we can access unconscious material through its conscious manifestations. It is a powerful but also a dangerous process, capable of yielding extraordinary insights into human motivation; but it is also a dangerous process which, when abused, can lead to false and potentially destructive conclusions. It is a process that cannot be reduced to a number of simple steps, but requires practice and experience. It is a process whose outcomes are virtually always provisional, open to refinement, correction and re-evaluation. Throughout this book, we shall offer numerous examples of interpretations. We shall interpret individual actions and ideas, some organizational stories and symbols and some wider cultural practices and institutions. None of these interpretations will be definitive and all must be accepted as conditional.

Interpretation is used not just in psychoanalysis, but in many fields when small signs are taken as the basis for inferences. The art critic Giovanni Morelli, for example, established a way of authenticating works of art based on the way in which different artists dealt with small details; for instance, the painting of ears or hands. Instead of seeking to identify a painting as the work of Raphael or Titian by looking at the general composition, Morelli was successful at deducing authorship through the interpretation of tiny details. Likewise, detective work as practised by Sherlock Holmes and his less famous imitators relies on interpreting small clues and trying to construct a general picture from the meaning of tiny details. The similarity of psychoanalysis to detective work has often been pointed out (Ricoeur, 1970; Ginzburg, 1980; Shepherd, 1985). But Freud was even keener on the parallel between psychoanalysis and archaeology, a discipline which held an acute fascination for him. Like an archaeologist, Freud imagined himself as someone who extrapolates latent structures from manifest ones by undoing the work of time. Yet, what Freud also realized, as some archaeologists also do, was that the material he was starting with – the dream, the neurotic symptom, the returning memory – had not just deteriorated with the passage of time, but had been deliberately tampered with in order to frustrate and mislead the attempts at interpretation.

In interpreting dreams, Freud postulated the existence of a mental censor, an ingenious mental agent which not only erases what it finds objectionable but, through omissions, changes in emphasis, careful substitutions and other subtle tactics, distorts the text's meaning. This made the work of interpretation both harder and easier; it made it harder because in the minds of patients, dreamers and people in general, psychoanalysis was facing an enemy determined to confuse and mislead, an enemy which operates in the mind of the dreamer as well as that of the interpreter. At the same time, however, it made it easier, once the purposes of this cunning adversary, its character and its methods of operation became known to the interpreter. Thus, Freud was led to make a 'bold hypothesis', namely that *dreams represent fulfilments of unconscious desires and that they are censored to the extent that they may contradict the contents of consciousness* (key idea 3).

AN EXAMPLE OF PSYCHOANALYTIC INTERPRETATION: THE 'UNCLE JOSEF DREAM'

Given the importance of the process of interpretation in depth psychology, we shall present a detailed example of an interpretation of a dream, as discussed by Freud in *The Interpretation of Dreams*, the book that introduced a systematic method for interpreting dreams in 1900. Later, Freud and others used a similar method for interpreting neurotic symptoms, slips of the tongue, fantasies and day-dreams, works of art, jokes, rituals, myths, stories and other items of folklore and culture.

The dream discussed below is one that Freud had in the spring of 1897, shortly after he was nominated for an appointment as professor extraordinary at the University of Vienna. The news surprised him and delighted him, as it marked the esteem in which he was held by those who had recommended him. He had no hopes, however, of being appointed, since earlier nominees, including his friends R and N, had failed to be appointed due to 'denominational considerations', i.e. the fact that they were Jewish.

Freud had the following dream on the night following a meeting with R. 'I. . . . My friend R was my uncle. – I had a great feeling of affection for him. II. I saw before me his face, somewhat changed. It was as though it had been drawn out lengthways. A yellow beard that surrounded it stood out especially clearly' (1900: 218). On recollecting the dream next day, Freud 'laughed aloud and said: "The dream's nonsense!"' But the dream refused to go away, and Freud began to suspect that his dismissal of the dream was itself significant, i.e. a sign that he was putting up an internal *resistance* against interpreting it for fear that it might reveal something painful or embarrassing. He therefore set about its interpretation.

The text above is referred to as the dream's 'manifest content'. It is relatively compressed, containing a thought combined with a feeling, followed by an image. In interpreting the dream, Freud starts with the overlap between his friend R and his uncle. This is an example of *condensation*, a dream process whereby two or more ideas (for example, the faces of two people) merge into one. But why should this happen? We learn from Freud that his Uncle Josef had, some thirty years earlier, been punished by law for a financial transaction that he had carried out in his eagerness to make money. Freud's father (Josef's brother) had been very upset about it, and his hair had turned white in a few days. He had tried to excuse his brother by saying that he was not a bad man, only a simpleton. The condensation of the two people seemed to transfer the quality of being a simpleton from Josef on to R, a person who was neither a simpleton nor guilty of any major offence.

Why, then, was Freud unconsciously seeking to view R as a simpleton? At this point, Freud remembered another conversation with a different friend of his, N, who, like R and Freud himself, had been nominated for the professorship. This is an example of *free association*, a process fundamental to psychoanalytic technique, whereby seemingly unrelated thoughts are allowed to reach consciousness and given voice. Frequently, the relations between these thoughts lead to some unconscious associations. In this case, Freud recollected a conversation with N in the street. N had offered his congratulations to Freud on his nomination, but Freud refused to accept them, saying 'You are the last person to make that kind of joke; you know what such a recommendation is worth from your own experience.' N then proceeded to tell Freud that in his own case an unsubstantiated scandal may have been held against his appointment, whereas no such factor could be used against Freud. This led Freud to his first interpretative conclusion:

> My uncle Josef represented my two colleagues who had not been appointed to professorships – the one as a simpleton and the other as a criminal. I now saw why they were represented in this light. If the appointment of my friends R and N had been postponed for 'denominational' reasons, my own appointment was also open to doubt; if, however, I could

attribute the rejection of my two friends to other reasons, which did not apply to me, my hopes would remain untouched. This was the procedure adopted by my dream: it made one of them, R, into a simpleton and the other, N, into a criminal, whereas *I* was neither the one nor the other; thus we no longer had anything in common; I could rejoice at my appointment to a professorship, and I could avoid drawing the distressing conclusion that R's report of what the high official had said to him must apply equally to me. (1900: 220–1)

A small and seemingly insignificant dream was thus interpreted as a fulfilment of wish, Freud's wish to be appointed to a professorship. In fact, it is the interpretation of the dream that brings this wish to the surface. It will be noted that Freud had initially disowned such a wish, along with other similar ones, in a slightly disingenuous manner: 'So far as I knew, I was not an ambitious man; I was following my profession with gratifying success even without the advantages afforded by a title' (1900: 217). What the dream and its interpretation did was to disabuse him of this self-deception, i.e. that he did not care for titles and honours. Not only did he care for them but, in order to achieve them, he was in his dream willing to dismiss one of his friends as a simpleton and the other as a crook.

But the interpretation of the dream is not yet complete. There are too many loose ends, which must be accounted for. The 'great feeling of affection' present in the dream seemed odd. Freud had never felt great warmth towards his uncle and his feelings towards R were far more tempered than those experienced in the dream. Moreover, the warm feeling was inconsistent with his dream's attempt to cast R in the part of a simpleton. Freud came to the view that the feeling was meant to foreclose the task of interpretation or at least to hamper it by introducing a distortion.

If my dream was distorted in this respect from its latent content – and distorted into its opposite – then the affection that was manifest in the dream served the purpose of this distortion. In other words, *distortion* was shown in this case to be deliberate and to be a means of *dissimulation*. My dream thoughts had contained a slander against R; and, in order that I might not notice this, what appeared in the dream was the opposite, a feeling of affection for him. (1900: 222–3)

Freud goes on to generalize and argue that, as in the case of political censorship, censorship and distortions in dreams 'are given their shape in individual human beings by the operation of two psychical forces (or we may describe them as currents or systems); and that one of these forces constructs the wish which is expressed in the dream, while the other exercises a censorship upon this dream-wish and, by the use of that censorship, forcibly brings about a distortion in the expression of the wish' (1900: 225). The task of interpretation is to undo the effects of the censor, reaching at the latent dream thoughts which find their disguised expressions in the manifest dream content.

There are still loose ends in the dream. There is, for example, the beard – yellow, surrounding the face and 'standing out'. Freud made a somewhat half-hearted attempt to account for the yellow beard as a sign of the passing of youth, though clearly the interpretation of this part of the dream is left incomplete, perhaps because Freud felt that he had already got what he wanted out of this dream (the illustration of the wish-fulfilling character of the dream and of the opposed mental forces which determine its form) or because he did not wish to share this part of the interpretation with the reader. Some commentators have suggested that the dream also reveals a disguised wish not to be Jewish or, at least, to have the power to eliminate Jewish rivals – an interpretation which finds some support in three other dreams reported in the same book (Schorske, 1961: 187). In any event, the interpretation of a dream is almost always incomplete, although in the majority of cases of successful interpretation, new lines of interpretation tend to reinforce earlier ones.

In summary, then, the interpretation of the Uncle Josef dream illustrates:

1 The link between the manifest content of the dream and the unconscious wish or desire which it expresses.
2 The way that the manifest content of a dream is a compromise formation between the unconscious desire seeking expression and censoring forces.
3 The processes of condensation and displacement which are known as primary processes and characterize the changes undergone by unconscious ideas as they reach consciousness.

THE BIG PICTURE AND THE INTIMATE DETAIL

The intimate, personal details of dreams and the vast panorama of thousands of people working to put rockets into space seem to belong to different worlds. Dreams appear to spring from the irrational recesses of each individual's unconscious, whereas an organization such as NASA appears to be the epitome of technical rationality, science and order. And, yet, is it not the case that behind the massive resources mobilized by NASA lie the dreams of millions of people? How many children have not dreamt of becoming astronauts, of going to the moon or beyond? And how many adults did not share Kennedy's dream of putting a man on the moon and bringing him back safely by the end of the decade? How many did not shed tears as they lined the roads to give the early astronauts the welcome reserved for conquering emperors in antiquity? It would seem that, however rational and ordered organizations appear to be, they are often carriers of strong emotional forces, unconscious desires and hopes, similar to those expressed in dreams.

Notice again how some of the details of the Uncle Josef dream are drawn from the broader picture of social life, organizations and culture: the ambition of professional recognition, the presence of professional rivalry, discrimination on the basis of religious denomination, the oppressive clout of academic hierarchies and honours; these are all features in the dream which are found in a large measure with contemporary organizations. The clash between proud ambition and fear of failure lies squarely at the heart of both Freud's dream and of the NASA officials' treatment of the warnings of the alarmed engineers. In both instances powerful censoring forces stopped unpalatable or painful ideas from being voiced.

The two worlds, then, the public arena of technical and cultural achievements and the private world of dreams, are not as far apart as they seem at first. In both, we encounter human desires finding different expressions. It is true that in organizations some desires are expressed through action or failure to act, whereas in dreams the expression is through manifest content. Yet, in both areas interpretation can uncover hidden meanings and desires. Psychoanalytic interpretations are built on the premiss that things often stand for more than they appear. As Paul Ricoeur, one of the most persuasive commentators on psychoanalysis, has argued, 'to interpret is to understand a double meaning' (1970: 8). Conscious phenomena are thus often found to be compromise formations between unconscious wishes that are too troublesome to gain access to consciousness and the forces of repression that aim to censor them. Interpretation is for Ricoeur the 'systematic exercise of suspicion' (1970: 32), forever looking for meanings behind meanings and for clues as signs of a wider picture. In this way, interpretation can move quickly from tiny detail to sweeping inference in a way akin to the primitive huntsman who can detect the existence of prey from tiny disturbances in the ground. Like the primitive huntsman, the psychoanalytic interpreter may disregard vast areas of undisturbed terrain and focus on the seemingly trifling irregularities and oddities; his or her skill resides in his or her ability to make sense of these trifles, to reveal their meaning as part of the broader picture (Ginzburg, 1980).

How can we distinguish between valid and spurious interpretations? What corroborations may be offered to strengthen specific interpretations? Since the work of Barthes and postmodernist theorists, we have learned to look for double meanings not only in dreams, neurotic symptoms and fantasies but in virtually any cultural artefact, from blue jeans to spaceships and from businessmen's grey suits to AIDS. Are all interpretations equally valid? We do not believe so. Interpretation is an art owing as much to tacit skills and know-how as to scientific method. Specific interpretations may not be proved or disproved by conventional criteria, like those used in the natural or mathematical sciences. Yet this does not make every interpretation equally meaningful or valid. An interpretation may be original, clever, perceptive, incomplete, misleading or even plain wrong. In Chapter 11, a number of techniques for corroborating interpretations will be suggested.

CONCLUSION

In this introductory chapter we have tried to show that the distance between the concerns of psychoanalysis and the types of phenomena prevalent in organizations is not so great. We have suggested that people's actions, thoughts and emotions in organizations are expressions of wishes and desires similar to those in the rest of their lives. The meaning of these actions, thoughts and emotions is not always clear because powerful psychic as well as social censors are muffling and distorting them. In these circumstances, interpretations like the ones pioneered by Freud in his discussions of dreams and neurotic symptoms can help reveal the hidden meanings of organizational phenomena. In the chapters that follow we shall see how such interpretations can initiate insightful explorations of organizational phenomena, such as leadership, group behaviour, symbolism and culture. We shall also introduce a number of key psychoanalytic ideas, concepts and theories which will further enhance these explorations.

NOTES

1 In fact, of nine flights in 1985, O-ring erosion occurred in seven, with blow-by occurring in six. This compared with four instances of erosion and three of blow-by for the six flights of 1984, when the problem began developing on a regular basis (Report of the Rogers Commission, 1986: 130–1).
2 It may be useful to cite here what the Rogers Commission wrote about NASA management's use of the term 'safety margin'. 'From the beginning, [contractor Morton-] Thiokol had suspected the putty was a contributing factor in O-ring erosion . . . In April 1983, Thiokol

reported on tests conducted to study the behavior of the joint putty. One conclusion of the report was that the STS-2 erosion was probably caused by blow holes in the putty, which allowed a jet of hot gas to focus on the primary O-ring. Thiokol discovered the focused jet ate away or "impinged" on portions of the O-ring. Thiokol calculated that the maximum possible impingement erosion was .090 inch, and that lab test proved that an O-ring would seal at 3,000 psi when erosion of .095 was simulated. This "safety margin" was the basis for approving Shuttle flights while accepting the possibility of O-ring erosion' (Report, 1986: 133). It is also important to note that, as investigation revealed, NASA's problems were by no means limited to the solid rocket boosters, but affected every aspect of their activity. They had hardware problems in other areas, and had lost technical, financial and operational control over what they were doing (Schwartz, 1990). The Rogers Commission, who observed that 'an assessment of the system's overall performance is best made by studying the process at the end of the production chain: crew training', cited this from astronaut Henry Hartsfield: 'Had we not had the accident, we were going to be up against a wall; STS 61-H . . . would have had to average 31 hours in the simulator to accomplish their required training, and STS 61-K would have to average 33 hours [note normal time was 77 hours]. That is ridiculous. For the first time, somebody was going to have to stand up and say we have got to slip the launch because we are not going to have the crew trained' (1986: 170). There can be little doubt that NASA's problems were systemic.

1 CORE PSYCHOANALYTIC IDEAS AND THEORIES

In the Introduction, we emphasized the importance of interpretation in unravelling the deeper meanings of organizational events. In later chapters we shall explore different psychoanalytic interpretations of organizational phenomena, including myths, fantasies and jokes. A large and important part of the psychoanalytic task is interpretative. Interpretation, however, is not an end in itself in depth psychology; rather, it is a technique leading towards an understanding of deeper psychic, organizational and cultural realities.

In *The Interpretation of Dreams* (1900), Freud provided the prototype for most types of psychoanalytic interpretations; in this work, he moved from interpretations of individual dreams to a study of the transformations of ideas and desires in the unconscious and the nature of unconscious processes. The interpretation of dreams was for Freud not an exercise in literary criticism, but the 'royal road' to the unconscious, the privileged but not exclusive path to the secrets of the human psyche. The final chapter of *The Interpretation of Dreams* is not a synthesis of all the interpretations which have been offered earlier, but a presentation of the theoretical yield of his interpretations, a *metapsychology*. This is a complex of concepts, principles, theories and models of the mind, the philosophical underpinning of a psychology of the unconscious, which, like metaphysics, lies once removed from empirical reality. This chapter presents most of the important elements of this metapsychology, including the emergence of the different agencies of the mind through each individual's early childhood experiences, the functions and dynamics of these mental agencies. Readers who are familiar with the core ideas of depth psychology will wish to skip this chapter. Those, however, with only a sketchy understanding of these ideas will find in this chapter a systematic presentation of concepts and theories sometimes used in a casual and imprecise way, which denies them their vitality and explanatory power.

METAPSYCHOLOGY: THE THREE POINTS OF VIEW

Freud's metapsychological investigations continued throughout his life; they are organized around three general 'points of view' or three distinct levels of analysis. These three points of view are seldom incompatible; at times they support each other and at times they proceed independently of each other, making use of different assumptions and imageries. The object of metapsychology is to provide complementary accounts from all three points of view.

The *topographic point of view* is essentially *descriptive*, a kind of mental map displaying different areas of the mind. The fundamental qualities and properties of ideas and processes in different areas are different. This point of view lacks a causal imagery: it does not seek to explain why an idea crosses a boundary; why, for example, a conscious idea becomes repressed in the unconscious; or why an unconscious one re-surfaces in consciousness at some particular point of an individual's life. It does, however, yield valuable information about the itinerary of different ideas as they travel into different mental locations being processed by different mental agencies, as well as their properties at different stages in their journeys.

The *economic point of view* deals in the currency of *energies*. Ideas and desires become charged with energy which is, essentially, in limited supply. Different events may be accompanied by the discharge or binding of energy, its investment ('cathexis') into different objects or ideas, its transformation or sublimation into different aims or its dissipation in different mental activities. The economic point of view becomes very important in explaining outcomes of mental conflicts or mental events in which different factors are pitched against each other, or in accounting for sudden surges of overpowering emotions or desires.

The *dynamic point of view* examines how and when different wishes and desires manifest themselves, how they are acted upon or are defended against. It focuses on mental *conflict*, its origins, which may lie in clashing desires or in the demands made by external reality, and its resolutions, which may lead to fresh conflicts, symptoms and inhibitions. This is the point of view which directly deals with different currents within the individual psyche and examines how and when unconscious material surfaces into consciousness.

Freud argued that 'when we have succeeded in describing a psychical process in its dynamic, topographical and economic aspects, we shall speak of it as a *metapsychological* presentation' (1915b: 184). This way of looking at mental processes from three different points of view may puzzle some; it is not, however, so unusual. It is a procedure that empirical scientists employ regularly in accounting for natural or historical phenomena. The discovery of a new set of historical artefacts, such as human remains, weapons or cooking implements, would lead to different examinations and hypotheses, draw-ing from the resources of different disciplines, including biology, chemistry, archaeology, geology, palaeontology and so on. Different scientists may bring their knowledge to bear in analysing such findings. Only when the hypotheses provided by different disciplines point in the same direction can we say that we have an understanding of the nature and meaning of the findings, their origins and their functions. In a similar way, a psychological process, such as the repression of a particular idea, may be approached from different points of view, each furnishing its own explanatory insights, each testing, qualifying or modifying the insights of the others.

A TORN SELF: THE DYNAMICS OF INNER CONFLICT

Undoubtedly, the dynamic point of view is the driving one in most psychoanalytic investigations, becoming over the past hundred years increasingly dominant. It is the one that builds most directly on to interpretation, and yields some of the most interesting insights, by addressing *conflict* – a fundamental feature of the psychoanalytic conception of the individual, culture and society. As Rieff has argued, Freud

> conceives of the self not as an abstract entity, uniting experience and cognition, but as the subject of a struggle between two objective forces – unregenerate instincts and overbearing culture. Between these two forces there may be compromise but no resolution. Since the individual can neither extirpate his instincts nor wholly reject the demands of society, his character expresses the way in which he organizes and appeases the conflict between the two. (Rieff, 1959: 29)

The unity of the self in the face of such conflicts is problematic. Individuals may at times experience themselves as wholesome, unified and centred; in reality, however, such unity is the result of psychological *work* in the presence of forces which seek to break the self apart, to decentre it. Freud's image of the self as something achieved rather than as something given has had a profound influence on twentieth-century culture, becoming one of the core features of postmodern theorizing. The individual psyche, the psychical apparatus as Freud often referred to it, is composed of different mental agencies, each one of which draws the individual in different directions. Between these mental agencies, there can be compromise, accommodation or strife, but no permanent harmony.

The id, the instincts and the pleasure principle

The oldest and least accessible mental agency is referred to as the *id*. The id is substantially unconscious, containing

> everything that is inherited, that is present at birth, that is laid down in the constitution – above all, therefore, the instincts, which originate from the somatic organization and which find a first psychical expression here in the id in forms unknown to us. This oldest portion of the psychical apparatus remains the most important throughout life; moreover, the investigations of psychoanalysis started with it. (1940: 376)

The id, then, is this large area of the psyche which is inaccessible to consciousness, untainted by culture or civilization, with no sense of time and no sense of reason, whose influence on our mental lives can only be studied indirectly, through its manifestations in conscious activity. The id, that 'cauldron full of seething excitations' (1933: 106), is the source of internal stimuli, which, unlike external ones, may not be avoided by running away from them, through flight. 'It is filled with energy reaching from the instincts, but it has no organization, produces no collective will, but only a striving to bring about the satisfaction of the instinctual needs subject to the observance of the pleasure principle' (1933: 106).

The concept of *instinct* or *drive* whose province is the id is one of the richest, but also one of the most problematic in depth psychology. It has been rejected or disregarded by many depth psychologists, who view it as a remnant of nineteenth-century biological thinking. Freud, for his part, was adamant that it is an indispensable concept for explaining stimuli originating from within. Much of his psychology was dedicated to an exploration of one major instinct, *sexuality*. Throughout his life, however, he argued for an instinctual dualism. In his early writings, he argued for a dualism of sexuality and self-preservation; later, he modified this view, arguing that self-preservation is itself a modification of the sexual instinct. He finally proposed a dualism of life instincts, which include sexuality, and death instincts, which include destructiveness and a tendency towards inertia and ultimately death.

While he viewed these instinctual forces as characteristic of all organic life, instincts in human beings have some totally unique properties. They are almost infinitely complex, malleable and changing, developing throughout an individual's life and manifesting themselves in a hugely diverse array of wishes and desires. Sexuality, for instance, develops from a simple force in early life into an increasingly complex force, which may be manifested in sexual desires, social bonding and solidarity, artistic creativity, scientific enquiry or spiritual longings. What is constant behind such different manifestations is *libido*, the life energy which drives them, an energy which becomes easily deflected, re-oriented or modified. Libido is the force that converts a mere idea into a vital urge, something that demands satisfaction or at least action. A satisfied desire is, at least temporarily, drained of its energy, reverting to its status as an idea. In this sense, Freud identified the *pleasure principle* as the principle of mental functioning which dominates desires in the id, a principle under which pleasure is the result of a fulfilled desire, a desire which, when left unfulfilled generates an unpleasant excitation. The importance of the pleasure principle in mental functioning cannot be exaggerated. No amount of civilization, morality or constraint can alter this. 'In the theory of psychoanalysis we have no hesitation in assuming that the course taken by mental events is automatically regulated by the pleasure principle' (1920: 275). The pleasure, according to this view, is no abstract ethical principle of how to achieve a good and happy life, but rather a lived experience associated with the fulfilment of our most basic strivings:

> The feeling of happiness derived from the satisfaction of a wild instinctual impulse untamed by the ego is incomparably more intense than that derived from sating an instinct that has been tamed. The irresistibility of perverse instincts, and perhaps the attraction in general of forbidden things finds an economic explanation here. (1930: 267)

Yet, the programme of the pleasure principle is 'at loggerheads with the whole world, with the microcosm as much as the macrocosm. There is no possibility at all of its being carried through; all regulations of the universe run counter to it' (1930: 263).

The ego, the reality principle and the mechanisms of defence

The life of an organism ruled exclusively by the pleasure principle would undoubtedly be colourful; it would also be extremely short. From a very early age, each one of us learns that some pleasures are out of bounds, forbidden or unattainable. The pursuit of such pleasures is bound to produce disappointment or damage, physical or psychological. Hence it is postponed, modified or relinquished, in exchange for what is attainable. This is described as the *reality principle*, the principle of mental functioning served by the *ego*, the second major mental agency.

> Under the influence of the real external world around us, one portion of the id has undergone a special development. From what was originally a cortical layer, equipped with the organs for receiving stimuli and with arrangements for acting as a protective shield against stimuli, a special organization has arisen which henceforward acts as an intermediary between the id and the external world. To this region of the mind we have given the name of *ego*. (1940: 376)

The ego performs a number of vital functions for an individual. It is responsible for receiving stimuli both from inside and outside and for establishing whether things are real or imaginary through *reality testing*. It interjects *thought* between the experience of a need and its fulfilment, frequently postponing or qualifying the gratification of instinctual impulses. It is responsible for *motility* and *action*; above all, the ego is the seat of *consciousness* and controls the movement of ideas from the preconscious to consciousness. It is also the mental agency responsible for keeping the individual together.

> What distinguishes the ego from the id quite especially is a tendency for synthesis in its contents, to a combination and unification in its mental processes which are totally lacking ... To adopt a popular mode of speaking, we might say that the ego stands for reason and good sense while the id stands for the untamed passions. (1933: 108)

The ego, then, is the mental agency specifically responsible for the sense of unity and integrity, which we each experience as 'self'. This is something that is accomplished at considerable cost and constant vigilance. How does the ego seek to maintain the integrity of the self in the face of inner and outer threats? In the first place, as we saw in the Introduction, it does so through the *defence mechanisms*, i.e. by initiating a set of psychological processes aimed at averting the danger. The process of repression, as a form of psychological defence against pain, embarrassment or disappointment, has already been examined in some detail. Freud came to regard repression as being triggered by a 'signal of anxiety', a very unpleasant feeling accompanying the recognition of a danger, inner or outer. Repression, however, is not the only type of defence available to the ego. Other defensive mechanisms, to use the term proposed by Anna Freud (1936), include the following:

1 *Regression*: the wholesale replacement of a set of instinctual impulses and desires by one which characterized an earlier stage of development; for example, reversion to childhood or adolescent configurations.
2 *Reaction-formation*: the obliteration of powerful impulses (especially hostile ones) through a transformation into their opposites; for example, an angry person manifests exaggerated care, a hateful person exaggerated love.
3 *Projection*: the attribution of one's own desires (especially destructive ones) to another person.
4 *Introjection or identification*: whereby one identifies with another person either as an object of admiration or as an object of persecution.
5 *Denial*: the refusal to acknowledge external reality or stimuli, however threatening.
6 *Isolation*: whereby an idea or memory is acknowledged in consciousness, but the accompanying emotion is rejected; alternatively, an idea or a memory, however painful, may be acknowledged but only if it is dissociated from other related ideas.

Subsequent theorists have added other defensive mechanisms against anxiety, some of which are deployed at an individual level, while others may be deployed in groups or larger social collectivities. Some of these will be examined in future chapters, but we should note now the following two:

1 *Splitting*: an object or indeed the ego is split into two, each part possessing qualities at odds with those of the other; for example, one is totally good and one is totally bad.
2 *Rationalization*: plausible or rational reasons are provided for explaining one's actions or feelings, but which in reality conceal the real reasons.

All of these mechanisms may involve the repression of particular ideas or desires, the dissociation between an instinct and the object to which it is attached, or the dissociation between two closely related ideas or desires which are kept apart. They may, sometimes, lead to behaviour which is recognized as 'pathological', involving a weakening of reality testing and thinking processes. One process which may also function as a defence mechanism is called *sublimation*, and this is of great importance for the study of group and organizational phenomena. Sublimation operates not by altering the relation between instinct and object, but by radically modifying the energy of the instinct itself, in a way analogous to the chemical process whereby a solid is directly transformed into a gas. Sublimation, an idea which Freud inherited from Nietzsche, involves the desexualization of libido and its transformation into a creative, bonding or spiritual energy, re-oriented towards non-sexual aims, such as artistic, scientific or spiritual pursuits. The transformation of libido from a pleasure-seeking force into a force towards cultural, economic and political achievement makes sublimation a vital process in the service of civilization.

> To the contributions of the energy won in such a way for the functions of our mental life we probably owe the highest cultural consequences. A repression taking place at an early period excludes the sublimation of the repressed impulse; after the removal of the repression the way to sublimation is again free. (1910: 54)

The discussion of the mechanisms of defence underlines the fact that the ego, in some of its manifestations, is itself unconscious. The mechanisms of defence are not conscious strategies of coping with stress or difficulties (as is sometimes assumed) but *unconscious processes*, which can only be established through painstaking interpretative work. This is what forced Freud to reconsider the nature of the ego in his later work. Contrary to his earlier views that psychic conflict is between unconscious impulses and the conscious forces of repression, in his later work Freud came to appreciate that defensive processes initiated by the ego are themselves unconscious. The analysis of the ego's defence mechanisms forms the central focus of a tradition in depth psychology known as *ego psychology*, which has flourished in the United States since the 1930s. In some versions of this tradition, the ego emerges essentially as an agent of adaptation, employing the defence mechanisms to ensure the survival and well-being of the individual: 'The term "mechanism" is unfortunate here; they are purposeful strategies, consciously or unconsciously designed to make life easier and more manageable, not mechanical routines with causes but no purposes' (Jahoda, 1977: 66). In this context, 'purposeful' must be understood as fulfilling an important psychological function, rather than as 'consciously purposeful'. Yet such functionalist readings of the ego do not do full justice to the complexities of the concept in psychoanalytic theory. In particular, they disregard a major feature of the ego, the fact that 'from a dynamic point of view it is weak, it has borrowed its energies from the id' (1933: 109). In a famous simile, Freud argued that

> the ego's relation to the id might be compared with that of a rider to his horse. The horse supplies the locomotive energy, while the rider has the privilege of deciding on the goal and of guiding the powerful animal's movement. But only too often there arises between the ego and the id the not precisely ideal situation of the rider being obliged to guide the horse along the path by which it itself wants to go. (1933: 109)

Narcissism and the ego-ideal

The concept which crucially shifted the psychoanalytic ego from its position as agent of adaptation is *narcissism*. The theory of narcissism is one of the most original and far-reaching concepts in depth psychology, which has made enormous contributions to the analysis of organizations as well as contemporary culture in general. The term 'narcissism' is drawn from the ancient Greek myth of Narcissus, the young man who fell in love with his own image in a lake's calm water, not realizing that the image was his own. The importance of the concept of narcissism for the study of the ego lies in the fact that it casts the ego not in its usual role as agent deploying defensive strategies, but as an *object*, an object of instinctual impulses. If libido may be directed outwards, towards the objects of the world, the theory of narcissism proposes that it may also be re-directed inwards by adopting the ego as its object.

The idea of narcissism was introduced in an important essay published by Freud in 1914. Reflecting on certain pathological conditions in which an individual withdraws all interest from the external objects, Freud proposed that these conditions are the result of an individual adopting him or herself as a love-object. Object libido is in this way converted into ego libido. But, as in other areas of psychoanalytic enquiry, pathology is not qualitatively different from normality, but rather marks an exaggerated preponderance of certain tendencies at the expense of others. A healthy individual is one who combines sturdy self-esteem with an ability to channel his or her interest, attention and love to objects of the natural and social world.

> [W]e may even venture to touch on the question of what makes it necessary at all for our mental life to pass beyond the limits of narcissism and to attach the libido to objects. The answer which would follow from our line of thought would once more be that this necessity arises when the cathexis of the ego with libido exceeds a certain amount. A strong egoism is a protection against falling ill, but in the last resort we must begin to love in order not to fall ill, and we are bound to fall ill if, in consequence of frustration, we are unable to love. (1914a: 78)

This extract highlights the importance of the economic factor in determining pathology as against mental health. Some of the libido must be *cathected*, i.e. channelled on to and invested in the ego, in order for the ego to function properly; if, however, an individual's libido is exclusively oriented towards the ego, then the individual will suffer from a kind of self-obsession, accompanied by an inability to form meaningful relations with the world around him or her and exaggerated feelings of self-importance. In fact, in choosing objects on which to focus their sexual and emotional interest, individuals may adopt one of two characteristic stances, the *narcissistic* and the *anaclitic*. In the former, individuals choose objects 'like themselves', while in the latter the object embodies certain attractive qualities associated with a person who once looked after them or protected them. Through narcissistic object choices, individuals strengthen their own feelings of self-esteem, provided that the object of their interest reciprocates the love and admiration. Anaclitic object choices, on the other hand, may leave the ego weakened; in extreme cases of falling in love, an individual may feel totally drained of self-interest or esteem as he or she exalts his or her lover to an idealized, sublime state.

How does the ego make itself an object of narcissistic admiration and love? The answer to this question rests on the concept of the *ego-ideal*, an amalgam of attractive qualities which are abstracted from admired persons, notably the parents as perceived in early life, cultural and personal heroes and other individuals or ideas that inspire respect. Against this ego-ideal, the ego continuously measures itself, and to the extent that it can draw itself close to the ideal, the ego can attract libido on to itself. Narcissism then restores some of the self-love which was enjoyed in early childhood by the ego before a distinction between the inner and the outer worlds was made. It must be noted that the ego-ideal is itself an unconscious representation; most people would deny that they idealize a particular individual or hero-worship another. Such admissions may expose them to ridicule or embarrassment. Instead, the ego-ideal may very well absorb disparate and at times contradictory qualities from different role models, provided that these are kept below consciousness.

From its earliest postulation, the importance of the ego-ideal for group and organizational psychology was evident to Freud:

> The ego ideal opens up an important avenue for the understanding of group psychology. In addition to its individual side, this ideal has a social side; it is also the common ideal of a family, a class or a nation. It binds not only a person's narcissistic libido, but also a considerable amount of his homosexual libido, which is in this way turned back into the ego. (1914a: 96)

Individuals may thus derive narcissistic fulfilment from the cultural, economic, military and even sporting achievements of their nation or group; as members of the group, they too can feel that they have played a part in the achievement, their ego drawing close to the cultural super-ego.

To recapitulate, then, the ego in psychoanalysis stands for the reality principle, the demands of natural and social reality, and seeks to curb the impulses from the id in the name of psychological unity and synthesis which is one of its major preoccupations. It commands the thinking, reflecting and testing faculties and initiates various defensive processes in response to anxiety which signals a threat, from inside or from outside. The ego, however, is weak and must use energies which it draws to itself from the id through the process of narcissism. To do so, it seeks to make itself lovable and attractive by emulating the ego-ideal which is composed of all the perfections with which the parents and other admired persons were once invested. Yet, in drawing libido to itself, the ego risks losing its ability to invest it in meaningful objects and forming relations with the world outside. Besides, the task of emulating the ego-ideal and making itself attractive and lovable is by no means unproblematic.

The super-ego, conscience and guilt

Just how problematic it is for the ego to adopt the attributes of the ego-ideal and attract libido on to itself is highlighted by the third major mental agency, the *super-ego*. The super-ego, in another of Freud's famous metaphors, is the ego's third harsh master, the other two being the id and external reality. The super-ego can be seen as part of the ego which becomes differentiated from the ego in childhood, just as the ego becomes differentiated from the id. But if the ego becomes separate from the id under the realization of the opposition between an outer and an inner world, the super-ego becomes separated following one of the major psychic episodes of childhood centring around what is referred to as the Oedipus complex. The super-ego embodies the authority of the child's father as a representative of broader moral and social laws, strictures and prohibitions. It is the super-ego which ensures that the moral demands of our society are not experienced as external but as part of ourselves. The chief qualities of the super-ego are vigilance, rigidity and harshness; it continuously monitors the ego, enforcing the social regulations through conscience and feelings of guilt. It also constantly measures the ego against the ideal and punishes cruelly any perceived shortfalls.

Where does the super-ego derive these properties from, whose social usefulness is quite evident but which make the ego's task even more problematic? We shall presently examine how the super-ego inherits many of the harsh, critical qualities with which the father was associated by the child during the Oedipal phase. From an economic point of view, however, the super-ego represents a re-orientation of aggressive impulses against the ego in the interest of morality.

> From the point of view of instinctual control of morality, it may be said of the id that it is totally non-moral, of the ego that it strives to be moral, and of the super-ego that it can be super-moral and then become as cruel as only the id can be. It is remarkable that the more a man controls his aggressiveness towards the exterior the more severe – that is aggressive – he becomes in his ego ideal. The ordinary view sees the situation the other way round: the standard set up by the ego ideal seems to be the motive for the suppression of aggressiveness. The fact remains, however, as we have stated it: the more a man controls his aggressiveness, the more intense becomes his ideal's inclination to aggressiveness against his ego. (1923: 395–6)

It will be noticed that in *The Ego and the Id* (1923), the work in which Freud first proposed the idea of the super-ego, it is used interchangeably with the ego-ideal. In the *New Introductory Lectures* (1933), however, the ego-ideal is treated as one of three core functions of the super-ego, the other two being self-observation and conscience. Subsequent writers have sought to draw these two concepts, the ego-ideal and the super-ego, further apart. Nunberg (1955), Chasseguet-Smirgel (1985) and several theorists interested in organizations, including Schwartz (1990), have argued that while the super-ego is associated with the qualities of dreaded figures, the ego-ideal is fundamentally formed on the model of loved objects, most especially the mother, of the very first life experiences. To appreciate these differences, it is now important to move from a relatively static presentation of the metapsychology to an examination of the development of the mental personality through some of life's early experiences.

THE STAGES OF SEXUAL DEVELOPMENT

One of Freud's most original and controversial theories is and has remained his theory of infantile sexuality. His book *Three Essays on the Theory of Sexuality* (1905b) caused a considerable scandal at the time of its publication. In it, he revolutionized the conception of sexuality by disengaging it from overtly sexual acts involving the genital apparatus, and re-orienting it towards a broad range of activities, sensations and experiences entailing pleasure and involving many different parts of the body.

> The detaching of sexuality from the genitals has the advantage of allowing us to bring the sexual activities of children and of perverts into the same scope as those of normal adults. The sexual activities of children have hitherto been entirely neglected and though those of perverts have been recognized it has been with moral indignation and without understanding. (1925a: 222)

Freud's conception of the development of sexuality involves a series of transitions through several stages, beginning with the child's earliest experiences. Each stage revolves around a particular bodily area which becomes the focus of pleasure-yielding sensations but also of disappointments and frustrations. The closure of each stage signals the arrival of the next, yet each stage bequeaths the individual a certain legacy which will remain with him or her for the rest of life. This includes a new range of meanings and distinctions, such as inner/outer, good/bad, me/not me; a new range of mental agencies or institutions, such as the ego and the super-ego; and a new range of repressed longings and desires which will surface later on in life, under diverse guises. It is largely through these subsequent manifestations that much of our understanding of the early transformations of sexuality are studied.

Primary narcissism and the oral stage

The infant's early experience is one without boundaries: there is no boundary between the child and the world; instead, the child experiences the mother's love for it directly and without mediation. And the mother is, at least in the beginning, the whole world to the infant; and the infant is, at least at the beginning, the central focus of her attention. The infant thus experiences itself as being continuous with the world, which itself appears to be made out of love. This early experience of being continuous with a loving world is shrouded in mystery, almost obliterated by the major trials that life places in the child's path. Yet, if we reflect on it, we may discover that in it lies the kernel of some religious experiences in later life, when the religious believer loses him or herself in a religious community, experiencing an 'oceanic' feeling of love, peace and complete fusion. In our nostalgic frames of mind, when we have the idea that once life was perfect, as in the Garden of Eden, or in our organizations before the despised present regime gained power, we are tapping into this substratum of our experience (Gabriel, 1993). This experience of fusion was described by Freud as *primary narcissism*, when self-love precedes the realization that there is a recalcitrant reality which does not automatically yield to our wishes.

The first realization that this blissful state of affairs is not going to last occurs when the mother's breast fails to be present when it is wanted. This, at once, establishes the mouth as the centre of pleasurable sensations but also as the centre of separation. It establishes the first core opposition in the child's universe of meanings, that between the ego and the object. The experience of separation defines us as specifically different from the rest of the world, and is marked by the first feelings of *anxiety*. Pleasure, on the other hand, is associated with the incorporation of the object, which is the dominant relational mode of this phase of sexual development. Later in life, the mouth and incorporation may re-surface as the focus of sexual pleasure. During the oral stage, and especially as the child starts teething, it begins to bite the breast. Melanie Klein, following Karl Abraham, placed much importance on what she viewed as the first display of infantile sadism, the first manifestation of destructive impulses:

> The destructive instinct projected outwards is first experienced as oral aggression. I believe that oral-sadistic impulses towards the mother's breast are active from the beginning of life, though with the onset of teething the cannibalistic impulses increase in strength – a factor stressed by Abraham.

> In states of frustration and anxiety the oral-sadistic and cannibalistic desires are reinforced, and then the infant feels that he has taken the nipple and the breast *in bits*. (Klein, 1946/1986: 180)

Klein attributes greater importance to the oral phase for the future development of the child than Freud did. The child, immersed in its narcissistic sense of self-importance, is unable as yet to understand the significance of the withdrawing breast or its own feelings of anxiety. It attributes the cause of the anxiety to powerful forces outside itself, which are arrayed against it. It attempts to defend against them with the idea of a return to the state of fusion in which there was no separation between it and the world, and hence no anxiety. Putting the whole matter in terms of the infant's relations with the mother, the infant *splits* its relations with the breast into two parts: one is a good breast, belonging to a perfect mother who loves it absolutely; the other is a bad breast, belonging to a malevolent, withholding, dangerous mother. In this way, the infant establishes the root of a view of the world which divides it into elements that are all good, filled with love, with which it may perfectly fuse, and elements that are all bad, filled with hate, seeking to destroy it (see Klein, 1946/1986, 1956/1986; Segal, 1964, 1979).

This conflict between perfect goodness and irredeemable badness can be seen as the second core opposition which comes to dominate our mental functioning. It is characteristic of what Klein calls the *paranoid-schizoid position*, a mode of *object relations* (i.e. relationships between ourselves and the important objects of our universe) during the first four or five months of life (Klein, 1946/1986). Our tendency to see the features of our world, including our organizations, our groups, our leaders, our co-workers and so on, as either all good or all bad is a consequence of this position. But the paranoid-schizoid position is superseded, before the first year of life is over, by what Klein calls the *depressive position*, built on the realization that the object of love and the object of hate is one and the same, the mother. This becomes part of a broader realization that others, and ourselves, are not either all bad or all good, but both (Klein, 1940/1986). The world is full of complexities, relations are transient and contingent, love is not something we are absolutely entitled to, but something that may be earned. Thus primary narcissism gives way to *mutualistic relations* with others.

Klein's contribution to an understanding of the oral phase, based on her work on children's play, has had profound implications for psychoanalytic theory. It has highlighted the complexity of the child's relationship with its world, the discovery of the world of objects, the experience of emotional *ambivalence* (i.e. simultaneous strong positive and strong negative feelings about the same object) and the early manifestations of aggressiveness. It initiated a psychoanalytic tradition known as *object relations theory*, which shifted the focus of understanding of early childhood development and subsequent mental functioning away from the world of instincts, sexuality and pleasure, towards the modes of relating to others. This tradition, which has prospered in the United Kingdom, has made notable contributions to the study of group and organizational phenomena, including those of Bion, Jaques and Menzies Lyth, some of which will be explored in later chapters of this book. In many of these contributions, the child's early emotional relationships, especially the distant memory of the perfect fusion with the mother and the desire to recover it, will continue to act as a powerful force whenever feelings of anxiety are experienced. Chasseguet-Smirgel (1985) has argued that memory of the child's perfect fusion with the mother is preserved in the ego-ideal, which seeks to restore the ego as the centre of a loving world, an idea which has proved of great value for the study of leadership and other organizational processes, as shown in the work of Schwartz (1990).

The anal-sadistic stage

Freud's interest, unlike that of the object relations theorists, remained firmly focused on the oral phase as a phase of *sexual* development, characterized by incorporation, its unique mode of deriving pleasure. In his very last work, *An Outline of Psychoanalysis*, Freud wrote: 'The baby's obstinate persistence in sucking gives evidence at an early stage of a need for satisfaction which, though it originates from and is instigated by the taking of nourishment, nevertheless strives to obtain pleasure independently of nourishment and for that reason may and should be termed *sexual*' (1940: 385).

Between the ages of two and four the child enters a new phase of sexual development, which is characterized by the anus as the centre of pleasurable sensations; this coincides with the strengthening of the child's muscular apparatus and its increasing control over the sphincter functions. The sexual nature of the excretory function may come as a surprise to those who regard it, like feeding, as a straightforward physiological function. For Freud, however, defecation, like eating before it, opens a new range of pleasurable sensations, associated with controlling the processes of evacuating and retaining. It is during this stage that the opposition of *activity* and *passivity* comes to the fore, as the child's wishes to control its bowel movements bring it into opposition with the parents' attempts to toilet-train it.

During the anal stage, the faeces assume an extraordinary symbolic importance as objects of sexual interest and value. They are, in the first instance, a part of the child that is detachable, and, in the second place, something that is of concern and value to the parents. The parents' apparent delight when the child succeeds in taming its excretions, producing faeces in the chamber pot, leads to a symbolic equation in the child's unconscious mind, one that will persist long after it has accepted the view that faeces are something quite disgusting and useless, the equation faeces = gift = money. Deferring to the parents' wishes is viewed by the child as an act of generosity on its part; alternatively, the child may deny its parents satisfaction, displaying an obstinacy which may re-surface in later life, as one of a triad of character traits which frequently occur together, orderliness, parsimoniousness and obstinacy, the traits of the so-called 'anal personality'. The anal phase, even more than the oral phase, displays a pronounced *sadistic* quality. This originates in the child's refusal to please the parents – a refusal which comes to be associated with the denial of another person's pleasure or even more intensely with the inflicting of pain on another person. Karl Abraham distinguished between two sadistic qualities in the anal stage, one succeeding the other. The earlier one is linked to the destruction of the object through evacuation, the later one to possessive collection and controlling of objects and a simultaneous frustration of the other's wishes (Abraham, 1973: 422ff). Both of these qualities may re-surface in later life in sadistic personalities.

As with the oral stage, the anal stage is usually concluded with the child accepting the frustrations and disappointments of external reality, surrendering some of the pleasures of early life and repressing most of its impulses. At the same time, the child emerges from the anal stage with a vastly increased symbolic universe, one that includes objects invested with a wealth of different meanings and nuances and a wide variety of emotional experiences. It has become aware of the enormity and recalcitrance of the external world that surrounds and confronts it, but at the same time has started to discover the limited but effective control that it can exercise over others if not yet over its own life.

THE PHALLIC STAGE AND THE OEDIPUS COMPLEX

The child has not yet discovered the difference between she and he (hence we have referred to 'it' through the neutral pronoun thus far). This polarity between feminine and masculine will come to dominate the third stage of libidinal development, the phallic stage. The arrival of this stage is signalled by the child's discovery of yet another area of bodily pleasure, the penis for the boy, the clitoris for the girl. The child's attitude towards this new discovery is coloured by its prior experiences with breast and faeces; from the start, the phallus is experienced as a detachable object, an object that may be lost. Two events mark the development of the phallic phase: the parents' admonishments against juvenile masturbation (at times accompanied by threats or innuendoes) and the discovery of the anatomical differences between the sexes. From this point on, the mental and sexual development of boys and girls will follow different paths. This is how Freud describes in a single sentence the great Oedipal adventure which lies in the path of every boy:

> The boy enters the Oedipus phase; he begins to manipulate his penis and simultaneously has phantasies of carrying out some sort of activity with it in relation to his mother, till owing to the effect of a threat of castration and the sight of the absence of a penis in females, he experiences the greatest trauma of his life and this introduces the period of latency with all its consequences. (1940: 386)

The Oedipus period or episode represents the climax of early childhood development, obliterating sexual feelings with a mass of repressions from which they will only re-surface, radically altered, in adolescence. The myth of Oedipus, hero of two great tragedies by Sophocles, provided Freud with the key to unlocking the complex mental dynamics of this fated episode in a person's life, an episode whose outcomes play a major part in subsequent mental life.

Oedipus was a child abandoned in his infancy on a mountain by his parents, Laius and Jocasta, the king and queen of Thebes, who had been alarmed by an oracle which claimed that the child would grow up to kill his father and marry his mother. The child's life was spared, however, by the shepherd who had been assigned to abandon him; instead, he handed him to another shepherd serving the king and queen of Corinth. They were childless and adopted the boy, naming him Oedipus, 'sore-footed', after the dreadful sores in his ankles, which had been pierced to allow for a rope to be put through them. The boy grew up not knowing his true origins, until he too heard of the prophecy, whereupon he left his foster parents to escape the dreadful fate, thinking that the prophecy related to them. During his travels he quarrelled with a rich man riding a chariot, who set his slaves upon him. In the fight that followed he killed the man and all but one of the slaves, little realizing that the first half of the prophecy had already been fulfilled.

Oedipus's wanderings took him to Thebes, a city ravaged by the Sphinx, a wild beast which tormented its inhabitants by setting a famous riddle: 'What is the animal which walks on four legs in the morning, on two at mid-day and on three in the evening?' Oedipus answered the riddle with the 'power of his intellect alone' and rid the city of its tormentor. The answer to the riddle was, of course, 'man', who walks on all fours in infancy, later on two legs and finally adds a third in old age in the shape of a walking stick. Little did Oedipus realize that he, the solver of riddles, was ignorant of the biggest riddle, that of his own roots and destiny. The people of Thebes rewarded Oedipus by crowning him king of their city; after all, had their king not recently been set upon by robbers and killed? The dead king's widow, Jocasta, was then offered to King Oedipus as his wife, thus completing the prophecy. Oedipus lived for many years with Jocasta, having four children with her. But his past caught up with him when he was at the peak of his powers in ripe middle age. It was then that sickness and hunger struck his city, a sure sign of a terrible insult to a god, the presence of miasma in the city. Oedipus set about to find the person responsible for the insult, not knowing that hunter and prey were one. In Sophocles' *Oedipus Rex*, he is the last person to realize the truth about his actions, his origins and the terrifying forces that had driven his life. In despair, he blinds himself and leaves the city, the most wretched and reviled of men.

Freud was taken with this myth long before he turned it into the centrepiece of his psychology. Jones, his friend and biographer, tells of an incident on his fiftieth birthday when he was presented with a medallion, which bore the inscription from Sophocles' *Oedipus Rex* 'He who divined the meaning of famous riddles and was a man most mighty.' On seeing the inscription, Freud became pale and agitated; he explained to those present that as a young student at Vienna University, he would stroll around the Great Hall, examining the busts of famous professors. 'He then had a phantasy, not merely seeing his own bust there in the future, which would not have been anything remarkable in an ambitious young student, but of it actually being inscribed with the *identical words* he now saw on the medallion' (Jones, 1955: II. 15). Undoubtedly, then, Oedipus was a mythical character with whom Freud had already identified; yet, it was in a letter to his friend Fliess written on 15 October 1897, a few days before the first anniversary of his own father's death (and six months after the 'Uncle Josef' dream examined in the Introduction), that Freud came upon what he viewed as his greatest discovery. The reason why the story of Oedipus has held such a powerful emotional grip over people across the ages, he ventured, is that it awakens memories of wishes which once dominated our mental lives but were subsequently repressed and obliterated from memory.

> Being entirely honest with oneself is a good exercise. Only one idea of general value has occurred to me. I have found love of the mother and jealousy of the father in my own case too, and now believe it to be a general phenomenon of childhood, even if it does not always occur so early as in children who have become hysterics . . . In this case, the gripping power of *Oedipus Rex*, in spite of all the rational objections to the inexorable fate that the story presupposes, becomes intelligible, and one can understand why later fate dramas were such failures. Our feelings rise against the arbitrary, individual fate . . . but the Greek myth seizes on a compulsion which everyone recognizes because he has felt traces of it himself. Every member of the audience was once a budding Oedipus in phantasy, and this dream-fulfilment played out in reality causes everyone to recoil in horror, with the full measure of repression which separates his infantile from his present state. (Freud, 1954: 227)

Like Oedipus, we are blind to our past, and only the fact that he acted out in deed what we all experienced as phantasy sets us apart. But why would one want to kill one's father and marry one's mother? That the child wants to be one with the mother comes as no surprise at the outset of the phallic stage, when for a brief moment it sees in the phallus the promise of reclaiming a union that characterized its early narcissistic experiences. It is then that the child comes to view the father as a barrier between itself and the mother, a blockage between the child and the realization of its desire of re-establishing a perfect fusion. The child feels rage at the father, wants to get rid of him, to kill him. After all, why not? Could the father not be made to disappear, just like the faeces? It is then, however, that the boy is seized by an extraordinary anxiety attack. How can he compete against the father? In such a conflict, is it not more likely that the fate of the faeces will befall that prized possession of his, the penis? The boy's *castration anxiety* is facilitated by any threats which have been made in connection to his juvenile masturbation, but even more by the discovery that there *are* indeed individuals who have already lost their penis, girls. For the boy, castration anxiety assumes existential proportions, a terrible fear of being mutilated by authority, of being deprived by authority of his means of re-connecting himself to all that is good and desirable. Under these circumstances, the boy resorts to the psychological process which will mark his entire future, repression. He represses both the desire to be united with the mother and the desire to rid himself of the father into the deepest recesses of the unconscious, from which they may never surface again. All memory of these desires disappears – most 'normal' men will rightly deny that they ever harboured such desires and will experience shock and disgust on first being exposed to the psychoanalytic idea of the Oedipus complex.

But repression is only one part of a remarkable transformation in the psyche, a transformation which thereafter makes it unnecessary to fear the father for transgression. The boy undertakes to punish himself for activity, or even impulse, that the father would have punished. In this way, he establishes the basis of an adult conscience and substitutes self-control for control by others. This is how the super-ego is established through a *split* within the ego – thereafter, each individual is at the same time observer and observed, accuser and accused, judge and judged. The super-ego then represents the internalization of the father's authority by the individual, setting up an enduring sense of obligation, responsibility and, above all, morality. The super-ego inherits some of the harshness with which the father was invested; this is not direct transformation. The boy's actual father may have been kind and loving, yet only by perceiving him as a harsh enforcer, the wielder of great powers, can the boy accomplish the repression of his Oedipus complex. How does the super-ego become associated with *guilt*? Having overcome his antagonism for the father, the boy rediscovers his love for him. His feelings, as noted earlier, are ambivalent, combining strong love with strong hate. Hate has been repressed along with the desire to dispose of him. Now love has a free reign – the child feels guilty of having wanted the father's demise. To be sure some of this guilt becomes repressed along with most other desires and ideas making up the Oedipus complex. As an unconscious factor, however, it remains available to the super-ego, whenever it seeks to admonish the ego for its social transgressions.

What gives the Freudian super-ego extraordinary rigidity and severity is its apparent disregard of whether the individual is actually guilty or not (after all, he did not kill the father, he only wished him dead) and its equal disregard of whether the individual is happy or not. Faced with this severity, which he observed in many of his patients and evidently concerned him greatly about his own feelings, Freud proposed that the harsh qualities of the super-ego do not owe their existence to the circumstances surrounding the actual unfolding and repression of the Oedipus complex, circumstances which may be altered by a more enlightened attitude towards juvenile masturbation or milder expressions of paternal admonishment. Instead, they are the result of the unyielding association of the super-ego with the death instinct: the unconscious sense of guilt is economically fuelled, so to speak, by the primary force of destruction when it assumes the ego as its object. This internalization of the death instinct is the source of much suffering for the individual and its function is purely social: it deflects the individual's aggressive energies from being directed against his fellow human beings and bolsters social controls. Thus, human suffering, as Ricoeur has argued, 'is no mere accident which the individual might be spared by a better social organization or a more suitable education; human beings can experience entry into culture only in the mode of conflict. Suffering accompanies the task of culture like fate, the fate illustrated by the Oedipus tragedy' (1970: 196).

The implications of these formulations for social and organizational life will become clear when we come to discuss the phenomenon of culture. At this point, however, it is important to observe that the conclusion of the Oedipus complex for the boy includes, in addition to renunciations, guilt and splitting, a *promise*: the promise that he may one day inherit the father's power, acquire a wife of his own and perhaps even restore himself to the centre of a loving world. This promise, omnipresent in all fairy-tales and children's stories in which the young prince must go through numerous adventures and trials before marrying the princess of his dreams, will become a very powerful feature of the boy's strivings and ordeals during adolescence. The promise leads the boy to *identify* with the father, adopting what he believes to be his characteristics, treating him as a role model and using his idealized qualities to enrich his own ego-ideal. Being like the father implies that one day he will enjoy the father's privileges. In this way, identification emerges as the second major way in which we form meaningful relations with those around us (the other being object cathexis), treating them not as objects to be possessed but models to be emulated.

The resolution of the Oedipus complex marks one final transformation in our mental functioning and our relations with those around us. By bringing the father into ourselves to form the super-ego, we bring along with him the pattern of exchange relationships and reciprocations which are part of the external world. To identify with the father is to see ourselves as being embedded in this pattern of exchange relationships, which includes us but does not revolve around us. To see oneself from the standpoint of that framework, then, is to define social demands upon us as legitimate and justified. Following the super-ego means being able to stand with others on the basis of moral equality. The super-ego represents the readiness to see oneself from the standpoint of those with whom one is in interaction, and brings with it the principles of organization on which this interaction is based. It thus represents the internalized component of the exchange relationships, the mutual obligations, which structure society and define its roles and requirements.

The Oedipus complex and the girl

For some time Freud believed that the girl's experience during the Oedipal stage was symmetrical to that of the boy, substituting the father for the mother. This view, however, was fundamentally flawed since at the outset of this stage boys and girls have been through the same experiences. The young girl enters the Oedipus stage in the same way as the boy. She too loves her mother; she too perceives the father as an obstacle in her relationship with the mother.

What impressed Freud was that the experiences of many of his female patients indicated a far greater hostility towards their mothers than those of his male patients; this hostility often assumed the form of a lasting alienation from the mother, very rarely encountered among male patients. Many female patients reported strong feelings of resentment towards their mothers, often centred on oral frustration, as though the mother had deliberately denied them nourishment in early infancy, and also feelings of jealousy for the love and care that the mother lavished on their siblings and on other children. Freud sought the origins of these feelings and the divergent paths followed by the boy and the girl following the Oedipus episode in a unique factor, which distinguishes the boy's experiences from those of the girl. In his *New Introductory Lectures* (1933), Freud gives one of the clearest descriptions of this factor:

> I believe that we have found this specific factor, and indeed where we expected to find it, even though in a surprising form. Where we expected to find it, I say, for it lies in the castration complex. After all, the anatomical distinction between the sexes must express itself in psychical consequences. It was, however, a surprise to learn from analyses that girls hold their mother responsible for their lack of a penis and do not forgive her for their being thus put at a disadvantage.
>
> As you hear, then, we ascribe a castration complex to women as well. And for good reasons, though its content cannot be the same as with boys. In the latter the castration complex arises after they have learnt from the sight of the female genitals that the organ which they value so highly need not necessarily accompany the body. At this the boy recalls to mind the threats he brought on himself by his doings with that organ, he begins to give credence to them and falls under the influence of fear for castration, which will be the most powerful force in his subsequent development. The castration complex of girls is also started by the sight of the genitals of the other sex. They at once notice the difference and, it must be admitted, its significance too. They feel seriously wronged, often declaring that they want to 'have something like it too', and fall victim to 'envy for the penis', which will leave ineradicable traces on their development and the formation of their character and which will not be surmounted in even the most favourable cases without a severe expenditure of energy. (1933: 158–9)

We have quoted this extract at length because it presents one of the most highly contested Freudian concepts and arguments, that of *penis envy*, a concept that has become a taboo subject in its own right. Feminist critics have argued that it is at best the product of Freud's biased understanding, shaped by the subordinate position of women accorded by his cultural milieu, at worst the result of his own misogynism. For why should girls envy something they can do very well without? Why should the clitoris or indeed the rest of their sexual equipment be viewed as inferior? And why should their body and their ego be viewed as inferior on account of their sexual equipment? The practical issues raised by Freud's argument generate further questions. What if the girl has not learnt from sight the difference between her own genital equipment and that of the male? Even if we allow for penis envy to have been present among his female patients, why should this be a characteristic of the Oedipal stage in all women?

Psychoanalysts themselves are divided on the issue. (For an admirably clear exposition of the different approaches and some of the key texts on the subject, see Minsky, 1996.) Most orthodox Freudians continue to make use of the concept of penis envy, growing out of the girl's unconscious realization that she is 'deficient' in respect of her anatomical equipment ('already castrated'). Penis envy does not imply some objective evaluation of the merits of the male's genital apparatus, merely the desire (hence it is often also referred to as 'penis wish') for something that the girl does not possess. It is not a conscious desire, and along with most other Oedipal desires it is repressed in most people, so it is unrealistic to expect that it may be observed directly in individuals' conscious mental lives. Klein supported the view of the preponderance of feelings of envy, jealousy and resentment in women, and made use of the concept of penis envy in the therapy of her patients, but looked at it not as a primary psychic formation but as something derivative from an earlier and deeper envy. Laying great emphasis on the earliest stages of life, Klein argued that the original object of envy is the mother and especially the mother's breast as the source of all creativity (Klein, 1956/1986). One of the strongest defences of the Freudian position against the charges of feminist writers, like Friedan, Firestone, Millet and Greer, is offered by Juliet Mitchell in her book *Feminism and Psychoanalysis*, in which she maintains that Freud's arguments regarding the psychological distinction of the sexes represents a true understanding of the processes through which individuals enter a culture ruled by patriarchy. In such a culture, the phallus is the symbol of power. It is the power rather than its symbol that the girl wants, and only when she realizes that this will be denied to her does she develop envy. In arguing that girls 'at once notice the difference and, it must be admitted, its significance too', Freud allows this interpretation.

If the girl at the age of about five realizes that her gender denies her the power enjoyed by her male siblings, she develops a resentment towards her mother for failing to provide her with that which makes her different from the boys. Initially, she may see this shortcoming as a personal misfortune, but soon she realizes that this is not the case. Until now there have been no males and females in her universe; now she realizes that she has been short-changed in the arbitrary fact that she belongs to the subordinate sex. The discovery that the mother too, like herself, has no penis is almost as traumatic as the boy's realization that the father stands in the way of his desire. For the girl's

> love was directed to her *phallic* mother; with the discovery that her mother is castrated it becomes possible to drop her as an object, so that the motives for hostility, which have long been accumulating, gain the upper hand. This means, therefore, that as a result of women's lack of a penis they are debased in value for the girls just as they are for boys and later perhaps for men. (1933: 160)

This undoubtedly direct statement may be read as simply sexist – a pseudo-scientific account purportedly explaining the inferior position of women in society as determined by their anatomy. 'Phallocentrism' is a more polite word for expressing the same thing. Alternatively, however, it can be read as a profound psychological observation, accounting for the sexual devaluation of women in a culture dominated by men, which consigns the boy to a predicament of anxiety lest he should lose the power and the girl to envy for what she is excluded from. The girl's 'task' in overcoming her Oedipus complex (i.e. the complex of feelings, desires, phantasies and painful discoveries present in the Oedipal stage) is, if anything, even harder than the boy's. The girl can only overcome these painful experiences by exchanging her desire for the mother with the desire of being wanted, and the desire for a penis with the desire for a baby. The girl must, therefore, replace active desires with passive ones, while at the same time adding another factor, baby, to the unconscious equation faeces = gift = money that we examined earlier. The girl enters her Oedipal phase with the transference of her wish for a penis–baby on to her father. That the girl's interest turns towards the father, following her disappointment with the mother, comes as no surprise; the replacement of active desire, however, with passive desire is something that will take the girl much effort to accomplish. The girl's sexuality must undergo a transformation 'from the active wanting of her mother to the passive wanting to be wanted by the father' (Mitchell, 1974: 108), marked by a loss of interest in the clitoris as a source of sexual satisfaction. Ultimately, the girl, like the boy, will compensate for the disappointments of the Oedipal phase with a promise, in her case the promise that one day she may have a baby of her own. Thus the burning desire for a baby in later life, a desire whose strength seems to surprise future companions and husbands, is but the desire for that promise to be realized.

Like the boy, then, the girl experiences entry into culture, as signalled by the Oedipus stage, as a conflict between her desires and a superior law. But while the boy stumbles into the incest taboo, whose enforcer he perceives the father, the father who embodies that law, the girl directly encounters the law of patriarchy, the law which consigns her to a subordinate position to that of the male. The boy constructs a punitive super-ego which turns him into an enforcer of the law of patriarchy, driven to achievement and activity in order to gain a place he assumes to be rightfully his, the place as a future father and husband, a patriarch. The girl's super-ego, on the other hand, is likely to be less severe – in the absence of a fear of castration, the resolution of the Oedipus complex lacks the decisiveness of its male counterpart.

> The fear of castration being ... excluded in the little girl, a powerful motive also drops out for the setting-up of a super-ego and for the breaking-off of the infantile genital organization. In her, far more than in the boy, these changes seem to be the result of upbringing and of intimidation from outside which threatens her with loss of love. (1924: 321)

The girl, like the boy, will repress a large part of the desires that surface during this stage, notably the desire for her mother, the desire to have a penis and at least the sexual component of her desire to be wanted by the father. At the conclusion of the Oedipal stage, however, she has entered a very distinct path from that of the boy:

> The *confirmation* of his first love-object for the boy *which is his Oedipus* complex is renounced till he grows up like his father whom he meanwhile internalizes as his superego by identification. The *contradiction* of her first love-object for the girl, *which is her Oedipus complex*, never really need be renounced, for that is her feminine destiny. She may feel some rivalry with the mother for the father, but its strength will not be commensurate with the boy's rivalry with the father for the mother because, in a sense, the father is only second-best anyway, and furthermore, how much point is there in competing with another one of the same 'castrated' sex? Identifying with and thus to some degree internalizing the mother does not provide for the formation of a strong superego, for it is not she who, in a patriarchal culture, ever has the final word. (Mitchell, 1974: 111–12)

Latency

In discussing the paths of the girl and the boy through the Oedipus phase, we have presented the 'normal' course of events, a set of events which for all individuals assumes unique qualities, depending on the particularities of their upbringing, the existence of siblings and other close relatives, important family events and so forth. One important question regards the behaviour of the parents themselves. To what extent can they affect the outcome of the Oedipus complex through their own behaviour and the way in which they relate to their children? Many authors, since Freud, have argued that the parents' own behaviour is of vital importance, determining whether the child can emerge from the Oedipal phase as an outward-looking, active and competent person or one ridden by overwhelming anxieties, psychologically stunted and unable to lead a normal life. It should not be forgotten after all that the drama of Oedipus began with his cruel treatment at the hands of his parents and his abandonment. Parents who withhold love, who discriminate among their children, who ruthlessly thwart the child's desires, are undoubtedly not laying the foundations for a future happy life. Nor too are parents who indulge their children's every desire and favour, failing to impress upon them the indifference or even hostility of the world outside the home.

The truth, however, is considerably more elaborate than a simple parallel between parental behaviour and resolution of the Oedipus complex. There are children who will triumph against the most adverse upbringing, just as there are severe neurotics whose upbringing carries the marks of loving and caring. The reason for this is that, between the parent's actual behaviour and its effect on instinctual impulses and desires, the child interposes a thick layer of *phantasy*, one which is undoubtedly shaped by its earlier experiences, but not one that can be reduced to them. Thus, a loving and caring father can be experienced as a threatening and even a castrating one – his kindness but a part of his dreadful duplicity. Likewise, a generous, giving mother can be experienced as a withholding, rejecting one, where no change in her actual behaviour will convince the child otherwise. Besides, however, the parents are not free agents in their attitude towards their children; on the one hand, they are acting as members of the society to which they belong, adopting and adapting its criteria of how to bring up children, criteria which frequently change. The mother's decision whether and for how long to breast-feed her child, whether to breast-feed on demand or at fixed intervals, are matters influenced by the demands of work, husband and other children upon her time as well as by fashions and ideas on good parenting. On the other hand, the parents' behaviour towards their children carries the strong stamp of their own childhood experiences, either in the form of imitation or as a reaction-formation against those things for which they reproach their own parents. Finally, as Chodorow (1978) has pointed out in *The Reproduction of Mothering*, the parents', and especially the mother's, own behaviour towards her female child is different from that towards her male child. The particulars, therefore, of each individual's heritage from the Oedipal stage will vary. More importantly, as most of these particulars are repressed, they are not available for direct analysis, but require the intervening task of interpretation.

Reviewing this survey of the child's early development, we can make the following observations:

- Each stage is associated with pleasure deriving from one particular erotogenic zone.
- The stages of development merge, the conclusion of each signalling the arrival of the next.
- Each stage leaves permanent marks on the child's developing mental apparatus;

the major agencies of the mental apparatus, including the ego, the ego-ideal and the super-ego, emerge during this period.
- At each stage, the child's sexuality is frustrated by external reality; most of the desires which characterize each stage are renounced and repressed.
- At the conclusion of each stage, the child emerges with an enlarged universe of meanings, many of which are organized in polarities, such as inner–outer, good–bad, male–female, or in symbolic equations, such as faeces=gift=money.

The child now reaches a stage known as *latency*, the period from about five to eleven, during which many of the trials and disappointments of the earlier period are laid to rest, the child's sexuality assuming the form of intense curiosity and creativity. During this period, the child continues to experience sexual excitations, but he or she has now learned how to block his or her libido through repressions and reaction-formations or to channel it into non-sexual aims. It is during this period that children begin to discover the wonders of the world as well as their own creative powers; they may spend much time drawing, painting, reading and writing and begin to embark on grandiose projects and ideas. Their imagination blossoms and their games assume great variety and flair. It is also during this period that many children display extraordinary precocity in applications such as music, chess or mathematics. It is a period in which they may learn to sublimate sexual impulses into 'higher and finer' aims, replacing sexual objects with spiritual, artistic or cultural ones.

Yet, the child's earlier tribulations may continue to influence his or her life and may re-surface later in accentuated forms. Three particular mechanisms through which this may happen must be noted. Some individuals fail to repress totally the desires associated with a particular stage of libidinal development or acquire exaggerated reaction-formations against them. Such individuals may be said to have a *fixation* to the oral, anal or phallic stages, displaying either certain sexual aberrations or specific character traits, some of which will be explored in future chapters. Secondly, some individuals who seem to have successfully overcome the early stages may nevertheless regress to one of them under conditions in later social life which generate feelings of anxiety or frustration. *Regression*, as was seen earlier, is a type of ego defence. This phenomenon is especially important in the study of organizational phenomena, since later relationships with an organization's leaders may result in the individual regressing to modes of mental functioning characteristic of childhood. Thirdly, desires repressed in infancy and early childhood may at some later stage overwhelm the forces which keep them repressed and may re-surface in the form of *neurotic symptoms*, such as phobias, compulsions or psychosomatic disorders. These too are of interest to organizational studies as acutely pathological organizational environments may trigger off the collapse of individual defensive structures and their replacement with collective equivalents.

PUBERTY AND MATURE GENITALITY

As girls and boys enter puberty, their paths will diverge further, leading to a wide variation in sexual habits, desires and patterns. Many of the early instinctual impulses will find legitimate expression in mature sexuality; for example, oral impulses may seek gratification in kissing, phallic impulses in adolescent masturbation. It is at this stage that young women may re-orient their sexuality from the clitoris to the vagina, their development becoming still more asymmetrical from that of young men:

> Puberty, which brings about so great an accession of libido in boys, is marked in girls by a fresh wave of *repression*, in which it is precisely clitoridal sexuality that is affected. What is thus overtaken by repression is a piece of masculine sexuality. The intensification of the brake upon sexuality brought about by pubertal repression in women serves as a stimulus to the libido in men and causes an increase of its activity. Along with the heightening of libido there is also an increase of sexual overvaluation which only emerges in full force in relation to a woman who holds herself back and who denies her sexuality. When at last the sexual act is permitted and the clitoris itself becomes excited, it still retains a function: the task, namely, of transmitting the excitation to the adjacent female sexual parts, just as – to use a simile – pine shavings can be kindled in order to set a log of harder wood on fire. (1905b: 143)

In the course of puberty, women and men will face several new psychological tasks: rediscovering their sexuality and reconciling the pursuit of pleasure with the formation of lasting emotional commitments, the search for identity and self-esteem, the emotional distancing from the parents and the discovery of new role models to draw into their ego-ideal, the balancing of narcissistic self-absorption with the outward investment of libido. Numerous dangers lurk throughout a person's subsequent development: unresolved conflicts, fixations, denials, narcissistic self-obsession; in most (though not in all) cases, these dangers represent a return of troubled episodes from the past, which threaten to disrupt mental life in adulthood. Psychoanalysis envisages a state of *mature genitality* which is regarded as the desirable destination of a person's psychosexual development. This is a state in which the individual may experience sexual pleasure with his or her chosen partner, a pleasure which involves many component instincts but is nevertheless firmly centred in the genital area, a pleasure which enhances rather than inhibits emotional and affective commitment to the partner. This is also the time when the two early promises, in the name of which so many sacrifices and denunciations were made, the woman's desire for a baby and the man's desire for a woman of his own, will be tested. Will they rediscover the happiness of their early fusions with the mother, the happiness which was so brutally interrupted?

CONCLUSION

Having reached the topic of mature sexuality, whose organizational manifestations will be addressed in later chapters, we can conclude this chapter, which has introduced some of the core psychoanalytic theories and concepts, by observing that, while the importance of the sexual factor may recede in later life, it never disappears. Depth psychology views people in and out of organizations as sexual beings, which means beings with a sexual past, sexual desires and sexual phantasies. Moreover, it approaches sexuality in a broad and developmental manner: many of its manifestations are of a non-sexual nature and a large part of its history is repressed within each individual. As we shall see in subsequent chapters, it is a force of great value to the generation and sustenance of wider social relationships and yet, at the same time, it presents culture with an unpredictable, obstinate force which is difficult to tame, let alone control.

2 PSYCHOANALYSIS, CLINICAL PRACTICE AND THE HUMAN SCIENCES

The reader who has patiently followed the presentation of psychoanalytic theories and ideas in Chapter 1 may rightly ask 'What is the evidence for the existence of these concepts, for the validity of these arguments?' Readers who are introduced to psychoanalytic ideas and theories for the first time usually respond with a mixture of *déjà vu* ('Aha! I did not know that this is where the idea came from!') and astonishment ('How can this possibly be so?'). Some find that their impatience with these ideas eventually turns into hostility, at which point they give up any attempt at further understanding and join the now fashionable chorus of ignorant criticism. More receptive readers may give psychoanalytic concepts and theories the benefit of the doubt while they become familiarized with them. Some of these readers may intuitively grasp the power of these ideas and the paths which they open for understanding oneself and others. A few may embrace psychoanalysis with a fervour approaching faith, requiring no further proof or evidence than the fact that they have seen the truth and it works, at least for them. The majority, however, will rightly wish to evaluate the evidence and assess for themselves the claims of psychoanalytic ideas and theories, establishing those which are more useful, relevant or meaningful to them.

Assessing the claims of psychoanalytic theories and ideas, however, is far from easy. Since its early days, psychoanalysis has met with a reception which embraces both extremes, idolization and vilification. Few doctrines in the past hundred years have generated as much hostility as well as commitment as psychoanalysis, and few thinkers have attracted the rancour as well as the reverence that has surrounded Freud. In a way, hostility and commitment, adulation and rancour have fed on each other – the greater the accusations levelled against psychoanalysis and Freud, the greater the claims made for their perfection, and vice versa. Freud himself is cast in roles verging on the caricature, either as an infallible super-hero who revealed the inner secrets of mankind or as a charlatan who conned virtually everybody with his preposterous fabrications. Exaggerated claims from all sides are common, and the assessment of the theories themselves difficult. Another difficulty arises from the fact that Freud has been attacked simultaneously from many different quarters, and his defenders have had to fight on many fronts. For example, Freud is vociferously attacked for not believing his patients' accounts as truthful, and yet at the same time he is accused of entirely fabricating these self-same accounts as a projection of his own fantasies.

This chapter cannot begin to unravel the complexities of the claims and counter-claims of what have become known as 'the Freud Wars' (see Grünbaum, 1984; Frosh, 1987, 1997; Crews, 1993/1995; Forrester, 1997) or to address all the criticisms, personal, professional and academic, raised against Freud. It will, however, present some of the grounds for taking psychoanalysis seriously as one of the major traditions in the human sciences, whose theories, even if incomplete or flawed, can infinitely enrich the depth of our understanding of human actions and emotions. In doing so, we shall examine the complex relation of psychoanalysis as a body of theoretical arguments with the therapeutic practice centring on the relation between analyst and analysand. For, at the heart of most charges levelled at psychoanalysis lies a concern about the psychoanalyst's use of his or her patients' utterances as research material on which theoretical arguments are based. This material is easily presented as at best unreliable, at worst tampered with, contaminated or even fabricated.

The fact that Freud has become the object of not one but many wars is in itself an interesting sociological question. With the possible exceptions of Marx during the Cold War period and Darwin in his collision with creationist fundamentalism, few other theorists and their doctrines have generated as much passion as Freud. It is telling that, in 1995, an exhibition in the Library of Congress of its holdings from the Freud archives was postponed indefinitely. The decision was ostensibly attributed to financial reasons, but friends and critics of Freudian therapy were certain that it was the result of an outcry against the exhibition, spearheaded by a number of academics, who claimed that the exhibition would endorse psychoanalysis, which they saw as entirely without therapeutic or scientific value (see Irvin Molotsky, in *The New York Times*, 6 December 1995). Interestingly, earlier that year critics forced the revision of a Smithsonian Institution exhibition on the atom bomb in the Second World War and the resignation of the director of the National Air and Space Museum who had planned the exhibition. Psychoanalysis may not be quite as dangerous as the atom bomb, but as liable to stir up scientific sensitivities.

Most criticisms against psychoanalysis fall into four general arguments:

1 Psychoanalysis does not work as therapy.
2 Psychoanalysis is not scientific.
3 Freud was guilty of grave errors, misrepresentations and lies.
4 Freud exaggerated the novelty or importance of his discoveries.

Arguments 1 and 2 are almost invariably seen as reinforcing each other; argument 3 is often used in support of 2; argument 4 is used as a catch-all argument whereby, to the extent that psychoanalysis contains any truths, they are supposed to have been already known. Virtually all of the criticisms levelled at Freud derive from the way in which he treated his patients and the use he made of clinical material in developing his theories. To be sure, clinical material is not the only research material used by psychoanalysis as the basis of its theories. Works of art and cultural artefacts, routine experiences and actions of everyday life, religious and political practices, group and organizational phenomena and, of course, dreams, all offer testing ground for psychoanalytic ideas and hypotheses. Occasionally, psychoanalytic applications in these non-therapeutic domains attract criticism, so that Marxists, for example, have long criticized psychoanalysis for 'reducing' political behaviour to interpersonal politics, rebellions against the father and sibling rivalry. Yet, such criticisms are as nothing compared to the vociferous attacks aimed at the clinical material on which psychoanalysis is based. To address these attacks, it is necessary to introduce the reader to some of the main features of psychoanalytic treatments.

There is another reason why the reader interested in organizational processes may wish to familiarize him or herself with some of the ideas underpinning the clinical work of psychoanalysis. As we shall see later, some of the pathologies that afflict individuals, such as narcissistic, phobic or compulsive disorders, can at times take hold of organizations; organizations then become subject to particularly dysfunctional processes, delusional thinking and potential decay and collapse. It is then argued that psychoanalytic interventions at the level of organizations may restore their sense of reality and ability to function effectively, in a way not dissimilar to that of psychoanalytic interventions operating at the level of the individual. To assess these claims, it is important to introduce more generally the nature and objectives of psychoanalytic treatments.

THEORY AND THERAPY

Resistance, transference and suggestion

The existence of psychoanalysis is the result of Freud's early attempts to make sense of mental disorders, on the one hand, and dreams, on the other. As an ambitious physician (remember the Uncle Josef dream and his fantasies at the Grand Court of the Vienna University), Freud was evidently interested in discovering an effective method of treating neurotic disorders, radically different from earlier ones, which would bring him fame and money. By the late 1890s, he was claiming to have discovered just such a method. Having tried hypnotism, he opted for the technique of free association, whereby the patient reports freely, and without straining his or her thoughts during the analytic session as they spontaneously occur. This technique was adopted at the prompting of one of his early patients, Frl. Elisabeth von R, whose case is described in *Studies in Hysteria* (1895). The analyst then gradually proceeds to make interpretations of these reports, which in turn generate further associations. At times, the patient may be silent or angrily reject the analyst's interpretations. It is then that the analyst may interpret such behaviour as constituting *resistance*, an attempt by the patient to block access to his or her unconscious. This observation of resistance is a sure sign for the analyst that he or she has hit upon a repressed idea; the interpretation threatens to breach the repression and is, therefore, resisted by the patient. In the course of analysis, the patient may 'work through' these resistances, realizing that the repressions (for example, of a painful memory or a shameful desire) served by them are no longer necessary, or that the price in anxiety and disability paid for them is excessive. Part of the analyst's skill lies in offering interpretations at appropriate moments, not risking premature or wild interpretations which would raise powerful and justified resistances that would lead to an inhibition or termination of treatment.

The therapeutic process is not merely a process of identifying and working through resistances. These operations take place within a broader interpersonal phenomenon that characterizes the therapeutic relationship, *transference*. The concept of transference is one of the most significant and useful features in psychoanalytic theory and treatment. What Freud observed is that, in the course of treatment, patients do not merely recollect various events or experiences from their earlier lives, but seem actually to 're-live' them. A feeling or a desire, which once was directed against a particular individual, may re-surface within analytic treatment, displaced on to the person of the analyst. Thus a feeling of envy or resentment towards an older sibling may not be merely remembered but actually re-experienced towards the therapist. Transference, like the strong feelings in an individual's past, is almost invariably ambivalent, combining positive and negative feelings towards the analyst, which fight for predominance. Initially, Freud viewed transference as an impediment to therapeutic progress, as something that interfered with the recovery of repressed memories and brought about the patient's regression to a less mature and less rational mode of behaviour. By 1912, however, Freud had changed his view on this matter. He now viewed transference as a powerful instrument aiding the analyst in two indispensable ways. First, it enabled him or her to observe first hand, as it were, the actualization of the repressed: infantile experiences, long disappeared in time, may suddenly re-surface in the present, offering the analyst an opportunity to see at first hand the pathogenic process in the making. Secondly, to the extent that transference assumes positive (friendly and warm) as well as negative (hostile and distrustful) forms, it may be mobilized to aid the therapeutic process. The patient is thus encouraged to get better out of a love for the analyst, which revives earlier warm and positive experiences.

How then are psychoanalytic cures brought about? Freud insisted that the key to psychoanalytic cures is self-understanding; recovery is brought about through self-knowledge. This is epitomized in his programmatic aphorisms: 'Making the unconscious conscious' or 'Where id was, there ego shall be.' Recovery, for psychoanalysis, coincides with the lifting of pathogenic repressions and the restoration to a person of some of his or her unconscious wishes. This, he insisted, is what distinguishes psychoanalysis from *suggestive* treatments that are characteristic of other therapies, including hypnotism that he himself had practised. By analogy to Leonardo da Vinci's contrast between painting, which adds material to a canvas (*per via di porre*) and sculpture, which removes material from the block of stone (*per via di levare*), Freud argued that suggestive treatment 'superimposes something (a suggestion) and expects this to be strong enough to restrain the pathogenic idea from coming to expression. Analytic therapy, on the other hand, does not seek to add or to introduce anything new, but to take away something, to bring out something' (1904: 260–1).

In line with this, he insisted that psychoanalytic patients must not be bullied or in any way pressured into accepting the analyst's interpretations. 'The psychoanalytic treatment is founded on truthfulness . . . It is dangerous to depart from this sure foundation' (1915a: 164). The analyst is not a moral figure, respected or revered by the patient, as Rieff (1966) and MacIntyre (1981) have correctly remarked. The analysand is not asked to suspend his or her critical or enquiring qualities during the analytic session; nor is he or she asked to have faith in the analyst or in the treatment. 'The relationship between analyst and patient is based on a love of truth, that is, on the acknowledgement of reality, and that it precludes any kind of sham or deception' (1937: 248).

During the analytic session, the patient is invited to reveal all his or her thoughts, irrespective of how trivial, absurd or offensive they may seem. Contrary to disclosure under hypnosis, when the patient's resistances have been overcome by the hypnotist, in free association the patient's resistances operate both consciously and unconsciously to conceal, disrupt and distort his or her thoughts. The analyst must therefore interpret the hidden meanings of the patient's utterances, recollections and silences in a way analogous to the interpretation of dreams. These interpretations are gradually fed back to the patient, as he or she learns to overcome the resistances that have kept these pathogenic desires repressed. Thus, the neurotic is not seen as merely ignoring the truth but, as was suggested in our discussion of the NASA officials in the Introduction, actively as resisting it:

> The idea that a neurotic is suffering from a sort of ignorance, and if one removes this ignorance by telling him facts he must recover, is an idea that has long been superseded, and one derived from superficial appearances. The pathological factor is not his ignorance in itself, but the root of this ignorance in his inner resistances . . . In combating these resistances lies the task of therapy. (1910: 255)

In overcoming these resistances, the analyst finds a strong ally in the positive transference experienced by the patient, which provides the patient with a motive for recovery and release from his or her symptoms and anxiety. Negative transference, on the other hand, undermines this process since it leads the patient to regress to precisely those types of experiences which caused his or her condition in the first place. He or she may become irrational, spoilt, argumentative or hostile and may break off the treatment. Negative transference may give clues to the analyst as to the nature of the pathogenic factor, but undermines the gains made under positive transference.

But what is there to stop positive transference inducing the patient into accepting the analyst's interpretations, irrespective of their merit and truthfulness? This is an issue which Freud addresses in one of his last works:

> The therapeutic successes that occurred under the sway of the positive transference are open to the suspicion of being of a *suggestive* nature. If the negative transference gains the upper hand, they are blown away like chaff before the wind. We observe with horror that all our trouble and labour hitherto have been in vain. Indeed, what we might have regarded as a permanent intellectual gain by the patient, his understanding of psychoanalysis and his reliance on its efficacy, suddenly vanish. He behaves like a child who has not power of judgement of his own but blindly believes anyone whom he loves and no one who is a stranger to him. The danger of these states of transference evidently lies in the patient's misunderstanding their nature and taking them for fresh real experiences instead of reflections of the past. If he [or she] becomes aware of the strong erotic desire that lies concealed behind the positive transference, he believes that he has fallen passionately in love; if the transference changes over, then he feels insulted and neglected, he hates the analyst as his enemy and is ready to abandon analysis. In both these extreme cases he has forgotten the pact that he made at the beginning of treatment and has become useless for continuing the common work. It is the analyst's task constantly to tear the patient out of his menacing illusion and to show him again and again that what he takes to be new real life is a reflection of the past. And lest he should fall into a state in which he is inaccessible to all evidence, the analyst takes care that neither the love nor the hostility reach an extreme height. This is effected by preparing him in good time for these possibilities and by not overlooking the first signs of them. Careful handling of transference on these lines is as a rule richly rewarded. If we succeed, as we usually can, in enlightening the patient on the true nature of the phenomena of transference, we shall have converted dangers into gains. (1940: 411)

This extract is quoted at length because it demonstrates both the strengths and the potential vulnerabilities of the analytic method of treatment. The patient is fully conscious of the analyst's conceptual apparatus, which includes the concept of 'transference' itself. In this sense, analysis invites the analysand fully into its professional secrets, asking that he or she adopt the attitude of analyst *qua* scientist *vis-à-vis* him or herself. Philip Rieff, in *The Triumph of the Therapeutic* (1966), makes the point very clearly. Suggestive treatments derive from faith in the therapist and personal commitment to him or her as a healer. They are derivative of religion:

> Commitment therapies . . . operate by returning the individual to the cosset of his natal community with a more effective pattern of symbolic integration; the therapeutic effort is transformative; the therapist is characteristically either a sacral or an exemplary figure. Analytic therapies, on the other hand, are uniquely modern and depend largely on Freudian presuppositions. The therapeutic effort is not primarily transformative but informative. The assumption of analytic theory is that there is no positive community standing behind the therapist. (1966: 76)

An analytic treatment offers no promise of healing or salvation; instead of proffering a dream of a better future, personal, political or religious, analysis offers a new orientation towards life, one that accepts its pains and disappointments and seeks to maximize the potential for achievable satisfaction and happiness. Recovery can only be based on true knowledge of ourselves, and true acceptance of ourselves, our wishes and our deeper feelings. Nevertheless, Freud acknowledges that some spectacular cures can be the result of suggestion, even in analytic treatment. He warns against this by proposing that successes achieved through suggestive treatments may easily be reversed, a phenomenon familiar in hypnotic treatments, whose success recedes as the patient's dependence on the hypnotist declines. Thus, Freud proposes that the analyst must walk a tightrope between positive and negative transference, in order to effect a lowering of resistance and a will to recover without bringing about suggestive influences.

The social factor in the aetiology of neurosis

In discussing the aetiology of neurosis, i.e. the complex sets of interacting causes which precipitate it, one refers to those factors which account for the fact that some individuals experience incapacitating anxiety, disabling symptoms and an inability to lead a 'normal' life. Among those factors, the demands of society and culture cannot be overlooked; and, by this, we do not only consider the demands of societies and cultures distinguished by their brutality and irrationality, but virtually all societies and cultures in which there are relations of domination and subordination, injustices and restrictions on individual wishes which set in motion repressions and other defensive mechanisms. Different cultures have different definitions of normality or neurosis. Different cultures offer different collective substitutes for individual neurosis. Yet, as Marcuse argued: 'Behind all the differences among the historical forms of society, Freud saw the basic inhumanity common to all of them, and the repressive controls which perpetuate, in the instinctual structure itself, the domination of man by man' (1955: 235).

Marcuse, Brown and other theorists have argued that neurosis is a uniquely human condition because it is a uniquely social condition, one which derives from the nature of the demands that culture makes on our instinctual natures. Culture does not only require that we tame our more extreme impulses, namely those of a sexual or destructive nature, but also generates deeply seated anxiety and guilt for which it offers socially acceptable consolations. But these consolations, coming as they do in the shape of substitute satisfactions, ideals and illusions, merely reinforce the discontents for which they ostensibly offer consolations. Freud was keenly aware of the extent to which culture as a whole can be said to be neurotic. In a famous passage in *Civilization and its Discontents*, he noted:

> There is one question which I can hardly evade. If the development of civilization has a far-reaching similarity to the development of the individual and if it employs the same methods, may we not be justified in reaching the diagnosis that, under the influence of cultural urges, some civilizations, or some epochs of civilization – possibly the whole of mankind have become 'neurotic'? (1930: 338)

This, of course, leads to the fundamental tension which underlies the entire psychoanalytic discourse, the tension between the pragmatic concerns of therapy, those of returning the patient to a 'normal' life and the recognition that normality is itself an evasive ideal. 'While psychoanalytic theory recognizes that the sickness of the individual is ultimately caused and sustained by the sickness of his civilization, psychoanalytic therapy aims at curing the individual so that he can continue to function as part of a sick civilization without surrendering to it altogether' (Marcuse, 1955: 224).

This argument has several important implications. Neurosis should not be seen as an exceptional condition afflicting a few particularly vulnerable individuals; its existence is coextensive with the demands made by our civilization upon our instinctual nature. Different cultures may make different demands, but as we shall see in Chapter 8, what characterizes all of them is an underlying restriction of instinctual gratification accompanied by a provision of substitute satisfactions in the form of ideals and illusions. The discontents and illusions generated by different cultures may vary, but the facts of repression, mental conflict and substitute gratifications remain. This is why Norman O. Brown argues with Freud: 'The essence of society is the repression of the individual and the essence of the individual is the repression of himself' (1959: 4).

THEORIZING THE PATIENT

Neurosis and normality

The reader will by now have a basic understanding of the therapeutic claims made by psychoanalysis. Its aim, recovery through self-understanding, is meant to restore to the patient some of his or her own unconscious wishes and ideas, enabling him or her to accept them and learn to live with them, rather than suffer the consequences of keeping them repressed. From a philosophy of science perspective, this account of the nature of clinical interventions raises several difficulties. The first question that may be raised is 'How can a psychology rooted in the treatment and study of neurotic disturbances represent a valid theory of mental functioning?' The psychoanalytic answer to this question is unambiguous, even though it took Freud many years of work to reach it. Normality and neurosis are not characterized by different psychological processes, but represent different outcomes of similar psychological processes. 'Neurotics have approximately the same innate dispositions as other

ANOREXIA NERVOSA: A CONTEMPORARY MENTAL DISORDER

Different historical epochs have their characteristic types of mental disorders. Freud's *fin-de-siècle* Vienna had its unique *mélange* of phobias and compulsions, anxiety neuroses and 'neurasthenias', but the predominant type of neurosis in Freud's milieu was hysteria. The symptoms of hysteria were diverse but usually included bodily manifestations, such as the paralysis or loss of sensation of a limb or a perennial sore throat. The expression 'conversion hysteria' is meant to denote the transformation of a mental conflict into physical symptoms and the corresponding detachment of libido from a painful desire or idea and its channelling into a physical manifestation. The word 'hysteria' itself originates in the ancient Greeks' mistaken belief that it was a condition exclusively afflicting women and associated with disorders of the womb (*hysteron*). Freud sought to 'read' meaning into the (male or female) hysteric's symptoms as expressions of repressed ideas through the medium of the body.

Hysteria is a far less common type of disorder in contemporary society, though one suspects that many of today's myriad psychosomatic disorders would have been classified as hysterias one hundred years ago. In her provocative book *Hystories: Hysterical Epidemics and Modern Media*, Elaine Showalter (1997) has argued that chronic fatigue syndromes, recovered memory syndromes, the Gulf War syndrome and various other 'imaginary illnesses' and rumour panics of our end of century represent contemporary waves of mass hysteria, far more contagious than the hysterias of Freud's age. If official diagnosis of hysteria has declined precipitously, other disorders, notably eating disorders, have increased as substantially. By the late 1980s, it was estimated that over one million American women suffered from anorexia nervosa and bulimia. Male anorexia was hardly known until the 1980s, but by the 1990s males accounted for 5–10 per cent of anorexics. Compulsive over-eating and obesity appeared to afflict still greater proportions of the populations of developed countries, though the point at which being overweight turns into pathological obesity and becomes an eating disorder is not clear.

As social phenomena, anorexia nervosa and bulimia have attracted many different theories. In her pioneering books *Eating Disorders: Obesity, Anorexia Nervosa and the Person Within* (1973) and *The Golden Cage: the Enigma of Anorexia* (1978), Hilde Bruch argued that anorexia represents an adolescent's struggle for control of her life in a society dominated by images of slender women. Bruch argued that anorexics were generally obedient and over-compliant children, eager to please yet susceptible to family tensions, especially in their relations with their mothers. Susie Orbach, in her celebrated books *Fat is a Feminist Issue* (1978) and *Hunger Strike: the Anorectic's Struggle as a Metaphor for our Age* (1986), took a different view, arguing that anorexia represents not over-compliance to the images of consumer society, but a rebellion, especially by women, against the consumer society, a refusal of the poisoned chalice. Anorexics go on hunger strike, highly motivated one-person campaigns against a system which they see as denying them control over their bodies and their lives. Showalter, for her part, views anorexia nervosa as a fashionable disease of our time (which does not make it any less disturbing or painful), an epidemic which spreads as it acquires its celebrities, heroes, martyrs and gurus, through the stories and narratives propagated and sustained by the mass media. Various other sociological theories have been propounded about the nature and causes of the condition, highlighting various factors such as the identity problems of adolescence and the breakdown of the nuclear family unit.

At the individual level, however, it is difficult to generalize and impossible to identify a common pathogenic factor for all those susceptible to the condition. To be sure, certain symptoms, mechanisms and processes will be shared by many sufferers, though the precise development of the condition in each case is the result of a unique combination of factors. Treatments for anorexia include hospitalization or institutionalization in special treatment centres; there the patient is presented with a variety of weight restoration and resting regimes which may involve medication as well as a wide range of psychotherapies. Given that anorexia nervosa can be a life-threatening condition, it is hardly surprising that many practitioners view weight gain as the first priority. Even staunch advocates of psychotherapy, like Bruch, argue that psychotherapy cannot be effective if the patient's physical and mental functions are severely impaired and she faces imminent death.

> The psychotherapist's unease and anxiety will interfere with his therapeutic effectiveness, and the patient's continuous rigid pre-occupation with food, characteristic of the starvation state, will make exploration of relevant dynamic factors virtually impossible. Furthermore, during this extreme state of starvation, anorexics live in such social isolation that the interpersonal experiences explored in psychotherapy are completely absent. (Bruch, 1978: 97)

Yet, as Orbach has shown, hospitalization and force-feeding a person whose entire will and identity are focused on the denial of food can only be experienced as a profound violation, thus reinforcing the very factors which cause the condition.

> Confined to bed or to a cubicle, she is re-fed with calorie-enriched food under the controlled conditions where she may be watched, accompanied to the toilet, denied access to her own clothes, books, friends and the telephone until she has reached the weight that the doctor has designated as safe. While there may be some attempt to provide therapy, this is compromised by the fact that the institution involved in the re-feeding – the act that can feel so abusive and intrusive to the anorectic – is the same as the one providing the therapy. It's hard for an anorectic to feel that those who make her eat are also helping her. (Orbach, 1997)

While weight may be gained during hospitalization, it is often swiftly lost upon discharge, when the anorexic can re-claim control over herself. Such treatment focuses on the symptoms without addressing their causes. It treats the loss of weight as the problem, disregarding the fact that anorexia (along with other mental disorders) is itself a solution to a problem, a flawed solution perhaps, but a solution all the same.

Some types of psychotherapy, such as behaviour modification treatment, also address the symptoms; this treatment involves the cooperation of the patient in as much as she is offered various deals, whereby weight gain is rewarded by various privileges and loss of weight checked by the withdrawal of the privileges. Other types of psychotherapy seek to go deeper, establishing the causes of the condition and helping the patient overcome them; these include cognitive and personal construct therapy and family therapy. Hilde Bruch (1978) advocates a therapy which seeks to restore the patient's self-esteem, and dispel various self-deceptions to which she desperately clings.

> [The patient's] whole life is based on certain faulty assumptions that need to be exposed and corrected. Deep down every anorexic is convinced that her basic personality is defective, gross, not good enough, 'the scum of the earth', all her efforts directed toward hiding the fatal flaw of her basic inadequacy. She is also convinced that the people around her, her family, friends, and the world at large, look at her with

disapproving eyes, ready to pounce and to criticize her. The picture of human behavior and interaction that anorexics form in their smooth-functioning homes is one of surprising cynicism and pessimism.

Therapy must help the patient to uncover the error of these convictions, to let her recognize that she has substance and worth of her own, and that she does not need the strained and stressful superstructure of an artificial ultra-perfection . . . Treatment with anorexics involves the great problem of establishing honest communication. As a group they are manipulative and deceitful; anything goes in their effort to defeat a weight-gaining program. You have to establish from the beginning that psychotherapy deals with their inner self-doubt, not with weight and dieting. (Bruch, 1978: 136–7)

Bruch rejects psychoanalytic treatments of anorexia as ineffective and potentially harmful:

Many therapists in approaching an anorexic patient are tied to outmoded concepts of psychoanalytic treatment, even those who otherwise work with contemporary concepts. Many stress the symbolic meaning of the non-eating and the underlying unconscious problems, fantasies, and dreams, and interpret their unconscious meaning to the patient. (1978: 123)

But anorexics

experience 'interpretations' as indicating that someone else knows what they truly mean and feel, and that they themselves do not understand their own thoughts. The goal of individual therapy should be to help them develop a valid self-concept and the capacity for self-directed action. The therapist's task is to assist patients in uncovering their own abilities and resources for thinking, judging, and feeling. 'Giving interpretations' contradicts this goal. It does not matter whether or not an interpretation is correct; what is harmful is that it confirms a patient's fear of being defective and incompetent, doomed to dependence. (1978: 123)

Whether psychoanalysis in its different therapeutic variants is an efficacious treatment for anorexia is a debatable point. It is quite possible that it is not a suitable therapy for the majority of anorexics, for one reason or other. Some psychoanalysts may object to Bruch's argument, however, by pointing out that the effects she describes are those of 'wild' or 'premature' interpretations, which are harmful in treating every type of disorder, not just anorexia. Interpretations need not be intrusive and may involve a collaborative effort between analyst and patient. Psychoanalysts may also view Bruch's attempt to help the patient strengthen her 'self-concept' as a form of suggestive treatment which ultimately leaves the deeper causes of the disease untouched. Why should an anorexic swap a 'self-concept' organized around the palpable struggle against fat for one based on the recognition that 'she has substance and worth of her own'? Where does this substance and worth come from? Does this type of therapy not begin to sound much like the consolatory imposition of the therapist's view (the same therapist who regards the patient as manipulative and deceitful) over the patient's?

That the anorexic suffers from serious delusions is not doubted by any of the therapeutic authorities. Even the staunchest advocates of her rights to control her body acknowledge that an anorexic's perception of her body is severely distorted as indeed are several other aspects of her self-image. In a period when virtually any self-belief or opinion easily masquerades as self-discovery, growth or development, the anorexic's stubborn insistence on seeing her skeletal self as overweight alone stands as a warning of the extent to which we can all deceive ourselves, often with the collusion of others. When the concept of 'reality' has become so flexible or relative as to accommodate virtually any eccentric opinion or argument, the anorexic's 'reality' of her body is still viewed as less legitimate than that of the parental, medical or therapeutic authorities that surround her. A psychoanalytic approach to anorexia nervosa, too, views the anorexic's image of herself as distorted. Neither interpretations nor facts, however, can restore her sense of reality or indeed her sense of worth and identity. Instead, it would seek to address the unconscious material which expresses itself in the disease as well as the resistances which prevent recovery.

Unlike humanistic psychotherapies, however, a psychoanalytic treatment refuses to console the patient with platitudes about her worth and substance, and views the strategies which sustain her self-starvation (i.e. her deceitfulness and manipulativeness) not as character failures but as resistances to the analyst's attempts at probing what are well-organized repressions. The analyst's refusal to offer consolatory illusions to whitewash the damaging delusions of the condition does not make his or her task any easier, nor is there any guarantee of its success. In contrast to the optimistic outlook of the humanistic psychotherapies, the outlook of psychoanalysis is more measured. Many conditions are too deeply embedded in the individual psyche to be overcome: the relief offered to the patient by his or her symptoms, especially the relief from anxiety, guilt and inner conflict, is such that the patient cannot relinquish them, even when his or her physical survival is called into question. Furthermore, the patient derives a 'secondary gain' from his or her condition: the practical advantages of making him or herself the centre of attention, attracting the sympathy, concern, flattery or even the anger of others, and avoiding the ordinary wear and tear of everyday life. Thus, Freud argued that 'the expectation that every neurotic phenomenon can be cured may, I suspect, be derived from the layman's belief that the neuroses are something quite unnecessary which have no right to exist' (1933: 189).

Freud's observation does not offer much solace to the parents, friends and relatives of those suffering from life-threatening conditions like anorexia. It signals the limits of psychoanalysis in treating mental disorders, some of which are altogether outside its therapeutic orbit. More importantly, it suggests that eating disorders, like all mental disorders, have 'a right to exist', something which may seem old-fashioned and defeatist in the days of Prozac. Mental disorders, argued Freud, are complex phenomena resulting from a combination of social, family and constitutional factors, over which any therapy has but limited or no power. The human predicament is not an easy one: not least because of the aggressive, destructive and self-destructive drives that operate within each one of us, because of the pressures and restrictions imposed on us by our culture, and because no family can adequately contain all of the explosive feelings that family life generates. Under these pressures, human suffering is not the exception, but rather part of what Freud saw as the tragic fate of humanity. Inner conflicts are unavoidable, leading to more or less severe mental disorders with their allied symptoms, feelings and self-deceptions.

For certain disorders, psychoanalysis offers a quietly effective treatment. For others, it offers temporary relief. Others are beyond its powers. To the extent that mental disorders reflect the underlying conflicts and contradictions of culture, psychoanalysis can only provide limited relief. In closing his first major book, *Studies in Hysteria* (1895), co-authored with Josef Breuer, Freud addresses a common complaint of his patients:

> 'Why, you tell me yourself that my illness is probably connected with the circumstances and events of my life. You cannot alter these in any way. How do you propose to help me, then?' And I have been able to reply: 'No doubt fate would find it easier than I do to relieve you of your illness. But you will be able to convince yourself *that much will be gained if we succeed in transforming your hysterical misery into common unhappiness.* With a mental life that has been restored to health you will be better armed against that unhappiness.' (1895: 393, emphasis added)
>
> If in Freud's times sexual frustration was precipitating an epidemic of hysteric attacks, it would be hard to deny that eating disorders are among the preferred disorders of our own culture, a culture that combines riotous consumption with an iconic idealization of the emaciated feminine image.
>
> **Further reading**
>
> Bemporad and Herzog (1989); Bruch (1973 and 1978); Brumberg (1988); Farrell (1995); Johnson (1991); Kaplan (1986); Orbach (1978); Orbach (1986); Orbach (1997).

people, they have the same experiences and they have the same [psychological] tasks to perform' (1940: 417).

The conclusion of Freud's early investigations into neurotic disorders convinced him that human life abounds in neurotic symptoms. Some of these are recognized as such, notably if they inhibit the 'normal' functioning of an individual, while others may go unnoticed. Dreams are, *par excellence*, neurotic symptoms, common among 'normal' people, as indeed are various kinds of religious or organizational rituals, which involve compulsive repetition. Each individual displays myriads of neurotic traits, including compulsions, superstitions, phobias, nervous tics and twitches, psychosomatic pains and aches, inhibitions, irrationalities, violent likes and dislikes and other 'little crazinesses', which are an important part of his or her mental functioning, though hardly classifying him or her as a neurotic. What singles out the neurotic from the normal is his or her inability to lead a life recognized as normal by the majority of society. Thus, the line between normal and neurotic is a not just a blurred one, but one which is socially constructed: highly 'neurotic' individuals may function quite 'effectively' in severely 'neurotic' environments, in which normal individuals may become quite dysfunctional.

Helping individuals to lead a 'normal life' is the task of *adjustment*, a task which enabled psychoanalysis, that pessimistic doctrine of humanity, to be accepted and eventually become an important part of the fabric of American society. With Freud's therapeutic pessimism, American psychoanalysis juxtaposed a humanistic outlook, in which mental disorders can be fixed, opening the way for personal growth, development and happiness. The more disturbing features of psychoanalytic theory, including destructive and self-destructive drives, the unavoidability of psychic conflict and the burden of social restrictions upon the individual, were suitably forgotten or corrected to support the view that mental health, like physical health, resides in eliminating the pathogenic agent, the painful memory, the bad parent, the low self-esteem and restoring to the individual the happiness that was rightly his or hers. It is for this reason that, as Bettelheim (1983: 40ff) and others have noted, psychoanalysis in America has remained closely allied to medicine, which conferred on it the scientific legitimacy of a reputable profession. Psychoanalysts enjoyed considerable prestige and power, as an ever-widening range of mental disorders was brought within its therapeutic orbit.

It is not altogether surprising, then, that when the efficacy of analytic treatments is challenged by superior and cheaper technologies of the soul, notably anti-depressant and tranquillizing drugs and, potentially, neuro-psychiatry and genetic engineering, much of their legitimacy is undermined. That psychoanalysis is experiencing a sharp institutional decline in the United States is not in doubt. Critics, like Frederick Crews (1993/1995), are arguing that at long last people have realized that psychoanalysis does not work as therapy and can even have damaging effects. Crews, one of Freud's most intemperate critics, contends that Freud's 'therapeutic successes, supposedly the chief warrant that his psychological theory was correct, appear to have been non-existent and . . . he lied about them brazenly and often' (1993/1995: 109). Crews's polemic against psychoanalysis in *The Unknown Freud* rallied some of Freud's defenders, whose contributions, along with Crews's, were subsequently published in *The Memory Wars: Freud's Legacy in Dispute* (Crews, 1993/1995). Some of Freud's defenders (see the contributions by Olds, Ostow and Luborsky) argued that the decline of psychoanalysis as therapy is mostly due to the promise of cheap, quick and painless cures proposed by drug treatments, which predictably find favour with medical insurance companies. They provide some evidence of the beneficial effect of analysis on a range of mental disorders, which Crews dismisses as the placebo effect, i.e. being of a suggestive nature.

A different type of defence, however, can be staged not by strengthening the claims of psychoanalysis as an alternative to Prozac and other technologies of recuperation and adjustment, but by abandoning the criterion of therapeutic success as a test of the validity or value of psychoanalytic ideas. This is the position taken by Jonathan Lear:

> It is a mistake to think of psychoanalysis and Prozac as two different means to the same end. The point of psychoanalysis is to help us develop a clearer, yet more flexible and creative, sense of what our ends might be. 'How shall we live?' is, for Socrates, the fundamental question of human existence – and the attempt to answer that question is, for him, what makes human life worthwhile. And it is Plato and Shakespeare, Proust, Nietzsche and, most recently, Freud who complicated the issue by insisting that there are deep currents of meaning, often crosscurrents, running through the human soul which can at best be glimpsed through a glass darkly. This, if anything, is the Western tradition: not a specific set of values, but a belief that the human soul is too deep for there to be any easy answer to the question of how to live. (Lear, 1995: 24)

Freud himself was not a therapeutic enthusiast, in spite of some exaggerated claims that he made in his early writings, and, contrary to Crews's view, did not see therapeutic success as a test of scientific validity or value. He certainly saw it as less effective than some other therapies, notably those based on faith:

> Psycho-analysis is really a method of treatment like others. It has its triumphs and its defeats, its difficulties, its limitations, its indications . . . And here I should like to add that I do not think that our cures can compete with those of Lourdes. There are so many more people who believe in the miracles of the Blessed Virgin than in the existence of the unconscious. (1933: 188)

The 'contamination' of clinical material as research material

As the above extract makes perfectly clear, Freud was also quite aware that even when psychoanalytic treatments work, they may work in a suggestive way, people 'believing' in the unconscious is in a way similar to 'believing' in the Virgin Mary. This placebo effect is the key to Crews's attempt not only to discredit psychoanalysis as a therapy, but more importantly to destroy its credentials as a valid and valuable body of scientific knowledge. Crews (1993/1995) with the help of Grünbaum (1984), resuscitates an argument first put forward by Popper (1965), namely that clinical observations used by Freud and those after him to develop psychoanalytic theories are so tainted by suggestion that they are entirely without value as research material. The argument operates at two levels. The patient who has been put through psychoanalytic treatment internalizes many of the concepts and ideas of psychoanalysis and begins to have Freudian dreams, make Freudian slips and display Freudian symptoms. The analyst, for his or her part, projects his or her own psychoanalytic fantasies on to the patient, proposing psychoanalytic interpretations, which the patient, in his or her suggestible state, accepts as valid. Conversely, if the patient rejects these interpretations, he or she is seen as resisting, therefore ostensibly confirming their validity. The analyst has therefore discovered as sure a way of supporting his or her claims as medieval judges in convicting witches. '"Clinical" observations which analysts naively believe confirm their theory', concludes Popper, 'cannot do this any more than the daily confirmations which astrologers find in their practice' (1965: 37–8). Hence the vast amounts of material collected by Freud and other analysts during their long hours of clinical work are 'contaminated' – quite useless as research material (for a critique of this view, see Fischer and Greenberg, 1996).

Popper's critique of psychoanalysis (along with Marxism and Darwinism) as a pseudo-science because of its failure to meet his criterion of falsifiability has been widely discussed. This criterion, i.e. the ability of a discipline to provide a set of tests which it may fail, is what in Popper's view distinguishes proper sciences from other bodies of faith, belief and superstition. His argument is essentially that these are closed bodies of doctrine which do not permit independent validation of their claims. In the case of a Freudian interpretation, for example, if the patient agrees with it, it is seen as valid, but if the patient rejects it, it is still seen as valid since the patient is said to be resisting the interpretation, which proves its validity. More generally, Popper charges psychoanalysis with an inability to state what evidence would falsify any of its theories, for example the existence of the unconscious, the Oedipus complex or infantile sexuality. The debate on whether psychoanalysis can claim to be a science has been one in which the two sides have progressively hardened their positions, almost invariably turning into *ad hominem* charges: an argument is seen to be invalid if its author can be shown to have an axe to grind or an ulterior motive (itself an indirect acknowledgement of unconscious processes at play).

It is interesting that when debates in the philosophy of science have moved beyond Popper's falsificationism, this criterion is still widely used to discredit psychoanalysis. Popper's own critics, like Feyerabend and Kuhn, argued that many of his requirements (for example, no *ad hoc* sub-explanations, no inconsistencies between standards of proof and standing of theories, no contamination of observation by theory) are not only untenable, but also if really adhered to would grind the production of scientific knowledge to a halt. Many if not the majority of 'hard' scientists proceed in counter-intuitive, counter-falsificationist, counter-methodical ways and some of the best discoveries have been made in this way (see Sokal and Bricmont, 1998, for an account of this argument by natural scientists who are no methodological anarchists). If every new theory or creative idea were submitted to Popperian criteria it would be nipped in the bud before it had time to develop or test itself. It is now widely accepted that new disciplines create new ways of observing the world and new ways of relating observations to theories. Observations and theories are not separate entities but often interacting ones, contrary to the strictures of logical positivism and its off-shoots.

Freud, like many scientific pioneers, was also quite a good propagandist for his theories. Anticipating many subsequent criticisms, he tried to present his theories as a hard-and-fast science, as he supposed physics and medicine to be. He believed that the main danger facing psychoanalysis was a descent into mysticism and believed that medicine and physics were important correctives. Yet, he was perfectly clear (at least after the mid-1890s) that psychoanalytic method and theories differed in many ways from a positivist model of scientific theory. Interpretations and inferences about unconscious mental processes cannot be made along similar lines as medical diagnoses of physical disorders. The standards of validity of interpretations and the nature of inferences are different from those of other disciplines. This does not mean that all psychoanalytic inferences and interpretations are valid and anyone who has studied psychoanalysis knows that interpretations are submitted to various tests before being accepted, and even then their acceptance is almost invariably provisional and qualified (see Introduction).

Towards the end of his life Freud explicitly recognized the futility of pretending that psychoanalysis was a true off-shoot of medicine. In the 'Postscript to "An Autobiographical Study"', he wrote:

> After a lifelong detour over the natural sciences, medicine, and psychotherapy, my interests returned to those cultural problems which had once captivated the youth who had barely awakened to deeper thought. These interests had centered on 'the events of the history of man, the mutual influences between man's nature, the development of culture, and those residues of prehistoric events of which religion is the foremost representation . . . studies which originate in psychoanalysis but go beyond it. (trans. in Bettelheim, 1983: 48)

Trying to defend psychoanalysis as a natural science does it little justice, although Fischer and Greenberg (1996) have diligently reviewed 800 empirical studies and have found extensive support for some, though not for all, psychoanalytic theories. Nature does not communicate meanings, human beings do. It is, however, true that in current Anglo-Saxon culture, where much else sinks to the standing of 'mere opinion' or 'story-telling', science alone, in the idealized model of physics or biology, has come to be viewed as rational, legitimate knowledge. There scarcely seems to be room for wisdom, for common-sense, for savvy or for intuition as legitimate types of understanding. This is one of the enduring paradoxes of our culture – our view that science provides the only sure and objective knowledge of anything, alongside a simultaneous suspicion of scientists as excitable, morally retarded obsessives, who should not be trusted with their discoveries.

Freud was writing within a different cultural milieu, one which took for granted a deep distinction between natural and human sciences, *Naturwissenschaften* and *Geisteswissenschaften*, the latter encompassing not only psychology and sociology, but also history, ethics and other areas of philosophy. Meaning, will and motives, as well as a lasting preoccupation with the nature of the good life, are the vital concerns of the *Geisteswissenschaften*, which generally deal with the peculiarities and singularities of unique, unrepeatable events rather than predictable regularities. Max Weber, one of Freud's great contemporaries, approached sociological understanding (*verstehen*) as a type of understanding which addresses the meanings and motives of social action, one which necessitates not only observation, but also interpretation (Weber, 1913/1947: 94–7). For Weber, the ways in which individuals make sense of their actions and those of others is an essential part of explanation in the human sciences, yet not one that can be taken 'directly', since individuals often have clashing or hidden motives; interpretation is as central a feature of his sociology as it is of Freudian psychology:

> Every interpretation attempts to attain clarity and certainty, but no matter how clear an interpretation as such appears to be from the point of view of meaning, it cannot on this account alone claim to be the causally valid interpretation. On this level it must remain only a peculiarly plausible hypothesis. In the first place the 'conscious motives' may well, even to the actor himself, conceal the various 'motives' and 'repressions' which constitute the real driving force of his action. Thus in such cases even subjectively honest self-analysis has only a relative value. Then it is the task of the sociologist to be aware of this motivational situation and to describe and analyse it, even though it has not actually been concretely part of the conscious 'intention' of the actor; possibly not at all, at least not fully. This is a borderline case of the interpretation of meaning. Secondly, processes of action which seem to an observer to be the same or similar may fit into exceedingly various complexes of motives in the case of the actual actor . . . Third, the actors in any given situation are often subject to opposing and conflicting impulses, all of which we are able to understand. In a large number of cases we know from experience it is not possible to arrive at even an approximate estimate of the relative strength of conflicting motives and very often we cannot be certain of our interpretations. (1913/1947: 96–7)

Social sciences in the United States and Britain have, throughout the twentieth century, pretended that there is no difference between themselves and the natural sciences. At worst, they saw themselves as less-developed versions of the natural sciences which, given time, would approach the same degree of objectivity and rigour as the established natural sciences. Behaviourist psychology and empirical sociology, among other human sciences, aspired to the types of subject-free generalizations propounded by the dominant scientific model. In popular culture social scientists did not attain the status of natural scientists, either as great pioneers or as dangerous freaks. Yet, concerned not to be branded as charlatans peddling glorified common-sense, social scientists sought to stay as close to the narrow model of science, that of natural science, as possible. Abandoning this model seems to many friends of psychoanalysis to be forsaking any claim to legitimacy, validity or value. Yet, as Lear (1995: 25) has argued:

> If psychoanalysis were to imitate the methods of physical science, it would be useless for interpreting people. Psychoanalysis is an extension of our ordinary psychological ways of interpreting people in terms of their beliefs, desires, hopes and fears. The extension is important because psychoanalysis attributes to people other forms of motivation – in particular wish and fantasy – which attempt to account for outbreaks of irrationality and other puzzling human behavior. In fact, it is a sign of psychoanalysis's success as an interpretive science that its causal claims cannot be validated in the same way as those of the physical sciences.

From a similar perspective, John Forrester (1997) has developed a series of interesting arguments responding to some of Grünbaum's (1984) criticisms of the scientific claims of psychoanalysis. Forrester suggests that the monolithic conception of 'science' as an entity that can be identified via a single criterion, such as Popper's falsifiability, is itself misleading and untenable, even in the case of the natural sciences. Instead of 'science', he adopts Ian Hacking's (1990) concept of 'scientific reasoning', which comes in six varieties: postulation and deduction; experimental exploration; hypothetical construction of models by analogy; ordering of variety by comparison and taxonomy; statistical analysis of regularities of populations; and historical derivation of genetic development. Different sciences make use of different combinations of such reasonings, rather than consistently aiming at fulfilling a particular criterion. While psychoanalysis makes use of observational techniques, it cannot use them in the same way as astronomy or chemistry, since the observing subject and the observed object coincide. In these circumstances, it makes no sense to talk of contamination of the research material, since the contamination is itself part of this material and the process of contamination is itself what is being investigated.

The claims of psychoanalysis

If psychoanalysis cannot be defended as a natural science what would its claims to validity and value be? In the first place, as we have argued in the Introduction, psychoanalysis can be defended as an interpretative discipline, which can reveal the meaning behind opaque phenomena. In this respect, psychoanalysis offers not only a systematic way of examining symbolic transformations of ideas in the human mind but powerful insights into human motivation and the meaning of human actions and experiences. Of course, one does not need psychoanalysis in order to interpret one's own behaviour or that of others for that matter. Everybody is ceaselessly involved in interpretation and self-interpretation. Psychoanalysis, however, enables one to go beyond 'innocent interpretations' and probe for self-deceptions and double-meanings. Interpretation does not mean jumping to conclusions, but on the contrary 'the systematic exercise of suspicion' (Ricoeur, 1970: 32) in every respect, including suspicion over the interpreter's own motives and the merits of interpretations themselves. In this sense, the constant probing of Freud's own motivations as well as those of his critics and supporters and the ensuing *ad hominem* arguments are themselves features of what amounts to a psychoanalytic discourse.

Some theorists and therapists are content to defend psychoanalysis as just that, a sophisticated hermeneutic technique whose main claim is as a sense-making device. In this way, they argue, psychoanalysis and its core concepts have become part of contemporary culture, which can no longer be denied, rejected or avoided. In W. H. Auden's memorable lines, written after Freud's death, he 'is no more a person now, but a whole climate of opinion under whom we conduct our different lives'. Thus, Forrester suggests that what now passes as common-sense is continuous with psychoanalytic discourse.

> Psychoanalysis has always started from and opposed the fact that we are all experts on ourselves and each other. It is the science of that individual expertise – both for and against it. And . . . [furthermore] psychoanalysis is popular culture, the popular culture not only of films and TV, not only of detective stories and avant-garde art (because today the

avant-garde is also popular culture), but also the popular culture of gossip, of sorting out relationships with employers, spouses, and children. (1997: 246)

The sophistication in Forrester's argument lies in his ability to maintain psychoanalysis both as part of popular culture and as a critical engagement with it. After all, if psychoanalysis consisted of only gossip and everyday explanation, material for chat-shows and films, a discourse for making sense of our and other people's lives, it would not be so different from astrology; many people make sense of their lives through that set of ideas. What sets psychoanalysis apart is that it provides a comprehensive body of theoretical concepts and propositions, fallible, conditional and capable of further development, which account for the infinite variety, depth and uniqueness of human experience, emotion and desire. Lear (1995: 23) is quite right in pointing out that:

> there is something that would count as a global refutation of psychoanalysis: if people always and everywhere acted in rational and transparently explicable ways, one could easily dismiss psychoanalysis as unnecessary rubbish. It is because people often behave in bizarre ways, ways which cause pain to themselves and to others, ways which puzzle even the actors themselves, that psychoanalysis commands our attention.

Accepting psychoanalysis as a set of ideas which enable us to make sense of irrational and bizarre forms of behaviour and experience dictates that the idea of 'making sense' itself cannot be taken for granted. If interpretation is the systematic exercise of suspicion, as Ricoeur insists, psychoanalysis reserves the greatest suspicion for consciousness itself:

> The philosopher trained in the school of Descartes knows that things are doubtful, that they are not such as they appear; but he does not doubt that consciousness is such as it appears to itself; in consciousness, meaning and consciousness of meaning coincide. Since . . . Freud, this too has become doubtful. After the doubt about things, we have started to doubt consciousness. (Ricoeur, 1970: 33)

What psychoanalysis, following Freud, has done is to challenge the contents of consciousness, without resorting to the concept of lying. A person may genuinely claim to feel something ('I love him', 'I do not envy her') or to believe something ('He insulted me', 'Popper has proved that psychoanalysis is a pseudo-science', 'Freud discovered the unconscious') and yet, at the same time, be expressing something else besides, something which is unknown to themselves. At the level of human experience, unlike the realm of natural science, truth and lies are not opposites; one may be lying while telling the truth and telling the truth while lying. A true science of meaning is not reducible to the consciousness of meaning, but is concerned with the systematic understanding of the movements, distortions and metamorphoses of meaning as it moves in and out of consciousness. For this to happen, we must take seriously the implications of the unconscious.

The idea of the unconscious is ridden by paradox. While popular culture now acknowledges at every turn that people are driven by inner forces which are not always clear to them, it also places a high price on raw experience and on the value of personal testimony. While constantly preoccupied with destructive or 'evil' powers at work in people, popular culture refuses to accept these powers as part of our psychological make-up, clinging on to the rhetoric of growth, self-help and development, which views happiness as a technical matter. As Lear (1995: 25) has argued, this is what attacks on Freud amount to:

> The real object of attack – for which Freud is only a stalking horse – is the very idea of humans having unconscious motivation. A battle may be fought over Freud, but the war is over our culture's image of the human soul. Are we to see humans as having depth – as complex psychological organisms who generate layers of meaning which lie beneath the surface of their own understanding? Or are we to take ourselves as transparent to ourselves?

The same issue, unconscious motivation, lies at the core of scientific attacks on psychoanalysis. Most criticisms of psychoanalysis amount to direct or indirect refusal to acknowledge the implications of the unconscious (see Mitchell, 1974: 5ff). Interestingly, this happens even with critics who use psychoanalytic types of argument against psychoanalysis, as in the case of Esterson, who accuses Freud of 'projecting' his own phantasies on to his patients (1993: 133). If Freud had no unconscious, how could he be projecting its content?

The major complication in scholarly disputes on the unconscious arises from the fact that science itself, both in the broad and in the narrow sense, is not separate from or unrelated to the workings of the unconscious. The search for truth or for new scientific or philosophical theories is itself liable to unconscious motives, especially when we consider the passion with which creative scientists invest their work. The creative imagination of science, the scientist's commitment and loyalty to some theorists and their ideas, his or her consuming envy and hate of others, these are not processes that may be analysed and adjudicated through the clinical power of reason alone, irrespective of the scientist's protestations to the contrary. They are in part emotional and, at times, irrational processes, which stray into the domain of the unconscious, hence the importance of rhetoric and presentation in scientific discourse (see Feyerabend, 1975, 1978; Edmondson, 1984; Billig, 1989; Simons, 1989). Science is itself the product of human passion, whose understanding invites us to delve into the scientist's unconscious motivation. Few scientists are likely to abandon a lifetime's commitment to particular theoretical or methodological attachments simply because there are claims to the effect that they have been 'falsified' or because there are charges that they are 'unscientific'. It then becomes clear why arguments for and against psychoanalysis so easily end up as *ad hominem* arguments. The motives of those arguing in support of or against psychoanalysis are themselves part of the argument. The scientific consciousness, like all consciousness, is liable to systematic suspicion for ulterior motives and double-meanings.

A 'difficulty in the path of psychoanalysis'

The question may legitimately be asked why Freud has generated so much controversy, so much adulation but also venom. After all, few theorists would get excited about revealing the 'hidden Max Weber' or, for that matter, accusing Robert Millikan of being a fraud. What is it about psychoanalysis that generates so much passion? In a paper called 'A Difficulty in the Path of Psycho-Analysis' (1917), Freud argued that the psychoanalytic theory of the unconscious had inflicted a blow on our narcissism as human beings, on an even greater scale than two earlier scientific discoveries. If Copernicus's heliocentric theory shattered the view that the earth was the centre of the universe and Darwin's evolution destroyed the myth of man's uniqueness among animals, psychoanalysis added a third blow, which was probably 'the most wounding' for man's narcissism because it showed that 'the ego is not master in its own house' (1917: 189). Instead of a sovereign consciousness, moving on to ever higher achievements, psychoanalysis argues that the human soul is at odds with itself, fragmented, systematically deluded.

Arguing that the entity to which we each refer as 'self' is not only substantially unknown, but also deeply fragmented, fragile and fractious, poses big threats to our self-esteem and confidence. Some humanistic off-shoots of psychoanalysis, along with self-help and growth psychologies, have sought to cushion this blow to our narcissism, by re-defining the unconscious as an essentially benign, noble territory at the core of our being, oppressed and distorted by external forces which have little to do with it. For these traditions, with their echoes of Rousseau and the young Marx, men and women can re-discover their essential humanity by shaking off the layers of artifice, self-deceit and alienation, which culture, materialism, consumerism or any other suitable social scapegoat can be said to have inflicted on them. Freud, however, offers no such consolation to our narcissism, since the forces that oppress and distort are themselves part of our inner being as well as part of the world in which we live. The Freudian unconscious has little that can be described as noble or benign and contains much that is selfish and destructive.

> Men are not gentle creatures who want to be loved, and who at the most can defend themselves if they are attacked; they are on the contrary, creatures among whose instinctual endowments is to be reckoned a powerful share of aggressiveness. As a result, their neighbour is for them not only a potential helper and a sexual object, but also someone who tempts them to satisfy their aggressiveness on him, to exploit his capacity for work without compensation, to use him sexually without his consent, to seize his possessions, to humiliate him, to cause him pain, to torture and kill him. Homo homini lupus. (1930: 302)

Such arguments do not make Freud popular with New Age theorists or most theorists for that matter. Whether he was conceited and arrogant in placing himself on a par with Copernicus and Darwin is debatable. Yet it is not accidental that they, like psychoanalysis, generated enormous controversies and passions. Like heliocentrism and evolution, psychoanalysis poses a threat to our psychological well-being, in as much as it threatens deeply held convictions. The result is that psychoanalysis is resisted, just like other forms of unpleasant knowledge.

THE VALUE OF THE UNCONSCIOUS IN THE HUMAN SCIENCES

The concept of resistance is one that infuriates critics, since virtually any rational objection to psychoanalytic arguments may be put down to resistance. Freud's argument may be valid, though it is not a defence that serves psychoanalysis especially well. It may be true that some of the opposition which it generates has this narcissistic origin, just as some can be put down to fashion, misinterpretation or guilt by association. A stronger defence of psychoanalysis concentrates on the understanding that is made possible through the concept of the unconscious in illuminating countless phenomena that are otherwise opaque, as distorted expressions of hidden desires. Ultimately, even when repudiated, the unconscious is an indispensable concept for most human sciences. The Marxist concept of ideology and the sociological concept of norm would lose their bearings without the implicit or explicit assumption that there is an unconscious in which they become internalized.

The unconscious is equally indispensable in linguistics, in which it is argued that people can learn a language without knowing its grammar in a conscious way – the unconscious is 'a way of explaining how [the system of linguistic rules] can be simultaneously unknown and yet effectively present' (Culler 1976: 76). The study of mythology, folklore, fairy-tales, symbolism and magic is equally dependent on the concept of the unconscious for a decoding of the meaning of these phenomena. In all of these areas, cultural elements (like linguistic structures, symbols, moral constraints and so on) become constitutive of the individual by becoming engraved in unconscious areas of his or her mind, from where they can regulate his or her behaviour and shape his or her conscious perception and understanding. As we shall see in Chapters 8 and 9, human sciences encounter the unconscious not only as the psychic layer in which culture becomes constitutive of the individual but also as the source of fundamental wishes and desires which cultural institutions seek alternately to frustrate, modify, tame or gratify.

It is not an exaggeration then to argue that the unconscious is not a concept conveniently invoked by the human sciences on disparate occasions, but a theoretical foundation on which many of their theoretical concepts are anchored. Thus Foucault (1970: 364) insists that

> the problem of the unconscious – its possibility, status, mode of existence, the means of knowing it and bringing it to light – is not simply a problem within the human sciences which they can be thought of as encountering by chance in their steps; it is a problem that is ultimately coextensive with their very existence ... an unveiling of the non-conscious is constitutive of all the sciences of man.

Before the unconscious, man did not exist within Western science; he was the forever absent spectator of Velasquez's great painting, *Las Meninas*, whose presence is only glimpsed in the distant reflection of a mirror. 'In classical thought, the personage for whom the representation exists, and who represents himself within it ... he is never to be found in that table (or picture of representation) himself. Before the end of the eighteenth century, *man* did not exist' (Foucault, 1970: 308). Thus, concludes Foucault, psychoanalysis paves the way for the human sciences to pursue their 'project of bringing man's consciousness back to its real conditions, of restoring it to the contents and forms that brought it into being, and elude us within it' (1970: 364). But also, by making this process of unveiling possible, psychoanalysis functions as 'a perpetual principle of dissatisfaction', a critical agency within the human sciences, constantly questioning and undermining their final claim of having discovered 'what is'. It is here that psychoanalysis parts company with the other human sciences, leaving the realm of representation for the darker grounds of thought, which some call ideology or social critique.

Having revealed the depths of humanity's frustrations and discontents, having delved into the repressions and the self-deceptions and illusions in which we seek consolation, the Freudian discourse faces a choice, between utopia and tragedy, between a programme of social transformation towards a better future and an acceptance of a painful, flawed social reality. In the theories of Erich Fromm, Wilhelm Reich, Norman O. Brown and especially Herbert Marcuse, psychoanalysis, that most pessimistic doctrine of humanity, develops into a launching pad for powerful utopian visions, in which self-knowledge and fulfilment are achieved in a culture that has finally transcended the discontents and illusions of the past. By contrast, theorists like Rieff, Bettelheim, Ricoeur and Lear have reaffirmed the tragic message of psychoanalysis, the message that conflict, suffering and a measure of self-deception are inevitable features of all cultures – sorrow, suffering and destructiveness are central elements of human life. As Bettelheim (1983: 110) suggests: 'A good life denies neither its real and often painful difficulties nor the dark aspects of our psyche; rather, it is a life in which our hardships are not permitted to engulf us in despair, and our dark impulses are not allowed to draw us into their chaotic and often destructive orbit.' In these discussions, psychoanalysis addresses the core questions of morality, human existence, life and death, as well as the influence and scope of knowledge in human affairs. These are not issues which science, in the narrow sense, addresses. Psychoanalysis can offer some enlightenment to those wishing to explore them and discover some answers to the questions which they raise.

CONCLUSION

In this chapter, we have explored the psychoanalytic theory of neurosis and the nature of treatments offered by psychoanalysis, distinguishing analytic treatments from suggestive ones and indicating some of the limitations of each. We have also examined how Freud developed some of his theories on the basis of his clinical observations and discussed some of the criticisms levelled against him. Many of these criticisms derive from the allegedly closed nature of psychoanalytic thinking, its unwillingness to submit itself to an independent confirmation of its claims, and to its elimination of all criticism by discounting it as psychological resistance and defence. In discussing these criticisms, we have suggested that many of them stem from a far too restrictive conception of science, one that does not take into account the unique challenges facing the human sciences, in which observation must be accompanied by interpretation. Some criticisms are rightful responses to rhetorical or exaggerated claims proffered by psychoanalysis and its friends and some merely reproduce *ad hominem* types of argument, which result from the fact that observer and observed, known and knower coincide.

This chapter has offered a number of counter-arguments which can be summarized as follows:

1 Psychoanalysis does not work as a therapy in the way that psycho-pharmacology and neuro-psychiatry may work in reducing human suffering; nor is it a form of faith-healing or suggestive treatment, although it may occasionally work this way (as may orthodox medicine). It was never meant as part of a therapeutic technology of adjustment, even though this was the use made of it, especially in the United States. Instead, psychoanalysis works as a form of self-reflection and, in some cases, self-enlightenment, a 'therapy for the healthy, not a solution for the sick' (Rieff, 1959: xiii).
2 Psychoanalysis cannot be defended as a natural science; it can, however, be strongly defended as a domain of testable, rational, evolving and provisionally truthful knowledge (rather than as closed, frozen doctrine) which may be submitted to critical evaluation, correct mistakes, learn from these mistakes and develop (like other disciplines) more robust forms of theoretical knowledge.
3 Freud often proceeded in counter-intuitive, counter-methodical ways; his

observations were often 'tainted' by theory; he certainly made mistakes and was not always willing to recognize them or learn from them; as an enthusiastic propagandist for his approach, he sometimes made exaggerated or extravagant claims for his theories or his practices; in all of these ways he is not unlike other major scientific pioneers.

4 Many criticisms against psychoanalytic theories are the result of an inability to accept scientifically, or acknowledge at a more personal level, darker, destructive and aggressive forces which are part of us, yet of which we are unconscious. In the last resort, most criticisms against psychoanalysis derive from an unwillingness, both personal and theoretical, to accept the implications of the unconscious. Yet, the concept of the unconscious is of vital importance for many different fields of the human sciences and all-important in addressing deeper moral and existential questions. We concluded by suggesting that psychoanalysis enables us to address questions regarding the meaning of our lives, the causes of human suffering and the systematic distortions undergone by consciousness, which inevitably lead it into speculations of a utopian or tragic nature.

3 INDIVIDUAL AND ORGANIZATION

with Howard S. Schwartz

In this chapter, we enter at last the world of organizations. It is customary to treat organizations as 'facts'. After all, what can be more factual than hospitals, businesses, schools, armies, governments or prisons? It is curious, then, that in the past hundred years scholars have failed to come up with a satisfactory and generally accepted definition of an organization. In seeking to define them, different authors highlight different features of what is meant by 'organization', features such as goals, boundaries, cooperation, interaction, rules or division of labour. Consider the following definitions:

> A social relationship, which is either closed or limits the admission of outsiders by rules, will be called 'corporate group' [i.e. organization] so far as its order is enforced by the action of specific individuals whose regular function this is, of a chief or 'head' and usually also of an administrative staff. (Weber, 1913/1947: 145–6)

> A collectivity with a relatively identifiable boundary, a normative order, ranks of authority, communications systems, and membership-coordinating systems; this collectivity exists on a relatively continuous basis in an environment and engages in activities that are usually related to a set of goals; the activities have outcomes for organizational members, the organization itself, and for society. (Hall, 1987)

> An organization is
>
> 1 A plurality of parts
> 2 Maintaining themselves through their interrelatedness, and
> 3 Achieving specific objectives,
> 4 While accomplishing 2 and 3 adapt to the external environment, thereby,
> 5 Maintaining their interrelated state of the parts. (Argyris, 1960: 27–8)

> A consciously co-ordinated social unit, composed of two or more people, that functions on a relatively continuous basis to achieve a common goal or set of goals. (Robbins, 1998: 2)

> Social arrangements for the controlled performance of collective goals. (Huczynski and Buchanan, 1991)

> Structures of mutual expectation, attached to roles which define what each of its members shall expect from others and from himself. (Vickers, 1967: 109–10)

> Organizing . . . is defined as a *consensually validated grammar for reducing equivocality by means of sensible interlocked behaviors* . . . Organizations keep people busy, occasionally entertain

them, give them a variety of experiences, keep them off the streets, provide pretexts for story-telling, and allow socializing. They haven't anything else to give. (Weick, 1979: 3, 264)

Organizations are nets of collective action, undertaken in an effort to shape the world and human lives. The contents of the action are meanings and things (artifacts). One net of collective action is distinguishable from another by the kind of meanings and products socially attributed to a given organization. (Czarniawska-Joerges, 1992: 32)

Faced with such diversity of opinion, some scholars of organizations (for example, Sims et al., 1993; Hatch, 1997) avoid definitions of organizations altogether and content themselves with loose descriptions of the meanings assumed by the term 'organization'. Beyond individual differences between scholars, it is easy to recognize that definitions of organizations go through phases. Each historical period seems to recognize organizations according to its own concerns and outlooks, some through their goals, others through their social relations, others through their politics, yet others through their cultures, and so on.

Disagreements on the definition of organizations are not 'just academic': quite a lot hangs on the way organizations are defined.

1. What social groupings or collectivities should be referred to as an organization? For instance, should religious congregations or football crowds be treated as organizations? Families and clans? Social clubs? Small firms or partnerships of a couple of individuals? Are informal groups, such as those that can be found within all organizations, organizations in their own rights?
2. The definition of organization establishes what the essential features of these entities are, features from which much else derives. Is it their goals which confer on organizations their vital qualities, their political systems, their presumed rationality or their distinct emotional qualities?
3. Subsequent classifications of organizations, such as successful/unsuccessful, strong/weak, efficient/inefficient, moral/immoral, voluntary/involuntary, profit-making/non-profit and so on, depend on the way that organizations have been defined.
4. The definition of organizations indicates the extent to which a particular individual or party (an executive, a consultant, a labour union, a consumers' group, an environmental regulator) may intervene in the way in which they function, and seek to control them, change them, improve them or destroy them.
5. And this *is* academic, the definition of organizations influences the ways in which organizations should be studied, the assumptions that scholars can make about them and the approaches which they should be taking in their researches.

The inability to agree on what is meant by organization is not restricted to academics debating finer nuances of meaning. It extends to managers, workers, governments, shareholders, customers and virtually anyone who has dealings with organizations. As Harry Levinson has argued, this inability leads to numerous misunderstandings and conflicts regarding an organization's boundaries, purpose and responsibilities: 'Many of the difficulties encountered by organizations and their members derive from this lack of understanding, or, more probably, from a misunderstanding: we think we know what is meant [by 'organization'], but on closer examination it turns out that we do not' (1968/1981: 3). Organizations may have a material substance, yet their meaning is by no means fixed, clear or uniform. It would be accurate to describe 'organization' not as an abstract 'concept' but as a *construction*, an entity whose meaning is subject to continuous debate, argument and change. In time, the concept acquires new meanings and new nuances, losing some of the older ones. Different individuals approach organizations differently, some as effective instruments of administration, some as impersonal jungles, some as organic communities and so on.

Depth psychology is not perplexed by such a diversity of meanings. If organizations mean different things to different people it is because they are not just given, the same to all individuals at all times, but constructed. The way we perceive organizations, the way we try to find our place in them, the way we submit to or question their requirements, are influenced by our psychological development. Different individuals, working side by side in the same organization, may be working in organizations that are in effect different – one person may experience the organization as a hostile and malevolent force, bent on destruction, while a second experiences the same organization as a model of everything that is good and right and a third 'is only doing a job' and does not care one way or another for the organization.

In this chapter, we will argue that the psychological significance of organizations, the ways in which we each construct organizations, depends on our *character*, itself a product of our psychological development. The concept of character was originally developed by Freud, in connection with the 'anal character', to denote a relatively stable organization of libido. Anal characters were found to possess a triad of traits – orderliness, parsimony and stubbornness – which arose as reaction-formations during the toilet-training stage (1908); these traits colour an individual's entire outlook on others and shape the nature of his or her relations to his or her environment. Anal characters will generally favour well-defined, orderly relations which they feel they can control. Karl Abraham, in a series of influential papers published in the 1920s, explored the features of characters which are rooted in different episodes of the child's early development: the oral, the phallic and the genital characters. Abraham defined 'the character of a person to be the sum of his instinctive reactions towards his social environment' (1973: 408) and systematized psychoanalytic thinking on character formation, the different types of character, the traits associated with them, and the ways in which particular characters relate to others (Abraham, 1973).

Subsequent theorists, such as Wilhelm Reich and Erich Fromm, developed the concept of character further in different ways, until it became a centrepiece of ego-psychology. Character, initially the product of our sexual development, influences our whole outlook on life and the way in which we relate to other people. How is character shaped? Two processes central to the formation of character are sublimation and reaction-formation. *Sublimation* preserves the desires that characterized a particular stage of development, but redirects them towards new objects, usually stripping them of their sexual qualities. Thus, the oral desires for sucking or biting may be sublimated from the breast on to a pipe. *Reaction-formation*, on the other hand, leaves a trait diametrically opposed to that exhibited at the early developmental stage; thus, a pleasure in inspecting or playing with faeces is replaced by disgust towards them. In the course of their early development, individuals build up sublimations and reaction-formations; some of these may manifest themselves in specific types of behaviour later in life, or, more generally, they may become traits more or less integrated into the overall character. Thus, each stage of development is associated with a distinctive range of character traits. While character evolves throughout life, some of its core features remain stable – the traits associated with different characters are grouped together. Thus, for example, oral characters display heightened concern with giving and taking, dependence–independence and tend to be excessively pessimistic or optimistic. Likewise, anal characters display all three traits noted earlier. Fischer and Greenberg (1996), following their review of over 800 empirical studies, found 'ample and consistent verification' for this view. This stability of character structures (which in Reich's theory become 'character armours') is helpful in identifying how different individuals experience organizations and how they relate with others within organizations.

Some individuals become *fixated* in particular stages of development, consistently relating to others in a manner which they adopted during their oral, anal or phallic stages. Such individuals display a uniform set of character traits in virtually all social and interpersonal interactions. Others display a wider repertoire of traits, their characters involving combinations of reaction-formations and sublimations from different stages. Such individuals, however, may tend to *regress* to a particular character under the influence of specific factors, such as surprise, trauma or sudden feelings of anxiety. Our character continues to develop throughout life as we identify with different role models, initially parents, later other influential figures. Other important relations and experiences (including successes, disappointments and traumas) in our lives leave 'precipitates' or 'residues' on our individual characters, which can be either active or latent influences in our later lives. None of these transformations is either total or final. Resolutions are never complete, but are always liable to coming apart, re-awakening earlier conflicts. The mind, as Freud remarked, is like the city of Rome, whose various layers all co-exist one layer upon another.

STAGE ONE: ORAL STAGE AND NARCISSISTIC CHARACTER

For the child at the outset of life, the mother's breast *is* the entire world. The child at that moment experiences desire and satisfaction of desire; there is nothing else. The world is experienced as being in perfect accord with desire. It exists for the purpose of loving the child, of being incorporated by it, thereby satisfying its desire. Whatever is not incorporated has no meaning. The name given to this stage is *primary narcissism*. The child reacts with rage when it discovers that there is another side to the world, one that interferes with its gratification and calls its desire into question. This is the world of external, recalcitrant objects, which will bring about the end of primary narcissism. The child has not yet understood that the world does not revolve around it. It understands only that some things do what they are supposed to do: they satisfy it, love it and permit fusion with it. Other things do not do what they are supposed to do. Pure love and hate, then, applied without balance or measure, mark the child's orientation towards the world and whatever is in it. Melanie Klein and her followers refer to this orientation as the *paranoid-schizoid position*, and to the division between objects that are loved and those that are hated as *splitting*. It is the tension of this splitting, between the perfectly good world which one may engage with love, and the absolutely bad world which one must destroy or risk being destroyed by, that structures psychological life at this stage. Loevinger (1976) calls this stage 'impulsive'. We prefer the Freudian term 'primary narcissism' and shall refer to the character who becomes fixated to this stage as narcissistic character.

Primary narcissism must not be confused with the far wider range of psychological processes referred to as narcissistic. Most of these processes, both 'normal' and 'pathological', derive from *secondary narcissism*, the attempt to attract sexual energy on to the ego by increasing its attractiveness. While primary narcissism is rooted in the experience of fusion which precedes the discovery of a separate reality including other people and the separation of the ego from the id, secondary narcissism derives from the recognition of attractive qualities in objects; through identifications with such objects, especially objects which have to be abandoned as love-objects, individuals seek to enhance their self-love:

> When the ego assumes the features of the object, it is forcing itself, so to speak, upon the id as a love-object and is trying to make good the id's loss by saying: 'Look, you can love me too – I am so like the object' . . . The libido which flows into the ego owing to the identifications described above brings about its 'secondary narcissism'. (Freud, 1923: 369)

Organization, work and the narcissistic character: the personalized organization

The idea of an organization as a separate and autonomous sphere of social relations is alien to an individual fixated at the narcissistic stage of development or the individual who regresses to it. All relations are experienced as personal, focusing on the self, and assume extreme forms. Narcissistic characters' experience of the organization is strongly coloured by their emotional relations to a few people, such as their co-workers or their managers, and they are unable to visualize it as something apart from these people. Such relationships tend to be extremely intense and emotionally simple, admitting of no nuance. Narcissistic characters are also liable to rapid changes of mood and emotion, from love to hate or hate to love. They view the actions of managers and supervisors as personally aimed at them and have difficulty understanding that they represent a broader organizational agenda. They take everything personally. They are dependent on others for support and admiration, something that extends to their relations to organizations. Yet, they are also incapable of acknowledging their dependence, and they are likely to respond by denying it. For both of these reasons, they have frequent conflicts with authority, for which they blame a hated manager or supervisor.

Supervision of these individuals has to focus on the maintenance of a close personal relationship through the careful management of interpersonal relations. The requirements of the organization have to be expressed in personal terms, the supervisor using the leverage afforded by a tight emotional bond. The employee, after all, is emotionally wide open, fused with the supervisor, and is therefore acutely sensitive to the disapproval or disappointment of the supervisor, so long as this is experienced within the relationship, and not as coming from a separate source or authority. At the same time, unless the supervisor can maintain some emotional distance from this relationship, he or she will be in danger of getting caught up in it, losing track of his or her wider organizational responsibilities.

One of the characteristics of narcissistic characters is an emphasis on spontaneous experience and creativity. They live predominantly in what Lacan (1977) has called the *imaginary* order, a prelinguistic domain in which our image of the world is structured by our spontaneous feelings. Narcissistic individuals often display a creativity, mixed with an interpersonal freshness and vivacity, an unwillingness to submit to impersonal regulations or stand by ceremony. They can be quite attractive, engaging and, under certain circumstances, productive. We often think of such individuals as spoilt or childish, yet this childishness is not without either its appeal or its usefulness. In roles requiring spontaneous interaction, their independence from organizational strictures can be usefully channelled. Creative work, by definition, cannot be done by simply following procedures. Creativity can also take artistic forms, vital in many organizations concerned with innovative design, style or fashion. In such organizations, we may also find individuals testily defending their personal autonomy and resisting the organizational demands that they tame their spontaneity to the bureaucratic ways of doing things. It would be inaccurate to label all such individuals (often described as having 'artistic temperament') as narcissistic characters. Those, for instance, who are driven by a sense of creative duty and a heightened sense of organizational responsibility do not fit the narcissistic character, a character which is fixated to a pre-Oedipal stage, one in which experiences of duty and responsibility are virtually absent.

Narcissistic characters can often be found in organizations described as charismatic (Biggart, 1988), which are imbued by a collective belief in the organization's supreme beauty, goodness and power. Such organizations range from religious and political sects to direct selling companies. They generate tremendous devotion, excitement and unity. Within such organizations individuals may find their primary narcissism restored in an 'oceanic' feeling, a feeling of oneness with the world and with others, a feeling which may be rooted in a re-creation of the distant experience of fusion with the mother (see Chapter 1). Within such organizations followers may find themselves exploited by unscrupulous leaders, who can take advantage of the members' reliance on the organization to sustain their own feelings of omnipotence, beauty and goodness. Alternatively, such organizations may lose all checks from reality, ending up as mutual admiration societies, unable to engage constructively with their environment, achieve a task or deliver a product.

There is one more important mode in which we encounter narcissistic characters in organizations, namely as leaders. It is not uncommon for highly narcissistic individuals to rise to leadership positions, by stimulating the narcissism of their followers and inspiring them with their ambitious visions and schemes. Leaders and followers in such organizations embark on an adventure where they reinforce each other's dependency, the leader's dependency on an adoring followership and the followers' dependence on an alluring, ambitious and charismatic leader, capable of making them feel good. These situations, which often come to unfortunate conclusions, will be examined in greater detail in Chapters 7 and 11.

STAGE TWO: THE ANAL STAGE AND OBSESSIVE CHARACTER

The world of the narcissistic character is structured around impulses. Social rules, roles and norms – the primary means through which society controls behaviour, and through which social reality is structured – are experienced as alien and arbitrary. What marks the development of the next stage is that the individual comes to understand the operation of rules, although without yet comprehending their meaning or the function they serve. The engagement with these alien structures, uncomprehended as they are, creates a high degree of anxiety concerning one's spontaneity. This anxiety can only be assuaged by submitting oneself to the rules, taking them as compulsions, as things that one has to do, without questioning why. Individuals at this stage, driven to escape the danger that awaits following their impulses in an alien world, require and demand rules as guides to action. The tension that characterizes this stage, then, is that between the anxiety of being in an uncomprehended world and uncomprehending, compulsive adherence to the rules of that world.

If persons and organizations at the narcissistic stage may lose contact with reality, the opposite may be said to characterize this next stage of development, which is associated with the *anal character*. Its primary traits are orderliness, parsimony and obstinacy. The anal character develops his or her traits either as modified expressions (sublimations) of anal impulses or as ways of denying them by invoking their opposites (reaction-formations). Thus, orderliness is a reaction-formation against dirt, i.e. matter in the wrong place. Obstinacy arises from the learned necessity to control oneself at that stage of sexual development. Parsimony, i.e. extreme interest in money, is understood as a socially acceptable transformation of the child's interest in faecal material itself. Thus, the repression of anal sexuality, by learning or being forced to control its excretory activity, signals the child's first encounter of the clash between its own impulses and organized social prohibitions. While the term 'anal character' has a long pedigree in psychoanalytic studies, we prefer to use the term *obsessive character* which shifts the emphasis away from the stage in which this character is shaped and towards the qualities which make this character distinct.

Control is the trademark of obsessive characters, just as impulsiveness is that of narcissistic ones. One often sees the compulsively neat person, afraid that anything out of place represents a deep danger. One sees the deeply controlled person, without discernible joy or pleasure in anything, who often treats others with the same need for control, as if all spontaneity anywhere must be obliterated. And one sees the person who hoards and accumulates, often without apparent pleasure in possessing, as if their only identity were in the size of the pile of their money or possessions. The obsessive character's destructive impulses can have a sado-masochistic quality, his or her satisfaction deriving from the suffering or humiliation inflicted on others or on him or herself. This is quite different from the narcissistic character's experience of blind rage. While the narcissist may wish to annihilate an object that stands in the way of his or her satisfaction, the obsessive character can actually enjoy the careful and protracted ministration or experience of pain. Violence and physical suffering may hold a great fascination for him or her.

Obsessive characters, however, have a different means of venting their destructive impulses, one whose consequences are less anti-social. This consists of total subordination to mechanical routines and a behaviour based on repetition. Compulsive repetition represents a very primitive force in instinctual life, a conservative force that seeks to reduce stimulation and return life to a condition of total inertia. By adhering mechanically to their routines, which echo the toilet-training routines, obsessive characters are reaching for a state of extreme inertia and relative security in a complex and bewildering world, a state that could be likened to institutional suicide as a mode of personal survival (see Freud, 1921; Gabriel, 1983, 1984).

Organization, work and the obsessive character: impersonal order stage

The narcissistic character may find a place in organizations, but engages with them rather fitfully. The same cannot be said for the obsessive character, who finds him or herself perfectly at home within the world of organizations, or at least organizations of a certain sort. Organizational rules and regulations, routines, timetables, accounts, records, regularity and predictability, those features of bureaucracy, offer a highly controlled environment, which constitutes the obsessive character's very idea of organization. Driven by anxiety, obsessive characters find comfort in structure. They are at their best in the application of predetermined rules to bring order. The amount of energy that they bring to the creation of order is often quite prodigious. They glory in discovering minute inconsistencies in records, rules and procedures or indeed specks of dust or dirt. In the interest of order and consistency, obsessive characters venerate precedent and tradition and view every departure from it as potentially catastrophic. Hence, they resist change and innovation with a stubbornness that is entirely characteristic of their entire personality. Equally, obsessive characters find it quite difficult to work together with impulsive narcissistic ones. Creativity, emotion and spontaneous interaction are profoundly threatening phenomena, generating acute anxiety, which they seek to contain by ever more elaborate and impersonal rules and regulations.

The value of obsessive characters for most organizations is hard to over-estimate. They are, after all, 'natural' organizers, capable of incredibly detailed plans, seeking to contain disorder and unpredictability. They are assiduous record-keepers, makers of lists, drafters of timetables and spotters of irregularities. They operate happily in impersonal bureaucratic orders, which shelter them from having to engage in emotionally demanding relationships or interpersonal negotiations or bargains. They can always be relied upon to apply rules with no concern for the feelings of those affected, not even their own. In this sense they are the embodiment of the bureaucratic official who discharges his or her office in a highly 'professional' manner, *sine ira et studio* (Weber, 1946). At the same time, they are systematic economizers, always looking for ways of reducing inefficiencies and waste, capable of impressing their superiors with great feats of husbandry and frugality.

The ease with which obsessive characters carve themselves a place in organizations can obscure some of their negative influences. They tend to thwart initiative and creativity, they stand in the way of innovation and progress, they systematically annihilate new ideas and they are capable of incredible lack of care and cruelty (see the discussion of 'Authoritarianism' in Chapter 7). In observing minute details of regulations and procedures, they often disregard the spirit in which these were introduced, leading to organizational rigidities, injustices and inefficiencies. They are often capable of implementing, in the most methodical and efficient ways, the most irrational, counter-productive and inhuman policies.

Individuals at the anal stage, unlike their narcissistic counterparts, can relate to organizations as organized collectivities, existing independently of themselves, as impersonal orders. They can find a place for themselves in large-scale bureaucracies with relative ease and do not mind impersonality, routine and tight, explicit controls. Still, their engagement with organizations tends to be non-affective; they form few attachments with their colleagues and their loyalty is directed to the office they hold rather than to the organization which they serve. Obsessive characters who can meet the demands of their office, can maintain order and control and can enforce the rules to the letter experience considerable self-satisfaction and pride, a form of narcissistic fulfilment which echoes the experience of the well-trained and well-groomed child. It should not be thought, therefore, that obsessive characters (or any of the subsequent characters we shall examine) are without narcissism. But where all psychological characters have narcissistic strivings deriving from attempts to make their ego attractive and lovable, the narcissistic character alone seeks to transcend the divisions of ego and id, ego and other, and restore the ego to the centre of an all-encompassing universe. Where the narcissistic character, therefore, tends to deny the existence of recalcitrant objects, the obsessive character seeks to maintain control over them.

STAGE THREE: PHALLIC STAGE, THE OEDIPUS COMPLEX AND COLLECTIVISM

The anal stage is succeeded by the phallic stage, which signals the approach of the Oedipus complex. The phallic stage is characterized by the erotic primacy of the genital organs, the discovery of the anatomical differences of the genders and the subsequent divergence of the psychological development of boys from that of girls. Some of the features of the phallic stage become part of character only after they have been through the dramatic changes which follow the resolution of the Oedipus complex and the start of the child's moral development. During the Oedipus complex, the child discovers that not only is the mother someone separate from him or her (the realization that obliterated primary narcissism) but that he or she, the child, is not everything for the mother, that someone else has a claim on the mother that supersedes that of the child. The fact that mother and father have a relationship independent of the child, and its corollary, that the child has a rival for the affection of the mother, leads to a sequence of dramatic transformations, different for boys and girls, which will bring infantile sexual development to an end, most sexual desires disowned or repressed in what is known as *latency*.

During the phallic stage it is common for children to become fascinated with epic stories, myths involving heroic deeds, dragons, magic weapons, princesses and so on. Power becomes a major preoccupation in the child's fantasy life, and in many societies power comes to be associated with the possession of a penis. In later life, phallic elements may re-surface in people with 'burning' ambition, mainly preoccupied with issues of power and control over others, the achievement of grandiose objectives and the implementation of ambitious visions. These will be discussed presently as features of the *heroic individualistic character*. First, however, it is important to explore another character, who also emerges in the aftermath of the Oedipus complex, a character often referred to as *collectivist*. Feelings for a group of people, as opposed to feelings aimed at specific individuals, appear at the latency stage, which Freud viewed as succeeding the resolution of the Oedipus complex. 'It is during this period of total or at least partial latency that the psychic forces develop which later act as inhibitions on the sexual life, and narrow its direction like dams. These psychic forces are loathing, shame, and moral and aesthetic ideal demands' (1905b: 93, trans. from Brill, 1938: 583). These forces do not stop sexuality but

> its energy is deflected either wholly or partially from sexual utilization and conducted to other aims. The historians of civilization seem to be unanimous in the opinion that such deflection of sexual motive powers from sexual aims to new aims, a process which merits the name of *sublimation*, has furnished powerful components for all cultural accomplishments. We will, therefore, add that the same process acts in the development of every individual, and that it begins to act in the sexual latency period. (1905b: 94, trans. from Brill, 1938: 584)

As we saw in Chapter 1, two significant events take place at this point. First, children internalize the authority of society embodied by the father into a new mental agency, the super-ego; they accept that life is full of social restrictions and prohibitions and no longer need external threats to impose them but impose them on themselves. Secondly, children discover that life holds a promise. Boys can become men, like their fathers, and discover love in a relationship with some-one like their mother. Girls, in the traditional configuration, can become women, like their mothers, enjoying the love of a man, like their fathers, and having babies of their own. For both boys and girls, to aspire to adulthood means being ready to give up their childish ways, at the command of the super-ego, in exchange for the promise that their desires will be satisfied when they become adults. Growing up involves this act of faith, an idealization of the adult world. On this basis, we learn to discipline and check our impulsive nature, our desires and our feelings. Driven by the unrelenting repression of those desires, which until the onset of the Oedipus period ruled our mental life, we throw ourselves enthusiastically and uncritically into our groups, the social world around us.

On one level we discover, for example at school, a wide open world, one far larger than the small family milieu in which Oedipal dramas were acted out. This is a world with restrictions and prohibitions, but also with rewards for those who comply. On another level, we do not merely discover this wider world, but actually construct it through our joint acts of faith, our mutual readiness to believe in it. And it is largely this idealized world that we create through our faith, a world that exists because we believe in it, that provides the basis for the group psychology of this period. Thus, idealization of the group, identification with its members and shame over the individual desires which make us different from the rest of the group, become the defining characteristics of this stage.

Loevinger (1976) calls this the *conformist* stage. Conformist characters do not distinguish between trivial matters of etiquette and deep moral principles. Everything comes under the sway of the group, which precludes spontaneously acting on our desires and the individuality and initiative that grow out of that spontaneity. But if this stage represses spontaneity, it provides a powerful base for group and organizational cohesion and integration. The root of this cohesion, as of all cohesion, is love. In this case, though, love assumes the form of sublimated, de-sexualized bonds of identification. As long as they identify with the other members of the group, as members of the group, each individual will be experienced as being like everyone else. Then they can all feel part of this idealized entity, and feel proud, loved and included. It is easy to see the power of this bond if everyone is eager to maintain it.

The negative side is exclusion, scapegoating and intolerance of individuality and difference. For this character, the group's judgement defines what is right or wrong. There is no other authority that he or she can appeal to. This type of conformity underlies phenomena such as 'groupthink' (Janis, 1972) and submission to authority that psychologists such as Milgram (1974) have described. The idealized group of which its members feel so proud, after all, exists only in fantasy. Members are aware that their lives are not perfect; this imperfection is experienced as a personal failure and results in feelings of shame, which makes members powerfully sensitive to exclusion and scapegoating. Since shame of one's own individuality leads to the repression of spontaneity, imagination and individuality are suppressed at this stage. Conformists are not creative people, and find themselves strained by situations that are ambiguous or novel and permit of different interpretations and opinions. This lack of individual imagination is made up as the group collectively constructs a new entity, a union, a 'we' within which individuals find a new way of relating to the world, as members of a group rather than seeing the world as revolving around their individual selves.

Organization, work and the collectivist character: the perfect group

If organization at the early narcissistic stage is experienced as personal relations, and at the impersonal order stage as formal rules, organization at the collectivist stage is often experienced as the perfect group. Individuals fixated at this stage often experience their organizations as deities, and do their bidding as if it were a sacred mission. As members of their organizations, such individuals are full of confidence, pride and self-esteem; outside their organizations, they can be consumed by doubt and insecurity. It is the organization that lends them its perfection, while imperfections are seen as arising from out-side influences. They are loyal, dependable and tractable. The fact that they do not have much capacity for sizing up individual situations and responding to them is part of the same package.

For such individuals, the organization represents their best self, and they will respond to its dictates with a sense of high moral purpose. They have little sense of their own individual worth, as opposed to their organizational role, and will therefore make few demands. Tendencies to disagree with the organization will be experienced as unacceptable and will be repressed. Their approach to authority is one that combines deference with undying loyalty, akin to what Max Weber (1946) referred to as 'traditional authority'. Management seen as embodying the whole organization is held above reproach. Conformist characters will do what management wishes them to do, without question or qualification.

At one level, it would seem as if individuals at the collective stage are perfect employees. They give everything they have to give, and appear to demand little in return. They will make personal sacrifices and act in what they regard as the interest of their organization, even if they place themselves at risk. They will compromise their personal values and beliefs in discharging their organizational responsibilities. And, what is more, they will do all these things without questioning the reasons for doing so. At a deeper level, however, the needs of such individuals to feel continuously integrated in a group tests organizations, especially large and impersonal ones. Their phantasies of organizational perfection, projected on to their supervisor, is one that many supervisors find attractive and seek to maintain. If this could be accomplished without the distortion of reality, there would be little harm to it. But none of us is perfect, and the attempt to maintain the fiction of our perfection can easily lead to dysfunctional consequences, when the appearance of perfection can no longer be sustained.

Conformist characters operate within a very simple psychological contract: they undertake to serve the organization with complete loyalty in exchange for the organization's total loyalty to them; they will do anything for the organization, so long as the organization offers to protect and succour them. In some cases, they may steal, lie and even kill in the name of their organization, never wishing anything in return other than the organization's willingness to have them as members. This leads to a scenario, common in periods of 'downsizing', when such individuals find

> ## GROUP CONFORMITY
>
> A classic experiment by Solomon Asch (1956) illustrates the dynamic of conformity to the group very well. In that experiment, subjects were required to make the simple perceptual judgement of whether lines were the same or different lengths. But they were confronted with the question in a group situation in which the other members of the group had already unanimously made their judgements in an erroneous way. Unbeknown to the subject, the other members of the group were confederates of the experimenter. The question was whether the real subject would contradict the clear evidence of his senses and go along with the group, or whether he would go along with his senses and differ from the group. Strikingly, most of the subjects – approximately three-quarters – conformed.
>
> Thomas Scheff (1990), analysing this experiment, argued that the response which occasioned the conformity, a response felt, incidentally, both by those who conformed and those who did not, was shame: 'the fear that they were suffering from a defect and that the study would disclose this defect' (1990: 90). Thus, he quotes Asch on the subjects who conformed:
>
>> They were *dominated* by their exclusion from the group which they took to be a reflection on themselves. Essentially they were *unable* to face a conflict which threatened, in some undefined way, to expose a deficiency in themselves. They were consequently trying to *merge* in the group in order not to feel peculiar. (Asch, 1956: 45; cited by Scheff, 1990: 90–1; emphasis added by Scheff)

themselves dispensed with as 'dead wood', a scenario explored in Arthur Miller's play *The Death of a Salesman*. When they are made redundant (often receiving a compensation package and some counselling on starting a new career), not only is their ego destroyed (since it depends to such an extent on membership) but also their moral sense of justice (since their loyalty is betrayed) can be shattered. The incapacity of such individuals to respond individually and creatively to new situations puts them at a disadvantage in conditions of rapid change which undermine the value of loyalty and conformity and place a premium on flexibility and imagination.

Individuals at the collective stage do not always idolize their employing organization. Their collectivism may equally be fulfilled in their attachment to some other organization, a trade union, a professional association, a club, a society or a department of a larger organization. They then display the same unswerving loyalty and solidarity to these different collectivities, identifying with their fellow members and idealizing the collectivity.

STAGE FOUR: INDIVIDUALISM

Like collectivism, *individualism* can be traced to the dissolution of the Oedipus complex and the institution of the super-ego. Both collectivism and individualism are attempts to placate the super-ego, the former through submission to the social order, the latter through distinction, excellence and achievement. Conformity alone cannot satisfy the super-ego – after all, it is not by being one of the crowd that the boy will win the ultimate prize, the woman of his dreams; nor does being part of the crowd win for the girl the 'happy-ever-after' life of her dreams. One looks in vain for fairy-tales about lemmings, working together to accomplish collective tasks. Achievement, distinction and excellence are what grip the child's imagination, which idealizes the heroes and heroines of fairy-tales and casts him or herself in the starring role (Bettelheim, 1976: 111). It is by slaying dragons, answering riddles and accomplishing the impossible that the child achieves the fulfilment of the promise which concluded his or her Oedipal drama.

The super-ego, it will be recalled, is not merely society's fifth column within the individual. It is also the product of identification with the parents, who 'at the time at which the Oedipus complex gives place to the super-ego . . . are something quite magnificent' (Freud, 1933: 96). Later identifications with role models bring fresh idealized elements within the individual's personality. Hence, the punitive, conformist function does not exhaust the super-ego's character:

> One more important function remains to be mentioned which we attribute to this super-ego. It also carries the ego ideal by which the ego measures itself, which it emulates, and whose demand for ever greater perfection it strives to fulfil. There is no doubt that this ego ideal is the precipitate of the old picture of the parents, the expression of admiration for the perfection which the child then attributed to them. (Freud, 1933: 96)

This, then, is the ambiguity of the super-ego: it is the mental agency which dictates at once conformity and distinction. It decrees both sameness and difference. It is both conservative and progressive. In its very ambiguity, the super-ego lies behind the higher cultural achievements, individual and collective. Achievement is what promises to raise the child once again above the anonymity of a largely indifferent world, restoring him or her to the centre of loving attention which was once experienced in the arms of the mother. Achievement is one of the processes whereby the gap between ego and its ideal is bridged, thereby silencing the super-ego. The elation of success or victory, the liberation of libido which comes from this silencing of the voice of criticism and admonishment, may not last long, but it produces some of the greatest experiences in a person's life, and acts as the aim towards which the individualist's future efforts are aimed.

The stage of development revolving around individualism, with its emphasis on respect, status and reputation, is marked off from the conformist stage in that the function of conformity may be taken for granted. The person is now a socialized individual, in whom concern for others is built into the very structure of the personality. What now emerges is the need to have a special place within the social order. Individualism, then, takes on two distinct forms, depending on whether the emphasis is placed on standing out or on the social connections within which one stands out. The first form is what we will call *heroic individualism*, in which the ego, under the urge of the super-ego, strives towards an ego-ideal which contains relatively simple epic qualities. It is a form that acknowledges neither pain nor suffering, neither compromise nor cost; it revolves entirely around victory and defeat, noble deeds and villainy. The other is a more complex form, *civic individualism*, in which the ego-ideal becomes fragmented and composite, and the ego's repertoire of dealing with the demands of id, super-ego and external reality becomes more varied. The ego-ideal continues to exercise an influence on mental functioning, within a broader picture of social functioning, a picture that entails relations of mutuality, responsibility and obligation.

For the heroic individualist, narcissistic rewards, such as status, fame, recognition and power, are all of prime importance. He or she views the world as an arena for noble and heroic deeds, drawing admiration and appreciation. This narcissism of the heroic individualist can easily be confused with the narcissism of the narcissistic character. They both have a deep need to be admired and loved. They both need an audience and rely on external affirmation. They are both possessed of an extreme sense of their own importance, which exercises a powerful influence on their mental life. Finally, they may both attain leadership positions in groups or organizations, attracting mass following and loyalty. Yet, in spite of these similarities, as psychological characters they are far apart. The narcissist, whose mental development is highly influenced by the oral stage, is generally passive, temperamental and moody. He or she does not wish to relate to others (other than as an admiring audience), let alone dominate them. By contrast, the heroic individualist, whose development is highly influenced by the phallic stage, is outward-looking, active and domineering. The narcissistic individual wishes to be admired for who he or she is, the heroic individualist wishes to be admired for what he or she has achieved.

The ego-ideal is a source of endless frustration for the narcissistic individual, who, in contemplating his or her own image, invariably finds him or herself inadequate, seeking to lay the blame for such inadequacy on others or collapsing into catastrophic depression. The ego-ideal is a cause of frustration for the heroic individualist as well, but in this case it is a spur towards achievement. This is a matter that deserves further elaboration.

The ego-ideal can never become a steady state of reality. As Harry Levinson argues:

> The ego ideal, like a mountain peak, is beyond one's capacities so that it continues to serve as a goal toward which one is constantly striving. Various social models ranging from presidents, artists, scholars, and saints on the one hand, to con men and drug dealers on the other – depending upon the cultural milieu from which the child comes – serve as the raw material for the ego ideal, and their function as models is reinforced by history, literature, myth, and folklore. (1968/1981: 20–1)

It is important to appreciate this point. The ego-ideal is not merely a conscious formation, but involves a wide range of unconscious images, drawn from diverse sources. Some of these may be at odds with each other, the way in which other unconscious formations are. In our ego-ideal, for example, we may aspire to be, at once, victors and victims, dominating and dominated, young and old, male and female, infant and mother. But even in its early, relatively simple stage, when the boy's ego-ideal is predominantly heroic and the girl's predominantly narcissistic, it cannot be realized. Within the stage of heroic individualism, the hero or heroine can never rest on his or her laurels but is forever drawn to new achievements and new peaks.

In reality, not many of us continue to pursue forever the heroic life. Instead, we discover a constructive and socially useful way of understanding why this ego-ideal can never become a reality, without experiencing continuous frustration. The key to this lies in a dimension of the super-ego which we typically come to understand only later in life: the framework of mutual obligations which it introduces into our mental personality. As we grow up, provided that we do not become fixated in an earlier stage of development, our ego develops a growing repertoire of ways to deal with the demands of the id, the super-ego and external reality. At some point, we lose interest in the heroic life; the fascination of myths and fairy-tales declines as we begin to realize that social life is far more complex than an endless series of exciting adventures. Instead, it entails a nexus of mutual obligations and compromises, rights and responsibilities, deals of all sorts to which we must all commit ourselves in order to be able to live our lives together. The father himself ceases to be perceived as a powerful hero and comes to be seen as the embodiment of this system of mutual obligations to which he is himself subordinate – his role is part of this mutually defined system and does not exist apart from it. This is the system of rules of exchange that operates in society and even defines society as an entity in its own right – akin to what Lacan (1977) calls the 'symbolic order' – which, of course, includes language.

Our emotional connection with others, established at the collective stage, can now develop in a new direction, which includes participation, involvement, tolerance and acceptance of difference. The currently fashionable concept of 'stakeholder' seeks to capture the structure of the world as it is seen at this stage. The old concept of 'citizen' does better justice to the idea, though it is somewhat tainted by its long-standing association with exclusion of all those to whom citizenship is denied. Citizenship grows out of a recognition of an entity, a *polis*, a civilization, existing above individuals, capable of turning its constituents away from their narrow self-interests, but in which the pursuit of the collective interest is left to the differentiated but complementary activity of individuals. The concept of citizen is currently being rediscovered in environmental and moral debates, notably as distinct from the concept of 'the consumer', driven by less noble ideals (Gabriel and Lang, 1995: 173ff). By contrast, the concept of citizen is consistent with a civic ideal, neither heroic nor conformist, which combines social responsibility and altruism without sacrificing the individual.

Citizenship generates a new idea of self-respect: we earn our moral standing, neither as conformist automata nor as heroes, but as unique and valued members of a community, with rights and obligations. Thus, the rules of the super-ego encoded in our own minds dictate what we need to do in order to sustain our moral standing and maintain our self-respect. Others have given something to us, not because they owe it to us, but with the expectation that we shall return it. What do we have to give to them in order for them to feel that their expenditure was justified? Take too much, give too little, and they are likely to condemn us. Take their condemnation into ourselves and we will feel guilty, the feeling that we are in moral debt. Give what the situation calls for, and we feel that we have earned what we received, that we are on a solid moral footing with others, and are free of guilt. In all of this we can see the importance of the framework of mutual understanding, which is the only way in which we can agree on what the situation calls for, and therefore be secure in our freedom from guilt.

Through this development, the importance of narcissistic rewards in motivating the achievements of the heroic individualist is replaced by a sense of social responsibility. What emerges is a type we call *civic individualism*. The heroic individualist wishes to be admired for who he or she is, seeing his or her achievements as uniquely valuable because they are manifestations of him or herself. The civic individualist wishes to be admired for what he or she has achieved within a framework of diverse valuable roles, all of whose occupants are worthy of admiration.

Organization, work and individualism: idealized hierarchy and moral commonwealth

The two forms of individualism lead to quite distinct experiences of organizations and work. At the extreme, heroic individualists may experience organizations as arenas for epic exploits, such as rescue missions, bold initiatives, momentous battles and noble sacrifices. Such individuals occasionally attain leadership positions and may manage to infect some of their followers with a commensurate appetite for heroics. The memoirs of some famous business leaders, like Lee Iacocca, with their villains, heroes, fools, sleeping princesses, dragons, magic weapons and other mythic ingredients, read like sagas of quasi-epic proportions. From the 1980s, it became quite fashionable to argue that successful businesses were those which enabled each and every one of their employees to feel like a super-hero involved in a sequence of heroic adventures (see Deal and Kennedy, 1982; Hirsch, 1986). More sceptical commentators have questioned the scope that business organizations offer for heroism, though there can be little doubt that they offer ample opportunities for stimulating and even acting out of heroic phantasies (Gabriel, 1991a, 1995). Meeting deadlines with bursts of frenetic activity, striking deals against seemingly impossible odds, turning round moribund firms, talking back to abusive supervisors or clients, receiving prizes and awards, and numerous other episodes of organizational life can be readily infused with heroic meanings.

Whether life in organizations can ever be consistently heroic is highly doubtful. Heroic leadership (see Burns, 1978) can inspire individuals to enormous feats of achievement, sacrifice and change, yet, in the long term, as Weber recognized, charisma is not as reliable a principle for leading organizations, ensuring discipline and consistency, as a rational system of rules and a bureaucratic hierarchy of officials. Within this context, heroic individualism loses some of its wildness, adopting the hierarchy as the route to the ego-ideal. Look into the mind of a heroic individualist within an organizational setting and you are likely to find that everything he or she does is geared towards promotion. Heroic individualists long to be recognized as special within the corporate setting, and this means being elevated within the hierarchy (Jackall, 1988; Schwartz, 1990). Of course, they will never get to the ego-ideal, no matter how high they climb, but this does not deter them. There are always, after all, more levels of hierarchy, or more prestigious organizations, or lines of work, or whatever it takes to keep the spirit alive.

It is easy to see why organizations are keen on individuals of this type. The fact that they are constantly looking for promotion out of the position that they are in means that the actual characteristics of that position are relatively unimportant to them. They can therefore be counted on to put great enthusiasm into any activity, whether they like it or not, so long as it leads to promotion. By stipulating how promotion may be attained, organizations can exercise extraordinary control over such individuals. This control is accepted as perfectly legitimate, since it is seen as an expression of the hierarchy, the heavenly ladder, which heroic individualists need to idealize. So fine is the fit between such individuals and corporate life that they are often referred to as 'corporation men', as portrayed in Wilson's classic novel, *The Man in the Grey Flannel Suit*.

For heroic individualists, rules are experienced as conditions for 'getting ahead' in a structure of upward mobility. This is quite different from the meaning of rules in the impersonal order, where they function as routines for mechanical adherence or, in the perfect group, as principles for moral allegiance. It is also different from the meaning which rules have to the civic individualist, who experiences them as setting the parameters within which individuals engage in relations of mutuality, a framework of mutual responsibilities which is greater than any single individual. Obsessive characters experience bureaucratic rules as unconscious defences against the threat of disorder and chaos. Conformist individuals experience them as moral principles to be defended against infractors. By contrast, civic individualists interpret them, modify them and bend them to serve a superior organizational order. In this way, they form a more elaborate psychological contract with the organization than conformist individuals. They understand and accept that no organization is faultless and no rule is perfect. Justice, fairness and success require constant vigilance, within a nexus of rights and obligations. They will not simply observe the rules but seek to understand them, criticize them and improve them. For them, the rules are justified by the purpose they serve in organizing useful and valuable work, and are subject to revision on the basis of how well they serve their function. In this, they are giving life to the term 'rational' in Max Weber's idea of legal-rational authority. They will not merely work to order because their performance is being monitored and evaluated, but will seek to excel at what they do and enhance their organization. In extreme forms, they may almost see organizations as embodiments of the ancient *agora*, inviting their members to participate as citizens, honouring them, and relying on them for its continuing prosperity and well-being.

Life without illusions?

It is easy to idealize the character of the civic individualist, as indeed many authors do. Yet it should not be overlooked that, like his or her predecessor, this character too builds his or her experiences of organizations around a web of phantasies acting as fulfilments of unconscious wishes. The civic individualist imagines that the organization, and society more generally, are places where conflicts of interest, opinions and belief can be harmonized within a tolerant commonwealth, which gives everybody enough opportunities to achieve his or her objectives, without inhibiting the objectives of others. By denying aggression in him or herself, the civic individualist can only conceive destructiveness as the consequence of social pathologies and problems, calling for social measures to overcome. In this respect, this character is not unlike the others. His or her dominant illusion is that conflict can be resolved through reasoned argument. This is often seen by others as unfeeling and inappropriate.

Each of the characters we have discussed (see Table 3.1) constructs organizations in distinct ways: the narcissistic character as a set of interpersonal relations from which they can extract admiration and love; the obsessive character as an impersonal system of rules which eliminates disorder; the conformist character as a set of immutable moral dictates which stand for collective perfection; the heroic individualist character as an arena for heroic exploits where distinction and excellence may be achieved; the civic individualist as a commonwealth of sovereign individuals who can be relied upon to act in the interests of collective welfare. Yet, as critical readers will not fail to notice, all of these images of organizations are thinly veiled phantasies which act as wish-fulfilments, fulfilments of those wishes that are fundamental to each character. The narcissist envisions the organization as something that will fulfil his or her strivings for love and appreciation; the obsessive character as something that will meet his or her deep need for order and control; the conformist as something that

TABLE 3.1 Characters and organization

Character	Main vicissitudes of libido	Main vicissitudes of death instinct	Main type of relation with others	Main character traits	Predominant meaning of organization	Favourite illusion
Oral/ narcissistic	Being loved and admired; centre of attention; inability to form object love	Rage/hate against anything frustrating desires; annihilation of the other	Emphasis on the personal; using others; fusing with others in 'oceanic' feeling	Impulsive, egocentric, moody, extreme, optimistic–pessimistic, spontaneous	Organization as *people*; charismatic	Fusion
Anal/ obsessive	Some object love, often sadistic; puritanical self-control of sexuality	Sadistic; compulsion to repeat; 'institutional death' in total bureaucratic inertia	Impersonal, controlling, manipulative, sometimes sadistic	Orderly, parsimonious, stubborn, clean, eye for detail, manipulative	Organization as *bureaucracy*; impersonal, unemotional, rational	Control
Collectivist	Idealization; identification with the group	Shame for personal shortcomings; scapegoating 'deviants'	Imitative, conformist	Compliant, co-operative, timid, cautious, respectful	Organization as *perfect group*; loyal, idealistic	Group perfection
Heroic individualist	Object love, sublimation into achievement and adventure	Super-ego guilt for perceived failure	Competitive; others perceived as villains, victims, heroes, fools	Proud, strong sense of justice, adventurous, risk-taker	Organization as *arena for distinction* or as *game*; ambitious	Victory, success
Civic individualist	Object love, identification with commonwealth	Super-ego guilt against aggression	Fellow citizens; reasonable people	Tolerant, conscientious, controlled, altruistic	Organization as *symbolic order or normative community*; pluralistic	Harmony

hierarchy; a

will enable him or her to disappear within a highly cohesive social whole; the heroic individualist as something that will express his or her desire for epic achievement; and the civic individualist as something that will allow him or her to be respected and valued within a diverse totality. All of these characters invest organizations with meanings and symbolism, imbuing them with ideals and their close relatives, illusions (Schwartz, 1983). We have seen how each set of phantasies is articulated in an uncomfortable but potentially productive way, resulting in different psychological contracts between the individual and his or her organization. Phantasies, and especially illusions, can undoubtedly sustain individuals in organizations, enabling them to overcome difficulties, to cope with adversity and to infuse their activities with meaning. Illusions can be defended against reality, often at considerable cost. In order to maintain an image of an organization as generous, heroic or orderly, an individual must be prepared to overlook much evidence that clashes with such images. Yet, as we saw earlier in the case of the conformist individual, there are times when this may become untenable. It is then common for all of these characters to lapse into cynicism or despair, as they discover that their psychological contracts with their organizations have been built on false premises.

This raises the question of whether illusions are psychologically necessary to sustain life. Is life in general, and organizational life in particular, without illusions possible? Does an organization have to be made out of fantasy, and do fantasies within organizations need to be preserved or should they be checked and even punctured? Opinions here diverge. Some argue that organizations without illusions are impossible. All life entails phantasy, and all organizations have a phantasy life. Rationality itself grows out of a commitment to a set of phantasies which can be described as objective, scientific and so on. Chapter 9 explores the phantasy life of organizations, examining many of the contributions made in this area. Other theorists, including Maslow, Erikson and Rieff, however, argue that there is a stage of psychological development which transcends all earlier ones, one in which the individual learns to live a productive life without illusions, one in which his or her emotions come under the benevolent tutelage of reason. In this stage, the individual ceases to look for substitute gratifications for his or her repressed desires, accepts the harsh realities of life and seeks to attain those satisfactions that are available. This is what Rieff (1959, 1966) calls the 'analysed man', a mental personality who no longer looks for culture, religion, politics, institutions or organizations to provide meaning in his or her life. The individual neither rebels against social institutions, nor becomes dependent on them for his or her psychological well-being. The 'analysed man'

> is active and outgoing. Expedient normal attitudes lead to some achievement in the outer world. The brisk managerial ego of the normal personality devotes itself to aggression against the environment, to the practical use of objects; it does not fixate upon them ... Again, the economic metaphor discloses Freud's ideal of health as well: a fully employed libido. (Rieff, 1959: 388)

Using insights from *The Future of an Illusion* (1927), a late work in which Freud criticized religion as an illusion which merely reinforces the discontents it causes, Rieff, like Freud, advocates a life based on reason and science. At this point, organizations, institutions and culture in general cease to function as a source of consolation for unrealizable desires and become resources to be used by mature individuals seeking to maximize their satisfactions. Many criticisms have been voiced at Rieff's articulation of the Freudian ideal. Some have argued that it represents a lapse to the earliest stage of psychological development, narcissism, in which the individual is unable to develop meaningful relations of mutuality with others and is only capable of using them in an instrumental way. Questions have also been raised as to whether organizations, groups and even society, composed of such individuals, are at all possible. What would bind them together (see Gabriel, 1982)? Yet individuals searching for an ideal of reason which may be used as a control over irrational emotions will find in Rieff's work the clearest and most level-headed of such presentations.

Organizational theorists are not in agreement as to whether an individual can achieve transparency in his or her relations to organizations and their leaders. The majority accept that it is impossible to rid organizations of what Fineman (1996) calls 'the demon of irrationality', which creeps in through processes of transference, regression and fixation. Irrational, emotional forces will always surface in organizational life. Yet the majority of psychoanalytic authorities writing on organizations, writers such as Levinson, Zaleznik, Hirschhorn, Diamond, Baum, Kets de Vries and others, suggest that these forces may be tamed and controlled by the forces of reason and rationality. Reason may never establish a benevolent dictatorship in organizations but, like Rieff's 'brisk managerial ego' which keeps the id and the forces of passion and desire under control, so too can an organization's management keep under control the forces of irrationality which threaten to seize organizations. They do so by being ever-vigilant, by resisting attempts by their subordinates to either idolize them or vilify them, by being critical and self-critical.

Other writers express reservations about the possibility and even the desirability of ridding organizations of impulsive and emotional forces. They argue that a mature organization, like a mature individual, is not to be found in one that has transcended all earlier stages by advancing to a new stage, in which reason reigns supreme. Instead, they view the mature individual as one who does not become fixated to any one stage of his or her development but embodies all of the stages, in a relatively integrated unity. He or she may experience occasional narcissistic strivings and may at times find solace in routine and habit; he or she may conform in some groups while seeking to fulfil his or her heroic strivings in sport or some other appropriate arena; he or she may be the epitome of citizenship in some of his or her capacities, yet he or she is able to detach him or herself from an organization when necessary. In short, the mature character is one who draws from a wide repertoire for his or her emotional and cognitive responses to his or her environment. In an analogous fashion, it is possible to argue that an organization can be successful, not by ridding itself of emotion and irrationality, but by being able to call on members with a variety of character structures in different positions. In such an organization, no single character and no single set of phantasies or illusions predominates, but there is a constant discourse between them. Individual characters are consistent with the requirements of their work, so, for instance, accountants may be in the impersonal order stage, salesmen in the heroic individualist stage and leaders in the narcissistic stage. In such organizations, emotions are easier to control because they do not all drive the organization in the same direction, but to an extent they check and control each other. By contrast, organizations in which a particular set of phantasies predominates makes itself a hostage to fortune. For a time, these phantasies may serve the organization well, but when circumstances change it may be difficult or impossible for an organization to free itself from them. These issues will be discussed further in Chapter 11 which deals with organizational pathologies.

PSYCHOLOGICAL DEVELOPMENT AND ACADEMIC TRADITIONS OF STUDYING ORGANIZATION

If different individuals experience organizations in different ways depending on their psychological development, it is also true that different academic traditions of studying organization reflect these same stages of development. Since the late 1970s, it has become commonplace to assert that organizational theory is composed of a set of incommensurable paradigms, each one of which contains its own assumptions, problems and methodologies (see Burrell and Morgan, 1979). Morgan (1986) carved up the entire terrain of organizational studies in terms of certain dominant 'images of organization', each image driven by a certain metaphor of organizations as machines, biological organisms, cultures, political systems and so on. Others joined in the debate, either supporting the view that different approaches to organizations cannot communicate with each other because they are talking about different things, or to claim that this compartmentalization is a symptom of academic parochialism and territoriality (see Carr, 1997). It now seems increasingly difficult to defend the view of incommensurability, since there are many common concepts, concerns and assumptions shared by several paradigms. Yet, it is surprising how easily the dominant traditions in organizational studies can be mapped against the stages of psychological development discussed here.

The narcissistic character's perspective is that of *postmodern theories* of organizations. These theories essentially deny that organizations have a separate existence, and approach them primarily as they feature in language, narrative and symbolism. Methodologically, postmodern theories of organization often seem to share the narcissist's belief that 'anything goes', and that most disciplines, whether organizational or academic, can be overcome through the playful use of irony, wit and spontaneity (see Boje and Dennehy, 1993; and, for a critique, Schwartz, 1995). There is in this an incapacity to anticipate and cope with matters that do not yield immediately to spontaneity, and which therefore have to be split off and attacked as the work of hated and evil objects, in accordance with the form that paranoid ideation takes at the time. Modernism and some of its supposedly hallowed ideas ('essentialism', 'progress', 'objectivity', 'quality') become targets of caustic commentaries and criticism.

The obsessive character's perspective corresponds closely to the classical theories of organizations, above all Max Weber's ideal type of *bureaucracy* and F. W. Taylor's *scientific management*. These approaches emphasize the need for total control through the application of impersonal routines, which rid the organization of emotion and passion. They emphasize conventional Protestant ethic values, like frugality, cleanliness, emotional control and renunciation of bodily pleasures, all of which echo the preoccupations of the obsessive personality.

The collectivist character's concerns correspond fairly well to the tradition initiated by the human relations tradition and much management theory dating from the 1950s and 1960s, which emphasized *teamwork*, *groups* and *synergy*. This is a tradition that acquired a new lease of life with the 'discovery' of Japanese management in the late 1970s and 1980s, whose phenomenal successes at the time were attributed to the prodigious commitment of Japanese workers to their organization.

The heroic individualist character's outlook is admirably reflected by the *corporate culture* literature represented by authors such as Peters and Waterman (1982), Deal and Kennedy (1982), and so on. This literature rediscovered the heroic heritage of capitalism and argued that successful organizations are those which offer the opportunities to their members to emerge as cosmic super-heroes. The emphasis of this tradition lies in the myths, stories and other phenomena of organizational symbolism (badges, prizes, logos), through which the heroic achievements of the organization are honoured and celebrated. Also worthy of mention here are those vast tracts of organizational writing devoted to informing readers of how to 'get ahead' in organizational life.

The civic individualist character's outlook can be traced to *pluralistic* perspectives on organizations, drawn from political theory in the 1950s and 1960s. Some institutional theories of organizations develop the view of organizations as commonwealths of diverse interests and values, which different *stakeholders* seek to influence, without, however, undermining the essential value which they embody. In recent years, this perspective has been revived as a result of interest in environmental and ethical issues affecting corporate governance.

These analogies do not mean to imply that theoretical traditions in organizational studies do nothing but reflect the meanings of organizations rooted in character structures and early psychological development. They do, however, suggest that academic clusters of meanings related to organizations are continuous with the meanings, conscious and unconscious, of organizations held by laypeople.

CONCLUSION

In this chapter, we have introduced the individual in his or her relation to organizations, arguing that the difficulties of defining organizations stem from the fact that organizations are constructs rather than concepts; as constructs they carry symbolic resonances which, we have argued, are linked to different individuals' psychological character. Each distinct character represents a distinct experience of organization. Narcissistic characters tend to dismiss the idea of organization altogether, preferring instead to approach them as collections of individuals, who can provide an appreciative audience. Narcissistic characters can be difficult to accommodate within organizations, being impulsive, undisciplined and unpredictable. Obsessive characters, on the other hand, are in their element in organizations; the more bureaucratic the organization, the more impersonal and standardized, the better it seems to suit them, as they rely on mechanical procedures to eliminate disorder and unpredictability. Collectivist individuals tend to idealize the organization, and idealize themselves in as much as they belong to it, suppressing their difference and individuality. They are great team players, capable of considerable self-sacrifice, but will often act irrationally or immorally in following the crowd. Heroic individualists tend to approach organizations as terrains for noble exploits, achievements and victories. They too are capable of sacrifice, but only in pursuit of individual glory and fame. They are constantly driven towards distinction and excellence, seeking to stand out from the crowd through their accomplishments. Finally, civic individualists are those who experience organizations as normative communities, involving a legitimate plurality of interests and points of view; they adopt the stance of citizens who contribute to a broad commonwealth, not because they have to, but because they see the virtue of doing so; they can act altruistically without melodramatic self-sacrifices.

In all of these instances, an individual's experience of organizations is shaped by his or her desires and the phantasies through which he or she seeks to realize these desires. At the core of the way in which different individuals relate to organizations is emotion – emotion which can range from loyalty, commitment, responsibility and pride to fear, contempt and hate. In concluding the chapter, we have examined the possibility of an organization whose members are free of phantasies and illusions, who go about their business in a rational manner. In spite of the arguments, notably by Rieff, suggesting that this is possible, we suggest that it is unlikely for reason to keep emotion and phantasy out of the realm of organizations. Instead, we propose that it may be possible for emotions and phantasies to be tempered by reason, provided that a variety of character structures and their attending phantasies can be found in the same organization.

4 ORGANIZATION AND INDIVIDUAL

In Chapter 3 we examined how different individuals experience organizations depending on their character and their psychological development. We argued that, while organizations appear as objective, factual features of an external world, they can represent very different psychological realities. This makes the definition of organization difficult, as different individuals highlight those aspects of organizations which reflect their own concerns, in a positive or negative way. In this chapter we will present the opposite picture. We will concentrate on the demands which organizations make on individuals and the ways in which individuals deal with these demands. In the course of our discussion, it will become clear that some of the demands made by organizations are similar to those made by other collectivities or associations. In some respects, therefore, organizations are like groups, crowds, families and so forth. In other respects, however, they make quite different and unique demands. It is for this reason that organizations merit a special treatment from depth psychology, distinct, say, from the depth psychology of groups, crowds or families.

Most theorists of organizations agree that organizations are relatively recent historical phenomena, which have grown in size and power in the past 150 years of so. Of course, some organizations have existed for a long time: armies and the Catholic church, for instance, go way back in history, as do some universities and some sectors of government. But organization as a dominant social institution is usually seen as a product of modernity, the growth of capital, cities, communications and rationality. Western society is frequently referred to as an organizational society; it is certainly true that most of our daily activities take place within organizations, such as companies, government departments, schools, hospitals, universities, political parties and so on. Most of the goods and services we consume are products of large organizations, as indeed is much of the information that daily comes our way. Most of us are born in hospitals; increasingly, we also die in hospitals. Even when we think that we are at a safe distance from organizations – for instance, in the privacy of our own homes – we are still directly or indirectly enmeshed with organizations, as consumers of their products or recipients of their outputs. When we leave the hectic spaces of the city to visit the countryside or go mountain-climbing, we carry with us obligations, commitments and resources linked to organizations. In this way, it would not be untrue to say that organizations have colonized our lives. The ways in which we forge our identities are inextricably linked to the organizations that employ us, support us or supply us.

At this point, we shall refrain from providing a definition of organizations. In assessing their sway over our lives, we will examine, in a somewhat piecemeal fashion, some of their main features and compare them to those of other types of human collectivities. The idea of *collectivity* is meant to capture any social whole, within which individuals relate to each other in some way, however weak or ephemeral: a family, a crowd, a caste, a race, a professional association, a community, a business organization, a cinema audience, a minority group, or even the whole of humanity, are collectivities. What are *not* collectivities? Social aggregates – for instance, all individuals born in June or all individuals who like pastrami on rye – are not collectivities, though under some circumstances (for example, the government decides to ban pastrami) they could become collectivities. Collectivities can be long term (the civil service) or short term (a theatre audience), they can be large (the Catholic church) or small (a couple living together), they can be linked together by powerful emotional bonds (religious sects) or very weak ones (a bus queue), they can have leaders (a business firm) or not (four friends meeting for a game of bridge), they can have hierarchies (an army) or not (a family), they can be impersonal (a large university) or personal (a clan), they can have a collective task or set of tasks (a hospital) or not (tourists lying on a beach), they may seek to control membership (a golf club) or be open to all (an Internet discussion group).

What, then, are the characteristics that accord organizations a special place among collectivities? In the discussion that follows, we will concentrate on some specific features which give organizations their uniqueness among collectivities. These include impersonality, hierarchy, size, goals, concern for efficiency, boundaries, control and the nature of work.

IMPERSONALITY

Consider the beginning of an academic session when a group of first-year undergraduates go to their first lecture. The students have probably never met each other before. They come from many different countries and have many different backgrounds. A year earlier, they were doing very different things, little realizing that they would all be in the same place at the same time. Twenty years later, they are likely to have gone their separate ways, perhaps keeping in touch with a few of their classmates, but hardly remembering the names of the majority. During the lecture, students listen attentively to their lecturer. Yet they do not know her. They would certainly not be able to know if an impostor had suddenly taken over the class; they take it on trust that she is the right person, doing the right thing. Nor does the lecturer know her students. To her they may appear as an undifferentiated mass, not unlike those she taught in previous years. Outside the lecture theatre, she will have difficulty identifying them. Over the next four years, she will be unable to put with certainty a name next to a face for the majority. Walking around the campus, she may identify some individuals, like close colleagues or outstanding students, but most remain faces, strange or vaguely familiar.

In organizations, most of the people we meet are unknown to us. Many are entirely unknown, i.e. we cannot even identify them by name or function. Some we may be able to identify by name, though most of the personal details, their families, their histories, their feelings and desires are alien to us. A few may be closer to us; we may care for them, spend time with them, love them even. Yet even then we are often surprised when we find that a major event in their lives, or a major decision, was entirely unknown to us. For instance, we suddenly learn that they are about to leave the

TWO ILLUSTRATIONS

The red lines

Monica is a female school teacher; she is married to Alan, a personnel manager for Fixx and Partners, a medium-sized light engineering company. They have lived together happily for six years, in spite of their political and ideological differences. Monica often talks to Alan about her daily experiences at school, although Alan is less inclined to share his experiences with Monica. One evening, while marking her pupils' assignments, Monica noticed Alan absorbed in a computer print-out. Going down the document carefully, Alan was drawing thick red lines across some of the writing.

> MONICA: Not like you to bring work back home, Alan. What is it that you are doing?
> ALAN: I am going through the list of redundancies. Fixx will announce the package next week, and I have been given a list of staff, their jobs and their salaries. My job is to reduce our payroll by 20 per cent, or else the company will go to the wall.
> MONICA: How can you do such a thing, Alan? Do you know any of these people?
> ALAN: Of course I don't know most of them. What does it matter anyway? It would make my job far harder if I knew them.
> MONICA: Alan, don't you see – you may be throwing people on the scrapheap, people with families to support, people who have given their lives to the company?
> ALAN: Monica, it's easy for you to feel sorry for all these poor souls. But don't you see? The company is losing money; if it does nothing it will be curtains for everyone, from the top to the bottom. This is a recession – our order books are empty, we can hardly keep going. This is a business, not an agency to keep people employed.

Monica reported this conversation with her husband, observing that it had had a great impact on her outlook on organizations. It had forced her to confront the fact that an organization is not truly like a family. After all, no family would cast out some of its members to ensure the survival of the others.

Sorry Joyce!

Joyce, a departmental head, arrives for an early start at the head office of a chemicals multinational; she is met by a guard, whose name she has never managed to learn but whose face is very familiar:

> GUARD: Good morning, Joyce, your security pass, please.
> JOYCE: Sorry, I accidentally left it in my office yesterday.
> GUARD: Sorry, Joyce, I can't let you in.
> JOYCE: But you know me, I am the head of sales . . .
> GUARD: Sorry, Joyce, a rule's a rule.
> JOYCE: Can you phone and have someone send my pass?
> GUARD: Sorry Joyce, you're first in this morning and I'm not expecting anyone for another hour.

Where but in a modern organization could incidents like these take place? A visitor from a pre-organizational society would find it more difficult to make sense of it than Western anthropologists studying primitive cultures. What is more, Alan and Joyce themselves

> are unlikely to make a special effort to make sense of the incidents. 'People must be sacrificed for the survival of the company', 'A rule is a rule': these are assumptions which we automatically make in thinking about organizations. Organizations seek to control human behaviour in a quite unique way, through a multiplicity of highly specific and impersonal bureaucratic regulations. Various restrictions are placed on individuals' freedoms which would be intolerable in a different context. Their time is regimented, their performance continuously monitored, their emotions curtailed and their relations to their fellow human beings substantially stripped of spontaneity, affection and passion. Their private joys, their sorrows, their worries and their histories are effectively excluded.

organization to take up a job elsewhere, and yet we did not know that they were applying for such a job.

Contrast these impersonal relations with the personal relations that bond us to our relatives or our friends. Dealing with them, we are responsive to their personality, their feelings, their histories. We interpret their mood and facial expressions. Our transactions are part of a historical process, a history of creative commitments and bonds, moulded by subtle emotional dynamics of giving and taking. Not so when we relate with strangers as members of organizations. There, our transactions are mainly governed by our organizational *roles* and the *rules* that pertain to different situations. Who we are matters much less than what we do. What brings us together with other individuals are not our spontaneous desires or wishes, but impersonal arrangements, made by people whose identity and existence may be unknown to us. Some writers in the past, following an argument of Max Weber, saw impersonality as leading to a total exclusion of emotions from organizational life. We now know that this is inaccurate, and in Chapter 9 we shall examine how emotions are constructed, expressed and controlled in organizations.

Impersonality is a key ingredient of our experience of organizations from our first day at school when we become one of many, a number on the register, a face among unknowns. To be sure, impersonality is a more general feature of modern life, not merely a product of organizations. Living in large cities, surrounded by millions of unfamiliar faces, people in the twentieth century have had to learn to live as unknowns in the midst of unknowns. Impersonality is a fundamental affront to our narcissism. From being unique members of a family, a clan or a group, we are consigned by organizations, and urban life in general, to the status of cogs, important or critical perhaps, but dispensable and replaceable. In compensation, we seek to develop identities of our own, to distinguish ourselves from the crowd, to establish our own individuality and uniqueness. We also tend to exaggerate the importance of the personal in our organizational lives, overstating our own importance for the organization and those of our narrow circle of associates. Sometimes we relate to organizations as though they were surrogates of our family and, indeed, in some cases they can function as such. However, this does not change the fact that most individuals in organizations are replaceable.

The impersonality of organizations is not only a psychological burden. It also has advantages. It strips unpleasant decisions which are liable to upset others of the personal element. It offers some psychological protection against guilt and anxiety. It shelters us from having to examine the moral and political implications of our actions. It guards us from the violent emotions of others and guards them, in turn, from our own violent emotions. Finally, it liberates us from a nexus of mutual obligations and entitlements which can become overbearing and paralysing.

Discussing depersonalization, as economic activity shifted from family businesses to large corporations, Levinson makes an interesting observation:

> The relationship between employee and manager became depersonalized and the relationship between employee and organization became animated instead. The work organization has taken on psychological significance in the way that an old school might: because people relate to it in the manner of children to an adult, it assumes a significance that would be obscure to an outsider. (1968/1981: 77)

Thus organizations, as single entities, may enter our emotional and fantasy life because of the very impersonality of our relations with each other. In effect, our loyalties, commitments, resentments and hates are addressed at this entity, through which early emotional experiences are revived. We may thus invest it with meanings and significance which have little relationship to reality, but serve important psychic needs.

HIERARCHY

Impersonality is an important characteristic of organizations but, as we saw, it is also a feature of crowds and urban life in general. The second feature of organizations, hierarchy, is also not unique to organizations. It can be observed in pecking orders throughout the animal kingdom; it can also be observed in the status and power hierarchies of nobility as well as those of street gangs and political elites. Finally, within families, the order of birth establishes a subtle hierarchy of privileges and obligations which may play a defining role in a person's psychological structure (Sulloway, 1996). Yet, organizational hierarchy is combined with impersonality and this presents our psychological functioning with some very special challenges.

Organizational hierarchies represent hierarchies of both authority and accountability. Within such hierarchies superiors hold certain rights over their subordinates, which include the rights to issue particular types of command, to reward and to discipline. At the same time, superiors are accountable both for their own actions and those of their subordinates to their own superiors. Subordinates, for their part, are obligated to carry out the commands of their superiors, provided that they accord with the organization's impersonal system of rules and regulations. Thus, authority and accountability, from the organization's point of view, are not attached to individuals but invested in the positions within the hierarchy.

The hierarchical principle has been essential for the growth of organizations on a colossal scale, requiring the collaboration of thousands or hundreds of thousands of disparate individuals. Without hierarchies, it is hardly conceivable that massive organizations would have come into being. And yet, hierarchies wreak havoc on our psychological experiences of leadership, power, responsibility and accountability. If impersonality is an affront to our narcissism, hierarchy distorts our experiences of authority, which are rooted in the resolution of the Oedipus complex and the institution of the super-ego. The super-ego prepares us to obey and respect strong leaders, who carry the authority with which we once invested our father. In Chapter 6 we will establish that there is a second principle of leadership, one in which we follow leaders who inspire us with the self-love and self-confidence we once experienced in our early fusion with our mother. In every case, our allegiance to the leader is part of a mutual relationship, whereby the leader undertakes to protect us, guide us and uplift us. However, the hierarchical principle demands that we obey individuals who are merely appointed officials, like ourselves, who are themselves weak and vulnerable, accountable for their actions to their own superiors, whose only claim to legitimacy is their holding of a position and whose ability to protect us is as tenuous as their own hold over their position. Some organizational leaders may succeed in inspiring the loyalty of their followers, by supplementing their formal authority with considerable personal authority. Many, however, are ill-equipped for doing so, both in the technical and the personal sense:

> Because of the way that the hierarchical model distributes authority, people may find themselves in positions of power without having had any training in the use of authority. Well-trained in other areas, for other tasks, they are nevertheless ill-prepared for managing the people they supervise. It is as if an engineer unusually skilled in designing engines for power boats were suddenly to find himself as a captain of a large freighter: commanding the freighter calls for coordination management and decision-making skills that are quite different from the skills needed to design an engine. (Levinson, 1968/1981: 84)

Baum (1987) has argued that organizational hierarchies become embedded in each individual's psychological structure, leading to what he calls an 'invisible bureaucracy'. The psychological structure of bureaucracy is characterized by chronic anxiety, insecurity, guilt and shame. Organizational hierarchies disperse responsibility while centralizing authority, leaving a wide area of ambiguity in relations between superiors and subordinates. A divisional vice-president requests a set of figures of one of his departmental directors. She is unsure about the purpose or exact nature of the figures requested, she is overworked and overwrought; she passes the request down to one of her subordinates who is even less sure about the purpose or nature of the figures requested. The request is thus passed down until it reaches someone who, for some reason or other, may compile *some* figures. The figures will then start travelling up the hierarchy, possibly being changed at every stage to suit the interest of the relevant official, until eventually they reach the VP. In many instances, they will no longer be relevant or needed, in which case the entire exercise has been for nought. Even more often, the figures are not the ones the VP believes them to be or expects them to be. If the figures prove to be false or misleading, who is to blame? Within hierarchies, individuals find themselves unsure about the limits of their power

---

People want to live and have to sell themselves; but they despise him who exploits their necessity and purchases the workman. It is curious that the subjection to powerful, fear inspiring and even dreadful individuals, to tyrants and leaders of armies, is not at all felt so painfully as the subjection to such undistinguished and uninteresting persons as the captains of industry.

Nietzsche, The Gay Science

and responsibility, assessed by superiors who know little about their work, and confronted at all stages by unpredictable factors which they cannot control. A psychological gulf develops between leaders and followers, where individuals deny their subordinates the very protection which they demand of their superiors. This gulf is filled by the products of fantasy or reverie which subordinates develop towards their superiors, which in turn exacerbates mistrust and anxiety and further undermines authority.

Organizational hierarchies produce a related psychological consequence: a chronic rivalry among officials competing for promotion. Promotion is one avenue available to individuals for restoring their narcissistic sense of value and self-worth which impersonality undermines. There are others, including cynical distancing and nostalgic idealization of the organization's past, yet a successful climb up the hierarchy holds much promise, notably for younger employees. Promotion is a powerful motivator. In response to this, organizations seek to create new layers, new distinctions and new status markers with which to give individuals a sense of movement and progress. This, in turn, fosters infinitesimal comparisons among officials about pay, title, position, fringe benefits and status symbols, which promote envy and depression. These have their roots in early experiences of sibling rivalries, which are exacerbated by unequal treatment by the parents. In organizations, 'the hierarchical model, with its penchant for creating more defeated people than victorious ones, makes for a self-fulfilling prophecy. There is a pile-up of "career" people who are destined to stay in their grade and are often depressed' (Levinson, 1968/1981: 88). Like impersonality, hierarchy is a feature of organizations which does not only leave individuals with significant psychological burdens. It also offers certain advantages, three of which merit special note. First, organizational hierarchies create the illusion of progression, growth and development. If this is joined with the illusion of fair competition, this can be a powerful illusion, galvanizing the new employee to great feats of achievement and self-sacrifice. By contrast, an organization where power is invested directly in a powerful central leader like Haile Selassie (*see* Box) drives new recruits in a different way, as they seek to make themselves noticed by the leader through acts of personal devotion and loyalty.

THE PECKING ORDER IN THE COURT OF HAILE SELASSIE

This is how the eminent Polish journalist Ryszard Kapuscinski describes the struggles of court officials to rise in the pecking order of the Ethiopian royal court.

> Those who were lower were determined to rise. Number forty-three wanted to be twenty-sixth. Seventy-eight had an eye on thirty-two's place. Fifty-seven climbed to twenty-nine, sixty-seven went straight to thirty-four, forty-one pushed thirty out of the way, twenty-six was sure of being twenty-second, fifty-four gnawed at forty-six, sixty-three scratched his way to forty-nine, and always upward toward the top without end . . . Our palace was a fabric of hierarchies and if you were slipping on one you could grab hold of another, and everyone found some satisfaction and reason to be proud of himself. Everyone spoke with admiration and jealousy of those who had made the list: 'Look who's going!' (Kapuscinski, 1983: 61, 62)

Secondly, hierarchies enable individuals to acquire power quickly without having to prove themselves on a continuous basis. They eliminate the need for costly tests of power, where individuals challenge each other in order to maintain their position in the pecking order. Thus, in spite of the limitations noted earlier, organizational hierarchies do accord some legitimacy to individuals' use of power and enable them to do their work. At times, they may offer opportunities to highly talented individuals to rise rapidly and assume positions of power and responsibility, without having to wait for earlier incumbents of senior positions to retire or drop out of the race.

Thirdly, hierarchies offer some measure of protection for each individual against demands and interference from people other than their direct superior. They reduce the conflicts of allegiance that may afflict individuals who serve several masters at the same time and reduce the attendant anxiety.

SIZE, POWER, WEALTH AND DURATION

Organizations do not have to be large, but they are capable of growing extremely large. Some of them are geographically spread on five continents, employing hundreds of thousands of people. Their economic and political powers can be formidable, at times overwhelming the powers of individual nation-states. The sheer scale of their operations is colossal. They are also long term, giving the impression of permanence and even immortality. Faced with such scales, an individual can easily feel insignificant and overwhelmed.

Like impersonality and hierarchy, size is not the exclusive preserve of organizations. Other collectivities, including nations, television audiences, social classes and crowds can number many thousands or even millions of individuals. But in organizations alone are such large numbers to be found working together, interacting with each other and earning their livelihoods from a single source. Size is thus compounded by complexity of structure, diversity of membership and a detailed division of labour.

The effects of size on other organizational entities, such as structure, culture and technology, have been discussed widely by organizational scholars. Since early studies by the Aston Group in the United Kingdom and Peter Blau in the United States, strong correlations have been found between size and structural variables, such as complexity, formality and density. A substantial amount of literature has been devoted to the question of the effects of size on performance, economies and diseconomies of scale. However, the psychological effects of size have not been studied nearly as extensively. In his classic critique of our 'almost universal idolatry of giantism' (1973: 54), Fritz Schumacher has argued that large organizations foster dependency and unwillingness to take responsibility:

> Nobody really likes large-scale organization; nobody likes to take orders from a superior who takes orders from a superior who takes orders... Even if the rules devised by bureaucracy are outstandingly humane, nobody likes to be ruled by rules, that is to say, by people whose answer to every complaint is: 'I did not make the rules: I am merely applying them.' (1973: 202)

Schumacher may have been rash in arguing that *nobody* likes large-scale organizations, as is evident from the excitement that mergers and acquisitions cause in the stock markets. His observation, however, that being a member of a vast organization makes people feel like insignificant cogs is not far off the mark.

Psychoanalysis would, in the first place, seek to approach the psychological realities of being a member of a huge collectivity through the concepts of impotence and omnipotence. Following the pioneering work of Gustave Le Bon, Freud explored the sense of omnipotence experienced by individuals as members of crowds and large groups.

> A group impresses the individual as being an unlimited power and an insurmountable peril. For the moment it replaces the whole of human society, which is the wielder of authority, whose punishments the individual fears, and for whose sake he has submitted to so many inhibitions. It is clearly perilous for him to put himself in opposition to it, and it will be safer to follow the example of those around him and perhaps even 'hunt with the pack'. (1921: 113)

Clearly, an organization is different from a crowd, not least in respect of the intensification of affect, which is Freud's focus in the above extract. Yet, the same contrast between the collectivity's infinite power and the individual's infinite vulnerability characterizes the experience of being a member of a large organization. One of the distinct features of psychoanalytic approaches is an attempt to interpret experiences of later life as re-creations, at least in part, of formative experiences of early life. In this respect, omnipotence, whether bestowed to a crowd, an organization or indeed a deity, is seen as deriving from the great powers we accord our parents, and especially the father, in contrast to our early childhood dependence and vulnerability. Just as the child tends to exaggerate the freedom, power and autonomy of the father, so too we tend to exaggerate the same qualities of large objects in future, experiencing ourselves as weak and vulnerable by contrast.

There are different ways in which we attempt to cope psychologically with the size and power disparities between ourselves and our organizations. One common way is to subordinate ourselves to them, exchanging our freedom for their protection. In such cases, we may exaggerate further their omnipotence and size. But the similarity with our early childhood experience can go still further. Every child discovers at some point that the father is neither omnipotent nor invulnerable. In some instances, this discovery leads to a profound sense of disillusionment and mourning, as when a child sees his or her father humiliated and insulted by someone wielding a larger stick. The child may then feel betrayed – he or she agreed to obey and love the father in exchange for the protection the father affords him or her – but the father has proved himself to be an unworthy protector, weak like the child. In a similar way, the respect and even love that as adults we have for our organizations may turn into disillusionment, mourning and betrayal when these organizations are beaten or defiled.

Of course, not all of us experience feelings of insignificance and impotence as members of large organizations. Such organizations may provoke in us feelings of pride and excitement, as though their grandeur and power were our own. Schwartz (1990) has argued that being a member of a large organization can re-awaken in us a different experience from that of being powerless and in need for protection. Instead, it can lead to invulnerability and grandiosity which re-create the condition of primary narcissism. Using Freud's concept of the ego-ideal, as elaborated by Chasseguet-Smirgel (1985), Schwartz (1990) has proposed that the vehicle for restoring primary narcissism is the organizational ideal, a set of organizational fantasies which colonize the individual's ego-ideal. In as much as he or she is a member of the organization, the individual imagines him or herself endowed with all its perfections, including power, wealth and immortality. The organization's size and glamour, in this way, support the individual's identity while loosening his or her grasp of reality and morality. On occasion, individuals will engage in profoundly anti-social or irrational acts in support of the organizational ideal, without which they would be reduced to non-entities. In extreme situations, individuals may experience towards their organizations a religious devotion, akin to an 'oceanic' feeling (Freud, 1930), a feeling of being part of an immense entity which is nourishing and unthreatening and which dissolves all boundaries and all strife. The organization in such cases may become an omnibenevolent mother with whom the individual fuses.

To be part of a large, supra-individual entity is an important demand made by organizations on our psychological functioning. Unlike crowds, which tend to be ephemeral, organizations appear as long standing and even permanent. It would not be an exaggeration to say that in addition to fuelling fantasies of omnipotence (as crowds can do), organizations fuel fantasies of immortality (Sievers, 1990, 1994). Unlike nations or classes, organizations are not only large, they generally have a sense of purpose or objective.

GOALS

It is a strange feature of organizations that, while virtually all their members agree that they have goals, any random survey of their members reveals wide discrepancies in their assessment of the nature of those goals. A hospital porter, a secretary, a physician, a personnel manager, a nurse and a patient may have very different notions of what a hospital's goals are. Even individuals in similar positions frequently find themselves at odds over the precise goals of their organizations or, at least, the priority ranking of such goals. Is a hospital's goal to cure patients, to relieve pain, to improve the health standards of people, to carry out large numbers of operations, to offer a very high quality of medical care, to carry out world-class research, to make patients feel happy or to make profit?

In spite of grave difficulties in establishing organizational goals, there can be little doubt that most of our time in organizations is spent being conscious of certain goals which are to be achieved. We go about our affairs in a business-like, no-nonsense manner. Unlike our actions in other collectivities, our actions as organizational employees are aimed at some objectives, however dim or ill-defined they may be. They are certainly not governed by the pleasure principle, unless this too is turned into a business proposition, as in theme parks, where pleasure must be pursued with the utmost seriousness. Organizations can be seen as areas where rationality, efficiency and the reality principle rule supreme. Few of us can function in organizations without being constantly aware of the need to be efficient, consistent, rational and, perhaps above all, continually busy. To be sure, as this entire book seeks to establish, emotional forces, fantasy and irrationality are constantly at play within organizations. Yet our actions in organizations would make little sense to us without the sense that they are linked to some collective aim to which individual will must be subordinated.

Organizational goals are not the same as a leader's vision or even a sense of mission. Visions and missions, as we shall see in Chapter 6, can characterize many different collectivities, including nations and classes. Noble visions may involve great sacrifices, waste and suffering. They may lead to action (including war) or may lie dormant in the hope that one day they may be fulfilled. Not so goals, which are meant to be pursued in a no-nonsense, methodical way which minimizes the use of resources and effort. There can be little doubt that organizations can be massively wasteful and inefficient. Yet no organization can be thought of which would proclaim that its object is to be wasteful and inefficient. Efficiency may in the case of many organizations be a fiction, but it is a fiction in front of which everyone must bow and in the name of which large amounts of resources and efforts are expended. In the first place, the continuous monitoring of performance, its detailed recording, measurement and regimentation, its obsessional comparing, are all legitimized by recourse to the needs for efficiency. And efficiency makes little sense without an implicit assumption of goals. A family, a crowd, and even a nation could hardly be imagined priding themselves on their efficiency – an organization certainly can.

Psychoanalytic writers frequently approach organizational goals through the concept of a *primary task*, a fundamental task which each organization must carry out in order to survive (Rice, 1963). The idea of working groups performing a fundamental task has its origins in the pioneering work of W. R. Bion (1961). Bion studied relatively small groups, initially in the army and later at the Tavistock Clinic in London, on the basis of which he proposed a highly influential theory of the mental functioning of groups. His theory will be examined in greater detail in Chapter 5, which addresses groups in organizations, though for the purposes of this chapter the organization may be addressed as a large work group. Bion argues that:

> when a group meets, it meets for a specific task, and in most human activities today co-operation has to be achieved by sophisticated means. As I have already pointed out, rules of procedure are adopted; there is usually some administrative machinery operated by officials who are recognizable as such by the rest of the group, and so on. The capacity for co-operation on this level is great, as anybody's experience of groups will show. (1961: 98)

Bion likens the work group to the healthy individual ego, which is in command of its resources and is capable of responding to demands from the environment, without being overwhelmed by anxiety or other powerful emotions. By contrast, under conditions of intense anxiety, often precipitated by the task itself, groups may lapse into what Bion calls 'basic assumption functioning', which is dominated by powerful emotional forces. In contrast, then, to basic assumption groups, Bion argues that the work group can keep its sights on the task, preserves its critical abilities, is capable of development and has 'accepted the validity of learning from experience' (1961: 99). Its members act as individuals rather than as an undifferentiated mass. Organization is not something superimposed on to the work group, but constitutes its very essence:

> Group organization gives stability and permanence to the work group, which is felt to be more submerged by the basic assumptions if the group is unorganized. Individual distinctiveness is no part of life in a group that is acting on the basic assumptions. Organization and structure are weapons of the work group. (Bion, 1961: 170)

Thus, in Bion's view, organization is not a new historical phenomenon, except in its size; instead, it is a feature of all groups that are task-oriented, differentiated and capable of keeping their emotions and fantasies under control. Like the idea of organizational goals, the concept of primary group task has proved difficult to pin down in all but the cases of the most focused and single-minded organizations; for example, an army immediately before battle or a sports team before a cup final. Gordon Lawrence (1977/1985) has proposed that within organizations there are different types of primary tasks: there is a *normative primary task*, which is usually a set of publicly stated goals, what the organization says it does; there is an *existential primary task*, reflecting the actual beliefs and experiences of those working in the organization; and there is a *phenomenal primary task*, which is mostly unconscious, and which addresses deeper psychic needs. Obholzer (1994) has argued that, at this deeper level, the primary task of the health service is not to cure disease or care for patients but to support the fantasy that pain and even death can be overcome.

These psychoanalytic ideas suggest that organizational goals can become part of our psychic structure; in doing so, however, they undergo transformations, which bring them ever closer to our own desires and anxieties, and further away from the aims defined by some external stakeholders or organizational leaders. In this way, the primary task, as defined by each individual, or as it is experienced at the unconscious level, may be at variance with the organization's official claim.

EFFICIENCY

The discrepancy between an individual's perception of an organization's primary task and that embodied in organizational functioning itself is often tested over the issue of efficiency. As we saw earlier, whatever organizations seek to accomplish, they seek to do it in a methodical, business-like, efficient manner. Efficiency is raised to the standard of a universal value: one to be compared with altruism, love and independence. At a psychological level, these, as we saw earlier, become entrenched in the ego-ideal, which becomes the carrier of national, class and group ideals.

How can the ideal of efficiency assume the same status as these other ideals? One way of addressing this question is through the notion of economy. This is something that we often admire, for instance, in a well-managed household (the word 'economy' originates in the Greek for household management); mathematical proofs are described as 'elegant' when they rely on minimal resources, while physical movements are described as graceful if they are devoid of waste. Recycling waste is another instance where economy is apparent as a value. Sociologically, the value of economy is central to that cluster of values, which include frugality, temperance, cleanliness and hard work, referred to as the Protestant work ethic. Psychologically, these have been linked to the anal character who is a compulsive economizer of time, resources and effort. Economy in this form is the product of methodical thinking, husbanding of resources, comparing alternatives and discovering marginal improvements in the way things are done.

But there is another type of economy. This is the product not of method, but of intuition, inspiration or magic. Thus, a few magic words will move the boulder that several sturdy men cannot budge. This is the economy which lies at the heart of jokes and insults, where a punch line delivers a massive effect in mirth or anger. It is also the economy of the shortcut, the chance discovery which alleviates much drudgery and toil. This type of economy is unlikely to appeal to the anal characters, but it is sure to grasp the imagination of the impulsive narcissistic character and the heroic individualist; the former will view it as an aesthetic delight affording him or her narcissistic pleasure, the latter as a tool towards enhancing his or her power and reputation.

INDIVIDUAL IDENTITY AND ORGANIZATIONAL POWER PRACTICES: PSYCHOSTRUCTURE AND POLITICAL LANGUAGE

Sharon Mason and Adrian Carr

Sharon Mason and Adrian Carr develop the concept of 'psychostructure' which highlights the ego-ideal as the meeting point of organizational structure and mental dynamics.

In recent years we have heard people speak frequently of 'organizational identity' as though, like individuals, organizations have discernible traits. The problem that has arisen in such a discourse is one of being able to explain coherently how such an organizational identity is created and thus be potentially capable of transformation. Psychoanalytic theory, and particularly the derivative concept of 'psychostructure', developed by Maccoby (1976), La Bier (1986) and Carr (1993, 1998), provides a very useful linkage. In the following discussion, we elaborate the usefulness of 'psycho-structure' in understanding the relationship between individual and organizational identity, and the importance of language in such a dynamic. We then use a case example to illustrate these dynamics and conclude with some implications for organizations.

Freud (1921) used the term 'identification' to describe a psychological process in which the ego seeks to identify an aspect of itself with some other object in keeping with the constraints of social acceptability. These 'rules' of society were seen by Freud as being the province of the super-ego, and were really those rules of conduct demanded by parents and *other significant authority figures*. Badcock states that:

> the super-ego provides a sense of moral and aesthetic self-judgement (conscience and values, in other words), both in a positive sense as acting as an *ego-ideal* and in the negative one in performing the role of censor of the ego's wishes . . . Failure to meet the demands of the super-ego creates feelings of moral anxiety. (1988: 122; emphasis added)

It is through a series of identifications that this ego-ideal is formed and re-formed, thereby constituting an individual's personality (Laplanche and Pontalis, 1988). Identity emerges from the integration of such identifications in what is, largely, an unconscious process. Freud (1914a) viewed the generation of the ego-ideal as an attempt to recover some of the narcissistic perfection enjoyed in childhood. This quest for narcissism is not the pathological condition that is an exaggerated concern for power and self, but is rather a healthy quest for wholeness, perfection and positive self-esteem.

The work organization is an important stage on which these psychodynamics are played out, particularly in a world where self-worth and identity are increasingly gauged by the paid employment that an individual undertakes. Freud (1921: 161) suggested that, in a group context, individuals may seek to identify strongly with the leader such that they would disregard the prohibitive/censor aspect of the super-ego, and replace the ego-ideal with that group ideal embodied in the leader. The narcissistic gratification (and simultaneous avoidance of the psychological punishment for non-compliance) that comes through such identification is a potent psychodynamic. Viewed in this context, the individual is, in a way, psychologically 'seduced' into compliance behaviour, abandoning the ability to stand outside the dynamic and make 'rational' decisions about the relationship.

Studies in work organizations (see Maccoby, 1976; La Bier, 1986; Carr, 1993) provide evidence consistent with these psychodynamics. The term 'psychostructure' is used by these researchers to refer to the cluster of traits or values that represent the ego-ideal (or personality profile) found to exist in an organization or some part thereof. The collective voice from these studies is that the subject's personality becomes, to some degree, transformed by internalizing specific components of psychostructure and identifying with them. As the underpinning of such psychodynamics, narcissistic gratification represents a significant vehicle through which power can be exercised, particularly, but not only, through the use of language.

Language in all its forms, verbal, written, symbolic and behavioural, can be thought of as a signal to another party. In the context of the psychodynamics outlined above, the forms of language used, and by whom they are used, are scanned for psychological 'meaning'. The 'clues and cues' are decoded for meaning, intended or otherwise, albeit unconsciously. In the organizational context this searching and decoding activity may lead to a cumulative 'picture' that, through the psychodynamics of forming and re-forming the ego-ideal, is embedded as a psychological phenomenon as a psychostructure to be realized. Viewed in this manner, one can start to appreciate how, in particular, *political language* is a signal of authority, and at the same time a psychologically potent phenomenon. Edelman (1964) viewed political language as symbolic language, evocative and motivating, but not producing an accurate or unbiased assessment of self-interest. When functioning on an expressive (versus instrumental) level, political language operates primarily with and on symbolic outcomes and sentiments, including attitudes, beliefs and social perceptions; in other words, the elements comprising organizational psychostructure. Let us look at a case example to illustrate this usage.

The following examples of political language were taken from an employee handbook produced for a large Canadian financial institution. While consistently making record profits, the company was simultaneously engaged in relentless lay-offs. The expressed purpose of the handbook was to articulate the 'new work habits required of employees in a radically changing world'. It seems likely that a change in the organization's psychostructure ('*new* work habits') rendered more salient efforts at constructing psychostructure than might otherwise have been visible. Our intent in the accompanying interpretations was to illustrate the psychostructure 'clues and cues' contained therein. Our rendering was *not* intended as any kind of definitive statement about the organization.

Social perceptions about 'careers' and the 'world', as well as beliefs and attitudes towards management and self, were prescribed for employees remaining after the lay-offs:

> Careers have already quit working like they used to. That's not really *anybody's* [emphasis in original] fault . . . It does no good whatsoever to complain or be bitter about what's happening . . . We waste precious energy if we resist, get angry, or give in to grief . . . We jeopardize our future if we cling to old assumptions and expectations about how careers should operate . . . Frankly, the world doesn't care about our opinions. Or our feelings.

In this text, management absolves itself of responsibility for the lay-offs, disparages normal emotional responses as a waste of energy (taboo in relation to the psychostructure), exerts a subtle threat to those who resist this interpretation and paints the world, rather than itself, as an uncaring, capricious place. In sharp contrast to the lack of accountability of management, employees are told: 'Organizations are insisting on new levels of accountability. And you can't get off the hook by rationalizing, "I tried . . . I really worked hard . . . I did high quality work . . . I did *my* part".' Working hard, quality work and doing one's part are a rationalization, an attempt to 'get off the hook' and duck appropriate responsibility. What might be described as an over-exaggerated sense of responsibility is thus a prescribed component of the organization's psychostructure. Managers are rendered blameless, and responsibility for lay-offs and accompanying changes is shifted to the employees and an uncaring world. Even if employees adopt the prescribed *mea culpa* attributions, however, they may still lose their jobs: 'Granted, this drive toward an ever-improving performance doesn't guarantee job security, raises or promotions. *You still can be a victim of circumstances, even in strong, financially successful organizations* [emphasis added].'

Once again, the authors of these circumstances are obscured and the prescribed perception by and about managers – 'we are blameless' – is reinforced. In contrast to the ascribed powerless position of 'victims of circumstances', employees are simultaneously attributed full power to determine their career success: 'But if you've passionately practised *kaizen* [continuous improvement] . . . you'll at least find it easier to resume your career in another setting.' If these 'victims of circumstances' do not resume their careers, it is their own fault for not being passionate enough in practising *kaizen*. Employees are further instructed to: 'Think of it [*kaizen*] as the daily pursuit of perfection.' The organizational psychostructure thus seems to prescribe a mechanistic, perfectionistic personality without space for trial and error, experimentation or creativity. While unrealistic self-expectations, perfectionism and self-blame do not seem conducive to long-term work performance or individual well-being, these characteristics do deflect attention away from the agents of the above 'circumstances'. The prescribed attribution of self-blame ironically assumes an almost grandiose power in sharp contrast to the inherent powerlessness of a 'victim' of circumstances.

While a lack of passion in practising *kaizen* is the prescribed 'reason' for career problems, job commitment 'characterizes' those who experience career success. The 'committed' are described as 'those who work from the heart . . . who invest themselves passionately in their jobs'. Being 'committed' not only includes 'far more satisfying' work but is also described as 'therapeutic, an excellent antidote for stress and a fine cure for the pain of change'. If people are experiencing stress and pain at the prospect of being laid off by a record profit-making employer, or dissatisfaction with increased workloads, for example, their own lack of job commitment is the prescribed causal attribution. A little more 'commitment therapy' (i.e. stronger identification with the organization's psychostructure) is the prescribed antidote. Effecting a personality transformation into the image of the psychostructure may indeed lead to narcissistic gratification and 'work satisfaction'. But at what cost?

Conclusion

We have proposed that the concepts of 'psychostructure' and 'political language' provide useful linkages in understanding the connections between individual identity and organizational power practices. The desire for narcissistic gratification was suggested as rendering individuals susceptible to being psychologically 'seduced' by and assimilated into the organization's ego-ideal.

A case example was used to illustrate the role of political language as both a signal of authority and elucidator of the ego-ideal reflected in a company's psychostructure. The cumulative 'picture' that emerged was the result of our searching and decoding activity. However, the primarily unconscious nature of the psychodynamics presented may suggest the usefulness of an 'outside' perspective. A disturbing implication is the potentially pathological nature of psychostructure characteristics, such as those of perfectionism and self-blame seen in the text analysed. As the harmful consequences of such traits are well established, individuals may be paying dearly with their well-being for narcissistic gratification. In addition, the indirect injunctions against behaviour necessary for creativity and innovation may ultimately undermine organizational survival. What then can be done to avert the potential harm of such potent dynamics?

One possibility is the use of 'psychostructure audits'. An organization, through its structuring and reward systems, may potentially produce a psychostructure or a tension towards a psychostructure that encourages or promotes 'abnormal' personality profiles. In this context, we ask the question whether an organization has an ethical obligation to have a psychostructure audit and an obligation to make such results public? We are all too familiar with some employers using a battery of psychological tests to vet potential employees and also the notion of industrial inspectors ensuring that a workplace is ergonomically safe. The idea that the workplace should be audited for its psychological effects on employees seems to have largely been ignored. Such audits cannot be conducted by simply focusing on statistical information about the number of absences from work due to medically diagnosed work-related stress. The mere presence or absence of stress does not in itself indicate the psychological health of the work environment. The suggestion of psychological audits must not be construed as advocacy of another battery of psychological tests for the employee. The notion of psychostructure inherently conceives of the employee in an interactive relationship with the leadership and organization structure and processes. In this context the psychological audit needs to include a psychological appraisal of the leaders of the organization, for there is a significant amount of accumulated evidence that organization structure and processes themselves may simply be an extension of the 'self' of the leader(s) (see Kets de Vries and Miller, 1991, for an appraisal of this literature).

The organizational predilection for economy of both types is one that can easily be accommodated in the individual's psychic functioning, especially those of a narcissistic, obsessive or heroic individualist character. Yet, when economy comes up against another value or another element of the organization ideal, it becomes a cause of anxiety, frustration and guilt. This is the case when professionals complain that they cannot do their job properly for lack of resources, something especially common in public sector organizations, like hospitals, universities or the police (Stokes, 1994). In the private sector, the organization's ceaseless drive for efficiency has still more dire psychological consequences when employees' livelihoods are disrupted or ruined through relocation, restructuring or redundancy.

An important test of the strength of a collective value in our lives is the extent to which we are willing to defend it, even if, in doing so, we disadvantage ourselves. Individuals throughout the ages have been willing to sacrifice their own happiness and even their life in the interest of a group with which they are strongly bonded, its interests and values. This is what Durkheim (1951) defined as 'altruistic suicide', a type of suicide common among soldiers and religious zealots. Psychoanalysis approaches the same phenomenon as an instance in which the group, under the influence of a messianic leader, is inspired to acts of self-denial and self-sacrifice as the individual's ego becomes depleted of the libido that is channelled in the creation of powerful bonds of identification and as each individual's identity becomes submerged into the identity of the group. Organizational participants may at times be similarly inspired to sacrifice their personal interest in the name of the organization they serve. More commonly, however, individuals do not sacrifice themselves, but are sacrificed by their organizations in pursuit of efficiency and competitiveness; thus, profit-oriented organizations will readily shed individuals in order to remain profitable. This generates formidable psychical problems, not only for those directly affected but for others too. In Chapter 3, we examined how individuals who have developed dependence on their organization are shattered when, after many years of loyal service, they are discarded. But those left behind are also faced with formidable tasks of mourning for their departed colleagues and of dealing with their own anxieties about the future. Mourning for those who sacrifice themselves to a noble cause is a lot easier than mourning for those sacrificed by an organization on the altar of profit and efficiency. Survivors' guilt is liable to combine with realistic anxiety about the future, undermining group bonds and promoting scapegoating and cynicism.

BOUNDARIES

Downsizing and forced expulsions highlight another characteristic of organizations which makes special demands on our psychological functioning – boundaries. Like other features examined in this chapter, boundaries are not unique to organizations, but the ways in which they function are. All collectivities have boundaries; in the first instance, there is a physical boundary regarding who is in and who is out. Some collectivities make no attempt to control their boundaries – individuals may join and leave at will. Others mark the entry of new members and the departure of others with rites of passage, which symbolize a significant change in a person's life: a child has become an adult, a non-member has become a member. Most organizations patrol their borders with their customary method and diligence, employing gate-keepers to keep strays out. New members are appointed, often after elaborate selection procedures have been observed, and are then asked to undergo training and socialization, formal and informal (see Chapter 8). New members may not be admitted to full membership, but may be put on a probationary period, when they are neither in nor out, but on trial. Departing members may be given an official farewell function, or may be escorted out of the building 'unceremoniously' with no time to empty their desks or take their belongings, but left in no doubt that they have been put outside, in the wilderness. Visitors to organizations are often supplied with lapel badges to denote their temporary status, as having been allowed to cross the organizational boundary after suitable vetting and for an appropriate term.

Organizational boundaries have become increasingly complex in recent decades, as organizations form strategic alliances with each other, erasing boundaries which separated them, or alternatively setting up internal markets and agencies which erect new internal boundaries. Increasing use is made of contract or agency staff, workers who may perform vital duties for a company (telephonist, security staff, consultant, nurse), while being employed by a different one. Companies contracting out some of their productive operations set terms and conditions for their suppliers which, to all intents and purposes, dictate the conditions which they must observe within their own boundaries. The idea that an organization is separated from its environment by a fixed line has become increasingly unhelpful under such conditions.

Boundaries have been a major feature of systems theory, an approach which enjoyed great currency in organizational studies in the 1950s and 1960s and is currently enjoying something of a comeback, notably in versions informed by ideas of autopoiesis, instability, complexity and chaos. Boundaries continue to feature prominently in these versions, though they are now approached as less fixed, more negotiable, more vulnerable and more permeable than in classical open-systems theory. Psychoanalysis, for its part, teaches us that boundaries are internal as well as external (Hirschhorn, 1988; Schneider, 1991; Roberts, 1994). The first boundary we discover is that which separates us from an external world. This is the boundary of our own ego, at a stage when it is undifferentiated from the id. The discovery of this boundary, its assertion and its defence, in the late oral stage, are a driving motive in what is referred to as the 'terrible twos', when 'No' becomes the child's main weapon in its new-found independence. Later, the ego itself acquires internal boundaries, boundaries which separate unconscious from conscious mental activity, and set it apart from the other mental institutions. The ego is coextensive with boundary. It establishes itself as that part of the mental personality which stands at the boundary with the external world. It also builds up boundaries against inner threats, wild desires, overpowering anxieties. The defence of boundaries is vital for the ego; the onset of neurosis is invariably alluded to by Freud through an imagery of boundary violation: the ego's defences, like those of a besieged city, are broken, the ego is visited by 'unwelcome guests' (1917: 141–2), or the 'dams' are broken and the ego is flooded (1937: 227). The mature ego, then, is, among other things, a manager of boundaries, inner and outer; it learns to redraw boundaries by incorporating external objects or rejecting internal ones. It learns to re-arrange boundaries and to mistrust them.

Let us try to deepen our understanding of the psychological meaning of boundaries. Picture a line, a line without ends. This side of the line, order and security; the other side of the line, danger, insecurity, unpredictability. Then take a closer look beyond the line. How far beyond the line can you see? Is there a second line further out, which you cannot even see, hiding a *terra incognita* of utter unpredictability and strangeness? Then look at the line itself. How thin is the line? A pencil line, perhaps, or a thick line, like the Great Wall of China? How near the line would someone need to be before becoming a threat? What keeps strangers out? Under what conditions are they allowed to cross it? Is the line perhaps not a line at all, but a no-man's-land, where different rules obtain or no rules at all? Is it a dead space or is it a space brimming with life and activity, where strangers can meet and where strange deals may be struck? The closer we look at the boundary, the less clear-cut it becomes. And, yet, the fundamental psychological reality is clear; this side of the boundary is home, where uninvited intruders are violators to be resisted; the other side of the boundary is a source of threats and opportunities. It is interesting how easily this imagery can travel from the individual, to the household, to the clan, the group, the organization, the nation.

Psychoanalytic thinkers, such as Hirschhorn (1988) and Roberts (1994), have argued that the maintenance of boundaries involves a great deal of psychological work. Boundaries offer a defence against anxiety, at a cost of generating an anxiety all of their own. Consider the expression 'It is not my job' frequently heard in organizational spaces. This is a statement defining the boundary of one's responsibilities and duties, a statement meant to protect one from unreasonable demands, yet also generating anxiety, in case someone should decide to test the boundary. 'Oh, yes, it is your job.' Hirschhorn has argued rather ingeniously that individuals operating near an organization's boundaries (i.e. close to customers, suppliers, competitors, potential members) experience acute anxiety from two quarters: external risks and inner

ORGANIZATIONAL ROLES AND THE MANAGEMENT OF CHANGE:
A SYSTEMIC APPROACH

Robert French and Peter Simpson

In this case study, Robert French and Peter Simpson discuss the consequences of a major re-organization in a department of the British civil service. The re-organization did not change the boundaries so much as seek to redefine the meaning of boundaries, leaving members of the department in confusion about the nature of their roles and the source of authority.

An action research project was undertaken over the period of a year with the senior management group of an organization in the British civil service. Like much of the UK public sector in recent years, this organization has experienced a period of radical change, including restructuring, delayering and projected staff cuts of approximately 20 per cent. The challenge has been to manage the transition from a traditional bureaucracy to a new organizational form (Cravens et al., 1996). One of the consequences of the fast pace of change has been a series of role re-definitions, following or promoting restructuring, and a consequent blurring of role relations. This research project was established to investigate the contribution that could be made to managing the change by focusing on *organizational role*.

Our approach has been to work with managers' experience of role and relationships in the workplace. Our work can be located within the fields of group relations (Trist and Sofer, 1959; Colman and Geller, 1985; Gillette and McCollom, 1990) and socio-technical systems (Miller and Rice, 1967; Emery and Trist, 1969; Miller, 1993). In particular we combine systemic thinking and psychodynamic theory (see, for example, Lawrence, 1979; Hirschhorn, 1988; Menzies Lyth, 1988, 1989; Trist and Murray, 1990; Obholzer and Roberts, 1994). This account describes the insights gained from undertaking four activities: (a) one-to-one work on role with the chief executive; (b) individual interviews with all eleven members of the senior management team; (c) developmental work on role with a sub-group of senior managers; (d) exploration with the whole senior management group of the way in which the experience of 'representation' affects their work.

The project

This is a case study of an organization in transition. For most of this century the organization has operated as a traditional bureaucracy, characterized by clarity of roles and lines of authority and communication, and rules for the settlement of disputes. However, external pressures for improved effectiveness with a lower level of resource have necessitated a search for radical solutions. Prevailing organizational wisdom suggests new organizational structures that have fewer layers, are more flexible and responsive and are based on empowered teams and individuals with the expertise to modify and develop ways of working in response to changing circumstances and demands.

We became involved with this organization twelve months after a major restructuring had been initiated. At this point, the presenting problem among the senior managers was that of role confusion. It was our hypothesis that the bureaucratic concept of role, based on a clear description of tasks and procedures for reporting within a well-defined hierarchy, was no longer adequate. In the more complex organizational form that was developing, managers needed to find new ways of managing. The chief executive was the primary sponsor of this project, and was himself experiencing particular difficulties in defining his role at a manageable level, as pressures and demands came from all directions, along with advice about what he should and should not be doing.

One-to-one work on role with the chief executive

The work undertaken was based on a process entitled 'organizational role analysis' (Reed, 1976; Lawrence, 1979; Quine and Hutton, 1992). This involved a series of eight monthly sessions of approximately two hours. The aim was to work with the chief executive 'to make a bridge between his consciousness of his experience and the realities of the institution' (Reed, 1976: 96). Thus, rather than starting with a list of activities in the form of a job description, we sought, through reflection upon particular issues, hopes, problems or stresses, to frame and reframe his understanding of his role within the changing organization. This involved paying particular attention to the aim of the organization and working relations with others, both internal (other senior managers, senior civil servants, staff) and external (clients, the public, MPs and so on).

Individual interviews with the senior management team

We were interested in the possibility of working with this different concept of role more widely within senior management. The chief executive appeared to be very comfortable with the ideas and able to work with them readily. Would the same be true of others? In order to explore this question and to get a broader picture of the problems that were being experienced in role, we interviewed the other senior managers. Each interview lasted approximately two hours. The aim was to work together to explore each manager's image of his role (they were all men) in relation to the organization and the wider system. These interviews revealed the wide diversity within the senior management team in understanding the nature and importance of role and of its relation to authority. It also became clear just how strongly conceptualizations of role influence are in turn influenced by the *culture* of the organization.

Work on role with a sub-group of senior management

The largest operational area in the organization involved five of the eleven senior managers. The interviews indicated the existence of a number of differences that appeared to cause specific difficulties for these five in clarifying their roles and role relations within the senior management group. These included differences in function, history, perceptions and size, and the fact that four out of five members of this sub-group were not included in the strategic management group, which included all other senior managers and was seen to influence major strategic decisions. We worked with the group for a day on the theme of 'Managing Oneself in Role'. The day was designed to provide this group of senior managers with the opportunity to explore their shared and different perceptions and experiences of working in role.

The experience of 'representation' in the senior management group

As the project progressed, we found ourselves paying increasing attention to the relationship between the senior managers' roles and the complex management structure which comprised a range of formal and informal groupings, sub-groupings and steering groups. It appeared to us that a critical difficulty within the emerging organizational structure was linked to what we saw as the 'representational' dimension of role.

In contrast to a bureaucratic organization, where role definition and clarity are externally imposed, there exists in the new organizational forms greater potential for confusion in knowing what role an individual is taking in a particular interaction. We designed and facilitated a workshop with the primary aim of enabling senior management collectively to experience and reflect upon the practice of representation in the context of the senior management structure.

What did the focus on role reveal?

The focus on organizational role proved to be effective in two ways: first, in revealing the patterns of interaction and perception among senior managers; secondly, in helping senior managers to see the possibilities inherent in developing new ways of working in role.

Patterns of interaction and perception

The early interviews and meetings presented us with a view of an organization dominated by what approximated to 'basic assumption mentality' (Bion, 1961; Pines, 1985), where the primary task is obscured by emotional states arising from anxiety. At the level of system, the experience of senior managers was of separation and division. This was most clearly captured in the notion of a 'patch', a relatively 'closed system' where the 'senior manager is squire of his domain'. What had once been functional, at a time when boundaries were carefully policed, had become dysfunctional because the primary focus of the senior managers had shifted to the whole organization.

There was also evidence of the counter-tendency, Bion's 'work' mentality. Individuals who welcomed the changes demonstrated the desire to get to grips with the new, broader concepts of role and system and the new forms of representation that these require. However, the general role confusion had supported a culture of distrust, expressed in terms of micro-political manoeuvring, with gossip and rumour as the dominant mode of communication, and negative competition over resources and access to power. Interactions tended to occur at the level of *person* not *role*.

These dynamics may always have existed within the organization, but the nature of control within a bureaucracy would have been sufficient to ensure that the required organizational tasks were undertaken despite these potential problems. However, within the new organizational form the control of rules, procedures and lines of accountability were neither explicit nor enforced from above. The primary source of organizational control came from the ability of organizational members to maintain for themselves an attention to the task. We found some support for the contention that this might be achieved by working constantly at the experience of role in oneself and in others, as it is revealed in action and interaction.

New ways of working in role

The critical shift that we saw occurring for some of the managers was a decreasing dependence upon clear job descriptions and a growing awareness that role can be utilized as a method to access authority in a range of situations. Working with role in this way helped managers to make judgements about priorities within the system. Within the new organizational forms they needed to be able to make these judgements for themselves moment by moment, meeting by meeting, in contrast to bureaucratic organization where stability is a design feature. The dynamic nature of role became clearer for some, leading to an awareness that priorities could and would change over time, and in relation to different tasks and contexts.

Work on the relatedness of role and system enabled a growing sense that the ranking of roles, i.e. the level of emotional identification with different aspects of one's role, needed to be addressed, both individually and collectively. Historically, the perception of managerial priorities had involved a hierarchy which placed divisional management at the top, followed by functional and, finally, corporate responsibility. In the new organizational form, a new ranking of senior management responsibilities needed to emerge, giving primary importance to the corporate, followed by responsibilities at functional and divisional levels. However, working this out in practice is not straightforward. For example, is it always possible for a corporate decision to be taken by a divisional manager in a manner that fully acknowledges both divisional and organizational responsibilities? A systemic approach to organizational role directs attention to the importance of managerial judgement but this does not mean that the judgement will be easy to make.

This relates to the most difficult area of work, for us as well as for the managers, on the representational dimension of role. It is our proposition that in any interaction an awareness of who each party is representing will facilitate more effective work on the task. However, the nature of the new organizational forms was such that all managers had a complex array of roles. The discussion above has indicated that it can be difficult enough to decide for oneself which role takes priority within a particular situation. How possible is it also to establish clarity in relation to others? In the limited work that we were able to undertake on this issue, a greater level of clarity was achieved by working on two specific strategic tasks while, at the same time, giving conscious attention to the representative membership within working groups. However, some managers appeared to find aspects of this process threatening or difficult to appreciate. As a consequence, some chose deliberately to avoid giving attention to issues of representation in the latter part of the workshop on this theme. It appears to us that this is an aspect of organizational experience that is currently under-theorized and requires more work.

Conclusion

The project has shown how experience in role can be used both to make sense of and to work with change in relation to system and task. If the understanding of role and role relations does not develop to keep pace with change, the authority of management within the organization may become overly dependent upon interpersonal relationships, and structures may evolve that are founded on basic assumption mentality despite the appearance of being task-related.

inhibitions against the use of aggression against those risks. The tendency then becomes to retreat to the safety of the centre, away from the boundary towards a comfort zone, a niche, far away from the hurly-burly of the boundary. In doing so, however, they risk hurting their co-workers and the organization as a whole. An avoidance of responsibility, an ever-increasing raising of boundaries, a stolid disregard for what goes on outside and a compulsive search for niches become endemic in what Kanter (1983) has referred to as a 'fragmented organization'.

Are organizations unique among collectivities in the way in which they handle boundaries? In some respects, they are not; in other respects, however, they are. First, their hierarchical and impersonal nature makes the creation of boundaries easier; secondly, these and other characteristics are more likely to place individuals in a position where they feel driven to erect boundaries around them. Finally, organizations are places where boundaries are policed not only diligently, but with the utmost method, through security passes and gatekeepers, through signs and warnings, through spatial arrangements, through the use of elaborate language and jargon and, above all, through the use of rules and regulations. This brings us to the next characteristic of organizations that calls for special responses from our psychological apparatus – control.

CONTROL

The concept of control lies at the core of most discussions on organizations. It has featured prominently in management literature since Taylor and Fayol and has been a central pillar of organizational theory since Max Weber's pioneering work on bureaucracy. Standing for order, predictability and reliability, control is virtually coextensive with what many understand by organization. Some theorists, like Edwards (1979), define organizations by virtue of the particular mode of control which they employ – administrative control, based on impersonal rules, which camouflage the underlying power relations within business organizations. More recently, theorists inspired by the work of Foucault have argued that control is even more pervasive than the Weberian 'iron cage', since the very subject, the prisoner inside the cage, is not a 'pre-given entity which is seized on by the exercise of power' (Cousins and Hussain, 1984: 251), but is itself the product of ubiquitous discourses of power. Whichever guide one chooses to follow through the elaborate discussions of control, there is little doubt that organizations elevate control to undreamed of heights, colonizing every nook and cranny of human experience. One of the most recent preoccupations in this regard is the massive current interest in organizational controls over emotion, which will be addressed in Chapter 9.

Freud's strictures on the ego, in particular his view of it as not being master in its own house, has readily yielded the decentred subject, the fragmented self, which is currently so popular with postmodernist theorists. The unity of the self as executive agent, as thinking and feeling subject or even as suffering victim, is currently questioned. Power is omnipresent and unavoidable, especially where we imagine it to be absent. In some extreme postmodernist accounts power is the only thing actually to exist, all else disintegrating into merely its effects. Some more temperate voices have been raised, arguing that power inevitably implies opposition and resistance. In the days when control was exercised primarily through impersonal rules, opposition and resistance took both individual and collective, organized and disorganized, militant and accommodating forms. Workers joined trade unions, they vocally opposed the rule of the bosses, went on strike, engaged in sabotage, arrived at work late, cut corners, tried to get away with doing as little work as possible and sought to create niches which were kept outside management control; in Edwards's (1979) terms, they converted the workplace into a contested terrain, where the rule of management was challenged and checked. Since the 1980s, however, the scope of management control has expanded phenomenally. Programmes of organizational re-structuring and re-engineering, the intensification of competition and new possibilities for monitoring and observation offered by digital technologies have blunted the workers' appetite for resistance and opposition. Increasingly, they are seen as willing, self-regulating agents, embracing their organization's culture without complaining.

Formerly, in traditional organizations, workers were under no illusions about the rules which governed their behaviour at work. It is essential here to distinguish between administrative regulations deriving from social norms and deeper moral values. Regulations had no moral stature deriving from a group's communal life or from deep ethical principles. In no way did they become lodged in the super-ego, nor was transgression accompanied by feelings of guilt or shame. Administrative rules and regulations, as Gouldner (1954) accurately observed in his gypsum-mining study, could be experienced in one of three ways: as disciplinary devices functioning in the interest of the owners (punishment-centred bureaucracy), as useful and rational devices of regulation, ensuring the welfare of all at work (representative democracy) or as redundant measures dreamed up by out-of-touch administrators (mock bureaucracy). Some of the time, employees observed these rules in a ritualistic, resigned manner; at other times, they disregarded them, even with the collusion of management. In other circumstances, they tested them and sought to redefine them. Bureaucratic rules make very different psychological demands from those made by moral laws. To the extent that they are observed, they amount to an acting out of a repetition of routinized behaviour, through which individuals achieve the safety of inertia (see Gouldner, 1954). The same compulsive adherence to routines of behaviour are the hallmark of the mindless administrator and the robotic factory-floor worker immortalized by Charlie Chaplin in *Modern Times* (1936). In both of these cases, behaviour becomes depersonalized and uniform, devoid of meaning and life, an expression perhaps of the death instinct as a compulsive repetition.

But such traditional forms of control are, in the view of most organizational writers, being displaced by new, more sophisticated forms, which turn the employee into an agent of his or her own regulation. If earlier bureaucratic controls concealed the underlying power relations, contemporary controls conceal themselves, embedding themselves in the words we use, the associations we make, the images we present. Where bureaucratic controls drained behaviour of meaning, under contemporary controls, behaviour rediscovers meaning, the employee acquires once again a sense of personal responsibility for the organization; the rules of the organization, to the extent that they exist, re-acquire a moral stature. Instead of seeking to legislate minutely every aspect of workplace conduct, the new types of rules demand flexibility and discretion, and rely on the employee's commitment to these aims. In the case of one company, Nordstrom, this trend has gone to such an extreme that its rulebook is reduced to the following :

WELCOME TO NORDSTROM

We are glad to have you with our company. Our number one goal is to provide
outstanding customer service.

Set both personal and professional goals high.

We have great confidence in your ability to achieve them.

Nordstrom Rules:

Rule 1: *Use your good judgment in all situations.*

There will be no additional rules. Please feel free to ask your departmental manager any question at any time.

It takes considerable confidence for a company to produce a statement such as the above, entrusting its operations to the good judgement of its employees. Some may see it as a hollow, disingenuous statement, concealing the existence of ever-vigilant managers and elaborate procedures. Others, however, may recognize it as part of a trend whereby organizations rely increasingly on the training, socialization and psychological manipulation of each individual employee rather than detailed impersonal rules to achieve control. Some psychoanalytic writers, such as Schwartz (1990), Sievers (1994) and Casey (1996), have argued that organizations have managed to induce among their employees a new state of infantile dependence, a state where employing organizations provide a surrogate for the family and community, supporting their employees' egos and self-esteem. Hard work, total commitment and flexibility are what employees offer, in exchange for egos inflated by the organization's power and ego-ideals enriched by its allure. In this way, the old dream of human relations theorists, that of a business enterprise replacing family, neighbourhood and city as a moral community, is realized, albeit through the mobilization of infinitely more sophisticated machinery than Mayo and his colleagues had in mind.

Authors who have studied workplaces at the technological cutting edge, like Kunda (1992) and Casey (1996), have been struck by the suppression of all critical and enquiring faculties on the part of employees and by the use of oblique expressions such as 'golden handcuffs' to express a profound ambivalence between admiration for and commitment to the firm and a simultaneous feeling of entrapment and despair. Employees who stay with the company both identify with it (and to this extent they act as its agents with no sense of imposition) and yet are also aware that the company extracts a heavy toll from them, in the shape of stress, tiredness, alcoholism, obsessive compulsions and unfocused anxiety. It is difficult to know the extent to which these more pervasive control devices characterize today's organizations. It is also difficult to know how well they have survived the downsizing wave of the 1990s, when the image of the organization as caring surrogate family has been tested to the extreme. Some authors (Gabriel, 1988; Watson, 1994) have argued that the employees' acquiescence and obsequiousness are skin-deep, a front presented to outsiders, including academic researchers, behind which loom dissatisfactions that are capable of being articulated and explained.

In any event, it is premature to argue that new controls eliminate the deeper experiences of power inequalities and injustices at the workplace, or that to the extent they succeed they are without costs. In my own work (Gabriel, 1995; Gabriel and Lang, 1995), I have explored fantasy as providing an avenue in which individuals create unmanaged spaces within organizations, spaces where they can remould reality in the interests of pleasure. They turn facts into stories and cast themselves into worthy roles of hero, survivor, victim or object of love, thus affording themselves some consolation and pride. Instead of relying on organizational supports for their narcissism, they may feed it by distancing themselves from the organization, which is seen as exploitative and corrupt. Through myths, stories and jokes, individuals may sometimes challenge organizational controls directly, by celebrating the blunders of their superiors and ridiculing the pompous fads and fashions of contemporary management. At other times, the unmanaged spaces of the organization do not directly challenge organizational controls, but allow individuals and groups to affirm themselves as independent agents, heroes, survivors, victims and objects of love, whose subjectivity is not derivative of the organization they serve.

WORK

The final feature of organizations which we shall examine in this chapter is their emphasis on work and the ways in which they help us to define work. Work, as we are endlessly and rightly reminded, does not only take place in workplaces and is not always rewarded with payment; it is also a large part of our domestic lives, and is part of the voluntary sector. Work can be pleasurable and life-enhancing or it can be alienating and oppressive. What is characteristic of most organizations is their emphasis on visible, measurable work, work that can be monitored and assessed. It would be fair to say that much organizational activity, even when it entails lavish lunches and rounds of golf, is thought of as work, at least by those engaging in it. What is more, much of it is constructed as *hard* work. It is scarcely imaginable that individuals in organizations would, even for short periods of time, describe themselves as relaxing, playing, politicking, plotting, socializing, gossiping, daydreaming, story-telling, experimenting, enjoying themselves or worrying themselves sick, though undoubtedly they do all of these things at different times. Instead, they would describe themselves as working, working hard.

What is paradoxical is the contrast between what goes on in organizations and what people from previous eras might have recognized as work. True, a time-traveller from five centuries ago may have readily identified as work the hammering of heavy metal, the carrying of large loads or, at a stretch, the dextrous assembling of microscopic components. But workers accustomed to the back-breaking work of Roman *latifundia*, Attic mines and Southern plantations, women worn to the bone by hand-milling corn for hours on end, would have been perplexed by the claims of hard work by people talking gently into telephones, tapping the keys of keyboards, conversing while seated on comfortable chairs, or sitting behind steering wheels while listening to gently soothing music. Within organizations, work can stretch to encompass almost any activity, however pleasant or physically undemanding. When seeking to cross an organization's boundary as future employees, individuals routinely extol themselves, not for being clever, competent or even flexible, but for their ability to work hard. This is the best that many people, across occupational, gender and class divides, seem able to offer prospective employers.

How, then, is hard work to be measured? If sweat and physical exhaustion are no indicators of hard work, the common measures are output, as measured by some quasi-objective indicator, and hours in the office, on the shopfloor or on the road, as measured by the hands on a clock. Both of these measures involve comparisons and competition: individuals may be seen as producing more output or working longer hours than their fellow workers. Hard work frequently means a belief that one is working harder than one's peers. There is another, far more subjective, measure of hard work, one that has to do with an individual's ability to cope, to survive in spite of the stress and exhaustion he or she experiences. Hard work, then, means to keep one's head above water, just; anything less than that means that they are not working hard enough. Work, in this way, often becomes reduced to a rather one-dimensional entity, a quantity rather than a quality, a quantity reflecting commitment to the organization and self-denial rather than productive output.

Many theorists from diverse disciplines have explored the meaning of work for human beings and have reached different conclusions. Marx, for example, regarded work as a species-activity, an activity whose dependence on imagination, intelligence and consciousness makes it uniquely human. Others, including many postmodern theorists, have argued that the psychological meaning of work in our culture is eclipsed by other meaning-generators, including the mass media, the world of consumption and life-styles. Psychoanalysis belongs to that humanistic tradition which distinguishes between two types of work. On the one hand, there is creative, life-enhancing work through which we express our desires and visions; this type of work enables us to grow psychologically and emotionally, and through it we develop meaningful relations with our social environment. On the other hand, there is work undertaken from a position of need, which is undertaken purely for the purposes of securing our livelihood. This work, too, may have useful psychological consequences but it can easily become stultifying and alienating.

The unique contribution of psychoanalysis to the psychology of work is in exploring not only the conscious meanings that work has in our lives (whether as members of organizations or not) but also the unconscious, symbolic dimensions of work. Thus, psychoanalysis would look sceptically and with disbelief at the 'rational man' concept of work, where individuals seek to obtain work which maximizes their gain and minimizes their effort. Instead, even if such purely economically driven individuals exist, psychoanalysis would seek to understand why for these individuals a job is merely a source of money and nothing else. Money, after all, as Shakespeare and many other writers recognized long before Freud, is a richly symbolic entity, one in which unlimited freedom and filthy corruption are condensed. Even when work appears to be purely instrumental, it may, therefore, be entailing deeper unconscious meanings (for a discussion of the psychoanalytic approach to work, see Czander, 1993).

As a highly productive individual, it is not surprising that Freud approached work in the first instance as a creative activity, exemplified in the work of the artist. In *Civilization and its Discontents*, Freud argued:

> One gains the most if one can sufficiently heighten the yield of pleasure from the sources of physical and intellectual work. When that is so, fate can do little against one. A satisfaction of this kind, such as an artist's joy in creating, in giving his phantasies body, or a scientist's in solving problems or discovering truth, has a special quality which we shall certainly one day be able to characterize in metapsychological terms. (Freud, 1930: 267)

Freud believed that the key to understanding the psychological significance of creative work is contained in the concept of *sublimation*, the ability to redirect libido away from sexual aims, towards spiritual, scientific or aesthetic ones. Individuals with the ability and the opportunity to sublimate may transcend the discontents of civilization and produce work which survives them and enriches the lives of others. In a famous footnote following the above extract, Freud placed two qualifications on the ability of work to supply such consolations for life's sufferings: first, the satisfactions that it affords (even for creative geniuses) are relatively modest in comparison with the satisfactions offered by the sating of primary instinctual impulses; secondly, people 'do not strive after it [work] as they do after other possibilities of satisfaction. The great majority of people only work under the stress of necessity, and this natural human aversion to work raises most serious social problems' (1930: 268).

The Freudian view of creative work as sublimation does not seem to suit the work that most people do in organizations especially well; it is possible that some individuals in managerial, artistic, creative or entrepreneurial positions may be able to sublimate their libido into their work, but for the majority this possibility is severely restricted. The corollary which views work as the product of economic necessity, which people do under compunction, evidently has wider applications. This work, too, has deeper psychological meanings, even if it is not enjoyable or creative. As Levinson (1969/1981) argued:

> By concentrating on their tasks, people push out of consciousness many thoughts and ideas they would rather forget. Work, then, is a way of being 'on top'. To work is to be in control of oneself and of a part of the surrounding world, to have some idea of what the future holds and to be prepared for it. It is also to be in touch with the changing world, and to grow more competent and secure in it. (1969/1981: 29)

These ideas are easily compatible with Weberian views on the Protestant work ethic and vocation. Creative work, like a vocation, proceeds from the individual's need to express him or herself, to produce worthwhile work through which he or she stamps his or her mark on the environment. Under the Protestant work ethic, much work does not have the character of vocation, but of duty, i.e. to work hard becomes one of the super-ego's strictures; guilt is experienced whenever one feels that one is being idle, and a great effort is made to present oneself as working all the time to allay one's super-ego. As Lang and I have argued, it is highly doubtful whether the Protestant work ethic held sway for anything but a minority of individuals, which certainly excluded many working-class people (Gabriel and Lang, 1995). In any event, neither the conception of work as creative expression nor that of work as duty seem to accord especially well with the emphasis on display, i.e. appearing to be busy all of the time, which was noted earlier.

Display is linked to experiences of shame, especially shame about having been caught in the wrong. Thus, public displays of repentance are often used as a way of repairing earlier damage. This suggests an alternative approach to the psychological significance of work, one which derives from the work of Klein and has been considerably elaborated by Hirschhorn. Klein sought to replace many of Freud's drive-based propositions with propositions emerging from the relations which we form with important objects throughout our lives. In contrast to Freud's heroic vision of work summed up in the extracts given above, Klein's conception of work is more feminine, highlighting the nurturing, caring qualities of work. Work for Klein (1935/1986) expresses a need to care for and repair an object that we have earlier maltreated in practice or in our phantasies. Hirschhorn (1988) has generalized this idea, arguing that work is a characteristic of the depressive position, the position that grows out of a realization that the world is imperfect, that good and bad exist in combination, and that where we earlier (in the paranoid-schizoid phase) imagined some objects as pure evil, we did them grave injustice. We then seek to undo this injustice by tending and repairing the damaged object, to appease our feelings of anxiety, shame and guilt. The meaning of work in this conception is that of healing, restoring and revitalizing an external object.

While creativity for Freud is a manifestation of an individual's ability to sublimate his or her libido, for Klein and Hirschhorn it is the result of the anxiety of the depressive position. The two approaches would seem to describe rather different types of work and could certainly co-exist. Hirschhorn has made extensive use of Klein's ideas in his work as consultant, and it would seem that this type of work, like the work of teachers, nurses and community workers, can be elucidated using this perspective. As a description of a more general mechanism of the psychological significance of work in contemporary organizations, it seems less well-suited. For example, one could hardly argue that young careerists or ageing workaholics are driven by reparative urges, any more than we could argue that they are driven by work as duty. Drawing on other psychoanalytic approaches, Schwartz (1990) has developed a theory that is quite successful in describing the driven character of the work done by such people. For Schwartz, the majority of people most of the time work under compunction; work becomes embedded in the super-ego, not because it is a moral imperative, but because many organizations have succeeded in making individuals feel chronically guilty, by lavishing resources on new recruits, training them and indoctrinating them. The discontents that such organizations generate (stress, anxiety, chronic overload) lead to greater urgency to work hard, since employees are likely to experience these discontents as their own personal failings and seek to compensate by working still longer hours, which, of course, further exacerbates their symptoms.

The ingenious twist that Schwartz gives to this argument (which, after all, amounts essentially to a psychoanalytic rendering of orthodox theories of socialization) is to claim that behind organizational claims of the importance of hard work lies a devaluation of work. What organizations value is not work as output, but work as displays of loyalty, something that converts work from a creative activity into a ritual. The cause of this is a pervasive dysfunction that afflicts many organizations, one of narcissism. It is epitomized in the predicament of NASA as it transformed itself from a heroic organization committed to single combat against the Soviet space programme into a 'Disneyland in Space' organization, committed to sustaining America's narcissistic delusions about itself. Such organizations, argues Schwartz, devalue work. Disney, for example, does not refer to its employees as workers but rather as a cast; their function is not work, but entertainment, even if they are sweeping roads and tossing hamburgers. To the extent, then, that such organizations succeed in infusing an ethic of hard work into their members, it is as a display of loyalty and love, a love that is returned in narcissistic self-aggrandizement for the employee.

Psychoanalytic accounts suggest that it is vain to try to establish a single set of meanings, conscious or unconscious, for work in organizations. The heavy emphasis on work placed by most organizations generates demands which different individuals handle differently. Some individuals may be fortunate in discovering ways of doing life-enhancing creative work within organizations by sublimating their libido into creative outlets. Others may endure hard and dangerous work, consistent with the depressive position's outlook of reparation and caring. Yet others may work under moral compunction, feeling that hard work is an ethical principle or even a divine decree. Yet others may work in an ostentatious, display-oriented manner, unconsciously believing themselves to be paying back their dues to their organization and sustaining a psychological contract with it. Some may go through the motions of work in a ritualistic way, caring little about the value of their work and thinking only of what their pay-packet does for themselves and their families. For these last people, who may be the majority in most organizations, work may be a less important source of meaning than other aspects of their lives.

CONCLUSION

Our discussion in this chapter has examined many features of organizations in connection with the demands they make on our psychological functioning. Although none of these features is unique to organizations, the combination of features and their interaction make for very specific demands on our mental functioning, demands which differ from those made by other collectivities, such as crowds, families or groups (see Table 4.1). We respond to these demands in our different ways, seeking to infuse our lives in organizations with meaning, to cope with the pain and the anxiety we experience and to discover outlets for our creative and social impulses.

Is it possible to capture the essence of organizational experience (as distinct from that of group experience or crowd experience) in terms of a single set of interconnected propositions? This is a question that has haunted organizational studies ever since Weber sought to produce a unified and general theory of bureaucracy, whose scope and coverage included all organizations and whose essence was to be found in a single cluster of conceptually linked ideas, deriving from his principle of rational-legal authority. Today, the Weberian project has floundered. Under contemporary capitalism, organizations have moved further and further from Weber's bureaucratic ideal, diversifying, discovering new ways of conducting their affairs, frequently violating basic principles of management. It seems futile to seek to provide such a unitary conception. Depth psychology provides a way of studying the diversity of demands that different organizations make on our diverse lives. Some of us may serve organizations loyally, identifying with them and deriving our sense of self-esteem from our association with them. Others may keep a critical distance from the organization which employs them, hardly thinking twice about deserting it for another organization which offers a better compensation package. Still others work for companies in spite of feeling desperately trapped in them. Some challenge different facets of organizational life, others do not.

Nor should we imagine that organizations are the only vital social influence on our mental lives, as though, once we enter their space, we become detached from other

TABLE 4.1 *Features of organizations and collectivities*

	Impersonal	Hierarchical	Durable	Large	Goals	Efficiency	Boundary controls	Formal control	Work
Organizations	+	+	+	+	+	+	+	+	+
Groups	−	+/−	+/−	−	+/−	+/−	+/−	−	+/−
Family	−	+	+	−	−	−	+	−	−
Queue	+	−	−	−	−	−	+	−	−
Club	−	−	+	−	+	−	+	+	−
Crowds	+	−	−	+	+/−	−	−	−	−

emotional and social attachments. Organizations may have a pervasive effect on our sense of identity and selfhood but they can hardly be thought of as determining it. In fact, many theorists are currently arguing that our identities are more likely to be shaped by other cultural experiences, notably those as consumers, rather than by the organization which employs us. Consumption, life-styles, sexual preferences are, in the view of postmodern theorists like Baudrillard (1988) and Bauman (1988, 1992), more likely to support fragile and multiple identities than the work we do or the employer we serve. While work remains for most individuals an ultimately unfulfilling activity, consumption provides us with opportunities for developing our identities and nurturing our self-esteem. Yet, consumption itself, as a sphere of human activity, is far from unproblematic. At present, claiming that the consumer represents a single principle of choice, pleasure or identity-creation is as short-sighted as arguing that organizations may be reduced to a single essence, as Weber bravely tried to do one hundred years ago.

5 WORK GROUPS

with Marion McCollom Hampton

As members of an organization, we have the sense of being part of a large aggregate of people, mostly unknown to us, who go about their business without directly affecting us. From time to time, our business brings us together with other individuals, in mostly impersonal transactions or in political conflicts and alliances. Our relation to the organization is one to a supra-individual entity, capable of symbolic and emotional qualities, but generally devoid of personal character. By contrast, as members of a group, our experience is much more personalized, our emotions more immediate, focused on particular individuals. Our sense of responsibility for the group's performance is more direct, our involvement more intimate. Within a group, what each individual does, how he or she feels, is of great interest to us and affects us directly. Being denied some information in an organization is unlikely to be experienced as a personal threat or as an insult. We recognize that it would be impossible to know everything that is going on. In a group, however, being excluded from some information or from some important decision is much more likely to lead to feelings of bitterness, frustration and anger. In an organization, we accept that a large part of the organization's reality does not concern us. In a group, however, it is much more likely that we regard everything that goes on as our business.

Our experiences as members of groups can be overpowering. Feelings of being valued, of belonging, of contributing, can be off-set by anxieties about being intimidated, excluded or swamped. There are moments when we can observe ourselves behaving irrationally as members of crowds or audiences, yet we are swept by the emotion, unable to check it. In smaller groups too, like committees or teams, we may experience powerful feelings of loyalty, anxiety or anger. The moods and emotions of those around us seem to have an exaggerated effect on our own moods and emotions. In this chapter, we examine the psychoanalytic contributions to our understanding of the psychological meanings of groups, the dynamics of groups and the impact of groups on an individual's mental life. We will also address the influences of groups on an organization's performance, seeking to identify different modes in which groups operate.

Much of the work that goes on in organizations takes place in groups, teams, squads or crews. Such collectivities are generally defined through collective tasks that require collaboration among their members to accomplish. The tasks may be carried out on a one-off or a continuous basis, but they require cooperation, the sharing of information and the division of labour. Above all, the tasks require *interaction* among the group members; they cannot be accomplished by members going about their jobs independently of the others. Interaction generates *relationships* among group members. These relationships come in many varieties. They may address the task or may be more personal and even intimate; they may be egalitarian or may involve power and subordination; they may be harmonious or conflictual; they may involve fixed roles or diffused ones. Groups themselves can be cohesive, their members held together by a common bond, or may be hardly more than a collection of individuals that circumstances have temporarily thrown together.

Within management literature, groups occupy an ambiguous position. On the one hand, business culture, especially in the United States, has extolled teamwork at least since the Hawthorne studies of the 1920s. As Zaleznik has argued:

> While Americans admire the hero', the individual who has the 'right stuff,' they worry about his recklessness, his willingness to take risks that endanger others. Frequently the 'hero' is suppressed in favor of the team player who values the performance of the group over individual recognition. (1993: 180)

Groups embody many important cultural values of Western society: teamwork, cooperation, a collective that is greater than the sum of its parts, informality, egalitarianism and even the indispensability of the individual member. Groups are seen as having a motivating, inspiring influence on the individual, drawing the best out of him or her, enabling him or her to perform feats that would be beyond him or herself as a detached individual. Groups can have a healing influence on individuals, bolstering their self-esteem and filling their lives with meaning (Swogger, 1993). Yet groups are also endowed with a darker side, one which is highlighted in mobs and crowds. They are seen as taking over the individual's mind, depressing intelligence, eliminating moral responsibility and forcing conformity. They can cause their members a great deal of suffering and despair and can perpetrate acts of great cruelty. If groups are capable of great deeds, they are also capable of great follies.

AN ILLUSTRATION

A small group of middle managers is selected by the president and founder of an educational publishing company to develop a mission statement for the organization. The company has operated successfully for twenty years, and has ten distribution and support offices around the United States. The president, Joseph, has recently decided that he wants to see middle managers take more responsibility for decision-making, and has created an assortment of 'project teams' to tackle organization-wide issues. The Mission Statement Project Team (MSPT) has the most high profile and high status of these teams.

Joseph appoints Terrence, a softly spoken and genial marketing manager, to chair the MSPT. Others on the team include: William, the comptroller; Greg, a regional sales manager; Bob, a production project manager; and Jeanne, a curriculum content manager. The group has six months to complete a project that has been defined to involve polling all of the major constituencies of the organization (customers, employees, board members) as well as crafting the statement itself. The group is to present its draft statement at a board meeting, with the understanding that the board will use its work to create the final 'official' mission statement for the organization.

Jeanne finds herself, from the first meeting, fighting with Terrence to get more structure, more direction and more resources for the project. Between meetings, others in the group express concern with Terrence's leadership style. But during the meetings themselves, it is always Jeanne who seems to press for structure and accountability. Jeanne finds herself in an exhausting role: effectively running the meetings when Terrence lapses into a passive 'what do *you* think we should do?' position, organizing the team's work between meetings, and confronting Terrence off-line about his inadequate management style. Her regular work is suffering. She feels the project is impossible, and that the group is being set up for a high-visibility failure. To add to her anxiety, three months into the project, Joseph calls Jeanne into his office and, indirectly, tells her not to undermine Terrence's leadership of the team. He expresses his confidence in Terrence, calls her attention to the tight deadline, and tells her, effectively, to 'get in line'. Completely confused and demoralized, Jeanne goes to Terrence to offer her resignation from the team.

Terrence is shocked: she is the most valuable contributor he has, the team couldn't function without her! He tells her that the team will surely miss its deadline if she resigns. Completely at a loss, Jeanne then protests to him that her behaviour has been counterproductive and unprofessional and that she can't seem to find a way to participate competently on the team. To her amazement, Terrence responds by confessing that she is right about his weak points as group leader. After this conversation, she decides to stay on the team for at least a little longer. Work at the next meeting flows as never before, as Jeanne and Terrence seem to share the leadership role.

What is going on here? Who is responsible for the problems this team has had in functioning? Is Jeanne over-zealous, controlling, obsessive and anxious? If so, perhaps Terrence should have accepted her resignation. Or is Terrence abdicating responsibility, leaning on Jeanne for the decisive leadership he cannot provide? If so, the rest of the team should ask Joseph to replace him with Jeanne. We need an understanding of group dynamics to sort through this situation; otherwise, we run the risk of holding individuals responsible for the complex combination of collective forces that shapes the effectiveness of teams and the experience of team members. In the sections which follow we shall introduce some of the core psychoanalytic theories of group dynamics, using them to elucidate different aspects of the case we have presented.

GROUP DYNAMICS AND UNCONSCIOUS PROCESSES

Organizational theory has addressed group phenomena from different angles, including leadership, decision-making processes, communication processes, group roles and the relative merits of task and process. The term 'group dynamics' identifies the psychoanalytic tradition of studying group phenomena in and out of the workplace. The contribution of this approach lies in its emphasis on the complex emotional forces which shape group life, the unconscious wishes and desires that influence group processes and the delicate networks of relationship that members form with each other.

The application of psychoanalytic theories to group phenomena requires the navigation of a difficult problem: how can the term 'unconscious processes' be used to describe what happens in groups? Didn't Freud describe the unconscious, after all, as a domain of the mind of the individual? Carl Gustav Jung (1964, 1968), Freud's most controversial and creative disciple and, later, critic, argued that the individual unconscious is at least in part a manifestation of a deeper collective unconscious, through which all members of the human species are linked spiritually and psychically. This collective unconscious comprises the spiritual and mythical heritage of humanity, instincts and archetypes. Jung departed from the psychoanalytic tradition which views the individual's mind as a carrier of physical, bodily demands and developed a theory in which the individual psyche is part of a transcendental entity that defies time and space. His theory views the unconscious as a force of creativity as well as a force of destruction, but above all as a force of psychic union for mankind. Most psychoanalytic writers have shied away from this view, fearing the non-scientific or mystical implications of Jung's thought. Yet, in different ways, they have incorporated Jung's seminal idea of symbolic archetypes into psychoanalytic thinking, generating great insights for the understanding of group processes (one such example is the discussion by Paul Moxnes later in the chapter).

Instead of approaching archetypes (such as the archetype of the wise old man, the woman warrior, the innocent fool, the *puer eternus* and so on) as being stored in a collective unconscious, psychoanalytic writers view these archetypes as primal phantasies shared by a large number of people, products of humanity's shared predicament across the ages, as it faces the eternal realities of birth, growth, separation, loss and death. Following Freud, psychoanalytic writers prefer to view group processes as having their own distinct unconscious dimensions which must be studied empirically, and which are directly reducible neither to individual unconscious phenomena nor to the collective unconscious.

> It is not easy to translate the concepts of individual psychology into mass psychology, and I do not think that much is gained by introducing the concept of a 'collective' unconscious – the content of the unconscious is collective anyhow, a general possession of mankind. (Freud, 1939: 381)

The core idea, then, is that unconscious processes occur at the group level; that is, members of a specific group share an emotional experience which often obliterates individual experience, triggered off by unique unconscious processes, unlike those that characterize the mental life of the individual in isolation.

LE BON

This idea can be found in the work of the French psychologist Gustave Le Bon, often regarded as the founder of the study of groups. In his classic book *The Crowd* (1895), Le Bon first proposed that crowds are psychological entities in their own right, more than collections of individuals:

> The psychological crowd is a provisional being formed of heterogeneous elements, which for a moment are combined, exactly as the cells which constitute a living body form by their reunion a new being which displays characteristics very different from those possessed by each of the cells singly. (Le Bon, 1895/1960: 27)

Le Bon's use of a biological metaphor anticipates some of the core concepts of twentieth-century group theory:

- The group as a distinct level of analysis in a kind of nested hierarchy of human systems (the individual, the group, the organization, the society), each level

requiring its own theories and means of analysis and not being reducible to its constituents.
- The 'boundaries', mostly invisible, psychological, but also spatial and temporal, features that differentiate groups from each other and from their environments.
- The temporary character of groups, which implies that these social systems have a lifespan, with a beginning, a maturity and an end.

At the heart of Le Bon's theory lie two ideas: first, that the individual's mental processes are radically altered when he or she finds him or herself as a member of a crowd, sharing the emotional experience of others; and, secondly, that, within crowds, emotional and unconscious forces predominate against the forces of reason:

> Whoever be the individuals that compose [the crowd], however like or unlike be their mode of life, their occupations, their character, or their intelligence, the fact that they have been transformed into a group puts them in possession of a sort of collective mind which makes them feel, think, and act in a manner quite different from that in which each individual of them would feel, think, and act were he in a state of isolation. (1895/1960: 27).

Le Bon argued specifically that crowd members, under the influence of the collective mind, yield to instincts that would otherwise be restrained, absorb emotions from others in a kind of contagion, and become highly suggestible, as if in a hypnotic trance. All of these processes mark the predominance of unconscious, irrational forces over the forces of reason and rationality. Writing in the very year that Freud and Breuer published their *Studies in Hysteria* (1895), Le Bon argued that:

> Crowds, doubtless, are always unconscious, but this very unconsciousness is perhaps one of the secrets of their strength. In the natural world beings exclusively governed by instinct accomplish acts whose marvellous complexity astounds us. Reason is an attribute of humanity of too recent date and still too imperfect to reveal to us the laws of the unconscious, and still more to take its place. The part played by the unconscious in all our acts is immense, and that played by reason very small. The unconscious acts like a force still unknown. (1895/1960: 7)

FREUD

Freud took Le Bon's ideas on the psychology of crowds as his starting point in his book *Group Psychology and the Analysis of the Ego* (1921). Freud's ambivalence towards Le Bon is admirably captured by Robert Merton, in his introduction to Le Bon's work:

> The upshot of Freud's ambivalence to Le Bon amounts, then, to this: Le Bon had a remarkably apt sense of hitting upon salient aspects of crowd and of group behavior, but he did not satisfactorily account for them. On this estimate, Le Bon emerges as a human counter-part to the truffle-dog, who somehow pauses at just those places of social psychology beneath which lie the theoretically significant truffles, unseen by others. And Freud, in projecting his self-image in contrast to this image of Le Bon, sees himself as the master who can dig below the surface, find the truffles of social psychology, and serve them up as piquant intellectual dish. (Le Bon, 1895/1960: xiii)

What Freud sought to do was to use his insights into the workings of the unconscious to elucidate the dynamics of groups. In so doing, he highlighted the importance of *leaders* for the psychological functioning of groups. For Freud, leaderless groups are highly transient, ephemeral arrangements. It is leaders who hold groups together, not so much through their actions and decisions, as through the position which they occupy in the unconscious life of groups. Using the church and the army as examples, Freud argued that members of each group experience 'an intense emotional tie' (1921: 123) to their leader (Christ, the commander in chief) and also to each other. The power of unconscious dynamics in groups is illustrated with the example of panic on the battlefield: when the leader falls, group members forsake the very relatedness that brought them together, as well as the task of battle, lose their minds, and flee in fear.

Freud also proposes that the shared emotional experience of group members comes from a shared *identification* with the leader. Each group member identifies with the leader, who is placed in the individual's ego-ideal; in so doing, each individual identifies with all other group members, who share the same relationship to the leader as themselves. This leads to a definition of 'group' which has at its core the shared unconscious experience of group members: 'A primary group . . . is a number of individuals who have put one and the same object in the place of their ego ideal and have consequently identified themselves with one another in their ego' (1921: 147). What joins members of a group to each other, then, are libidinal ties. Groups represent a special type of love bond, one in which the sexual element has been replaced by an emotional attachment; in short, one in which libido becomes sublimated into social ties. Overt sexual attraction or activity threatens the cohesion of a group, in Freud's view. Thus individuals in a group sacrifice the prospect of direct sexual gratification, but also their uniqueness and individuality, in return for the stability of love relationships, belongingess and group power. In their relationships to their leaders, individuals sacrifice their independence for protection, order and authority. The Freudian group is dominated by his conception of the omnipotent leader, the leader who embodies the qualities of the feared father of the mythical primal horde, whose will is never questioned and whose power is absolute. Groups, in this view, represent not merely a state of intensified emotional ties but something involving psychological regression to a child-like dependence:

> Some of [the group's] features – the weakness of intellectual ability, the lack of emotional restraint, the incapacity for moderation and delay, the inclination to exceed every limit in the expression of emotion and to work it off completely in the form of action – these and similar features, which we find so impressively described in Le Bon, show an unmistakable picture of a regression of mental activity to an earlier stage such as we are not surprised to find among savages or children. (1921: 148)

Yet Freud, along with Robert McDougall, believed that the regressive aspects of a group's mental life may be tempered by organization and task. The extract above continues as follows: 'A regression of this sort is in particular an essential characteristic of common groups, while, as we have heard, in organized and artificial groups it can to a large extent be checked' (1921: 148). In this, there is in embryo an idea that characterizes much subsequent thinking in group psychoanalysis, which reaches its mature formulation in the works of Bion: groups are liable to act in primitive, regressive ways, which may be controlled by appropriate interventions.

KLEIN AND OBJECT RELATIONS THEORY

Originally a follower of Freud, Melanie Klein struck out on her own, creating theoretical links between our earliest experiences as infants and our adult responses to life's emotional challenges, one of which relates to group membership. In Klein's view, young children relate to their world through phantasy; when their emotional state is happy and contented, they experience the world (and adults) as sustaining and nurturing. When they are distressed and angry, they can experience the world as attacking and dangerous. Klein proposed that humans at a very early age utilize two psychological defences to cope with unpleasant emotions: splitting and projective identification. In order to 'preserve' the experience of a caring, attentive mother in those situations in which the mother is not fulfilling all the infant's needs (to eat or to feel dry, for example), the infant mentally creates two mothers: a bad one and a good mother; the first is denying and threatening, the latter all-caring and loving. The same mother that holds the infant at one moment yet refuses to pick it up the next is experienced as two separate beings, or objects (hence 'object relations'). This psychological mechanism, called *splitting*, is 'an action undertaken in fantasy which can be used to separate things which belong together' (Segal, 1964: 36); splitting allows the infant, and later the adult in stressful situations, to cope with fears about survival by separating the 'self' from painful feelings. *Projective identification*, the second mechanism, is closely related. Klein proposed that infants learn to distance themselves from their own destructive feelings by disowning them and actively 'placing' those feelings in someone else.

> Projection can be thought of as perceiving someone else as having one's own characteristics: projective identification involves a more active getting rid of something belonging to the self into someone else . . . Projective identification involves a very deep split, where the aspects of the self projected into others are very deeply denied in the self. (Segal, 1964: 36).

Klein's theories outlining the basic mechanisms of splitting and projective identification have provided, for several group theorists, the link between the individual unconscious experience and an experience that is 'shared' at the group level. Essentially, a large part of group dynamics literature proposes that group membership evokes the strong, contradictory wishes that individual members have had in response to their mothers: on the one hand, to be fused with and indistinguishable from her; on the other, to be distinct and differentiated from her. This common emotional 'history' causes all group members to share an ambivalent emotional response to a group, based on a fantasy of the group as an overwhelming, undifferentiated entity like the mother. Individuals fear being swallowed up and lost in that undifferentiated mass; on the other hand, they fear the isolation and abandonment of being left out or rejected.

It can be seen that the existence of a leader is not as vital in Klein's theory as it is in Freud's. If the Freudian group leader stands for the feared primal father, it is the group itself which assumes the role of the split mother in the Kleinian conception. Both approaches view experiences in groups as triggering off primitive phantasies whose origins lie in the earliest years of life. But while Freud focuses these phantasies firmly in the Oedipal triangle, where mother and father feature as whole objects, Klein focuses on still earlier unconscious material, built around part object relations.

BION'S BASIC ASSUMPTION THEORY

Current group dynamics theory is highly indebted to the work of psychoanalyst Wilfred Bion. Bion observed the dynamics of groups of military personnel, whom he treated for mental traumas sustained during the Second World War. He subsequently codified these observations into a framework widely used now to describe unconscious elements of group interaction. Like Klein, he placed great emphasis on pre-Oedipal experiences, especially in dysfunctional groups:

> The more disturbed the group, the more easily discernible are . . . primitive phantasies and mechanisms; the more stable the group, the more it corresponds with Freud's description of the group as a repetition of family group patterns and neurotic mechanisms. But even in the 'stable' group the deep psychotic levels [can] be demonstrated, though it may involve temporarily an apparent increase of the 'illness' of the group. (Bion, 1961: 165)

Bion observed that the groups he treated seemed to keep their task in focus only some of the time; at other times, the groups seemed intent on avoiding the work that had brought them together. He referred to these diversions as 'basic assumption' activity. By this, he meant that the group members were acting as if they held certain shared assumptions about each other, about the therapist/leader or about the subject they were discussing. When the group was in 'work group' modality, members were intent on furthering the task; they maintained close contact with reality and used rational means to address the demands of the task. In basic assumption mode, on the other hand, members seemed focused primarily on easing anxiety and avoiding the painful interactions or emotions that continued task work would bring. They lost touch with reality and embraced collective delusions that might amount to virtual psychosis (see Lawrence et al., 1996). The casual observer may have the impression that the group is working smoothly and even efficiently, yet in reality the group has lost its ability to interact with the outside world, to test its ideas against the evidence and to act rationally.

Bion identified three types of basic assumptions – dependency, fight/flight and pairing – each with a characteristic set of behaviours and emotions. In basic assumption dependency (baD) mode, group members act as if a leader in the group (who may be formal or informal) is possessed of almost supernatural powers to protect the group and make its decisions. The group members, in contrast, are without knowledge, essentially powerless and dependent on that leader. In this state, the group quickly becomes frustrated as subsequent events prove the leader all too human and fallible. Disappointment then often leads the group to 'depose' the former leader and 'elect' another.

In fight/flight (baF) mode, the group acts as if there is a great danger that must be attacked or fled from. This fantasized danger can spring from inside the group or outside and is typically identifiable only in the apparent panic of group members. The baF is typically led by group members who, in Bion's terms, 'have a valency for' (or 'specialize' in) fight or flight. Thus, one member may be regularly mobilized to fight with the group's leader, while another may lead a group 'excursion' into a nostalgic discussion of 'how we used to do things'.

Basic assumption pairing (baP) is readily identified by the feeling of hopefulness that infuses the group. In this mode, the group acts as if two members of the group, in getting together, can generate an idea or give birth to a person who can solve the

JURIES AS PSYCHOLOGICAL GROUPS

Herman Bingham

In criminal cases, juries have the primary task of determining – in simplest terms – whether the state has met its legal obligation to prove 'beyond reasonable doubt' the guilt of a defendant. At the beginning of each trial, the judge specifies the charges brought against the defendant, educates the jury on the laws applicable to the charges, and instructs the jury members on what evidence and testimony are appropriate for the jury to know. At the end of a criminal trial, before the jury leaves the courtroom to deliberate, the judge describes to them the legal procedures they must use to determine whether the state has met its obligation.

I was on a jury in a criminal trial. The charge brought against the defendant, a medical doctor, was that he had practised medicine without a licence during a specified two-week period. During questioning, the state asked the defendant whether he had practised medicine on such-and-such a day. He answered 'Yes.' Then the state asked if he had had a licence to practise medicine on that day. The defendant answered 'No.' This type of questioning continued for each day of the two-week period. At the end, the defendant had answered that he had practised medicine on twelve of the fourteen days of the two weeks, and had not had a medical licence on any day during that time. The state brought forth other evidence, including the testimony and records of an undercover officer who had faked an illness in order to receive treatment from the defendant. At the end of the trial, the judge instructed us to consider the facts of the case and to determine whether the state had shown, through evidence and testimony and 'beyond a shadow of a doubt', that the defendant was indeed guilty of practising medicine without a licence during those two weeks. The judge went on to tell us to select a foreperson first. This foreperson had the role of directing the discussion towards a verdict, and was the only jury member authorized to speak directly to the judge with any questions from the jury.

I entered the deliberation room confident that we would render our verdict quickly and be out early. After all, the defendant confessed to the charges during questioning. Instead, we spent twelve hours in deliberation over two days. Our deliberation was longer than the trial itself! And, while no two juries can be said to be cut from the identical cloth, we can safely assume, I think, that juries are subject to the same covert processes we see in other groups.

We chose a foreperson without much fanfare. There was an anxious unanimity in selecting as foreperson the only man on the jury wearing a suit and tie. He turned out to be reasonably effective as a leader. On a conscious level, he and two other individuals took up leadership roles, keeping the group on task. While each member of the jury is authorized by law, none the less these three members took a 'greater' authority from the judge's instructions: they were 'following the rules' and in doing so, borrowing the authority of those rules.

Once the foreperson was selected, he polled the room for verdicts. To the surprise of many, three on the jury voted 'Not Guilty.' This was perplexing to say the least, as the defendant himself admitted his guilt. How, then, could anyone find otherwise? The foreperson asked the three who voted 'Not Guilty' to explain how they came to their conclusions. Two of the three said that it was simply too difficult for them to find a doctor guilty. He was, after all, doing good and not hurting anyone, and to find him guilty could ruin his chances of practising medicine for ever, at least in our state. After all (the reasoning went), the good doctor had only allowed his licence to lapse. It was not as though he were an impostor, without training or qualification. No. Rather, this 'once-licenced' doctor was simply too busy helping others to be bothered with bureaucratic formalities. The last of the three – who for clarity's sake I will call no. 12 – explained that he was convinced that the state had set up the doctor in a kind of sting operation. This member cautioned us that he was prepared to 'hold out' as long as necessary because he wanted to send a message to the state that they couldn't treat private citizens in such a reprehensible manner.

With this, the jury-as-a-whole began testing ways to avoid the anxiety inherent in our primary task: determining whether the state had made its case of guilt. The foreperson highlighted the split within the jury by asking only the minority to 'explain' themselves. On an unconscious level, this was a test, a trial, of the baF as a viable solution to the anxiety of finding guilt in another. He might have asked all jurors to explain ourselves. Instead, the three were identified by the leader of the majority as holding a position that required explanation. Presumably, the 'Guilty' position was self-evident, needing no explanation.

This effort to establish the baF failed for a number of reasons. Briefly, we understood that we had to render a decision, and would leave the room only if as a group we were 'unanimous' in our verdict or 'hung'. The anxiety not to render a decision, I believe, became greater than the anxiety of rendering judgment. This produced a significant shift in our own understanding of our primary task, a shift away from (mere) determining guilt to that of unanimous verdict. How and why we were able, as a group, finally to achieve our task, was determined by this shift, this redefinition by the group of its primary task.

I suspect each of us on the jury entered the deliberation room with the conflicting anxieties of, first, being responsible for rendering a verdict and, secondly, being responsible for that verdict being unanimous. For my part, I too experienced conflict about passing judgment, but the task was clear and the defendant's confession incontrovertible. The conflict was in part due to the fact that I could see the face of the defendant, and could understand the potential harm of a guilty verdict. I could not see the face (or faces) of the state, even when one face was my own. Also, my own experience with unfeeling bureaucracies disinclined me to take up their cause; after all, he was but one doctor – weren't there other villains far more worthy of the state's attention? On the other hand, I wanted to please the judge, to be found righteous myself; that is, good, dutiful in the execution of my task, loyal to The Law, obedient to our instructions.

With these feelings, I was in the majority, and we now had a new task: that of complete incorporation, that is a oneness of mind. In making converts, the majority first tackled the objects of those two jury members whose objections seemed most vulnerable. These jury members, nos 10 and 11, held strong but personal objections leading them away from judging another person who was also a doctor. We met those objections through open discussion of our feelings (imagine that!). We talked for some time of the consequences of our collective verdict. Though it was clear we would not level the penalty, we were none the less well aware that our verdict would, in fact, determine whether or not there was a penalty. Given the known realities of medical school and unconscious feelings about doctors and their 'power' to heal and/or kill, there was perhaps more anxiety in passing judgment than if the defendant had been, say, a tobacco company executive or someone else who had become rich at the expense of others. It must be recalled that this doctor did have a valid licence at one time.

After discussing our feelings about both verdicts, we then began to question why a 'Not Guilty' verdict seemed at all acceptable. This reasoning process took only about thirty minutes. One member asked whether, had the doctor been a specialist, would we feel different? Had he been an oncologist or gynaecologist – the two specialties I recall being mentioned – would it make a difference to us whether he had a licence to practise or not? Indeed, it would, and the practical consequences of our verdict began to surface in the discussion.

There was additional speculation revolving around the fantasy of a person remaining silent while knowing unlicensed practitioners were going about their business. We reasoned that this was not merely a small and obscure case. Indeed, were we to turn the other way, we would not only be setting legal precedent, one that could be used in every subsequent case of this kind, but in so doing we would be choosing to unleash a scourge of quacks within our own state and possibly the nation. This argument carried the day. Thoughts of unlicensed obstetricians, gynaecologists and oncologists were abhorrent and frightening to all of us, with the biggest shock being the shock of recognition by both nos 10 and 11. There was an emotional appeal by several jury members for nos 10 and 11 to consider their own guilt. This was an appeal to one's terrible responsibility when knowing about practitioners so careless and unprofessional that they would allow their licences to lapse, yet doing nothing to stop their potential harm. The objections of these two jurors were thus silenced, and each changed her vote to 'Guilty.'

The next vote, this time via secret paper ballot, was eleven to one 'Guilty.' At this point, we did not know who the hold-out was and asked for a voice vote. Predictably, the last hold-out was no. 12, the man who wanted to send a message to the state that private citizens could not be treated in such a manner as the defendant.

The management of this second crisis was quite different from that of the first. This time, no. 12 was more than eager to explain his viewpoint, his philosophy of the state and its abuse of citizens. He was not in the least intimidated or, seemingly, conflicted in his position. The two members who had first voted 'Not Guilty' and then converted did so for personal reasons. It was their own personal anxiety that drove them, and not the group's anxiety.

For no. 12, things were quite different. There were indicators that his behaviour was a group-level solution. For one, his position was a reversal of the majority's. Where we considered only 'pertinent' information, no. 12 elevated the 'impertinent' to a viewing position. Another indicator was his grandiose zeal. No. 12 attempted to persuade all the other members of his position, and actually succeeded with one other member for a brief time. In our final secret ballot of the afternoon, the result was ten 'Guilty', two 'Not Guilty.' With this result, we asked the judge – through the foreperson – to permit us to leave for the day and return the next to continue deliberations. He did and we left for the day.

In retrospect, I see no. 12 as holding up for our attention the unconscious split within the jury (the Guilty/Not Guilty anxiety) and showing us that our redefinition of the primary task was, in fact, an abandonment of it. By considering only one bit of evidence, i.e. the confession, as relevant, we as a jury ignored the motives of both the doctor and the undercover officers. We were instructed by the judge to consider all the evidence in the case and this we failed to do; for certainly motives are – if not evidence – at least relevant data. Instead, what we wanted most was to flee the deliberation room and put the case as far behind us as possible, all the while assuming the postures of good and reasonable persons.

On the second day, the first order of business was another secret ballot. To everyone's surprise the vote was now eleven to one. A voice poll was again taken. No. 12 continued to hold out. It was at this point that individuals other than the foreperson emerged as task co-leaders.

No. 12's argument was fundamentally that the state was as guilty as the defendant they were prosecuting. He argued for the unconstitutionality of the so-called sting operation, calling it entrapment. The two individuals who emerged as leaders pointed out, in different ways, that it was not our task to determine the guilt or innocence of the state, but of the defendant. Referring to, or perhaps relying on, the judge's instructions, these two reiterated what we were supposed to do in this trial. Questions of constitutionality and determinations of entrapment by law enforcement personnel were outside the bounds of the judge's instructions to us. Conceding that argument, no. 12 countered with a technicality. As the doctor did not practise on either Sunday, could it be said that he practised medicine without a licence for the entire two-week period? His question was as frustrating as it was ludicrous. The majority of our 'deliberations' over ten hours had been, in reality, argument and counter-argument with him.

Suddenly, no. 12 came up with what seemed at the time a reasonable, if utterly irrational, way to break out of our impasse. His question was whether the dates specified in this case were 'inclusive' or 'exclusive'. I recall us glancing at each other a little embarrassed. He said that the state had shown that the defendant practised medicine without a licence 'inclusively', which is to say, for every day of the two weeks (except the two Sundays). He stated that if the charge was 'inclusive', he could reconsider his vote. However, if the dates were exclusive, that is not including the beginning and ending date, he could not change his vote. It should be noted that no juror challenged this way out of our gridlock. Confident that we would at last arrive at unanimity, we proceeded to obtain the answer to no. 12's question.

We spent a few minutes writing the question to be posed to the judge. We reached a unanimous agreement on the wording of the question. There was a fleeting sense of relief in knowing that it was indeed possible for us to reach a unanimous decision. It was comforting to know that we could, after all, do such a thing. With that, the foreperson brought the question to the judge. Forty-five minutes later, we were called back into the courtroom. On the tables before the prosecution and defence were stacks of books. The judge mentioned that our question was curious to him, adding with a gesture that it sent both sides 'scrambling to the law books'. He then answered our question, stating that the dates of the charge were inclusive dates, and then dismissed us again to the deliberation room. We took another vote and announced to the judge that we finally had a unanimous decision and were ready to return to the courtroom.

In these two days, we had gone from our initial timidity and counter-phobic unanimity (electing a foreperson), through amazement and frustration (the initial objections), and on to enjoy the spoils of minor victories (winning over nos 10 and 11). The group responded with panic at the prospect of complete unanimity, of coming together too quickly, in the form of no. 12's expressed scepticism and paranoia. In him the group found a container for its anxieties until such could be processed. This was done by working towards a small unanimous decision and then using the authority of the judge (in the inclusive/exclusive question) to move us to the larger unanimous verdict of 'Guilty.'

In the end, I believe no. 12 acted as a kind of conscience for the group. The undisguised irrational nature of his arguments and his 'inclusive/exclusive' remedy suggest strongly that he was serving the group unconscious. By embarking on a seemingly superfluous sub-task – getting an answer to the 'inclusive/exclusive' question – we were sure to feel better about our judgment. We would, at the very least, return to our homes believing that we had looked into every little thing, no matter how insignificant, and that we did everything we could to be just and fair.

group's problems. This hope can have a religious (messianic), sexual (pregnancy) or reparative (world peace) theme, but in all cases the focus of the group turns from immediate, difficult issues to a fantasized future in which all such difficulties will be overcome. Again, certain group members may have a valency for pairing, but the group may use any combination of members, depending on the issue at hand.

MORE RECENT DEVELOPMENTS

Bion's basic assumption theory has been acknowledged and incorporated by every major contributor to the group dynamics field; it has proved one of the most theoretically robust and heuristically useful set of ideas in depth psychology. A number of theoretical developments and refinements have been made. Gould (1997) has recently taken up a challenge offered by Bion, namely an intuition that group and individual psychoanalysis 'are dealing with different facets of the same phenomena. The two methods provide the practitioner with a rudimentary binocular vision' (Bion, 1961: 8). Gould argues that there is a one-to-one correspondence between Bion's basic assumptions and Klein's developmental positions. Thus, the paranoid-schizoid position, like the baF, is associated with acute fears of prosecution and destruction; the major defences are splitting of good from bad, denial of the bad within the group or the self, and idealization of the self or the leader. The depressive position, with its characteristic acceptance of dependency and fear of aggression lest it destroys the care-taker, corresponds to the baD, with its denial of the aggressive impulses towards the leader, its submission to authority and its general feelings of depressed powerlessness. Somewhat more contentiously, Gould associates a Kleinian reading of the Oedipus complex with the baP. The Oedipus complex starts with fears of exclusion from the pair, develops through fears of retaliation and punishment and concludes with a repression of one's own sexual desires and their replacement with a promise for the future. The pair becomes an exalted combination in this phase, as indeed it is characteristic of the baP group.

An interesting feature of Gould's argument is his attempt to elucidate a rather undeveloped area of Bion's thought, the sophisticated use of basic assumption. Bion maintained a sharp distinction between basic assumption group functioning and work group functioning geared towards the group's task. In his view, basic assumption groups cannot deliver task ('basic assumption mentality does not lend itself into action' (1961: 157)) since they are incapable of focusing on anything beyond their own emotional needs. But, he did recognize that groups can make sophisticated use of basic assumptions, by 'mobilizing the emotions of one basic assumption in the constructive pursuit of the primary task' (Stokes, 1994: 25). Basic assumption can have adaptive value if subordinated to the group's task. Gould observes that baF can act as the basis of sensitivity to dangers and threats as well as the force for loyalty, commitment and self-sacrifice. BaD offers a principle of submission to authority, learning from authority and acknowledging gratitude to the leader. Finally,

> *pairing*, when utilized by a group in a sophisticated manner, allows for the possibility of mobilizing productive and creative forces in the service of W [work group] by selectively recognizing and supporting special relationships (pairings). When these are permitted, or better yet actively encouraged by the group, such pairings can provide hopeful, realistic and creative leadership in the service of required change, renewal and continuity. (1997: 26–7)

It is currently becoming more acceptable to acknowledge potentially beneficial effects for groups, resulting from sophisticated use of basic assumptions. Stokes has offered some illustrations of how this may be accomplished:

> An example of such sophisticated use of baD can be found in a well-run hospital ward. An atmosphere of efficiency and calm is used to mobilize baD, encouraging patients to give themselves over to the nurses or doctors in a trusting dependent way. BaF is utilized by an army to keep on the alert, and, when required, to go into battle without disabling consideration for personal safety. In social work, baF supports the task of fighting or fleeing from family, social and environmental conditions or injustices which are harmful to the client. BaP finds a sophisticated use in the therapeutic situation, where the pairing between a staff member and a patient can provide a background sense of hope in order to sustain the setbacks inevitable in any treatment. (1994: 25)

The issues of whether and how basic assumption behaviour may be constructively channelled are not conclusively resolved. Purists would prefer to keep the line sharp, though practitioners, such as consultants and therapists, undoubtedly encounter group situations where basic assumption behaviour may be constructively directed.

Another development in Bion's theory has been the identification of other types of basic assumption groups. To Bion's three basic assumptions, Pierre Turquet (1974) has added a fourth, the basic assumption 'one-ness', which draws its inspiration from Freud's discussion of the 'oceanic' feeling. Under the grip of this basic assumption 'members seek to join in a powerful union with an omnipotent force, unobtainably high, to surrender self for passive participation, and thereby feel existence, well-being, and wholeness' (1974: 357). More recently, Lawrence et al. (1996) have hypothesized a fifth basic assumption, the basic assumption 'me-ness', which is almost the opposite of the basic assumption 'one-ness', a denial of the existence of a particular group because all groups are seen as impure, contaminating and oppressive (Lawrence et al., 1996). It is still unclear whether clinical and consulting practice will confirm these theoretical developments, though they provide evidence of the lively discourse that Bion's theories have sparked off.

Some writers have challenged Bion's view that groups swing, pendulum-style, from work mode to basic assumption mode, with no change in this pattern over time. Instead, they adopt a developmental view of groups. Philip Slater (1966), for example, drew insights from developmental psychologists like Piaget, in observing his Harvard undergraduate class. In his book *Microcosm* (1966), he proposed that unconscious dynamics in groups change over time in predictable ways as group members gradually substitute conscious bonds for the unconscious links that dominate group life in the early stages. Slater's argument is based on a now widely accepted assumption that the fantasy of the group-as-mother is strongest when members first join or create the group. When faced with unfamiliar settings and people, group members' behaviours towards each other tend to be driven by transference. Individuals must make some assumptions about who the others are, about how the group will function, and about what role the leader will play and the only source of information which they have is past experience. However, Slater observes, 'as time goes by, more and more reality begins to intrude itself gratingly into their perceptions of each other' (1966: 172).

Following Freud, Slater argues that the leader emerges first out of the undifferentiated group mass, in part to meet the group's basic assumption dependency needs. This initial dependency allows members of the group, in staking out positions of identification with or rebellion against the leader, to follow in their own gradual differentiation from the group. Eventually, conscious bonds are substituted for the transference:

> A conscious attachment is based, by definition, on an awareness of differences, whereas unconscious ones always entail mystical fusion. Group development is thus the gradual encroachment of light on shadow, with the various 'basic assumptions' being techniques applied at different points to defend against whichever shadows seem most fearsome at any given moment. (1966: 176)

Bion's framework has been extended in similar ways to form the basis of current group dynamics theory.

LEADERLESS GROUPS?

Is it possible for a group to function without a leader? Psychoanalytic writers, including Obholzer, Gould and Hirschhorn, are generally mistrustful of leaderless groups. On close inspection, such groups usually reveal ineffectual leadership taking cover behind the rhetoric of collegiality and equality, unwilling to face up to its responsibilities, emotional and practical. Two writers who have taken a different approach are Diamond and Allcorn, who, like Slater, have offered a developmental theory of groups (Diamond and Allcorn, 1987; Diamond, 1991). Diamond and Allcorn are keenly concerned about the dilemma noted by Klein – that between the need for independence and the need for belonging. They have developed their theory of group regression, drawing on Freud's and Kernberg's core insight that group affiliation makes demands on an individual's narcissism, emboldening it in some ways, frustrating it in others.

> Group membership can give many a feeling of omnipotence – being part of a group gives individuals a sense of being larger, greater, and better than they really are. Group membership is a way of fulfilling their ego ideal – that is, the sense of oneself at one's future best. Therefore, some affiliation with others is important in that it provides them not only with a defense, but also with a sense of being greater than themselves. (Diamond, 1991: 192)

But group affiliation creates an acute anxiety of rejection by the group which may be experienced as tantamount to self-disintegration. This prompts a regressive group action:

> a protective reaction, preserving the self from annihilation by withdrawal into a safe and secure inner space . . . Persecuted work groups, ethnic groups, and even nations have been known to withdraw from an external world they perceive as hostile and dangerous . . . Like lemmings, the work group reacts in order to preserve itself – but in doing so is rendered ineffective and may die. (Diamond, 1991: 194–5)

On the basis of their clinical and consulting experience, Diamond and Allcorn identify three degrees of group regression, each having its own unique political and psychic configuration. The most extreme regression is represented by the lemming-like 'homogenized work group', a leaderless, thoroughly homogeneous group, which is quite incapable of performing work, and may be represented by the Freudian description of the mob. The psychic mechanisms which characterize this extreme form of regression are those of the earliest schizoid splitting, 'group members perceive themselves as ideal and all-good, and others as persecutory and all-bad' (Diamond, 1991: 199; see also Diamond and Allcorn, 1987: 531). Less extreme forms of regression are characteristic of the other two groups, the institutionalized and the autocratic ones. The former usually assumes a bureaucratic structure and the latter an autocratic/patriarchal structure, with commensurate leadership configurations.

Diamond also observes a non-defensive and non-neurotic group which he refers to as the intentional group, which has participative leadership and is capable of double-loop learning. This is, *par excellence*, a work group, in which task assumes priority, without eclipsing defensive patterns characteristic of the regressive groups. Diamond argues that:

> it should be noted that the intentional group differs from traditional humanistic organization theories of sophisticated, collaborative work relations by emphasizing the need to attend to regressive and defensive actions. These actions underlie all group and organization dynamics. The intentional group represents a qualitative difference from more traditional prescriptions for collaborative work groups, in that it stresses the necessity for understanding and explaining cognitive and affective work dynamics in order to achieve effectiveness and intentionality in the work group. (1991: 208)

Of considerable interest in Diamond's argument is the view of the lemming-like homogenized group as a pre-Bionic configuration, one in which the group is unable to tolerate the idea that one of their lot would be able to emerge as a leader. This group is reminiscent of Turquet's basic assumption 'one-ness' group, a state where there is no differentiation of the constituents which form a fluid mass. To such a group, Bion's basic assumptions, argues Diamond, are *progressive* steps, representing a collective escape from the total paralysis of the homogenized group towards the less regressive configurations of either the institutional or the autocratic group. Further progressive steps may see a group move towards the intentional group, a group in which the individuality of each member is accepted as a valuable resource for the group.

> The secret to emotionally healthy and organizationally effective work groups may be uncovered in individuals' attempts to strike a balance between needs for independence and belonging. Regressive work groups are characterized by an imbalance that favors group membership and affiliation over and above personal identity and autonomy. In fact, critical organizational incidents trigger regressive group responses, which suppress and, in some cases, destroy the self-identity and independence of members. When autonomy is forfeited for group membership, the lemming syndrome becomes a dangerous possibility. (Diamond, 1991: 212)

Let us see now how helpful psychodynamic theory can be in analysing the dynamics of the group in our earlier illustration.

CASE EXAMPLE: THE MISSION STATEMENT PROJECT TEAM

The first thing to note about the Mission Statement Project Team (MSPT) is that it is faced with a relatively ill-defined and potentially difficult task. The group is composed of middle managers who for the first time in the organization's history, are entrusted with what is framed as a crucial task. The task itself may be conceived as involving little more than a few token interviews, a brainstorming session and the gradual polishing up of a simple set of statements; but such a definition can hardly accord with the importance of the task and the ceremony with which the group has been set up. Members of the team feel anxious. Can the task be achieved in the given time-frame? This triggers off a set of alarming possibilities. Could the team have been set up for failure? Could it be that Joseph, the founder of the organization who is moving towards retirement, is not fully in support of the creation of a mission statement, but has acceded to the wishes of the board in setting up this project team? The new mission statement, after all, could mean that his own personal vision for the organization is no longer appropriate. Could it be, then, that he will abandon the team at the crucial moment, blaming them for the failure? Why has the board the final word if the team is ostensibly empowered to devise a mission statement? Has the team been framed?

Under these circumstances, it could be that Jeanne has become the group's 'fight leader': the group, in not stopping her from fighting with Terrence, the formal leader, is endorsing the need for this defence against danger. At different moments, the group lapses into 'flight' mode, avoiding the task: no one but Jeanne, apparently, is willing to look at the logistical realities of the project. So, the group is experiencing anxiety verging on panic, as if their work entails a devastating danger. The failure to deliver the mission statement is experienced as a total catastrophe threatening their very being.

But the team's frustration may have a deeper source. In the uncertainty of the group's start-up, the group has not found adequate protection from the danger in Terrence's leadership and has not been able to face the anxiety of this situation. Here, object relations theory can contribute. Faced with these feelings of rage and frustration, group members have perhaps disowned them (split them off) and projected these feelings on to Jeanne. From this perspective, Jeanne is expressing the rage of others, but experiences herself as acting alone. Significantly, Joseph contributes to this dynamic by telling Jeanne that she is 'the problem'. Jeanne understands that she is at great risk of being scapegoated; that is, loaded with the group's negative projections and then treated as if she is the source of all the group's difficulties. If she stays in the group, then she runs the risk of being ejected from the group, as all collude in a desperate effort to be rid of their anxiety. Thus, she announces her intention to leave.

What happens next is a complete surprise to Jeanne. Terrence, instead of treating her as his enemy, views her as a valuable ally. Of course, from the object relations perspective, this makes sense. She has been absorbing the negative feelings in the group that otherwise would have been directed at him. If she leaves, would he not have to face the group's rage alone? The two, in Slater's (1966) terms, substitute a conscious understanding of each other's strengths and weaknesses for their former transferential relationship. (It is important to note here that this transference is as much a product of the group's unconscious activity as it is of the personal experience of Jeanne and Terrence.)

Thus, Terrence and Jeanne form a pair. Apparently their pairing has a salutary effect on the group, at least initially, allowing the group to soothe its anxieties in basic assumption pairing mode. Surely, the coming together of the former rivals is likely to generate the winning idea which will enable the team to discharge its duty successfully. But how long will the hopefulness represented by the repair of their relationship sustain the group? We cannot answer this question, nor can we say for sure that this analysis is correct. Certainly, it cannot be proved conclusively. However, it can be tested; we can check the details of the group's previous and subsequent interactions to see if the patterns fit this formulation. Thus, we have a framework to offer some hypotheses about what has happened in the group and why.

This framework also allows us to problem-solve, if we are in a position to intervene in this group. For example, understanding that basic assumption 'solutions' are temporary salves to anxiety, one would look for ways to bring to the surface the source of the group members' panic. Is it based on a fantasy of being asked to do an impossible task? If so, then the fear should subside as the group grapples successfully with the assignment. Or are there real dangers to group members in taking on this assignment? If there are real dangers, what actions should be taken? Should Terrence re-negotiate the deadline or scope of the project? Should he explore Joseph's level of support for the project? Should they consider reconstituting the group to include board members, as the board of directors will, finally, decide on the statement?

Good managerial decisions in this case will spring from an informed understanding of the forces affecting the team. And, as we have shown here, this understanding can be enhanced by using group dynamics frameworks derived from psychoanalytic perspectives. In the next part of this chapter, we will see how some areas of group psychology can be better understood through the use of psychoanalytic perspectives.

APPLICATIONS TO GROUP TOPICS IN MANAGEMENT

Group dynamics theory adds an unconscious dimension to the analysis of the common group topics in management curricula, which tends to highlight emotional forces at play. These forces can have a critical influence on group process and effectiveness.

Group decision-making

Almost all management students participate in some kind of group decision-making exercise. Most commonly, students are given a scenario and asked to work alone to rank certain items in order of importance. Then each student group is asked to develop a common ranking of the items. Typically, the exercises are designed to allow comparison of the performance of individuals versus the performance of the groups (a 'right' answer is typically provided as part of the exercise). And, typically, the group decisions are better. From this, students are supposed to learn that working in groups produces synergies.

However, some groups do not achieve better results than those achieved by individual members. In such cases, the 'groupthink' phenomenon is often used as an explanation. This term was introduced by Janis (1972) to describe the behaviour of President Kennedy's senior aides in 1961, which led to the disastrous attempt to invade Cuba at the Bay of Pigs. In that case, competent senior cabinet officers suppressed their internal doubts about the invasion and went along with the group, producing a spectacular military and policy failure. Janis attributes this behaviour to group arrogance, in which the moral and intellectual superiority of the US over the Cubans was taken for granted, and also to the group's culture, in which loyalty to the president was prized above everything else. 'How could we have been so stupid?', Kennedy remarked later. Group stupidity is the outcome of defensive postures which encourage the unthinking adoption of wish-fulfilling illusions.

'Groupthink' offers a plausible description of some group dysfunctions without, however, explaining the reasons why it takes sway or the mechanisms through which it operates. These become much clearer when we identify the underlying mechanisms, whose visible outcome is 'groupthink'. In the case of the Kennedy team, using Janis's (1972) own analysis, we can surmise that the group lapsed into basic assumption Dependency (baD) mode; experienced senior leaders were acting as if they did not have the expertise to think through or reason with the decision. What the president said was right; after all, he was the infallible leader who would save them from this crisis. The feelings of incompetence were split off and projected on to the Cubans who, in the minds of the Kennedy team, could not possibly mount an effective military response. Members of the group who experienced some doubts (and a few consciously did but suppressed the urge to express them) understood that to raise these doubts would be to become the target of the projected feelings of incompetence, and therefore to become the 'disloyal' scapegoat of the group.

Thus, 'groupthink' as a concept does not go far enough in explaining why a collection of otherwise competent individuals would, under pressure, behave so incompetently. In some cases, as in the one above, it is the outcome of a dependency basic assumption. In other instances, it can be the visible outcome of a fight/flight or pairing assumption. Only by examining the unconscious processes underlying the onset of 'groupthink' is it possible to account for its grip over the members' minds and perhaps to obviate its most adverse effects.

Task/process roles

Most management textbooks discuss 'task' and 'process' in groups: *task* is what the group is doing and *process* is how the group goes about doing it. Students are advised that they must, as group members or leaders, pay attention to process. The decision-making exercises described earlier are sometimes used as illustrations of how the task suffers when process is deficient; for example, when members decide to vote instead of arguing through their differences, or when the views of certain group members are systematically ignored. Discussions of group process tend to identify certain 'task roles' and 'process roles', which group members must fulfil in order for the group to function effectively. *Task roles* include 'information-seeker', 'finisher' and 'discussion leader', while *process roles* include 'mediator' and 'time-keeper'. The lesson is that the group cannot effectively accomplish its task without adequate attention to process. But such analysis focuses on the rational aspects of group life, and assumes that group members are both aware of their thoughts and willing to share them. The psychoanalytic perspective shows that this definition of 'process' barely skims the surface. Admonishments to be conscious of process and of the psychological needs of group members cannot succeed without a systematic understanding of the forces that supplant the conscious processes in group functioning.

Thus, a group facing disagreement between two vocal members may move into Bion's basic assumption fight/flight mode, and decide to vote as an avoidance of the conflict. Or a group may spend precious time attempting to reach consensus on one point and not complete the exercise. Again, in fight/flight mode this group may have unconsciously wanted to avoid a situation where one of its members wins over another. From this perspective, there often is no 'correct' process, just the process that each group has felt itself able to mobilize at the moment.

DEEP ROLES: TEMPLATES OF THE GROUP MIND
Paul Moxnes

Paul Moxnes uses his insights from animal ethology and Kleinian analysis to develop a matrix of deep roles in human groups. His discussion reaches a conclusion remarkably similar to Jung's theory of archetypes, without however making the assumption of the collective unconscious.

People have fantasies about one another, these are not always experienced as fantasy, but as reality. People need phantasies. Phantasies serve our emotions, and are used in games of power and influence. 'Darlings' and 'scapegoats' were two needed phantasies for hospital personnel I studied some years ago. Later on, they turned out to be only two of twelve needed roles in the group. These roles, the *deep roles*, were the result of collective projections of unconscious phantasies; they were vital in maintaining, channelling and legitimizing primary interpersonal feelings and needs, such as hate, love, admiration, dislike, anxiety and pride. Without primary feelings, we would be robots. Deprived of deep roles, the group would be a machine. The players in the group are living people, and the group itself is a pulsating interaction of powerful phantasies, consisting of victory and defeat, peace of mind and fear. In the phantasy world of groups, individuals must assume roles, some as friends and others as enemies, some as helpers and others as opponents, some as winners and others as losers. These roles are what I shall call 'deep roles'. Far back in the chain of events, they are the result of 'splitting'. When the results of the splitting in individual members of the group are projected on to certain people (who for some reason or other attract these projections), the group is in the process of building up group deep roles. When, in addition, members of the group identify with this role – more precisely, when they become 'containers' for projective identification processes – the deep role is established as a common collective, a reality of the mind. It is still, however, a phantasy, a phantasy which has become a reality.

It is claimed that every mind is populated by many people, a statement often made by artists and scientists. 'In every soul are thousands of souls imprisoned', writes the Swedish poet, Gunnar Ekelöf. The poet August Strindberg was thinking along similar lines when he wrote: 'Everything is in all. And likewise everybody is in all.' The great Strindberg biographer, Olof Lagercrantz, says that Strindberg at certain moments could see that those human characteristics that he despised in others were really his own. If this is so, even at a general level, and this is my belief, it suggests that the human characteristics we see around us are within us. Our 'personality' to a greater or lesser extent creates the roles of others. The actress and movie celebrity Liv Ullmann writes: 'I am full of fairy-tales, of trolls, elves, and goblins, and of legends. The fantasy world of childhood invades my reality with intense force.' We have to recognize the pull of archetypal forces in our own psyche. The contact with the archetypes in us creates energy and power – not only in us, but also within the group. Every individual carries everything within him or herself: all personalities, feelings, mental health and illnesses, peace of mind and anxiety. We are containers with many feelings. In creating our social environment, we choose to retain certain roles for ourselves and project some on to others, thus creating a social reality consisting of 'trolls, elves, and goblins'. This is a symbolic reality, which can be destroyed when an outsider who does not share the fantasy enters, an outsider who cannot or will not be cast in the group's system of deep roles.

Primary deep roles: the family

Finding deep roles is like looking for elements: it is assumed that a certain number of them are waiting to be discovered. I believe that there are altogether twelve of them, perhaps more. They fit into a single pattern, almost like the elements in the periodic system. Deep roles exist where people are together in a meaningful community; for example, individuals in a group or organization. Deep roles serve as protection against confusion, anxiety and group dissatisfactions. In order to find them, I start from the most basic features in both the individual and the group: the initial defence mechanisms of the individual, and the allocation of roles in the earliest type of group. What is, then, the earliest form of group? This is a more difficult question. My belief is that the earliest group is the *family*, with its nucleus of deep roles: mother, father (or father substitute) and children. I cannot see any group earlier than this one. If it can be established that the family also exists among animals, particularly among those animals which are genetically close to man, then there is reason to believe that the family is more or less a phylogenetic group. I believe that all deep roles, in the meaning of archetypal roles necessary for the survival of the species, are present in some form or other among animal species. We shall, therefore, pay another visit to the world of animals.

Not all animals live in families. Many types of animals, such as certain reptiles, are born alone, and live their lives without any particular role distribution other than that of male and female, in addition to certain degrees of dominance–submission. However, these roles, being among the earliest and most basic in the animal world, are not in themselves sufficient to create a group, but they none the less constitute two important parameters also in the family group.

In contrast to reptiles, all mammals are born close to their mother. The mother–child relationship is beyond doubt a basic psycho-biological relationship. But not even the mother–child dyad is sufficient to be termed a group. A true group must consist of a minimum of three, preferably four, role bearers. Most of the higher forms of monkeys are born into a social system in which they are immediately in contact with other individuals, in addition to the mother. Observations have been made which indicate that the family, as we know it among humans, has a biological basis among other mammals as well. There are monogamous types of primates which live in a sort of family structure; in certain gorilla tribes the female is tied in a long-lasting relationship to a single male, albeit in a harem system. In this way, she gains better protection, better access to resources and, not least, can ensure that her children are better protected. The dominant male may maintain a long-lasting relationship with his 'child' during its growing years and, when this child grows up, it may 'inherit' the older male's throne, taking over the leadership of the group (Whitten, 1987). In most primates, including gibbons and brown capuchins but not chimpanzees, the roles of father and protector coincide. In such primates, the children become equally tied to the father as to the mother. The fact that such primates have a sense of who is their father, mother or close relation creates a developmental biological advantage in that they avoid incest with them. (Elgmork, 1988). These three roles – mother, father and child – are sufficient to constitute a group, complemented in most mammals by a fourth one, that of siblings. In the human family, this creates four primary roles: mother, father, sister, brother. Together they constitute an elementary form of group: a group which has a clear and biologically determined programme – to survive.

In the human psyche, though hardly in that of the animal, these four primary roles have the possibility of multiplying from the moment splitting or differentiation begins, following Klein's model of the splitting of the mother. The same process occurs in what we may call the natural 'tetrad', consisting of mother, father, son and daughter, as the Danish psychologist Pia Skogemann (1987) does. When these four elements are combined with the splitting process, we obtain the *eight* basic elements of the psyche. The contents of this mental matrix are determined by three parameters: *sex* (female and male), *evaluation* (good and evil) and *power* (dominance and submission). Together they yield eight primary archetypal roles: good and evil father, mother, son and daughter. These are projected on to individuals in groups and can also be recognized in fairy-tales, films, literature, myths and religions.

Secondary deep roles: the helpers

Family members are not the only ones who occupy our minds, even if they occupy a considerable part of it. We think of our mother, father, sister and brother all our lives for better or worse – and often, when they are gone, they emerge more strongly, sometimes, even towards the end of our lives. There is time for reconciliation, for discussion, for forgiveness, for gratitude. There are no other archetypal roles as central as these. We call them the *primary* deep roles.

Are there roles outside the primary family which are significant for its survival and maintenance, roles which could be called archetypal? An ancient English prayer says: 'God save the family and its helpers.' Here we are on the path which leads us to what I should like to call the *secondary* deep roles. Most families have *helpers*, who more or less form a circle around the family in order to protect or help it in different ways. Helper behaviour has both genetic and social antecedents, and we recognize them in the entire animal world, where it has been observed in more than 150 types of bird and more than 30 types of mammal (Goldizen, 1987). This suggests a phylogenetic nature for the role. One example is the suricates in Australia, living in packs on the plains, where one of them always keeps watch. Without this solitary sentinel at the top of some high point on the landscape, the suricates would not survive. Other animal helpers may show willingness to delay reproducing their own families, to feed the offspring of others, to 'babysit' them (taking time off from their own time for hunting and the gathering of food) and to put their own lives at risk in order to protect the children of others.

In the old hunting and farming societies the helper was indispensable. But among people today, the helper is an equally important person, often appearing in the form of 'network', 'contacts', 'friends' and 'advisers'. We can recognize the archetypal helpers in myths, and especially in fairy-tales, where they play key roles, often as animals or old people. In fairy-tales, the helper has a magical power which he or she uses to help a family member; the king, for example, searching for his abducted daughter, or the youngest child performing a difficult task and gaining happiness, and thereby bringing honour and wealth to himself and his family. Another form assumed by the helper is as a mentor figure, Mentor being the wise old man to whom Odysseus entrusted his son when he left for the Trojan War. Good helpers can assume two forms, spiritual and material, and are the key to the survival and welfare of the family.

The helper role also splits into good and evil. The family and its good helpers must constantly be on guard against bad helpers. These bad helpers may initially appear, Iago-like, as good ones or may remain on the sidelines. Establishing the goodness or badness of helpers requires extensive efforts of surveillance and tests of loyalty. A group does not, of course, need evil helpers for its existence, but it absolutely needs to be on the look out for them. It may also make psychological use of evil helpers as scapegoats.

The transformation roles: winners and losers

I have now introduced ten group deep roles: the eight primary roles (the family), and the two secondary ones (the helpers). There are two more. These are the *transformation* roles, roles connected to metamorphosis, to change. They relate to having a major goal and achieving great happiness by becoming a member of a family; or, suffering a great disaster by never achieving this or by ceasing to be a family member. This is the basis of the two last archetypal roles: *winners* and *losers*.

Whereas the primary and secondary roles are static, the transformation roles are dynamic. The winner achieves greatness by leaving his original home and becoming raised to a place almost among the gods. From his previous position outside his new family, he achieves a place as a father figure within it. The loser, on the other hand, loses his original position, and is deprived of his membership within the group. He has by accident or by lack of ability more or less 'fallen outside'. We may pity him, but we may also laugh at him out of malice. He is the exact opposite of the winner. The winner has many names that will long be remembered. The loser is nameless.

Can we trace these transformational roles back to a psycho-biological origin? This origin, I believe, is to be found in the behaviour of primates, which ethologists call 'transfer' behaviour, where a member leaves its tribe or group in order to go out into the world to seek a new group. Sometimes this might lead to defeat and death, at other times to victory and acceptance by the new group. It was a pleasure for me to discover the similarity between *transfer* and the *transformation* role. Transfer takes place in all species of group-living monkeys and apes (Pusey and Packer, 1987). In most species of primates, the males leave the group in which they have grown up at the age of puberty; in others, such as chimpanzees and gorillas, it is the females that do so. Animal ethologists have little doubt that transfer is a universal phenomenon among primates and have proposed a number of reasons why this is necessary for the survival of the species; without transfer, a species would degenerate. Going out into the world to join other groups – fighting, winning, becoming accepted as a member of the new group and mating – become biological necessities (in order to 'live happily ever after'). My conjecture is that they also furnish the raw material for fairy-tales and myths. In one widely found version, the youngest son is constantly ridiculed by his brothers. They, not he, are entitled to the princess. He is left without a mating partner; he is left with the poorest jobs and the poorest care. He is therefore forced out of the group, into the world, to seek his fortune. If he is lucky and able, he overcomes all difficulties and wins a princess, the gold and half of the kingdom – while his brothers languish at home.

I am not going to tire the reader by providing further parallels between traditional fairy-tales and the behaviour of apes. My intention has been to argue in support of biological roots for the transformation roles so as to support the claim that they are deep roles. Like the other deep roles, transformation roles split up. Both the winner and the loser divide up into good and evil roles, but there is a redundant quality about the negative roles (bad winner and bad loser). Winners and losers have already been divided. The loser is the winner's shadow. The 'evil winner', if we may use this term, is one who destroys, one who becomes famous for his evil actions. The world he conquers is the underworld, whose inhabitants view the evil winner as 'good'. Evil winners do not exist in our primitive world of ideas. A winner is, by definition, good. Good eventually has to conquer evil. All human existence and society is established according to this universal psychological credo. It is easier to imagine a bad loser in contrast to a good loser. The latter knows his or her predicament, accepts it and behaves accordingly. In some instances, he or she is a tragic figure or a victim. Victims may command respect but are easily forgotten, characters without a name or a face. Bad losers, for their part, are those who do not accept their defeat, ending up disparaged as fools or clowns.

This, then, is the matrix of the deep roles of the group mind (see Figure 5.1). Viewed this way, the deep roles are collective and necessary perceptions of people. Certain people become 'containers' into which we can throw our unconscious phantasies. The sex of a carrier of a deep role may be irrelevant. Whether the carrier of a deep role is actually physically present in the group may also be irrelevant. Our mental images can be tied to people outside the group, as long as these people have significance for the phantasy life of our in-group and therefore serve the function of deep roles. The negative father can, for instance, be a person in a rival group. If the negative daughter is not physically present in the group, she might none the less fill a deep role function in the group as long as people know of her, think of her and talk about her. Our mental images can also be related to objects which, in such cases, would appear as powerful symbols. An artefact, an icon, a mascot or the like can sometimes attract to itself the group's projections, and become the object of strong feelings.

The deep role matrix has its origins in the family tetrad, but it possesses mythological power in all groups – not just in the family group. Groups may function without deep roles for some time, but a group which – in a wanting situation – is unable to create

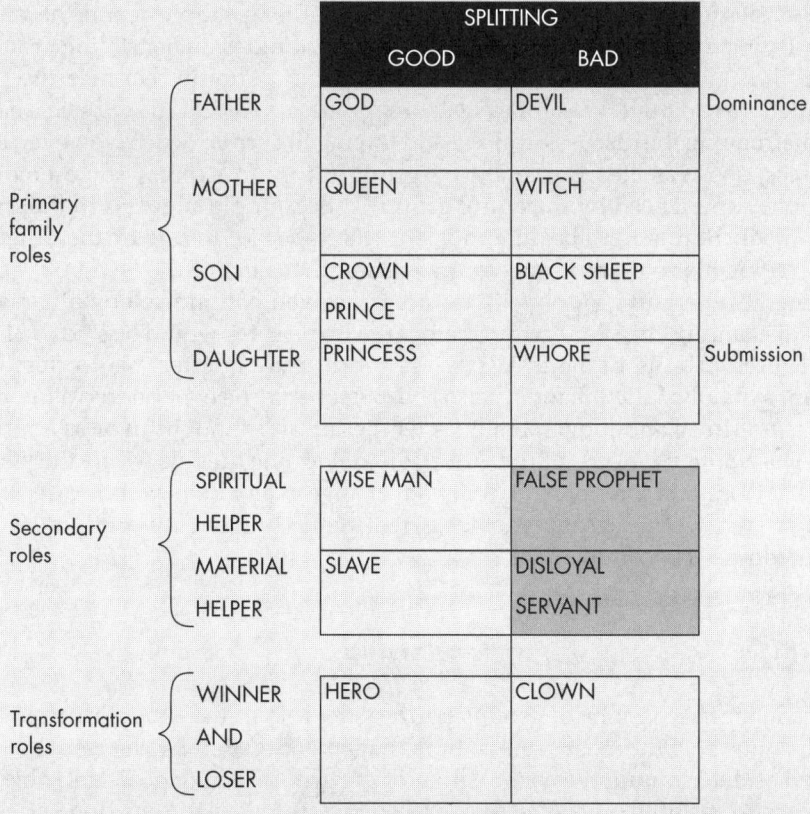

FIGURE 5.1 *Matrix of the deep roles of the group mind*

> primary deep roles because its members' projections go out in different directions could be in disequilibrium and even in crisis. Without these roles in their appropriate places, without value agreements as to who is 'good' and who is 'evil', who is 'father' and who is 'mother', who is 'winner' and who is 'loser', the group will have problems both with its daily internal adaptation and with its survival on a long-term basis. A group living in competitive surroundings cannot exist for long without making 'real', i.e. externalizing, the various forms of the mental matrix. The alternative is mental group chaos, which can often be the beginning of a new group.
>
> Adapted from P. Moxnes, *Hjältar, häxor, horor och andra djuproller i mänskligt samspel.* Stockholm: Natur & Kultur, 1995.

If the group dynamics theories described here all offer a richer and more complex definition of 'group process', they also offer a more sophisticated understanding of the *roles* that group members play. Bion's concept of *valency* is helpful here. While it is true that group members may consciously assume the roles necessary for their group to accomplish its work, as group members they are also moved by unconscious forces and phantasies to assume emotional roles. In our earlier example, Jeanne became the fight leader in the MSPT, perhaps because she was the oldest in her sibling group and thus familiar with the role in her own family, but certainly because the group 'nominated' her to do it. Was this a task or a process role? On the surface, she took a task role, moving the discussion along and forcing the group to act. However, below the surface, she was clearly moved by group forces to express some emotional frustrations experienced by the entire group. This example suggests that the task/process distinction is not absolute, nor are roles specific to one or the other. The concept of 'visible role' itself may be less useful than that of the 'symbolic role' in describing how certain group members are conceived of and used by others in the group. For example, the silent group member, who perhaps would be said to play the neutral 'observer' role in the task/process rubric, may in effect be serving a very important symbolic function for others. This person may be experienced as aloof and arrogant, as critical and judgemental, as temperate and thoughtful or as angry and hostile. The emotional needs of the group will determine the role, while the person's actual behaviour and intentionality may not change at all. 'Role', in this case, is more defined by what other group members feel than by what the individual 'role-occupant' does – it becomes a *'deep role'*.

Leadership

Most academic discussions of groups address the role of the group leader. This is, after all, a vital role for most groups. In management textbooks, the leader's role is described as determining the composition of the group, setting goals and objectives for the group, establishing effective procedures for decision-making, clarifying expectations (between him or herself and the group as well as among group members), negotiating with the outside environment for resources and support, setting and enforcing deadlines, promoting clear and open communication among group members, and maintaining a group climate of trust and teamwork. This leadership agenda is consistent with the task/ process model of activities and roles in groups; the leader's role is to make sure essential task and process activities are carried out, either personally or through delegation. Less conspicuous in such discussions is the leader's influence on the group's emotional life: or, more specifically, the essential role of the leader as the transferential and projective target of the group's feelings of dependency, fear, envy, love, rage and so forth. The psychoanalytic perspective can help leaders appreciate how such powerful feelings are unleashed in others and in themselves.

As we have shown here, Freudian, object relations and basic assumption theories are all built on the premises that leaders play an essential role in the unconscious life of groups. Leaders become enmeshed in the group's emotional processes. However competent a leader may be, the group's emotional needs will affect how well he or she is able to do his or her work. If we develop this perspective to find out what a leader can actually do to enable the group to function effectively, we emerge with a list of attributes that is quite different from the task-focused one cited above. The leader's 'survival kit' list would look more like this: develop a group culture in which emotions and thoughts can be discussed; stop the group occasionally and pursue a collective assessment of the emotional dynamics at play (especially when the group lapses into basic assumption mode); share your experience of the emotions being projected on to your role, and your own participation in those dynamics; be aware of the changing developmental needs of the group; be conscious of the emotions projected on to the group from the outside environment and be willing to intervene if necessary; be aware of the complexity of the feelings of group members for you; and many more.

The psychoanalytic approach does not ignore the importance of task in the operation of a group or in the priorities of a leader; what it does is to underscore the unity of task and process in the group's mental life, as well as the active participation of both leaders and followers if the task is to be accomplished. The emotional dynamics between leaders and followers will be examined in Chapter 6. What is important to emphasize here is that leaders do not accidentally find themselves at the vortex of emotional turbulence in groups, something that may be avoided through better management or better selection of group members. As Obholzer (1994: 43–4) has argued:

> Task performance requires active participation on the part of the followers as well as of the leader. A passive, accepting, *basic assumption* state of followership, such as one might find in a demoralized organization, is quite different from a state of mind of exercising one's own authority to take up the followership role in relation to the task. The latter implies clarity about the organization's task, and about where one's role fits in with others.
>
> In order to manage oneself in role, the fundamental question is 'How can I mobilize my resources and potential to contribute to the task?' This requires recognition of where one's role ends and another person's begins, the scope and limits of one's own authority, and a readiness to sanction that of others. Rivalry, jealousy and envy often interfere with the process of taking up either a leadership or a followership position. Staff rivalry is a ubiquitous phenomenon. In a misguided attempt to avoid fanning rivalry and envy, managers may try to manage from a position of equality, or, more commonly, pseudo-equality, often presented as 'democracy'. This term is used as if everyone has equal authority. The hope is that rivalry, jealousy and envy will thereby be avoided; the reality is the undermining of the manager's authority, capacity to hold an overall perspective and ability to lead.

Leading a group, then, is an activity that requires skill, sensitivity and self-understanding. When confronted with unpleasantness resulting from group 'process', it is all too easy for the leader to retreat to the task by admonishing the followers or to withdraw altogether behind a veil of collegiality and egalitarianism (see Hirschhorn, 1988, 1997). In these ways, leaders may collude with the forces that stand in the way of the task and inhibit effective group functioning.

CONCLUSION

In this chapter we have presented some of the major psychoanalytic accounts of group behaviour. Throughout this discussion we have acknowledged that group experiences cannot be reduced to phenomena of individual psychology and require their own level of analysis. Since the pioneering work of Le Bon, psychology has recognized the quite unique demands placed by groups on individuals and the powerful emotional forces that groups are likely to unleash. The study of organizations has maintained a guarded attitude towards groups. To be sure, groups can be friends of organizations, enhancing motivation, bringing about cross-fertilization of skills and talents, stimulating creativity and generating commitment. But groups can also undermine organizational performance and cohesion. They can give free reign to wild emotional impulses, promote conformity and dull individuals' critical and intellectual qualities. The psychoanalytic tradition enhances our understanding of these characteristics of group life by exploring the unconscious processes, notably regression, splitting, defence, identification and idealization which underlie them. In Bion's theory of basic assumption and its subsequent elaborations, we have one of the most convincing explanations of numerous group dysfunctions and also a powerful instrument for explaining the great power which groups have over our lives. The group's frequent excursions into psychosis, with its attendant distortions of reality and the predominance of fantasy over rationality, is made very clear.

Less successful have been attempts to define the healthy group, as one which balances emotion and rationality, independence and belonging, task and process. To the question 'How can groups be helped on the way to psychological health and effective task performance?' psychoanalytic approaches can hardly offer ready answers. Psychoanalysis enables us to diagnose, often with remarkable accuracy, group processes, warning us of the onset of psychotic delusions, overwhelming emotions and incapacitating splits. Counteracting these trends, however, requires more than diagnosis. The difference between health and illness, cohesion and fragmentation, truth and delusion is often accounted for through one of the most problematic ideas of all – leadership, to which we shall now turn our attention.

6 LEADERS AND FOLLOWERS

with Larry Hirschhorn

The literature on the subject of leadership is vast. Students of leadership can read the biographies of great and failed leaders, they can read the social science literature on different types of leadership, they can read psychological theories on the attributes of good leaders, they can read the organizational development literature to discover techniques for effective leadership. This chapter presents a psychodynamic perspective on leadership; it examines the nature of the bonds between leaders and followers and the dilemmas we face in following leaders who offer us visions of the future.

The focus of this chapter is on leaders, not on managers. Of course, leaders can manage and managers can lead. But a by-now well-established argument treats leadership as an organizational and psychological process distinct from management (Zaleznik, 1977, 1991; Burns, 1978). Managers help us focus on the present situation. They help us organize our current resources so that we use them effectively. They have a keen eye for detail; they cut deals; they think of ways of stretching resources further. They are the quintessential 'profit maximizers' of microeconomics. Leaders, by contrast, help us to focus on the future. They invent an image of the future so persuasive that we are willing to commit our efforts, time and resources to turn the image into reality. In this breach between the present and the future we face all the excitement as well as dangers of leadership. It is possible to manage inanimate objects – a diary, a farm, a stamp collection – but it is only possible to lead people.

LEADERS AND DREAMS

Consider the following example. The chief executive officer (CEO), Will, and chief scientist, Marc, of a biotechnology start-up company are meeting with potential investors. They need to raise capital to fund the next two years of research. Like most start-ups, the company has lost money in each of its six years of existence. Will, the CEO, presents the history of the company emphasizing its roots in the brilliant discoveries that Marc made while working as a lone researcher in a university laboratory. He shapes the story of the firm as an unfinished epic tale.

As a result of Marc's breakthrough, he recounts, the company developed a new class of compounds and a promising medicine based on their biochemical properties. But when the medicine was tested, the results were ambiguous. Company employees, Will notes, were devastated, and the value of the company's stock fell dramatically.

Marc then made a second discovery, resulting in another set of compounds which promised to be doubly effective. Marc argued that the firm should re-focus its efforts and commit most of its resources to developing this new class. Some senior executives of the company, however, did not want to change direction so suddenly. They argued, Will reports, that by improving the first medicine, the firm could still develop effective and profitable healing agents. Marc, however, seems inspired, indeed driven, and after threatening to quit, the firm's executives support his plan. The CEO who opposed it leaves. The firm's scientists quickly characterized this new set of compounds; even more importantly, the larger scientific community took note, suggesting that these compounds could indeed prove revolutionary. Will concludes his talk with the proviso that, of course, a long chain of events links discovery, development and the launch of a successful product and often brilliant ideas never result in safe and effective new drugs.

As Will tells his story he weaves in the history of his own career, its idiosyncratic quality, his unconventional rise to senior-level positions in the pharmaceutical industry and his learnings about life. He emphasizes how he started as a salesman, a detail man and rose to the top by dint of his 'street smarts'. He is proud that he does not have an MBA. Throughout the presentation, Will's manner and mood becomes infectious. The potential investors appear to be swept up in his story. At the end of the meeting they put $5 million on the table.

Why did the investors put up the money? If we assume that the investors act rationally, we would say that they compared the risks of not investing with the risks of investing and decided that $5 million was a reasonable bet. But how did they determine the risks associated with the investment? How did they know that the bet was 'reasonable'? After all, the company had not made any money, its first product had not passed scientific trials, and all present knew that most biotechnology start-ups fail. Marc's evident genius was important but, as Will acknowledged, there is only a tenuous link between a discovery and a profitable enterprise.

Noting these uncertainties, we must conclude that Will was a great salesman. His enthusiasm, his infectious manner, his story of defeats and triumphs led investors to discount in some degree the probability of failure. But what was Will selling? He had no product to offer them, nor was he guaranteeing them any income. As shareholders, they had no legal claim on the firm's revenue stream. We want to suggest that they bought a dream. They were enchanted by Will's vision, his implicit story of the future – that investments now would make them all rich later.

Leaders first and foremost spin dreams. But they are no mere salesmen of visions, tricksters exploiting the gullibility of those willing to follow them. In launching new projects or taking big decisions, they take stock of their followers' desires and potential. As Burns (1978) has argued, a great leader can understand the unconscious motives of the followers better than the followers understand them themselves. Thus, leaders can mobilize people to work hard, to perform above what they think they are capable of, to put in extra effort even though the outcome is far from certain. Leaders step in when the standard contractual mechanisms based on self-interest prove insufficient. An employee comes to work everyday to get paid, but what simulates him or her to stay late to do unremunerated work? The employee who shares in the leader's dream invests his or her own effort and time in the hope that the dream will come true. In that sense, he or she is similar to the investors who gave Will money. When Steven Jobs of Apple Computer recruited Apple engineers and technicians to build the Macintosh, he housed them all in a separate building and placed a pirate flag with skull and cross-bones on the roof. The flag invoked a particular fantasy: men with derring-do who succeed by operating outside the law. The Macintosh, Jobs was suggesting, would break the rules, flout the establishment and take enemies by surprise. Jobs, of course, had a good track record; he had succeeded with the first Apple computer but one success does not guarantee another. To mobilize his employees, to extract that extra effort he needed, he created a dream, a tale of the future. His employees worked day and night for two reasons. The dream, if believed, promised fame and fortune, while working to make the dream come true was exciting in its own right.

DREAMS AND FANTASIES

The role of the dream illuminates an important dimension of leadership. The leader stands at the boundary between rational and non-rational decision-making or, in psychodynamic terms, between realities and fantasies. Because the future always contains uncertainties and because no person is guaranteed a return on their efforts, people invest effort, attention and feeling in an undertaking because they believe in the leader's fantasy and its ability to turn into reality. To understand leadership we must turn once again to an understanding of fantasy.

As we saw in Chapter 5, fantasies are fundamental to the mental life of both individuals and groups. Our fantasies both console and excite us; in the midst of the difficulties and tensions we face everyday, our fantasies give us hope and propel us forward. Freud suggests that fantasies are compromise formations, the outcome of a conflict between wild desire and the forces of reason, morality and social responsibility. In this way, desires can find fulfilment, possibly surrogate fulfilment, in the fantasy. In Chapter 5, we examined how each of Bion's basic assumptions represents a distinct group fantasy fulfilling deep psychological needs. Seeking to translate a fantasy into reality, making it the driving force for collective action, is different. Some people may derive enough fulfilment by dreaming as they flick through the pages of popular magazines or by watching movies. But leaders do not remain dreamers; they are possessed of a *will*, a drive to turn vision into reality, something that requires the assistance of others. So, they embark on the complicated and realistic venture of acting on the real world, through hard work, their own and that of those they lead. They endure pain, they make sacrifices, for the sake of the vision which they desperately want to see materialize.

It is here that leaders are tested. Many writers (for example, Zaleznik, 1989; Schwartz, 1990; Hirschhorn, 1997) and theorists have observed that, in leading others, leaders run the risk of becoming trapped in delusions of grandeur and omnipotence, fuelled by narcissism. Such leaders become so absorbed in their fantasies of success and power that they lose touch with reality. They become like the day-dreamers who derive satisfaction purely through fantasy. Their followers, having purchased a share of the leader's vision, are unwilling to abandon it. They have, after all, endured hardships and made sacrifices, they trust the leader's assurances that the final success will be the sweeter for all the adversities which have been overcome. Since the vision flows from the leader's inner life, preserving its persuasiveness, its power to mould attention and action, is linked ultimately to the leader's sense of power. Followers then play a special role: protecting the leader from reality so that the leader's faith in the vision is never threatened. The leader him or herself becomes the most important reality; questioning the leader's vision or wisdom becomes tantamount to betrayal. In this manner, organizations may inoculate themselves against reality, disregarding all signs of imminent disaster and marching happily and blindly to their doom.

It is important to distinguish here between narcissistic leaders and heroic leaders. As we saw in earlier chapters, all individuals and all leaders have narcissistic desires: desires to be respected, recognized and admired. Our super-ego constantly acts as a spur on our narcissistic strivings, seeking to bridge the gap between our ego and our ego-ideal. Most leaders have strong narcissistic strivings, relishing the prospect of success and victory. What distinguishes the narcissistic leader from the heroic leader with a strong narcissism is the focus of attention. Where the heroic leader looks outward for opportunities for distinction and achievement, the narcissistic leader looks outward for opportunities for admiration and love. The heroic leader has a strong ego, capable of handling the super-ego's criticisms and reproach. The narcissistic leader, by contrast, suffers from constant self-doubt and insecurity, needing to prove him or herself at every opportunity, relishing the admiration of others and unable to stand criticism.

Unfortunately, in studying leaders it is virtually impossible to draw a hard-and-fast line between narcissism and heroism. Heroic leaders who find themselves surrounded by sycophants and rest on their laurels may lapse into narcissistic regression when, later on in life, they are called upon to repeat their earlier accomplishments. Equally, leaders with strong narcissistic tendencies, lucky enough to be supported by strong and competent associates, may find the inner strength for genuine heroic accomplishment. Regression to narcissism is a permanent danger for leaders, the more so as their followers find themselves uplifted by their leader's narcissism and collude with it.

THE CASE OF *USA TODAY*

Consider the following case. In 1989 Gannet Inc., the communications conglomerate and parent company of the newspaper *USA Today*, funded the development of a television news show to be called *USA Today*. Steven Friedman was hired as the show's director and creator. He envisioned the show as breaking new ground by integrating news and entertainment to create what he called then 'infotainment'. Like the newspaper, the show would broadcast news to busy Americans in a way that demanded little concentration and was fun to watch. The show was to be produced by Grant Tinker, who had recently retired as NBC's chairman, and it was supported by an ultra-modern production studio costing $40 million. It flopped after its first airing.

Interviews with the show's staff highlighted the particular role that narcissistic processes play in linking leaders to followers. Friedman was a charismatic but temperamental leader. Portraying himself as a rebel and outsider who would transform television news, he helped create a climate of excitement in which subordinates felt they were corporate outlaws ready to destroy the establishment. They were the modernizers, the good guys, ready to attack the 'bad' producers and directors who did not understand what the public 'really' want.

But, in purchasing a share of Friedman's self-image as an outlaw, his followers also reinforced his apparent arrogance, his disdain for the work and thinking of others. Convinced of his superiority and brilliance, he overlooked some of the most common practices of television production. Moreover, in advancing his vision of 'infotainment' as simple-minded news, the kind of news the public 'really' wanted, he developed a basic contempt for his audience. As an outlaw he disdained 'bureaucracy', so he appointed no coordinator to control story development nor did he hire any professional writers. He believed that his audience, at least in the first year, would be satisfied simply with glitz. Caught up in this adventure of proving others wrong, his subordinates stopped using their own common sense. As one subordinate said, 'We were like a family of alcoholics, some of us saw what was happening but no one wanted to hear about it.'

Like Steve Jobs, Friedman created an exciting vision of outlaws on the high seas of television news. Unlike Jobs, however, he could not create a successful product, a product that was based on a realistic understanding of the TV viewers he hoped to attract. As this short case description suggests, his vision became too fantastical, it led him to ignore the self-evident practicalities of producing broadcast news. The dream did not simply define a future, it distorted his understanding of the present. His contempt for his prospective audience is telling here. People feel contemptuous of others when they imagine them to be weak, pitifully easy to exploit and easy to manipulate. While some leaders fit this description, it is dangerous to assume that all your prospective customers lack an independent capacity for judgement. When a person makes this assumption, as Friedman apparently did, he is assuming that reality – in this case, the marketplace for television viewers – can be manipulated at will. This is fantasy run riot. Instead of the fantasy pointing the way to hard work, we act as if simply by fantasizing we can create the reality we want – until, of course, it strikes back at us.

The subordinate's statement, 'we were like a family of alcoholics', gives us added insight into narcissistic processes. When the mother or father of a family is an alcoholic, its members mobilize to suppress the truth. They pretend to one another that nothing is wrong, they cover up the parent's alcoholism from neighbours and relatives, and they protect the alcoholic from the truth of his or her own condition. They collude with the alcoholic's fantasy that his or her drunken stupors are aberrations and that he or she could stop drinking any time. The family takes on the work of protecting the alcoholic's and their own self-esteem. Reality goes out of the window. The subordinate is suggesting that Steve Friedman's followers mobilized to protect his self-esteem by hiding the truth from him, that is by colluding in his own denial of reality.

THE NARCISSISTIC LEADER

Why does one leader turn a dream into reality by working on reality, while another presumes that the dream is already reality? It is first of all important to recognize that any division of leaders into good and bad is naïve. Successful leaders and even great leaders can suddenly encounter failure, just as mediocre leaders may enjoy unexpected boons of fortune. Innumerable factors may account for the difference between success and failure, victory and defeat; not all of them may be anticipated and most of them remain outside the leader's control. Steve Jobs's touch seemed to desert him following his great success with the Apple Mac. Highly successful military leaders famously turn into great failures when they turn to politics and vice versa. Psychoanalytic theory cannot provide a blueprint of leadership success, any more than any other theory can. It does, however, draw attention to the delicate balance between feelings of omnipotence and feelings of impotence which leaders must achieve, in order to enhance the chances of turning vision into reality. Lapierre describes it admirably:

> Leaders must both imagine a future and develop a vision while also remaining vigilant and careful. If they fail in the former task, they cannot develop the organization. If they fail in the latter, they cannot protect it. But each of these abilities is rooted in primitive or primal feelings. The capacity to imagine is linked to the capacity to idealize and has its roots in feelings of omnipotence. The capacity for vigilance is linked to feelings of vulnerability and thus has its early roots in feelings of impotence. (1989: 187)

Narcissistic leaders have a particular aptitude in getting this balance wrong. In essence, then, the self-esteem of narcissistic leaders is low. While their bravado helps them to win some initial victories, their aversion to the truth is such that they deny real obstacles and threats. Even if they are talented in their field, their judgement increasingly fails them. This is compounded by the collusion of their followers. Narcissistic individuals can exercise remarkable influence over others. As followers, we are easily attracted by the narcissistic leader's allure, his or her seeming disregard for mundane matters, his or her willingness to think the unthinkable and speak the unspeakable. Instead of dismissing these as markers of regression to a state of spoilt childhood, we allow ourselves to be seduced by the apparent simplicity, beauty and effortlessness of it all. Narcissistic leaders can appear remarkably 'cool' individuals, self-possessed yet impulsive. For a brief while their touch can seem truly magical. They can get things done simply by pronouncing them. In this way, as we shall see shortly, they are apt to generate among followers feelings akin to the infatuation of being in love. In doing so, the followers gratify the narcissistic leader's very evident wish for approval, offering an admiring audience, which further stimulates his or her narcissism. In short, drawn into the psychological orbit of a person who, despite his or her bravado has a fragile ego and low self-esteem, they collude with this person's delusions of grandeur.

In following leaders we are always at risk of following narcissistic ones. As we have argued, the leader must supply a vision if we are to mobilize ourselves to work hard, to sacrifice, to give our best. There is no other way for us to justify the irrational risks we take, irrational in the sense that we can never satisfactorily justify the risk. No amount of data, research or enquiry can tell us if the leader's forecast of the future is wrong or right. We have to purchase a share of his or her dream. Narcissistic people are talented at spinning dreams. Because they experience reality as psychologically injurious, they are driven to escape from it. And because they often develop a contempt for reality as a way of denying its power to frustrate fantasy, they overlook the actual obstacles to succeeding.

Detecting the narcissistic process

How can we identify when a leader's dream has become a narcissistic fantasy? We need to establish that organizational process and performance depend more on protecting the leader from reality than in working on and through reality. We can point to four indicators.

First, we can assess the balance between what Abraham Zaleznik (1989/1997) calls 'real work' and organizational process. When the leader helps us identify obstacles and charges us with working to overcome them, then we are engaged in real work. We must summon up our talents, efforts and powers of judgement. By contrast, when we find ourselves engaged in the management of organizational processes, when for example we spend an inordinate amount of time writing internal memos, preparing for meetings, creating the right appearances, crafting speeches that use the 'right words', then we have signs of a narcissistic process. We commit an inordinate amount of time to sustaining the leader's image of how the organization should be working, as opposed to actually working. As a result, while we are often overworked, we actually feel under-utilized.

Secondly, we can assess the ways in which personal ties as opposed to merit shape who gets resources to do what. In the narcissistic process, leaders are particularly dependent on those who can bolster their self-image. They draw these people close to them. While some of these people are deliberately manipulative, others are drawn into the leader's psychological orbit without being aware of what is happening to them. They may, for example, be drawn in because they naturally feel protective, or they feel guilty, when confronted with someone who looks hurt. Whether their motives are conscious or unconscious, it is unlikely that these people are among the most independent-minded in the group or organization. They are thrown into situations where they lack the will to make good decisions. They will often hire consultants to improve these processes. But, at bottom, no amount of tinkering can make up for the fact that such followers are not up to the task.

Thirdly, we can assess whether on balance the leader protects the followers or the followers protect the leader All projects entail some uncertainty. The 'good enough' leader carves out pieces of the work to subordinates, charging them with accomplishing particular sub-tasks while he or she takes up the work of worrying about the overall risks and uncertainties. The 'good enough' leader relieves the followers of the burden of excessive worry. He or she wants them to ignore part of the reality, so that they can focus on their particular piece of the work. He or she promises them, however, that reality will not go unattended; that he or she will bring his or her best talents and skills to the task of assessing, managing and containing the total risks the organization faces. When the leader functions in this way, we say that he or she creates a 'containing' psychological space in which people feel protected enough to accomplish their piece of real work.

By contrast, as we have seen, in the narcissistic process it is the leader who needs protection. While on the surface he or she appears to offer people powerful images of the future and plans for their implementation, the followers consciously or unconsciously seek to protect him or her from any sense of defeat. They will never, for instance, report failures or major obstacles, lest they be seen as being defeatist or disloyal. Followers who are talented or influential themselves may be able to 'make the boss look good' while not jeopardizing the enterprise and its functioning. But if they are not, they protect the leader at the risk of exposing the enterprise to defeat.

Fourthly, we can assess the extent to which individuals feel that they are linked together as a group, facing a common task, as against being divided by competition and jealousy. The 'good enough' leader divides up the important work, while ensuring that each person or division understands the link between their part and the organization's goal. This understanding helps people coordinate their plans and actions with others, without having to draw on the leader excessively to resolve conflict. By contrast, narcissistic leaders are frightened by talent. They worry that talented subordinates will undermine their version of the dream, or will, by virtue of their capabilities, take the organization out of their own control. Such leaders are only comfortable when they monopolize the right to dream and will, often unconsciously, weaken the talented, by setting up competitors, by assigning them impossible tasks, by depriving them of resources, or by obfuscating the actual purposes and goals of the enterprise. Followers will then feel confused and rudderless and will prove unable to resolve their own conflicts. The leader may in turn castigate them for being poor team players and, unaware of the situation they have helped sustain, they may indeed blame themselves. Such leaders often resort to calling in consultants to help 'build the team', but no amount of team-building hocus-pocus can overcome the divisiveness that the leader has created him or herself.

In sum

A leader's major role is to give us a dream. Without the dream there is no basis for us to mobilize the extra effort, attention and skill we need to achieve a goal fraught with risks. Many of us, perhaps most of us, would rather sit on the sidelines, do our daily work and hope that we can participate in the gains that others have sweated for. The dream, by contrast, excites all of us.

The 'good enough' leader, however, cannot just spin dreams; he or she needs to stand between the dream and reality, helping us assess the obstacles we face and the plans we need to overcome them. But we are vulnerable here. It is unfortunate but true that narcissistic people are adept at spinning dreams because they need dreams or fantasies to bolster their self-esteem. These people develop a contempt for reality as a way of denying its severity and often intractability. This contempt may allow them to appear at first courageous but, in fact, it is based on flight from what is hard and difficult. Ultimately, narcissistic leaders value self-image the most. Consequently, they draw followers into their psychological orbit who, for a range of reasons, bolster the leader's self-esteem. As we saw in the case of *USA Today* this process can lead to egregious failure.

It is possible, however, to detect when we might be in the throes of a narcissistic process. We need to monitor four indicators: the balance between real work and organizational processes; the balance between merit and personal ties as criteria for allocating resources; the balance between the leader's protection of followers and the followers' protection of the leader; and the balance between the experience of integration and the experience of divisiveness.

FOLLOWERS

We have seen how leaders' fantasies can turn into visions galvanizing their followers into action or alternatively, turn into delusions of grandeur drawing their followers to destruction and defeat. Followers, however, have their own fantasies, many of which revolve around the leader. We now turn to the followers' experiences in order to establish the nature of the psychological bond which links them to their leaders.

To many people in the lower echelons of organizations, top leaders do not appear altogether human, not at least in the sense that colleagues or immediate superiors are. The 'Big Boss' is the object of acute curiosity, fascination and gossip, the more so when followers rarely catch sight of him or her, and then only on ceremonial occasions. A physical and psychological gulf seems to separate top leaders from ordinary organizational members, who often fantasize about their leaders. In these fantasies, leaders can feature in different ways: as benevolent, father-like figures, as demonic schemers engaged in plotting and machination, as cunning wheeler-dealers who strike clever deals for the organization, as impostors who attained their position by deception and so forth.

Meeting the leader in a face-to-face encounter tests these fantasies. Such meetings echo the archetypal Christian scene of meeting God as supreme ruler on the Day of Judgement, and are fairly regular episodes in works of literature and the stage. In Tolstoy's *War and Peace*, for instance, we meet young Nikolai Rostov, who, having fantasized countless times the moment when he might meet his Emperor, finally gets his chance on the morrow of a military defeat:

> But as a youth in love trembles and turns faint and dares not utter what he has spent nights in dreaming of, and looks around in terror, seeking aid or a chance of delay and flight, when the longed-for moment arrives and he is alone with *her*, so Rostov, now that he had attained what he had longed for beyond everything in the world, did not know how to approach the Emperor, and a thousand reasons occurred to him why it would be untimely, improper and impossible to do so. (Tolstoy, 1869/1982: 334)

In organizations, the theme of meeting the leader may be the subject of a conscious fantasy or day-dreaming, when members of organizations imagine what would happen if they had such an encounter. They may then muse, for example, on the favours they might ask for, the grievances they might express, the enlightenment they might seek, the advice they might give or the violence they might perpetrate. Alternatively, the theme may assume the form of a story, i.e. a wish-fulfilling embellishment of a meeting which actually took place. Such meetings have a memorable quality, often becoming landmarks in individuals' personal histories. Accounts of such meetings lead us to some of the unconscious phantasies which subordinates spin around the figure of the organization's top leaders. These phantasies, in turn, reveal a great deal about the nature and dynamics of leader–follower relations as well as the emotional needs of subordinates fulfilled by leaders.

It is important now to introduce a distinction, drawn by Isaacs (1948), Rycroft (1968) and others, between conscious fantasy or day-dreaming and unconscious phantasy. The spelling 'phantasy' is restricted to unconscious constellations of ideas, whereas 'fantasy' is used in a more generic way (see Glossary). The contents of phantasies are not directly accessible to consciousness but may be approached indirectly through dreams, stories, emotions or conscious fantasies. We shall examine some of the core phantasies that followers have *vis-à-vis* their leaders by interpreting and analysing two texts supplied by students following six-month internships. These texts have been discussed in great detail elsewhere (Gabriel, 1997). It is, of course, impossible to discover the full variety and richness of followers' phantasies in two texts; what is possible, however, is to identify certain elements on the basis of which a wide variety of phantasies may be constructed and seek to establish what these elements reveal about the bond between followers and leaders.

THE LEADER AS REINCARNATION OF THE PRIMAL MOTHER

In the first text, Anna, a Greek student, recounts her meeting with the director of a publishing company.

Anna's story: the most precious experience of my placement

Is it really possible to capture the essence of an organization through a single event? This sounds quite scary, though it is a pretty attractive idea. For three or four days now, my mind has been travelling back to Athens, where I had my placement, trying to revive my working life and experiences . . . There is indeed so much to write about and thus it is very confusing to try and select just one thing to refer to. Yet, after a lot of thinking, I have decided on something that truly deserves to be written down. It is probably the most precious experience that I had during my placement.

As most people do when they find themselves in a new environment, I kept on observing and thinking. I was analysing people's actions and reactions, attitudes and overall behaviour. The theories we had learned at the university, about roles, hierarchy, working groups etc., seemed to come alive right in front of my eyes, leaving me satisfied and even more interested in the subject of my studies. But what about this 'myth' of management? What is the top person's role in all that? What is it to lead people? These were the questions that I needed the answers for. After much wondering, I decided to try and have a discussion with my top manager, a conversation which would, hopefully, help me to solve the 'mystery'.

As the manager was extremely busy for days and days, I was becoming even more obsessed with the idea that I had to talk with her and ask her to reveal to me all the secrets that had guided her to success. Finally one afternoon she was free and pleased to talk to me. I then realized for a moment that my request was difficult. I wanted to find out about *everything*. Was this feasible? I explained most of my thoughts to her, she understood all the worries that had been in my mind all this time. We discussed a lot of things involving managerial concepts and attitudes.

The first issue was that of managerial style, in particular the ways in which a manager imposes him or herself on his or her subordinates. Can one win the trust of others by fear or by personal respect? The answer was respect. If you have knowledge of the work subject, and if what you want is the involvement and cooperation of your subordinates, then you have found a sure way to get what you want from your department. A successful manager must first of all have passion for his or her work. This is the basis for transmitting your personal enthusiasm to the people you are working with and to inspire them to work with you to reach the organizational targets . . .

A good manager must also be accessible to his or her subordinates in both business and personal terms. People are indeed the most important issue within the organization and the art of handling them should be one of the major abilities a manager should be endowed with. Nobody starts his or her career as a manager. And if this is the case, they are bound to fail. Only by understanding and considering the position of a subordinate – this is by taking his or her place at least once – can the management of the people and the department be fair and effective.

The discussion continued for a long time and all the issues were mainly connected with the human aspect of the organization. My satisfaction from listening to my manager talk about these issues was indescribable. All these theories I had seen applied in our department with great success, were now reconfirmed to me by my manager, a person whom I respect and admire enormously. I consider myself very lucky to have worked as a subordinate for this particular manager. I hope that one day I will have the chance to practise all that I have learned and I am still learning, becoming a successful manager.

Anna recounts her meeting with the director in almost religious terms. Meeting her leader was a moment when she made important decisions about her future and distilled a new set of meanings regarding her university studies, authority relations and, possibly, life as a whole. Things which had been bookish theories or, more tellingly, 'mysteries' and 'myths' before the meeting became clear and full of meaning afterwards.

Idealization

Anna's professed 'indescribable' satisfaction appears out of proportion with the views on management which she describes, views which are not especially profound or original. Yet, the very fervour with which she reports these views provides evidence that banalities can sound extraordinary, and clichés can appear like wisdom, when uttered by 'great' leaders, whose endorsement turns mere ideas into 'gospel'. In fact, everything touched by the leader acquires a glowing aura. This is a characteristic of the psychological process of *idealization*, which imbues the whole text. Not a single negative word or critical comment is allowed to spoil an image of sheer perfection and bliss. This transformation of the commonplace into perfection has been singled out as a crucial feature, common to relations with both leaders and love-objects. (Freud, 1921; Gabriel, 1983, 1984, 1993; Schwartz, 1985, 1987, 1990; Lindholm, 1988). Leaders as well as objects of infatuation become endowed with 'all' the perfections, forming part of an individual's ego-ideal, the set of idealized images against which he or she measures him or herself. Anna's vivid description of her nervousness before the eagerly anticipated meeting, as well as her feeling of relief that her manager had understood 'all her worries' in a flash, have a romantic quality, reminiscent of the lover's inhibitions before meeting his or her beloved. Having the manager's undivided attention for 'a long time', in which 'all the issues', 'all the secrets' and 'all the worries' are gone through suggests both a process of initiation and the consummation of a love affair, meriting indeed the 'indescribable satisfaction' noted. In this sense, Anna is part of what Krantz (1989) has entirely appropriately described as the *managerial couple*.

Identification

Psychoanalysis distinguishes two seminal ways in which we relate to objects of our environment – object-love and identification. In contrast to object-love, which involves a mixture of both sexual and sublimated or aim-inhibited desires, *identification* involves desexualization of libido and its transformation from a pleasure-seeking force into a bond-building life force. Three distinct types of identification were singled out by Freud (1921: 137), all of which have a bearing on group phenomena. The first type of identification is rooted in the earliest life experiences before an individual's ego has taken shape in opposition to an external world. This identification, which coincides with the phase of primary narcissism, is irredeemably broken with the realization that the mother is a separate person, yet the memory of fusion with one's environment may persist and re-surface in ecstatic phenomena, such as 'oceanic' feelings and so on. The second type of identification occurs as a replacement for object-love. If the object of desire cannot be enjoyed, it may become instead an object of identification, losing its sexual attractiveness but becoming a role model. There is a third type of identification in which two or more individuals identify with each other by virtue of a common quality, trait or predicament. This is characteristic of the bond which siblings establish with each other, by virtue of their shared relation towards the parents (provided that the parents treat them equally). The stronger this shared quality is the more powerful the identification.

Anna's identification with her leader, someone she 'respected and admired enormously', is clear; her leader is a role model, someone she wants to emulate as a successful woman in a business culture dominated by men. The fact that this outstanding woman took the time to talk to Anna in person, to address her worries and answer her questions, was very important for Anna. 'Only by understanding and considering the position of a subordinate – this is by taking his or her place at least once – can the management of the people and the department be fair and effective.' In this revealing sentence, she indicates both the extent of her identification with her leader and also the way in which this identification serves as the basis of a promise – that she too will become a leader one day, just as her manager, who was herself once a subordinate, did. It is noteworthy how Anna stresses *accessibility* as an important leadership attribute, and sees her leader as an accessible one, notwithstanding the difficulties she had in meeting her. The leader is accessible but, as a very 'busy' person, her time is priceless; a single meeting establishes the accessibility of the leader, without at the same time suggesting any undue familiarity. The leader is at once accessible and distant, her gifts of time, wisdom and care to be accepted with gratitude rather than taken for granted.

Anna's description, resonant with narrative elements of both religion and romantic love, contains in a nutshell several features of the psychoanalytic approach to leadership: idealization, identification with the leader, identification with other followers, suspension of most critical faculties and sublimation of libido. What this narrative does not contain is any echo of the leader as the harsh and omnipotent primal father, dominating his followers and enforcing social values. Instead, it is redolent with a quality of satisfaction and self-satisfaction which are characteristic of narcissistic gratification. The leader neither punishes nor judges, but gives time, wisdom, affection and faith. This is consistent with a more recent psychoanalytic line of thinking about leadership, which maintains the view that we transfer on to leaders feelings we experienced towards parents in early life, but replaces Freud's emphasis on the leader as father-substitute with the leader as reincarnation of the mother of primal narcissism, the mother who recognizes no boundaries and no conditions, the mother who meets *all* needs and fuses everything in one. Chasseguet-Smirgel (1976) was an early advocate of the view that some leaders do not function psychically as father-substitutes, in the manner Freud envisaged, but as reincarnations of the primal mother, as agents through which illusions are achieved. She noted that this type of group

> desires illusion more than leadership, and chooses as master the one who promises to reunite the ego and the ego ideal. No absolute leader is without an 'ideology'. He is, in fact, the intermediary who negotiates between the people and the ideological illusion. Understanding the ideology, there is always a fantasy of narcissistic triumph. (Chasseguet-Smirgel, 1976: 362)

Instead of the aloof paternal leader, who rewards and punishes, leaving his followers with weakened egos, this accessible, primal mother leader restores her followers' narcissism and provides a considerable boost to their self-esteem by achieving a fusion between each individual follower and the wider group. Kohut (1985) further developed the distinction between the two types of leadership, by arguing that resurrection of primal narcissism and fusion with the mother defines charismatic leadership, while the prototypical Freudian father-surrogate type of leadership is messianic. Unlike the followers of charismatic leaders, who are prone to ecstatic phenomena and overflow with both self-regard and libido, the followers of messianic leaders are depleted of self-regard, stand in awe of their leader and are ever-willing to sacrifice themselves in the interests of a superior cause.

THE LEADER AS REINCARNATION OF THE OMNIPOTENT PRIMAL FATHER

In order to gain an understanding of the relation between followers and messianic leaders, we turn now to another text by a student internee, one which introduces a vital new phantasy element, omnipotence. In this text, the leader features not as a primal mother figure, caring, supporting and recognizing, but as a figure of authority, reverence and fear. The phantasy of the leader's omnipotence (and the associated phantasy of the leader's omniscience) is one of the commonest phantasies about leaders. As we saw earlier, it is often consciously furthered by leaders themselves, whose own narcissism is enhanced in this way, though followers tend to project truly super-human powers on to them. One of the most potent organizational experiences, spawning numerous stories and myths, centres on the discovery that leaders themselves are only human and fallible, that they too are afraid and that they too may be driven by someone standing above them. In the story which follows, Steve vividly describes how his faith in his own leader, in a large transnational corporation, was shattered when he realized that he was but a puppet on someone else's string.

Steve's story: the day I lost faith in Mike McKie

DACRO UK is an affiliate of DACRO International based in the US; [yet], it is officially a separate entity with its own management, culture and vision. DACRO UK is split into seven major product divisions, each of which functions independently of the others. The division to which I was assigned is called the Consumer Appliances Division (CAD) and deals in the traditional appliances. CAD is headed up by an executive named Mike McKie.

When I joined DACRO the demands on McKie appeared to come from two sources. I have already mentioned the US connection, but DACRO UK prided itself on its independence, its distinct culture and its ability to outperform its US parent company. If the British subsidiary's independence was genuine, McKie should be answerable to the demi-gods of DACRO UK (i.e. the Board of Directors). Perched on the 17th floor of DACRO House, these mythical creatures are reputed to rule from sumptuous quarters of mahogany and leather. Nobody you meet within the company has actually entered the 17th floor and nobody is quite sure what goes on there. However, most people have their own story of a personal encounter with Zeus himself – Erroll Bates, CEO of DACRO UK.

This report describes the events surrounding December 9, the day I lost faith in McKie. McKie had stressed on frequent occasions that CAD needed a radical change in structure in order to become more 'customer focused' – a condition he believed to be essential if DACRO were to remain successful in the 1990s. He had developed his own plans to this effect and had begun to implement some of them with considerable ceremony. However, all these plans were laid to rest on December 9, when Peter Kellner, Head of CAD world-wide in corporate headquarters in Boston, announced *his* global strategy for change. DACRO UK senior management were told of the announcement a fortnight before the event. They spent two weeks anticipating what Kellner would announce and how his 'decree' would affect CAD UK. Indeed, they were so anxious that they arranged a satellite link-up with the US so that they could listen to Kellner 'live'. However, there was little or no communication between senior management and the rest of the workforce during this period. The workforce sensed how significant the announcement was to senior management and began to speculate on what it would mean for the future of DACRO UK – negative rumour was rife. Incredibly, management did *absolutely nothing* to dispel these rumours: they must have known what scenarios were being discussed and yet they stuck their heads in the sand and pretended that it was business as usual.

December 9 came to pass and Kellner made his speech. His 'grand design' was swallowed hook, line and sinker – and McKie has made changes in line with the 'edict' ever since. No consideration has been given to the possible culture differences and market disparities between the US and the UK, or any attempt to 'interpret' the edict in line with the strategy of DACRO UK. In fact, McKie completely disregarded his own strategy for the future of the division and appears to have adopted enthusiastically Kellner's plans in their entirety.

Initially, I had a lot of time and respect for McKie. He was (in my mind) an unsuccessful [sic] executive who would in time turn CAD around by adhering to his principles and 'sticking it out'. He was very much a 'people' manager with a high profile – always encouraging, and seeing the silver lining in every cloud. All my preconceptions were shattered by the events of and around December 9. The way McKie and his management team acquiesced to Kellner's announcement was spineless. Why didn't McKie have the guts to continue with *his* strategy for the UK? The sudden change in vision and direction was detrimental to the division's morale and devastating on McKie's authority. Kellner had made the call and McKie had jumped. During the weeks preceding December 9, McKie frequently scurried off to Boston, presumably to ingratiate himself with US senior management (this only served to alienate him further from his UK workforce). I completely lost faith in his authority because it became so second-hand in my eyes. I also experienced a feeling of vulnerability as an employee. The security that a strong management provides had been removed – the UK management team appeared to lack the guts to lead – it was as if they would stick their heads in a fire at the whim of the US . . .

It would be worth mentioning that this incident was of much more significance to me than to others within the division. Those employees who had been with the company for a while had perhaps come to terms with the fact that their senior management were little more than puppets of Boston. However, because I was new to the company, I felt 'let down'. Initially, I had almost idolized the executives at DACRO UK, and when my image of them was shattered I became bitter and resentful. To cope with my feelings, I found myself turning my attention away from the UK senior management team towards the US for signs of where the company was heading. Directives which were endorsed by Boston became highly significant, while those of UK origin I dismissed as petty.

Finally, it is worth pointing out how the whole affair destroyed the 'magic' of the 17th floor myth. I had adopted the fantasy that surrounded Bates and the directors and it had become a form of motivation to think of these overseers controlling operations. However, the implication of the Kellner affair is that Bates and his Board are little more than figureheads, with no real power or purpose. This realization filled me with disillusion and the 17th floor became quite a pathetic spectacle.

Certain elements in Steve's narrative echo Anna's. It touches on the leader's caring, accessible qualities, embodied by McKie before his fall from grace ('A "people" manager'). But, unlike Anna, the image of leader as protector ('I also experienced a feeling of vulnerability') is central. Several other features set this narrative apart from the earlier one. In place of the earlier report's intimacy, this is altogether on a grander scale ('global strategy for change', 'Head of CAD world-wide'), revolving crucially around the power of leaders, who are invisible, mysterious and terrifying. Its language ('demi-gods', 'mythical creatures', 'spineless', 'guts', 'ingratiate' and so on) is overwhelmingly a language of masculine qualities, a language of rude power and raw fear. Leadership features in this narrative not as a unitary entity (a single leader) but as a fairly elaborate authority structure (McKie, the UK directors, the Head of world-wide CAD and, finally, 'Boston'). Moreover, unlike the earlier narrative, Steve is fully conscious of the fantasy of omnipotence he was projecting on Bates and the directors ('I had adopted the fantasy'). His loss of faith in the company's British leadership coincides with what he sees as the shattering of this fantasy. He therefore presents himself as one wiser and less gullible, like the longer-standing members of the organization ('Those employees who had been with the company for a while'), in contrast to his younger, more impressionable self.

If accessibility and caring form the two axes around which Anna's fantasy revolves, Steve's self-professed leadership fantasy revolves around a complex of ideas which include aloofness, indifference, power and mystery; these have been discussed extensively by authors like Sennett (1980) and Baum (1987). Baum, for example, argues, that

> the indifference of someone who is powerful simultaneously poses a riddle and increases that person's control. The riddle concerns the identity of someone who exercises such undeniable authority in virtual anonymity. How does this person do it? And what does he/she want from subordinates? Efforts to solve the riddle lead to greater attentiveness to and, consequently, dependence on the authority. (Baum, 1987: 66)

The mystery surrounding a leader's provenance and his or her personal circumstances, doubtless reinforces his or her psychological hold over his or her followers. Conversely, acquaintance with the mundane realities of a leader's everyday life (his or her marriage to an 'ordinary' spouse; his or her perfectly 'ordinary' bourgeois tastes and so on) severely dents the leadership mystique. Goffman (1959) recounts several instances when Sir Frederick Ponsonby, late equerry of the British court, advised monarchs to keep their distance from their subjects. The view that familiarity breeds contempt seems uniquely apt to people's attitudes towards leaders. Thus, in Steve's account, the mystery of the leader as well as the mystique of the unvisited 17th floor are sustained by his faith in the leader's omnipotence.

False messiahs

Steve's loss of faith in the leader is accompanied by distancing and disidentification; his feelings are those of contempt, expressed in scarcely concealed sarcasm, towards someone regarded as a false messiah, a leader who is not strong enough. Time and again in the narrative, we read that McKie's authority became 'second-hand', that the idolized demi-gods of DACRO UK turned out to be mere puppets of Boston.

If Anna's narrative casts the leader in the role of the primal mother, recognizing, fusing and restoring, Steve's narrative is much closer to the Freudian view of the leader as a father-surrogate, a person of formidable strength, at once judgemental and severe, protecting and punishing. Could, then, his leadership fantasy be described as messianic (Kohut, 1985) in contrast to Anna's charismatic leadership fantasies? Instead of highlighting fusion and unity, his report vividly depicts the great powers with which leaders are endowed in some followers' eyes and also the devastating consequences of discovering that they are only fallible after all. Leaders who inspired faith, commitment and awe are relegated to mere mortals and become targets for extraordinary hostility and contempt. Discovering that the leader is not omnipotent undermines his or her perceived capacity to protect the subordinates and to stand up for them. The leader's weakness makes the followers feel vulnerable and exposed, undermining the leader's legitimacy. More importantly, it makes them feel betrayed, as if the messiah has turned out to be an impostor.

It is hard to over-emphasize the importance of the impostor theme in our emotional lives, both inside and outside organizations. This theme may assume several forms, attaching itself both to an individual's self and to others. It may manifest itself as a crisis in self-confidence; we may fear, for instance, that a certain lack of knowledge or expertise, an inferior qualification, or an earlier failure will be uncovered, thus destroying our credibility. The impostor theme can also be found in the common fantasy referred to by psychoanalysis as 'the family romance': a child imagines that his or her real parents are king and queen, and his actual parents mere impostors, who seized him or her up at a young age. The theme is also rehearsed in numerous organizational stories, in which the legitimacy of an individual, and especially a leader, is questioned, for a wide variety of reasons, such as that his or her claims are false, his or her qualifications are fraudulent or even that his or her position has been usurped by an actual pretender. Goffman (1959: 77) has noted that Western culture regards an individual's performances as either authentic or fraudulent, so that a person can be either true or an impostor. He argues that this is logically far from true, though perhaps he underestimates the vital psychic needs fulfilled by this dichotomy. In our fantasy life, a claim is either true or false; this is especially so in the case of a leader's claim to be the messiah. One cannot be half a messiah or a different type of messiah; if the messiah is found to make fraudulent claims once, his entire credibility is destroyed.

In Steve's imagination, what turns McKie from messiah to impostor is not a major revelation about his mysterious past, but a relatively routine discovery, that he is not self-driven, but a cog in an organizational hierarchy. His fraudulence lies not in his qualifications or credentials but in his bravado, his closeness with his staff and his presumed power, all of which had encouraged Steve's faith in him in the first place. The standards by which Steve judged McKie may seem harsh and unrealistic. Yet they are not untypical of standards by which we often judge our organizational superiors.

Why do subordinates use such harsh standards when judging leaders? Why do they deliberately forget that they too are members of hierarchies, with superiors of their own? Why can they not merely treat leaders as ordinary humans, just like themselves, confused, fallible, capable of great deeds but also of great errors? Doubtless many leaders connive in the power mystique which surrounds them, by isolating themselves on 17th floors and in executive suites, awarding themselves awe-inspiring salaries (Krantz, 1990), wearing masks of unshaken certainty and conviction and eschewing all traces of humility, doubt or hesitation. Other leaders, possibly like

McKie, connive with the mystique by being defiant or disparaging towards the organization's top management in front of their subordinates, yet obsequious and subservient in front of their own superiors. Yet, what Steve's account suggests is that leaders, like McKie, are often invested with powers which are totally out of proportion with their actual position or personal qualities.

THE FOLLOWERS' CORE FANTASIES ABOUT THEIR LEADERS

Anna's and Steve's texts reveal a number of phantasies which subordinates construct around their superiors. These revolve around four axes:

1. The leader as someone who cares for his or her subordinates, either offering recognition and support or protection. The reverse of this fantasy is the leader who is indifferent to the plight of his or her subordinates and may even be an axeman, willing to sacrifice them in order to achieve his or her ambition.
2. The leader as someone who is accessible, who can be seen and heard, even if his or her appearances constitute special occasions. Conversely, the leader as someone who is mysterious and aloof, distant and inscrutable.
3. The leader as someone who is omnipotent, unafraid and capable of anything. Omnipotence sometimes extends to omniscience, especially an ability to read the minds of his or her subordinates and recognize true loyalty from flattery and sycophancy. Conversely, the leader as someone externally driven, afraid and fallible.
4. The leader as someone who has a legitimate claim to power; conversely, the leader as an impostor, someone who has usurped power and whose claims are fraudulent.

Phantasy fragments from different axes may combine or may turn into their opposites. Anna's narrative revolves primarily around the first two axes, the leader envisioned as the reincarnation of the primal mother, through whom, in Chasseguet-Smirgel's terms (1976), illusions are achieved. Steve's narrative, on the other hand, included elements from all four fantasy axes, though the last two had special prominence. Here, the leader was envisioned much more closely to the Freudian image of father-substitute, who rewards and punishes, arousing at once fear, loyalty, jealousy and suspicion. The former is close to Kohut's (1985) account of charismatic leadership phantasy, while the latter is closer to his account of messianic leadership phantasy. The phantasies that most followers have about their leaders can be seen as creative amalgams (condensations) of these two fundamental types. If most of us project on to leaders qualities of omnipotence, omniscience and wisdom we once attributed to our father, we also project on to them the fusion and unity which once tied us to our mother.

Instead of looking at the distinction between charismatic and messianic leaders as determined by the attributes of the leaders themselves, we would therefore be inclined to see it as the product of follower phantasies. A leader may be perceived as messianic by some followers, charismatic by others and as a mixture by yet others. He or she may be seen as an impostor, as caring or as aloof by different followers. In the course of rehearsing fantasies through jokes, stories and myths a few principal leadership phantasies may emerge, expressed in a shared folklore.

What the narratives in this chapter highlight is the key psychoanalytic insight that 'present relations are structured by and resemble past ones, most notably, those from early childhood with mother and father' (Oglensky, 1995: 1036). It is very difficult to relate to leaders in ways which are unaffected by our early relations with our mother and father; these early relations provide a core of primal political experiences which will forever colour our subsequent relations with authority. Different individuals will relate to authority in different ways, develop distinct fantasies and spin different stories about their leaders. As Oglensky points out, 'the role of the subordinate *does* actually depend upon his or her unique biography of attachment to parents as prototypes of authority' (1995: 1051), each biography unfolding around a specific 'authority template'. For some individuals, the legitimate–impostor axis may dominate their political fantasy life, for others the caring–persecuting axis may predominate. In Steve's story, the impotence–omnipotence axis overshadows the legitimate–impostor dimension. Even though his faith in McKie was shattered when faced with McKie's weakness, he quickly substituted Boston for McKie, and preserved his fantasy of leadership omnipotence. The loss of faith in one leader did not undermine his faith in all leaders, but rather the substitution of a false messiah by a supposedly true one.

In this, Steve is neither naïve nor untypical. His reaction reveals that most people find it difficult to accept working for an organization led by ordinary functionaries, appointed in bureaucratic ways and subject to both regulations and hierarchies. Max Weber's essential insight that impersonal hierarchies kill leadership (or at least what he saw as leadership based on emotion) cannot be reversed merely by elevating leaders to super-star status and according them the public relations treatment. At the same time, the Weberian insight cannot banish people's continuing psychic needs for leaders on whom to transfer emotion by turning them into objects of fantasy. Leaders must be endowed with superhuman qualities because only then can they really be perceived as real leaders, accepted and respected. Yet, at the same time, the entire apparatus of bureaucracy conspires against this illusion. Ordinary power-brokers cannot turn into messiah figures through the force of fantasy alone.

Yet, as Hirschhorn (1988, 1993) and Bennis (1989) have shown, opposition to leadership fantasies is not only external. Both authors have argued that the way many individuals relate to their leaders in contemporary organizations is affected by the predominant culture of narcissism. Narcissistic personalities both claim to long for 'strong leaders', and yet are uniquely unwilling to accept a leader's claim to authority for any period of time. To a narcissistic individual, any notion of leadership is both necessary and unbearable. It is necessary as a psychological defence against anxiety, yet at the same time it is unbearable since it threatens the autonomy and self-delusions of the ego. The only acceptable leader is one who not only has truly outstanding qualities but also one who must constantly 'prove' these qualities. Narcissists, therefore, find themselves profoundly ambivalent in their relations to their leaders. On the one hand, their exaggerated opinion of the huge and famous organizations which dominate our society, the organizations whose products, logos and advertisements are utterly necessary for sustaining contemporary narcissism, calls for the demi-gods featured in Steve's story. On the other hand, however, such demi-gods cast a fatal injury on narcissistic longings, and are eventually doomed to be brought down from their pedestals. This argument would suggest that in an organization peopled by narcissists all leadership romance is eventually doomed, ending in cynicism, with leaders seen as usurpers or impostors. In fact, the stronger the romance with specific leaders, the greater the final disappointment which they are likely to generate.

A FAILED MANAGERIAL COUPLE?

Ben Askew-Renaut

During the first few weeks of my placement in Germany I often found myself thinking about the 'best' relationship to have with my boss. Should I try to be the boss's friend or to impress him? What is the purpose of such an artificial relationship in any case? I gradually came to realize that my new relationship amounted to much more than a simple playing off of my boss's vanity in an attempt to flatter him and obtain a flattering report in return. I felt somewhat attracted to him, and was not able to understand why. I knew that he appreciated my work, yet sometimes I felt he was not particularly interested in me. In the psychoanalytic literature on leadership, I found many concepts which echoed my personal experience with my boss. Some fitted extremely well, others had to be interpreted in a certain way to provide the insights I had been looking for. This is an analysis of our relationship in two stages – one that brought us together, one that drew us apart.

With hindsight, I would say that my boss did have an overall interest in me, notably in what I could offer him; he relied on me for all the business he conducted with English-speaking customers. On a wider level, however, I often found him dedicating time to his entourage; he was never, for example, averse to discussing issues with his secretaries. His general attitude towards others, and me in particular, although I was often second on his list of priorities, leads me to believe that he depended heavily on the department's assurance and tended to use individual people for what they could offer him, symptomatic of a leader who loves no one but himself, or other people only in so far as they serve his need (Freud, 1921).

In fact, I strongly believe that he presented many of the traits of a narcissistic leader who consistently needs an admiring audience. For example, I could not help but think that his secretaries were pampering him a little too much. After all, he was a highly experienced manager. Yet, at the same time, I must admit that from the very beginning of my placement I found him both awe-inspiring and fascinating. How can I explain this attraction? The only answer I have come to accept comes in the form of Kohut's (1985) concept of follower narcissism, although at first I was quite resistant to its implications. Narcissism is an integral part of all personalities and, although self-analysis can lead to misinterpretations, I have tried to place my own experience under scrutiny. I would say without a doubt that I often rely on the critical eye of my family or friends in most of what I undertake, most especially in the field of my academic work. This, combined with the general pride I experience when I receive their recognition in a wide range of activities, suggests that my narcissism requires strong support from others. Were my boss and I operating in a miniature replica of a 'mutual admiration society'?

There was certainly a common identification with the company. This identification was strengthened by the fact that the company was family-run, and that the resulting atmosphere encouraged feelings of organizational unity. I was reminded of the argument put forward by Schwartz (1990) of the organization-ideal as a displaced ego-ideal. The glitter in my boss's eye each time he presented the company to potential customers, over the phone or face to face, was a clear expression of his idealized image of the company: in effect, the organization probably only existed in his mind in an idealized form, much as Freud's ego-ideal acts as guardian of goals and aspirations. In fact, his identification with the organization was so great that people around him would not have dared contradict his beliefs or presented any evidence of imperfection; perhaps this was what Weber described as the raw emotion of the charismatic, which seems to stimulate the onlooker into imitation or even submission.

Although I found my boss's love of the organization a little excessive, I openly admit that I found myself experiencing an equally inexplicable pride when monthly corporate results were published and laid on every employee's desk on the third of every month. I even ask myself today if the enthusiasm I expressed when talking about my placement activities to friends was not simply a scaled-down version of my boss's admiration for the company. Could my enthusiasm in time have led to the creation of an organization-ideal dominating the way I saw myself? On the whole, I feel that this common identification with the organization, although different in intensity, can explain the respect my boss and I expressed for each other: perhaps what linked us was the extent to which we were going along with the same system, with the organization itself.

Why, then, did I occasionally find him distant and detached, and end up arguing with him regularly? Surely, if we were both working towards a common organization-ideal, there would be no need for him to consider me a rival in even the weakest sense of the term. However, occasions such as these did arise, and I do not believe that they were exclusively due to my naïveté. I was often made to feel not morally inferior, but rather an obstacle, however small, to the overall objectives my boss had set himself. I have found that the theory of organizational narcissism provides further explanations as to why this reciprocal and increasing uneasiness arose in our relationship.

The first explanation for this climate of mistrust may have stemmed from the fact that over his working life at the firm my boss had developed a heightened sensitivity to those working for the organization, and was able to relate to them intensely, in as much as they accorded with his notion of the organization-ideal. However, this meant that it made it difficult to perceive and distinguish among individuals; in particular, he could not relate to me as a friend or colleague, but only as an ingredient in the organization-ideal. Furthermore, I have come to realize that when I made proposals which, largely due to my inexperience, lay outside the standard proceedings in the organization, he seemed to view them as *contemptible*. This may reflect the shortcomings of narcissistic personalities in crossing *cultural* barriers. Kohut (1971: 56) terms this '[the failure to] understand groups that are different from his own . . . which do not spring from the grandiose fantasies that they hold in common with [the narcissistic leader]' (Kohut, 1985: 56).

However, this may not be a one-sided issue. I have come to ask myself if my own narcissism did not feel threatened by my boss's charisma and his popularity within the organization; this is often the case, for example, when fellow students do better than I do. Was I also to blame for the climate of hostility through, for example, an uncompromising sensitivity to criticism? Perhaps my (by now) mature form of positive self-esteem could occasionally have been interpreted as a solipsistic claim for attention, or what Kohut terms the 'grandiose self'. Would this, combined with my tendency to compliment my boss a little too often to remain in his good books, not suggest the preponderance of narcissistic elements in my own personality? It may then be fair to say that we were unable to form a long-lasting relationship precisely because our respective desires to succeed and become the centre of attention were clashing.

If there was indeed this clashing of narcissistic motives, i.e. my striving to obtain rewarding tasks and eventually a favourable report, and his striving to use me to the full of my capacity to further his aims, then it may be justified to view this relationship as a remote manifestation of organizational narcissistic decay. We may have been involved in a pursuit to outbid our respective need for attention. This interpretation of our relationship came to me as I found unnerving similarities between the degrading of my relationship with my boss over time and the concepts of idealized transference (Kohut, 1971) applied to the organization (Schwartz, 1990). Although it would be exaggerated to claim that we had fallen prey to a narcissistic 'loss of reality', we were to a

> certain extent feeding off our own narcissisms. Had I been on a similar hierarchical footing to my boss, the risk that our relationship would further degenerate was clearly present. However, despite our difficulties and mutual recognition that we just would not 'get along', our relationship did remain relatively healthy. I believe our respective narcissism fell short of delusional grandiosity of the psychotic counterparts of healthy narcissistic configurations. Furthermore, I cannot believe that I possess enough personal aura for my boss to consider me a big enough threat. This leads me to believe that narcissistic leaders work best with followers whose narcissism does not clash with their own. I have also come to ask myself if I am not an earlier form of my boss, as I too would no doubt enjoy the stature he was accredited with.

ORGANIZATIONAL POLITICS

We have now examined how relations between leaders and followers are shaped by fantasy – the leader's fantasy or vision for the collective and the followers' fantasies about what the leader represents. Psychoanalysis is sometimes criticized for reducing all politics, including organizational politics, to the acting out of fantasies, dismissing economic or political factors as mere mirages. Revolutions are seen not as insurrections against economic exploitation or political oppression, involving organization, ideology and strategy; instead, they are approached as a re-enactment of the primal murder, where the sons turn against the tyrannical father, kill him and replace him by a collective rule. Wars are, likewise, seen as having their causes in processes of splitting, projective identification and externalization of aggression, rather than as having any political or economic causes. At a more mundane level, conflict within organizations is seen as the product of psychological splits and group processes, which may be overcome through better containment, more willingness to address process and more efficient communications.

Psychoanalytic writers are sometimes guilty of encouraging such criticisms by disregarding power and rational interests driving political processes and highlighting irrational, emotional and primarily group factors. This characterizes a large section of consultation literature in which power is conspicuously absent, except in the context of transference, but also the work of some of the profoundest philosophical commentators of psychoanalysis. Norman O. Brown, for example, through a sequence of spectacular arguments, reaches the view that all politics is illusion, a mere super-structure on the twin psychoanalytic pillars of brotherhood and fatherhood: 'Political power is a web woven, a political well-wrought veil; a veil of deceit, the veil of Maya. It is non-existent cloth, the Emperor's new clothes' (1966: 76). For Brown, politics is the superficial image, the shadow of the great psychological powers, Eros and death, as they eternally confront each other, endlessly building and destroying. Writing from the other end of the political spectrum, Philip Rieff (1959, 1966), another outstanding commentator of psychoanalysis, views all revolutionaries as neurotics, pursuing chimerical projects, driven by personal inadequacies and reinforcing those social forces of oppression which they purport to destroy.

Freud was himself responsible for fuelling charges of reducing everything to psychological processes. After all, in works like *Totem and Taboo* (1913a) and *Moses and Monotheism* (1939), he put forward quite audacious psychological explanations

IT IS NOT WHAT YOU KNOW, IT IS WHO YOU KNOW

Seth Allcorn

In this case study, Allcorn gives an example of the insights which may be gained by cross-fertilizing psychoanalytic insights with sharp political analysis. At no point is Allcorn seeking to reduce the political manoeuvring to psychological process, though he identifies some of the psychological processes which underpin the intricate and devious game which is being enacted.

The phrase, 'It is not what you know, it is who you know that matters' is very often mentioned in the context of the public political process. In and of itself the phrase appears to offer little hope that local, state and national governments can be operated in a manner consistent with logical, informed and participative decision-making processes. These dynamics are illustrated by the following case study that the author participated in.

Case study

A colleague's wife, Jane, was elected to the city council of a city of 50,000 population. During an office conversation with my colleague I suggested the idea of convening a group of citizens who had expertise in many different management areas for the purpose of reviewing the city's operations to locate possible improvements and cost savings. He conveyed the idea to Jane who liked it and subsequently researched the use of such groups in other cities. It was found that a number of other cities had tried similar strategies with success. Jane asked me to write an ordinance to be passed by the city council to initiate the process, which I did. The ordinance was passed without mention of my name. Jane then called a lunch meeting of myself, the mayor and one other council member to discuss how to act upon the ordinance. I briefly reviewed the ordinance as I understood it with the group, emphasizing the need for open participation of citizens who would volunteer their time and expert skills. Having completed my overview, the mayor pulled from his pocket a list of people he wanted to appoint to the group. This list was immediately matched by a list produced by the other councillor. I pointed out that the lists were inconsistent with the intent of the ordinance and its successful implementation. The lists were then taken off the table; however, as the discussion continued they re-emerged and ultimately proved to be an irresistible force.

The assembled work group was based entirely upon the lists with one exception. Jane managed to have me appointed to the group, a role that I assumed with an attitude of participant observation. The group ultimately contained three past mayors and a number of local activists, volunteers and political 'wannabes'. The group, upon meeting, reviewed its purpose as described by the ordinance and eventually discovered that its members had none of the requisite skills to carry out the ordinance. This quandary was discussed at length by the group. Eventually, I suggested that the group could open the process up to participation by all citizens with the interest and expert skills required to fulfil the intent of the ordinance. Group members were to each chair a sub-group with a specialized focus, such as information systems, finance, accounting, purchasing and so on. After completing this work at one meeting, the next meeting commenced with most members of the work group producing lists of whom they wanted to serve on the various sub-groups. The entire meeting was given over to discussing the various lists from the point of view of who knew these individuals. A typical interaction might include the mention of a name followed by another person saying that he or she also knew the individual or perhaps a parent, relative of workplace colleague. People who were not known to others were invariably rejected. I pointed out on several occasions that the lists would not lead to the sought after outcome; however, once again the process seemed to be irresistible.

These sub-groups were eventually assembled to work on their assigned tasks and predictably discovered that they also lacked the skills to do the work. At this point the work group began to feel that the ordinance was at fault and that it needed to be changed to fit the skills and interests of the members of the work group and sub-groups. This implied abandoning the original purpose and changing the work group into a group focused on more familiar politicized turf such as planning the future of the city in terms of park development and use, new roads, and so on. Despite the group adopting the notion that the ordinance needed to be changed, I steadfastly advocated that the ordinance needed to be complied with as it was the basis for having developed the group in the first place.

My solitary role of advocacy eventually created gridlock within the group. It could not do the work and nor could it change it. The gridlock and accompanying frustration was eventually blamed on Jane who had insisted on my being appointed to the group. Pressure was brought upon her to have me change my position. As it was not my purpose to undermine her role on the council, I obliged and rewrote the ordinance in a manner consistent with the group's wishes. The next meeting commenced with a lengthy monologue by the chair about how the group appeared to be hopelessly gridlocked. I eventually interrupted and handed out the revised draft of the ordinance which was applauded by the group as a job well done. The entirely new draft was submitted to the city council for adoption which occurred at the next meeting of the council. Upon passage I resigned from the group.

This brief case study omits descriptions of many group dynamics and interpersonal clashes of wills, one of which led to an anger-filled public self-humiliation of one past mayor and his resignation. The case, however, does describe what is an all too familiar aspect of the operation of the public political arena, one that does not inspire confidence or, conversely, inspires a sense of dread, foreboding and cynicism – depressive realizations to be certain. One may also understand that the story is one of irrational process run amok. How can this staple of public politics be better understood?

Analysis

At first glance the text of the story is about a group of insiders (mayor, council members, group members) who acquire power. They want it their way which is assured by selecting others who they know and trust without regard for accomplishing the task at hand. These dynamics are familiar, as illustrated by Saddam Hussein who appoints family members and close friends to roles of power and authority. Tactics such as these for acquiring and conserving power are centuries, even millennia old. However, there are other aspects to the situation that also contribute to understanding the case study.

Another pervasive and powerful aspect of human nature is trying to make others over into one's own image – inseminate them with oneself. This is often done through careful selection and mentoring and a system of rewards and sanctions. The usually younger and more junior person is seemingly promised everything if only he or she will assume the identity offered. Here I am reminded of the proverbial selling of one's soul to the devil for personal gain. In many cases the political arena is filled with wannabes and hangers-on, people who either want power and glory or who desire to bask in the radiance of others who possess them. These individuals 'suck-up' to powerful others in the hope of replacing them one day or receiving other forms of gratification not the least of which are power and wealth. Sycophants are all too common in history as illustrated by those who basked in the Führer's bright, shining light.

On a darker note, if that is conceivable, the possibility of a hidden agenda may also have been at work. I eventually learned that the city manager was opposed to the ordinance from the outset as he did not want to have his administration inspected and evaluated by knowledgeable outsiders not under his control. As a result, he may have convinced the mayor and the other council member present at the original meeting to undermine the ordinance by the process described while, at the same time, creating a group that would fulfil partisan political purposes. This scenario implies a conspiracy on the part of a few to undermine the majority vote – certainly another all too familiar aspect of the political arena where rules of fair play and civility are all too often suspended. Once again, throughout history, one finds many horrific examples of a state controlled by a few key individuals who sponsor bureaucratized terrorism, with Nazi Germany representing the archetype.

These three dynamics I hypothesize explain much of what happened in the case. I certainly do not rule out others that did not come to my attention. My own personal reaction to this experience that spanned but a few months was that, while I did not hold high regard for the political arena, the experience vastly exceeded my worst fears. This perspective may well shed light on how others (outsiders) experience participation or more often non-participation in the political arena. The reality may well be worse than the darkest fantasies of being disfranchised in the name of democracy. This analysis may have additional light shed upon it by exploring the contribution psychoanalytic theory makes to understanding the dynamics discussed.

Psychoanalytic insights

The case study may be interpreted from many different psychoanalytic perspectives. The following insights are provided as but a few of the ways in which the political and psychological dynamics may be appreciated psychodynamically.

Narcissistic process

Narcissistic deficits are comprised of the painful self-experience of not being worthy of admiration and love. These individuals are highly motivated to achieve powerful public or organizational roles that make them the centre of attention. Their grand visions and seductive, competitive and manipulative interpersonal relations pave the way for their success. Maintaining oneself in role to acquire narcissistic supplies from others becomes a self-defeating preoccupation aimed at overcoming the deficit arising from within. This individual surrounds him or herself with unquestioning and loyal followers. They, in turn, have their narcissistic needs (needs that are aggravated by the unidirectional flow of positive feelings towards this powerful individual) met by a similar process relative to those who seek relationships with them, thereby creating a narcissistic organizational culture as illustrated in this case.

Persecutory anxiety

Persecutory anxiety and accompanying elements of paranoia are present within the case. Those who hold power (individuals and groups) fear being attacked and stripped of their power. This dynamic may be understood from two perspectives. First, the person's or group's aggression towards others is denied to exist, split off from self or group and projected on to others who are then known with pathological certainty to possess aggression towards them. Secondly, the out-group's dynamics, accentuated by introjection of the projected aggression and lack of power, invariably stimulate a fight/flight response most often centred on resisting the in-group thereby fulfilling the in-group's fears. Certainly these dynamics are often present in democracies as well as dictatorships where the opposing party or rebels have to be contained, controlled, dominated and disposed of, as occurred to myself and eventually the ordinance and, by extension, the city council in the case.

Mirroring, merger and idealization

Follower dynamics that compensate for the leader's narcissistic deficit and support the sense of persecutory anxiety may also be understood to include unconscious desires held by followers to merge with the idealized greatness of the leader, thereby vicariously experiencing his or her power and glory. This unconscious dynamic of projection of meritorious aspects of self on to the leader who introjects them creates a self-sealing system of power and perfection where problems are denied and attributed to others. This is essential to sustaining the unconscious dynamics of idealization which may be defended at the cost of complete loss of reality testing.

Morbid dependency

The creation of an idealized all powerful leader is frequently accompanied by the wish to assume roles of morbid dependency in service to this great person who rewards those who support the idealization with powerful roles of their own or other organizational resources such as wealth acquired through corruption. Those who do not go along to get along (question the leader and challenge the idealization) must either submit or leave the group.

Projection, transference and sameness

The case study includes a striving for homogeneity of members and opinions. This tendency is supported by the projection of aspects of the self on to others who are then known to have much in common. Projected aspects of the self also promote transference on to others related to the feelings held for those aspects of the self, thereby creating a powerful unconscious affective bond. Questioning these cognitive and affective bonds is experienced as a threat to the dynamic and ultimately to oneself. As a result, diversity, which implicitly may call these dynamics into question, is not readily tolerated.

False self

A false self may arise as a child strives to receive parental love and approval. Loss of true self through lack of development, other and self-suppression and repression creates existential anxiety. The above-mentioned and often powerfully motivated desire to change others to be like oneself merely perpetuates these childhood tendencies. The result is that those with the greatest loss of true self most readily adopt new attributes, thereby creating a group of chameleon-like individuals who all share these tendencies. Awareness of these self-destructive dynamics of submission is necessary in order to avoid experience of a profound sense of loss of self.

Arrogance and vindictiveness

In the case, one crusty, old (arrogant) past mayor erupted with vindictive public statements when his point of view was challenged by the author. Many, when confronted with vindictive rages such as this, yield rather than stand their ground, thereby rewarding and encouraging the behaviour in the future. A challenge to the individual's arrogant pride required vindication which escalated until self-destruction occurred. This all-or-nothing, win–lose dynamic, when placed in the context of a powerful public figure, offers yet an additional reason why powerful positions are sought by these individuals.

Missionary zeal

A last element of the case study is the missionary zeal which many of those involved possessed for accomplishing their self-identified public good. Those who steadfastly and with great energy and self-sacrifice seek to rescue the poverty stricken, lame or any other sub-group identified as needy may be understood to involve projection, transference and therefore identification of needy parts of oneself in these others. Saving or healing them saves or heals these parts of oneself. Conversely, there are those who wish to cut the public dole. They redefine the needy as in need of a dose of honest work and personal responsibility. For this group, undesirable, irresponsible, dependent and helpless aspects of self are located in others who must be whipped into shape by this now strong and resolute individual or group that no longer possesses these attributes. In either case, these unconscious aspects of daily life provide exceptional polarizing emotion-filled motivations to act on behalf of or against others.

Conclusion

The case is filled with many conscious and unconscious behavioural motivations for the individuals and groups involved. What must be appreciated is that the ability to address any of these dynamics as a member of the group is almost certainly doomed to fail as a result of the pervasive group culture, values and dynamics. Those who do not go along to get along must get out. Also to be appreciated is that, while psychoanalytically informed perspectives provide much needed understanding and appreciation of group processes such as these, they ultimately offer little basis for intervening in the dysfunctional individual and group dynamics. Pointing out dysfunctional repetitions of group process and offering interpretations of individual and group dynamics are experienced as threatening to the group which promotes regression and greater reliance upon these familiar individual and social defences.

for social and political developments. Yet, Freud was no political simpleton. In the Introduction, we saw him in his machinations to gain the academic chair he longed for. Neither as a professional nor as a Jew was Freud unaware of the independent political processes, which involve social classes and factions, material and political privileges, conflicts, compromises, alliances, crises, democracy, dictatorship, warfare and so on (for a fascinating discussion of Freud's politics, see Schorske, 1961). He was certainly a fairly accomplished wheeler-dealer himself, within the highly politicized organization which he founded and would have laughed at the idea that all tactics and strategy, all political posturing, alliance building and marginalization can be reduced to the unconscious phantasies of the participants.

Depth psychology does not do justice to itself if it reduces all social and political processes, including organizational conflict, to deep psychological conflicts and desires. What psychoanalysis can, however, do is explain the psychological processes which underpin political ones. The two levels of explanation, psychological and political, may each enlighten the other and must seek to be consistent with each other, but they can certainly not replace each other. Personal rivalries may be unconscious re-enactments of sibling rivalry or may be the outcomes of structural or ideological factors in organizations, such as the location of boundaries, the criteria for promotion, the distribution of resources and tasks or deeply held values and beliefs.

CONCLUSION

In this chapter we have examined some of the psychodynamic contributions to the analysis of leadership relations. We have seen that leaders can inspire their followers through compelling visions which span the present and the future. We have also seen that leaders awaken in their followers fantasies and desires first experienced in childhood in those early relations with parents, which act as templates for our subsequent encounters with authority and power.

The leaders themselves are moved by fantasies of changing the world, having to tread a very delicate line between delusions of grandeur and omnipotence and feelings of impotence and fatalism. Leaders must have a highly developed narcissism, relishing the fame and glory which comes with success. They are, at the same time, highly vulnerable to narcissistic disorders, where approval and admiration is all they crave for, and in the interests of which, they are capable of distorting reality, disregarding obstacles and indulging in wishful thinking.

Finally, we have warned against reducing political relations to interpersonal relations, arguing that structures of political and organizational control cut across mental dynamics, without being reducible to them. Individuals may be driven to rebel against leaders by powerful fantasies that at one point they may have directed at their father or at some other figure of authority. Yet, such fantasies would remain dormant if they were not accompanied by actual experiences of exploitation, oppression and despair.

7 PSYCHOANALYSIS AND CULTURE

In 1799, in the French region of Aveyron, an unusual animal was discovered. A dirty, naked creature, he turned out to be the most famous of several 'wild children'. These are children lost or abandoned in early infancy, brought up by animals, usually wolves or bears. The wild child of Aveyron was about twelve years old. He appeared to have had no contact with humans, living alone in the forest. Victor, as he became known, generated much curiosity in French society. Trotting and grunting 'like a beast', terrified, unable to communicate and impervious to changes in temperature, the child did not meet then common criteria of a 'noble savage' and was dismissed as a congenital idiot.

A physician, Jean-Marc-Gaspard Itard tried to educate the child, to restore him to human civilization. The moving diary of his modest successes and overall failure is the basis for François Truffaut's great film *L'Enfant Sauvage*. Although he lived to an advanced age, Victor never really became a member of human society. It will never be known what Victor might have become had he grown up in an 'ordinary' family. Biologically, Victor and other wild children are recognizably human, yet their behaviours are distinctly unhuman (Singh and Zingg, 1942; Humphrey and Humphrey, 1932; Curtiss, 1977; Hicks and Gwynne, 1994). It is not just that they lack something, which they may later gain through training and teaching. Such children may eventually learn to eat cooked food with a knife and fork; they may eventually learn to walk on two legs; they may even learn to control their bowel movements. They are not able, however, to learn to speak, to write, to sing or to believe in God. Unlike their fictional cousin, Mowgli, Victor and other wild children who miss the boat cannot catch up later.

The journey which such children have missed is *socialization*, the long, hard and forced process whereby children are turned from little bundles of flesh and bone into male and female members of society. The driving force as well as the destination of the journey is *culture*, this uniquely human kingdom to which every new recruit to the human race (with few notable exceptions, like Victor) must willingly or unwillingly enter.

CULTURE, CIVILIZATION AND NATURE

Etymologically, the word 'culture' derives from cultivation. Its roots are truly in the soil, in nature. And yet culture is a uniquely human creation, it is the result of human work applied on nature's resources. Just as agriculture works on the natural landscape, tames it and humanizes it, culture works on human beings themselves, turning them from physical, animal beings into members of societies.

Culture is sometimes contrasted to *civilization*. The word 'civilization' has been strongly linked with the idea of progress and development, opposed to the uncivilized, the savage, the wild. It is a term loaded with assumptions about the supremacy of certain types of human achievement over others. Culture, as a more neutral term, has kept its attachment to the primitive and primeval. It is perfectly possible to talk of pre-literate or primitive cultures, but it would hardly make sense to talk of tribal civilizations. Civilization generally stresses the technical, economic and political achievements of humanity and presupposes a certain minimum advancement in these areas; etymologically, the word is related to civil society, to the world of the ancient *polis*, the city-state.

Culture, on the other hand, stresses artistic, religious or legal forms which characterize different societies. It presupposes no minimum achievement, nor does it prejudge which forms deserve greater value and recognition. The rock etchings and stone circles of prehistoric people are accepted as cultural forms, comparable to Gothic cathedrals or the Statue of Liberty. Nor does culture discriminate against the mundane, the everyday and the here and now. Tools and utensils, eating implements, clothes and tattoos, advertisements, musical instruments, religious rituals and linguistic slang are all accepted as elements of culture.

When we think of the great cultural accomplishments of humanity, of the sciences, the arts, the political and legal institutions, the great religions of the world, we tend to forget the biological, animal part of our nature. This is perhaps why the wild child of Aveyron generated so much interest at the time and would doubtless generate even greater interest today. It was Darwin's great achievement to establish that behind our civilized, cultured veneer we remain creatures of nature, products of evolutionary development. Freud's work complemented Darwin's by establishing that our biological nature is not obliterated by culture, but continues to be a vital force in our lives. The battle between nature and culture, with its crises and compromises, forever shapes our lives.

Three important characteristics of culture

1 *Culture becomes 'second' nature to us*. Having gone through socialization, we find that our culture's requirements come to be regarded as natural. Eating with a knife and fork, refraining from spitting on pavements, or marrying for love, these are things which we take for granted in Western society and can hardly imagine doing differently. Through socialization, each individual absorbs culture, not only becoming a part of culture but allowing culture to become part of him or herself.
2 *There is a bewildering diversity of cultures*. Even though we all imagine our culture to be 'natural', anthropologists have discovered enormous differences in the ways in which human societies are organized. Whether studying economic behaviour or religious beliefs, marriage arrangements or sexual behaviour, political systems or the use of language, the rule of thumb seems to be that what is forbidden by one culture is tolerated, permitted or encouraged by others.
3 *Exposure to other cultures enables us to recognize our own cultural assumptions*. It is only when we realize that other people live their lives very differently that we realize some of our own cultural assumptions. We then recognize that what we regard as 'natural' behaviours (such as grieving over a death and rejoicing over a birth, marrying for love or allowing our elderly parents to spend their last years in institutions, working hard for success and social recognition) are merely conventions of our own Western culture.

Why study culture?

The study of culture in organizational studies has increased dramatically in the past fifteen years. Culture has now become a very fashionable topic among organizational scholars. Why? In the first place, today's organizations operate increasingly on a global scale, venturing beyond their own national cultures into unfamiliar cultural environments. They draw their resources from such environments, and into them they channel their outputs. Different national cultures make different demands on organizations and offer them different opportunities. Recognizing and building on cultural particularities, adapting organizational products and policies to local cultures and managing employees in a manner appropriate to their culture become vital ingredients of organizational success.

Secondly, organizations have become themselves a core feature of most contemporary cultures, especially in industrialized countries. Whether we look at manufacturing, health, education, politics or the arts, organizations like firms, hospitals, schools and universities, political parties and mass media dominate the scene. Our personal daily lives are continuously woven around organizations, as members, as employees or as consumers of their products. The majority of people we meet and interact with are not personal friends or acquaintances, but people whom we encounter as members of organizations. The ticket collector, the university lecturer, the shop assistant, the nurse, the union official, the manager, the fellow-worker, these are people with whom we come into daily contact not as a result of the personal relations we have with them, but as a result of the roles which they and we perform within different organizations.

It is not accidental that Western society has often been referred to as an organizational society (see Chapter 4). Many features of organizations such as their impersonality, their formalism, their emphasis on rules and procedures, become features of our culture as a whole. How did this organization-dominated culture emerge? How does it affect the nature of the work we do? What demands does it make on us? How does it influence our social and emotional lives?

A third reason for studying culture is that there has recently been an increasing recognition that organizations are themselves cultures. This view emerged from an attempt to explain the reasons for the phenomenal success of Japanese manufacturing organizations in the 1970s and 1980s. Looking for the secret of Japanese success, scholars focused increasingly on the culture of these companies and its relation to the wider Japanese culture. Studying organizations as cultural phenomena has substantially altered our views of what organizations actually are, how they affect individuals' lives, what the role of leadership is, and what distinguishes successful from less successful organizations.

The idea that organizations do things differently as a result of their different cultures is nicely summed up in a joke told by an executive of a European computer manufacturer:

> There is a ravine. The distance between two cliffs of the ravine is 8.9 m, the distance of the world's longest jump, the legendary jump of Bob Beamon. Between the two cliffs, chaos. IBM has to get across the ravine, so they get their think tanks to work, and after a month they decide to build a bridge. A few months later they've built the bridge and they cross the ravine. Digital have to cross the ravine, so the executives give a pep-talk to their staff, convince them that they are all winners and can do it, so they all jump across, landing safely.

Hewlett Packard are next to cross the ravine. They figure that the ravine can't be the same width all along so they send scouting parties to find where the gap is smaller. They eventually find the place and they all follow their leader jumping across the narrower gap. Finally, it's our turn to cross the ravine, so our chief executive says, 'OK, you jump the first foot, you jump the second . . .'

What this self-deprecating joke suggests is that organizations, like societies, have cultures. What makes this proposition especially intriguing is that current approaches have not emphasized those features of culture which we normally associate with our technologically advanced civilization, i.e. features like automation and information technology, urbanization, mass media and so on. Instead, they emphasize what is primitive and archaic in culture. The result has been to introduce to the study of organizations ideas and words borrowed from ethnography, like myth, ritual, tribe, clan, taboo and, above all, symbols and symbolism. The resulting images of organizations in current discussions have as much in common with primitive, pre-literate tribes as with the rational models of organizations devised by Max Weber and his followers. Chapter 8 discusses in detail this view of organizations as cultures. In this chapter we shall look at the wider culture, especially the cultures of industrialized societies, and present some psychoanalytic contributions to this field.

WHAT IS CULTURE?

Norms and values

Culture, like many other core concepts of the human sciences (power, role, personality, intelligence, class), is notoriously difficult to define. In a widely cited book on culture, Krober and Kluckholn (1952) identified 164 distinct definitions of culture proposed by different anthropologists. One of the simplest ways to approach culture is to equate it with the *norms* and *values* of a society. Norms are specific standards of behaviour to which we generally adhere, while values are wider beliefs about what is right and what is wrong. Norms govern numerous aspects of our behaviour, often without our conscious knowledge. One group of social norms, for example, governs how close we physically approach people. Americans generally feel comfortable in the following buffer spaces: 0–18 inches for intimacy; 18–48 inches for talking with friends; 4–12 feet for talking with strangers; more than 12 feet for standing in public areas. Adults tend to keep more distance than children; men more distance than women. The differences, however, are more pronounced across different cultures. Cultures near the equator, for reasons unknown, prefer less social space; they also make much more physical contact.

Evidently, social norms do not only govern how close we stand to each other when we talk. They affect our drinking and eating, our leisure activities, our preferences as consumers, aspects of our sexual behaviour and so on. While norms may vary from one culture to the next, cultures seek to enforce their norms, with a greater or lesser degree of severity, through the use of negative and positive sanctions. A student who goes to a lecture dressed in tie and suit may attract sarcastic comments from other students, or may be excluded from their social activities or may be simply accepted as an eccentric. A person, however, who goes to a funeral wearing a funny hat is likely to cause a scandal, angry words or receive a request to leave.

FITTING THE CULTURE

In the story that follows, Paul, an accountancy intern describes an incident at a professional function which he attended. The incident illustrates the consequences of breaking social norms.

It so happened that the invited guest speaker at this event was Jonathan Fox, the well-known TV weatherman. He delivered a very entertaining and enjoyable speech which pleased Eric very much – he laughed and cheered. All pretty normal behaviour you may be thinking. At the end of Mr Fox's speech he asked his avid recipients if they had any questions that they would like to put to him. Eric, with an excited look similar to that of a nine-year-old school boy who knew the answer to teacher's very difficult maths question, thrust his hand into the air. Now Jonathan, who, it has to be said, was rather lacking in the hair department, looked across at Eric. Eric, in an eardrum-bursting voice, shouted: 'Jonathan, does the glowing sheen on the top of your head reflect the current economic climate?'

The room fell silent as 400 unamused accountants looked first at Eric and then Jonathan. The look on the faces of all the partners, students and senior management from the company said it all. It was then worsened by the fact that, five seconds later, Eric clapped his hands and laughed, with rather more gusto than was strictly necessary, at his very funny joke (as one imagines he supposed it to be).

Earlier in the evening we had all taken part in a sweepstake guessing how long Jonathan Fox's speech would last. Just after Eric's slight blunder one of the senior managers turned to me and said 'The next sweepstake will be on how long Eric Minton will stay on the Branfeld's payroll.' It was said in jest but contained a strong element of threat.

This incident, although extreme, is a prime example of how everyone, in all aspects of life, is being judged at Branfeld – and the effect this has on their career. During the incident, I could not help the overwhelming feeling of embarrassment at our table, or for that matter the whole room. It was as if I was willing Eric to stop because I was realizing that, from this moment on, he will have been judged. People who have worked with Eric will lose respect for him, and people who have yet to work with him will have preconditioned ideas.

From the moment one enters Branfeld as an organization, every move you make is being observed, whether it be academic, in work or social. I would liken it to being back at school. Academically you are being observed closely, penalized for failing exams, rewarded for passing. Failure can also result in being asked to leave the company. From the results of formative academic examinations, high-flyers are already being plucked out. Weekly judgements in the form of staff reports render this monitoring a constant aspect of one's position. These reports contain grading systems and a space for personal comments from seniors. This staff reporting system is pay-related and continues all the way up the hierarchical structure.

In the incident above, Eric was being judged in the social aspects – as, indeed, we all were – at the dinner. I was sitting with partners either side of me. I hope I was being positively judged, unlike Eric, surely. During the incident, it was so obvious from the reactions of senior members of staff that his behaviour was not producing positive thoughts: 'Eric Minton is not fitting in to the Branfeld culture.' When a student's whole career within Branfeld balances upon his or her ability to 'fit in' to this culture, or way of life, one can see the importance of not breaking the rules.

Adapted from Fineman and Gabriel, 1996.

If norms are the standards which guide our behaviour, values are profoundly held beliefs about what is right and wrong, good and evil. Like norms, values vary widely across different cultures. Western culture places great value on individual effort and achievement as well as on material possessions. A good life may then be seen as a life of hard work, rewarded through material well-being and affluence. Other cultures, by contrast, place greater value on community and asceticism, honouring a life of spirituality and tranquillity.

Culture and meaning

Norms and values are important elements of any culture. They are part of the processes of *social control*, whereby individuals behave in particular ways, which they come to regard as natural and normal. In Paul's story (see Box), social control seems to be temporarily broken by Minton's norm-breaking outburst. This is signalled by the embarrassment felt by all concerned. Yet, the subsequent isolation and exclusion of Minton and the negative implications of his offence on his career, reinforce conformity to the company's main culture. In this way, culture can unite and integrate people who share in their disapproval of norm violation, just as it can unite and integrate a group of people who share a successful joke.

In due course, the story of Minton's *faux pas* and his subsequent come-uppance may become part of the organization's folklore, helping to deter future recruits from similar temptations. Culture includes all the material and spiritual heritage of an organization or a community, its myths and stories, artistic and craft artefacts, buildings, tools, laws, institutions, rituals and customs. What makes these ingredients cultural products is not their physical substance, but the *meanings* attached to them and the ways in which they infuse people's lives with meaning. A wedding ring, for example, is seen as a *symbol* of loyalty, love or commitment. Within a particular culture, everyone recognizes the significance of a ring on a person's finger, just as the personalized parking space is seen as a sign of an executive's status and importance. Hofstede (1991) has offered the metaphor of culture as 'the software of the mind'. Just as software turns inert machinery into sophisticated thinking machines, so too does culture turn biological beings into sense-making, sensible human subjects.

Culture and religion

Traditionally, the meanings of most cultural objects and practices have been underpinned by religion, humanity's major source of meaning. Rituals and ceremonies, myths and legends, eating, drinking, healing and growing-up practices, taboos and prohibitions, values and norms have all traditionally grown out of religious systems. Religion not only infused everyday life with meaning, but it also answered humans' awe-inspiring questions about the origin and nature of the world, their past and future, the mysteries of life and death.

As religion has declined in Western civilization, other institutions have assumed major cultural significance, supporting some of the same functions. Science as well as political and economic institutions have assumed an important cultural role. Gradually, culture has become secularized. And with greater secularization has come greater pluralism. Meanings and symbolism no longer flow exclusively from the ceaseless fountain of religion. Scientific institutions, political organizations, the mass media, businesses, schools, professional bodies, lobbies, fashion leaders, advertisers as well as religious organizations all have a part in the cultural polyphony of modern societies.

To summarize, anthropologists and sociologists acknowledge that culture stands in opposition to nature, as 'everything acquired by human beings which is not physically inherited' (Worsley, 1970: 24). They acknowledge the wide varieties and richness of human cultures. Yet they also agree that, in spite of all their differences, all cultures must fulfil certain fundamental functions, without which social life becomes problematic or impossible. One such function of culture is that of social control, ensuring that people behave in accordance with social norms and values. A second function, sometimes referred to as the *symbolic* function, is that of infusing human life with meaning. A third function, known as the *epistemological* function, is that of answering people's questions about the nature of the world they live in.

FREUD'S THEORY OF CULTURE

Psychoanalysis lifts the discussion of culture to a higher level altogether. First, at the level of *interpretation*, psychoanalysis unlocks the deeper meanings of cultural phenomena, ranging from advertisements to religious rituals, by linking them to the unconscious desires and processes of individuals. Secondly, it casts the *relation between the individual and the social whole* under a powerful new light, which reveals that individuals both submit to and resist culture, both depend upon culture and yet pay a major price for its sustenance. Finally, it enables researchers to compare the *demands and contributions* made by different cultures, without losing sight of the underlying similarities of all cultures.

In the first place, psychoanalysis approaches cultural phenomena neither in terms of their causes, nor in terms of their functions but, symbolically, in terms of their meanings. Whether discussing a work of art (like Sophocles' *Oedipus Rex*), a myth (such as Prometheus stealing fire), a religious practice (circumcision) or even an advertisement, psychoanalysis initially seeks to interpret them. In short, psychoanalysis begins by treating cultural phenomena as if they are collective equivalents of individual phenomena, like dreams, slips of the tongue or neurotic symptoms. This is an imaginative and provocative undertaking. But what is the justification for doing so?

In an early paper called 'Obsessive Actions and Religious Practices' (1907b), Freud identified certain striking similarities between religious rituals and obsessional symptoms.

At a formal level, both religious rituals and obsessional symptoms display an exaggerated attention to detail, they share a compulsive repetitive quality, they exhibit a degree of detachment from rational considerations, and they both seem to be dictated by powerful 'unwritten rules' (1907b: 33–4).

At the symbolic level, certain religious rituals, such as circumcision (symbolic castration) and the Christian Eucharist (symbolic eating of the murdered leader's flesh and drinking of his blood), seem to re-enact unconscious desires or fears which, at an individual level, lead to neurosis.

INTERPRETING SOPHOCLES' KING OEDIPUS

On numerous occasions, Freud described his view of humanity as 'tragic'. This is something that many of his successors tended to disregard. Tragic is the fate of people who are driven by forces beyond their comprehension, suffering for crimes they have not committed and pursuing goals which often end up in dead ends. Nothing illustrates this view better than the myth of King Oedipus, which so fascinated Freud and which provided psychoanalysis with its core text. The story of Oedipus and its psychoanalytic interpretation give us an insight into how psychoanalysis can offer interpretations of cultural artefacts, in this case a myth.

The story of Oedipus, as it is presented in Sophocles' great tragedy, is a detective story in which Oedipus is detective, criminal and victim rolled into one. Oedipus became king of Thebes when he delivered the city by answering the famous riddle of the Sphinx, through the power of his 'intellect alone'. But Thebes is afflicted by disease and starvation. Oedipus sets out to discover who has brought this evil on the city. Unlike classic detective stories but just as in all tragedy, the hero is the last person to discover the truth. He, Oedipus, is the culprit; he killed a man who turned out to be his father, King Laius of Thebes, and he was honoured by marrying the widowed queen, Jocasta, his very own mother.

Laius and Jocasta, worried about an ancient oracle which foretold the death of the l king at the hands of his son, ordered the child to be killed; only, as often happens in myths, the shepherd entrusted with killing the child spared the child's life. Young Oedipus was brought up by the king and queen of Corinth, whom he considered his real parents. The tragic irony was that he left Corinth precisely because he learnt about an oracle foretelling the death of his father at his own hands. All the tragic characters in the story, Laius and Jocasta, the shepherd, Oedipus himself, appear to be doing exactly what is required to evade the tragedy, and yet achieve precisely the opposite. And Oedipus, the great solver of riddles, turns out to have failed with the most basic truth – his own identity.

For Freud, the story draws its sweeping power from the fact that Oedipus acts out in deed, what every male child has dreamt of doing – kill his father and sexually possess his mother. The myth lays bare the fundamental human desires, which the whole of culture conspires to keep repressed. Of course, a price has to be paid in order for such dangerous wishes to find public expression. Oedipus acts out his deeds *unknowingly*. As he says in the tragedy's noble follow-up, *Oedipus at Colonus*, 'As for my deeds, I hardly acted them at all, rather they happened to me.' In this way, the myth emerges as a compromise between desire and the censoring forces that keep desires repressed.

The story, however, has many additional layers of meaning which resonate with each individual's specific desires and wishes. Bruno Bettelheim pointed out that the entire story is built on the cruelty of the parents, who want their child killed. No child, however gifted and noble, can ever escape from the injuries caused, knowingly or unknowingly, by his or her parents. Herbert Marcuse unveils yet another line of meaning by arguing that 'reason alone' cannot be the driving force in human affairs. Oedipus pays for presuming that humans can be ruled through the force of reason, disregarding the political realities of the city he rules. Other writers have provided yet more layers of interpretation. Are all these interpretations 'right'? There are some interpretations which are more coherent, more convincing and more rigorous than others. Claude Levi-Strauss, the great French anthropologist, has argued powerfully that all versions of the story of Oedipus and all interpretations are part of the same underlying unity, a unity that must be read not

> linearly, like a story, but vertically, like an orchestral score, with different voices speaking together, in harmony or in counterpoint. With every great cultural masterpiece each epoch discovers those nuances and connections that address its own anxieties and desires. And every individual must arrive at an interpretation that leaves no loose ends for him or herself.

At the psychological level, both religious rituals and obsessional symptoms (such as the compulsive washing of hands), if not observed, generate a sense of acute discomfort or guilt, they both breed intense dependency and they both appear to exorcise anxieties as acts of defence. Jaques (1955), Menzies (1960), Baum (1987) and Hirschhorn (1988) have argued that organizational rituals and ceremonials which become embedded in bureaucratic routine represent a similar type of social defence against anxiety.

Culture and repression

These similarities suggested to Freud (1907b) that many cultural phenomena, just like neurotic symptoms, are products of the repression of instinctual impulses and may therefore be interpreted using a similar methodology. Repression, as was seen in Chapter 1, is a core concept of psychoanalysis. 'In the new Freudian perspective, the essence of society is the repression of the individual, and the essence of the individual is the repression of himself' (Brown, 1959: 3). Whenever the ego threatens to be overwhelmed by powerful desires from the id which stand in opposition to the demands of the super-ego or the realistic opportunities on offer by the external world, it prevents these desires from reaching consciousness by restricting them to the unconscious.

This inaugurates a continuous struggle between those desires seeking to reach consciousness and fulfilment and the ego striving to keep them repressed. One usual result of this struggle is the *symptom*, a compromise formation, which reaches consciousness and which embodies the original desire in a distorted form. An alternative is the religious ritual. Both phenomena are compromise formations between two warring forces of the psyche, the instinctual impulses demanding fulfilment and the forces of repression imposing censorship. And both reproduce, often in distorted or symbolic forms, 'something of the pleasure which they are designed to prevent' (1907b: 39). Result:

> In view of these similarities and analogies one might venture to regard obsessional neurosis as a pathological counterpart of the formation of religion, and to describe that neurosis as an individual religiosity and religion as a universal obsessional neurosis. (1907b: 40)

Eventually, Freud came to regard neurosis and religion as mutual substitutes: 'The neuroses themselves have turned out to be attempts to *individual* solutions for the problems of compensating for unsatisfied wishes, while the institutions seek to provide *social* solutions for these same problems' (1913: 52).

The importance of these formulations on religious phenomena cannot be over-emphasized. They represent a dimension which complements the classical theories of

Weber and Durkheim. Culture, as embodied in religion, is not merely a source of meaning in people's actions, it is not merely a force for social cohesion and identity – it is a *substitute gratification* representing society's solution to a psychic problem and reflecting the underlying structure of this problem. Freud's discussion of culture is dominated by his conception of the twin functions of religion as *prohibition* and *consolation*, a source of discontents and a provider of substitute gratifications in the form of illusions. In this, Freud was not far from Marx's famous view of religion as at once 'the opium of the people' and 'the sigh of the oppressed creature, the sentiment of a heartless world, the soul of soulless conditions'.

Having accepted the premiss that religion and other cultural artefacts fulfil broadly similar psychic functions as neurotic symptoms, psychoanalysis proceeds to interpret them after its model of dream interpretation. In fact, religious beliefs will reveal their secrets rather more easily than most dreams. Behind the Christian religion looms the wish to be loved and protected by an almighty father. This need grows out of every infant's early helplessness, and is revived and reinforced every time the mature individual is dealt one of fate's cruel blows. Beliefs in divine retribution and the immortality of the soul are for Freud so scarcely concealed as wish-fulfilments that their character is almost infantile.

Interpretation is the point of entry of psychoanalysis into the discussion of culture. But it is not the limit of its contribution, which goes on to address two century-old debates: that concerning man as a social animal, and that concerning the causes of human suffering and the pre-conditions for potential redemption.

Freud's earlier writings leave little doubt that he regarded culture as an external source of prohibitions and renunciations for the individual. These could be relaxed under a more enlightened social organization and some purely technical breakthroughs, such as in the area of contraception. Gradually, however, he moved to the view that culture itself is founded on instinctual energies. Far from being the declared enemies of culture, instincts, when tamed and civilized, become the material on which culture is based. To the concept of repression, Freud added the concept of *sublimation*, as the instinctual vicissitude through which the sexual instinct

> exchanges [its] sexual goal for one more remote and socially more useful. To the contributions of the energy won in such a way for the functions of our mental life we probably owe the highest cultural consequences. A repression taking place at an early period excludes the sublimation of the repressed impulse; after the removal of the repression the way to sublimation is again free. (1910: 54)

Culture, narcissism and the death instinct

Culture, then, is a force that works inside each person, rather than something forced from the outside. It redirects and tames sexuality, but it also offers *narcissistic compensation*. People identify with their culture's greatest achievements as well as its minor idiosyncrasies. They each incorporate into their mental personality a 'cultural ego-ideal', a symbolic nexus which includes elements of family, class or nation, against which they measure their own ego. The nearer they perceive themselves to it, the greater the sense of narcissistic satisfaction they obtain. While the cultural ego-ideal may be dominated by grand ideals of patriotism, religion and so on, it may equally include allegiance to specific groups or organizations. At the group level, this leads to what Freud called 'the narcissism of small differences' (1921: 131; 1930: 305), the pride of football supporters and their petty antagonism towards supporters of a club from an adjacent territory. At the organizational level, it leads to the incorporation of an organization-ideal into the individual ego-ideal. This is a process whereby, as Schwartz has shown, an individual's narcissism feeds on an organization's corporate delusions of grandeur. While this makes for highly cohesive organizations with very committed members, it also leads to a sense of invulnerability and aversion to criticism which can have disastrous results for organization and individual alike (Schwartz, 1990).

In Freud's early work, sexuality as an unpredictable, blinkered and wild force was seen as an enemy of culture. In his later work, however, sexuality as Eros, a power which 'unites all things' rather than a pleasure-seeking force, came to be seen as the great ally of culture, forming the basis for group and social bonds, altruism and togetherness. While, however, the uneasy alliance of Eros and culture, with its resulting costs to the individual, was taking shape, a force threatening the fruit of this alliance was coming to the forefront of the Freudian stage, the death instinct. This concept was introduced tentatively (Freud, 1920) to explain a variety of puzzling phenomena, yet Freud's commitment to the concept stems from the remarkable theoretical yield of the cross-fertilization of this concept with that of the super-ego.

Importance of the super-ego in Freud's mature theory of culture

The convergence of the death instinct and the super-ego, in Freud's view, accounts for the power of conscience and the cruelty and unreasonableness of the super-ego. Through the super-ego, the death instinct turns inward and attacks the individual as an unconscious sense of guilt and as tyrannical conscience. The super-ego is the vital concept which mediates between culture and mental personality. It inherits the ruthlessness of the paternal imago during the Oedipal phase; it is entirely indifferent to the well-being of the individual on whom it makes entirely unreasonable demands. In extreme cases, referred to as 'saintlihood syndrome', the more an individual controls his or her aggression the greater the aggression unleashed by the super-ego against the ego.

The internalization of the death instinct is the source of endless sufferings for the individual and cannot, properly speaking, be said to have any psychological function. Its function is purely cultural: it prevents the individual's aggressive energies from being directed against the social whole and fortifies the control over the ego held by the society fifth column within the individual, the super-ego.

Discontents and illusions

The implications of these ideas for the relationship between individual and society are studied in Freud's mature masterpiece *Civilization and its Discontents* (1930). Although the theme of the conflict between individual and society remains central, the discovery of an instinct working towards dissolution and death casts this conflict in a dramatically different light. In the earlier formulations, the paramount problem of culture and of the ego was the domestication of sexuality, which was seen as a rebellious force, noisy, short-sighted and altogether unreliable. In the new formulation, the relation between the individual and society becomes more complex and the costs of culture far more painful. The central problem is now the deflection of the aggressive forces away from the social bonds; the solution is more costly – the channelling of aggression against the individual ego.

What Freud found especially disturbing was that the amalgam of factors which favour the survival of culture and the formation of stable and cohesive groups, namely the sublimation of Eros and the internalization of the death instinct, may ultimately be leading to the demise of the individual. For by suppressing aggressive impulses according to the edicts of the super-ego ('love thy neighbour'), the ego adds to the latter's supplies of destructive energies which will sooner or later be targeted against itself. On the other hand, by de-sexualizing the sexual instinct, the ego weakens the ability of these instincts to neutralize and defuse aggression.

Although Freud recognized many varieties of human suffering (1930: 261ff), he regarded *guilt and sexual frustration* as inevitable discontents resulting from the demands made by the culture on our instinctual nature. What makes the fate of mankind truly tragic is that the consolations are worse than the discontents. People espouse numerous illusions, whose net result, like that of opiates, is to reinforce the condition which they purport to cure. Some of these illusions are of a private escapist nature (like fantasies of winning the pools or marrying a prince) and may provide some consolation. Yet, illusions of romantic love, dreams of escape to desert islands, are quickly frustrated. Just as the androgynous men in Plato's Symposium were too powerful for the comfort of Zeus who decided to split them into men and women, the blissful self-sufficiency of the couple is not compatible with the purposes of culture which quickly puts an end to such illusions.

In their place, culture provides its own socially sponsored illusions, celebrated in communal ceremonials, illusions which justify human suffering, allow for innocent narcissistic satisfactions and, above all, offer consolations and comfort for the individual. While religion has been the primary source of human illusions, in advanced cultures it is supplemented and even supplanted by other types of illusions – political, organizational and even marketing ones.

Criticisms of Freud's cultural views

To summarize, Freud argued that culture is built on a systematic suppression and re-orientation of instinctual energies. Eros is sublimated in establishing bonds of identification among different individuals. The death instinct turns inwards to pursue the individual as an unconscious sense of guilt, ensuring adherence to social norms and prohibitions. These processes involve considerable conflict between the individual and society and the individual within him or herself. The individual both submits to and resists in different measure culture's demands, suffering as a result from various discontents. A substantial part of his or her desires is repressed in the unconscious, from where it will forever seek to reach consciousness.

As compensations, culture offers a range of substitute gratifications. It provides institutions which protect each individual from the destructive qualities of others; it offers explanations for the mysteries of life and death, giving a measure of security against an unpredictable environment. It offers legitimate love-objects with whom to establish long-lasting bonds and relations. To some, it provides creative work and the enjoyment of artistic outputs of others. It also proffers ideals and illusions which grant

> ### AN ORGANIZATIONAL STORY AS CONSOLATION
>
> Older recruits in closed organizations, like army camps, boarding schools or police academies, enjoy unnerving new arrivals with terrible stories about the ordeals of their predecessors. In a Greek naval camp, older recruits told stories about a vicious officer who found various twisted ways of tormenting the conscripts. According to one of them, the officer was inspecting the conscripts before granting them their furloughs. After inspecting their uniforms, he asked them to lower their trousers to inspect their underpants. On seeing that they were not wearing regulation navy underpants, he cancelled their leave.
>
> Such alarmist stories make the new recruits uncomfortable, but they also warn them of trials that lie ahead. They unsettle them, but also reassure them that, like their seniors, they too can survive these ordeals, if they can take the rough with the smooth. At a symbolic level, the pants story may hint that underneath the uniformity of the navy, each recruit can keep a part of himself as he likes it (his underpants), even if he occasionally has to pay a price for it. Older recruits may identify with the officer, enjoying the distress which the story causes them, just as the officer supposedly enjoyed his antic. The story helps them overcome their own feelings of powerlessness, by casting them in the role of survivors (adapted from Gabriel, 1991c).
>
> Many organizational stories have similar consolatory qualities, helping individuals come to terms with the stresses of organizational life, enabling them to have a laugh at the expense of feared superiors or the organization itself and turn victimhood into victory. In this way, they open valuable windows into the emotional and fantasy life of organizational members.

some narcissistic satisfactions and consolations for the individual. Yet, in the long run, illusions deepen the discontents of the civilization by imposing additional burdens on the individual. Just as the neurotic obtains some comfort from his or her symptoms, unconscious of the fact that this only worsens his or her condition, individuals espouse illusions unaware of the attendant costs.

Freud did not ignore other sources of suffering which nature, society and fate inflict on individuals. Poverty, disease, political oppression, injustice, inequality, the loss of loved ones, stultifying labour, all add in different measure to the burdens of humanity and call for consolations. Yet sexual discontents and guilt were seen as the unique costs of culture. At this point the reader may legitimately begin to suspect that what Freud regards as the inevitable sufferings of civilization reflect the anxieties and discontents of a slender section of humanity, that of his own milieu and that of his patients – *fin-de-siècle*, guilt-ridden and over-repressed Viennese middle class. If so, what can the relevance of his theories be for the study of a very different culture, one dominated by large-scale organizations, in which sexual repression and overwhelming guilt no longer seem so important?

This has been a long-standing criticism of the psychoanalytic approach to culture. Both friendly and hostile critics have questioned whether concepts such as repression, castration anxiety and penis envy are not specific to the narrow, male-dominated, sexually restrictive culture of Vienna at the turn of the twentieth century rather than universal characteristics of human kind. One of the earliest critics was the Polish anthropologist Bronislaw Malinowski (1884–1942), who carried out a seminal piece of research (1914–18) with the Trobriand islanders in the South Pacific. Trobriand society was a matrilinear society, built around extended family networks and characterized by permissive sexual morality, which even sanctioned sexual activity for children. Malinowski, whose views on psychoanalysis were generally sympathetic, proposed that in societies like the Trobrianders', castration anxiety, penis envy and the entire Oedipus complex simply do not exist (see Malinowski, 1922/1961, 1927). Freudian theory of personality development, he contended, is the product of a particular cultural and family organization, specific to his cultural milieu. Ernest Jones, Freud's English disciple and biographer, and other anthropologically versed psychoanalysts countered that the Oedipus complex is universal (even the Trobrianders have prohibitions against mother–son incest), even though it may assume different forms in different cultures.

Malinowski's charge of the cultural limitations of psychoanalytic theory has more recently been taken up by feminist critics, such as Betty Friedan:

> Freud, it is generally agreed, was a most perceptive and accurate observer of important problems of the human personality. But in describing and interpreting these problems, he was a prisoner of his own culture. As he was creating a new framework for our culture, he could not escape the framework of his own. (Friedan, 1965: 93)

Freud's defenders have, in different ways, countered that, far from being a prisoner of his culture, he managed to get to the heart of all culture and its effects on individuals. Feminist defenders of psychoanalytic theory, like Juliet Mitchell, have argued that 'matrilineages only present us with a variation on the theme of the law-of-the-father' (Mitchell, 1974: 415); Freud's theories will continue to hold as long as societies are expressions of the father's law. Herbert Marcuse, the radical social philosopher and guru of the 1960s' youth movement, argued that 'behind all the differences among the historical forms of society, Freud saw the basic inhumanity common to all of them, and the repressive controls which perpetuate, in the instinctual structure itself, the domination of man by man' (1955: 235).

The debate regarding the cultural specificity of psychoanalytic theories has been polarized in doctrinaire invective. Who is right and who is wrong totally obscures the issues which demand elucidation and understanding. Yet critics and defenders of the psychoanalytic approach converge on the same point, without acknowledging it in their opponents. Cultures differ in the specific demands that they make on individuals, on the discontents they inflict and the consolations that they provide. But beyond idealized golden ages and future utopias, there are no cultures which can spare individuals misfortune and suffering. What is vital is to establish the ways in which specific cultural attributes become embedded in the mental personality; how, in other words, each culture becomes part of the mental life, conscious and unconscious, of individuals. This is an undertaking in which psychoanalytic writers have made considerable contributions.

PSYCHOANALYSIS AND FASCISM

In discussing fascism and Nazism, for instance, psychoanalytically informed writers have argued that these phenomena were not merely political or economic, as historians or political theorists argue. Fascism was under-written by a type of personality which has some very specific traits. In this way, fascism was a cultural and political as well as a psychological phenomenon. In his pioneering book *The Mass Psychology of Fascism*, Wilhelm Reich argued that the family was the true factory of German fascism. Reich, a Marxist and psychoanalyst of outstanding courage and originality, argued that, under 'authoritarian patriarchy', the family exercises an asphyxiating sexual repression on children, which

> makes the child afraid, shy, fearful of authority, obedient, 'good', and 'docile' in the authoritarian sense of the words. It has a crippling effect on man's rebellious forces because every vital life-impulse is burdened with severe fear; and since sex is a forbidden subject, thought in general and man's critical faculty also becomes inhibited. In short, morality's aim is to produce acquiescent subjects who, despite distress and humiliation, are adjusted to the authoritarian order. Thus, the family is the authoritarian state in miniature, to which the child must learn to adapt himself as a preparation for the general social adjustment required of him later. *Man's authoritarian structure* – this must be clearly established – *is basically produced by embedding of sexual inhibitions and fear in the living substance of sexual impulses*. (1970: 64)

Reich saw authoritarianism not as a healthy respect for authority but as the product of psychological crippling, by an authority which is divorced from love, rationality or concern for the other's well-being. In his opinion, the victims of authoritarianism, those psychologically crippled individuals, form the psychological infra-structure of fascism. This argument, that an oppressive social order becomes embedded in the human psyche, led him to conclude that human liberation requires not only a political revolution, but a personal one too; not only a socialist revolution, but also a sexual one. This view pleased neither his Marxist nor his psychoanalytical friends. He was forced to leave both the Communist Party and the Psychoanalytic Association in 1933, the same year Hitler came to power. His fundamental insight, however, that authoritarian, exploitative and exploited individuals are sexually repressed individuals has enormously deepened our comprehension of this most unfathomable, most atrocious, twentieth-century cultural phenomenon.

Authoritarianism

Reich's arguments on authoritarianism have received substantial support from the work of Adorno and his colleagues. Adorno, an eminent member of the Frankfurt School of Social Research, which pioneered attempts to integrate psychoanalysis with a humanist Marxism in the 1930s, was an émigré from Nazi Germany, who carried out research seeking to establish the psychological make-up of individuals holding racist beliefs and capable of racist violence. His research was part of the output of a department at the University of California at Berkeley, set up by the American Jewish Committee towards the end of the Second World War, led by Max Horkheimer, a fellow Frankfurt School theorist.

Adorno and his fellow workers carried out an extensive survey of over 2,000 individuals using a variety of mostly empiricist research techniques, including interviews, questionnaires, thematic appreciation tests (TAT), as well as clinical techniques. Their findings were published in *The Authoritarian Personality* (Adorno et al., 1950) which identified clusters of mental attributes correlating with racist beliefs. This study confirmed Reich's speculation that racism is the outcome of authoritarian personalities, which combine 'a mechanical surrender to conventional values; blind submission to authority together with blind hatred of all opponents and outsiders; anti-introspectiveness; rigid stereotyped thinking; a penchant for superstition; vilification, half-moralistic and half-cynical, of human nature, projectivity' (Horkheimer, 1950; quoted in Jay, 1973: 240). This research suggested that authoritarianism on a massive scale provided the psychological underpinning of fascism. It also supported 'the psychoanalytic axiom that the first social relationships to be observed within the family are, to a large extent, formative of attitudes in later life' (Adorno et al., 1950: 376).

Authoritarianism is transmitted intergenerationally as hyper-critical, disciplinarian parents, unable to display affection and love, weighed down by stereotypical thinking and conventionalism, ashamed about their own sexuality and that of others, reproduce these very same qualities in their children.

> The most crucial result of the present study ... is the demonstration of close correspondence in the type of approach and outlook a subject is likely to have in a great variety of areas, ranging from the most intimate features of family life and sex adjustments through relationships to other people in general, to religion and to social and political philosophy. Thus a basically hierarchical, authoritarian, exploitative parent–child relationship is apt to carry over into a power-oriented, exploitatively dependent attitude toward one's sex partner and one's God and may well culminate in a political philosophy and social outlook which has no room for anything but a desperate clinging to what appears to be strong and disdainful rejection of whatever is relegated to the bottom ... Conventionality, rigidity, repressive denial, and the ensuing break-through of one's weakness, fear and dependency are but other aspects of the same personality pattern, and they can be observed in personal life as well as in attitudes towards religion and social issues. (Adorno et al., 1950: 971)

The authors of *The Authoritarian Personality* also identified an 'anti-type', 'characterized chiefly by affectionate, basically egalitarian, and permissive interpersonal relationships' (1950: 971).

In a fascinating book called *On the Psychology of Military Incompetence*, Norman Dixon (1976) identified the familiar personality structure of authoritarianism in numerous military leaders, who distinguished themselves by their cruelty, their bloody-mindedness, their total disregard for common sense, and above all their ineptitude. Authoritarianism is a common affliction of military outfits. Dixon sees the authoritarian personality as having many of the character traits of the anal obsessive character (see Chapter 3); these become institutionalized in military hierarchies and ritually reinforced by the culture of most military organizations. Dixon singles out one of the traits of the Berkeley research for special attention, the 'vilification of the human':

> This was the trait which was manifested to such an extreme degree by the members of the Nazi SS that they could commit wholesale murder, not just without guilt or shame but, perhaps more surprisingly, without the slightest evidence of revulsion. This cool detachment and complete incapacity for empathy with other human beings was not only reflected in the bleakly unemotional title for their task – 'the final solution' – but also a sine qua non of its tidy execution. At first sight, this mixture of brutality and bureaucracy is strange to say the least. After all, it is one thing to shoot helpless prisoners in the back ... but quite another to plan such operations down to the minutest detail, to make ledger entries of hair and calcium, wigs and artificial limbs; to stack corpses and extract the gold from their teeth. In fact, of course, this horrific concatenation of traits is an extreme example of the relationship between ... authoritarianism and the anal obsessive personality. (Dixon, 1976: 275)

THE MALE FIGHTING BAND

Lawrence Rosenthal

Lawrence Rosenthal makes a strong case for the fact that authoritarianism, at least in the variant that is associated with fascism, entailed a large measure of both collectivism (the idealization of the male fighting band) and heroism (the rejection of political process in favour of direct action). It also represented a rebellion against the civic individualism which underpins conventional democratic politics, a politics viewed by the authoritarian fascists as irrevocably tainted, emasculated and corrupt.

As the Frankfurt School established, the authoritarian personality is a type that appears in many societies. In a sociological sense, it represents a potential available to be tapped by political movements of a similarly authoritarian character. Reich's seminal work on the authoritarian personality was an account of the rise and appeal of fascism, which flourished in Europe between the two world wars. No subsequent authoritarian movements in the West have managed to equal fascism's feat of mass organizing. Another look at fascism's rise can help specify the conditions needed to activate the authoritarian potential Reich discovered to the level of mass political participation.

The first condition needed is great social disruption and displacement. Dwarfing anything the world had seen before, the First World War caused the combatant nations of Europe to conscript millions and millions of men. This meant tapping huge numbers from what sociologists call the 'traditional' sectors of society – those sectors not yet caught up in the industrial world. Men from the countryside were one prime example, men whose lives till then promised to be essentially similar to the lives their fathers had led, and their grandfathers before them. Beyond the family, these men would intersect with a small number of institutions in their lives: the church, the landlord, perhaps a school. They would work hard with their hands, in the fields or a trade, marry from within the village, speak a dialect understood only in their province, and perhaps not understand the national language – German or Italian, for example. They might never travel more than a village or two away from home, and their relationship to their nation-states would be abstract and far away, as if to a foreign country.

Suddenly, millions of these men, still youths, were ripped from their villages, and thrown in with fellows from throughout the nation. In this perverse cosmopolitanism, they were in a fundamental way closer, more intimate, with these fellows than with anyone back home: they depended on one another for their very lives. The young men died in huge numbers, often after months of unfathomable miseries in the trenches. They were maimed in huge numbers. When the war was over, both the villages they had come from and they themselves were altered in ways that could never be undone. Traditional roles no longer existed as they had. The returning veterans could not fit back into civilian life.

Fascism as a political movement was made up almost entirely of war veterans. Fascist movements offered them something to repair their displacement, and this was the secret of fascism's success in mass organizing. It offered a new and suitable community, an alternative community, for men whose traditional communities were shattered by the war and subsequent social disruption. This alternative community can be called the 'male fighting band'.

What did it mean to be a fascist in, say, the Po Valley in Italy in late 1921? It meant to dress in a black-shirted uniform, assemble with your fellows at night, ride a truck to another village, lynch the socialist mayor, pour castor oil down the throats of officers and members of labour unions. As a new social organizing principle, the male fighting band not only replaced traditional communities in post-war life, it made sense of life for men whose own identities were now tied to their experience in war.

Perhaps above all else, fascism was the discovery that the wartime camaraderie of the trenches could be transferred to a political movement. Such a movement would have some quite particular characteristics. Rigid hierarchy would be one – a clear sense of who was above you, who was to be obeyed, and who could be ordered about. Demands for loyalty would be another, and they would be uncommonly demanding. Members would be judged against a scale of heroic action. Heroism, the doing of daring deeds, is the moral coin of the realm of the male fighting band, conferring prestige and honour which, like capital, could be hoarded, invested, spent, squandered.

At the top of the heroic heap was the leader, a man so revered, a hero so great, that his followers believed his very presence was like a gift from providence. His was the appearance of a man with superhuman qualities, the agent of deliverance. He confirmed the historical rightness of what the movement stood for, which otherwise was ill-defined. He was a lightning rod for the emotional transformations his followers experienced in their new communities. Dispossession turned into entitlement. Resentment of those with power and position and jobs turned into contempt for them and their ways. They needed to be swept away.

From the point of view of politics, perhaps the most significant novelty introduced by fascism's male fighting bands was the transformation of the political opposition into an enemy. This freed fascism to engage in politics in the way most suited to the male fighting band – as a paramilitary force. Importing the tactics and mentality of war into the wholly unprepared parliamentary arena was politics by blackmail: either we get our way or we will beat you and kill you in the streets till you cry uncle.

All organizations contain components of structure and community. By structure, we refer to the goals of the organization and the rules and procedures devised to accomplish its goals. By community, or the organizational 'culture', we refer to the social relations that grow up among organization members as they carry out their assigned roles. In most formal organizations, and certainly in political parties, structure has primacy over community. Take fascism's opposition, the socialist and communist parties. People joined those parties because of belief in their goals: the advancement of the industrial working class. The community one felt part of in these parties flowed from this goal-orientation. Fascism reversed the primacy of organizational structure over community in the political party. Men joined for the community, to belong to the male fighting band, to participate in the band's 'expeditions'. What the expeditions accomplished was secondary to the action itself.

In the end, the male fighting band, like the authoritarian personality, is a sociological potential. It is a principle available for organizing collective behaviour in many different times and places. Fascism seized on both the authoritarian personality and the male fighting band community to build the most aggressive political movement in the twentieth century Western world, fusing a political party with a paramilitary organization. In less trying times authoritarian personalities are expressed in prosaic activities. So, too, the male fighting band can lay low. Functioning institutions, and their attendant social relations, keep it in check. But when institutions fail, and its members are cast adrift in large numbers, the male fighting band has the capacity to make many feel it is the ticket to right what has gone awry.

Authoritarianism, in this conception, is a cultural–psychological complex which may account for both brutalism and bureaucracy, the hottest, most abhorrent violence combined with the coldest, most dispassionate calculation. How does the authoritarian personality relate to the character types identified in Chapter 3? As Dixon indicates, the obsession with order, the preoccupation with cleanliness and purity in matters sexual, racial and physical and the sadistic qualities of the authoritarian personality indicate that it grows out of the obsessive character structure, as identified in Chapter 3. However, simple equations of psychological character structures with socio-cultural personality types are misleading. While authoritarianism entails pronounced anal obsessive characteristics it cannot be reduced to them. This would make authoritarianism a pre-Oedipal psychological configuration, something that flies in the face of the distorted relation with authority, which gives this personality type its name.

The concept of authoritarianism, a creative amalgam of psychoanalysis, empiricism and democratic ideology, assumed much importance in the 1950s and 1960s. One of the earliest modifications to Adorno's conception was to postulate an authoritarianism of the 'left' on a par with fascist authoritarianism. This was soon commandeered by Cold War rhetoric to demonstrate the supposed superiority, both technical and moral, of the Free World's democratic values over the authoritarian values represented by the Soviet Union and its allies. Management education in the West extolled the values of openness, teamwork, human relations and self-realization, even as assembly lines consigned large numbers of employees to working lives of stultifying boredom.

Motivation as surrogate for meaning

Throughout the quarter of a century following the publication of *The Authoritarian Personality*, one of the most popular topics of organizational theory was referred to as 'motivation theory'. To this day, the motivation theories of Abraham Maslow, Frederick Herzberg, Douglas McGregor and others continue to haunt introductory organization behaviour textbooks, like ghosts from a bygone era, stubbornly refusing to leave the scene. Generations of managers were tutored on the merits of theory Y, of a highly motivated workforce and of human relations at the workplace. Yet, at the same time, mass production technologies and vast impersonal hierarchies drained work of its meaning, its fulfilment of human needs and its ability to express human creativity. This is the period described by Gabriel and Lang (1995) as the high-noon of the Fordist deal, the implicit bargain of well-paid, though meaningless jobs in exchange for a quiescent labour force. Never before had living standards improved so rapidly; never before had work, whether in offices, factory floors or public spaces, been depersonalized and dehumanized to such an extent.

The promise of the Fordist deal was to compensate for the meaninglessness of work through the rich meanings springing to life from commodities. Television sets, motor-cars and all the comforts of suburban living, rather than the old values of creative work and achievement, were the new carriers of personal and social meaning, identity and prestige. Yet, while employees appeared to embrace the Fordist deal at least as far as spending was concerned, they never seemed to deliver their part of their bargain with great enthusiasm. This is where motivation theory came in. As long as the Protestant work ethic, hunger and fear delivered a hard-working workforce no one had thought of turning motivation into a science. But in the 1950s and 1960s the time was ripe to bring science into such questions as: 'What makes people tick?' 'How can the worker's or the manager's appetite for work be enhanced?' 'What motivates people at the workplace?'

To their credit, most psychoanalysts did not join the pursuit of the psychological chimera of those decades – the key to how to motivate workers. The resulting motley of ideas and theories, endlessly promising, yet endlessly flawed, endlessly criticized, yet endlessly reproduced, owe little to depth psychology. (By contrast, there were attempts to recruit psychoanalysis to the cause of deciphering and taking advantage of the consumer's motivation; these were not altogether fruitless, though their success is often exaggerated.) One of the most powerful critiques of these motivation theorists has been offered by Burkard Sievers, whose arguments will lead us to the psychoanalytic study of contemporary culture.

Sievers (1986, 1994) argues that the motivational theories of the 1950s and 1960s were built on a number of assumptions, whose interest lies not in the fact that they are invalid, but in the fact that they reveal the deeper rationale of the theories themselves. These theories focused on the micro-perspective and favoured causal explanations, treating human beings essentially as mechanical entities to be driven by pushing a simple button or two. Human beings are seen in static, non-developmental terms, as though they had neither personal histories nor social attachments. The theories have no real interest in learning and development. The question of what drives human action is of interest only in as much as it may be applied by managers as a substitute to power and coercion. Organizations themselves are seen in narrow instrumental terms, where rational means are deployed to maximize output. Finally, despite their concern for supposed universal truths, these motivation theories are surprisingly naïve about culture and politics; in fact, they are hardly theories at all, but rather 'an expression of the extreme individualism, self-interest and masculinity that are characteristics of American culture' (Sievers, 1994: 7).

These theories are themselves, therefore, cultural artefacts and legitimate targets for interpretation. Sievers (1986, 1994: 9) offers the hypothesis that:

> motivation only became an issue – for management and organization theories as well as for the organization of work itself – when meaning disappeared or was lost from work; that the loss of meaning of work is immediately connected with the increasing amount of fragmentation and splitting in the way work has been and is still organized in the majority of our western enterprises. In consequence, motivation theories have become surrogates for the search for meaning.

Drawing on formulations from numerous psychoanalytic and non-psychoanalytic writers, Sievers builds considerable support for his hypothesis. The need to 'motivate' is not a property of human beings but the product of deskilling, fragmenting and alienating organizations. 'It seems as if management were saying to the workers: "If you don't know why you are doing what you are doing, we'll give you good reasons. And these reasons are good because science offers sufficiently convincing models and explanations to let your actions appear meaningful!"' (1994: 28). Managers, then, according to this formulation, emerge unconsciously as 'merchandisers of meaning', whose attempts at creating meaning are futile as long as the deeper questions of life and death, creation and destruction remain unanswered.

CULTURE AND NARCISSISM

As we enter the period variously referred to as post-industrial, late capitalist or postmodern, the fragmentation of social values and the general erosion of meaning structures become exacerbated. Sievers himself notes that the fragmentation of meaning structures between work and leisure activities (the fundamental consequence of the Fordist deal) has devastating consequences for meaning in general. 'The meaning of work one does and the meaning of one's life cannot be regarded as two pairs of shoes for different occasions' (Sievers, 1994: 33).

If organizational theorists, like Sievers, have studied in considerable depth the destruction of meaning at the workplace, social commentators have addressed the same issue at the social level and many of them have reached an even more pessimistic view. Postmodern writers, like Baudrillard, have gone as far as to argue that Western culture has become one of simulacra, full of images and totally empty of meaning. The television commercial serves as an archetypal illustration of the point. It presents a commodity, a perfume, a brand of beer or a motor-car, in a way which the contemporary viewer recognizes as unreal, yet in a vital way it is more real than reality. Television personalities are more real than the anonymous faces which we encounter in the flesh. What is real about contemporary political or cultural events are the images which are carried on television screens, printed media or the Internet rather than the lived experience of individuals. In a world increasingly dominated by image, signifiers (whether they be material objects, politicians or other 'personalities', organizations, causes or public issues) become spasmodic transmitters of transient meanings which no sooner reach consciousness than they are overwhelmed by the clutter that surrounds them.

In such a cultural context, the arguments of earlier psychoanalytic commentators regarding disciplinarian parenting, a ruthless super-ego, guilt and authoritarianism begin to look out of date. Many of the psychopathologies associated with asphyxiating cultural controls, like those which preoccupied Freud and the first generation of analysts, notably transference neuroses and especially hysteria, have declined. Instead, a new type of psychological disorder, associated with feelings of emptiness, meaninglessness and depression, have become much more prominent.

The psychoanalytic concept which has assumed pivotal importance, both in accounting for individual disorders and, more generally, for explaining numerous contemporary cultural phenomena has been *narcissism*. In his seminal book *The Culture of Narcissism* (1980), the American cultural historian Christopher Lasch has argued that contemporary culture breeds a new psychological personality, the narcissistic one, whose primary characteristics include 'a dependence on the vicarious warmth provided by others combined with a fear of dependence, a sense of inner emptiness, boundless repressed rage, and unsatisfied oral cravings' (1980: 33). At the conceptual level, narcissism performs a similar function in linking personality structures with socio-political configurations as authoritarianism did for the previous generation of psychoanalytic discussions. Narcissism has also come to the forefront of debates on the qualities and pathologies of today's organizations and some of these will be discussed in Chapter 8. But, above all, narcissism appears to have captured the spirit of an age preoccupied with images and consumption, an age which has become disillusioned with politics, religion and science as forces of social progress, and above all an age obsessed with intimacy and approval, yet fearful of emotional commitment and responsibility.

If authoritarianism presented an image of selfhood almost obliterated by culture, drawing its content from social and political ideologies, narcissism represents an uncoupling of social and personal meanings. For the narcissistic personality, living in a constantly shrinking public world, a world devoid of meaning and value, identity becomes an all-consuming yet ultimately futile preoccupation.

> The 'authoritarian personality' no longer represents the prototype of the economic man. Economic man himself has given way to the psychological man of our times – the final product of bourgeois individualism. The new narcissist is haunted not by guilt but by anxiety. He seeks not to inflict his own uncertainties on others but to find a meaning in life. Liberated from the superstitions of the past, he doubts even the reality of his own existence. Superficially relaxed and tolerant, he finds little use in dogmas of racial and ethnic purity but at the same time forfeits the security of group loyalties and regards everyone as a rival for the favors conferred by a paternalistic state. (Lasch, 1980: xvi)

Unlike Narcissus, his mythological counterpart, the contemporary narcissist is not lost in self-love but depends on an admiring audience. This is something which contemporary culture stubbornly denies anyone without a 'celebrity' status. Building on work by Kernberg, Kohut, Grunberger, Laplanche and others, Lasch argues that contemporary narcissism should not be mistaken for selfishness or egoism. Referring to Sennett's (1977) arguments, Lasch contends that, unlike selfishness, narcissism 'has more in common with self-hatred than with self-admiration' (1980: 31). This self-hatred is the result of the narcissist's disturbing inability to love him or herself, the way he or she believes he or she should be loved, narcissist's inability to drive his or her ego into the space occupied by his or her ego-ideal.

In Lasch's view, the ego-ideal is as crucial a psychic agency for the narcissist as the super-ego is for the authoritarian. The distinction of the ego-ideal from the super-ego has been the focus of important theoretical work carried out by Janine Chasseguet-Smirgel and her husband Bela Grunberger into the nature of narcissism.

> It is noteworthy that a fundamental difference exists between the ego ideal, inheritor of primary narcissism, and the superego, inheritor of the Oedipus complex. At least initially, the former is an attempt to repossess the lost omnipotence. The latter, in a Freudian perspective, stems from the castration complex. The first tends to restore illusion, the second to promote reality. (Chasseguet-Smirgel, 1976: 358)

The ego-ideal represents an attempt to recreate, in later life, the condition of primary narcissism, the period of our infancy when we imagined ourselves the centre of a loving and admiring world. This primary narcissism is doomed to receive numerous blows, starting with the realization that the world is generally not a loving place and that, contrary possibly to the impression created by our mother, we are not its centre (Freud, 1914a; Schwartz, 1990: 17ff). We may still cling to the fantasy that we are unique and special, but this too will receive a cruel blow during our first encounters with schools and other impersonal organizations, which consign us to the status of a number on a register (Mannoni, 1971; Gabriel, 1993). Thereafter, we discover that admiration is hard to come by and love even harder. With every injury to our narcissism, the need to erect an ego-ideal becomes more pressing. The ego-ideal, then, emerges as a wishful fantasy of ourselves as we wish to be in order to become once more the centre of an admiring and loving world.

> What man projects before him as his ideal is the substitute for the lost narcissism of his childhood in which he was his own ideal . . . To this ideal ego is now directed the self-love which the real ego enjoyed in childhood. The narcissism seems to be now displaced on to this new ideal ego, which, like the infantile ego, deems itself the possessor of all perfections. (Freud, 1914a: 94)

NARCISSISM AND CONSUMPTION

At times our ego-ideal merges with our ego; these are moments of triumph and joy when admiration and love is lavished on us, either for our individual achievements or for the achievements of groups, organizations or cultures with which we identify. Traditional cultures supported individual ego-ideals with cultural ideals, powerful role models and overbearing symbols. Members of religious or political sects, today, may derive total narcissistic fulfilment through their membership of these organizations, which promise them not only omnipotence and salvation but also immortality in one form or another. For the rest of us, however, the ego-ideal presents much more of a problem. As Gabriel and Lang (1995: 85) have argued:

> Contemporary culture not only exacerbates the need for an ego-ideal by inflicting numerous injuries to our narcissism, but it also places formidable obstacles to its formation. Gone are the days of sweeping cultural ideals and moral certainties. Gone are the powerful role models, untouched by scandal and corruption. Gone are the stirring symbols. Gone too are the great cultural accomplishments, artistic, scientific or military, in which we may take unalloyed pride. In a world where heroes are forever cut to size and perfection remains elusive, the gleaming surfaces of material goods, their pristine packaging and virginal existence inevitably attract our attention, even before the image makers get down to work.

The world of objects, then, material and human, appears to hold the promise of delivery to our ailing narcissism. A riot of consumption reflects the vain hope of bridging the distance between the actual and the ideal. 'If only I could buy that car I would be what I would ideally like to be.' The car becomes a phantasy bridging the actual and the ideal. The less accessible the car, the greater the promise it holds. As focal point of a phantasy, the longed-for car becomes a magnet for displaced meaning; the flawlessness of the paintwork, the power inside the bonnet, the overwhelming sense of perfection which it radiates, are thinly disguised narcissistic delusions transferred on to the idealized object. Once acquired, the object may at least temporarily act as a powerful narcissistic booster. Grown-up men have been known to cry in the arms of their mothers, on seeing a tiny scratch on that gleaming bodywork. In such cases, the car is incorporated in the ego-ideal, its every problem experienced as a personal inadequacy. In as much as it provides a reason for self-love and the respect of others, such an object can be said to support the consumer's identity quite effectively. Yet, as McCracken (1990: 112) argues, once acquired, often at considerable sacrifice, the spell of the commodity is exposed to falsification:

> The possession of objects that serve as bridges to displaced meaning is perilous. Once possessed these objects can begin to collapse the distance between an individual and his/her ideals. When a 'bridge' is purchased, the owner has begun to run the risk of putting the displaced meaning to empirical test.

Once the fantasy built around the product has accepted the test of reality, its value to the ego-ideal decreases; almost invariably, it is bound to be found lacking, not because the product is not good, but because such extraordinary expectations had been built on it. A new fantasy will already start to develop around some new product.

Behind the consumer's quest for identity lurk more fundamental cravings for respect and self-love, born out of the injuries that contemporary modern life inflicts on us. These generate anxieties which cannot be allayed by image alone or narratives spun around commodities; they demand far more radical measures. These anxieties are the result of injuries sustained by our narcissism, whose healing requires nothing less than the formation of an idealized fantasy of the self, an ego-ideal, commanding admiration, respect and self-love. In a culture shorn of role models and ideals, consumerism throws up ephemeral images to identify with (pop stars, sports people, TV celebrities) and a promise of boosting our ego-ideals by proffering commodities around which fantasies of perfection, beauty and power may be built. These fantasies are wish-fulfilments which transform mundane, everyday objects into highly charged symbols.

How successful is consumerism as the means of restoring our ailing narcissism? Cultural critics like Christopher Lasch are in no doubt that consumerism merely reinforces the discontents for which it promises consolations. Individuals become constantly more insecure and image-conscious, looking at themselves in mirrors.

> A culture organized around mass consumption encourages narcissism – which [we] can define, for the moment, as a disposition to see the world as a mirror, more particularly as a projection of one's own fears and desires – not because it makes people grasping and self-assertive but because it makes them weak and dependent. (Lasch, 1980: 33)

In a subsequent work, Lasch argued that Western consumerism, sustained by mass production and celebrated in the mass media, amounts to a mechanism of addiction.

> 'Shop till you drop.' Like exercise, it often seems to present itself as a form of therapy, designed to restore a sense of wholeness and well-being after long hours of unrewarding work. 'I feel like hell and I go out for a run, and before I know it, everything's OK.' Shopping serves the same purpose: 'It hardly matters what I buy, I just get a kick out of buying. It's like that first whiff of cocaine. It's euphoric and I just get higher and higher as I buy.' (Lasch, 1991: 521)

At this point, we rejoin the great Freudian theme of culture as the opiate of the people, reinforcing the very discontents for which it purports to offer consolations. A culture of narcissism may well mark the transcendence of sexual frustration and over-powering guilt; it may also mark the transcendence of traditional religious and political illusions, promising salvation. Instead, a culture of narcissism generates it own vicious circle of discontents and illusions.

Having turned the contemporary individual into an infinitely gullible and malleable consumer, unable to tolerate pain or generate joy, constantly preoccupied with the protection of his or her precarious self and in constant need of having his or her individuality and identity affirmed, capitalism consoles the consumer with what he or she needs – a world saturated with commodities and devoid of risk. Meaninglessness and insecurity may have replaced sexual frustration and guilt as the dominant modes of human discontents, yet the underlying situation has not changed: culture remains both the cause and the consolatory treatment of the disease called man (Gabriel, 1983: 259–60). As we shall see in Chapter 8, the study of culture, and phenomena such as authoritarianism and narcissism, are of great value in understanding organizational culture, its demands and offerings.

CONCLUSION

This chapter has explored the psychoanalytic study of culture and has highlighted certain key ideas. An understanding of culture is indispensable in understanding organizations, since organizations are dominant cultural institutions and have cultural properties of their own. Cultures embody systems of meaning and signification, which are expressed in cultural artefacts, such as material objects, myths, stories, rituals, traditions and so on. These cultural artefacts may be interpreted using a psychoanalytic technique similar to that used for interpreting dreams, which enables us to reach at their underlying symbolism. Psychoanalytic interpretations of cultural products reveal a partly antagonistic relation between individual and culture, where the individual both suffers from culturally inflicted discontents but also enjoys consolations and narcissistic satisfactions provided by culture. Culture provides consolations for the discontents it causes, yet in doing so it deepens these discontents. Different cultures generate distinct configurations of character structures. Fascism, for example, was substantially sustained by the authoritarian personality. Contemporary Western culture favours the narcissistic personality, characterized by inner emptiness, need for reassurance and anxiety over an inability to create a meaningful world with which to establish relations.

8 ORGANIZATIONAL CULTURE

The view that Western culture is in its very essence an organizational culture seems commonplace. Organizations dominate every aspect of social life in Western societies. This chapter explores a somewhat more paradoxical view: that organizations themselves can and must be studied as cultures. This view was at the core of organizational discourses and debates throughout the 1980s and 1990s, forcing a radical re-thinking of the nature of organizations, the demands they make on us and the different ways in which they affect our lives. As Chapter 7 showed, psychoanalysis has, since its early days, offered numerous insights into the interplay between culture and the individual. Some of these insights may be extended to the study of organizational cultures and the relationship between individuals and their organizations. Yet, while the literature on organizational culture has flourished, psychoanalytic contributions have been scarce. This chapter seeks to explore some of the possibilities and establish bridges between psychoanalysis and existing traditions of research in this field.

THE CURRENT POPULARITY OF ORGANIZATIONAL CULTURE

The idea that organizations are cultural phenomena has only recently been taken up systematically by researchers. Most older academic traditions of organizations were profoundly anti-cultural. They approached organizations as forces opposed to culture, rather than forms of culture. Organizational theory itself grew as a by-product of an idea of modernity, in which the actions of men and women were related to rationality, calculation and profit rather than cultural values and norms, meanings and symbolism. Modernity and its chief representatives, science, the state, business enterprises and organizations of all forms, were seen as sweeping away cultural forms from bygone ages, such as folklore, rituals, superstitions, kinship systems, ceremonies and so on. Knowledge rather than belief, calculation rather than emotion, interest rather than commitment, were seen as the forces behind modernity by the founding theorists of the social sciences, Adam Smith, Karl Marx and Auguste Compte. Max Weber, who viewed bureaucracy as the core institution of modernity, portrayed it as a symbolically emaciated institution, part of what he saw as the 'disenchantment of the world'. Organizations, in this view, were 'anti-cultures', uniquely modern collectivities quite unlike families, clans, communities, crowds, tribes, cults or sects.

Interest in organizational culture was kindled by the rise of Japan as an industrial superpower. By the 1970s, it had become clear that Japanese companies were outperforming their Western counterparts in many different sectors. Looking for the secret of Japanese success, the Weberian theory of bureaucracy, its off-shoots and most management theory proved of little help. Several early studies of Japanese management concluded that the decisive reason for the Japanese advance lay not in technology or structure but in Japanese culture and the way this is embedded in Japanese companies (see Ouchi, 1981; Pascale and Athos, 1981).

Subsequent discussions of Japanese organizations have moved away from simple explanations of their economic success in terms of their culture. Structural and technical factors, such as 'lean production', flexible production techniques, the reduction of inventories and close relations with suppliers (Womack et al., 1990), as well as Japan's institutional and educational set-ups have come into prominence. More recently, much emphasis has been paid to the ability of Japanese organizations continuously to generate new knowledge and innovation (Kenney and Florida, 1993; Nonaka and Takeuchi, 1995). Culturalist explanations of Japanese success have come to seem increasingly naïve, not least in the light of the subsequent ups and down in the Japanese economy (see Wilkinson et al., 1995; Wilkinson, 1996). In spite of such developments, the study of Japanese organizations has highlighted the importance of the cultural dimensions of organizations:

1 Organizations operate within a national culture, whose values and norms crucially affect the orientations and attitudes of employees towards their work and their employers.
2 People's actions within organizations are not purely instrumental, based on calculation and utility, but can be value- and norm-driven.
3 Organizations, like nations, have distinct cultures, with specific symbols, values and norms. Becoming a member of an organization implies a process of socialization, analogous to becoming a member of a society.
4 Like societies, organizations do not have fully homogeneous cultures but are composed of overlapping and fragmented symbolic clusters, including sub-cultures and counter-cultures. Some organizational cultures are more uniform than others.

From the 1980s, organizational culture became a very fashionable topic among organizational scholars. Cultural concepts, such as stories, symbols, rituals, ceremonies and legends, were used extensively in analysing and understanding organizations. In addition, there was a concerted attempt to promote organizational culture as the key to corporate success and failure. 'Bureaucracy is dead! The future belongs to those with strong cultures' proclaimed numerous management best-sellers. For a period in the 1980s organizational culture was presented as a management panacea; a strong culture was the royal road to 'excellence'. 'Strong culture' implies strong commitment to a set of shared values and meanings. Management gurus argued that, while many companies may claim to possess such values, few are genuinely committed to them. The majority take a short-term view, opting for 'quick-fix' solutions; they easily compromise their values in the interest of profit or become fixated on quantifiable objectives, like sales growth, earnings per share or profit. Employees soon lose sight of the company's values or become disenchanted as they realize that the company preaches one thing and practices another. The genuinely excellent companies, on the other hand, display real commitment to values such as service to the customer, technological innovation, superior quality and care for their employees, even when these values do not accord with short-term financial expedience. The roles of leaders and managers were accordingly redefined as people who, among other things, guide, fashion and manage an organization's culture.

THE CULTURE OF JAPANESE ORGANIZATIONS

Japanese companies recruit staff for life-time employment. They progress slowly through company hierarchy mainly on the basis of seniority, following non-specialized career paths. Organizational controls are frequently informal with relatively few rules and regulations, but a strong sense of group responsibility and collective decision-making. The work life and home life of Japanese workers are strongly integrated. Workers often live in company-owned houses, shopping in company-owned shops. If the company as a machine has dominated the thinking of Western managers, the company as an extended family is of paramount importance in the minds of Japanese managers. Akio Morita, the founder of Sony, one of the world's most successful companies writes:

> One old style of management that is still being practiced by many companies in the United States and by some in Japan is based on the idea that the company that is successful is one that can produce the conventional product most efficiently at cheaper cost. Efficiency, in this system, becomes a god. Ultimately, it means that machinery is everything, and the ideal factory is a perfectly automated one, perhaps one that is unmanned. This machinelike management is a management of dehumanization. (1987: 185)

Morita's own assessment of the success of Japanese companies is clear:

> There is no secret ingredient or hidden formula responsible for the success of the best Japanese companies. No theory or plan or government policy will make a business a success; that can only be done by people. The most important mission for a Japanese manager is to develop a healthy relationship with his employees, to create a familylike feeling within the corporation, a feeling that employees and managers share the same fate . . . The emphasis on people must be genuine and sometimes very bold and daring, and it can even be quite risky. (Morita, 1987: 130–1)

The Japanese stress on unity is no mere rhetoric or rationalization but a core value to which even profit, efficiency and rationality must be subordinated. Morita again:

> Americans pride themselves on being rational in their business judgements: the total logic of the American business schools seems to be cold, deemphasizing the human element. We in Japan see the bases for success in business and industry differently. We believe that if you want high efficiency and productivity, a close cordial relationship with your employees, which leads to high morale, is necessary. Sometimes it is more important to generate a sense of affinity than anything else, and sometimes you must make decisions that are, technically, irrational. You can be totally rational with a machine. But if you work with people, sometimes logic often has to take a backseat to understanding. (1987: 202)

Looking more closely into the management of Japanese companies, Western writers were shocked by what they saw as the unreasonable demands made by Japanese companies on their employees. Far from just 'doing a job', Japanese employees were expected to adopt their company's philosophy and closely identify with its products, its principles and its values. Matsushita Electric Company, Japan's largest electrical firm, derives its company philosophy from the seven 'spiritual' values developed by its founder. These are:

- National service through industry
- Fairness
- Harmony and cooperation
- Struggle for betterment
- Courtesy and humility
- Adjustment and assimilation
- Gratitude

Commenting on Matsushita, Pascale and Athos (1981: 50) write:

> The Matsushita philosophy provides a basis of meaning beyond the products it produces. Matsushita was the first company in Japan to have a song and a code of values. 'It seems silly to Westerners,' says one executive, 'but every morning at 8:00 a.m. all across Japan, there are 87,000 people reciting the code of values and singing together. It's like we are all a community.' Matsushita foresaw that a lifetime's organizational experience shapes one's character indelibly. It was unthinkable, in his view, that work, which occupies at least half of our working hours, should be denied its powerful role. The firm, therefore, had an inescapable responsibility to help the employees' inner selves.

Culture raised many hopes for both theorists of organizations and practising managers. As a catch-all solution to the problems of management, culture has disappointed. It soon became apparent that, like earlier and subsequent management panaceas, organizational culture was ineffective, confusing and self-contradictory. More recent research continues to link culture and performance, although a simple connection between the two is not tenable (Denison, 1990; Bate, 1994). Yet, if the study of organizational culture has not produced the practical recipes for which many managers were yearning, it has made significant contribution to the study of organizations and to the practice of some managers. It enabled theorists to observe and analyse phenomena that had remained previously invisible and it has forced managers, especially those at the top, to rethink their own role within organizations. Above all, it has enhanced a concept of organizations as less unique, less distinct and less modern than earlier images. Organizations may indeed be different from crowds, families and groups but, like them, they harbour irrational forces, they fulfil emotional needs, they evolve in a more organic, more random and less controlled manner than was previously envisaged.

ORGANIZATIONAL SOCIALIZATION

One of the first consequences of approaching organizations as cultures is that the fundamental relation between the individual and his or her organization must be redefined. At the core of this relationship is neither a free contract (Weber), nor a bond of oppression and exploitation (Marx). Instead, the relation between individual and organization evolves as a complex and dynamic process of socialization. Through this process, the values and beliefs of individuals are transformed by their involvement with organizations.

Cultural approaches to the study of organizations suggest that entering an organization is in some ways similar to visiting a new country; one sees a lot of unfamiliar things and many familiar things have unfamiliar meanings. Making sense of things is difficult; getting simple things done is difficult. If mailing a letter in a foreign country can be a difficult operation for the first-time visitor, obtaining a computer password can be a daunting task for a new organizational recruit. The first few days and weeks in a new organization are days of learning and absorbing, as well as 'unlearning' past assumptions.

This process of organizational socialization, i.e. of assimilating an organization's culture and becoming part of it, takes place through a sequence of sanctions, pressures and rewards, similar to those of childhood socialization. An employee who infringes organizational norms is made aware of it through direct or subtle pressures. Initiation rites are not uncommon for recruits to new organizations, from police academies to business organizations, from schools to college fraternities and sororities. This is how Kelvin, a trainee accountant with an accounting company, described an incident which occurred shortly after he had started work:

> That morning, my train arrived late at the station. I sprinted to the office (annoying several shoppers and getting rather hot in the process!). I was an hour and a half late for work. Having composed myself and my 'sorry I am late speech', I entered my department to deliver it to my senior manager. He looked at me sternly and instructed me to see Lynn Taylor (a partner's secretary) in order to sign the 'Late Book'. For a moment, I felt angry, tempted to retort 'Don't be ridiculous, I'm at work, not at school', but I controlled myself and gullibly followed my superior's instructions.
>
> I soon discovered that I was the subject of a practical joke – the 'Late Book' did not exist, and I was met with much good-humoured laughter when I returned to my department. I soon learnt that the practical joke epitomized that open, informal management style of the organization, together with the light-hearted, humorous aspect of the office culture – practical jokes were a common, normal behaviour pattern aiding the cultivation of a friendly working environment. Despite the fact that the company exudes professional competence and seriousness to the client, the office culture was invariably friendly and informal.

Such initiation rites are organizational equivalents of the rites of passage which are a feature of every culture. A person crossing an important threshold, such as reaching adulthood, getting married or being accepted to a special group, must undergo some ceremonial trial. Likewise, new members of organizations must often prove themselves by passing a test. Initiation rites can be relatively innocuous or more severe. Kelvin's was a minor ordeal, which he survived by not blowing his cool. Yet socialization to a new culture, like all socialization, can be a painful and unpredictable process.

In a well-known article, Schein (1968/1988) argued that individuals respond to the socialization process in one of three ways:

1 *Conformity*: the individual accepts the organization's culture, absorbs its norms and values.
2 *Rebellion*: the individual rejects the organization's culture and rebels against it in tacit or overt ways.
3 *Creative individualism*: the individual selectively accepts and rejects the organization's culture, adapting it to his or her own personality.

The distinctions between the three are not so clear-cut. Creative individualism combines a quality of improvisation, a healthy scepticism concerning the rationality of organizational rules but also a deeper acceptance of the organization. It may lapse into conformity, token rebellion or may disintegrate into cynical detachment. Current organizational theory sees compliance and resistance not as opposites but as complementary. Individuals may be resisting even as they give all outward appearances of compliance. Orders, social norms and regulations may be obeyed in many different ways – with exaggerated zeal, grudgingly, ritualistically, inaccurately, sarcastically or, above all, inappropriately. In all such cases, a member of an organization may give the impression of conformity while simultaneously expressing opposition. But what are the psychological processes which characterize different responses to socialization?

One of the main psychoanalytic arguments presented in Chapter 7 is that individuals both submit to culture and also experience it as an alien external force. They submit to culture which offers them a set of consolations for the privations and hardships which they put up with. This proposition casts an illuminating light on the relations between individuals and their organizations. Depth psychologists use the concept of the ego-ideal to paint a richer picture of socialization. Through socialization, the individual becomes a part of the organization; but so, too, does the organization become part of the individual. At the heart of it is a deal. The organization offers individuals something of the power, the glamour and the glory which surrounds it. The size of its buildings, the gleaming surfaces of its products, the allure of its logos, the Olympian power of its leaders, these are qualities in which an individual can have a stake as soon as he or she joins. In exchange, the individual must compromise his or her freedom, work to someone else's orders, and espouse the organization's values and norms.

The transformation undergone by individuals as they join a new and prestigious organization can be spectacular. This is how a college senior described her interview and subsequent offer of a job by IBM.

> I went to the interview feeling nervous and intimidated. The company's reputation, its prestige and size made me feel small and insignificant. Those inside the company seemed to me like giants, ultra-clever, dynamic, invincible, incredibly privileged. Even the receptionist seemed to me almost super-human. I can hardly remember anything of the interview, other than it was one of the most concentrated experiences in my life. I do remember, however, the moment a couple of days later when I opened the letter with the offer of a job. Definitely one of the greatest moments of my life. I also remember the effect that it had on my classmates. They all seemed to take me more seriously than before, they wanted to be my friends, people who had hardly spoken to me during four years at college. In their eyes, I was a different person; I supposed that in my own eyes, too, I was a different person.

How can such a transformation be achieved? Schwartz (1987, 1990) has suggested that what we perceive as an organization's glamour and might becomes part of our ego-ideal once we see ourselves as part of it. He has proposed the concept of an organization-ideal, a complex set of idealized images, fantasies and illusions, with which we can identify, as long as we are part of this organization, thus enriching our own ego-ideal. The imagined perfection of the organization thus becomes our own attribute. The closer we identify with the organization, the closer our ego-ideal gets to the organization-ideal and the closer our ego gets to our ego-ideal, the greater the narcissistic satisfaction we derive. The argument exactly parallels Freud's (1914a) view that the great artistic, scientific and other achievements of our nation or culture offer us narcissistic satisfaction because we build our ego-ideal around these achievements as if they were our very own.

The organization, then, can act as the mother of an individual's fantasy, who is able to restore her children's narcissism simply because they are her children. Likewise, members of organizations can feel themselves to be invincible, omnipotent and even immortal simply because they are members. The organization will never die – hence those who believe in it will never die (Sievers, 1990, 1994). It is now possible to understand why organizations spend lavishly on the induction of their new members. New recruits are often flown to exotic destinations, housed in lavish hotels far beyond their private means and exposed to what is not so much a training programme as a regime of corporate fantasy. This is how a participant described his induction programme at Arthur Andersen and Co., professional services firm:

> The firm is very image-conscious, careful to promote itself both to its clients and its own staff. During my period of induction training, this image was constantly reiterated. Part of my seven-week induction programme was spent in a residential course in Segovia, Spain. Here the 'one firm' concept was everywhere. In evidence were AA & Co. mugs, stationery, sports equipment, even boxer shorts and T-shirts, everything bearing the logo 'AA & Co., the class of '89'. I must admit that this apparent indoctrination was beginning to worry me. After seven weeks, an off-hand comment made by a friend of mine who worked for another of the 'big eight' accountancy firms came to mind: 'They are a bloody good company, but beware of being turned into an Andersen Android.'

Similar stories by new recruits are often less critical, the young people being dazzled by the opulence, resources and style of their employer. The company's omnipresent logo appears to become embedded in the new member's unconscious, symbolizing everything that is good about the company. In such situations, psychoanalytic writers such as Levinson, Kets de Vries and Schwartz warn us, companies can be taken in by their own fantasies, imagining themselves to be invincible, infallible and immune to all threats. The result: organizational decay and even collapse. The individual, too, faces dangers in identifying too closely with the fantasies of his or her employer. One of the severest problems is that such identification makes people morally blind, unable to distinguish between right and wrong. If the organization is a surrogate for the all-good mother of fantasy, then all that is done in its name is good. What is not good is questioning her commands, criticizing her or doubting her. This is how a fast-food manager described her resignation from the company in order to enrol on an MBA course.

> I spent most of the night crying. I felt awful, like I was letting down my fellow workers, my team and my managers. I was a traitor. The next day, I just could not bring myself to sign my resignation letter. My father had to do it for me. For me the company was home and family and religion and work, all rolled into one. Looking back at myself now, I just can't believe how naïve I had been.

Participants displaying such levels of commitment and identification have been described as acolytes. They may engage in anti-social or immoral actions if they perceive them to be in the interests of the organization against those who threaten it. A danger of extreme identification with the employing organization is eventual loss of faith and the conversion of an idealized image into a persecuting one. This phenomenon is quite well known, and is sometimes a feature of 'burn-out', suffered by the most idealistic and dedicated employees. The transformation is characteristic of the paranoid-schizoid position (see Chapters 6 and 10), which splits the world into good and bad parts, recreating the infant's early attempts to master his or her destructiveness. This change-over from extreme loyalty to total demonization of an organization recalls the loss of faith in a messiah, whose claims have proved false (See Chapter 6).

AMBIVALENCE AND RESISTANCE

The majority of organizational members, however, feel more ambivalent. They rely on their organization not only for their livelihoods, but also for a set of idealized images around which they can construct their ego-ideals. They may also have reservations and seek to distance themselves from the organization through a variety of individual and collective strategies. They may resist management's indoctrination, even if they affect to espouse the company's core values. Resistance against an organization and its culture can take many forms. It can be overt and militant. Employees who take their employers to court on grounds of discrimination or harassment rebel against the organization. Going on strike or other industrial action is also a form of direct resistance. Whistle-blowers who seek to embarrass organizations by revealing disagreeable aspects of their operations rebel in a more covert, yet more radical, way. They are often individuals who were once loyal members, even acolytes, and then become disenchanted by what they see as the organization's betrayal of its mission, its customers or its staff. Instead of supporting their narcissism, the organization threatens it. Such individuals construct their ego-ideals out of a rejection of the organization and all it stands for. For them, the organization is an object of demonization – all that it touches is tarnished, and all that opposes it is good.

Jokes

Much resistance in organizations does not take direct forms, like litigation, industrial action, sabotage or whistle-blowing. Instead, it takes a more ambiguous, symbolic form. Individuals who do not 'buy' their organization's culture may challenge or ridicule their organization's symbols, expressing cynicism and detachment at managerial attempts to whip up commitment and enthusiasm (Sims et al., 1993). They mock organizational acolytes and celebrate the behaviour of employees who defy the organization's values and rules. Perhaps the most widespread and powerful form of symbolic resistance are jokes. In *Jokes and their Relation to the Unconscious*, Freud (1905a) argued that jokes provide a temporary liberation of repressed energy. Through a joke, an idea that was kept repressed suddenly finds a way of reaching consciousness, releasing those feelings which were blocked or censored. 'My boss is a very ambitious man – his greatest ambition is how to draw a salary without doing any work' is an often-heard joke at the workplace. It allows repressed resentment, envy and hostility toward's one's superior to be expressed in an exhilarating moment. But jokes are a way of dodging not only inner censors, notably the super-ego, but also outward censors. Challenging the joke at the factual level ('But your boss works quite hard, he comes to the office on Saturdays and Sundays') allows for a face-saving retreat ('I was only joking') or for a further attempt at a joke ('This is to play games on his computer/ escape from the clutches of his wife').

What jokes do, then, is to provide the teller with a partial amnesty, a licence to express something uncomfortable and risky. The reception of the joke (polite chuckle, boisterous laughter, embarrassed silence) enables the teller to gauge the feelings of the listeners and adjust his or her behaviour accordingly. Shared jokes undoubtedly reinforce social bonds among individuals, very often at the expense of a third party. In organizations, jokes can strengthen the organizational culture, especially if they celebrate the achievements of a 'character' or channel aggression against outsiders, such as competitors. Alternatively, jokes may be part of a sub-culture or a counter-culture which may exist side by side with the culture of the organization as a whole, undermining it or fragmenting it (Gabriel, 1991b). A new student arrives at a prestigious university, expecting to have to work hard for academic success. This message may be reinforced by her professors and by official university documents. Yet she notices early on that her classmates make pitiless fun of anyone preferring to stay in and work rather than go out every night. She quickly learns the organizational norm: academic success perhaps requires hard work, but social success requires that you should not appear to work hard.

Stories

Jokes are one type of narrative which sustains organizational culture. There are many others. These include gossip, nicknames, legends, cartoons, graffiti and, above all, stories. Stories are symbolic elaborations of 'facts', in which accuracy is sacrificed for the purpose of effect. Omissions, exaggerations, embellishments, shifts in emphasis and all kinds of distortion are common in stories, which become more detached from facts with every telling and re-telling. Events as diverse as the breakdown of an elevator, an altercation with an angry customer or a worker losing part of his finger in a sausage-making machine can spark off fireworks of organizational story-telling, elaborated with every re-telling.

As avenues to the truth, stories are of questionable value. As signs of what people believe to be true and what they want to be true, stories are absolutely invaluable. Instead of offering us 'facts as information', stories offer us 'facts as experience', merging wish-fulfilling fantasies with reality. Hence, the truth of stories is not to be found in the events which they describe but in the meanings which they contain (Gabriel, 1998a, b). Psychoanalysis, with its techniques of interpretation for dreams, symptoms, works of art and other cultural phenomena, is uniquely equipped to reveal some of the meanings of stories, using them as windows into an organization's culture.

Not all stories fulfil wishes in the same manner. Some of the main types of story are the epic stories, the comic stories, the tragic stories and the romantic stories.

- *Epic stories*, which generate pride and enthusiasm, focus on the achievements of heroes and allow for identification with their courage, strength and ingenuity. In many companies, epic stories surround the exploits of the early founders, heroic employees who defy the elements to discharge their duties or teams which keep their cool in a crisis and prevail against the odds. At times, epic stories are features of counter-cultures within organizations, where subordinates stand up against the bullying behaviour of their superiors.
- *Comic stories* generate amusement and mirth and are often associated with the deserved come-uppance of disliked individuals. The humbling of a pompous or pretentious manager, whether caused by an accident or a crafty ruse, generates much mirth among his or her subordinates; an arrogant executive reversing his expensive car into a lamp-post generates similar feelings. The hero of such stories

is often a 'trickster' who deflates a more powerful figure by using cunning against force.
- *Tragic stories* focus on undeserved misfortune and suffering and generate feelings of compassion and fear. The central character of such stories is a victim, whose sufferings have nothing funny or heroic about them. Instead, these sufferings go to unmask an evil party, such as a fellow employee, a manager or a superior power like 'bureaucracy' or 'fate'.
- *Romantic stories* centre on love affairs, romantic attachments, gifts or acts of unsolicited kindness. These are stories which express love, gratitude and appreciation and are sometimes associated with feelings of affection but also nostalgia or self-pity.

The power of organizational stories lies in their ability to refashion actual events in a remarkably broad manner. For instance, an accident may generate a tragic story (someone got hurt), a comic story (he deserved it because he is such a pompous fool), an epic story (he went on with the performance in spite of his injury) or a romantic story (he looked so embarrassed he was positively 'sweet'). Often the same 'events' may generate several different stories, sometimes hybrids of the above types, such as tragi-comic or epic-romantic. Hence, the ways in which 'events' are turned into stories can give us some of the deepest information about an organization's culture and the psychological needs of its members.

Organizations differ in the number, type and variety of stories which they spawn. It is clear that in organizations with more uniform cultures, many stories will be shared across different levels and departments. The feelings generated by these stories will also be shared across different organizational levels and departments. By contrast, in organizations with fragmented cultures or strong sub-cultures, the same events will lead to different accounts. For example, an employee's mental breakdown may be presented as evidence of management evil by his co-workers or as evidence of his fellow-workers picking on him by managers. A new product may be presented as a great success, the result of heroic teamwork by some managers. Other employees may attribute it to good luck or the gullibility of the company's customers or to clever advertising. Yet other employees may deny that the product is successful and ridicule its poor reliability record or the high cost of repairs under warranty.

To conclude, stories express collective fantasies, imparting meaning and value to organizational life. They can be seen as attempts to humanize the impersonal character of bureaucratic organizations and to allow the expression of different emotions. As carriers of shared symbolism, they are features of an organization's culture and contribute to the formation of bonds of identification among organizational members. Alternatively, they can be features of a counter-culture or a sub-culture subverting or challenging an organization's dominant values, as expressed in official stories and symbols. In such circumstances, it is understandable why managers may claim that it is easier to slay a dragon than to kill a myth.

Material culture

Companies devote huge resources to erecting and promoting such symbols as corporate logos and mottoes. In recent years, in the wake of the corporate culture vogue, many companies have sought to highlight their values by emblazoning them

STORY INTERPRETATION: TWO EXAMPLES

I used to work for a company where we had regular bomb practice. The security chief would hide a package with a sign saying 'BOMB' to see how quickly people got out of the building and how quickly his boys would locate the 'bomb'. They carried out this exercise many times and were pleased with their response times. Until eventually the bomb was hidden under the mainframe, where it proved impossible to locate; for hours they searched all over the building, but nobody thought of looking under the machine!

This story, recounted light-headedly over lunch by a computer executive, generated much amusement among his audience, fellow executives of a British computer manufacturer. The story-teller invites the listener to speculate why the security staff failed to check under the mainframe. Was the machine seen as being above suspicion or was it a taboo object? Did the men perhaps fail to see the computer altogether, regarding it as a fixed part of the building, in the same way that our untrained eyes fail to distinguish the dozens of types of snow apparent to the Inuit. What made this a good story? Does the story try to tell us something more general about computers and organizations?

The meaning of the story (at least as far as the story-teller was concerned) is unlocked when we learn that it was recounted in response to a casual comment that, to the non-expert, computers are mystifying and threatening. The story came as an amplification and embellishment of this rather trivial point, as if to say that even security men, hardened men who will go after bombs, share in the general malaise when confronted with computers. They didn't dare touch the computer or even get close to it – as if that were the real bomb. And, given that the teller was a man working constantly with computers, is the implication of the story not that computer experts are the real hard men of the organization, dealing with the truly dangerous objects? And did his audience not appreciate the story because they, as computer experts, could identify with the teller, sharing a joke at the expense of non-experts.

Such an interpretation may find some support in a subsequent story related by the same individual:

I had been doing consultancy for the launch of a US software product, called Soft-tool. With a name like this, you don't stand a chance, I told the manufacturers. You have to change the brand name. No luck, it was company policy to use the same name in all its geographic divisions. My job was to come up with a logo for this product. Imagine now, 'Buy Soft-tool to increase your performance.' When they realized their gaffe, they changed the name to . . . Hard-tool!

In spite of its very light-hearted nature, this story is especially telling, in many different ways. The *double entendre*, stemming from the sexual connotation of the word 'tool' which is evident to a British person but lost on an American, creates an imaginary conspiracy between the teller of the story and his audience at the expense of the American company, which thought naïvely (and with a degree of imperial disdain, perhaps) that it could force its brand name on other people, disregarding their culture and language. The imaginary logo 'Buy Soft-tool to increase your performance' strengthens the conspiracy with its implied questioning of American virility as well as the patently inadequate recipe for its restoration.

Would the story be as good if the object in question had been unrelated to computers, if 'Soft-tool', instead of being a piece of software, had been a photocopier or a new lighting system? The story could probably stand such transpositions, if a connection was

> made between the products and 'softness'; for instance, if the lighting was meant to be 'soft' as against the hardness of neon. Even so, however, the story would lose much of its punch, since computers (software and hardware) are far more plausible 'tools' for increasing company performance than lighting or photocopiers.
>
> The story's quality, then, seems to rest on the fact that 'Buy Soft-tool to increase your performance' sounds like an eminently plausible logo for a computer program to someone who does not understand the innuendo in the word 'tool'. It plays on the widely accepted and yet problematic notion that information technology is a key, or even the key, to performance and competitive advantage. The story's subtle irony (which runs in parallel with the coarse sexual allusion) seems to be something like 'Here is an American company which preaches high-tech recipes to competitive advantage and then proceeds to shoot itself in the foot through a brand name, whose absurdity would be evident to any simpleton in England.'
>
> What do the stories and their enthusiastic reception tell us about the culture of the company in question? Although by themselves they may not be enough to support generalizations, they do suggest certain possibilities:
>
> - computers are dangerous and exciting things, and those who can handle them are heroic people;
> - masculinity is equated with hardness and hardness with computers;
> - Americans are arrogant and their arrogance leads them to shoot themselves in the foot.
>
> The stories suggest a hard, xenophobic, fairly closed culture, in which manual workers (like the security men), foreigners (Americans) and women (who flinch at talk of hard-tools) would feel out of place. It also suggests a considerable degree of narcissistic self-admiration on the part of the teller and his audience, who imagine themselves above the foibles of lesser mortals.
>
> *Adapted from Gabriel, 1992.*

on publicity materials and celebrating them in official stories, corporate functions and rituals. Official organizational stories, dealing with the company's founders, its early struggles, its crises, its triumphs, its great characters may find their places in organizational culture or may be subverted and undermined by counter-cultural stories.

One of the most interesting cultural ingredients of an organization is the architecture of its buildings. A bureaucratic theory of organizations may lead us to think that corporate buildings are essentially a utilitarian feature, dictated by rationality, expedience and the need to minimize costs. Yet, since the industrial revolution, capitalist companies have invested heavily in their buildings, seeking to turn them into statements about themselves. They have modelled their factories on the palace of Versailles, as did the nineteenth-century English industrialist Sir Titus Salt, and have outreached Gothic cathedrals, as in the Chrysler building in New York or St Pancras Station in London. Other architectural features of organizations, the gleaming glass exteriors, the open plan office, the vast atrium at the heart of the building, the plush carpeting, the opulent decor, have totemic qualities, acting as icons of corporate identity.

Visible aspects of an organization, such as buildings, logos, products, are sometimes known as material culture. Some anthropologists, like Douglas and McCracken, have argued that material culture, which includes things like tools, clothes, food, cars and buildings, is similar to a language system, making statements about ourselves, as if words were being used. Sometimes, material culture may speak louder than words. A gleaming glass tower may appear to provide stronger evidence of a firm's might than many spreadsheets of accounts. It invites respect and communicates authority. At an emotional level, it persuades more than many words.

Yet material culture can also deceive and its symbolism can resonate differently with different people. Like official organizational stories, the material artefacts of an organization may be challenged or subverted. Such challenges can be material, as when a piece of graffiti spoils the effect of a gleaming surface. Alternatively, material artefacts may be challenged symbolically, by attaching subversive meanings to them. When is a mighty building a sign of well-deserved grandeur and when is it a statement of arrogance and conceit? When is a bright new logo a sign of dynamism and youth and when is it a waste of corporate money at a time of supposed economies?

To conclude, then, many of an organization's symbols are contested. They emit different messages and generate different emotions in different individuals. At times, people are content with their meanings and their interpretations and let others hold on to their interpretations. At times, interpretations and meanings clash vigorously, sub-cultural or counter-cultural meanings and interpretations seeking to subvert or undermine dominant meanings and interpretations.

TYPES OF ORGANIZATIONAL CULTURE

Various attempts have been made to identify the predominant types of organizational culture. The benefits of a convincing classification are numerous. First, the analysis of the cultures of specific organizations is greatly simplified if they can be neatly placed within a particular type. Secondly, a relationship may be found between type of culture and other crucial organizational variables, like leadership style, structure and performance. Thirdly, a number of generalizations may be made about the work experiences of those working in each type of culture, such as job satisfaction, career prospects or prevalent emotions. Several attempts have been made by organizational psychologists to identify the chief types of culture in organizations, though none has proved totally convincing.

Deal and Kennedy (1982), for example, identify four types of culture: (a) the tough-guy, macho culture, a risk-taking culture, which is tough, uncompromising and decisive; (b) the work-hard/play-hard culture, which emphasizes both hard work and also fun and enjoyment; (c) the bet-your-company culture, which emphasizes long-term planning, thorough thinking and the spread of responsibility; and (d) the process culture, which is low-risk, rule-driven and highly ordered. They argue that these cultures are related to the nature of the risk faced by different organizations. Yet few organizations falling neatly into one of these four types and it is very hard to relate these types to different psychological personalities. A more influential typology was developed by Charles Handy (1988), following work by Roger Harrison (1972), who argued that organizational cultures can be classified into four major types: the power culture; the role culture; the task culture; and the person or support culture. Individuals, they suggested, feel more comfortable in the culture which best suits their personality.

INTERPRETING A BUILDING

One of Britain's leading chemical companies decided to refashion radically its 1930s' headquarters in London. The company decamped across the Thames for a number of years, while the works were in progress. When the staff moved back, the building's interior was unrecognizable. This is how a senior executive described it:

> The old building was like a gentlemen's club, long dark corridors, heavy oak doors, but during the seventies' recession we had lost a lot of staff and the rest of us were rattling like peas in a pod. When we moved out, I found people I didn't even know existed and I'm supposed to know everyone in the building. Everyone at that time worked in their distinct little cells, and the idea was to make the culture of the organization much more open; we would have an all-glazed environment, so that it would appear more open. I have my own personal views on whether it happened, but I'd rather not risk them . . . As for my staff, a lot of them don't like the modern architecture, can't open windows, we have a high incidence of sickness, headaches. Don't know if this is psychological, psychosomatic or the 'sick-building' syndrome, but the staff personalize their work environment a lot more than they did in the old building. They didn't use to have all these fluffy toys around.

His views were reinforced by numerous staff who spoke nostalgically about the old building and complained about what had been done to it. A supervisor with thirty years' experience said:

> I hate this building, I loathe it. It's a lovely building to come in and walk around and say 'Isn't it wonderful!' To work in it is hell, nothing goes right. The idea was that there should be an atrium, where there used to be just a light well, sort of white lavatory tiles on it, an unused space, just open. They decided to turn it into useable space; originally they were going to have trees; they said it was going to be too noisy. So they carpet it, it's quite stunning if you look from the eighth floor, but from the working point of view it's no good. The idea was that we'd all feel part of a whole; you could see everybody, but you don't. All you can see is the people in the corridors, or you look at the fish-tanks, the offices that line up the atrium, half of the time they are empty, so that's depressing.

Several more employees had noted the gap between the intention of openness and the actuality of anonymity, impersonality and lack of character. For those working in the building, there seemed to be a contradiction between the outward opulence of the building and the lifeless, spiritually impoverished human environment within.

> I liked the look of the new building when I first walked in, very impressive. But the offices, the way they are organized, you don't see an awful lot of people. Where we are you might not see anyone all day. It is quiet. Conducive to work, but not conducive to gatherings or anything like that. The old building, well it was antiquated, but it had character, while this has no character, and this is also how I feel about people. There used to be birthday parties in our offices, whereas now, they don't have impromptu get-togethers any more.

To be sure, the new building carried a powerful symbolism, but for many the symbolism was far from that intended by the architects and the corporate image-makers. Outwardly

> the same, the building's new interior affronted the people's sense of authenticity and epitomized what they saw as a phoney rhetoric of openness. The atrium, instead of openness, was experienced as the spiritual void at the heart of the organization.
>
> *Adapted from Gabriel, 1993.*

Power culture

Handy illustrates the power culture as a spider's web, with the all-important spider sitting in the centre, 'because the key to the whole organization sits in the centre, surrounded by ever-widening circles of intimates and influence. The closer you are to the spider, the more influence you have' (1988: 86). An important ruler is central to the power culture; the organization appears to be the personal creation of the ruler who holds it together, animates it and leads it. He or she appoints officials, promotes and demotes, using his or her personal judgement and taking little notice of rules and regulations. In extreme cases, a power culture is a dictatorship, but it does not have to be. Great empires, both in politics and in business, are power cultures. Their leaders, whether Hitler, Alexander the Great, Walt Disney or Henry Ford, may be feared or loved; their personalities and character colour everything that happens in these organizations. The core value of power cultures is loyalty.

Role culture

The role culture is illustrated with a pyramid of boxes: 'Inside each box is a job title with an individual's name in smaller type below, indicating who is currently the occupant of that box; but of course the box continues even if the individual departs' (1988: 89). Role cultures are characteristic of bureaucratic organizations in which every official has a role which is closely defined by rules and regulations; the different roles are hierarchically organized. The importance of Handy's role culture is that it suggests that bureaucracy itself is not culture-free. Even the most ritualistic organization, frozen in time, has a culture; in fact, Handy's description would suggest that bureaucracy, with its supreme value, the adherence to impersonal rules, is itself a most pervasive culture.

Task culture

If role cultures insist that what has to be done must be done according to the rules, ceremonies and procedures, task cultures emphasize getting the job done, in any possible way. This is a culture which encourages improvisation, invention and resourcefulness. It flourishes in organizations which must deliver a product by a certain deadline, organizations that face a lot of unpredictability and change. Problem-solving is the core value of such cultures, which usually involve people working in non-hierarchical teams or groups. Tasks are not standardized; each presents unique challenges. Handy depicts the task culture as a net 'which can pull its cords this way and that and regroup at will' (1988: 90).

Task cultures are common among professional groups, consultancy agencies, advertising and the mass media, parts of journalism and publishing, surgical teams and teams in charge of one-off projects like organizing the Olympic Games or running a military campaign. The patron god of this culture, in Handy's view, is Athena, the protector of Odysseus, the chief of problem-solvers. Such cultures offer excitement and disappointment, victories and defeats but no long-term security. 'Task cultures ... tend to be full of young, energetic people developing and testing talents: people who are self-confident enough not to worry about long-term security, at least not yet!' (1988: 91). In task cultures, everything is subordinated to getting the job done; this involves inventiveness but also quite a lot of duplication and waste. Consequently, organizations which function on a pure task principle can be quite expensive. One example of a task culture is NASA, the American space agency. Its official task had been defined by President Kennedy: to put a man on the moon before the end of the 1960s and bring him back safely. Its unofficial task was to do so before the Soviet Union did. To this end no expense was spared, no resource untapped and no possibility unexplored. It was exciting, effective and expensive. Its success was the beginning of its demise (Wolfe, 1979; Schwartz, 1990).

Person culture

This type of culture is illustrated by a loose cluster or a constellation of stars. The individual, his/her development and well-being reign supreme; the organization exists to serve the individual rather than the other way round. Handy says: 'The person culture is very different from the previous three. The other three cultures put the organization's purposes first and then, in their different ways, harness the individual to this purpose. The person culture puts the individual first and makes the organization the resource for the individual's talents (1988: 92).

Harrison has re-examined person culture in a slightly different light. He argues that far from being a marginal culture, person culture dominates the outlooks of those organizations which develop a sense of true dedication to their clients and provide a strong supporting network for their employees. Seen in this way, person cultures are not only organizations in which each individual is a prima donna but also those organizations which emphasize their family-like quality. To be sure, the same company has also strong task features (involving all those groups of experts on project-work) as well as power culture (Morita himself at the centre of the web).

Most real-life organizations involve a mixture of cultures. However, the predominant culture of each organization, in Handy's view, depends on factors such as size, output and history. None of the four types can claim to be better or superior; they are each suited to different types of circumstances. They are also each suited to a different type of mental personality. Authoritarian personalities tend to be attracted to the power culture's emphasis on blind obedience and loyalty to the leader, respect for authority and dependence. Obsessive characters, on the other hand, find their natural home in the perfect routine of the role culture, its meticulous adherence to rules and unflinching devotion to order, planning and economy. Heroic individualists and collectivists are attracted to the task culture, which offers them a chance to shine and distinguish themselves in an egalitarian, unstudied environment. Finally, narcissistic personalities are at home in the person culture, which views the organization as the servant rather than the master of individuals, a place where individuals can be supported, admired and developed.

SOME PSYCHOANALYTIC TYPES OF CULTURE

Psychoanalytic researchers have not produced systematic typologies of organizational culture like those of Deal and Kennedy (1982), Handy (1986, 1987) and Harrison (1988). What they have done is to provide elaborate portraits of certain types of cultural pathologies, which are found quite regularly in a large number of organizations. These portraits are quite detailed and seem to capture the qualities of such organizations with admirable clarity.

Narcissistic cultures

One of the commonest organizational cultures encountered, especially in organizations suffering sudden reverses, is the narcissistic culture. Such cultures are largely peopled by individuals who believe that they can earn a living by resting on their laurels. Organizational achievement is replaced by a belief in the natural and indisputable superiority of the organization and an illusion of invulnerability. Self-congratulation is a regular phenomenon in such cultures, where rhetoric is confused with reality. As Schwartz (1990: 69ff) has argued, such cultures represent a magical flight away from reality and towards utopia, and may develop out of decaying 'task cultures', once the dominant task has been achieved, leaving every member self-obsessed and self-important.

At times, such organizations are led by a leader who triggers fantasies associated with the primal mother, ever-loving and ever-admiring towards her children, irrespective of their actual behaviour and achievement. Alternatively, narcissistic cultures may be the product of a chief executive officer who uses the organization as an extension of his or her own narcissism, glorifying certain workers who fit the ideal and disregarding others, denying the existence of pain, difficulties and conflicts (Hirschhorn, 1988). Narcissism is a perennial risk for contemporary organizations which are surrounded by professional image-makers, corporate publicity people and advertisers. These, wittingly or unwittingly, act as sycophants and courtiers, singing the praises of the corporate emperor, which the emperor can all too easily believe. An obsession with image and appearance is endemic in organizations like Disneyland and McDonald's but it also features in many others. Schwartz (1990) has argued that the transformation of NASA from a heroic organization doing battle for supremacy in space to a Disneyland in space marked the onslaught of narcissism and brought about corporate decay and space tragedy. Similar decay has been observed in other organizations where narcissistic self-delusions have taken hold.

Narcissistic cultures often breed cynical sub-cultures within their fold, where self-deception and idealization of the narcissistic establishment – the leader and his or her acolytes – is dismissed and ridiculed. Cynical sub-cultures rarely mount a direct challenge to a narcissistic culture. They disparage but rarely confront directly narcissistic delusions and self-deceptions. The moral indifference and defeatist ethos of cynical sub-cultures make them in some ways a suitable counter-foil to a narcissistic culture. The narcissist shines against the cynic, who in turn disparages without confronting the narcissist's delusions.

Collegiate cultures

In narcissistic cultures, the leader is held as an ideal by those below him or her, often reawakening fantasies whose origins lie in the imago of the good mother. A different type of idealizing culture is one in which the members of an organization stubbornly refuse to idealize or even to recognize anyone as different from the others. A leader, if recognized at all, is seen more as a coordinator, *primus inter pares*, rather than as someone who has the right to lead. Such cultures grow around egalitarian, co-operative and collegiate traditions and are to be commonly found in professional and academic organizations, gentlemen's clubs, professional societies and partnerships. Members of such cultures, instead of idealizing a leader, are proud of the ethos of equality and collegiality and are critical of anyone who may claim to be superior to others or to have a right to tell others what to do. In collegiate cultures nothing is as important as containing aggression and disagreement, or anything that threatens to spoil feelings of equality and fraternity.

Hirschhorn studied collegiate culture in a legal firm, where he observed that this culture acted as a defence against aggression or competition.

> Unlike other firms who dealt in the dirty world of money and business, the partners could imagine that they were special, that their 'noble experiment' was unique and precious, one that stood above the fray of streetwise lawyers fighting for money. As intellectuals, they imagined they could avoid this world, and if they failed, their stance had been worth the try. (Hirschhorn, 1993: 74)

Collegiate cultures are sometimes identified by what seems like a *laissez-faire* style of leadership, the leader being little more than a co-opted chairperson. It would be more accurate to say that they exist in a leadership vacuum. They can survive and even prosper so long as they operate in a benevolent environment, maintaining cosy relations with outsiders. When facing adversity, external or internal, they lack the fighting resources and can be easy prey for aggressive predators. The character most often associated with collegiality is that of the civic individualist.

Leaders' effects on organizational culture

Psychoanalytic writers have generally maintained that the personality of the leader has a strong influence on an organization's culture. What they mean is not, of course, that leaders can design or mould cultures at will, but rather that certain qualities of leaders, such as narcissism, paranoia or depressiveness, cascade down the organization, through processes such as identification, idealization and dependence. Moreover, leaders tend to appoint people like themselves to vital positions, thus reinforcing particular cultural characteristics.

Kets de Vries and Miller (1984) have argued that in dysfunctional, centralized firms a leader's neurotic style can be mirrored in the organization's culture and strategy. Pathological cultures reflect their leaders' neuroses. Highly suspicious leaders, like Harold Geneen, the former CEO of ITT, may thus influence the ethos of their entire organization, making it reactive, defensive and secretive. On the basis of their consultancy work with troubled organizations, Kets de Vries and Miller (1984) singled out five types of pathological culture, as follows:

1   *Paranoid culture* reflects a suspicious leadership style; its dominant fantasy is persecution.
2   *Avoidant culture* reflects a depressive leadership style; its dominant fantasy is helplessness.
3   *Charismatic/dramatic culture* reflects an uninhibited dramatic leadership style; its dominant fantasy is grandiosity.
4   *Bureaucratic culture* reflects a compulsive leadership style; its dominant fantasy is complete control.
5   *Power culture* reflects a detached leadership style which allows jockeying for position and influence; its dominant fantasy is detachment.

Kets de Vries and Miller argue that, in modest degrees, features of all these cultural types can be beneficial to organizations. For instance, a degree of paranoia helps protect organizations; a degree of avoidance forestalls conflicts over trivialities; a degree of charisma gives dynamism and drive to an organization; a degree of bureaucracy gives it stability and control; a degree of detachment encourages self-reliance and initiative on the part of the subordinates. Moreover, a certain style may be effective at a particular point in a firm's history, but may become dysfunctional under different circumstances.

> It is excess that leads to pathology, and the equilibrium between normality and pathology is easily breached. Holding on to a particular style when the circumstances have changed can lead to corporate disaster. It can be said, however, that the style of the leader or the dominant coalition may become modified through interactions with the evolving organization. (Kets de Vries and Miller, 1991: 260)

Psychoanalysis recognizes the effect of leadership on culture, whether at the level of an individual organization or of society at large. It also recognizes the possibility of influencing or changing organizational culture through interventions by leaders or consultants. Where depth psychologists diverge from other schools of cultural change is in the emphasis they accord to the overcoming of resistances, which are not only institutional but also psychological. Culture, even dysfunctional, decaying and oppressive culture, offers consolations to its members, to which they become strongly attached. Many of these consolations are in the form of wish-fulfilling self-deceptions and delusions which, as in the case of neurotics, reinforce the malaise and dysfunction. Seeking to change culture by introducing new sets of values or by putting it through a process of organizational learning is unlikely to be successful. Individuals become far too dependent on their delusions to give them up easily. Yet, under crisis conditions, a process of cultural change may be initiated, frequently instigated by a new agent, a consultant or a new leader who triggers off both a desire to learn and the will to recover. In this way, agents of cultural change act in a therapeutic mode. Rational analysis alone will flounder against organizational resistances, just as the will to recover will quickly dissipate in the absence of rational analysis of present and past. Psychoanalytic consultants work both at the analytical and at the emotional levels simultaneously, seeking to unfreeze some of the defensive postures and set in motion reparative processes.

Diagnosis is the consultant's early task. This is done not only on the basis of professed attitudes and beliefs of participants but equally through the interpretation of points of stress revealed in stories and jokes, silences and powerful emotions. Here is how Levinson (1991: 61) goes about organizational diagnosis:

There are some questions the consultant should always have before him: What is hurting this organization? How do I interpret what key people cite as their main problem? How do I interpret what other employees say is their main problem? The pain may be literally what the informants say it is or it may be symptomatic of something more deep seated. How does this organization experience its problems? That is, how severe do the problems appear to be to the organization? And how well does the organization relate them to basic causes? This is a vital question because the degree to which the organization acknowledges pain is one measure of how ready it is to accept help.

Even if the consultant gets the diagnosis right, interventions aimed at changing a company's culture can be quite unpredictable and even unmanageable. They may lead to a strengthening of organizational resistances, they may have no effect, the may have an effect opposite to the intended one or they may have the intended effect for the wrong reasons. Insensitive attempts by managers to introduce new values, new rituals and new symbols can easily backfire, being cynically dismissed as silly gimmicks.

New logos, buildings, mission statements, regulations and procedures, structure and strategy, staff development practices and reward systems will only be part of a process of cultural change if they lead to fundamentally new outlooks on the part of organizational members. Cultural change must be internal as well as external. The connections between culture and the psychic needs of individuals is the major contribution of depth psychology to the study of organizational culture. To be sure, as many other traditions argue, individuals in organizations yearn for meanings which organizational culture appeases. What sets depth psychological accounts apart is their view of culture as representing a symbolic means of coping with pain and of turning passivity into activity. The meanings which individuals read into events and characters by transforming them into stories are not arbitrary, but derive from deeper and frequently repressed wishes and desires. Unless agents of change can address these wishes and desires they will find that the possibilities for cultural change are blocked.

CONCLUSION

Depth psychologists, like other organizational theorists, look at organizational culture as a complex web of symbols, meanings and values, capable of driving action and unleashing emotion. Culture, including organizational culture, infuses everyday events with meaning and directs our emotional responses to the world around us; in doing so, it enables us to share meanings and emotional responses with others and it bonds us emotionally with them.

Where psychoanalysis goes beyond other approaches is in its ability to recognize unconscious needs and desires behind symbolic structures. Organizational culture is no chance supplier of meanings which may be arbitrarily generated by leaders and others. Instead, it seeks to provide a sequence of wish-fulfilments, offering symbolic avenues for conquering pain and converting victimhood into agency and powerlessness into control. In some organizations, culture may temporarily drive innovation, productivity and learning; in others, it may inhibit them. In every case, however, organizational culture drives and is driven more by irrational fantasies and emotions than by rational plans and calculations. It is to these irrational factors in organizations that the next chapter turns.

9 THE EMOTIONAL LIFE OF ORGANIZATIONS

> When fully developed, bureaucracy also stands, in a specific sense, under the principle of *sine ira et studio*. Its specific nature which is welcomed by capitalism, develops the more perfectly the more the bureaucracy is 'dehumanized,' the more completely it succeeds in eliminating from official business love, hatred, and all purely personal, irrational, and emotional elements which escape calculation. This is the specific nature of bureaucracy and it is appraised as its special virtue. (Weber, 1946: 215–16)

Written in the twentieth century, Max Weber's pronouncement has haunted the study of organizations ever since. Is Weber's vision of bureaucracy one of the profoundest observations in the social sciences? Or is it an extraordinary piece of blinkered thinking which consigned the study of organizations to fifty years of wasted effort? For there can be no denying that images of organizations as passion-free or at least potentially passion-free have dominated theory and practice alike. Some people define organizations as a type of human association from which feeling is excluded, where rationality reigns supreme. In the kingdom of rationality, observed Weber, with resigned disenchantment, 'the performance of each individual is mathematically measured, each man becomes a little cog in the machine and, aware of this, his one pre-occupation is whether he can become a bigger cog' (quoted in Mayer, 1956: 126–7).

Psychoanalysis has stayed at the margins of the discussions on bureaucracy initiated by Weber. In many of these discussions, emotions and passions (such as envy, hatred, anger, fear, anxiety) were seen as unwelcome intruders into the world of organizations, symptoms of pathologies, of which organizations had to rid themselves. Alternatively, they were referred to by a small number of euphemisms, like stress or job satisfaction, which ostensibly gave emotions some scientific weight and also offered the prospect of containing, managing and controlling them. As Fineman has argued, such euphemisms reinforced the view of people in organizations as 'emotionally anorexic' (1993: 9).

Yet one only has to scratch the surface of organizational life to discover a thick layer of emotions and feelings, at times checked, at times feigned, at times timidly expressed and at other times bursting out uncontrollably. Consider the following description offered by Andy, a computer operations manager at a chemical company.

> Wednesday morning. I'd had a very good evening; we've started a bridge club and I'd played remarkably well. I came in, it was a nice morning, I was in fine spirits, I got down and spent an hour and a half clearing a load of billing, which isn't the most interesting work, and

I thought 'This is really good, it's ten o'clock and I've got rid of all these horrible little tasks.'

I turned round and said to my colleague working in the same office 'I'm not going to complain about Simon today, I'll tell you about the bridge last night, it was really great' and in walks my manager [Simon], saying 'Still talking!' He sat down and said that he wanted to have a meeting at 11 o'clock. I asked him how long the meeting would go on, because I had another meeting later, his meetings go on interminably, and he turned to me and said: 'Why, are you playing squash at 11.30?' He continued to bait me, all because I smiled. Then, I burst out at him and used quite strong language. He was very angry and said to me that I thought I was the cleverest in the department etc. and the row went on for 25 minutes or so. The upshot was that I've been in a very good mood ever since, for no apparent reason.

The problem here is that you are pushed into positions where you can't win either way. If you answer back you are in the wrong, and if you sit there and take it you feel bad as well, because it's not right. Being the manager doesn't give him the right to shout at people for no apparent reason. This is my view of management.

In the space of a few hours, Andy's feelings changed from cheerful good humour, to relief at having done a whole lot of 'horrible little tasks', to defiant determination not to gripe about his manager, to irritation and anger at Simon's remarks, to emotional outburst, to sustained emotional warfare, to pride at having held his own. This description seems a world apart from the clinical, rule-governed relations between subordinates and superiors envisaged by Weber. Instead, the relation here appears riddled with antagonism, anger, frustration, fulfilment, resentment, defiance, envy, contempt, fear and many other emotional nuances. This suggests that passion is never entirely absent from organizational life and politics, just as it is never absent from life and politics in general.

THE RE-DISCOVERY OF EMOTION BY ORGANIZATIONAL THEORY

The view that organizations, like families, sporting events and religious ceremonies, are emotional arenas, in which different emotions are generated, displayed, shed and traded, did not emerge seriously until the 1980s. Since then, a number of theoretical and practical developments have brought emotion closer to the centre of the study of organizations.

Emotional labour

Emotion is now recognized as a key feature of the work that many people do. A display of friendliness, involving direct eye-contact and a smile, is not merely a bonus for sales or catering staff, but is an integral part of their job. Different occupations require different emotional displays or 'performances': nurses must show care and affection, sports coaches enthusiasm and drive, funeral directors dignified respect and professional wrestlers anger and hate. Hochschild (1983) used the term 'emotional labour' to describe those aspects of people's work which involve adopting an emotional attitude appropriate to their role. Since Hochschild's early work, emotional labour has been recognized as a core feature of a wide range of occupations (from secretaries to car mechanics, from computer analysts to Disneyland employees) especially in the service sector. Emotional labour also involves assessing and managing other people's emotions as well as one's own. (Hochschild, 1983; Fineman, 1993). A sales assistant must diagnose whether a customer's anger is real and serious and use his or her own techniques to defuse or redirect it.

According to this research, emotions and even feelings are no longer seen as dysfunctional or disruptive elements in organizations but as vital resources to be marshalled and controlled, in a manner not dissimilar to other resources, such as money, information or materials. This is how Putnam and Mumby (1993: 37) have put it: 'Through recruitment, selection, socialization and performance evaluations, organizations develop a social reality in which feelings become a commodity for achieving instrumental goals.' In this way, bureaucratic rationality expands to colonize affectivity and emotions. Mature bureaucracy need no longer be afraid of emotions; rather, it may commandeer them, control them and deploy them as it does other resources, like knowledge, money or technology. Writers, such as Ferguson (1984), Van Maanen and Kunda (1989), Mumby and Putnam (1992, Putnam and Mumby, 1993) as well as Hochschild herself (1983), then critique the resulting self-estrangement, inauthenticity and burn-out suffered by employees who, under pressure from management, adopt the emotions and even the feelings required by their roles. Others may seek to resist management's attempts to manipulate their feelings, through acts of defiance, resistance and escape.

Emotions and leadership

If emotions are part of the work people do, the right emotional attitude has come to be seen as a key feature of successful organizations. At a time when continuous change and uncertainty make traditional machine-bureaucracies less relevant, emotions such as commitment, trust, caring, enthusiasm, pride and even fun become necessary for organizational success. Business leaders are seen less as super-brains formulating policies and more as passion generators. Business people like Morita (1987), Carlzon (1989) and Roddick (1991) have written books which extol passion, commitment and enthusiasm as the basis of success, viewing themselves as heroic leaders of passionate followers, rather than managers of obedient functionaries.

As was seen in Chapter 6, following Zaleznik (1977) and Burns (1978) a distinction has been drawn between managers, who promote efficiency through clever deals and an eye for detail, and leaders, who stir emotion, provide vision and generate commitment. In so doing, organizational studies has rejoined a thread in Weber's thought which had remained forgotten, namely that leadership and administration are not merely different entities but diametrical opposites.

> *Sine ira et studio,* 'without scorn or bias,' [the administrator] shall administer his office. Hence, he shall not do precisely what the politician, the leader as well as his following, must necessarily do, namely *fight*. To take a stand, to be passionate – *ira et studium* – is the politician's element, and above all the element of the political leader. His conduct is subject to quite a different, indeed exactly the opposite, principle of responsibility from that of the civil servant. The honor of the civil servant is vested in his ability to execute conscientiously the order of the superior authorities, exactly as if the order agreed with his own conviction ... The honor of the political leader, of the leading statesman, however, lies precisely in an exclusive personal responsibility for what he does, a responsibility he cannot and must not reject or transfer. (Weber, 1946: 95)

Emotions as social constructions

The two discourses that we have introduced, emotional labour and leaders as visionary passion-stirrers, are closely intertwined with a third current discourse, according to which emotions themselves are cultural phenomena, whose meanings emerge through culture. We normally think of our own emotions as the outcomes of our own personal psychological states; we are happy when we are offered a desirable job, we are angry when we are slighted, we are envious when we desire something belonging to someone else. Yet, researchers into organizational emotion challenge this way of thinking about emotions, arguing that the meaning of emotions emerges through culture, that emotions themselves are communicated through culture and are even generated by culture. Specific cultural events, such as a funeral, a job interview, a downsizing announcement or a business deal, call for appropriate emotional performances of those participating. Inspired by the work of Goffman (1959), *social constructionists* argue that emotions can be learned, just as theatrical roles may be learned. And just as theatrical actors learn to experience anger, sorrow, joy or fear when their roles call for them, so too social actors learn to experience feelings appropriate to the social settings. Writers like Heller, Mangham, Flam and Fineman have studied the rules which govern emotional performances and have examined how emotion 'flows' by being symbolically constructed, communicated and disseminated, from each individual to his or her audience.

Social constructionists have relied on theories by Le Bon (1895/1960), Durkheim (1915/1961) and Simmel (1971), suggesting that 'human sentiments are intensified when affirmed collectively. Sorrow, like joy, becomes exalted and amplified when leaping from mind to mind' (Durkheim, 1915: 446). Thus when we find ourselves surrounded by sad people at a funeral, we feel sad, even if we do not have a great reason to feel sad; likewise, when we find ourselves surrounded by a cheering, laughing or jeering crowd we may become affected by these emotions, even if we have no personal reason for experiencing them. They recognize, however, that emotions change as they flow in different social settings. Despair can turn into anger, envy into pride, joy into hate. An individual's display of a specific emotion may generate the same emotion in his or her audience or it may lead to a different emotional response. A leader, for example, may discover that her attempts to share her enthusiasm or pride with her subordinates lead to indifference or suspicion on their part.

Limitations of social constructionist theories of emotions

Social constructionist theories are not yet able to account for transformations undergone by emotions as they are communicated or shared. They tend to treat most emotions in an undifferentiated manner, occasionally dividing them into positive and negative, hot and cold, active and passive, prescribed and proscribed, but rarely explore them in their infinite nuances and subtlety, vigour and vitality. For all the virtuosity that writers such as Mangham and Overington (1987) and Hopfl and Linstead (1997) bring to discussions of the rules of emotional micro-performances, they are a long way from establishing the qualities which make a performance a success with one audience and a failure with another. The reasons why a particular emotion is associated with a specific social occasion (say, grief at a funeral, anger or derision at an inadequate offer from the employer, nostalgia at a farewell function and so on) are not addressed.

Furthermore, social constructionist approaches add little to the study of the origins of emotions like rage, despair, boredom, envy or bliss, or their sudden modifications in the course of everyday experience. Why did Andy's 'high spirits' in the earlier example, suddenly change to uncontrollable anger? And why was his anger uncontrollable ('I burst out at him and used quite strong language'), while on other occasions it might have been tempered? And why was Andy in 'a very good mood ever since, for no apparent reason'? As no less a constructionist authority on emotion than Fineman has recognized, this approach has a total blind spot when it comes to identifying where emotions come from and how they fit into the overall biographies of organizations or individuals (Fineman, 1993: 23). This is where psychoanalytic theory can substantially enhance our understanding.

PSYCHOANALYSIS AND EMOTIONS

Psychoanalysis has always been absorbed in the study of emotion. It has opened new avenues in analysing the emotional life of individuals, in exploring the origin and meaning of different emotions and in accounting for the grip which emotions have on our lives. Human beings are approached by psychoanalysis not merely as emotional but as desiring, passionate beings. Emotions are no simple side-effects of mental life, no performances staged for the sake of audiences, no instruments of interpersonal manipulation, although they may under certain circumstances be all of these things. Instead, psychoanalysis approaches emotions as driving forces in human affairs.

For psychoanalysis, emotion lies at the heart of human motivation – emotion *is* motivation. It is not accidental that both words derive from the Latin *emovere*, to move. The drive for money, no less than the drive for power or the drive for work – they all derive from emotion and are liable to become passions. The drive for truth, too, is emotionally driven, rather than the expression of an abstract interest in knowledge and learning. Hence, too, illusion is no mere product of ignorance of error, but rather the product of fear, love, anxiety, desire and passion. For psychoanalysis, emotion is what holds groups together ('necessity alone will not hold them together': Freud, 1921: 120; 1930: 313), and emotion too is what destroys them. Being in love and being under hypnosis are the two closest psychological states to being a member of a group, according to Freud (though Freud was wise enough to limit his formulations to groups 'without too much organization' (1921: 116).

For this reason, the supposedly passion-free spaces of modern organizations (where there is precisely 'too much organization') were of relatively limited interest to psychoanalytic writers for many years. Groups, on the other hand, where emotion can be dominant, were of much greater interest (see Chapter 5). The attempts of writers like such as Jaques (1955), Menzies (1960; Menzies Lyth, 1988, 1991), Levinson (1972, 1976) and Zaleznik (1977, 1989) to introduce a psychoanalytic dimension to the study of organizations were respectfully received, but until recently were not integrated into the mainstream of organizational studies. But as the view of organizations as emotional arenas has gained currency, there are opportunities for re-integrating psychoanalytic scholarship into the study of organizational processes.

KEY PSYCHOANALYTIC PROPOSITIONS REGARDING EMOTIONS IN ORGANIZATIONS

Is it possible to talk of a single psychoanalytic approach to emotion in organizations, or indeed emotion in general? The study of emotions, feelings and affects has been an organic part of the development of psychoanalytic theory since its earliest days. A wide diversity of theoretical propositions has been made, not least by Freud, whose views on emotional life developed considerably in the course of his investigations. In *Psychoanalytic Theories of Affect* (1991), Ruth Stein sketches closely the development of Freud's ideas as well as those of other important psychoanalytic writers. In Freud's earliest works, emotion features principally as *affect*, and is generally seen as a cause of mental disorders. Ineffective emotional discharges ('abreactions') surrounding traumatic events in an individual's life were seen by Freud and Breuer as causes of hysterical and obsessional symptoms.

Drawing on the then current psycho-physiological theories, Freud envisaged affect as a physical, bodily quantity which operated as a psychological force. He used the concept 'quota of affect' to indicate the quantitative nature of the emotional charge that drives a particular idea. Increases in affect are experienced as unpleasurable, hence under the rule of the pleasure principle the mental apparatus seeks to discharge it. This idea remained sovereign in Freud's thought until *Beyond the Pleasure Principle* (1920), when the simple correlation of quantity of affect discharged and quality of pleasurable experience was abandoned. Yet, in spite of many subsequent elaborations, Freud never gave up completely the idea of 'quota of affect', though he increasingly came to regard it as a psychic rather than a somatic charge.

The discharge of emotions

A charge must eventually be discharged. And Freud and Breuer in *Studies on Hysteria* (1895) envisaged three basic forms that this discharge may take. In the first case, it may lead to physical action: when hunger reaches a certain level of intensity, one seeks food. When dissatisfaction with one's job reaches a certain level, one may quit one's job. Alternatively, discharge may take the form of verbal action. In Andy's description earlier, when his anger reached a certain intensity, it led to a verbal outburst. Afterwards, Andy felt unaccountably in a good mood, something that early Freud would explain by viewing it as the result of the sudden discharge of affect achieved by his outburst. Finally, the accumulated affect may shift from one idea to another. This is the case of phobias where the object of fear is displaced; it is also the case in scapegoating, where hate is transposed on to an innocent party. In organizations, it is common to blame consultants when things go drastically wrong. This prevents members of the organization from attacking each other, although at times it also stops them learning from their mistakes (see Box). One of the crucial discoveries of psychoanalysis concerns the mobility of emotion, whereby an emotion may move from one object to another. The distinction between an idea and its emotional charge is one that permeates much of depth psychology to this day.

The transformation of emotions

Based on his clinical investigations, Freud argued that emotions may not only change objects, but may be transformed into different emotions. The two most important

AN A TO Z OF EMOTIONS

How many different emotions exist? What are the commonest emotions? What are the main emotions expressed in organizations? These are not questions that existing research on organizations can answer with great confidence. One way of approaching them is to study emotion through the stories told in and about organizations. In a piece of research, I collected, classified, interpreted and analysed 404 such stories. One aspect of the analysis concerned their emotional content. The emotions generated and communicated by these stories were quite powerful, and go some way towards reinforcing the view of organizations as emotional arenas. In fact, the stories provide a fascinating window into a wide range of emotions which one may not normally associate with organizations.

It is not possible to bring to light every emotional nuance present in a story: the same story may evoke different emotions in different individuals, and the narrator him or herself may have ambiguous or confused feelings about his or her material. The emotional content of a story comprises the emotions recollected by the narrator, the emotions which the story seeks to communicate to the listener, the emotions which the listener experiences while hearing the story and the emotions which he or she later feels on recollecting it. Thus, a comic story which generates mirth and amusement in the teller may be based on events which at the time generated horror and panic, and are received with disgust by the listener. The complications resulting from any attempt to classify stories solely in terms of their emotional content are, therefore, formidable. Nevertheless, the following were found to be the most frequent emotions (Gabriel, 1998a):

emotion	count	emotion	count
amusement (present in 114 stories)		worry	13
disparagement	82	bitterness	12
pride	70	horror	11
disapproval	57	admiration	10
relief	20	disappointment	9
anger	19	diversion	9
pity	19	panic	9
reproach	17	irony	8
sadness	17	mockery	7
satisfaction	15	anxiety	6
affection	14	fun	6
approval	14	guilt	6
frustration	14	scorn	6
nostalgia	14	self-disparagement	6
derision	13		

It will be noted that certain important emotions, such as embarrassment, happiness and hate, are absent from the above list. Doubtless, by scrutinizing the stories in the database, one could discover stories in which such emotions are present. For instance, many of the stories whose principal emotional tone was identified as amusement focused on another person's embarrassment. This illustrates the shortcomings of using quantitative techniques in analysing *en masse* what is highly subjective, delicate material. Different readers, reading the same story will read different emotional nuances in the text. Nevertheless, it is possible through the study of organizational stories to identify a far larger number of emotions than those discussed by organizational theorists.

transformations of emotions are transformation into the opposite (love transformed into hate, gratitude into envy, fear into defiance) and transformation into anxiety.

Anxiety has, since then, occupied a privileged position in psychoanalytic studies of emotion. Initially seen as an emotional waste product, which offered an outlet for all poorly discharged emotions (including love and hate, anger and jealousy), anxiety, as we shall see, came to be seen increasingly in dynamic terms, either as the psychological state to be defended against or as a signal which alerts the ego to the imminence of danger, thus setting off defensive mechanisms like repression (Freud, 1926). Along with reassessing the nature of anxiety, Freud's later theory reconsiders the nature of pleasure and pain. Pain or unpleasure is no longer the mere accumulation of unwanted excitation but rather the result of inner conflict, signalled by anxiety. Some excitation can be pleasant, especially if it may be controlled. Window-shopping, for example, may afford pleasure provided that one is not overwhelmed by the desire to buy more than one can afford. Pleasure in Freud's later theory is not the product of a sudden discharge of all excitation but depends on the nature of the excitation itself and the ability to control it. In this way, pleasure and pain cease to be opposites: pain (as is the case in masochism) can be pleasurable and pleasure can be painful (for instance, if it is not going to last long). Developing this idea, Campbell (1989) has argued that virtually any emotion, including fear, horror, grief, sorrow and hate, can be a source of pleasure, provided that it can be controlled. Bungee jumping, horror movies, hard training, travelling, even going to war, can be sources of pleasurable experience, in spite of the dangers and hardships they entail.

Viewed from this angle, Andy's 'very good mood' in the earlier example is not the result of the discharge of emotion, but rather the outcome of his ability to turn a situation in which he is normally victim into one in which he is victor. The very danger entailed by his outburst (the risks to his career or even to his job) actually increase the thrill he gets from having spoken out and increase the theatrical effect of turning the tables on his aggressor. Likewise, Bill McAder (see Box, p. 219) can actually derive some pleasure in describing a 'traumatic crisis' by finding a way of ridiculing the consultants who 'came in like gladiatorial knights on white chargers and they ended up firmly with their tails between their legs'. Thus the size of the disaster, instead of accentuating feelings of guilt and despondency, strengthens the ridicule heaped on the scapegoat.

Emotional experiences, then, depend on the extent to which we are able to control excitations. Yet Freud never ceased to emphasize the partly involuntary character of emotions – the control of emotions by the ego can never be taken for granted. Emotions are liable to be unpredictable, inconsistent, unmanageable and even chaotic, in spite of the ego's continuing attempts to control them, tame them or isolate them.

The repression of affects

Is it possible to seek to control an emotion by repressing it? Can affects be repressed in the same way that ideas and desires can? Can we repress our feelings or emotions? This is a question which puzzled Freud over a period of many years. After all, if affects are experienced as feelings and 'it is the essence of a feeling to be felt', i.e. to be fully conscious perceptions, then it makes little sense to argue that a feeling can be repressed. As Ruth Stein argues, 'the notion of an unfelt feeling is inherently

SCAPEGOATING THE CONSULTANTS

A publishing organization with over a million subscribers had been through a traumatic crisis, trying to replace its outdated computer system with a new one. Numerous employees gave their version of what happened, mostly agreeing on two facts; this had been the most traumatic experience in the history of the organization and most of the blame lay with the consultants who advised the company on information systems. This is how Bill McAder, the company's deputy director, described the experience:

> Moving from the original computer system installed in 1977 to a single-customer database would allow us to develop much faster, more flexibly. Besides, the old system had already started to creak. I came into the computer replacement project in the middle of the crisis, when the project had started to hit the rocks and I stayed with it in crisis till we aborted it £5 million and four years later. This was the most expensive mistake the organization ever made.

What did the organization learn from this mistake?

> The lesson, that I had known all along, was that if you are going to try and re-write the software for your basic product and you have a complex system, as we undoubtedly did, don't try and do anything, no matter how desperate you are, until you've got somebody on board on your own camp that you can trust to lead that project. That of itself takes a bit of doing because the number of abortive attempts we had in the course of those 4 years, trying to identify such a person were legion. We were lurching from crisis of dependence to crisis of dependence – we became dependent on consultants. In the course of that, there were issues of matching the needs of the organization to the expertise of the consultants, but all of them [consultants] failed to appreciate the complexity of what we were trying to do. They all ran out of knowledge, partners like 'IGG' and Austers, they were the biggest two we used. They came in like gladiatorial knights on white chargers and they ended up firmly with their tails between their legs.

This account suggests much pain and guilt on the part of the narrator, whose career had been blighted by his involvement in the fiasco. But the final flurry is an attempt to shift the blame on to the consultants, as though they, rather than the company, were the subjects of the humiliation.

paradoxical' (1991: 21). In 'Negation' (1925b), Freud offered the suggestion that a repressed desire may enter consciousness only by being disowned. The repressed content is accepted intellectually but not *emotionally*. So an individual saying 'I can see why one may say that I am worried about losing my hair/job/youth; but this is absolutely not so' allows a partial lifting of the repression by entertaining the idea of being afraid but not the affect.

Anna Freud subsequently generalized this principle as the isolation of affect, a process where many repressed ideas may be expressed at the intellectual level, without being confronted emotionally (1936). It is possible, for example, to recognize having acted wrongly and even apologize without actually feeling any remorse. Discussing threatening or painful topics in a highly cerebral manner, like feelings of abandonment, failure or loss, may be a way of stopping oneself from experiencing these feelings. Thus, in Freud's later work, psychological defences can operate against unacceptable emotions just as against painful ideas. Sandler and Sandler (1994) have enlarged on this view by arguing that an emotion may be repressed very shortly after it has been experienced or felt and then disavowed. In this way it is suppressed, choked and unacknowledged, yet not entirely obliterated; an example of such a choked emotion is the 'unconscious sense of guilt' which Freud regarded as a fundamental cost of culture (see Chapter 7).

To sum up, then, psychoanalysis emphasizes the mobility of human emotion. Whether at the individual or at the social level, emotions may be diverted towards different objects, turned into their opposites or find new expressions; they may lead to action or to verbalization; they may be muffled and repressed or amplified into fully-fledged passions.

Transference

No single psychological process provides as sharp a testing ground for the transformation of emotions as *transference*. Transference is, in the first place, part of the complex emotional bond that develops between patient and analyst in an analytic situation. The seminal characteristic of this situation, and the one which provides vital leverage for psychoanalytic interpretations, is the repetition of earlier emotional experiences. The patient does not merely recollect these experiences but actually relives them emotionally, redirecting many feelings, like love, hate, fear, anger and envy, on to the person of the analyst. In this manner, emotions, qualities and symbols which once held a powerful grip over an individual, re-surface in the analytic situation to provide strong evidence as to the origins of mental disturbances.

If transference is the bed-rock of psychoanalytic interventions within the therapeutic situation, its significance extends beyond the couch. It has been recognized since Ferenczi's work in the 1910s that repressed feelings may be transferred on to non-analytic persons, for example political or religious leaders. In so doing, an individual may enhance positive feelings by introjecting them from external objects ('As a follower of Christ, I am virtuous') or cast out negative feelings by projecting them on to external objects ('It is not I who wishes to destroy him, but he who wishes to destroy me').

Kleinian theorists have moved a stage further by arguing that, through projection and introjection, the ego actually divests itself of unwanted parts of itself and incorporates desirable parts from the external world. In this way, an individual may gain some mastery over his or her emotions by manipulating objects. Instead of repressing threatening or painful emotions, the ego may project them on to external objects or split them off. Klein's concept of splitting is of considerable interest. She views it as a pre-Oedipal defence employed against persecutory anxiety, a fear of total annihilation of the self by the outside world, which results in the world being split into two, good and bad objects, heroes and villains, objects of love and objects of hate (Klein, 1946/1986). In such a Manichean universe, idealization and vilification take hold of mental functioning and may affect whole groups or even nations; scapegoats are charged with every conceivable fault and attract collective hate, while idealized love-objects are endowed with every perfection and, through introjection, result in narcissistic self-love.

Klein has sometimes been criticized for approaching all social life as a complex of emotion-driven fantasies and for reducing social and political contradictions to innate emotional conflict, and especially to feelings of envy, hate and destructiveness (see Frosh, 1991). The self emerges as the product of fantasy scenarios and conflicting emotions with little regard for the deeper political and economic realities. Yet, Klein saw the paranoid-schizoid position as a developmental stage leading to a position of greater emotional maturity, in which the world is accepted with its imperfections and difficulties, the depressive position.

The depressive position is not free from anxiety, though in this instance anxiety is not a fear of total annihilation by the object (as in the paranoid-schizoid position) but a fear of losing the object damaging it, as a result of one's own destructive tendencies. The depressive position accepts ambivalence in the self, just as it accepts both good and bad qualities in objects, and is accompanied by a guilt which represents one's own sense of responsibility for the harm done to an object. The result of the depressive position can be a complex of reparative, protective, altruistic and nurturing emotions (see Chapter 3).

Klein attaches affects far more closely to objects than Freud did and, in so doing, dissolves the distinction between desire and affect, as well as giving even greater primacy to feelings than Freud. If, for Freud, emotions derive from fantasies which, in turn, are compromise formations between desire and the forces of repression, for Klein, fantasies are derivatives, not causes of emotions. Bad feelings, bad emotions and bad objects become amalgamated together as do their good equivalents. Feelings, conflicts between feelings and the ability to tolerate them become the primary motive forces of mental life, encouraging or inhibiting development.

Feelings may trigger off other feelings; for instance, one may feel angry about feeling sad, powerless or even love; one may feel anxious about feeling depressed or about falling in love. As Ruth Stein and other writers have observed, feelings may become part of chain reactions, triggering off each other. These chain reactions may, in turn, form self-reinforcing emotional cycles:

> An example of such a cycle would be that of persecutory fears, which cause aggression, which causes anxiety, which in turn increases the need to project aggression and 'bad feelings,' which in turn, increase persecutory fears, and so on. Another example is that of guilt, which reinforces gratitude, which in turn diminishes envy. (Stein, 1991: 91)

These emotional loops, vicious circles of 'bad feelings' and 'magic circles' of 'good feelings', can take hold of an individual's mental life; mental life itself becomes a sequence of emotional stages of development, in which different emotional conflicts unfold, reach temporary accommodation or threaten to regress to the splitting characteristic of the paranoid-schizoid position. Through all of these stages, the underlying conflict is that between feelings of love and feelings of hate, which in Klein's work assume a primary importance, rather than be seen as derivative of other conflicts (such as between Eros and the death instinct or between the individual and society) and deeper psychic entities. The concepts love and hate, 'good' and 'bad', become themselves evaluative. Hate is bad, love is good. Manicheanism, i.e. the division of the world into pure good and pure evil, is therefore not only a characteristic of the phenomena addressed by Klein's theory, but becomes a feature of the theory itself.

This judgemental quality is entirely absent from the work of Freud, who believed that life and death instincts, love and hate, all have the right to exist, can all be good as well as bad. By contrast, many authors influenced by Klein, who have developed these ideas and used them to understand group and organizational processes, have been concerned with improving the way groups and organizations function, enhancing reparative, supportive and learning processes and containing the destructive ones.

EMOTIONS IN GROUPS

The emotional qualities of groups had fascinated conservative historians of the French Revolution and were of great interest to revolutionary theorists like Sorel. The psychology of group emotion received two important contributions in the early part of the century in the work of Gustave Le Bon and William McDougall. The observations of these two theorists form the starting point of Freud's investigations in *Group Psychology and the Analysis of the Ego*: the intensification of emotions in groups, the contagiousness of specific emotions, suggestibility, the lowering of critical abilities and moral restraints, the thirst for illusions, these were well-known emotional qualities of group life.

> There is no doubt that something exists in us which, when we become aware of signs of an emotion in someone else, tends to make us fall into the same emotion; but how often do we not successfully oppose it, resist the emotion, and react in quite an opposite way. Why, therefore, do we invariably give way to this contagion when we are in a group? (Freud, 1921: 117)

Freud's arguments, however, soon leave emotions behind, treating them as outcomes of deeper psychological vicissitudes, namely identification, group bonding and the formation of an ego-ideal. In contrast to Freud, Bion, following Klein's example, placed emotions squarely at the centre of his investigations into the mental life of a group. A group may be a 'work group' or 'sophisticated group', drawing on its own resources to carry out its task. Such a group is outward-looking, engaging in creative exchange with its environment, and recalls Freud's notion of the 'managerial ego' which is generally able to keep its 'harsh masters' satisfied. Yet, a group whose task causes anxiety may lapse into basic assumption functioning, in which it becomes overpowered by emotional forces. Basic assumption groups defend themselves against anxiety by closing themselves to their environment and allowing emotion, fantasy and delusion to take over from task (see Chapter 5).

Each of the three types of basic assumption group displays its own characteristic batch of self-reinforcing emotions. The dependency assumption revolves around blind faith in the leader, trust, reverence, loyalty, devotion, respect and submissiveness. The fight/flight assumption commandeers many of the emotions characteristic of the paranoid-schizoid position, rage, hate, envy, destructiveness and fear. The pairing assumption revolves around feelings of hope, optimism, confidence and self-assurance. In all of these instances emotions undermine the group's ability to think or reason, to plan, to control and to administer its task; in short, they represent pathologies, analogous to individual pathologies. Effective groups, therefore, may not lapse into basic assumption functioning. The leader, the group therapist or the organizational consultant, as much as the members of the group, must therefore be on guard for signs of basic assumption functioning.

Three things should be noted in connection with Bion's influential theory. First, each basic assumption precludes the other two, so that there are no hybrid possibilities. In fact, it is a feature of each basic assumption that members will function as if the other two basic assumptions are not merely absent, but inconceivable. Secondly, Bion viewed group and individual psychologies as essentially the same. 'No individual, however isolated in time and space, can be regarded as outside a group or lacking in active manifestations of group psychology' (Bion, 1961: 132). The qualities of groups are therefore carried in each and every individual and there is no question of a group mind or of a tension between the individual and the group. Thirdly, emotion in groups is generally seen as a negative force, deflecting a group from its task and inhibiting the achievement of group aims. The 'sophisticated group' is a group in which each individual keeps his or her mind on the task, cooperating with each other rather than emotionally consolidating together, requiring no comforting delusions of salvation.

Bion's theory has received extensive support from the work organizational researchers and consultants who have found in it a valuable key for unlocking the emotional tangles of work groups, especially highly ineffectual ones. Many authors writing from a psychodynamic perspective, have employed basic assumption theory first to analyse group functioning and then to effect change, restoring the group to its task (see, for example, Kets de Vries and Miller, 1984; Hirschhorn, 1988; Krantz, 1989; Diamond, 1993). Nevertheless, the sharp distinction between the basic assumptions and the 'sophisticated group' have been hard to maintain and certain authors, like Mant (1977), Gould (1977) and Stokes (1994) have suggested that under certain circumstances primary assumption functioning may be beneficial for the attainment of collective tasks.

ORGANIZATIONS AND EMOTIONS

While Bion's theory has found many applications in relatively unstructured groups, the emotional life of organizations is considerably more complex than that of single groups. The complex theories developed by Elliott Jaques, Isabel Menzies Lyth, Eric Trist, Harold Bridger, Eric Miller and other theorists associated with the Tavistock Institute in London have addressed directly the effects of bureaucratic forms, hierarchies and rules on the emotional lives of their members. Drawing from Klein's theories, Tavistock research has studied how individuals in large bureaucratic organizations, faced with uncertainty and anxiety, set up psychological boundaries through projections and introjections which seriously distort organizational rationality and task. The overall perspective is not dissimilar to Bion's, in as much as emotion is seen as both the cause and the result of defensive reactions, which undermine clarity of purpose and execution. But instead of looking for defences against anxiety in emotional group functioning, the Tavistock theorists have looked at how organizations themselves may furnish individuals with defensive devices.

Transposing the Kleinian theory of defences against anxiety on to the organizational and social levels, Elliott Jaques (1952, 1955) argued that individuals may collectively project bad objects on to a single member of an organization or a stigmatized social group, while introjecting the idealized qualities of a good object. The first officer of a ship, for instance, is usually held responsible for everything that is wrong on the ship, while allowing the captain to be seen as a kind protecting figure. Scapegoating is thus a feature of many societies and organizations, which enables individuals to deal with internal anxieties as though they originated from the outside, and may therefore be fought against or destroyed.

In his famous Glacier Metals study conducted in the early 1950s, Jaques observed how splitting, idealization and denial functioned within a factory on a massive scale. Workers split managers into good ones and bad ones, while managers idealized the workers and denied any conflict that might exist between them. By denying that workers may have 'bad' aspects, managers were defending themselves against their own 'bad' aspects. In this way, an emotional vicious circle, reminiscent of the ones singled out by Klein, ensued: 'The greater the concessions given by management to the workers, the greater was the guilt and fear of depressive anxiety in the workers and hence the greater the retreat to paranoid attitudes as a means of avoiding depressive anxiety' (Jaques, 1955: 493).

SOCIAL DEFENCES AGAINST ANXIETY

Jaques's view that organizations supply individuals with suitable defences against anxiety (which he has since repudiated, preferring to see anxiety as the outcome of organizational dysfunctions, rather than vice versa (see Jaques, 1995) was supported by Menzies Lyth's research on nurses in a London teaching hospital. This study has made a lasting contribution to the study of emotion in organizations and is still widely cited. Nurses confront many different emotions from patients and their relatives: gratitude for the care they offer, admiration as well as envy for their skills, resentment stemming from forced dependence. Their own feelings towards the patients, especially feelings of closeness and personal caring, are tempered by the knowledge that the patient may die. 'The work situation arouses very strong and mixed feelings in the nurse: pity, compassion and love; guilt and anxiety; hatred and resentment of patients who arouse these strong feelings; envy of the care given to the patient' (Menzies Lyth, 1988: 46). Faced with such an emotional cauldron, many nurses re-experience infantile persecutory anxieties, from which they seek to defend themselves, through the familiar mechanisms of projection, splitting and denial. Menzies Lyth's important contribution was to establish how an organization's own bureaucratic features – its rules and procedures, rotas, task-lists, checks and counter-checks, paperwork, hierarchies and so on – all of these impersonal devices act as supports for the defensive techniques. By allowing for 'ritual task performance', by depersonalizing relations with the patients, by using organizational hierarchies, nurses contained their anxiety.

Yet, in Menzies Lyth's view, such organizational defences against anxiety were ultimately unsuccessful: 'The system made little provision for confronting anxiety and working it through, the only way in which a real increase in the capacity to cope with it and personal maturation would take place. As a social defence system, it was ineffectual in containing anxiety' (1991: 363). The system's inadequacy is evidenced by its failure to train and retain nurses, a chronically low morale, high levels of stress and burn-out and absence of work satisfaction. By contrast, institutional health is testified not only by performance and output indicators, but also by morale indicators, and individual feelings of growth and maturation. Along with other psychoanalytically trained consultants, Menzies Lyth views the role of the consultant as one who may help restore an organization to health, by implementing a number of principles:

> These principles match quite closely the criteria for a healthy personality as derived from psychoanalysis. They include avoiding dealing with anxiety by the use of regressed

defenses; more uses of adaptations and sublimation; the ability to confront and work through problems; opportunities for people to deploy their capacities to their fullest, no more or less than they are able to do; opportunity to operate realistic control over their life in the institution while being able to take due account of the needs and contributions of others; independence without undue supervision; and visible relation between efforts and rewards, not only financial. (Menzies Lyth, 1991: 377)

Menzies Lyth's prescriptions have been taken up with greater or lesser success by numerous psychoanalytically orientated consultants. Countless instances of backfiring social defences against anxiety have been documented by writers working within this psychodynamic perspective, and outstanding contributions in establishing the crippling effects of such defences both on individuals and on organizations have been made by Diamond (1985, 1993), Hirschhorn (1988, 1993), Krantz (1989), Lapierre (1989), Gould (1993) and Hirschhorn and Gilmore (1993).

In *The Workplace Within*, Hirschhorn (1988) uses his experience as an organizational consultant to show how anxiety in organizations triggers off primitive fears of annihilation, which in turn call for social defences. To Bion's basic assumption, Hirschhorn adds two further modes of social defence: organizational rituals and covert coalitions. Following Menzies Lyth, Hirschhorn views *organizational rituals* as depersonalized routines, which create a distance between the individuals and their roles, screening out threatening emotional involvements and replacing them with a set of mechanical actions. *Covert coalitions*, on the other hand, constitute a kind of unconscious psychological deal, whereby members of an organization call a truce to conflict or disagreement by assuming roles drawn from family life, which provides them with a model for anxiety containment. The price of such a truce, observes Hirschhorn, is the creation of taboo subjects which may not be referred to and the perpetuation of dysfunctional arrangements within the organization.

Hirschhorn documents several instances where management training and socialization reproduce and perpetuate defensive techniques. Yet, eschewing the a-historical quality of much organizational theorizing, Hirschhorn devotes nearly half of his book to a discussion of the increasing ineffectiveness of such techniques in a post-industrial milieu. Numerous social and technological factors conspire to alter the fundamental configurations of emotions in organizations. If mature capitalism found its typical expression in feelings of narcissistic emptiness and anxiety associated with splitting, post-industrial society is rapidly running out of meaningful 'bad' objects and institutional defences against anxiety. Hirschhorn argues that successful organizations in future will need members whose anxieties are confronted and worked through, rather than members who look for suitable scapegoats to victimize. Recognizing the complexities and interdependence of organizations, accepting good and bad within and outside boundaries, a feature of Klein's depressive position, supports reparative processes and accepts interdependence. In this manner, Hirschhorn envisages the possibility of the emergence of a culture that accepts complexity and supports learning and growth processes, both at the individual and organizational level.

The psychoanalytic idea of social defences against anxiety has become increasingly accepted by numerous scholars, including those working outside depth psychology. One particular version of the argument presents rationality itself, the use of quasi-scientific procedures, such as forecasting, planning, monitoring, evaluating, testing and so on, as no more that emotional rituals whose function is entirely the allaying of managers' anxieties in a highly unpredictable and even chaotic environment (Cleverley, 1971; MacIntyre, 1981/1985; A. B. Thomas, 1993; Watson, 1994; Gabriel, 1998c). Of considerable interest is Stacey's (1992, 1995) pioneering contribution which combines the psychoanalytic theory of social defences, MacIntyre's critique of quasi-scientific managerial procedures with complexity theory to the study of managerial work. Stacey maintains that successful organizations are those which function in a state of bounded instability, a near-chaos state which is neither one of catastrophic disequilibrium nor one of static ossification and death. Functioning in this mode, organizations are unpredictable beyond a very small time-span, much like weather patterns. Learning, creativity and innovation, according to Stacey, are the result of operating at the edge of the abyss, which creates feelings of realistic anxiety, as numerous organizations, once thought invulnerable, collapse and others make large numbers of people (including executives) redundant. Using psychoanalytic theory, Stacey has argued that managers hold on to outdated and virtually useless procedures of control in an attempt to contain such anxieties, seeking to create islands of calm in a turbulent sea. Needless to say, such procedures have no more chance of success than ancient rites of weather control, as MacIntyre has memorably put it (for a development of these arguments, see Chapter 12).

ORGANIZATIONAL CAUSES OF ANXIETY

The study of the containment mechanisms offered by organizations for anxiety, and subsequent complications, distortions and dysfunctions, is one of the foremost contributions of depth psychology in this area and has attracted much attention. A smaller number of theorists, however, have focused on the obverse proposition, namely that organizations are also sources of anxiety. While the former position has preoccupied mainly theorists influenced by Klein and the object relations tradition in psychoanalysis, the latter has drawn more directly from Freud's own theory of anxiety as a signal of danger. A seminal contribution in this area has been made by Howell S. Baum in his book *The Invisible Bureaucracy*. Like Hirschhorn, Baum (1987) explores the matching of psychological and organizational processes, only the emphasis here is in the opposite direction. Bureaucracy, argues Baum, contains certain features which function as systematic generators of anxiety. Foremost among these is hierarchy which disperses responsibility while concentrating power. Responsibilities of individuals tend to be highly ambiguous, which is compounded by the endemic impersonality and distance between individuals across organizational ranks. Individuals then adopt a defensive attitude, seeking to cover their own back at all times.

Bureaucratic impersonality creates an empty psychological space between subordinates and superiors, which is filled with fantasies. Baum notes two especially common ones among subordinates: the 'moral paragon' and the 'superiority in competence and strength'. Each of these sets off its own type of anxiety – the former guilt anxiety, the latter shame anxiety. It is noteworthy that, unlike the object relations approach, Baum reverts to a more orthodox view of emotion as the product of fantasy, rather than vice versa. Yet, like Hirschhorn, Baum views blame and credit as the vital currency in which organizational participants continuously trade. Blaming, victimization and scapegoating are not only major ingredients of the emotional life of organizations, but derive from the nature of bureaucracy itself, rather than from maladministration. When wrongly accused, individuals frequently feel threats of annihilation out of proportion to the actual blame placed on them. The strong feelings of rage, anxiety and fear generated by such events are evidence of regression to an earlier, more vulnerable age.

Fineman and Gabriel (1996) have collected several stories which support the view that the psychological need for clear lines of responsibility is systematically frustrated by bureaucratic procedures. In one story, an intern accused of tampering with a superior's computer bursts into an almost inarticulate fit of rage: 'I left with awful feelings of frustration, angriness, uselessness and betrayal' (1996: 112), he says, feeling trapped in the role of scapegoat, where his protestations of innocence only serve to reinforce his victimization. In another story, a young trainee reports how he was cajoled by a senior and respected manager to become an accomplice in the cover-up of a £50,000 blunder. Yet another employee, who confesses a serious computer mistake to his manager is told 'Listen, *you* haven't made a mistake, but *the system* has. Whenever something is wrong you must come and tell me that the accounts system has screwed up. The system will lose prestige and value, whereas you have gained recognition because you spotted the error. You see, this company likes winners' (1996: 116). Echoing the views of Baum and Hirschhorn, Fineman and Gabriel conclude that

> Organizational hierarchies become highways along which blame travels: superiors blame subordinates for filling-in the wrong forms or pulling the wrong levers; subordinates blame superiors for designing forms and levers wrongly or giving the wrong instructions. Apportioning blame can become a highly unpredictable business. Under these circumstances, people may learn the simple, but demoralizing lesson, that the best thing to do is simply to protect themselves. (1996: 119)

In my own research (Gabriel, 1991a, c), I have noted how many organizations, especially oppressive authoritarian ones, maintain a continuous level of anxiety through alarmist gossip and horror stories of sadism, injustice and humiliation. In a naval camp, for example, the vicious pranks of officers at the expense of recruits were lodged in organizational folklore, being further embellished by older conscripts who used them to educate their younger colleagues in the iniquities of military life and keep them on their guard. If bureaucracy harbours unseen dangers, potential victimization, unexpected responsibilities and dormant or unknown regulations, anxiety warns the individual of such threats and offers a partial inoculation against injury when misfortune strikes.

EMOTION IN ORGANIZATIONS: A SUMMARY OF CURRENT VIEWS

In summary, depth psychology views the display, channelling, unleashing, containment, control and management of emotions as a set of core processes in organizations, which frequently account for the difference between success and failure. Feelings, emotions and fantasies shape the world of work, rather than being mere by-products of work process. Of course, work processes generate distinct feelings, emotions and fantasies, but these irrational phenomena become embedded in work processes, at times enhancing and at others inhibiting them. Many organizational emotions recreate instances from both personal and collective past. Superior–subordinate relations, for example, may be charged with emotions, especially anxiety, envy and guilt, first experienced within a parent–child relationship (Krantz, 1989; Lapierre, 1989; Gabriel, 1997); relations across race boundaries may be burdened by intergenerationally transmitted emotions, rooted in the experiences of slavery and racial exploitation (D. A. Thomas, 1993).

Organizations are complex mazes in which different emotions travel, mutate and interact, as individuals trade in resources, information and power but, above all, in credit and blame. Anxiety is a pre-eminent emotion resulting from the demands which bureaucratic settings induce, yet these same settings offer various defences against anxiety, which sometimes protect individuals, yet at other times exacerbate the very causes of individuals' discomfort. For example, a glamorous organizational image may reinforce individuals' sense of their own merit and perfection or even provide a partial consolation for their individual mortality, yet it may also generate feelings of powerlessness, dependence and resentment.

Leaders continually intervene in the emotional processes of their organizations, knowingly or unknowingly. Yet their interventions can be unpredictable. Hirschhorn and Gilmore (1993) have shown how a leader's attempts to initiate increased participation among the followers may lead to a vicious circle of vulnerability, withdrawal, anger and frustration among subordinates, which pushes the leader towards authoritarianism. Similarly, Lapierre (1989) has noted how leaders must walk an emotional tightrope between impotence and omnipotence in order to pass emotional tests laid by their subordinates. If they err on either side, they risk losing the respect of those whom they lead.

Some scholars continue to emphasize the dysfunctional consequences of fantasies and emotions for organizations, seeking to vindicate the primacy of rational, task-oriented processes. The majority of depth psychologists, however, view emotion itself as vital in breaking out of dysfunctional processes which inhibit performance and exacerbate anxieties and discontents. Organizational learning, far from being a dispassionate Socratic pursuit, is driven by some emotions and opposed by others. Learning is, therefore, no mere cognitive experience of gradual enlightenment, but a frequently painful process of 'unlearning' past defensive and dysfunctional postures and working against inner and institutional resistances.

CRITIQUE OF PSYCHODYNAMIC APPROACHES TO ORGANIZATIONAL EMOTION

Fineman (1996), an author who generally favours a social constructionist approach to the study of organizational emotion, is a sympathetic critic of psychodynamic theory at two levels. First, he observes that psychodynamic approaches, while paying lip service to the social-situational dimension of emotion, tend to disregard it in practice, treating emotions and feelings as virtually interchangeable entities. In this way, psychodynamic writers tend to ignore emotions which derive from the logic of a situation itself; for example, mourning at funerals, anxiety at job appraisals, and horror in horror movies. Furthermore, the emotions themselves are culturally defined, so that individuals may experience specific emotions because their culture and their language equip them with the means necessary to specify them. Different languages carve up the emotional landscape in different ways. In one language, jealousy and envy are not distinguished with different words; in another language, there are three or four words describing distinct emotions which in English are translated as anxiety; in yet another language there is no word at all to describe emotions such as embarrassment or stress.

There is some justification in the view that depth psychology has blurred the distinctions between emotional experience and emotional display, disregarding the social influences on emotions. This is especially relevant to organizations, which have their own implicit rules about emotional display. Individual members are aware that certain emotional displays are appropriate within the organization and others are not; this, in turn, affects the emotional experiences themselves. Andy, whose description of his emotional encounter with his manager was presented earlier in this chapter, explained very perceptively the different emotional codes that he followed in and out of work.

> My personality changes when I come to work. I am a much less easy-going character at work. In my personal life I am a very laid-back, spontaneous sort of character. At work I have to put that to one side. My emotional responses to things are suppressed. I tend to be more level, less inclined to get heated about things.
>
> You switch off the emotional side, you try and let comments which you wouldn't stand for outside the work ride, if they've been passed on by senior people. The reason why Wednesday's débâcle [the incident described above] was so bad, was that I had been in such a good frame of mind, I didn't have the old defence mechanisms up, so when he then attacked me for no apparent reason, instead of sitting and thinking 'Oh well, just sit here, it's just Simon again', I immediately flared back at him.
>
> The switch off mode is no frame of mind at all, really, it is one of the things that people class as professional behaviour, what the Americans would call 'a suit'; straight face, you show no opinions on anything, you don't laugh at jokes, you don't make jokes, neither do you get upset visibly about comments, you accept criticism and you always come back with a productive cooperative statement.

Numerous individuals talk of having to switch off their emotional side while at work, and yet recognize how emotions stored up at the workplace may be expressed at home. This suggests that psychodynamic approaches to organizational emotion must engage with codes of emotional display and control which link the individual's experiences in and out of organizations. In this, they can learn from the formulations of social constructionists, who in turn may learn from depth psychology that individuals cannot be approached as actors capable of virtually *any* emotional performance and *any* degree of emotional control (Fineman, 1993: 23).

A second charge raised by Fineman is that psychodynamic writers operate within the assumption that there is an ideal of emotion-free, task-oriented organization, casting themselves in the role of uprooters of 'the demon of irrationality' (Fineman, 1996). In contrast to current trends which view emotion as the secret weapon of rationality, psychodynamic thinkers are presented as crypto-Weberians, approaching all emotion as irrational and all irrationality as dysfunctional. Now, few psychodynamic writers would take such an extreme view, yet there is little doubt that many of them have adopted a clinical paradigm which emphasizes negative emotions as carriers of organizational pathologies. Yet, this paradigm has not succeeded in establishing a sharp distinction between positive and negative emotions. Love, for example, may be a negative emotion if it leads to jealousy or over-protectiveness, whereas hate may be a positive emotion in an army about to enter battle. Nor has it proved possible to establish a sharp line between organizational normality and pathological processes. When, for example, does healthy scepticism end and paranoid anxiety start? When does healthy pride become narcissistic self-delusion or megalomania? When does optimism for a future project become a delusion of invulnerability?

These questions permit different answers and psychodynamic authors approach them differently. Some argue that criteria of organizational pathology, like those of individual pathology, are relatively objective, to be found in the ability to work and express emotion freely. Others argue that organizational pathologies are distinct from individual ones, in as much as healthy and normal individuals may be parties to highly contorted organizational relationships. A few, however, have taken a more pessimistic view, inspired by Freud's tentative but sweeping conclusion (at the end of *Civilization and its Discontents*) that 'under the influence of cultural urges, some civilizations, or some epochs of civilization – possibly the whole of mankind – have become "neurotic"' (1930: 338). Thus, individual neurosis, far from being the enemy of organizations, may quite often be its ally, i.e. unhappy, neurotic individuals may be quite functional and even prosper within organizational environments. Conversely, our bureaucratic culture, far from merely tolerating individual neurosis, thrives on it (Lasch, 1980, 1984; Gabriel, 1983).

CONCLUSION

Emotions suffuse all significant aspects of an individual's experience, including all meaningful objects, activities and relations, and underlie virtually the entire edifice we call culture. Everything that is meaningful is also emotionally charged. Yet emotions do not surface ready-made from the depths of the individual soul, even if this is exactly what an individual experiences when suddenly gripped by a powerful emotion, like anger, self-pity or despair. Instead, they are, to different degrees, learned, cultivated, modified and suppressed throughout an individual's development. As such, they lie at the intersection between individual and culture and may be studied both horizontally, in terms of the simultaneous emotional experiences of several individuals in a group or an organization, and vertically, in terms of an individual's own psycho-history.

The challenge for the study of organizational emotions in the future lies in a *rapprochement* of psychodynamic and social constructionist approaches, a continuing exploration of the relations between social and psychological defences, a clarification of the vital differences between feelings, emotions and affects, and a critical appraisal of the issue of emotional repression. On this last issue hinge numerous methodological and practical priorities. Should emotions be interpreted, described or analysed? Should they be approached symptomatically, phenomenologically or causally? Should they be seen as outcomes, as causes or as signs?

An even greater task currently facing scholars, researchers and practitioners is the exploration of the relation between rationality and emotion in organizations. In spite of the current recognition of the importance of emotions in organizations, the claims of rationality and, allied with it, the claims of control must not be discounted. The Weberian chimera *sine ira et studio* may have finally been slain, yet the claims of rationality continue to haunt organizations. In spite of the emotional maelstrom which may at times overwhelm organizations, many of the day-to-day activities of organizational members continue to be rationally defined and justified. Forms are filled, reports are written, deals are made, alliances are struck, regulations are introduced, costs are cut, not because people act emotionally, but because they act instrumentally, driven by considerations which are perceived as rational.

The clashing complexities of emotion and rationality are aptly demonstrated in the following account by a computer analyst, as she describes the completion of a report recommending that two of her colleagues are no longer needed in their jobs.

> There are parts of my job that I hate; for example, today, I've written a report where I've almost suggested that there ought to be redundancies in certain areas. Now, I've just felt dreadful about it and it's the first time I've done anything like that, and I don't feel that it's like, I am not sure what I'm doing when it comes to that. I mean everything, I'm never 100% confident [about what I do]. With pieces of software I am [confident], some pieces of software that I use I know them like the back of my hand, but on the analysis side I don't always know what I am doing. Or why I am doing it. Some systems seem to be working perfectly well but there is some political motive behind you going in there and analysing it. I know there *is* a political motive. I've actually done that before and they've said 'But there are reasons . . .'. I am a bit anxious about the report that I have just written, because I am talking about people that I know, I am talking about a system that currently exists and keeps two people employed and saying this can be done by one part-timer and this makes me anxious and worried. I never thought that I'd be in a position where I would be making these recommendations. But it's just a recommendation, not a decision.

This account combines a strong expression of feelings (hate, guilt, anxiety, worry, insecurity), blame-shifting ('political motive'), rationalization ('almost suggested', 'just a recommendation, not a decision'), with a sense of being a Weberian cog ('I don't always know what I am doing. Or why I am doing it'). Yet, there is no attempt to challenge the instrumental motive that if one part-time employee can run a system currently run by two full-time employees, then these two people (who have families to support and emotions of their own) are 'redundant'. The writing of a report and the report's recommendations are not in themselves expressions of emotions; on the contrary, they are based on systematic attempts to suppress emotion from the discharging of an organizational task.

This acts as a timely check to the current tendency to privilege emotion in the study of organizations. Bureaucracy, as an emotion-free principle of administration, may no longer be a valid way of studying organizations. Yet, it is surely premature to bury Weber's insight that modern organizations have a unique quality of blocking emotion from driving the actions of their members – and, in so doing, depth psychology helps us to appreciate the quite unique and taxing strains that they impose on our emotional lives.

10 PSYCHOANALYSIS AND ETHICS IN ORGANIZATIONS

Glenn Swogger

There is an ethic embedded within psychoanalytic theory and treatment. Psychoanalysis shares with other healing arts a commitment to the relief of suffering, the restoration of function and the promotion of normal development. More unique to psychoanalysis is a belief in the role and value of reason, knowledge and understanding in this process. This is evident in the role insight is given in psychoanalytic therapy and in the process of inner change: 'Where id is, there shall ego be.' With this goes a special value placed on honesty and truthfulness. Psychoanalysis is in some ways a psychology of self-deception, as shown in the concept of the dynamic, i.e. repressed, unconscious, and the defensive distortion of reality that occurs regularly in all of us. Implicit here is the value placed on self-knowledge.

One ramification of the belief in the importance of self-knowledge is that a relationship is asserted between self-knowledge and knowledge of others, or more generally, between self-knowledge and an understanding of the human condition. Stated negatively, limitations in our self-knowledge result in blind spots which limit and distort our understanding of others. Given the laborious and sometimes painful process of overcoming our protective self-deception, it is not surprising that psychoanalysts came to understand and accept their own counter-transference as an important component of the therapeutic process much later than they developed their understanding of transference (Racker, 1968). Just as the emotionally driven blind spots of the analyst lead to impaired understanding and improper treatment of the patient, so too may these same processes lead to unethical behaviour in organizations and other arenas of life. This relationship between inner psychodynamic events, understanding of self and others, and action will be the primary focus of this chapter. Psychoanalysis makes important contributions to the understanding of emotional and cognitive processes, in individuals and groups, that eventuate in ethical and unethical behaviour. In this way, psychoanalysis will be shown to contain within itself both a psychology of moral behaviour and a moral doctrine. As a psychology of moral behaviour, it seeks to show how the sense of morality, of right and wrong, of good and evil, takes root in all of us. As a moral doctrine, it offers some enlightenment in the moral choices we face.

MORAL RESPONSIBILITY AND THE COMPLEXITIES OF HUMAN MOTIVATION

Psychoanalysis deepens our understanding of ethical behaviour in part by making us aware of the complexity of motivation involved in behaviour, beautifully illustrated in an example by Walter Kaufmann:

> No single explanation can really explain human behavior; it can at most illuminate human behavior and allow us to see something we had not seen . . . An accident may be considered a paradigm. Why did it happen? The road was icy at that point. And the driver of the small car was in a great hurry because he was late for a crucial appointment, because the person who had promised to pick him up had not come, and his reflexes were slower than usual because he had had hardly any sleep that night because his mother had died the day before. And just before the accident his attention was distracted for one crucial second by a very pretty girl on the side of the road, who reminded him of a girl he had once known. Yet he might have regained control of his car if only a truck had not come toward him just as he skidded into the left lane. The truck driver might have managed not to hit him, but . . . if we add that the truck driver had just gone through a red light and was, moreover, going much faster than the legal speed limit, the policeman who witnessed the accident, as well as the court later on, might discount as irrelevant everything said before and be quite content to explain the accident simply in terms of the truck driver's two violations. *He* caused the accident. But that does not rule out the possibility that the other driver had a strong death wish because his mother had died, or that he punished himself for looking at an attractive girl the way he did so soon after his mother's death, or that the person who had let him down was partly to blame. (Kaufmann, 1980: 279–80)

Kaufmann's vignette captures the multiple determinants and meanings of an emotionally charged (and ethically complex) event. The germ of the psychoanalytic understanding of the complexity of emotional life is contained in Freud's concept of overdetermination, which he used to describe the multiple meanings of the elements of dreams. This concept was systematized and elaborated by Robert Wälder (1936) in what he called 'the principle of multiple function'. Every piece of behaviour is conceptualized as reflecting the influence of drives, super-ego, external realities, compulsive attempts to master past traumas, and the ego's response to each of these and to its own attempts at mastery. Wälder concludes that 'psychoanalysis is a kind of polyphonic theory of the psychic life in which each act is a chord, and in which there is consonance and dissonance' (1936: 53–4). Wälder explored the implications of the principle of multiple function for what he called 'psychoanalytical hermeneutics', and asserted that a given human event has multiple, perhaps even infinite, meanings. The rich explorations of Kaufmann and Wälder anticipate more recent hermeneutic approaches (cf. Spence, 1987).

The reality of psychic complexity postulated by psychoanalysis gives both new depth and new dimensions to personal and ethical responsibility. While the Western legal tradition has always comprehended intent and state of mind as a fundamental component of the criminal act, its practice has been to consider more conscious and straightforward elements such as premeditation, blind passion or a gross impairment of cognitive capacities. The postulate that a myriad of unconscious factors might influence behaviour, and that both super-ego and ego can be products of a flawed process of development, makes the whole question of the criminal state of mind more complex.

Critics have claimed that the concept of psychic determinism makes the unconscious a generalized excuse for unethical or criminal behaviour. But the complexity of mental life makes this interpretation of determinism untenable. Freud saw self-understanding as developed through psychoanalysis as an extension of responsibility for oneself. He is said to have responded to the question 'Should a person be held responsible for his dreams which are the products of unconscious forces over which he has no conscious control?' with the comment 'Who else but the dreamer should be held responsible for his dreams?' (cited in Staub and Alexander, 1929/1962: 144). He added elsewhere that 'Those who have absolved successfully an education for being truthful with themselves will be protected permanently against the danger of immorality, even if their standard of morality should deviate in some ways from what is customary in society' (cited in Kaufmann, 1980: 79). Staub and Alexander (1929/1962), among the early commentators on this issue, also pointed out that the social expectation of personal responsibility is itself one of the determining influences on behaviour: 'This principle of holding a person responsible for his behaviour has a deep effect in shaping the personality and eventually results in making the person what he is' (1929: 146).

Freud's comment about the ethical implications of being truthful with oneself is of fundamental importance in understanding the relationship of psychoanalytic understanding to ethical behaviour. Freud's concept of defence was elaborated by Anna Freud (1936) through her conceptualization of *defence mechanisms*, and further researched and elaborated by Vaillant (1977, 1986) in his concept of *adaptive mechanisms*. Hirschhorn (1988) has conceptualized similar processes in groups and organizations as *social defences*. The multiple functions served by adaptive mechanisms feature, on the one hand, attempts to control and modulate strong tensions and affects such as anxiety, rage, guilt, frustrated sexual feelings and feelings of shame and low self-esteem. But these inner regulatory mechanisms also entail varying degrees of distortion of inner and outer reality, and a whole gamut of ethical and unethical behaviour (see Table 10.1).

In general, it can be said that adaptive mechanisms which preserve inner equilibrium at the expense of fidelity to reality, or via behaviour whose basic purpose is to distract and confuse, interfere with successful adaptation. In addition, blaming and scapegoating others (projection and splitting), denying responsibility, and impulsive and destructive behaviour are frequently, and sometimes grossly and violently, unethical. By the same token, the capacity to tolerate anxiety and weather the storm in dedication to task (suppression); to assuage personal hurts and losses through service to and identification with others (altruism); and the ability to decentre narcissistic preoccupations through humour, are often concomitants of wisdom and ethical behaviour. In between these are all of the neurotic forms of everyday lying and mendacity that we see so often in others, and in ourselves.

In reviewing the contributions of psychoanalysis to an understanding of ethical issues, we must be aware of the varieties of psychoanalytic thought. Sometimes the various psychoanalytic 'schools' are perceived as conflicting and contradictory camps, and, indeed, at times, the large group dynamics of inter-group relations and politics among psychoanalytic factions has supplied grounds for that perception. Mitchell and Black (1995), in their review of the varieties of contemporary psychoanalytic theory, make the point that these different approaches revolve around a set of common concerns and functions. While different psychoanalytic theories are not always complementary, it is fruitful to view them as supplying different perspectives

TABLE 10.1 *Adaptive mechanisms*

Immature	Neurotic	Mature
Fantasy/withdrawal	Repression	Suppression
Projection, splitting	Vagueness, intellectualization, rationalization	Anticipation
Passive-aggressiveness	Reaction-formation	Sublimation
Depreciation	Displacement	Altruism
Acting out somatization	Dissociation	Humour

Adapted from Vaillant (1977)

of value in understanding the human condition, and that is the approach that will be taken in this chapter.

The multiplicity of psychoanalytic perspectives is due in part to the wide diversity of psychoanalytic ideas and theories. In developing his theories, and in the process defining the scope of psychoanalysis, Freud included biological dimensions such as drives, affects, anxiety, sexuality, inherited predisposition and maturational processes, while at the same time focusing his attention on processes of individual psychological development, including the differentiation of psychic structures, early trauma, infantile fantasy and early object relations, along with interpersonal and family relationships in their dyadic and Oedipal forms, as well as extending his gaze to group and even cultural and anthropological levels. Various schools of psychoanalytic thought differ to some extent in which of these levels they give primary focus and emphasis. Mitchell and Black (1995) point out that psychoanalytic schools differentiate themselves in their response to a number of core polarities: the role of trauma versus fantasy in psychopathology; the emphasis given to internal conflict versus processes of arrested development and inadequate parenting; conceptualizations of gender and sexuality; and whether clinical and epistemological approaches are based on empiricism or hermeneutics. Similarly, Guntrip (1971), in his summary of psychoanalytic approaches asserts that 'Freud's ideas fall into two main groups, (1) The Id-Plus-Ego-Control Apparatus, and (2) The Oedipus complex of Family Object-Relationship Situation . . . The first group of ideas tends to picture the psyche as a mechanism . . . The second group tends toward a personal psychology of the influence people have on each other's lives, particularly parents on children' (1971: 28).

Super-ego and morality

It is clear that, in terms of a comprehensive understanding of the person, all of these elements must be accounted for. For our understanding of the psychodynamic dimensions of ethics, our focus will be first on the development of internalized object relationships and the super-ego. Freud understood the super-ego as an outcome of processes involving the young child's wishes and needs, in particular needs for the exclusive attention of the mother, and vaguely or concretely experienced sexual strivings and fantasies. These needs and demands, premature in terms of the child's actual development and maturation, meet the reality of the adult world, the authority of parents and the peculiarities of the demands made on each child by their specific parents, family and culture. The result of this clash, with its inevitable frustration, anger and the child's fantasies of retaliation by adult authorities, is a process of internalization which leads to the formation of the super-ego.

In this process, children free themselves from external conflict with parents, and allay their own fears and fantasies, by identifying with parents and internalizing their moral strictures. The particularly concrete and literal aspect of this internalization can sometimes be seen when watching children at play instruct other children, perhaps younger, how to behave. But in addition to its imitative and literal quality, the fact that the super-ego is born in frustration, anger and conflict may mean that a sense of guilt and aggression may also be internalized, and manifested as an excessive sense of culpability, unrealistic self-criticism or self-defeating behaviour. An aggressive super-ego may also be externalized as aggressive and unrelenting moral condemnation of others. Because the process of super-ego formation is significantly driven by the child's own fantasies, frustration and aggression, it will not necessarily be mitigated by a mild and understanding attitude on the part of parents, although parental attitudes, values and education have long-term importance and value in ways more complex than can be described here.

The development of the rudimentary super-ego, as described here, is not the end of the process that eventuates in conscience and in our ethical sense (the more conscious elements of the super-ego) in the adult. For one thing, the early stages of the development of the super-ego involve not only an angry clash of wills, but also the child's wish not to lose the love of parents and, indeed, to maintain and achieve that love, and, in reasonably normal families, the same feelings on the part of parents. Thus, alongside fear and aggression, the wish to be loved is a crucial element in super-ego formation. As a result, guilt, i.e. tension between super-ego demands and the wishes, strivings and activities of the person, is experienced as a loss of self-esteem, a loss of self-love. It is for this reason that both normal functioning of the super-ego as well as its pathologies are closely related to narcissism, as well as to aggression and projected aggression. Around these basic conceptual axes, the various contributors to be discussed in this chapter organize their descriptions of the subtle, intricate and varied interplay of psychodynamic factors in ethical decision-making and behaviour.

Hartmann's psychoanalysis of moral values

In *Psychoanalysis and Moral Values* and other publications (1960, 1964), Heinz Hartmann has carefully explored ethical dimensions of psychoanalysis and applications of the psychoanalytic approach outside the clinical sphere. In his view, psychoanalysis follows a professional ethic but should not be seen as positing a specific world view or values. But moral issues are central to what psychoanalysis studies: 'A person's moral behaviour is as much an essential part and a distinctive sign of his personality as is his character or his instinctual life' (Hartmann, 1960: 53). Hartmann traces the centrality of the role of moral codes in Freud's own thinking about the personality, and adds that 'there are moral motivations which have the full dynamic significance of independent forces in the mental economy' (1960: 40). A person's moral values are the outcome of a lifelong process of development, beginning with the development

FREUD: A MORALIST?

Yiannis Gabriel

The view that psychoanalysis is a moral doctrine seems to fly in the face of what many critics regard as Freud's glorification of immorality. Was he, after all, not the man who forever spoilt our assumption of childhood innocence, the man who saw sexuality in everything, the man who sought to vindicate the claims of our animal instincts, the man who, at a personal level, is accused of all kinds of ethical and scientific improprieties? More importantly still, was Freud not the man who encouraged us to seek to understand the unconscious mind of the criminal before censuring or sentencing him or her? Was he not the man who undermined the principle of moral responsibility by arguing that our actions are governed by subterranean forces over which we have no control?

Some of the personal criticisms of Freud's integrity were discussed in Chapter 2. What concerns us here are Freud's views on human beings as moral animals and the nature of morality in general. Freud's moral position stems from a critique of conventional morality, as a set of ill-thought-out but motivated principles and ideas, which, far from enhancing our lives and bringing them closer to an ideal of 'the good life', causes us surplus suffering and privations. In this respect, Freud is as powerful a critic of bourgeois morality as Marx and Nietzsche (Ricoeur, 1970). If Marx points out that what passes for transcendental laws of right and wrong are, in fact, expressions of class interest, if Nietzsche sought to establish that Christian morality is a quiescent, defeatist morality which protects mediocrity instead of celebrating excellence, Freud tried to show that many of the distinctions between right and wrong are the product of a post-Oedipal patriarchal law. This law becomes embedded in the individual through the institution of the super-ego and exercises tyrannical control over his or her actions through an overpowering sense of guilt. The super-ego also unleashes unremitting hostility and self-righteous aggression against those who appear to have transgressed the law of the father.

Freud did not maintain that all laws and all moral strictures are repressive; he certainly recognized that many constraints and prohibitions are necessary for civilized living. As someone keenly aware of the darker sides of our nature, he saw very well that rampant aggression and unrestrained sexuality pose a threat to any society and that culture has developed mechanisms for the containment of our wilder impulses. What he denounced were the costs at which this containment takes place – the illusions and privations which impoverish the lives of people and render them susceptible to neurotic and other disorders.

In his two great books *Freud: the Mind of a Moralist* (1959) and *The Triumph of the Therapeutic* (1966), Philip Rieff, the American cultural commentator of the 1950s and 1960s, regards Freud as the last great moral philosopher. Why? Because when the other philosophers lost interest in the great religious questions of suffering and redemption, Freud, like Marx and Nietzsche before him, placed them squarely in the core of his philosophy. What made Freud's moral philosophy uniquely suitable for the twentieth century was his proclamation of a 'therapeutic', an attitude to life, which did not seek consolation in illusions of eternal salvation. Earlier eras had tried to soothe the discontents they generated by offering faith – faith in religious, political and economic promises of salvation. These promises were embodied by great religious leaders, powerful political heroes or economic modernizers, all figures commanding allegiance and respect, offering social and personal transformation. The Freudian therapeutic, on the other hand, argued Rieff, is not transformational, but informational. It seeks to equip

> each individual with the self-knowledge necessary to achieve not salvation, but well-being:
>
>> That a sense of well-being has become the end, rather than a by-product of striving after some superior communal end, announces a fundamental change of focus in the entire cast of our culture – toward a human condition about which there will be nothing further to say in terms of the old style of hope and despair. (Rieff, 1966: 261)
>
> The 'psychological man' is, accordingly, the Freudian moral ideal. Instead of seeking refuge and consolation from the miseries of life in healing doctrines and identification with communal goals, psychological man adopts a scientific attitude towards himself, learns to live with his conflicts and contradictions and seeks to maximize his well-being through a careful management of his inner life, understanding his desires and keeping a close watch on the returns he gets from his libidinal investments. Within this scheme of things, the individual no longer needs someone on whom to place his or her faith – the analyst is no sacral figure, the font of moral truth and model rectitude. The analyst is merely a therapist, a consultant who may help us enhance our emotional investments, just as our financial adviser may help us enhance the returns on our capital.
>
> Rieff's arguments have been criticized in many different ways (Gabriel, 1982, 1983). His view of the 'psychological man' comes very close to that of a self-obsessed narcissistic individual who is unwilling and unable to form meaningful relations with others. Yet it represents a major intervention in the discourse on the moral implications of psychoanalysis, and in particular on the articulation of the two major values that underpin psychoanalytic doctrine, its strong (but not entirely unqualified) commitment to truthfulness and its struggle to restore pleasure, including both spiritual and physical pleasure, as a core pursuit of the human sciences. Other authors, including Hartmann, Kernberg and Lasch, have made major contributions to this discourse, but none has viewed psychoanalysis so closely and so exclusively as a moral doctrine as Rieff.

of the super-ego in early childhood and continuing in the further development of the ego-ideal in adolescence and adulthood. Hartmann contrasts 'imperativistic ethics', the ethics of moral prohibition which reflects early super-ego development, with 'goal ethics', manifested in a vision of the good and ideals. Later development of the super-ego also incorporates ego functions, such as coordinating means and ends, anticipating the outcome and consequences of actions, and 'a process of generalization, of formalization, and of integration of moral values' (1960: 30). The super-ego/ego-ideal is 'in constant interaction with the social structure and cultural values in which the individual lives' (1960: 31); at the same time, individuals have varying degrees of autonomy of their super-ego functions from conformism and social pressures.

Hartmann, like Kaufmann and Wälder, believes that psychoanalysis gives us greater insight into 'the complexities of moral reality', how individuals try to achieve a 'state of balance' and integration of conflicting inner and outer demands. Internal conflict between varying goals and urges, and conflict with the pressures and demands of the social and political environment, is inevitable in this context. These conflicts test 'the moral stability' and the 'vulnerability of the moral system of the individual' (Hartmann, 1960: 29). In this approach, Hartmann's penetrating analysis of 'rationality' and 'self-interest' shows that these concepts are frequently deficient because they exclude emotional needs and moral drives which are also part of the 'self-interest' of the individual. Conflict may occur not only between moral values and instinctual needs, but between one's values and ego interests, such as pride and ambition, and narrowly conceived selfish goals. Hartmann believes that while psychoanalysis and psychoanalytic therapy do not promote a specific value system, awareness of one's own moral values, and of their genesis and motivation, may be an important aspect of psychoanalytic insight. The result of this process of self-understanding (or 'value testing' similar to 'reality testing') may lead to what he calls 'authentic values' (1960: 50–1). These are values which go beyond lip service to ethics by an individual or culture, and are an integrated and dynamic factor in actual moral behaviour.

Hartmann returns again and again to the widespread yearning that psychoanalysis would mandate specific ethical and moral codes, and the 'hidden preachers' who use psychoanalysis to promote their causes. He criticizes the confusion of health ethics with moral values, pointing out that 'health ethics' can be as 'moralistic' as any other type of ethics (1960: 68–71). Similarly, there is a danger that psychoanalytic concepts, such as narcissism, aggression, passivity or maturity, may be used as pejoratives or as values. Hartmann, as others, affirms 'the high value placed on the facing and acceptance of outer and inner reality, on intellectual integrity, and on self knowledge' (1960: 70). But he adds that 'acceptance of reality does not imply, in the context of analytic thinking, passive submission to a given social system' (1960: 89).

In terms of ethical functioning, broadening of self-knowledge, which also includes an understanding of motivations which are commonly unconscious, can lead to a broadening of the sense of responsibility and the avoidance of easy rationalizations. The recognition of one's authentic values allows individuals to see much more clearly the moral aims, ideals and imperatives they actually adhere to and to understand them in the context of their own personality (Hartmann 1960: 91–2). Hartmann's views stand in contrast to stereotypes of psychoanalysis as a debunking or self-preoccupied approach to human life and society. He makes the interesting observation that denial, repression, rationalization and other defence mechanisms can be used against the super-ego, i.e. against one's own moral values, as well as against instinctual demands:

> It often happens that individuals will behave according to their moral codes . . . and still refuse to accept that these codes are their own. They would rather try to explain their behavior in terms of their self interests or in some other related way. . . . Such people find it easier to recognize as factual in man what has usually been called 'bad' rather than what has usually been called 'good'. Of Freud's statement that man is not only much more immoral than he thinks but also much more moral than he knows, they would rather accept the first than the second half. (1960: 43–4)

APPLICATIONS TO ORGANIZATIONS

Organizations raise very special questions to the student of morality and ethics. Like other spheres of human social activity, they present individuals with choices, some of which can be thought of as moral choices – choices between right and wrong. However, due to their impersonal structure, their overlapping lines of responsibility and also the peculiar qualities of emotionality that governs people's actions within them, organizations are quite unique moral arenas with peculiarities all of their own. Large bureaucratic organizations may promote efficiency, productivity and fairness, and allow the pursuit and realization of collective goals and ideals. They may also, however, turn into frightening, technologically efficient forms of collective madness, as exemplified by the regimes of Hitler, Stalin and Pol Pot. There can be little doubt that as soon as we find ourselves in an organization, many of our moral reflexes and judgements are affected by the organization's own morality and ethics.

In this regard, a helpful distinction can be made between those who focus on ethical issues in relation to the nature of an organization's primary task, and ethical issues as they affect the way the primary task is accomplished. The concept of the primary task indicates the goal or purpose of the organization, defined as the process by which products or services are produced and conveyed to consumers and other stakeholders constituting the 'environment' of the organization, who reciprocally supply the organization with the money, supplies, information and other forms of support necessary for its survival (Rice, 1963, 1965). Some consider the provision of high-quality, inexpensive goods or services to consumers, at a profit, to be the primary ethical function of an organization. Others see this activity as at best value-neutral and see the ethical functions of an organization as involving financial support for community and charitable organizations, support of social policies such as affirmative action and diversity, and provision of jobs and benefits for workers.

Clearly this is not always an either/or choice, and in fact many argue that the two realms are synergistic. Hirschhorn (1988) argues that work and the performance of the primary task become meaningful only when there is some sense of agreement on the broader purposes of economic activity and the value of goods and services produced. In terms of the ethical choices made by decision-makers within an organization, the hierarchy of goals and values and the priorities set are of crucial importance. This chapter will take the approach that, from a long-term perspective, focus on the organization's primary task is the primary ethical imperative for its leadership. But, as will be discussed later, Kernberg and others argue that critical analysis of the primary task itself is not inconsistent with this approach.

Governmental and non-profit organizations have their primary task set by legislation or charter. They face a more complex process of feedback from their environment, involving both their 'clients', the members of the public specifically and in general whom they serve, and the boards or political institutions which determine their funding and have the power to review and revise their mandate, presumably in response to communication from the public. In addition, political and charitable organizations are often faced with constraints on their activities and even the manner in which they conduct these activities. A governmental unit cannot declare bankruptcy, or change its product line and go into a new business. Details of mandated processes may conflict with larger goals. Thus the US Environmental Protection Agency's overall goal of protecting the public through regulating the appropriate use of pesticides was distorted by unscientific legislative restrictions such as the Delaney Amendment. Similarly, a governmental unit may carry out its mandate to the satisfaction of its clients, and nevertheless be opposed and criticized by other segments of the public who wield political power, such as a legal service department which carries out successful class action lawsuits and in the course of doing so antagonizes the business community or city government officials. In addition, the primary task mandated by legislation creating a governmental organization may be given in ambivalent fashion. For example, the department of agriculture may be given a public health responsibility but at the same time allotted inadequate funds for the inspectors and testing necessary to carry it out.

These considerations suggest that decision-makers in governmental organizations face additional complexity in their ethical decisions. In the face of confusion, ambivalence and even hypocrisy in their mandate, they may be forced to rely on their own personal ethical standards. They thus face the additional danger of being tempted to substitute their own political agendas for those mandated by sometimes confusing legislation. Or they may cynically abandon commitment to the primary task and focus entirely on their own continued existence and survival.

Leadership and the moral tone of organizations

While Hartmann's incisive analysis of ethical issues is of great value, his work is based on clinical and philosophical considerations rather than group and organizational experience. Much of the useful work that has been done in understanding how the emotional dimensions of the leadership role relate to ethical behaviour stems from the experience of psychoanalysts in organizational and group leadership. Interestingly enough, Rangell, Kohut and Kernberg, all of whom have made significant contributions to the understanding of the psychodynamics of leadership, relate their understanding of this phenomenon to their roles in leadership positions of psychoanalytic and hospital organizations.

Kohut (1985) describes how apparently intractable theoretical and ideological conflicts within psychoanalytic organizations sometimes originate in narcissistic slights and disappointments experienced in organizational life by individuals, who then rationalize their anger and humiliation as theoretical disputes. He also describes how some charismatic and narcissistic leaders have an exquisite sensitivity to the low self-esteem, and needs for idealization, of their followers. Rangell (1974) starts with the recurrent phenomenon of splitting of psychoanalytic organizations into factions, and from there describes the syndrome of compromise of integrity, with which he examines the political career of Richard Nixon. In a formulation similar to Hartmann, Rangell describes the compromise of integrity as a conflict between the super-ego and ego interests, powered by 'uncontrollable and unsatisfiable narcissism'.

Similarly, Renshon (1996, 1998), in his psychodynamically oriented biography of President Clinton, has articulated a concept of character relating the interplay of ambition, integrity and public persona. He comments that 'For people like Clinton – with the substantial talents, skills, and the success they bring – there is a danger that their success may reinforce their sense of being special and therefore entitled. In short, it may facilitate their grandiosity' (Renshon 1996: 40). Renshon uses Erikson's distinction between ego identity and ego-ideal:

> It is important here to distinguish between holding ideals and being faithful to them ... Character integrity does not involve a president's public identification with the virtues and ideals that most would find laudable. Nobody would expect him to say otherwise. Rather, a president's integrity or lack thereof is confirmed by examining his behavior, over time and through difficult circumstances, to see how he has handled the complex dilemmas involving ambition and ideals. (1996: 41, 43)

Otto Kernberg (1979, 1991, 1993, 1994a and b, 1998) has used his wide-ranging experience in leadership positions, consulting and group relations conferences to produce the most fully developed and consistent application of psychoanalytic concepts to organizational life. He began with efforts to integrate classical psychoanalytic thought with group relations and systems concepts in the 1960s, and has continued his efforts with papers on 'Regression in Organizational Leadership', 'Paranoiagenesis in Organizations' and 'The Moral Dimensions of Leadership'. Kernberg's approach begins with a description of how the reciprocal interaction between the emotional make-up of leaders and the regressive emotional pressures on leaders from subordinates and groups within the organization, combined with flaws in the organizational structure itself, disturb the effective functioning of the organization, i.e. the performance of the primary task of the organization. This approach then illuminates breakdowns in organizational leadership. For example, Kernberg begins his paper on the moral dimensions of leadership by saying that he wishes to:

> focus on the psychological pressures that may induce or reinforce corruption in organizational leadership. Such corruption is manifest in practices that clearly negate the ethical principles of leadership, that tolerate gross contradictions between public and confidential practices and leadership functions, and/or represent significant injustice to the members of the organization or to those who depend on the organization's products or tasks. A secondary effect of such corruption is a deterioration of the task-oriented function of groups, task systems, and the entire organization within which such groups and task systems function. I am interested in the forces that tend to undermine the moral dimensions of leaders in organizations, and the counterforces, including the leader's personality, that may control and reverse this process. (1991: 87)

Narcissism and moral failure

Kernberg describes a similar intertwining of failure in the performance of the primary task and ethical corruption when he discusses how a pathological level of narcissism in the leader, resulting in an excessive need to be admired and followed, is reinforced by the excessive idealization and flattery of followers. This process:

> gradually diminishes the leader's capacity for self-criticism and leads to a chronic narcissistic regression that may become maladaptive to leadership. This narcissistic regression fosters corruption in leadership, because the leader's emotional needs may now run counter to the demands of the organizational tasks. The protection of the leader's self-esteem and the reinforcement of his narcissistic gratifications take precedence over painful decision making, and favoritism may replace justice in dealing with colleagues and subordinates. (Kernberg 1991: 96)

Similarly, Horwitz's (1996) study of narcissistic traits in therapists, using the data of the Menninger Psychotherapy Research Project as well as other studies, demonstrates how an excessive need on the part of therapists to maintain their own self-esteem leads to a lack of empathy with patients, an inability to tolerate anger and criticism from patients, a tendency to choose therapeutic approaches on the basis of therapist needs rather than patient needs, and generally less satisfactory treatment of patients and their needs. Here, too, the interference of the therapist's excessive narcissism in the treatment of patients not only impairs the performance of the primary task of treating patients properly, but at times verges on unethical behaviour.

Persons with high narcissistic needs frequently tend to gravitate to positions of high responsibility and authority. When these needs are grossly excessive and pathological, the syndrome of *malignant narcissism* appears, as described by Kernberg (1998) and others. Here a pathological degree of narcissism is paired with intense ego-syntonic sadism and anti-social features, manifested in leaders capable of the grossest kinds of cruelty and slaughter of subordinates and rivals, as well as whole populations.

However, the leader's narcissism is not necessary for an organization to be gripped by an ethic of moral irresponsibility. Anxieties inherent in the roles of leaders and followers may also lead to unethical behaviour. In his studies of organizational functioning, Hirschhorn (1988) points out that work itself may be a source of anxiety. Individuals and groups may experience a wide range of difficult emotions as a result of their commitment to the primary task. Anxieties are aroused by the possibility of failure in the face of obstacles and difficulties, the need to coordinate one's efforts with others, and the burden of taking responsibility. Social defences may be erected against anxiety, guilt, frustration, conflict and discouragement experienced in work settings. Hirschhorn (1985) has explored what he calls the 'psychodynamics of taking the role', describing processes where individuals may abandon leadership functions out of anxiety and assume the role of coach, therapist, friend or egalitarian collaborator. Similarly, Zaleznik (1984) has described the characteristics of charismatic and consensus leaders, pointing out that consensus leaders may use an appeal to group participation and group decision-making as a way to escape the anxiety of taking responsibility for unpopular decisions. Charismatic leaders may seek to shift responsibility for their failures by processes of projection and scapegoating. Thus moral responsibility is replaced by an ethos of buck-passing which can pervade an entire organization.

Scapegoating and the ego-ideal

Some psychoanalytic thinkers have related the development of the ego-ideal to processes of identity formation. Erikson (1950, 1968) has described how in adolescence earlier super-ego structures and ties to parents are reworked in relation to peers, leaders and social and political ideals. These processes combine with the development of adult roles and attitudes in particular societies and cultures, and the formation in individuals of an identity which asserts them as a functional and valued member of a particular social and cultural group. Volkan (1988) also believes that identity formation and group membership are closely related. Both Volkan and Erikson are concerned that this process frequently, if not inevitably, defines a negatively valued outgroup. 'They' are not 'us', and, in fact, are not quite human or deserving of the ethical standards and behaviour reserved for 'us'.

Volkan (1988) believes that this process is a critical step in the development of intractable social conflict. Similarly, Erikson (1968) warns against what he calls 'pseudospeciation', the presumption that those outside the group are, somehow, fundamentally different and flawed, thus deserving treatment that would not be appropriate towards members of the group. The findings of Volkan and Erikson suggest that in strongly cohesive organizational cultures, commitment to the organization may become a rationale for unethical behaviour. Cohesive and value-driven groups and organizations may develop what might be called 'moral grandiosity', the belief that their ideals and purposes are so important that ordinary ethical rules and reality constraints do not apply.

The reciprocal interplay between group and individual psychodynamics is so intimate that no effort has been made here to separate the contributions of individual and group psychodynamics to our understanding of ethical issues. Introducing his exploration of group psychology, Freud commented that:

> Only rarely and under certain exceptional conditions is individual psychology in a position to disregard the relations of this individual to others. In the individual's mental life someone else is invariably involved, as a model, as an object, as a helper, as a opponent; and so from the very first individual psychology, in this extended but entirely justifiable sense of the words, is at the same time social psychology as well. (Freud, 1921: 95)

Freud believed that as individuals become members of a group, they identify with and merge their super-ego with that of the leader. As a result, individuals in groups may lose their sense of responsibility and experience a paralysis of critical and realistic thinking: 'Groups have never thirsted after truth. They demand illusions, and cannot do without them' (Freud, 1921: 107). The influence of a patriarchal leader may bring out moral and ethical extremes, from 'all the cruel, brutal and destructive instincts' to devotion to an ideal in which individual moral standards are raised by a group (Freud, 1921: 107). Chasseguet-Smirgel (1984, 1985, 1986), in her contemporary reworking of Freud's concepts, shares his beliefs about the moral extremes of which groups are capable. However, she believes that in modern society groups are experienced as matriarchal entities in which individuals wish to merge. Such a group, led by a 'master of illusion', permits and forces individuals to divest themselves of a frightening sense of individuality, aloneness, moral responsibility and the constraints of troublesome reality.

THE SOCIAL CONTEXT OF ETHICAL CONCERNS

The psychodynamic approach can be applied not only to the ethical dilemmas of individual decision-makers and organizations but also to an analysis of social concerns about ethical behaviour. While in every age there are those who bemoan the deterioration of morals and ethical standards, it is probably true that such concerns are intensified in periods of rapid social and economic change, social mobility and dislocation. During these times, traditional religious and social institutions that support norms and values are weakened. Change also induces a sense of helplessness and anxiety about the behaviour of others. These anxieties and concerns often eventuate in convictions about the unethical behaviour of others and about the need for greater social control. We say 'there ought to be a law'. The need to control the behaviour of others may also express envy, resentment and a tendency to moralize. As Mark Twain put it, in another era of rapid social change, 'nothing needs reforming like other people's habits!'

The psychological dynamic underlying convictions about the misbehaviour of others and the need for control often involves projection, with ascriptions of badness and harmfulness embodied in ethical judgements. Kaplan (1997) offers a detailed description of individuals for whom moral outrage and the assertion of virtue serve intrapsychic needs. Their endlessly repeated formula is 'My distress, anger, confusion, and sense of victimization is due to Them.' The guilty 'Them' are those who are greedy, selfish, unscrupulous, mistreaters of animals, subversive, outside agitators, Jews, capitalists, polluters, racial and ethnic minorities, and others in infinite variety.

That this dynamic is so ubiquitous lends itself to use as a political currency. Political rhetoric utilizes accusations of unethical behaviour as a tactic to discredit opponents. Accusations of wrongdoing and evil allow accusers to take the moral high ground and put their opponents on the defensive. In contrast to Kaufmann's over-determined accidents and Hartmann's moral complexity, such critics assert one rigid standard of morality and enjoy what one author calls 'the moral superiority of the uninvolved' (Pastin, 1986). Accusations, scapegoating and polarization allow those involved to avoid the hard work and responsibility of tackling difficult issues. Accusations of unethical behaviour can become a weapon in political life, rather than an effort to improve public morality.

The debasement of ethical concerns into political rhetoric and demagoguery should invite scepticism about such accusations, and allow for analysis for the psychological mechanisms involved and the psychodynamics of the exploitation of fear and prejudice. Such phenomena, however, do not obviate the importance of ethical issues in modern society. In a complex and interdependent society, with a high degree of division of labour, we are all exquisitely dependent upon one another, and upon the trustworthiness and integrity of people and groups whom we never see. When we are a passenger in an aeroplane, purchase a child's toy, use any one of the myriad products made with potent chemicals and eat our food, we are dependent upon a multitude of others for our safety and security. It is, in fact, this very dependency which generates some of the anxiety enumerated above. But our dependence upon the competence, integrity and ethical behaviour of others also highlights the importance of understanding what contributes to ethical behaviour.

THE PSYCHODYNAMICS OF ETHICAL BEHAVIOUR

Moral decisions in the complex world we inhabit rarely involve a right and ethical choice versus a wrong and unethical choice. Every choice or decision has many moral and ethical consequences. Most decisions have a degree of moral ambiguity that only become more apparent, the more thoroughly the matter is considered. Take, for example, a manager's decision to fire an employee. The manager's decision may reflect unfairness and scapegoating; or be impulsive and poorly thought out; or may be realistic and even courageous. The consequences of this decision to the employee may be devastating, psychologically and financially. There are other instances, however, where the consequences may be salutary – removing the employee from a position not appropriate for him or her, or functioning as a wake-up call, for example. There are consequences for the employee's family. The manager must consider the consequences of firing or not firing the employee for co-workers, the meaning of tolerating corrupt or uncommitted behaviour or incompetence (see, for example, Kernberg, 1998: 73). There are consequences for the organization in terms of its goals. How does one balance the consequences to an organization of firing a unique and highly talented individual who is at the same time abrasive and underhand in dealings with others? What does firing this employee mean in terms of standards of fairness and adherence to procedure in the organization? There may be wider legal or public relations consequences in firing the employee. What does this particular employee mean in terms of the organization's commitment to assisting troubled or underperforming employees towards better performance? Or tolerating divergent working and interpersonal styles? It is rare that the answers to all of these

ADAM SMITH AND THE MORALITY OF YOUR BUTCHER

Yiannis Gabriel

It is not from the benevolence of the butcher, the brewer, or the baker that we expect our dinner, but from their regard to their own self-interest. We address ourselves, not to their humanity but to their self-love, and never talk to them of our own necessities but of their advantages. (Smith, 1776/1970: 119)

Writing at the time of the American Revolution, Adam Smith envisaged the free market as the mechanism which turned individual self-interest into a principle of economic development but also the basis of moral order. Why would your butcher cheat you, why would he sell you inferior goods, why would he endanger your health, if he stood to lose you as a customer? Milton Friedman, Nobel Prize laureate and contemporary prophet of free markets, put it more trenchantly: 'The business of business is business', he declared (1970) in opposition to those who proclaimed the moral responsibilities of business and management. According to this view, it is not the business of enterprises to preach morality or to impose their ethics on the rest of the community. Their goal is to make profit for their shareholders, and, as long as they stay within the law, anything goes. The role of managers is to plan production and run organizations in a way which generates wealth for their company and society at large. It is not their responsibility to act as moral paragons of the community. This vision enjoyed particular popularity during the Reagan and Thatcher years. It not only appeared to exonerate greed, but it sought to vindicate self-interest as the only orientation in life compatible with economic progress.

Writing from a different ethical perspective, the philosopher MacIntyre (1981/1985) saw the manager as one of the three central 'characters' or cultural archetype of our era, the others being 'the rich aesthete' and 'the therapist'. All three embody a particular cultural dimension – that of the manager is as a dispassionate technocrat, a moral illiterate whose concern is with means, not with ends or values (1981: 74ff). Not only is the manager unconcerned about the moral quality of his or her decisions, but he or she stands as the exemplar of the moral illiteracy of our age. MacIntyre invites us into a thought experiment. Imagine, he says, a world after a nuclear holocaust, a world reduced to a new stone age, yet a world which still contains the vocabulary of our technological age. People may still use words from the cutting edge of science, without having the remotest understanding of what they mean. Such, he contends, is our actual predicament as regards morality. We live in a world where we still use the vocabulary of old morality, or right and wrong, justice and injustice, without any sense of what these words actually mean. The very notion that we can distinguish between right and wrong on the basis of cast-iron principles, which we can rationally defend, has been obliterated. Instead, we rely on what he calls 'emotivism', associating right and wrong with whatever emotion happens to grip us from one moment to the next. We happen to feel sorry for a homeless person; we regard this person as a victim of poverty and are prepared to denounce poverty as a social ill. We consider this same person as an unworthy recipient of our taxes – our pity turns into anger. It is not poverty that is evil but laziness. We then realize that this person is a drug addict. Our judgement changes yet again – it is not poverty or laziness that is a social ill, but drugs. In this pessimistic view, morality is reduced by our age to cheap sentimentality, our moral sense as liable to influence and manipulation by opinion-shapers and the media as our flippant consumer tastes. Moral fashions, including moral panics, succeed each other like any other fashion on the back of moral confusion and uncertainty. A pervasive cynicism fills the moral vacuum; anyone standing up for a particular idea or principle, no matter how much popularity he or she may temporarily enjoy, is liable to be cut down to size sooner or later.

Visions of moral apocalypse are not new; they seem to be especially bountiful as centuries and millennia reach their close. It would be historically inaccurate to regard unremitting cynicism and moral fickleness as the unique qualities of our *Zeitgeist*. Nor is MacIntyre's vision unchallenged. There have been numerous ways in which cultural theorists in general and scholars of organizations in particular have sought to re-introduce a moral dimension to the argument. There has been a growth in scholarship on business ethics and the moral responsibility of business, especially in what concerns environmental matters (see Swogger, 1994; Fineman, 1997). The currency of the concept of 'stakeholder' challenges the view that shareholders are the only ones that count. One of the most important counterpoints to the earlier arguments has been the renewed interest in the concept of leadership. In the late 1970s, Burns (1978) and Zaleznik (1977), in two major contributions, sought to restore a vision of leader, in juxtaposition to the manager–technocrat, as someone who can provide moral leadership, a leadership of value not merely a leadership of means.

These arguments suggest that our age is neither unique in its moral confusions nor has it lost its appetite for distinguishing between right and wrong. They have also cast some doubts on Smith's pronouncement and its Friedmanesque reincarnation. How many of us still visit a butcher for our meat, a brewer for our beer and a baker for our bread? What happens when competition is replaced by monopolies? What happens if we are not aware of the inferior or dangerous qualities of the products we consume? What happens if we have been conditioned not to care? What happens if a business pursues the interest of its shareholders with no concern for the welfare or even the survival of their children? What happens to a society when social bonds of belonging are replaced by market relations?

Numerous reservations can be raised against Smith's view, that the pursuit of individual self-interest guarantees ethical standards. This is especially so in a complex, interdependent society like ours, a society where wrong-doing can go undetected for a long time and small mistakes can have devastating consequences for large numbers of people in distant places. In travelling by aeroplane, undergoing a medical operation or entrusting our children to the care of a school, we do not merely rely on the self-interest of these organizations or even on their adherence to the law of the land or the ethics of their professions. We rely on them to act as responsible moral agents, who would not wish to harm us, even if in doing so they suffered no personal ill consequences.

questions will be congruent, i.e. will point towards the same decision. Thus the manager's decision to fire the employee will have many connotations, will be ethically ambiguous, and will probably elicit divergent responses from various stakeholders inside and outside the organization.

A useful distinction may be made here between 'bravado' and 'moral courage', entities which are frequently confused, yet could not be more different. Both are invoked when a decision is described as 'difficult' or 'unpopular'. Bravado is usually a product of moral weakness: it is the display of stubborn single-mindedness irrespective of the suffering it may cause to others or to oneself. It usually refuses to question the soundness of a decision and will commit more resources in seeking to defend the soundness of the original decision. Moral courage, on the other hand, is the quality of facing up to the ethical ambiguities and complexities of such difficult decisions; of attaining clarity over the true reasons for making a particular decision, even if these reasons can be misinterpreted and devalued. Moral courage also implies the willingness to face up to the consequences of a 'difficult' decision, however detrimental they are at a personal level to the decision-maker. Moral courage also entails the ability to acknowledge a mistake, to change course and to make reparation. Finally, moral courage involves the ability to live with uncertainty. Ethical judgements must include an ability to tolerate ambiguity, the cognitive capacity to sort out and organize details of a complex situation, personal values and a hierarchy of values that provide guidance in complex situations, and the emotional independence to withstand inevitable criticism and contradiction. It might also be said that decision-making in an ethically ambiguous setting requires an ability to see the context whole, including its temporal and process elements. Seeing situations and persons whole, i.e. as they are, in their full complexity, stands in contrast to those processes of projection, splitting and scapegoating which at a cognitive level amount to a radical simplification of events.

A recognition of moral complexity, by itself, is no guarantee of moral courage. Instead, it may lead to regression either to impulsive edicts or to obsessional indecision. Hartmann's (1960) distinction between the imperative and idealistic aspects of the super-ego may thus be reflected in the polarity between a tendency to dichotomize moral decisions and a tendency to respond to complexity by becoming lost in rationalization. The one extreme poses the danger of rigid, moralistic judgements and scapegoating, but excessive preoccupation with complexity may lead to rationalization of complacency and tacit support of chronic injustice or gross evil.

LEADERS AND MORALITY

Kernberg's contributions regarding the intrapsychic make-up of leaders, their moral standards, their professional ethics and competence, and the interactions of these with group, organizational and social structures, do not end with his descriptions of the psychodynamics of unethical behaviour. What emerges from Kernberg's perspective is that ethical leadership necessitates a delicate balance of characteristics. While the effects of pathological narcissism have been described, decision-makers must possess a significant degree of a more healthy narcissism, with sufficient self-esteem to give them the emotional independence to make difficult decisions, and relieving them of the need always to be loved by subordinates.

Similarly, while rampant paranoia may be grossly destructive, a degree of healthy paranoia is needed to be able to recognize the overt and covert aggression of others, their secret agendas, and competitiveness and envy of the leader. A leader lacking this will show dangerous naïveté in relation to the real dangers facing the leader and the organization. Confidence in the use of power and aggression must be adequate to meet the needs for assertiveness, focused work and difficult decision-making necessary for organizational leadership; too much leads to authoritarianism and its ethical consequences. Kernberg also emphasizes the importance of high intelligence in assimilating the cognitive demands and ambiguities faced by leaders. Levinson (1984) has emphasized that excessive guilt about power and aggression may lead to paralysis of decision-making and abdication of responsibility. Zaleznik (1984) emphasizes that leaders must be comfortable with power, in order to form stable political and leadership coalitions within the organization.

Kernberg also emphasizes the importance of moral support and nurturance from sources outside the organizational role: from the leader's professional identity and competence, and from moral convictions derived prior to and outside organizational roles, with luck somewhat independent of 'the slings and arrows of outrageous fortune'. While Kernberg sees the emotional relationship between organization and those in leadership roles as reciprocal, he notes that leadership that is corrupt and authoritarian will have ethical ramifications throughout the organization, resulting in a tendency towards corrupt behaviour at other levels of the organization that individual members would not carry out in their private, personal lives. Kernberg also points out that a leader's independent moral standards may allow for a critique of adherence to the primary task of the organization itself:

> This task-oriented ideology may run counter to other human needs and value systems that may be irrelevant to the specific goals of the organization, but are crucial to the members of the organization maintaining a sense of well being and dignity. If the needs of individuals and groups in an organization are a basic constraint to optimal organizational functioning, in other words, if one has to consider human factors as limiting the degree of efficiency of an organization, then it is important for the leader to be able to identify with ideologies or socially accepted value systems that are tangential to the interests of the organization itself. In other words, it is a function of the leader to protect individuals from poor working conditions, from arbitrariness in job assignment, from risks connected with the work, regardless of the impact of such protective measures on work efficiency.
>
> Under ideal conditions, such ideological contradictions may be minimal, but under less ideal conditions the leader's identification with a complex system of values may actually protect his decision-making process from the expediency of exclusive identification with rarefied organizational or other goals. (Kernberg, 1991: 103)

Many instances of conflict between the interests of the organization in pursuing its primary task and ethical considerations involving either individuals and groups composing the organization, or the larger society, can be resolved when one takes a long-term rather than a short-term perspective of the organization's primary task, interests and survival. While a short-term perspective is essential in times of crisis, such a perspective can also become anxiety driven, so that inner crises and fundamental problems become externalized, while basic long-term issues are ignored in the excitement. Conversely, while long-term planning can have a defensive function in ignoring serious and immediate problems, such planning, when appropriate, requires a certain stability and narcissistic calm, the ability to avoid over-reacting to transient ups and downs, and the capacity for a commitment not only to the long-term future of an organization but to the people and social needs surrounding it. These capacities parallel the polarity that Erikson described as generativity versus stagnation: the capacity to make emotional commitments to the next generations. Such a commitment requires an assertion of value in people, culture and institutions, and a capacity to communicate and transmit one's values.

Kernberg's emphasis on the psychological strengths of a leader necessary for ethical decision-making needs to be expanded to include a capacity for realistic dependency and collaboration, which is closely allied to a capacity to tolerate criticism and the examination of mistakes and failed policies. Not a few ethical lapses of leaders and leadership groups happen because a tight defensive boundary is set up which excludes the communication and criticism necessary to expand ethical perspectives and bring them more in line with the human and technical realities faced by the organization. Cohen and Gooch (1990: 195), in their sophisticated multi-dimensional analysis of failed military campaigns, comment, in discussing efforts to understand a failure to make use of military intelligence information, 'to make full use of such understanding military organizations must seek out the most difficult kind of intelligence – knowledge of themselves.'

To the extent that unethical behaviour is powered by pathological forms of aggression, narcissism and projection, the repair of leadership and organizational failings must involve processes of coming to terms with these destructive emotions, and overcoming our tendencies to deny or avoid awareness and responsibility for them. Using the Kleinian concept of reparation, Hirschhorn (1988) has described 'the reparative organization'. On the basis of psychoanalytic treatment of children, Klein and her co-workers concluded that children and adults struggle with tendencies to split images of others into good and bad, loved and hated. With the recognition that these segregated images and feelings are attached to the same person, feelings of guilt ensue with the realization that one hates and wishes to hurt a person one loves (the depressive position), and we seek to repair the damage done by our hatefulness (reparation) (Klein and Riviere, 1964).

Hirschhorn believes that in a reparative organization, working through the guilt and shame that are part of the depressive position allows managers and employees to 'experience their organization as an instrument for accomplishing valued purposes', to recognize the realistic technical complexity and constraints of their roles, and to develop

> a relatively non-narcissistic process in which the good and the bad are acknowledged and psychological splitting is limited. People acknowledge that aggression is necessary, that members' performances must be evaluated, and that certain members may fail to meet the demands of the task. In contrast to fanciful descriptions of modern managers who are urged to be prophets, visionaries, and cultural transformers, managers in reparative settings take actions that pain others while remaining emotionally connected to the resulting suffering. (1988: 228–9)

The reparative process allows a recognition of moral complexity at an emotional level, without losing sight of the organization's ethically meaningful connections to the larger culture.

The work of psychoanalytic thinkers such as Kernberg, Hirschhorn and Erikson suggests that the sources of the super-ego go deeper than a particular organization, culture or even generation. As Lionel Trilling puts it,

> How very strange is the super-ego! For we say of it that it is the surrogate of society, or of the culture, but one of its functions seems to be to lead us to imagine that there is a sanction beyond the culture, that there is a place from which the culture may be judged and rejected. (1955: 56–7)

11 PSYCHOANALYTIC RESEARCH INTO ORGANIZATIONS

Psychoanalytic research into organizations is an uneven, evolving, dynamic process. It proceeds on several fronts at once; developments along these fronts are not always consistent or compatible. Advances on some fronts can be seen as reversals on others, since they call into question fundamental assumptions, typologies or theories. Alternative theories occasionally confront each other head on, though most often they seek accommodation with each other, by discovering their own niches and constituencies. The field is full of points of tension and ambiguity, theoretical lacunae, territories left untouched for years and areas of feverish theoretical and field activity. While in all these respects psychoanalytic research into organizations is not unlike other types of research, it can leave the new or aspiring researcher perplexed and confused. In this chapter, we offer some help on theoretical and methodological issues to researchers who wish to study organizations using psychoanalytic ideas like those presented in this book. We examine the extent to which psychoanalytic research is distinct from or contiguous with other research traditions; we explore different types of research, including research which is combined with active interventions in organizational processes through consultation; we single out some crucial dilemmas and difficulties facing the psychoanalytic researcher of organizations; finally, we offer a rudimentary tool kit for the psychoanalytic researcher. The tone of this chapter is different from that of preceding ones; the emphasis lies more on 'how' than on 'why' or 'what', one of our aims being to offer some advice on the practicalities of research.

The similarities of psychoanalysis with forensic investigations have long been noted (Ginzburg, 1980; Shepherd, 1985). Sigmund Freud, like Sherlock Holmes, was an interpreter of symptoms; he was also an interpreter of dreams, of fantasies, someone preoccupied with the meaning of the trivial, the inexplicable, the irrational. As noted in the Introduction, interpretation lies at the heart of psychoanalysis both as a research activity and as a clinical practice. Interpretation, as Ricoeur (1970) informs us, is the systematic exercise of suspicion. Our suspicion concerns, first, the truthfulness of each story, each narrative, we encounter. More significantly, however, our suspicion extends to the meaning of the narrative, the motives of the narrator, and our own motives, as listeners and interpreters. Thus our suspicion extends to our own narratives, our own interpretations as researchers.

This, then, is the first particularity of doing research using psychoanalytic perspectives. Instead of amassing data, the psychoanalytic researcher looks for clues. The odd, the out of place, the significant exception provide far more insight than large volumes of uniform and unidirectional data. Of special interest is what may have been disturbed, concealed, tampered with. Psychoanalytic researchers must beware of instant conclusions. They must be especially suspicious of 'innocent', straightforward explanations, of undisturbed terrains, of dogs that do not bark. At times, an off-the-cuff remark at the end of a long interview may be of greater value for psychoanalytic research than the data of the interview.

This places the psychoanalytic researcher in opposition to the largest segment of researchers who use qualitative techniques. Most humanistic traditions in qualitative research, inspired by phenomenology, treat 'experience' as the final arbiter of truth. Within these traditions, which include symbolic interactionism, social constructionism and most 'new paradigm' research, a person's experience and his or her sincere account of it cannot be called into question *as experience*, although it may be questioned as an accurate account of events. Psychoanalytic researchers, on the other hand, mistrust experience, they mistrust verbatim reports and they especially mistrust old experiences whose recollection serve as explanations of current troubles. Experience, as previous chapters of this book have indicated, is tainted with unconscious elements, desires, phantasies, resistances, and cannot be accepted at face value. It cannot be taken as evidence of fact but, more importantly, it cannot even be accepted as evidence of meaning, since conscious meanings may act as subterfuges for unconscious meanings. Experience, then, for the psychoanalytic researcher usually represents the tip of an iceberg, whose mass in the unconscious must be slowly and painstakingly uncovered.

This, of course, creates numerous moral, political and epistemological dilemmas. On whose authority does the psychoanalytic researcher doubt the heart-felt testimony of his or her respondent? How can he or she doubt the tears, the piercing anger, the rightful indignation? On whose authority does he or she sit listening attentively, while engaging in all kinds of speculation regarding the unconscious reality behind the lived experience? On whose authority can he or she claim to understand the narrators better than they understand themselves?

Unless psychoanalysis as the exercise of suspicion, i.e. psychoanalysis as interpretation, is backed up by a sound body of understanding, an imperfect but correctable stock of concepts, theories and propositions, it lacks the moral and scientific authority to question experience. Only by maintaining his or her belief in the difference between truths and untruths can the psychoanalytic researcher pursue his or her quest for truth in lies or fantasies. For there is no doubt that psychoanalysis looks for the truth in lies. Instead of dismissing lies as willing falsehoods, psychoanalysis engages with them at the levels of meaning and desire, i.e. the levels where lies are not cognitive untruths but true wish-fulfilments.

The second particularity of psychoanalytic research is that it is enquiry against resistance. All scientific enquiry involves resistance – resistance to new ideas or to new ways of thinking. However, psychoanalytic enquiry works against additional resistances, which are invisible without the aid of the psychoanalytic stock of concepts and theories noted earlier. It is the psychoanalytic theory of resistance which raises psychoanalytic interpretation above literary criticism, story-telling or a clever meta-narrative. Psychoanalysis does not seek to create attractive parcels of meaning, seductive but ultimately unfounded stories to feed the fantasies of its constituents, but seeks to put its finger on the psychological truth, the true meaning of the phenomena it observes.

In this regard, psychoanalytic research could not be more dissimilar to postmodern research. In place of the postmodernist ironic detachment, psychoanalytic research tends to be very serious. While postmodern research assumes a stance of playful engagement with its subject matter, psychoanalytic research usually assumes the form of struggle against resistances, inner as well as outer. These resistances are a source of great strength for psychoanalytic enquiry, but they also have potentially disastrous consequences. The strength lies in the fact that in recognizing the aims of the resistance and the mechanisms through which it functions, the psychoanalytic researcher can make great strides in corroborating interpretations. The potential weakness has been well rehearsed. It lies in the fact that all too often resistance to interpretation is mechanically taken to imply confirmation of the interpretation. Untold damage has been done to psychoanalysis by the cliché that equates denial with truth. Furthermore, the psychoanalytic investigator is working against inner resistances; for example, those stemming from attachments to particular ideas or theories or, even more alarmingly, those stemming from a personal stake in a particular tradition. It is not accidental that so many quarrels in psychoanalytic research end up as *ad hominem* arguments. Even in this potential weakness, however, psychoanalytic research is keenly conscious of a problem of which many other traditions remain unconscious: the possibility that theories themselves can become defences against uncertainty and accompanying anxieties.

PSYCHOANALYTIC AND NON-PSYCHOANALYTIC TRADITIONS OF RESEARCHING ORGANIZATIONS

How does psychoanalytic research into organizations relate to other traditions? It is true that in its assumptions, its theoretical concerns and its research tools, psychoanalysis represents a unique tradition within organizational research. Its core set of ideas regarding the nature of the human predicament, experiences and suffering are fundamentally dissimilar to those adhered to by other traditions. Some theorists may go as far as arguing that, in fact, there is little that psychoanalysis can learn from other traditions; that it is incommensurable, for example, with positivistic, humanistic, new paradigm, evolutionary or postmodernist traditions. Such an approach would regard any attempt at a dialogue between psychoanalysis and other traditions as essentially a dialogue among individuals using different languages or, worse, using languages in which the same words have different meanings.

The view that psychoanalytic studies of organization have nothing to learn from non-psychoanalytic traditions invites the criticism of reductionism and esoteric theorizing. The opposite point of view is one which regards psychoanalytic research as continuous with other traditions, probing the points which other traditions are unable or unwilling to examine, but using essentially the same modes of reasoning, arguing and demonstrating. This approach is consistent with the view of Freud, who denied that psychoanalysis has a unique *Weltanschauung*; psychoanalysis, he argued, 'as a specialist science, a branch of psychology – a depth psychology of the unconscious – is quite unfit to construct a *Weltanschauung* of its own: it must accept the scientific one' (1933: 193). It is doubtful whether many scientists or philosophers of science today would defend such a uniform view of science. Even within psychology, different schools of thought have emerged making very different theoretical and epistemological assumptions. In the human sciences, fragmentation has resulted in increasingly small areas where sensical discourse can take place across schools of thought.

THE CHALLENGE OF POSTMODERNISM AND THE CASTING OF PSYCHOANALYSIS AS MERE HERMENEUTICS

Adrian Carr

Adrian Carr takes issue with friendly and hostile attempts to redefine psychoanalytic research as 'mere hermeneutics'. He critiques the tendency of both postmodernist defenders and modernist detractors to discard much psychoanalytic theory in favour of a technique of interpretation.

The notion of a postmodern world is increasingly being entertained throughout the social sciences and so too in the discourse of organization and administrative theory. One of the central themes of the various postmodernist formulations is that language is not an attempt at a rough sketch of reality – it is reality. With this focus, the self, or individual, is no longer conceived as a user of language to express inner feelings and intentions, but instead is the medium through which culture, in the form of language, gains expression. The notion of the individual becomes a part of the text and not first and foremost the subject of the text. Individuality and consciousness are conceived as verbally grounded experience where self-awareness can only be realized through hearing oneself and being acknowledged by others through discourse; 'man is decentered; the individual subject is dissolved into linguistic structures and ensembles of relations' (Kvale, 1992: 40). While this may, putatively, spell the end of fields such as psychology (see Carr, 1997), those in the vanguard of the postmodernist movement view psychoanalytic theory as a valuable form of hermeneutic enquiry. However, such a conception is 'misguided' and reveals some of the fundamental weaknesses of the postmodernist declaration that it is 'all-in-the-text', as we shall now discover.

The term *hermeneutics* can be defined as 'the art of interpretation which aims to disclose an underlying coherence or sense in a text, or text-analogue, whose meaning is in one way or another unclear' (Connerton, 1976: 102). It would appear to be an 'art' that arose in the seventeenth century, the prime focus was one of uncovering the message from God that was to be gleaned from scripture (see Steele, 1979). A number of writers, and not only postmodernists, have cast psychoanalysis as merely hermeneutics or 'depth hermeneutics' (for example, Ricoeur, 1965/1976; Habermas, 1970/1976; Lorenzer, 1970). These writers view incomprehensible acts and utterances as masking a hidden text; the exposure or revealing of this text makes self-emancipation possible. Lacan (1968, 1977b), in keeping with Derrida's view (1976) that it is all-in-the-text, goes further and charges psychoanalysis with engaging in some kind of delusionary activity in trying to recover repressed memories as though therein resides the 'truth'. The analyst, Lacan urges, should not attempt to go beyond or behind the text but accept the text as it is presented; thus the analyst needs to reflect upon 'the logic of the signifier, to the detours and swerves in the discourse of the patient which mark the irruption of unconscious desire' (Norris, 1987: 115; see also Løvlie, 1992: 129). States (1988) goes further still, rejecting as he does psychoanalysis as a causal theory. He argues that by sticking to the text we no longer need to have that part of the metaphorical fiction we have called the unconscious and, indeed, all those accompanying processes we had to hypothesize, as Løvlie aptly notes 'in one bold move repressions, displacements and transferences are lifted from the inside of the psyche to the "outside" of the text; the archaeology of the psyche is replaced by a kind of literary analysis, a teasing out of speech in the rhetoric of dreams and action' (1988: 129).

Some writers in the field have 'forcefully' rejected such a view. Grünbaum, for example, described Ricoeur's hermeneutic rendering of psychoanalysis as a 'mutilation' and an 'ontological amputation' of Freud's clinical theory (1984: 43, 44; see also Robinson, 1993: 196). Ottmann, with similar vehemence, chides Habermas's casting of psychoanalysis as 'depth hermeneutics', believing he 'overintellectualizes' the process of psychoanalytic reflection (1982: 86; see also Alford, 1988: 171). Saas (1992) pragmatically warns about the impact upon patients of this relativism and play with meaning when he argues 'how can a person be encouraged to acknowledge truly unpleasant truths . . . if one assumes that there is no distinction between truth and mere fiction – but only stories about stories? And what is to prevent psychotherapy from turning into an elaborate workshop rationalization, a place for spinning self-justificatory fantasies?' (1992: 177). The whole question of therapy would seem to be recast!

The collective voice of those who dissent from a hermeneutic view of psychoanalysis, particularly the version that tells us to stick to the text, is one that resonates with a call to recognize that psychoanalysis is a *causal* theory (see Robinson, 1993: 197) and it is in that context that language may be part of a constellation of indicators. Language and symbolism have to gain their meaning from the association that is made by the patient. It is in the dramaturgical setting of psychotherapy that the drama and trauma associated with recollections of what was previously buried has to be noted for its causal attribution. The psychoanalyst helps in the search for a consistency or theme that includes considering: compulsive behaviours; psychosexual development; pre-linguistic experiences; the analysand's silence; body 'language'; even the tardiness of the analysand keeping appointments.

Freud stressed that the symbolic meaning of events and words are *not in themselves* linguistic signs of universal or constant import. For example, the quip that 'a cigar is sometimes just a cigar' stands against the automatic interpretation of smoking being a 'sign' of auto-eroticism (see Freud, 1905b: 97–9). It is the inner history of the individual that brings differential significance to word forms and symbols. Freud, in his seminal work on dreams, similarly cautioned that 'one can never tell whether any particular element in the content of a dream is to be interpreted symbolically or in its proper sense' (Freud, 1901/1986: 124; see also Freud, 1900: 470, 477; Gay, 1988: 114).

Grünbaum, in his rebuff to Ricoeur's hermeneutic rendering of psychoanalysis, uses the analogy of footprints in the sand to highlight that the 'meaning' of symptoms should be conceived as causal traces rather than the material of a communicative model. He puts the argument as followings: 'The footprint is *not, as such,* a vehicle of communication; it is not a linguistic sign or symbol; it does *not* semantically stand for, denote, designate, or refer to the past pedal incursion' (Grünbaum, 1984: 64, emphasis added; see also Grünbaum, 1988). It is the turn of a phrase 'as such' that conveys the essence of the distinction Grünbaum is trying to highlight. Having prepared us in this way, he then presents us with a psychoanalytic understanding of paranoia to illustrate the inappropriateness of applying a communicative model of language to the field. In expressing repressed sexual desires in feelings of persecution, the paranoid is not trying to communicate that he or she is homosexual.

> Paranoid *behavior* may well be a *vicarious outlet* for repressed homosexuality, but in no case is it a verbal label for it! Thus, as we saw, aetiologically that behavior is the afflicted person's attempt to cope with the anxieties generated by his unconscious sexual urges, *not* his/her attempt to *communicate* these yearnings by means of persecutory delusions and behaviour. (Grünbaum, 1984: 66; see also Robinson, 1993: 197)

> Thus, postmodernists in their contention that it's 'all-in-the-text', and in promoting what is virtually a reification of language (language seems to acquire an ontological status of its own), would seem to miss the mark on a number of grounds (see Carr, 1997). But, in the appropriation of psychoanalysis as merely some form of hermeneutic enquiry, postmodernists distract and divert our attention away from a depth of analysis that would help to reveal how and why these texts are constructed and emerge in the first place and, of course, how these texts in organizations might be ameliorated.

The view expounded in this book has been that there is much that psychoanalytic researchers can learn from different fields of organizational theory; theories of bureaucracy, organizational culture and symbolism, emotion, complexity, labour process and control, open systems, organizational and management learning have provided rich insights for psychoanalytic scholars. At the same time, psychoanalytic research parts company from other traditions in its single-minded exploration of unconscious phenomena, its general suspiciousness towards the sanctity of experience and its reluctance to place much credence on quantitative techniques of corroboration and proof. Overall, the view put forward in this book is that the psychoanalytic researcher must make eclectic and critical use of non-psychoanalytic theory, using some of its concepts and theories, modifying others, disregarding some and challenging some. There is no conceivable reason why a psychoanalytic researcher may not draw concepts, ideas, theories and hypotheses from non-psychoanalytic research, seeking to probe, test, develop and transcend them. By the same token, many theorists whose essential outlook is not psychoanalytic make use of psychoanalytic ideas, concepts and theories, frequently adding valuable insights to them.

PSYCHOANALYTIC RESEARCH AND CONSULTATION IN ORGANIZATIONS

Another potentially problematic area of psychoanalytic research into organizations is its relationship to consultation and practical interventions in organizations. It is beyond all doubt that some of the most original and influential contributions to this field have been the result of research stemming from consultation. Within a consultation relationship, the consultant/researcher does not merely seek to discover what is going on, but to diagnose a problem and, possibly, to effect some interventions, with a view to enhancing organizational performance, well-being and harmony. Much of the work of Jaques, Menzies Lyth, Levinson, Gould, Kets de Vries, Hirschhorn, Sievers, Krantz, Diamond, Allcorn, Baum, Gilmore and most of old and new Tavistock theorizing emanates from consultation relationships in which the pursuit of knowledge and understanding is inseparable from the improvement of organizational life. In fact, only a minority of academic researchers in the area claim to conduct research outside consultation relationships. This has not been without consequences both for the nature of psychoanalytic research into organizations and for the type of knowledge that has been generated.

In the first place, it has resulted in a convergence of clinical and organizational research, with the consultant's interventions into organizations being equivalent to the clinician's practice within the therapeutic dyad. As Levinson has aptly put it, 'there are two reasons people approach others for help: either they have some kind of pain or they are causing others to have pain, who are in turn compelling them to do something about that problem' (1991: 45). The same logic applies to the patient who approaches a therapist as to a businessman who approaches a consultant. Psychoanalytically oriented consultants have sometimes been tempted to approach an ailing organization as though it were a patient. Expressions like 'neurotic organization' (Kets de Vries and Miller, 1984), 'organizational unconscious' (Diamond, 1993), 'narcissistic organization' (Schwartz, 1990) or 'psychotic organization' (Sievers, 1998) can easily end up being treated as literal descriptions of organizational phenomena, rather than as potentially helpful metaphors. This has fuelled criticisms of reductionism, like that levelled by Jaques (1995), who argues that the analogy of individual and organizational pathologies is a false one. Jaques has polemically proclaimed that 'the psychoanalytic approach to understanding organizations is dysfunctional' (Jaques, 1995: 343) because, instead of looking for organizational dysfunctions in matters of structure, hierarchy and communication, it focuses on interpersonal relations and personal pathologies. This criticism has some merit, though reductionism is not a necessary consequence of the position criticized by Jaques. Structural defects in organizations may or may not overlap with psychological dysfunctions. Jaques's criticism also disregards the argument put forward repeatedly in this book, following the small but persistent line of psychoanalytic writers who have argued that individual and organizational pathologies are not only distinct but counteractive: a successful organization may be staffed by profoundly neurotic individuals (see, for example, Marcuse, 1964; Lasch, 1980, 1984; Gabriel, 1983, 1984; La Bier, 1986; Hoggett, 1992; Sievers, 1998).

The centrality of consultation in psychoanalytic research into organizations undoubtedly strengthens the grip of the clinical paradigm, i.e. the assumption that there are collective pathologies which, even if not mirroring individual pathologies, may be addressed in broadly similar ways. Yet, in a paradoxical way, it undermines the purity of the clinical paradigm. As Gould has noted, there are

> marked differences in the culture of psychoanalytic clinical practice compared to that of organizational consultation. The core clinical modes in psychoanalysis are the *processes* that result in healing and transformation. In the organizational sphere an emphasis on *results* or *outcomes* is the prevailing norm – among practitioners as well as clients. What this means, in effect, is that in organizational work a more pragmatic attitude prevails, with little concern about process or the 'purity' of the intervention. Therefore . . . the psychoanalytically oriented organizational practitioner usually feels free to do whatever seems to work, using many sorts of nonpsychoanalytic techniques, strategies, and interventions, as well as invoking many nonpsychoanalytic viewpoints (open-systems theory, family systems theory, communications theory, a variety of sociological and social psychological viewpoints, and so on). (Gould, 1991: 26)

Gould's observations would suggest that a more appropriate analogy than the clinical practice of psychoanalysis for the practice of organizational consultants would be a more pragmatic type of therapy, one which does not aim to discover the truth of the situation at all costs, but rather to improve the patient's condition, by using any method and tactic that achieves results.

The process of consultation radically influences the nature of the psychological contract between researcher and researched. The pursuit of truth becomes subordinated to the pursuit of a solution to a problem or problems: it is thus directly influenced by personal and organizational factors. The consultant's psychological and material need of the client may lead to a desire to please the client or to employ methods whose effect is reliable but not understood. This may be reinforced by the client's desire to see results and even measurable results or by his or her psychological dependency on the consultant. Achieving results and managing a relationship become at least as important priorities in the consultant's mind as discovering the truth.

But the pursuit of truthfulness itself is problematic, regardless of these pragmatic considerations. Writing about the clinical practice of psychoanalysis, Freud insisted that 'the relationship between analyst and patient is based on a love of truth, that is, on the acknowledgement of reality, and that precludes any kind of sham or deception' (1937: 248). In warning against premature interpretations, however, Freud acknowledged that truth must appear at the appropriate moment – truth at the wrong moment can act as an occasion for falsehood, resistance and denial. Alternatively, falsehood at the appropriate moment can assume the appearance of truth, under the influence of suggestion. The same dilemma, only in more acute form, characterizes psychoanalytic research into organizations. The researcher who goes into the field with a completely transparent brief about his or her intentions and interests is likely in the first place to be denied access. Even if access is granted, such an approach is likely either to bolster the resistances which inhibit the pursuit and acknowledgement of truth or to set in operation a suggestive chain of events, where the research is guaranteed to mirror the preconceived ideas of the researcher. (For an example of a revealing instance where a consultant must re-frame or withhold the truth from his client, see Levinson, 1991: 64.)

The dilemma between the search for truth and the search for solutions creates serious difficulties for the psychoanalytic consultant of organizations, without, however, fatally undermining his or her mission. The same dilemma, after all, characterizes many other scientific enterprises. The engineer requires good-enough solutions which will work in practice, even if the physicist may not be able to understand exactly why or how they work. The physician will use a reliable form of treatment, even if the precise way it affects the body is not altogether clear. Psychoanalytic research in organizations (including psychoanalytic consultation), like all scientific research, is as much a craft and an art as it is an application of fixed principles or methods. Competent researchers must balance the need for truthfulness against other factors, pragmatic, theoretical and methodological. They may rely on hunches or intuitive impulses, they must be sensitive to unforeseen opportunities and prepared to deviate from their research plan when circumstances change. They must have a keen eye for detail without losing sight of their overall purpose. And they must be prepared to engage subjectively with their observations and data, trusting themselves to be able to make sense of their engagement at a later stage. They must be prepared to take wrong turnings and to develop theories and ideas which must be given up later. They must also be prepared to give up ideas, research material and earlier work, like artists who realize that some sketches must remain sketches which have to be destroyed. In all these ways, research is quite a time-consuming and even wasteful activity, one which does not easily tally with the pressures facing consultants.

Yet, the prospective psychoanalytic researcher into organizations should not despair in the face of these difficulties. Like all crafts, the craft of research is one that some people learn relatively rapidly, developing extensive competences and skills, among which must be counted the economical use of resources. Others need longer periods of apprenticeship, while some may never actually master the craft. In a paradoxical way, it is possible for a scholar to be a very original thinker and theorist without being particularly good at field research. Even more paradoxically, as we saw in Chapter 2, some excellent theories, both in the natural and in the human sciences, can be based on flawed or problematic research material, just as some high-quality research material may fail to provide any theoretical insights.

RESEARCH AND DIFFERENT TYPES OF THEORIZING

Some readers may feel uncertain about the meaning of the words 'research' and 'theory' in the context of this book. Broadly speaking, we refer to research as the activity of finding out different features of the inner and outer worlds. Theory, on the other hand, represents different attempts to explain these features, organize them, classify them, interpret them, make sense of them and, possibly, use them in action. Research and theory are closely inter-related processes: it is not possible to research or even observe the world, unless we have some frame of reference obtained from a tacit or an explicit theory. Nor is it possible to theorize without having some conceptual and methodological ideas of how theories may be corroborated through research. Thus, neither research nor theory are purely cerebral processes; they are social practices, subject to specific disciplines and controls, and involving communities of practitioners and traditions of testing and presenting.

One of the major difficulties facing researchers in organizations is that theories and knowledge of organizations come in many different varieties, from grand and highly abstract to applied and very specific. It is not possible to use the same criteria and tests to assess all of them. Some forms of organizational knowledge assume the quality of lore or practical understanding, others are intricate analyses of minute processes which can be observed with variations in different settings, yet others assume the form of broad generalizations that can be tested through new observations or even experiments. At times, lore may form the basis for more systematic theorizing, at other times it must be accepted as highly contingent and situation-specific know-how, which may be of great practical value but lesser theoretical interest. (Most of the remaining part of this chapter belongs to this category – relatively practical and grounded ideas on how to do research.) Even 'gossip', widely practised in academic and professional conferences, can represent a valuable and valid type of knowledge, where ideas are disseminated in a friendly and informal manner, without the rigour demanded of more systematic forms of knowledge. This relaxation of the demand for rigour allows for greater freedom to experiment with ideas and feelings through gossip (Forrester, 1991). The psychoanalytic researcher must be flexible in his or her understanding of what passes as theory and avoid dogmatic distinctions between scientific and non-scientific knowledge.

Broadly speaking, psychoanalytic research in organizations can be problem-driven or theory-driven. *Problem-driven research* is what consultants inevitably conduct; it starts from an appreciation of an undesirable situation, which calls for some action to repair it. The understanding and the framing of the problem require the collection of appropriate data, usually from interviews, questionnaires and direct observations. *Theory-driven research*, on the other hand, starts by formulating a theoretical question, a hypothesis or a paradox that emerges from existing theory. This is more commonly undertaken by academic researchers, though it is not uncommon for theory-driven research to address issues of practical importance.

There is a third type of research which I refer to as *data-driven*. This is very common in historical research when new data arise unexpectedly, calling for explanation and incorporation into existing theory. Here research is driven by an existing body of data which is either unused or has been inadequately utilized. Some research into organizations undertaken by myself and colleagues was sparked by the availability of a large number of critical incident reports and essays supplied by students (see Sims et al., 1993; Fineman and Gabriel, 1996; Gabriel, 1997 and 1998d). Sometimes, the data which drive research is a major event (for instance, an accident, a merger, a major business success or failure) which calls for elaboration and understanding. Freud's study of Dr Schreber can be regarded as an example of data-driven psychoanalytic research, though generally this type of research is not very common in depth psychology or in organizational research and will not be discussed in the rest of this chapter.

PROBLEM-DRIVEN RESEARCH

This type of research investigation limits the researcher's freedom but offers, in return, access to an organization and, at least in principle, the cooperation of some of the participants. Much of the effort is directed at identifying the nature and severity of a problem or problems, comparing the perceptions of different organizational members, studying the factors which contribute to the problem and, sometimes, arriving at some proposals for solutions. Diagnosis is a major element in this type of research – and, like medical diagnosis, the assumption is that behind manifest symptoms lie latent pathological processes.

Many writers have offered insights on how to carry out this type of research; one of the most systematic and rigorous accounts has been provided by Levinson (1968/1981, 1972, 1991) who has sought to codify the craft of the problem-driven researcher. His work offers methodical guidelines on (a) how to observe and diagnose organizations; (b) how to organize, interpret and analyse data; (c) how to validate and corroborate the analysis; and (d) how to handle the relationship with the client, from beginning to termination. Of special interest, is Levinson's tool-kit of probing questions, some aimed at the organization, some aimed at oneself, through which the researcher can search behind the surfaces and the rationalizations.

> What is hurting this organization? How do I interpret what the key people cite as their main problem? How do I interpret what other employees say is their main problem? The pain may be literally what the informants say it is or it may be symptomatic of something more deep seated. How does this organization experience its problems? That is, how severe do the problems appear to be to the organization? And how well does the organization relate them to basic causes? This is a vital question because the degree to which the organization acknowledges pain is one measure of how ready it is to accept help. (Levinson, 1991: 61)

Equally valuable are Levinson's questions which the researcher must bear in mind in conducting his or her interviews:

What are this person's sources of involvement or lack of involvement and dissatisfaction?

How does this person's work contribute to personal knowledge and evaluation?

How does the subject perceive and respond to others at work?

What personal significance does the interviewee's activity and productivity have?
What are normative stresses for this person, and what techniques are used to cope with them? (Levinson, 1991: 32–3)

THEORY-DRIVEN RESEARCH

In Levinson's work, researchers pursuing problem-driven research into organizations have an almost encyclopaedic compendium on how to carry out this type of investigation. In the works of Hirschhorn, Kets de Vries, Diamond and others, they have numerous models on which to base their own research. By contrast, researchers wishing to pursue theory-driven research in organizations have relatively little to guide them and few role models to follow. Of course, many of the insights of consultation-based research may be adapted to theory-driven research (and many of Levinson's diagnostic techniques are useful to all researchers on organizations). Yet, many of the issues facing these researchers are different. In the first place, it is they who must approach companies for access rather than companies approaching them for help. Secondly, their entire way of operating involves a freedom which generates problems of its own. They are lumbered with no expectation of providing solutions for an organization's problems and are unlikely to end up being scapegoated for its failings. Relieved of an obligation to diagnose a problem or to prescribe solutions, they must use their freedom to decide how to examine unconscious processes within organizations and their diverse effects, without the constant concern of the researcher-consultant, that of determining what is good, helpful and healthy and what is bad, dysfunctional and pathological. In this section, I offer some basic guidelines and some field-tips on possible research strategies in this area.

Generally speaking, theory-driven research can be exploratory, theory-testing or, more commonly, a mixture of the two. Exploratory research starts with a diffuse understanding of an area of study and seeks to generate ideas, concepts and theories which will elucidate it. The researcher may have little literature to guide him or her and the terrain under investigation is hardly known or understood. Alternatively, theory-testing research begins with a body of knowledge which invites improvements or modifications. The researcher may seek to expand the theory by testing it in previously untested circumstances or by exploring paradoxes or lacunae by appeal to field data. Replication studies fall under this category.

The first issue facing theory-driven researchers is framing the aims of their research. The initial framing of the research, including its title, a one-line summary and a two paragraph statement of its aims and objectives, is absolutely vital, as it will underpin the research programme which includes the phenomena to study, the ideas or hypotheses to test, the concepts to used. While the programme of research may change innumerable times in the course of the investigation, it serves a useful function and prevents the investigator from going off on tangents, unless there are very good reasons for doing so. The research must have some well-thought-through boundaries beyond which it will not venture, unless it becomes absolutely vital to do so.

Next, the researcher must choose the field which is going to be explored or in which a theory will be tested. This usually involves a decision on the unit of analysis and the

ACTION RESEARCH, PARTICIPATIVE ACTION RESEARCH AND ACTION LEARNING IN ORGANIZATIONS

Susan Long

Action research is a type of problem-driven research which diminishes the distance between researcher and researched; it emphasizes the active involvement of both researcher and researched in the process of knowledge generation through active interventions. Susan Long examines psychoanalytically informed action research and juxtaposes it to participative action research and action learning as applied to organizations.

Action research shares some techniques with traditional scientific methods. An action research project may incorporate, for example, controlled observations, surveys, experiments, interviews, quantitatively measured tests. Its uniqueness, however, lies more in the context of the total research process. Emphasis is on discovery rather than hypothesis testing, on inductive rather than deductive thinking, on field rather than laboratory work, as much on evaluation as on observation. Action research very often has a definite and overt change agenda. Adherence to a change agenda often follows the realization that the aim of pure objectivity, as a stance within social systems research (the general field for action research), is problematic. This is not because objectivity is not considered a useful aim, but because action research addresses those aspects of social systems that are dynamic and changing. Beyond a general social science approach, a psychoanalytic approach to action research has as its major focus the *experience* of those within the social system. It is interested in the effects of subjectivity.

An emphasis on *action methods* in learning and research amount to the same thing. The scientist in the laboratory, the researcher in a library and the student in a classroom all take actions, make judgements and evaluations, engage in observations and develop working hypotheses. The distinctive difference of action research and action learning methods is largely a matter of emphasis and a focus on an engagement with the more socially practical aspects of learning and research. Social action and its effects are studied.

More important, however, is the social or discursive context of the endeavour. The more 'participatory' the research, the less the distinction between the roles of 'researcher' and 'researched'. The roles become positions to be taken up in the process, positions that may both be occupied by one individual at different times, much as one may distinguish between the observing ego and the observed aspects of self. Hence, participative action research engages a capacity in the individual to find multiple positions within the self. An alternative would be splitting and projecting these multiple positions on to either 'researchers' or 'researched'. To avoid this process, which unconsciously leads to the creation of a new outgroup on whom to project fantasies and anxieties, requires psychological sophistication and maturity. When successfully done, a state of mind is engendered where collaboration and organizational development are possible – as is an increased capacity to tolerate anxiety, ambiguity and other forms of psychological and social pain. It is this aspect of action research methods that is revolutionary.

Action research

Social systems are dynamic and changing. Change comes about through the people who make up the system being open to changing circumstances both within the system and in its physical and social environment. Being open in this way means that any changes occurring in the system are potentially available to members as new information for further action. Hence, the system is potentially able to evolve. Consequently, a research method that studies not only the current state of an organization, but also its ongoing dynamics, conscious and unconscious, is required.

The process of knowing about the system is itself part of the social system. People continuously use their knowledge and their processes of 'coming to know' in order to make decisions and to act. The action researcher can aid organization members to develop knowledge in a systematic, thoughtful way. The alternative is to go about knowing in a practical, fragmented or biased manner, as may occur, for example, when knowledge is regarded as the prerogative of a particular person or group within the system such as 'management' or 'the union'. This fragmentation is often the result of unconscious splitting and projection, which requires interpretation within the research.

In social systems or organizational research, the researcher impinges on the system and becomes a source of change. This is inevitable, even when the researcher acts in no more of an interventionist way than by being present in the minds of other people. In traditional research, such impingement is often regarded as 'error'. This may seem an acceptable way of dealing with this process when the researcher simply wishes to gather information and do no further work in an organization. Action research, however, takes advantage of the relations between researcher and organization. His or her work is not regarded as a source of error, but rather as a focus of the change process, or some aspect of this. Any changes occurring due to the research are themselves available for study. The researcher thus aims both to study and understand the organization as encountered, and to study the effects of the interaction between researcher and researched.

A typical project might proceed in the following manner. Having decided a research focus or question, the researcher systematically gathers information about the organization through a variety of methods. This information is then collated and analysed appropriately. The results of the data gathering and analysis are then fed back to the organization, perhaps through a small group drawn from the organization membership as a whole, who have the authority to work on the research on behalf of the organization. More widespread feedback may then be monitored through this group.

During the feedback process, the meaning of the data is examined and those involved are able to reflect on it, in the light of their general experiences of the organization as well as from the perspective of their particular role. As meanings are developed, a new knowledge of the organization begins to emerge. From this new knowledge comes the possibility of new ways of acting. These may then be tried out in an experimental manner, each change being monitored and evaluated as it is implemented. The results of these further studies are then 'fed back' and reflected on as with the earlier cycle. Close collaboration between researcher and those within the organization is essential for this method to succeed.

In this process, the researcher is also able to study and document the changes that occur in his or her own relations with the organization as the research proceeds. The underlying assumption is that the experience of the researcher will be shaped by the system entered (now a system with a researcher). Like any newcomer to the system, the researcher will be subject to the effects of the system. The experience of the researcher and the relatedness of researcher/researched, through processes such as transference, mirroring and the activation of social defences, are available for study and feedback as is any other information gathered. If a research team is involved, the internal dynamics of the team is also available as data, the assumption being that the team will unconsciously reflect the dynamics present in the organization.

This brief description indicates the crucial points in the research process that need to be managed, notably the point of entry into the organization, the research contract or agreement entered into, the initial identification of research issues, the authority to represent the organization in the research, who will work with the data, ownership of the data and so on.

Participative action research

Participative and collaborative action research (Elden and Chisholm, 1993; Greenwood et al., 1994) involves (a) the members of a particular system, (b) in a collaborative research process with each other as a research team, (c) on an aspect of their own system. The processes involved in such research are complex and, on first sight, seem contrary to traditional research practices which rely on the independence and supposed objectivity of the researcher. Participative action research, on the other hand, is predicated on the observation that no social research can be objective or value-free, nor can the researcher remain outside the system. Researchers always work within a particular value system and, in social research, the data of the research arise from their interactions with the system (Berg and Smith, 1985).

Participative action research takes advantage of these aspects of social research. If no social research is value-free, values should be explicit – at least as much as possible. If the data generated in social research are not produced without the subjective dimensions of particular researcher/researched interactions, then the ways in which the data are produced should be carefully documented and the subjective reactions of research participants used as data about the system.

Moreover, the philosophy behind participative action research assumes that members of the system are ideally located to (a) have some knowledge of their own system, (b) have knowledge of where information might be gained and, (c) be able to utilize the results of the research for implementation and action to change the system. Such changes are then studied as part of the action research project.

Given that work organizations are dynamic, changing systems, they require research methods that capture flux and change rather than stasis. People within such systems create their own futures (Williams, 1982) through planning, observation, action, reflection and evaluation. These five processes are also present in the participative action research method. Participative action research is thus a highly appropriate form of research for identifying and studying the effects of planned change within organizations.

A benefit of participative action research is the 'richness' of the data produced. Not only is directly observable data obtained, such as interview and questionnaire material, organizational statistics, planned systematized observation, but, in addition to this material, data are generated in the system of 'participants as researchers'. An underlying assumption is that particular system dynamics will permeate all aspects of the system including the participants as researchers. The experience of the research, through its five phases is, therefore, part of the organizational system being studied. Consequently, the dynamics of the research project is an additional source of data.

Three basic conditions are present in most participative action research projects:

- *Active collaboration* between the researcher or research team and the organization in the development of the research, its implementation and evaluation.
- *An iterative cyclical process* where data are gathered, fed back to the organization (in summary form), interpreted and employed to form the basis for further data gathering and for organizational change.
- *A consultative process* where participants act also as researchers in their own system and hence develop their own capacities in the process. It is this process that is quite revolutionary in action research methods.

Action learning

Action learning in organizations brings together (a) knowledge of theory, (b) professional or craft expertise, (c) tacit and local knowledge, and (d) intrapersonal, interpersonal and group dynamics. Moreover, it brings these together in a context of continuing experiential learning. The person involved in an action learning project works on a 'live' project in real time, works with others through a questioning process, and carries through that work to implementation and evaluation (Lawrence, 1991). Traditional university programmes deal with theory and its practical applications. On-the-job training and professional development deal primarily with the development of expertise. Experience in living adds to one's knowledge, but most often in an *ad hoc* unsystematized manner. Bringing these together is extremely challenging. Most challenging, perhaps, is the development of a *container* (Bion, 1970) or facilitating environment whose structure, process, authority and legitimacy can allow this in a creative way. What is meant by 'container' is that which holds the learning and allows its development without either rigid constriction or unmanageable loss of focus. In practical terms, the container is the project that can promote action learning so that learning really does occur instead of a defensive confirmation of existing prejudices or heightened flight into opinions ungrounded in immediate and local reality.

Action learning is learning by doing. The term was first covered by Reg Revans in the 1940s (see Revans, 1983). Revans, through his work with managers, developed the idea that they best learned their work through (a) the posing of insightful questions about the problems they face in their everyday tasks; and (b) through acting, that is, carrying out the solution to the problems as identified. Between the questioning and action lie the tasks of clarifying the problem, seeking alternative solutions, observing the effects of action and reflecting on the whole process. Formal instruction is an adjunct to this process, but is not sufficient for learning about real-life management or organizational problems and their solutions in real time.

Revans's work has been adopted, developed and modified (for example, Pedler, 1981; Winter, 1989; Torbert, 1991). The essential aspects of learning through working on real-life problems in real time are present in all these developments; as are the ideas of systematically studying the learning process as it develops and observing and evaluating outcomes as they occur.

Conclusion

Engaging with 'living' action research or action learning projects is complex and involves some chaos and pain. What organizations experience is a need to deal with

> ever-increasing change and uncertainty in organizational life. This is stressful, anxiety-provoking and often leaves people feeling de-skilled. Although the accumulated knowledge of the past is available, whether institutionalized in work practices and strategies (the foundations of organizational culture) or in theories, case studies and research methods (the foundations of academic management studies), the need moves beyond knowledge, or at least beyond knowledge in its traditional sense. Theory provides a kind of containment of thinking, 'craft knowledge' and tacit understanding are also important (Nonaka, 1991). However, beyond all this, action researchers and learners need to develop personal capacities of an even more ephemeral quality. These include:
>
> - the capacity for making judgements when limited data are available;
> - the capacity to follow through on decisions when peer pressure is exerted to prevent this, or to recognize the validity of others' points of view;
> - the capacity to consult others and listen to them;
> - the capacity to take up authority and exercise it responsibly;
> - the capacity to know when one should have confidence in one's decisions, intuitions or knowledge and to know one's limitations.
>
> Many of these qualities emerge from wide experience and from self-development where assumptions, thinking, reflection and action are challenged and one has to face one's own emotional realities.

number of units to be researched. The unit of analysis can be an individual, an organization or an abstract entity, like a story or an accident. Numbers may vary from one (single case study) to several hundred or thousands. Psychoanalytic research is not especially suited to handling large numbers, although it is not incompatible with the use of census or survey statistics to provide some corroboration for its theories. For example, as was seen in Chapter 7, Adorno and his colleagues (1950) were able to use large amounts of quantitative data in supporting their theory of the authoritarian personality. More commonly, however, psychoanalytic researchers rely on a small number of case studies (individuals, groups, organizations) which offer contrasting vantage points into a similar range of phenomena.

Researchers must be able to justify or explain the use of case studies and account for the particular cases chosen. Several plausible explanations may be offered, including the following:

1 *The 'critical' case study*: this involves choosing a particular case which seems too extreme and unlikely to establish a particular argument. If the argument can be established for such a critical case, the argument is likely to be equally valid in less extreme cases. The opposite to this approach, i.e. the choice of the most likely case to corroborate an argument or a straw man case to refute it, is enough to invalidate virtually any piece of research.
2 *The 'typical' case study*: this involves establishing that the range of phenomena involved is virtually identical irrespective of which particular case is chosen. To study the basic structure of the human liver, dissecting any liver may be adequate. A single drop of water from a river may be enough to establish the presence and magnitude of pollutants.

3 *The previously unthought of or previously inaccessible case*: here the case is chosen either because it promises to provide useful triangulation for existing theory based on a very different case; alternatively, it is chosen because of pragmatic reasons, like access, proximity and so on.
4 *The outstandingly interesting case*: this can be a study based on a phenomenon which is unlikely to be repeated (for example, the unification of Germany in 1989) or a case which possesses uniquely fascinating qualities (for example, the only labour union to have a two-party system). Sometimes this may lapse into a critical case study.
5 *The juxtaposition of a modest number of strategically contrasted case studies*: this involves selecting cases which differ in respect of some key qualities and are identical in others. The nature of the qualities chosen depends on the type of research being pursued; for instance, for certain types of research two successful companies in electronics and textiles may be selected; for other types of research one successful and one unsuccessful company in the same field may be chosen. Clearly, the larger the number of cases, the greater the resources required and the lesser the depth and breadth of the research.
6 *The pragmatic use of case studies* up to the point where each new case study adds little to the overall picture.

The researcher must be clear in his or her own mind what the unit of analysis is and must be able to reassess this in the course of his or her research (Gabriel, 1998a). Very different strategies for collecting and analysing data are dictated if the unit of analysis is the individual, the organization or the abstract entity. For instance, if the unit of analysis is the organization, the voice of some individuals (who know more, matter more or care more) carries more weight than that of others. If, on the other hand, the unit of analysis is the individual, then each individual carries the same weight and must be treated accordingly.

The next issue facing theory-driven researchers is access. Unlike their counterparts doing problem-driven research, where the client comes and asks for help, theory-driven researchers must approach organizations and offer a deal which will allow them to carry out their research. The pursuit of knowledge, by itself, is hardly likely to persuade many companies to open their doors to curious researchers, allowing them access to confidential and potentially embarrassing material. Researchers must, therefore, offer organizations something in exchange; for instance, an executive summary of their findings across many companies, some information or insight which the organization can use for its own purposes. Negotiating access involves making commitments which researchers must honour later.

RESEARCH STRATEGIES: METHODS OF DATA COLLECTION

Psychoanalytic researchers generally rely on observations, interview and questionnaire materials and published sources for their data. These may on rare occasions be supplemented by experimental findings. Observations are extremely important and require delicate interpersonal and tacit skills. Observations are the product of a continuous, restless engagement with an organization and its members, the constant looking for clues, the sensing of importance in the trivial. Some observations are aimed at material things, the nature and size of buildings, the clothes individuals

SOME GUIDELINES ON ORGANIZATIONAL RESEARCH ETHICS

Things which researchers must not do

1 Gain access on false pretences. This includes:
   (a) failure to mention the overall object of the research, its coverage or population;
   (b) failure to mention any relevant personal affiliation;
   (c) failure to mention that the project has a sponsor (who may be a competitor of the organization into which access is sought);
   (d) failure to mention that the research will be published or examined;
   (e) making exaggerated claims about the importance of the research;
   (f) making exaggerated claims about other organizations involved in the research.

2 Put undue pressure on individuals to participate in research, even if access to their employing organization has been obtained.
3 Record participants on tape or film without their knowledge and approval.
4 Agree to conditions which cannot be honoured on practical or moral grounds. This includes the breaking of confidentiality pledges given to other individuals or organizations.
5 Carry out research which harms individuals or organizations, or risks harming them without explaining such risks in advance. This includes the conduct of experiments and the collection of personal information or discussion of psychologically or professionally upsetting topics. *Under no circumstances are research means sanctified by research objectives.*

Things which researchers must do

1 Honour all the promises they make. This includes the maintenance of the confidentiality of the company and the individuals included in the research, the holding of feedback sessions or presentation of reports, the delivery of a product.
2 Treat their subjects with respect. This includes not putting undue pressure on subjects to answer questions they do not wish to answer. It also includes not forcing their answers into artificial categories with which they do not agree.

Things which researchers may do, after proper reflection (and discussion with colleagues or supervisors)

1 Use of a 'piggy-back' project on top of one for which access has been granted. This includes the use of research questions which are of interest to the researcher but not to an organization which is offering access. It does not include or justify the use of a totally hidden research agenda which is at odds with expressed research.
2 Withhold part of the research agenda from the subjects (the use of legitimate subterfuge in psychological research) in the interest of not prejudicing their responses; where legitimate psychological subterfuge is used, proper explanation and counselling must be offered to respondents.

wear, the lay-out of departments, the appearance of the car-park and so on. Other observations are aimed at individual and group behaviour and interactions, not just what they do or say but how they do or say it. Small nuances or voice inflections, the use of slang or jargon, body language, displays of emotion, signs of deference or defiance, these are areas where important observations may be made.

Observing is an active process and a tiring one. It involves a constant movement from detail to general picture, and a constant redefinition of the general in terms of the specific and vice versa. It also involves a continuous attempt to make sense of what is being observed, by active probing and questioning of others and also by a continuous attempt to organize and classify observations into basic types and categories. Having a catalogue of items to observe makes observations more incisive; it also creates blind spots. Observing to a brief (for example, observing how individuals use their bodies, what elements of interaction generate laughter and mirth or what emotions are displayed) can be a double-edged weapon: it sharpens observations, but it may prevent the observation of significant events which fall outside the brief. Observational skills can be developed through practice. By contrasting the general and the particular, researchers can refine their self-briefing and focus their observations on issues and areas which will be of value for their analyses later.

Important as observations are, they are supplemented by data from interviews and/or questionnaires, both valuable methods for collecting research material. Psychoanalytic researchers must be especially aware that the communication occurring during a research interview is itself part of an interpersonal relationship, however fleeting, which frames and colours the information being communicated. Researchers must be careful in establishing a relation of mutuality, in which they examine the purpose and interest of their research to each and every interviewee. They must not patronize their respondents, but must express the interest and relevance of their research in terms which make sense to the respondent, making the respondent feel as though he or she is participating in something of general value rather than being an instrument enabling the researcher to pursue his or her personal hobby-horse. It is especially important not to lapse into ritualistic explanations of the research purpose with every succeeding interview. The researcher may acknowledge that respondents will have learned something about the research from informal discussions and gossip with earlier interviewees. Finally, the researcher must offer each and every interviewee reassurance of his or her impartiality and of the confidential nature of the interview.

Special care must be paid in avoiding an inquisitorial stance or one that implies that there are right and wrong, clever and dumb, answers. Psychoanalytic research into organizations undoubtedly requires some factual information, including financial data, evidence on important incidents, demographic and other statistics. But, more importantly, psychoanalytic research must stimulate fantasy in the respondents, through which the meaning of experience can be accessed. The safest way to block the expression of fantasy is by asking questions like 'Did this *really* happen? Why? Did anyone else witness it? When? Where? etc.' By contrast, questions like 'Have there been any similar incidents? How did your colleagues feel about this? Was this incident discussed on the shop-floor?' are likely to stimulate free-associations which may bring to the surface important unconscious material.

Listening skills are absolutely vital for psychoanalytic researchers, who must be prepared to abandon their pre-arranged order of questions if new, promising lines of investigation unexpectedly arise. A friendly probing with a follow-up question is usually likely to generate better data than a ritualistic move to the next question on the interview schedule. Listening requires considerable concentration and emotional engagement, from which researchers must not shirk. They must be sensitive to their own responses to what they hear, and must be willing to probe deeper in situations which generate strong feelings. Later, after the conclusion of an interview, the researcher must ask him or herself a series of questions, such as 'Why did I take such a dislike to this person?' 'What made me feel uncomfortable in what they said?' 'Why did I suddenly change my attitude at a particular point in the interview?' 'How could I have got nearer the heart of the matter?' 'Why does this comment or word jar with me?'

Questionnaires or written responses to questions have been less widely used in psychoanalytic research into organizations, yet the anonymity offered by questionnaires can be a considerable aid, if respondents are willing to cooperate. Open questions may be preferred (for example, 'Can you relate an incident that caused amusement/anger/sadness/embarrassment in your department?), but word-association techniques, like those used by Jungian analysts, may generate important material.

RESEARCH STRATEGIES: MATERIALS FOR STUDY

Research strategies and the nature of the material collected depend on the nature of the field to be investigated, the strength and density of existing theory and the researcher's own interests and strengths. Given that psychoanalytic research aims at discovering unconscious meanings and processes, it generally prefers to focus on fantasies, since they represent compromise formations between conscious and unconscious forces. We must again emphasize that fantasies alone are not enough for most types of research; establishing the distance between reality and fantasy requires knowledge of objective reality. 'They kill people here' represents a very different fantasy in a high-pressure organization where people are forced to quit from that in an organization where individuals actually commit suicide. It is important, therefore, that the researcher is able to juxtapose subjective experiences with some salient objective features about the organization in hand.

How can access be gained into unconscious contents and processes in organizations? Several options are available to researchers.

Stories

One of the most effective strategies for carrying out research is through the collection of stories. By collecting stories in particular organizations, by listening and comparing different accounts, by investigating how narratives are constructed around specific events, by examining which events in an organization's history generate stories and which ones fail to do so, we gain access to deeper organizational realities, closely linked to their members' experiences. In this way, stories enable us to study organizational politics, leadership, culture, change and other organizational phenomena in uniquely illuminating ways, revealing how wider organizational issues are viewed, commented upon and worked upon by their members.

In telling a story, the requirements of accuracy are relaxed in the interest of making a point. Poetic licence is the prerogative of story-telling. At the same time, by shrouding a point in symbolic terms, stories are able to evade censors, both internal and external, and express views and feelings which may be unacceptable in straight talk (see Chapter 8). A joke, a story or a tale is a way of 'testing the water' to see whether others feel like the story-teller, reading the same meaning into events. The teller of a joke or a story can always fall back on the defence 'It was only a joke/story!' Stories are emotionally and symbolically charged narratives; they do not present information or facts about 'events', but they enrich, enhance and infuse facts with meaning – they use facts as a springboard for fantasy. This is both their strength and a potential weakness. For stories will often compromise accuracy in the interest of pleasure; they may focus on the incidental details, remaining stubbornly silent about what a researcher may regard as vital clues; they may contain inconsistencies, imprecisions, lacunae, non-sequiturs, illogicalities and ambiguities. Ultimately, the truth of a story lies not in its accuracy but in its meaning.

The role of the researcher in story-based research is that of a *fellow-traveller* on the narrative, engaging with it emotionally, displaying interest, empathy and pleasure in the story-telling process. The researcher does not risk alienating the story-teller by seeming to doubt the narrative or by placing him or her under cross-examination, but conspires to detach the narrative from the narrowness of the discourse of facts, guiding it instead in the direction of free-association, reverie and fantasy. Contradictions and ambiguities in the narrative are accepted with no embarrassment. Ambiguity lies at the heart of many stories, displaying an individual's ambivalent feelings or partial knowledge or understanding. While the researcher may ask for clarification of particular aspects of the story, the story-teller must feel that such clarification is asked in the interest of increased pleasure and empathy rather than in the form of pedantic enquiry.

Psychoanalysis is not the only academic tradition making use of stories in organizational research. The story-telling perspective now permeates a large part of organizational studies, generating quite a formidable bibliography (see Boyce, 1996, who has diligently assembled five pages of references). Psychoanalysis alone, however, approaches stories as manifest symptoms of unconscious processes. These processes may be unique to a single individual or shared by several and have both wish-fulfilling and consolatory qualities, which can be revealed using psychoanalytic interpretations (Bowles, 1989, 1990; Gabriel, 1991a, c; Stein, 1994). Moreover, within stories, individuals cast themselves in particular roles, such as victims, heroes, heroic survivors or love-objects, offering vital insights into their emotional attachment to their organization, their peers, subordinates and superiors. This type of organizational research has generated considerable insights and has been extensively discussed (for detailed discussions, see Bowles, 1989, 1990; Gabriel, 1991a, b, c, 1992; Stein, 1994).

How to elicit stories? Researchers may elicit stories directly or indirectly. Direct questions which invite story-telling include the following:

- Can you recall any incident which was widely discussed between yourself and your colleagues?
- Can you recall an incident that made you laugh/concerned/sad/proud/angry etc.?

- Are there any special characters in this organization? Any stories about them?
- Are there any stories about the organization's leaders?
- Can you think of an incident which sums up to you what it means to be part of this organization?
- Can you think of an incident which sums up the stresses and strains of your job?

Many of these questions may generate factual answers rather than stories. Undoubtedly, there are some individuals who, at least in the early parts of an interview, stick to the facts, either because of defensiveness or for other reasons. Skilful researchers can often overcome resistances, steering the conversation in the direction of story and fantasy, with questions like:

- What exactly did this incident mean to *you*?
- Did anyone read the situation differently?
- What did the incident show about the way in which this organization treats its members?
- What would you have done if you were in the position of that person?
- What is the moral of this story?

How to corroborate interpretations? Throughout this book we have underlined the delicate and dangerous nature of psychoanalytic interpretations. Researchers, in particular, must exercise the utmost caution in offering interpretations for particular stories they collect, especially if they are not very familiar with the context in which they are told. Interpretation is an art and a skill owing as much to tacit understanding, sensitivity, empathy and know-how as to scientific method. Specific interpretations may not be proved or disproved by conventional scientific criteria. Yet this does not make every interpretation equally meaningful or valid. An interpretation may be original, clever, perceptive, incomplete, misleading or even plain wrong.

I would argue briefly that there are four corroborating techniques which may be used to strengthen interpretations or organizational stories. First, the internal consistency of the interpretation. In a successful interpretation, the interpretation of parts is consistent with the interpretation of the whole, different signs or clues pointing in the same direction. Secondly, in strong interpretations specific outcomes are over-determined, i.e. not only different signs point in the same direction, but different mechanisms can be established leading to the same outcome. Thirdly, strong interpretations, although not falsifiable on the grounds of individual pieces of evidence, do, nevertheless, make clear what evidence would lead to their refutation. Fourthly, strong interpretations will generally address, account for and supersede less strong ones. Overall, strong interpretations leave one with a sense of discovery, a sense of having penetrated something opaque and incomprehensible. This is in a sense the ultimate object of psychoanalytic interpretations, of making conscious what was real, yet unconscious. Even in the excitement of a particularly penetrating interpretation, the researcher must beware. One can all too easily become seduced by an interpretation which is wide of the mark – a clever or even a dazzling interpretation is not necessarily an accurate one. One must continuously ask not only 'Is there any other way I could make sense of this story?', but also 'Why is this particular interpretation so satisfying to me?'

Critical incident analysis

This strategy, extensively used by non-psychoanalytic researchers, can be used in conjunction with the story-telling approach outlined above. The researcher here focuses on a single incident in an individual's or an organization's history and seeks to untangle its emotional and symbolic associations. Such moments of crisis frequently leave long-lasting effects, shaping an individual's outlook. In organizations, crises become part of the folklore and collective heritage of its members. Yet, if one probes closely, one discovers that behind the general acknowledgement that a particular moment was critical, different individuals have different memories and interpretations of the precise significance of the event.

Individual and organizational critical incidents can easily become springboards for fantasy and free-association, through questions like:

- Why was this such an important event?
- Suppose you had been in charge. What would you have done?
- With the benefit of hindsight, what do you think that you/the organization/X should have done?
- What did you/the organization learn from this incident?
- Were there any unforeseen benefits from this crisis?
- Who was primarily to blame for the crisis? Was anyone unfairly blamed?

Once again, researchers may find that these questions generate well-rehearsed, safe, stock answers, generating few insights. They may then venture to discuss more directly the emotions generated by the crisis and its aftermath.

Emotions

Direct research on emotions in organizations is still very undeveloped. Both story-based research and critical incident research, however, can lead into an examination of feelings and emotions. The following questions can open up this type of investigation:

- What did you feel at the time?
- Thinking about this now, what feelings do you have?
- What emotions did this generate among your colleagues?
- Did you/they try to control these emotions? Why? How?
- How were these emotions expressed?
- How much did this experience have to do with your own personality?
- What other incident has generated similar types of feelings?

These questions may be followed up with questions like

- Do you often feel like this?
- Would you prefer to feel differently about this? What would it take?
- How easy do you find controlling your emotions?

Fantasies

Individual and collective fantasies can be triggered with 'What if . . .' types of questions or in conjunction with questions on emotions:

- What is your great fear (as far as your work/ the organization is concerned)?
- What is your greatest hope?
- If you could start all over again, what would you like to do? What would be your ideal work?
- If you could swap places with someone in this organization, who would that be?
- What would you do if you were in X's place?
- What is your biggest unrealized ambition? Could you achieve it yet? What would it take?

Once again, evasive or facile answers ('I hope to win the lottery', 'I would like to be a pop star') may be followed up with questions like

- What do you think it would be like to 'win the lottery'/'be a pop star'?
- What would you do with 'all the money'/'the fame'?

Metaphors

Research using metaphors is relatively recent, although the theoretical and heuristic value of metaphors in organizational research has been known for some time (Turner, 1974; Morgan, 1986; Grant and Oswick, 1996). In my research, I have found that the use of metaphors provides a ready prompt for free-association, fantasy and story-telling. The researcher may start by asking the respondent if a metaphor from a particular list applies to the organization under study. The list may include:

- a machine (well-oiled? creaky?)
- a family (what kind? who is the father/ mother? how do they treat their children?)
- a football team
- an episode from a soap opera (which?)
- a nest of vipers
- a castle under siege
- a dinosaur
- a conveyor belt
- a prison
- an orchestra (with conductor? who wrote the score?)
- a pressure cooker
- a rose garden

The researcher will notice how respondents react to each metaphor, perplexed about some, amused by others, strongly rejecting some, instantly alighting on others. It is then possible to explore the meaning of each metaphor and examine its applicability to a particular organization. Respondents may be invited to improvise their own metaphor and to discuss the feelings evoked by it; they may be asked to contrast their ideal organization with the actual one or to provide a story which supports their preferred metaphor. In so doing they may reach a better understanding of the unconscious meanings which the organization holds for them (Diamond, 1993).

Participant observation

This type of research can be pursued by closely observing the ways in which individuals relate to each other in a work environment, possibly supplementing observations with individual or group interviews. Generally speaking, this approach has limited value unless the researcher has a good understanding of the organization being studied; otherwise, the researcher may find him or herself, like the individual observing people in a country which he or she is visiting for the first time, unable to know what is significant and what is trivial. Ideally, this type of research should approach the ethnographic type, in which the researcher maintains an identity close to the group being observed but separate from it. Participant observation techniques depend a great detail on the ability of researchers to go almost unnoticed, yet ever noticing, in ways that true insiders find difficult. Keeping a careful record of observations is essential in participant observation: early observations, frequently invalidated or obliterated by subsequent ones, can provide valuable insights both into the organization being studied and the researcher's own mental habits.

The great value of this type of research is that the researcher will encounter all the phenomena introduced earlier – stories, critical incidents, emotions, metaphors and fantasies – without having to elicit them. It is, however, a time-consuming and all-absorbing activity, which makes considerable demands on the researcher. Even when properly practised, it may not yield the hoped-for great insights. Participants always have difficulty maintaining the detachment necessary to remain observers. Moreover, participant observers cannot easily ask the type of probing questions available to other researchers. As participants, they are assumed to know the answers already and their questions (which would be perfectly acceptable if they came from an outsider) may easily be dismissed as presumptuous, patronizing or stupid.

Dreaming matrix

Dream interpretation has long been one of the chief tools of psychoanalysis. Psychoanalytic researchers have on occasion used respondents' dreams as a route into unconscious processes in organizations (see Gabriel, 1995; Carr, 1998). Lawrence (1991) has developed a unique working method for researching organizations via the dreams of their participants. Instead of looking at dreams as the private property of individuals, Lawrence seeks to turn them into collective resources through the technique of the 'social dreaming matrix', a group within which individuals report and explore the social meanings of their dreams. The 'social dreaming matrix' 'asks for dreams that go beyond the individual and are focused on the environment' (Lawrence, 1991: 280). These dreams can hold many diverse meanings, or can be invested with different types of symbolism. This is why Lawrence prefers the term 'matrix' over 'group':

> The idea of the 'matrix' has been central. Whereas in a group we search for a universe of meanings, in the matrix a multi-verse of meanings can coexist. If you think about it, once a dream is offered there can be as many associations as there are people in the room. That's a lot of associations. (Lawrence, 1991: 282)

Research based on the 'social dreaming matrix' is still in its infancy. The practical and methodological problems which it generates are considerable. (How can it be framed to appeal to individuals or organizations? How many individuals or companies would be willing to participate? How can the findings be corroborated?) Nevertheless, there have been some promising applications. Biran, for example, used it with great effect in her work with educational psychologists and consultants dealing with 'problem children' in Israeli schools. She found that, in the course of discussing dreams in a group which met weekly, participants were able to identify their own perceptions and fantasies of their role, the difficulties which they faced and some of the unconscious meanings engendered by children's violent or destructive behaviour (Biran, 1998). The use of the 'social dreaming matrix' is most appropriate where a group of people with a basic level of trust and a friendly attitude towards psychoanalysis already exists. It would be rather far-fetched to hope that hard-driven business people or labour organizers would be able or willing to supply much material through this type of research.

RELATIONS BETWEEN RESEARCHER AND RESEARCHED

The psychological contract between researcher and researched is a complex one. The researcher may be experienced by the researched as an unwelcome intruder, as an explorer at sea deserving help and support, as a friend, a spy, an ally, a gullible idiot, an agent of liberation, even a deliverer. Researchers may be prepared for different attitudes on the part of their respondents, ranging from cooperation to stubborn refusal, from defiance to deference, from kindness to hostility. They may naturally feel gratitude towards compliant, cooperative and helpful respondents, and anger or even rage at recalcitrant ones. Yet recalcitrant respondents can be valuable sources of research material; their recalcitrance itself may be a valuable research finding.

The handling of the relationship between researcher and researched is one that requires considerable skill and can itself be an area of learning rather than a prerequisite for it. Undoubtedly, this relationship is one of power and subordination, but power and subordination are diffused between the parties. The researcher has the power of the outsider, the person who is not personally affected by the hardships and difficulties of the workplace, one who, in the eyes of the respondent, may sooner or later return to the Olympian heights of the academy, surveying the field with clinical detachment. Yet the researcher is also the person in need, in need of data, in need of stories and of cooperation. It is the researcher who is asking the respondent for a favour, not the other way round. The research interview granted by an interviewee may then be seen as a gift, and as all gifts it is part of a relation of mutuality. What does the interviewee require in return? In the first place, the interviewee requests the respect of the interviewer, a respect that must continue after the interview has been completed and the researcher has safely stored away his or her tapes. Secondly, interviewees may want a sympathetic ally in their opposition to other organizational members, someone who will see their point of view and will believe their story. Thirdly, interviewees may want feedback on the research – some knowledge or information about their own organization which they do not already possess. Finally, interviewees may ask researchers for particular favours, including representations to their superiors. In all of these respects, researchers must handle the relationship with tact, without compromising the undertakings which they have given to other parties.

Transference

It is difficult to conceive of the research relationship without considering transference and counter-transference. Some respondents may regard the researcher as mother or father substitutes, something that may colour the nature of their testimony. They may alternatively seek to impress the researcher and gain his or her approval; they may antagonize the researcher by withholding information or by acting in childish ways; they may patronize the researcher by affecting to know the questions before they are uttered and by refusing to listen; they may even seek to seduce the researcher through their testimony or demeanour. Researchers must be aware of such effects and be prepared to interpret or analyse them. Why is it that they are having this effect on the interviewee? Are they having the same effect on all interviewees or on some? How does gender influence the nature of this transference?

Clearly, the research interviewer does not have the same scope to explore transference as the clinician – his or her time with the interviewee is limited and the brief of the conversation limited by the research aims. However, some effort must be made to establish the nature of the transference through questions like:

- What do you think of the type of work that I do?
- Do you think I am doing a good job of this interview?
- Has anyone else taken an interest in the work which you do?
- Does this interview remind you of any other situation?
- From your point of view, what would be the best outcome of my research?
- Suppose we swapped parts, what questions would you ask me?

Acknowledging, confronting and analysing the transferential qualities of the research relationship will eventually pay dividends, when the researcher seeks to interpret the narratives of his or her respondents. To whom were these narratives addressed? A friendly listener, a visitor from a foreign planet, a mother/father/ son/daughter figure?

Feedback, interpretation and resistance

Possibly one of the most serious dilemmas facing psychoanalytic researchers of organizations is whether and how to present their findings to their respondents. In the case of problem-driven research, Levinson advises adherence to a very strict procedure, where the consultant reads his or her report to the client in person and follows it up by handing over a written version of the report. This is likely to generate such strong feelings and possible resistances in the client that Levinson insists that a follow-up meeting is arranged immediately for the next morning to deal with the fall-out (Levinson, 1972). The theory-driven researcher does not face the same acute problems and may easily avoid giving feedback altogether. In my experience, the majority of organizations offering access to theory-driven research are far too busy, threatened or reluctant to allow for a feedback session, even if they insisted on one as a condition for granting access. Yet feedback sessions are both important sources of research material in their own right and also opportunities to corroborate hypotheses and interpretations which are taking shape in the researcher's mind.

In presenting their findings, researchers thus take a great risk. What sense will their respondents make of these findings? Will they be pleased? Will they be angry? Will they reject them? And, furthermore, what is the meaning of such reactions? Is rejection an indication of error or is it a case where denial *may* indicate the success of an interpretation or a construction? In my experience, feedback which entails detailed theoretical arguments or highly speculative interpretations and constructions ('this organization is populated by highly narcissistic individuals', 'the failure of product X represents a symbolic castration of the research and development department') are unlikely to prove helpful in feedback sessions, unless the researcher is prepared to invest a great amount of work into them. More modest or tentative interpretations may be tried out, inviting alternative explanations or conjectures. The researcher may then have an opportunity to observe the respondents' reactions to revelations about themselves of which they were themselves unaware. These may range from uncritical acceptance (following a suggestive effect) to hostile rejection and resistance to critical engagement and qualification.

The complexities of resistance must once again be recognized. Resistance may be an outcome of transference, where respondents resist the research findings because of their hostility to the researcher, who may at that moment be cast in the position of a preposterous busybody, who believes that he or she understands them better than they understand themselves. Alternatively, however, resistance may be part of a political process, one in which the researcher is seen as an agent of oppression and colonization, who must be undermined and discredited. After all, the question of interpretation revolves around the issue of whether we acknowledge or grant someone else the right to understand us better than we understand ourselves. Rejecting an interpretation implies a withholding of this right.

CONCLUSION

Psychoanalytic research into organizations, like all research, is a practice which is closer to an art or craft than the practice of scientific theorizing. It cannot be reduced to a set of immutable rules of scientific method or even a set of heuristic rules of thumb. This chapter has offered a set of guidelines for different stages of the research activity, but they too must be accepted as conditional and relative. Part of the researcher's skill lies in knowing when it is worth taking a risk in departing from such guidelines and also knowing whether the risk has paid off. There are occasions when breaking a particular research guideline can offer unexpected insights. The new researcher must develop his or her own command of the art of research by doing it and seeking to learn from his or her experiences and mistakes. Doing half a dozen interviews with one's colleagues or friends can develop the interviewer's sensitivity to a greater extent than reading a whole volume on the subject.

There is one type of mistake that researchers must avoid at all costs, one type of rule which they must not break. This concerns the ethical requirements of doing research; no hoped-for outcome justifies the breaking of undertakings which a researcher has given, the carrying out of research which will be harmful to those participating in it, or the dissemination of lies and distortions. Such practices, which all too frequently corrupt the work of investigative journalists and reporters, can have absolutely devastating effects when indulged in by academic researchers. They certainly close the doors for future researchers and taint the reputation of the academic establishments to which the researchers belong – nothing can justify such a cost.

The final thing that psychoanalytic researchers into organizations must be prepared for is yet another quality of all research activity. They must be prepared to endure the anxiety and distress of not knowing, and not knowing whether they are on the path towards knowing. Acknowledging one's own confusion and puzzlement at different points of the research process can be more helpful than seeking comfort in existing answers and reassuring platitudes. Researchers must be prepared to endure periods of uncertainty, periods of profound doubt, if they are to arrive at original and substantial conclusions. Being organized in recording one's materials, filing them and analysing them is an asset which can all too easily turn into a liability. The perfectly organized mind is unlikely to arrive at highly original ideas. By contrast, the alert mind, the mind which is prepared to improvise and change its mental and practical routines, is more likely to arrive at original thinking and theoretical innovation. Above all, researchers must be willing to ask themselves questions: the hardest and most awkward questions – those questions that even the most perceptive inquisitor, the most demanding examiner may fail to ask, but also, the easiest, most straightforward questions which sometimes seem hardly worth asking at all.

12 CONCLUDING THOUGHTS: TOWARDS A NEW CONCEPTION OF MANAGEMENT

Since their earliest beginnings, theories of organizations and management have been preoccupied with control. Standing for order, predictability and reliability, control is an integral part of what most people understand by 'organization'. Control is what distinguishes organization from its opposite, chaos. Management itself has come ever closer to mean being in control – control over resources, information and people. Much of the theory of organizations is aimed at putting the manager ever more firmly in control. Throughout the twentieth century, the orbit of management has constantly increased to encompass ever more grandiose projects. It seems that nothing lies beyond the embrace of management: *Managing* X is the title of countless books, where X applies to virtually anything. These days it is not unusual to hear talk of management of the environment, management of the economy, management of the African elephant, management of emotion or, still more ambitiously, management of the planet.

The equation of management with control and control with organization must raise serious questions among readers of this book. How can we control others when can hardly control ourselves? How can we manage organizations when we can hardly manage our own unconscious desires? How can we remain organized in the face of crises, turmoil and unpredictability? In this concluding chapter, I shall develop some of the implications of the psychoanalytic theories and ideas presented earlier for an understanding of management, its scope and the tasks facing it in the future.

It is not accidental that faith in control rises with feelings of insecurity, uncertainty and impending chaos (Drucker, 1980, 1995; Watson, 1994). Among managers today such feelings are generated by volatile economies, global markets and technologies, revolutionary information systems and government policies, to say nothing of the tribulations of companies themselves, mergers, acquisitions, precipitous bankruptcies, massive redundancies and re-structurings. Under such conditions, managers' needs for reassurance and comfort become exacerbated as insecurity becomes chronic. Many of the theories of management, in both their academic and popularized variants, aim at providing such reassurance, through a variety of magic recipes and panaceas: how to maintain competitive advantage, how to create an excellent culture, how to thrive on chaos. Reading current popular management texts, one has the impression that the manuals are advising drivers to grip their steering wheels ever more tightly as their vehicles run out of control.

A very different approach is suggested by complexity and chaos theories, which emerged in the natural sciences in the 1960s, drawing on the study of non-linear dynamic systems, such as the weather system or the turbulent flow of fluids. Here chaos cannot be managed or controlled, certainly not through reliance on prescriptions and formulas. Complexity and turbulence are not higher orders of order, orders whose rules we have not (yet) grasped. They are situations where there is vital randomness and unpredictability which defy domestication within linear mathematical equations. Since its beginnings, complexity theory has found applications in natural and biological sciences ranging from the study of volcanoes and earthquakes to the study of the heart and the brain. More recently, it has found some applications in human sciences, in demography, geography and economics (for an overview, see Gleick, 1987).

Complex systems are systems which do not return regularly to a condition of equilibrium. Their behaviour in the long run is quite unpredictable. Small or accidental factors can have disproportionate effects on the overall system and cause–effect links observed once cannot be repeated (Thietart and Forgues, 1995, 1997). This is one point to which complexity theory invariably returns – the total impossibility of long-term forecasting, in spite of the possibility of modest short-term predictions. A second feature of complex systems is referred to as self-similarity, the occurrence of similar patterns across very different scales; in this way, one can 'zoom' in or out of a complex system discovering similar types of phenomena, irrespective of the scale at which the phenomena are observed. A third property of complex systems is referred to as self-organization (Gleick, 1987; Kaufmann, 1993, 1995; Stacey, 1992, 1995, 1996), a chance but not uncommon ability to break out of a disorderly pattern into a spontaneous and unexpected order. This is a phenomenon observed in the behaviour of gas molecules as they are exposed to changing energy sources or in certain types of turbulent flow. Self-organization does not mean that the system has lapsed from complex to stable equilibrium, since it is not achieved with the help of damping feedback; instead, it generates what have been described as 'islands of order from the sea of chaos' (Gleick, 1987; Von Krogh and Roos, 1995). These islands are subject to the earlier two properties of complex systems: neither their scale, nor their duration may be predicted.

In conditions of complexity, science loses its predictive prowess. It cannot anticipate the precise condition of the system at some future time, nor can it anticipate the effect of specific disturbances or interventions. Control of the system from inside becomes impossible, since the same interventions may lead to diametrically opposite consequences. Yet, complexity theory does not leave us in a position of powerlessness and confusion: it enables us to observe and analyse such systems, unravel patterns, establish boundaries, note similarities, identify areas of tranquillity and make short-term forecasts. It also gives us a reassurance that departure from stable equilibrium or linear change does not necessarily imply total collapse and disorder. Controlled change is possible, without anyone being in control.

In the past ten years, complexity theory has started to penetrate organizational and management studies beyond the level of the fashionable cliché, generating some promising ideas. Contrary to a binary opposition of organization with chaos, a number of organizational theorists have long viewed a measure of disorder and unpredictability as constitutive of ordinary organizations and some have even seen them as beneficial to them. It may be argued that, in contrast to complexity theorists who envisage islands of tranquillity in seas of chaos, the majority of organizational theorists have viewed organizations as areas of tranquillity with pockets of chaos. Even when discontinuity, crisis and conflict are brought centrestage, they are commonly regarded as 'exceptional' or 'abnormal' phenomena. The long social science tradition of presuming stability to be normal and instability abnormal is still potent. But, there are signs of change, especially in current ethnographic case studies and studies based on depth interviews (see, for example, Mangham, 1986; Van Maanen, 1988; Mangham and Pye, 1991; Kunda, 1992; Hirschhorn, 1993; Hirschhorn and Gilmore, 1993; Hirschhorn and Young, 1993; Watson, 1994). These suggest that for many organizational participants, confusion, uncertainty and even chaos are not marginal phenomena, but endemic to their organizations. Many managers report unpredictable and even chaotic features in their organizations. When they pull a lever, push a button or issue an order, they feel that several different things may happen. To the extent that they are in control, their control is a precarious, nervous one, threatened by numerous forces. Even if some organizational participants idealize a golden age of stability and order (Gabriel, 1993; Allcorn, 1997), such images simply do not accord with the experiences of many organizational participants today. Control is experienced as increasingly difficult, both at the personal and at the organizational level. As Gould has argued succinctly:

> Organizations were, to be sure, never closed systems, but in more stable times with much slower rates of change, they were experienced as self-contained and self-perpetuating. By contrast, contemporary post-industrial organizations often have quite the opposite character. They are experienced as unstable, chaotic, turbulent, and often unmanageable. (Gould, 1993: 50)

If we accept that many organizations are experienced as chaotic either because they operate in a chaotic environment for which they are themselves partly responsible or because their internal dynamics are those of complex systems, the implications for management are far-reaching. For these organizations, neither long-term planning nor central control is possible. Simple cause–effect chains do not obtain. Instead, such organizations must capitalize on virtuous circles set off accidental or serendipitous events. Such virtuous circles operate at different organizational levels, across scales, in a self-similar manner. A measure of stability in such organizations is not the product of control or rational management procedures, but rather the result of spontaneous self-organization, across scales. Within such organizations, managers try in vain to plan for the longer term, since the longer term for most organizations is unknown and unknowable, like the weather. Reverting to rational procedures, routine, cost and waste minimization, control and linearity undermines creativity and innovation, the very qualities necessary to survive and succeed.

Under such conditions of unpredictable change, successful organizations are those whose leaders and members do not seek to predict the future and control it, but rather those which can rapidly change course, redefine themselves and learn to live with uncertainty and even chaos. These organizations must be prepared at times to be wasteful, destructive and conflict-ridden in order to be creative and innovative. Looking for targets to apportion blame or give credit for successes may appear to be organizationally expedient, but has little justification – single individuals are not responsible either for success or for failure, these phenomena being the products of a multiplicity of chance and systemic factors. Seeking to repeat success by applying a 'winning formula' can be futile; organizational learning has little to do with learning formulas and much to do with experimentation, reasoning by analogy and an ability to question underlying assumptions and existing patterns.

Learning in such organizations means essentially being prepared to operate without the safety-net of received wisdom and knowledge, taking risks and never standing still. Feyerabend's (1975, 1978, 1987) strictures on methodological anarchism have become peculiarly apposite to organizations. Successful organizations, like innovative scientists, must observe opportunities and seize them; they must often proceed counter-intuitively or counter-inductively, stumble on discoveries by transgressing prescriptions or by forgetting method. As Feyerabend argued, 'Without "chaos", no knowledge' (1975: 179).

THE ILLUSION OF CONTROL

Feyerabend's dictum now seems increasingly less like iconoclasm and more like common-sense. Unpleasant common-sense, all the same. As psychoanalysis teaches, surrendering an illusion is an anxiety-provoking experience. And few illusions are more powerful and more useful than the illusion of control. Being in charge is a core belief for managers, no matter how much unpredictable reality frustrates them. They hold each other technically and morally responsible for the successes and failures of their divisions, departments and organizations. They plan, they articulate visions and they use analytical techniques based on 'if–then' chains of thought in order to control resources, people and information.

The scientific standing of these techniques has come under severe criticism (MacIntyre, 1981/1985; A. B. Thomas, 1993; Carr, 1997). Thomas, for example, argues that they are

> best seen, not as rational means of controlling employees' behaviour but as magical rites which take a rational form. Furthermore, managerial faith in the possibility of the control of uncertainty presented by human involvement in organizations reflects reverence for the sacred symbols of rationality and professionalism. (A. B. Thomas, 1993: 79)

Like Thomas, MacIntyre (1981/1985) viewed management control as a myth and the analytical techniques meant to bring it about as quasi-magical rites.

> The dominance of the manipulative mode in our culture is not and cannot be accompanied by very much actual success in manipulation . . . The notion of social control embodied in the notion of expertise is indeed a masquerade. Our social order is in a very literal sense out of our, and indeed anyone's, control. No one is or could be in charge. (1981/1985: 107)

Yet MacIntyre argued that the myth of management control and the accompanying techniques are crucial for sustaining the legitimacy of managerial authority. This is why managers demand obedience; this is why they are handsomely paid. Their technical competence is meant to enable them to steer their departments or their companies through harsh and unpredictable waters. If it were an easy task, neither their claim to be obeyed nor their rewards would be justified. Politically, therefore, it is vital for managers to claim the credit for organizational success; equally, it is vital to be able to pin the blame for organizational failure on a specific number of people (those meant to be in charge).

Besides its political function, in recent decades, the myth of management control has contributed to a broader cultural trend. The 1980s saw the lionization of the manager as a cultural archetype, capable of heroic deeds like turning around moribund companies, rescuing failing ones, launching apocalyptic campaigns and reaching vertiginous success. During this decade, business and management were not merely rehabilitated from the radical critique of the 1960s and 1970s, but also redefined as a terrain for brave exploits and glorious careers (Grey and Mitev, 1995). The wider discourse of organizations as arenas for dull bureaucrats and tame 'organization men' was swept aside by epic and romantic narratives of managerial quests and ordeals and a quasi-religious rhetoric of missions, visions and 'management of the planet'-style grandiosity. None of this would have been possible if management had been seen as employing arcane procedures on a hit-and-miss basis with little direct influence on outcomes (A. B. Thomas, 1993).

While politically and culturally expedient, the myth of management control, like all illusions, also fulfils vital psychological needs – fulfilling in fantasy wishes that cannot be fulfilled in actuality and reducing anxiety. This is where the psychoanalytic ideas introduced in this volume offer valuable insights. For some individuals, control represents a grandiose dream in which people, groups and organizations may be commanded with no fear of recalcitrance, like machines, or symbols on a computer screen. For others, it meets a dependency need, a reassurance that someone is in charge, even if he or she is not liked. For yet others, it fulfils a need for victimization and scapegoating – someone may be blamed, so long as someone claims to be in charge. Subordinates collude in the illusion, endowing leaders with truly super-human qualities, such as omnipotence, omniscience and total composure. If they were seen as confused, erratic, ordinary people, their ability to stay in charge, to control things would be called into question (Krantz, 1989; Lapierre, 1989, 1991). Pretending that the world (including the eco-sphere and the African elephant) can be controlled and managed helps us cope with the anxiety caused by the chaos that is threatening our lives.

Building on the work of Bion, Jaques and Menzies, Stacey (1992, 1996) has argued that long-term plans, mission statements and corporate visions are defensive techniques aimed at exorcising the fear of losing control. They are techniques which preserve the illusion of control when faced with a chaotic environment. *But the fear of outer chaos and the threats issuing from it are themselves a result of the anxiety over inner chaos, chaos which arises from our own disorderly desires, impulses and inhibitions.*

Here complexity theory joins an important point of psychoanalytic discourse, one that has been discussed at length in this book. Freud, a major figure of modernity, is often seen as siding with the forces of order and rationality to keep mental chaos and disorder under control. Psychoanalysis is often presented as a regime of mental management (Rieff, 1959), in which the ego performs functions not unlike those of managers. Freud's fanatical devotion to the scientific status of psychoanalysis reinforces the view that he sought to mobilize reason against the forces of chaos and disintegration. Yet this presents only part of the picture because his very conception of the human psyche is a disintegrated one. In a paper called 'A Difficulty in the Path of Psycho-Analysis' (1917), Freud argued that psychoanalysis had inflicted a blow on human narcissism, by showing that our ego is not master in its own house. If Copernicus's heliocentric theory shattered the view that the earth is the centre of the universe and Darwin's evolution destroyed the myth of man's uniqueness among animals, psychoanalysis adds a third blow; our own soul

> is not a simple thing; on the contrary, it is a hierarchy of superordinated and subordinated agents, a labyrinth of impulses striving independently of one another towards action,

corresponding with the multiplicity of instincts and of relations with the outer world, many of which are antagonistic to one another and incompatible. (Freud, 1917: 187)

Faced with such a situation, the ego, as we saw in Chapter 2, is like the rider who seeks to control a wild horse; the rider may stay in control, but may equally be overwhelmed. While safely in control, he would be wrong to dilute his vigilance. It is telling that the word 'to manage' originates in the French word *manege* and the Italian *maneggiare*, the training of a horse in its paces. If Freudian ego is a managerial ego, as Philip Rieff (1959) has argued, it is one constantly facing forces greater than itself: it may temporarily keep these forces in check or even exploit them to its advantage, but it can never overcome them.

What are these unpredictable and potentially overpowering forces? In addition to natural catastrophes, floods, earthquakes, crop failures and so on, people are threatened by the slings and arrows of everyday life, by illness, accident, death, loss of loved ones, loss of jobs, discrimination, warfare, poverty, hatred and much else besides. They are also threatened by inner disorder, overwhelming cravings, irrational fears and anxieties, loss of self-esteem, fear of ageing and dying, rejection, guilt and so on. These uncontrollable chaotic forces in human life are frequently referred to by Freud (1927, 1930) by the unscientific term 'fate'.

> There are elements, which seem to mock all human control: the earth, which quakes and is torn apart and buries all human life and its works; water, which deluges and drowns everything in a turmoil; storms, which blow everything before them; there are diseases, which we have only recently recognized as attacks by other organisms and finally there is the painful riddle of death, against which no medicine has yet been found, nor probably will be. With these forces nature rises up against us, majestic, cruel and inexorable; she brings to mind once more our weakness and helplessness, which we thought to escape through the work of civilization ... For the individual, too, life is hard to bear, just as it is for mankind in general. The civilization in which he participates imposes some amount of privation on him, and other men bring him a measure of suffering, either in spite of the precepts of civilization or because of its imperfections. To this are added the injuries which untamed nature – he calls it Fate – inflicts on him. (Freud, 1927: 195)

In Freudian discourse the image of the ego confronting fate is ever-present. In this confrontation, the ego may seek solace in illusions which promise to make it independent of fate, including religious beliefs or erotic infatuation. It may become superstitious, seeking to placate fate through private, arcane rituals. Or it may deny fate, pretending that reality is controllable, civilized, orderly and predictable. More pragmatically, the ego may seek to establish a measure of order, employing the resources of civilization to keep chaos at bay.

> Man's observation of the great astronomical regularities not only furnished him with a model for introducing order into his life, but gave him the first points of departure for doing so. Order is a kind of compulsion to repeat which, when a regulation has been laid down once and for all, decides when, where and how a thing shall be done, so that in every similar circumstance one is spared hesitation and indecision. (Freud, 1930: 282)

But, in its confrontation with fate, the ego may only create islands of order, which are forever subject to disorder. The Freudian ego is usually troubled; whether seen as a city under siege or as the servant of three harsh masters, the ego's need to be in control is every bit as powerful as the forces of disorder, inner and outer, which threaten to overwhelm it. Reading managers' accounts of their work experiences one is struck by the aptness of those Freudian metaphors. Rather than 'running business', 'making decisions', 'solving problems' and so on, managers manage more in the sense of seeking to keep chaos at bay (see, for example, Watson, 1994). They worry a lot. They do a lot of fire-fighting. Crisis management becomes chronic.

CHAOS AND ORDER

This argument should not create the impression that all is chaos or that all control is illusory. Far from it. Both complexity and psychoanalytic theories recognize the existence of areas of tranquillity, predictability and order in personal and organizational lives. There are periods in the life of an organization or an individual when everything appears to be going according to plan, so much so that the future may appear as nothing more than an extension of the present. The argument developed here, however, would suggest that such a course would be tempting fate. When everything appears to be under control, a small discontinuity may result in a collapse of what previously seemed unassailable.

Nor does our argument deny that our lives in and out of organizations are daily and continuously controlled by forces ranging from traffic signals and appraisal procedures in organizations to seductive media images and career opportunities. In fact, we accept that we are simultaneously over-controlled and inadequately controlled, since we may never be totally controlled. What our argument emphasizes is, first, that many of the controlling practices are resisted, subverted or simply dodged by those who are meant to be subjected to them and that their outcomes cannot be taken for granted. And, secondly, that even when these practices are not tested by those subjected to them, they are tested by a clamorous, capricious entity, akin to Freud's fate, an entity which the Romans envisaged as Fortuna, the bitch-goddess of unpredictability, to whom they dedicated more temples than to any other. Turner (1978) paints a vivid picture of our confrontation with Fortuna, in concluding his book *Man-made Disasters*:

> However comforting the promise of an infinite tidiness offered to man by the older rationalist notion of the possibility of arranging our affairs always on the basis of the anticipation which our conscious knowledge offers us, we must recognize that we are in a contingent universe, in which ultimately there are limits on our ability to reduce uncertainty, to master all of the open-ended and perverse qualities of our environment, and upon our ability to prevent disaster. If we start by recognizing that instability lies at the heart of the world, then we may come to realize that the optimism and the assertion of certainty which enables life to create and spread order cannot completely overcome instability. We may come to realize that, even when our strategies are successful, they are still dependent upon the munificence of the environment and upon the mutability of fortune. (Turner, 1978: 201)

Fortuna, dispensing malice and favours in equal and equally unexpected measure, is a goddess not unknown to us, whether as the mast-head of a chief business publication in the USA or as the divinity of those hoping for a win on the lottery.

The hubris of management is to pretend that Fortuna does not exist or that she may be permanently coaxed or placated into servility. Disregarding the chaotic qualities of life or seeking to control them, tame them or 'disqualify' them, through forecasting, planning and other law-like techniques, amounts to a set of wish-fulfilling illusions, which may in the short run relieve feelings of anxiety and powerlessness but, if anything, accentuates our long-run vulnerability. In the face of defeat and failure, leaders may react by suddenly blaming the unpredictable and arbitrary qualities of fate and adopting a fatalistic position. They may then act, as Lapierre has argued, 'as if they have no freedom, no liberty to choose and shape their environment, and so avoid responsibility for their failure to act, to take risks. 'Fate' precludes success' (Lapierre, 1989: 187). Between the hubris of omnipotence and the fatalism of impotence, Lapierre rightly argues that leaders must find a course, combining self-questioning with a healthy pragmatism, which recognizes the complexities of their task, yet seeks to capitalize on opportunities and minimize the reverses. This is almost exactly the project Machiavelli set for himself in his major political writings, *The Prince* and *The Discourses*.

CONCLUSION

In the early sixteenth century, a period of great political turmoil as well as peerless artistic glory, Machiavelli drew a sophisticated picture of governance, now sometimes obscured by facile equations of his philosophy with immorality and deceit. Machiavelli tried to show how rulers or managers may rule in an environment which alternates between disorder and order, not by pretending that everything can be controlled but by accepting randomness and arbitrariness. At the broad level, Machiavelli, like Freud, was operating within an implicit and occasionally explicit paradigm that life is at times chaotic, that sufferings and blessings are meted out arbitrarily and that it is futile to seek to find meaning in the capriciousness of Fortuna. This churns up turbulent, random, clamorous and senseless sequences of happenings, which we may try to handle (*maneggiare*) but can hardly ever hope to control. What Machiavelli, along with some of his contemporaries, counter-posed to Fortuna is neither wisdom nor knowledge, neither management nor control, but *virtu*. *Virtu* does not mean 'virtue' in the Christian or Greek traditions, but a personal and collective virtuosity in political, administrative, military and psychological terms. *Virtu* is not a methodical, scientific or technical force – no such force would stand a chance against the caprices of Fortuna. Instead, it is a force which combines vitality, opportunism, éclat, wit, alertness and ruthlessness with prudence, knowledge and wisdom. While *virtu* finds institutional expressions in systems of governance and decision-making (*Discourses*, ii.1), it is also a quality of leadership. The first quality of *virtu* is the ability to read the times (Machiavelli's '*i tempi*') and then 'to adapt oneself to the times if one wants to enjoy continued good fortune' (*Discourses*, iii.9).

'I believe that it is probably true', argues Machiavelli, 'that fortune is the arbiter of half the things we do, leaving the other half or so to be controlled by ourselves' (*The Prince*, xxv). It is precisely because fortune is implacable that the task of the leader is complex, his or her success uncertain, and skills non-reducible to simple laws, generalizations and formulas. Machiavelli goes on to use a metaphor which would not surprise many of today's managers: the metaphor of the river which may seem peaceable and predictable one moment, violent and unmanageable the next. *Virtu* means prudence and prescience at times of calm, decisiveness and impetuosity at times of storm. By such means can fortune be handled, its boons maximized and its adversities lessened. Nevertheless, Machiavelli is under no illusion that two people may succeed by using different methods or that two people may enjoy widely differing fortunes even as they employ the same methods. The goddess may be placated but her capricious nature can never be tamed.

If we accept that managers, just like the rest of us, must contend with unpredictability and chaos, we would be wise to recognize the ambiguity in the word 'to manage', which means equally to treat with respect, to cope in adversity, to combine modesty with generosity of spirit, to handle with consideration as well as to control. We must recognize that, like the rest of us, managers are most of the time confused, erratic and irrational – they deserve neither exorbitant praise for success nor total vilification for failure. Their successes are more likely to be due to good fortune, adroit handling or good judgement rather than the application of quasi-scientific theories and propositions.

Management skills and knowledge are, as Machiavelli reminds us, highly contingent upon times and circumstances. They are not likely to be based on generalizable propositions, after the paradigm of natural sciences; they are even less likely to be like the numerous paradigms which operate in organizational studies, which seek to inoculate themselves from each other under the cloak of incommensurability. As Carr (1997) has amply demonstrated, paradigm proliferation is itself a symptom of the inability to recognize that the management of public as well as private affairs is a moral art, rather than a scientific practice. It makes use, not of abstract theories, but practical rules of thumb which 'sometimes work', akin to what Ginzburg (1980) describes as 'common knowledge' or lore, in opposition to science. Viewing management as a scientific discipline capable of taming the forces of unpredictability and disorder represents one of the chief illusions of the twentieth century, an illusion that has sought to replace the moral discourse of values with a supposedly technical discourse of means. The disastrous consequences of this illusion, the nemesis brought about by the hubris of management, can be observed in most of the bleakest episodes the century which has just closed. Yet its grimmest legacy is surely the disfranchisement of large sections of the citizenry from issues of vital concern to them, issues which became defined as technical matters for physicians, educationalists, scientists and managers.

Anticipating the tidings of this new century runs counter to the argument presented here. It remains an open question whether the management of organizations will resort to ever more desperate measures of control generating extra disappointments and privations for all or whether it will redefine itself in a way which calls for leadership virtuosity, coping with adversity and handling others with respect and consideration. The only certain thing is that the wheel of fortune will turn yet again.

GLOSSARY

All scientific innovations generate new vocabularies and give new meanings to old concepts and ideas. Yet few traditions have spawned a number of concepts on the scale of psychoanalysis, something that can be daunting to the new reader. The situation is not helped by the translators of Freud's works who tended to adopt unusual or scientific-sounding terms in their intention to add to the scientific credibility of psychoanalysis. This is in contrast to Freud himself who opted, whenever possible, for using ordinary words (see Bettelheim, 1983). To the new English reader, words such as 'cathexis', 'ego', 'id', 'abreaction' and 'narcissism' can be a major obstacle to understanding psychoanalytic arguments. For these reasons, we have provided a glossary of some 100 core concepts and ideas. None of these concepts is fixed and almost none is unproblematic. Different writers have used them in different ways and their meanings can be the subject of contestation and argument. It is still hoped that this glossary will provide a basic understanding of each concept which the main text of the book will help develop and refine.

Readers interested in a deeper understanding of specific terms, their development and the ways in which different authors have used them can consult two invaluable sources, Rycroft's (1968) concise but very informative *A Critical Dictionary of Psychoanalysis* and Laplanche's and Pontalis's (1988) massive and highly authoritative *The Language of Psychoanalysis*. A similarly authoritative coverage of Kleinian and post-Kleinian theories is offered by Hinschelwood (1989) in *A Dictionary of Kleinian Thought*.

Cross-references in the entries below are marked in *italic*.

abreaction
Emotional discharge, especially the discharge of emotion associated with a painful or traumatic memory. Abreaction, whether brought about by psychotherapy or not, may have a cathartic therapeutic effect.

agencies (or mental agencies)
The name given to various institutions or locations of the mind, notably the *ego*, the *id* and the *super-ego*, each one of which represents certain functions and tendencies of mental life. If the mental apparatus is conceived as a system, agencies represent sub-systems. Agencies must be distinguished from mental processes, functions, objects and representations, although agencies may act in any one of these ways. Thus, the ego may become an idealized object under the process of *narcissism*; it then becomes the *object* of *love*, as though it were an external object.

aggression
There is no consistent approach to aggression shared by all depth psychologists. Freud's mature view on the matter was to regard aggressive behaviour and fantasies as manifestations of the *death instinct* and virtually unavoidable elements of the human condition. According to this view, aggression may be tempered through the fusion of the death instinct with the life instinct; alternatively, it may be directed towards less harmful aims or it may be introjected as an unconscious sense of *guilt*. Freud's mature formulations on aggression indicate that pleasure may be derived from acts of violence, without the presence of a sexual component. The containment of

aggression becomes a major problem for all human cultures. The majority of psychoanalytic writers have disregarded or rejected this view, preferring instead to view aggression as a derivative of frustration and anger. Klein, who highlighted the importance played by aggression from the earliest parts of life, has shifted the emphasis away from the instinctual origin of destructiveness to its appearance in response to the recalcitrance of the *object*.

ambivalence
A core but often misused term indicating the simultaneous experience of powerful but conflicting feelings and attitudes towards a single object. One range of feelings usually occupies the dominant position, though an important event may lead to its replacement in the dominant position by its opposite. Acute ambivalence is a cause of great anxiety and is usually resolved through the *repression* of one range of feelings. Psychoanalysis views ambivalence as fundamental in virtually all deep relations between human beings. Ambivalence is a major feature of *transference*.

anal character
The character of an individual fixated in or regressing to the *anal stage*. The main characteristics of anal characters are stubbornness, orderliness and parsimoniousness. Anal characteristics are often found to co-exist with sadistic tendencies. In organizations, the anal character assumes the form of the obsessive character.

anal stage
The stage of infantile sexuality which follows the oral stage and is rooted in the experience of toilet training. During this stage the child gives up some significant pleasures (like controlling his or her own bowel movement) and acquires some important new meanings, including the symbolic value of faeces, giving, giving and withholding pleasure to others and being rewarded for compliant behaviour.

analytical psychology
The branch of *depth psychology* associated with the work of Carl Gustav Jung and his followers; Jung coined the term 'analytical psychology' in 1913, when his views had moved away from those of Freud and he wanted to differentiate his discipline from Freudian *psychoanalysis*. Some of Jung's major contributions have found effective applications in the analysis of organizations. These include his theory of *archetypes*, his theory of psychological types (extraverted/introverted, intuitive/sensing, feeling/thinking) and his ideas on symbolism and the collective unconscious.

anxiety
Psychoanalysis usually distinguished between fear (which is associated with an object), fright (which is the result of a lack of preparedness) and anxiety which is relatively unfocused, yet can be prolonged and highly incapacitating. A number of different types of anxiety have been identified, including castration anxiety, separation anxiety, moral anxiety, realistic anxiety, depressive anxiety, paranoid anxiety and neurotic anxiety. There is no integrated theory of anxiety in psychoanalysis, although there is general agreement that it is a feature of many core psychological processes. Anxiety can act as a signal for *defensive* processes, although it can equally be a signal that defensive processes have failed or backfired. Neurotic anxiety, in contrast to realistic anxiety, involves feelings disproportionate to the magnitude of threat facing an individual and may result in inhibitions (avoidance of particular people, areas or types of behaviour) or symptom-formation. In groups, anxiety may lead to *basic assumption* mode.

archetypes
A concept developed by Carl Gustav Jung to describe inherited and deeply unconscious contents of the mind, which are common to all humans; these are essential primordial images and ideas, charged with emotion and *symbolism*, which manifest themselves in *fantasies*, *dreams* and people's emotional responses to external stimuli which happen to be associated with archetypes. They exercise a powerful influence on the way in which we experience and understand the world

around us and colour our perceptions. Jung viewed archetypes as part of the collective heritage of humanity and assigned them to the collective *unconscious* along with the *instincts*. While rivalries within depth psychology have inhibited psychoanalytic writers from making use of this concept, it has been used very effectively in analysing certain types of organizational phenomena (see Mitroff and Kilmann, 1976; Mitroff, 1984; Bowles, 1990, 1991, 1993; Gherardi, 1995; Moxnes in this volume, p. 134).

basic assumption
A mode of group behaviour in which the group is ruled by overpowering emotions and shared *delusions*, under the influence of which the group loses sight of the task and contact with reality. In addition to the three basic assumptions identified by Bion (dependency, fight/flight and pairing), two further basic assumptions have been proposed: basic assumption 'one-ness' and basic assumption 'me-ness'.

borderline
A term used to designate conditions on the border between *neurosis* and *psychosis*, displaying a combination of neurotic *symptoms* and quasi-psychotic delusions. Borderline conditions have become increasingly common throughout the twentieth century at the expense of the traditional neuroses, notably hysteria.

castration
An important feature of the *Oedipus complex*, castration anxiety may not be a literal anxiety of the loss of the penis but a more generalized anxiety of losing that which is a source of pleasure and/or power. Castration anxiety is liable to re-surface later in life, especially when an individual experiences protracted loss of power, virility or status.

cathexis
The investment of mental *energy* into objects of the world, including human *objects* (love-objects, sexual objects), material objects (motor-cars, clothes), *symbols* and images (film stars, advertising logos).

character
A relatively stable combination of traits, which have resulted from a fixation to a particular stage of sexual development or from a *regression* to the core experiences of that stage. The oral or narcissistic, the anal and the phallic characters are identified in this way. Character determines largely how an individual relates to his or her social environment and may assume the form of a highly defensive formation, a character armour, that stops stimuli from reaching or touching the individual. Mature characters combine features of all stages of sexual development in relatively harmonious combinations.

condensation

An unconscious process, whereby several images may overlap or combine to form a new image which combines the symbolic associations present in all the other images. Condensation is one of the core processes in *dream* formation; its untangling represents one important task of *interpretation*.

conflict
Mental conflict is one of the foremost features of psychoanalytic theories of mental functioning. Freud conceived of individual *desires* in conflict with a large segment of social and moral values; in addition, the first movers of mental life, the *instincts* can themselves be in conflict with each other. Mental conflict lies at the heart of defensive processes, notably *repression*, through which unacceptable, dissonant, painful or repulsive ideas and desires are kept out of consciousness. *Neurosis* represents a mostly unsuccessful attempt to resolve a conflict which backfires, causing fresh

and often more severe conflicts. Successful resolution of a conflict may involve the re-orientation of desires to new, acceptable (possibly symbolic) objects, the *sublimation* of desire into non-sexual activities, the adoption of a socially acceptable set of *symptoms* or the management of the conflict by an *ego* strengthened through analytic self-examination.

conscience
Psychoanalysis treats conscience as a set of conscious and unconscious processes which proceed from the *super-ego*. Some of the super-ego's imperatives are *unconscious* and may be in contradiction with moral values to which an individual consciously subscribes. Conscience functions by constantly comparing the *ego* with the *ego-ideal* and systematically censuring the ego for its shortcomings by directing against it aggressive energy in the form of *guilt*.

consciousness
The state of being aware of some element of outer or inner reality. Outer stimuli are brought under the realm of consciousness through the perception system which is continuous with consciousness. The origin of stimuli is established through the process of reality testing, whereby a hallucination or a *fantasy* is established as a different mental entity from a sense perception. Consciousness may contain sense perceptions, ideas, images, facts, fantasies, feelings and all entities to which we refer as being conscious of. A distinction is drawn between consciousness and the *preconscious*, which includes knowledge and memories that are not part of consciousness at any particular point in time, but may be recalled at will.

container
An idea developed by Bion (1970) to indicate the emotional experience of a relationship in which the subject's anxieties are neither eliminated nor allowed to disable mental functioning. The concept of the container is related to Winnicott's (1958, 1965) idea of the holding environment – an environment provided by the mother to the infant, in which the latter is separate from the mother, yet close enough to feel safe. Current psychoanalytic theories of organizations, notably those developed within the Kleinian and Tavistock traditions, have advanced arguments on how groups, leaders and entire institutions can function as containers of anxiety and have highlighted the importance of containment in all organizations.

counter-transference   *see* transference

death instinct
Following many changes in the psychoanalytic theory of *instincts*, the death instinct emerged in Freud's mature theory as the great adversary of the life instinct, *Eros*, which subsumed sexuality. The death instinct is in the first place a force driving all life towards inorganic inertia, i.e. death, whose programme is delayed and frustrated by the life instinct which introduces excitement, pleasure and social bonds into life. However, the death instinct may combine with sexual desire in masochism and sadism; it may assume the form of a *repetition compulsion*, which is highly conservative and eschews all innovation or change; it may, alternatively, turn into destructiveness or a desire to master externality; it may be sublimated in controlled aggression on the sports field or the business arena; finally, it may be introjected into a sense of guilt which cannot be accounted for by rational reasons of culpability. While many clinical commentators of psychoanalysis have tended to ignore the death instinct, the majority of philosophical and cultural commentators have continued to make extensive use of this idea. It is a concept which not only addresses the question of human *aggression* in a radical way, but also allows us to gain an understanding of the psychological costs at which aggression is curtailed and controlled.

defence and mechanisms of defence
A group of mental processes aimed at the reduction of unpleasure (notably *anxiety*) or the elimination of forces which are experienced as threatening the integrity of mental survival of an

individual. These forces may include highly painful memories of real or imagined traumas. Freudian theory recognizes numerous defences, including *regression*, *reaction-formation*, projection, introjection, isolation, reversal and identification with the aggressor, though it treats *repression* as the archetypal defence. Kleinian theorists have placed greater emphasis on the defences of *splitting* and *denial*.

delusion
A severe distortion in a person's sense of reality. Delusions are characteristic of psychotic phenomena (in extreme cases an individual assumes an identity entirely alien to themselves), though it is also a feature of dreams and group life. Delusions, like illusions, are essentially *wish-fulfilments*, though unlike *illusions* they are generally incapable of correction by appeals to reason or evidence.

denial
A *defence* process whereby a painful aspect of the world or an aspect of the ego is denied, without, however, being excluded from consciousness as in *repression*. Denial may be confirmed on occasion through *negation*, the persistent and repeated rejection of a particular idea which does not call for such an overt disavowal.

depressive position
A pre-Oedipal position reached by the child, when it realizes that love and hate are directed at the same object, the mother. Depression is the result of the realization that what was good is discovered to contain bad qualities and vice versa. This Kleinian concept is characterized by *ambivalence* and by a desire to make reparation for the damage done by hate. The depressive position is associated with a view that the world is a complex place, where good and evil, right and wrong are inextricably linked, both in the inner and the outer spaces. The depressive position is sometimes seen as characteristic of a contemplative attitude to life.

depth psychology
A branch of psychology which studies the *unconscious* and its effects. Psychoanalysis, the doctrine and clinical practice pioneered by Freud, is an important tradition within depth psychology, though by no means the only one or the earliest. Lancelot L. Whyte has traced depth psychology to the seventeenth century and the works of Leibniz and discovered numerous books written in the nineteenth century by philosophers, physicians and psychologists with the word 'unconscious' in their title. Freud himself acknowledged his debt to earlier depth psychologists, notably Charcot, Bernheim and other practitioners of medical hypnosis. In the twentieth century, depth psychology has developed with the growth of *psychoanalysis* and its different schools of thought, as well as the traditions established by Freud's early followers, Alfred Adler and Carl Gustav Jung, who broke away from psychoanalysis and established individual psychology and *analytical psychology* respectively. Other branches of depth psychology include existential, *gestalt* and humanistic psychology.

desire
A core psychoanalytic concept, also referred to as wish. Desires can be conscious or *unconscious* and set in motion most psychological processes. Desires may ultimately derive their energy from *instincts*, though, unlike instincts, they involve rich *symbolic* dimensions, in which objects, activities and images become endowed with vibrant meanings and generate powerful emotions. Desire may come in many forms, including the desire to possess, the desire to revenge, the desire to be liked, the desire to be noticed, the desire to hurt or to destroy, the desire to dominate and the desire to achieve. The instant gratification of desire is demanded by the *pleasure principle*, but this is usually controlled by the *reality principle* which tests the ground before the realization of desire. Desire may be repressed if it is unrealizable and causes hardship and frustration, in which case it may find substitute-gratification in a modified form. When unchecked, desire assumes the character of a passion, totally possessing an individual. Unchecked desires which run counter to

conventional social morality assume the form of perversions. Unsuccessful attempts to tame desires may lead to *neurosis* or even *psychosis*.

displacement
An unconscious process, whereby the energy invested in one idea is transferred on to another one. Like *condensation*, displacement is one of the core processes in dream formation; its untangling represents one important task of *interpretation*. Displacement represents a wider principle of psychoanalysis which generally regards the links between emotions, *desires* or *fantasies* and the objects at which they are directed as tenuous; objects may mutate or alternate within the same desire, emotion or fantasy, displacing each other.

dream
Mental activity which takes place during a part of sleep characterized by rapid movement of the eye muscles. Psychoanalysis has treated dreams as the archetypal mental phenomenon whereby unconscious ideas and desires reach consciousness, albeit in highly distorted states, mixed with ideas, thoughts and experiences which occurred during the previous day (the day's residues). Dream-work is the psychological process through which unconscious material (the latent dream thoughts) are turned into the manifest dream-content which the dreamer may recollect after waking up. Dreams are thus treated as both *wish-fulfilments* and as compromise formations between unconscious desires and the forces of repression. Dream *interpretation* aims at discovering the latent dream thought and the unconscious desires associated with them, by undoing the distortions of dream-work. Freud viewed dreams as ultimately helping to preserve sleep, by allowing partial fulfilment to wishes which would otherwise wake the dreamer. This part of his theory has not been confirmed by current physiological and psychological research into dreams which has leaned to the view that dreams represent attempts to process and come to terms with the experiences and conflicts of the previous day.

drive   see **instinct**

dynamic point of view
One of the three types of analysis which combine to offer a metapsychological account of mental phenomena (the others being the *topographical* and the *economic*). The dynamic point of view seeks to uncover mental conflict, i.e. the conflict between different *desires*, emotions and *instincts*, which underlie mental functioning. It often addresses the conflict between conscious and unconscious forces or the conflict between different mental agencies, such as the ego and the id, and examines the various compromises, consequences and costs of these conflicts. The concept of *resistance* is of central importance to the dynamic point of view. Resistance signals the erection of different types of barriers to the uncovering of *unconscious* materials – these barriers may be overcome through suggestive or psychoanalytic interventions.

economic point of view
One of the three types of analysis which combine to offer a metapsychological account of mental phenomena (the others being the *topographical* and the *dynamic*). The economic point of view examines the quantities of *energy* available to different mental agencies, the origins of this energy and its transformations. Although the economic point of view is sometimes dismissed as a relic of Freud's early theory which conceived of the mind as a type of hydraulic system through which neural excitations flow, it is of vital importance in accounting for sudden changes of mood and outlook, such as those occurring in manic depression or mourning and grief, as well as for sudden outpourings of emotion, such as those occurring in jokes and insults. Underlying the economic point of view is the assumption that mental energy is quantifiable (even if an accurate method for its measurement is unavailable) and that it obeys certain laws of continuity and transformation.

ego
An *agency* of the mental apparatus which assumed its clearer expression in the second topography (see *topographic point of view*), in its opposition to the *id* and the *super-ego*. The ego

becomes differentiated from the id in early infancy as the child comes to appreciate the existence of an autonomous external reality over which it has limited control. The ego represents many of the demands of external reality and assumes the functions of self-preservation and maintaining the integrity of the mental personality. To these ends, it mobilizes the mechanisms of *defence*, which qualify the demands of the *pleasure principle* under the influence of the *reality principle*. The ego is responsible for reality-testing (i.e. establishing whether a stimulus originates from within or from without) and is the seat of consciousness; yet, many of its functions, notably the mechanisms of defence, are undertaken unconsciously. Ego psychology is an important tradition in psychoanalysis, rooted in the works of Anna Freud and Heinz Hartmann, which emphasizes the adaptive function of the ego for mental functioning, i.e. the ego's role as an agent which ensures the smooth adaptation of the individual in his or her social environment. This tradition stands in opposition to traditions which emphasize *instincts* and *object relations*. It tends to downplay the degree of conflict experienced by the ego itself, due to the fact that the ego has limited energy resources with which to achieve its aims. Thus, the ego must attract *libido* on to itself by making itself attractive to the super-ego, through the process of *narcissism*. The ambiguous qualities of the ego are vividly depicted in two famous metaphors offered by Freud. The first looks at the ego as the rider who maintains a precarious control over an impetuous horse, which represents the id. The second looks at the ego as the servant of three harsh masters, the id, the super-ego and external reality, continually striving to meet or check their conflicting demands.

ego-ideal
A very important though problematic concept in psychoanalysis. The ego-ideal can be seen as a composite of desirable and often contradictory qualities and images which the ego seeks to emulate in its attempt to make itself the object of narcissistic self-love. The ego-ideal contains idealized elements of the parents and other role models as well as cultural, class and national ideals. Although parts of it are conscious, a substantial part of it includes unconscious elements. Some theorists, like Chasseguet-Smirgel, view the ego-ideal as an autonomous agency, distinct from the *super-ego*, whose functions are quite different. Freud, however, in his later works tended to view the maintenance of the ego-ideal as a function of the super-ego, which constantly compares the ego's actual attainments with the perfections invested in the ego-ideal. The theory of the ego-ideal is vital for an understanding of *narcissistic* processes, both in and out of organizations.

energy
The core concept of the *economic point of view*. Mental energy is the derivative of the *instincts*, *libido* being the mental energy associated with the sexual instinct. One of the core observations of psychoanalysis is that, under certain circumstances, mental energy is mobile, being capable of rapidly attaching itself on to different objects (see *cathexis*) or ideas; under different circumstances, mental energy can be bound, attached in a fairly organized and permanent manner on to specific objects and ideas. Mobile energy is characteristic of 'primary processes', unconscious processes (see *condensation* and *displacement*) where different ideas can easily replace each other as the focus of mental life. Bound energy, on the other hand, is characteristic of 'secondary processes', whereby ideas are invested with energy in a more controlled manner, allowing for rational thought and mental experiments. Some theorists have discarded the psychoanalytic idea of energy altogether on the grounds that it is impossible to quantify, observe or measure; others, like Rycroft (1968), view it as a 'theory of meaning in disguise', enabling the analyst to account for the transfer of meaning and emotion from one idea on to a seemingly unrelated one. Theorists, however, who take seriously the psychoanalytic theory of *instincts*, like Marcuse and Brown, keep the idea of psychic energy at the centre of their arguments. For these theorists, the build-up and discharge of energy, its sublimation, its mutations and vicissitudes are vital for an understanding of mental functioning.

Eros
The name given to the sexual instinct in Freud's mature works. While the sexual instinct is associated with the *pleasure principle* and the fulfilment of sexual *desire* in all its vicissitudes, Eros

represents a broader motivation principle, a life instinct, which maintains variety, stimulation and union in the face of opposition from the *death instinct*. Eros represents both sublimated and unsublimated, both sensuous and social variants of *sexuality*. It is seen as holding people together in groups and societies.

fantasy

A product of the imagination, which may involve an idea, a desire or a detailed scene or sequence of scenes. Fantasy may assume the form of conscious day-dreaming or conscious rehearsal of mental scenarios (e.g. imagining oneself holidaying on an island or exploring the implications of making a decision to follow a particular career path). Alternatively, fantasy may be unconscious, its contents being partly or fully excluded from consciousness for one reason or other (e.g. the fantasy of being a princess or of killing a rival). Primal fantasies are deeply unconscious fantasies which many individuals experience as they grow up (e.g. fantasies of castration and seduction, fantasies of being the child of noble parents rather than of one's real parents). Freud hypothesized that the universality of such fantasies may be accounted for by their being part of a phylogenetic heritage of mankind, passed from generation to generation. In this way, primal fantasies are not unlike Jung's concept of *archetypes*, though they do not require the assumption of a collective unconscious.

Many British psychoanalysts use the spelling 'fantasy' to refer to conscious day-dreaming and 'phantasy' to refer to unconscious mental representations. This is a helpful distinction but not always a sharp one, since conscious elements of a fantasy may be continuous with deeper unconscious elements. Conscious fantasies may be surrogates for action, especially when they concern unaffordable or impossible pleasures (e.g. living the life of the rich and famous or shedding several years of one's age); alternatively, fantasies may be a spur for action, in numerous ways, ranging from a leader's 'vision' for an organization which helps galvanize the followers into action to the day-dream of being young which may lead one to resort to plastic surgery or hair replacement therapy. In all of these instances, individuals are aware of the difference between fantasy and reality, the confusion of the two amounting to *illusions* or *delusions*.

Unconscious phantasies tend to be seen by psychoanalysis as compromise formations between *desires* and the forces which oppose their realization. Phantasies are, therefore, the products of desire distorted to a greater or lesser extent by defensive processes: thus, a desire for a particular activity or object may be discovered in an unconscious phantasy for a different object or activity. Within organizations, phantasies generally assume a clandestine existence, mostly censored by the forces of rationality, efficiency and order. They do, however, occasionally surface in jokes and stories, office gossip and lore, day-dreaming and banter, and can provide a good way of understanding the deeper relations among individuals or between individuals and their work.

femininity

The principal components of female *sexuality* and the role attributes of women. Freud saw a set of basic connections of femininity with passivity, masochism and narcissism, feminine desires being primarily passive – being loved, admired and desired. While Freud viewed all human beings as psychologically bi-sexual, and therefore endowed with both active masculine and passive feminine desires, his theory of female sexuality has often, and rightly, been criticized as displaying a phallocentric bias – the male being designated by presence, the female by an absence. Juliet Mitchell (1974), in her path-breaking book *Psychoanalysis and Feminism*, reassessed the psychoanalytic theory of female sexuality and used Freud's theories to argue that, from the *Oedipus complex* on, boys and girls follow, not symmetrical, but fundamentally dissimilar sexual developments. The boy's *masculinity* will initially grow relatively unproblematically out of the *desire* for the mother, the first object of his love. The girl's femininity undergoes a traumatic transformation 'from the active wanting of her mother to the passive wanting to be wanted by the father' (1974: 108). The 'making of a lady' is then inextricably linked with a *repression* of active desires and a re-orientation towards passive ones, embodied in the shift of sexual interest from the clitoris to the vagina. Chodorow (1978), in *The Reproduction of Mothering*, has moved away from the Freudian emphasis on sexuality but keeps the focus on the early mother–child relationship. The fact that the majority of both boys and girls have the same primary love object, namely the mother, leads to very different types of personality development, because mothers treat babies differently depending on their gender, projecting different emotions and attitudes. One significant contribution of feminist writings since the 1970s has been to demonstrate that patriarchal capitalist societies place greater constraints on female *sexuality* than on male, turning it against women and using it to perpetuate male privilege and domination.

genital stage
A stage of psychosexual development which follows the oral and anal stages and is marked by the pleasure-yielding qualities of the genitals. This stage signals the onset of the *Oedipus complex* and the conclusion of early sexual development with the arrival of the latency period, between the age of five or six and puberty, when sexual activity declines and *object relations* become desexualized. Mature genitality is the term given to normal adult *sexuality*; while this may involve numerous component *instincts* and *desires* (including oral and anal ones), it is marked by the predominance of genital sexuality, aimed at the achievement of orgasm.

guilt
An important emotion which follows the breach of a moral command. Psychoanalysis notes the numerous instances when guilt is experienced when no actual infringement has taken place and approaches guilt as the product of a *conflict* between *super-ego* and instinctual wishes regarded as morally repugnant. Guilt is then viewed as an instrument wielded by the super-ego through which the *ego* is forced to tame *desire*. The *energy* of the sense of guilt originates in the *death instinct*, hence guilt may be seen as a form of aggression directed against the ego. Guilt serves a social function, ensuring a degree of adherence to moral codes. Guilt is distinguished from shame, which is more easily observable through bodily manifestations, such as blushing. Shame tends to result more from public exposure rather than a private awareness of transgression and sinfulness. Some theorists have argued that shame is the result of an inability to attain the perfection of the *ego-ideal*, and view it as quite distinct from phenomena relating to guilt and the super-ego. Following Darwin, some theorists have argued that cultures themselves fall into two categories, guilt and shame cultures; the former rely for social control on inner restraint, the latter on the fear of losing face.

hermeneutics
The art of *interpretation*, the search for deeper and often hidden meanings in material and cultural artefacts (e.g. works of art, myths, stories), mental phenomena (e.g. dreams, fixed ideas, decisions) or action (neurotic symptoms, errors and slips, personal habits and routines). Psychoanalysis offers a system of interpreting mental phenomena by approaching them as observable outcomes of *unconscious* processes. The search for meanings then becomes tantamount to an understanding of the processes which distort and conceal meaning and the functions served by these processes. An underlying assumption of this approach is that the deeper meaning of our own actions and decisions are often unknown to us; the reasons we offer for our behaviour are often little more than convenient justifications or rationalizations.

hysteria
A form of mental disorder in which *symptoms* assume physical, bodily manifestations (e.g. uncontrollable twitches, paralysis or pains and aches). An early contribution of psychoanalysis was the discovery of the psychosexual origin of hysteria, i.e. hysteria is the outcome of unsuccessful attempts at repressing *desires*, often of a sexual nature.

id
Mental *agency* in the second *topography* which contains *unconscious* excitations and *desires*. The id is the term used by Freud's translators to render his concept of *das Es*, literally 'the it', a concept which Freud borrowed from the German psychiatrist, Georg Groddeck. The id represents that part of us which is and remains unknown and invisible. A portion of the id is constitutionally

given from birth, while another portion is acquired as a result of *repressions*. As an entity, the id is devoid of will and organization, famously described by Freud as a 'cauldron full of seething excitations' whose sole purpose is to achieve satisfaction, following the *pleasure principle*. The content of the id conforms to *primary processes*, and is not subject to contradiction, reality testing or considerations of space and time. Ideas in the id are charged with *energy* which is mobile, capable of migrating from one idea to another. In all of these ways, the id represents the instinctive part of our mental personality.

idealization
A mental process whereby an object acquires an aura of perfection and is stripped of all undesirable or negative qualities. *Identification* with idealized objects is vital for the creation of an *ego-ideal*. Kleinian theorists see idealization as a *defence* mechanism, the product of *splitting* of an object into two totally separate ones, one wholly good and one wholly bad. They also see idealization as calling for further defensive mechanisms, as the individual denies all imperfections in order to maintain the purity of the ideal. Many Freudian theorists, on the other hand, prefer to view idealization as not necessarily implying a vilification of the opposite, but rather as a way of enhancing the *ego*; in as much as the ego is like the idealized object, it may attract narcissistic *libido* on to itself.

identification
A mental process whereby an individual assimilates a quality of an object and incorporates it into his or her own constitution. Identification is one of the two core processes of relating to others (the other being *object cathexis*) and is vital in the development of our mental personality, much of which is built through successive identifications. Identification is central to the way in which individuals relate to their parents (especially to the parent of the same sex) and to their leaders; it is also a vital process in the creation of social bonds among individuals in a community or an organization, in as much as these individuals identify with each other in their struggles, their hopes and their sufferings.

identity
The sense of one's uniqueness and continuity in contradistinction to others. According to Erikson, identity is a difficult psychological process, liable to periodic crises, especially during life's major transitions. Identity incorporates both individual elements, such as features from an individual's biography, his or her tastes and desires, but also cultural characteristics shared with others, such as ethnic, class, race or organizational allegiances. One's identity is liable to contain idealized elements residing in the *ego-ideal* and precipitates of *identifications* with important figures from one's past.

illusion
A type of idea which is characterized by its *wish-fulfilling* qualities. Illusions do not represent the same drastic distortion of a person's sense of reality as *delusions*; while they are products of *fantasy*, they are capable of testing and modification, through rational discourse and appeal to evidence. The belief that one is a prince can be seen as delusion; the belief that one will one day marry a prince is an illusion. Some illusions may be socially sponsored by communities, classes or organizations; others have a private, personal character. Many religious beliefs are classified as illusions (representing fulfilments of wishes, for example, for paternal protection, for divine justice or maternal love). Many illusions have a hopeful, future-directed quality, as in winning the lottery or marrying a prince. Illusions offer substitute gratifications for the discontents of life, but at times they can have a paralysing effect which only goes to reinforce these discontents.

imago
A term used by Freud to describe *unconscious* ways in which real objects are represented in the mind. The mother imago, for example, may be endowed with qualities of perfection and nurturance which are at variance with the qualities of a particular mother; the phallus imago may

be endowed with qualities of power and privilege which are a far-cry from the actual penis. In this way, an imago can be seen as a symbolically enriched and distorted representation of an object of the real world.

instinct
Referred to more correctly as 'drive', instinct is one of the central yet most problematic concepts in depth psychology. Instincts represent the body's demands upon our mind and lie at the interface between body and mind; their source is a bodily stimulus, their aim is the elimination of the tension which results from this stimulus; their object is the means whereby the aim is achieved. Instincts can only be studied through their mental representatives, *desires*, impulses and wishes. One difficulty is the wide variety and multiplicity of human desires; this could end up suggesting that there is an infinity of instincts, including instincts of self-preservation, sociability, sexuality, learning, destroying and so forth. Psychoanalysts have sought to identify the basic instincts of which different desires are derivative. In his early work, Freud juxtaposed sexual instincts with self-preservation instincts. In his later work, he came to view both of these as manifestations of *Eros*, the life instinct, whose object may swing from the ego to external objects. *Libido* is the name given to the *energy* of the life instinct. The life instinct is opposed by the *death instinct* which seeks to drive life towards inertia and stillness. The two classes of instincts may merge to generate desires which combine erotic and destructive elements, as in masochism and sadism; they may also 'defuse' each other or cancel each other out.

interpretation
A procedure of bringing to light the hidden meanings of our actions, desires and fantasies. Psychoanalysis is not the only discipline seeking to interpret human action; it did, however, introduce a new type of interpretation, a new form of *hermeneutics*, based on the theory of mental conflict and its consequences in *repression* and other *defence* mechanisms, which systematically distort the meaning of our actions and experiences. It expanded the scope of phenomena subject to interpretation considerably, offering ways of interpreting dreams, neurotic symptoms, slips of the tongue, errors, day-dreams and fantasies, jokes, stories, insults, powerful emotions, eccentricities and idiosyncrasies, as well as cultural phenomena, including myths, works of art, religious beliefs and practices. Interpretation represents the starting-point of psychoanalysis, both as theory and as technique; most psychoanalytic treatments start with interpretation and most psychoanalytic theories of mental functioning and social behaviour are built on systematic interpretations of mental and social phenomena.

libido
The *energy* associated with *Eros* and, especially, *sexuality*. While libido is mental energy, its origins are somatic and Freud's early theory allows for conversion of mental energy into physical energy and vice versa. The movements of libido into different areas of the mind, its discharges, the ego's attempts to re-direct it or store it, its attachments and dislocations, its sublimation into social bonds and ties of affection or into creativity, these are highly speculative processes which cannot be directly observed and can only be tentatively corroborated. In view of this, many depth psychologists have given up this concept, along with much of *instinct* theory. The theory of libido does, however, offer some spectacularly interesting, if not always immediately plausible, explanations of otherwise obscure mental phenomena. These include phenomena with a bodily dimension, such as laughing, crying or displaying hysterical symptoms. It also seems to accord with the plausible hypotheses that (a) the mind does not have endless supplies of energy, and that, therefore, (b) energy must be quantifiable. In Jung's work, the concept of libido was broadened to denote all psychical energy, present in every appetite or tendency. It is not dissimilar to Bergson's idea of '*elan vital*', the vital energy of all living forms. In Freud's work, however, libido maintains its strong association with bodily pleasure and sexual aims.

life instinct   see Eros

love
There are two quite distinct traditions of viewing love in psychoanalysis. Freudian theory views love in its infinite variety as an expression of the sexual instinct in its diverse manifestations. Underlying all experiences of loving someone, something or oneself are vicissitudes of *libido*, whether the love is spiritual or sensuous, pure or mixed with hatred. According to this view, mature genital love combines two components: a sensuous and an emotional one. More generally, love is seen as a source of social ties, as the set of emotions through which *Eros* holds social groups together and maintains the claims of life against the *death instinct*. *Object relations* theory represents a different tradition towards love, viewing it as an expression of an innate need to relate to objects. In this sense, it reverses the Freudian argument: we do not relate to others as an attempt to discover outlets for our libido; instead our fate is to relate to others, something that calls for love. Love and hate, according to this tradition, are basic ways of relating to objects which can be traced in the infant's earliest responses to the breast, rather than expressions of instinctual forces.

masculinity
A term used, in juxtaposition to *femininity*, to refer to *desires*, attitudes and behaviours associated with the male gender. Classical psychoanalytic theory tended to view associated masculinity with activity, aggressiveness and a strong *super-ego*. Many dimensions of masculinity were seen as related to the *castration* anxiety. At the same time, Freud insisted on seeing both men and women as having both masculine and feminine psychological attributes. More recently, masculinity has been used to describe equally the major components of male *sexuality* and the role attributes of the male gender. The study of masculinity has lagged behind that of femininity, the assumptions being that (a) everyone knows what 'real men' are like, and (b) there is no problem about men being 'real men'. Many stereotypes of masculine behaviour are currently being questioned, leading to an increased interest in masculinity, notably in the United States. Books like Robert Bly's *Iron John: a Book about Men* and Sam Keen's *Fire in the Belly: on Being a Man* have argued that the attainment of real manhood is problematic for men as are stereotypes of macho masculinity. Such books have sought to promote a new vision of masculinity, at once caring and heroic, founded not on hate or contempt for women but on strong male bonding and a reappraisal of the relation between fathers and sons.

mechanisms of defence   see defence

mental agencies   see agencies

metapsychology
A term used by Freud to denote a level of abstraction 'beyond the psychological', in a way similar to 'metaphysics' as that level of abstraction that goes beyond physics. If psychology (including depth psychology) studies a range of phenomena that can somehow be observed or inferred, metapsychology addresses the structures which make psychological phenomena possible. Freud argued that a metapsychological account of a range of mental events must address three points of view, the *economic*, the *topographic* and the *dynamic*.

mourning
A type of psychological work through which one manages to detach oneself from a loved object that has been lost or has died. One characteristic of mourning is the loss of interest in all other elements of our social environment and the focus of all mental and emotional energies on the lost object. At the conclusion of successful mourning work, the *libido* is freed from the lost object and can become re-oriented towards new objects including the *ego*.

narcissism
The theory of narcissism represents one of the most original and fruitful contributions of psychoanalysis to an understanding of psychic processes. In the most general way, narcissism represents a range of phenomena in which *love* and *libido* are directed towards one's own *ego*; the ego is, in other words adopted as an object choice. Initially, Freud distinguished between two

types of object *cathexis*: anaclitic object cathexis is love directed to objects that are selected on the basis of their similarity with figures similar to the parents who once looked after the individual, while narcissistic object cathexis in love for objects similar to the individual him or herself. Subsequently, narcissism came to represent all phenomena in which the ego becomes an object of libidinal cathexis. Two forms of narcissism are distinguished. Primary narcissism is a very early state (before the discovery of an external world of objects) in which all of the infant's libido is cathected on itself. Secondary narcissism is the adoption of the differentiated ego as an object of cathexis. To this end, the *ego-ideal* is of critical importance, since it is by endowing itself with the ideal's perfections that the ego seeks to attract libido on to itself. Narcissism can become the source of *neurosis* if it inhibits an individual from forming meaningful relations with his or her social environment. The individual may then become excessively self-obsessed and use others as a means of reinforcing his or her own ego. Alternatively, an individual whose ego fails to attract sufficient qualities of libido on to itself may find him or herself depleted of self-esteem and self-confidence. Narcissism is of vital importance for the psychology of organizations, both as a source of organizational pathologies and as a vital dimension of the bond which links leaders with their followers.

negation
A process whereby an individual may allow *repressed* ideas to re-enter consciousness by disowning them or by denying that they are true. Thus an emphatic 'No' to a suggestion or an interpretation put forward by an analyst may indicate that the suggestion or *interpretation* has hit the mark. In such circumstances, negation may confirm the interpretation. It is, however, a grave mistake to regard all instances of denial as confirmation, without corroborating evidence. The process of negation is sometimes alluded to in the popular expression when someone is said to be 'in denial'.

neurosis
A range of psychological disorders resulting from unsuccessful attempts to deal with mental *conflict*. The classification of neuroses according to symptoms or causes has always been problematic, but they are generally seen as including *hysterias*, *obsessional* conditions, *phobias*, narcissistic and character disorders. Neuroses are generally characterized by feelings of *anxiety*, a distortion of reality and *symptoms* which may be more or less incapacitating. There is no hard-and-fast line between normality and neurosis; numerous neuroses may go undetected, in so far as they do not inhibit an individual's overall ability to cope with life. In his later writings, Freud moved towards the view that neurosis is an inevitable price of civilized life, resulting from the instinctual conflict, *repression* and renunciations made inevitable by culture. All the same, a distinction may be drawn between successful and unsuccessful repressions, the latter being more likely to lead to neurotic phenomena. A distinction is made between neurosis and *psychosis* which involves a far greater distortion to an individual's sense of reality and ability to lead an ordinary life.

object and object relations
The range of ways in which we relate psychologically to the objects of our environment. These objects are never purely external, since they become symbolically charged with qualities and attributes drawn from earlier experiences and *fantasies*. Freudian theory emphasized objects as the targets of an individual's *instincts*, for instance objects for libidinal *cathexis* or objects which generate *identification*. However, a subsequent psychoanalytic tradition rooted in the works of Klein, Fairbairn and Winnicott has shifted attention away from instincts to object relations as primary elements of psychological functioning. Within this tradition, objects are highly fashioned by phantasies and feelings, they are projected and introjected, they are split into good and bad and they constantly define and redefine the ego. Within the object relations tradition, pleasure and desire lose their sensuous, bodily associations and derive from a deeper need to connect with other people. Object relations theory has found numerous important applications in the theory of organizations, primarily through the works of Jaques and Menzies Lyth

in the UK, and, more recently, Hirschhorn, Gould, Krantz, Diamond and Schwartz in the US. Notable among these applications is the treatment of the whole organization as an object which is liable to become incorporated in psychic reality and towards which the individual may develop relations akin to early relations with significant objects from his or her environment. Other significant contributions originating from this tradition address the processes of scapegoating, idealization, demonization, splitting and reparation within organizations.

obsessional neurosis

A form of *neurosis* characterized by obsessive thoughts and compulsive behaviour, such as washing of the hands. Many qualities of religious ritual and ceremony have an obsessional character (crossing among Roman Catholics and Orthodox Christians, the observation of kosher by Jews); likewise, many organizational rituals (the meticulous filling of forms or the mechanical observance of procedures) have an obsessional character. It is with some justification that Freud argued that obsessional neurosis is like an individual's private religion, while religion is the universal obsessional neurosis of humanity.

Oedipus complex

A complex of fantasies, desires and feelings towards the parents, experienced by each child at around the age of four or five years, during the *phallic stage* of development. This complex takes its name from the Greek myth of Oedipus, who, unknowingly, killed his own father and married his own mother. The Oedipus complex involves powerful loving and aggressive desires towards the parents. After different transformations, these are *repressed* and forgotten with the resolution of the complex and the onset of latency; yet, they continue to influence each individual's later life as a major part of his or her repressed *unconscious*. The precise nature of the complex differs for each individual, being influenced by cultural factors (e.g. the nature of the family unit, the severity of upbringing, the roles of men and women in the family and in society at large), family factors (e.g. the relationship between the parents, the existence of siblings), socio-economic factors (e.g. the amount of time a child spends with the parents, the wealth of the parents), personal factors (including the behaviour and feelings of the parents, the child's earlier development) and constitutional factors.

Yet, there are some broad configurations in the Oedipus complex of each gender, from which individual cases may deviate to a greater or lesser extent. In boys, the Oedipus complex is signalled by a powerful desire for the mother and a desire to eliminate the father, who is seen as a rival for the mother's love and affection. Eventually, under the influence of *castration* anxiety, most boys relinquish their desires for their mother (at least the sexual element of these desires) and their jealous hatred of the father; instead, they *identify* with their father, whose authority they come to accept. Through the institution of the *super-ego*, which takes place towards the conclusion of the Oedipus complex, boys internalize external authority and begin to live with the promise of one day having a woman of their own.

In girls, the Oedipus complex starts with a similar configuration to that of the boys but soon develops in a different way. This is prompted by the girl's realization that she, like her mother, appears excluded from the authority embodied by the father and symbolized by the possession of a penis. In place of the boy's castration anxiety, the girl experiences an envy for this symbolically meaningful organ which accords power to its owner. In the classical formulation, the repression of Oedipal desires in the girl leaves her with a desire to be loved by the father and to have a penis 'within herself', usually in the form of a child of her own. While many girls may identify with their mother at the conclusion of the Oedipus complex, some may retain an envious or antagonistic feeling towards her. The Freudian account of the feminine version of the Oedipus complex is one of the most controversial of the psychoanalytic theories. Numerous alternatives have been put forward. Erikson (1950), along with many others, challenged the equations of penis with privilege and absence of penis with deficiency: girls may experience their genitals as a fertile inner space rather than as an inadequacy. Chodorow, in her different writings, has diminished the importance of anatomical differences in the psychological development of girls and has placed the emphasis on social and cultural arrangements, especially those which concern rearing and caring for children.

Freud viewed the Oedipus complex and its resolution as having a lasting impact on an individual's subsequent social and psychological development. While the content of the Oedipus complex (the desires, fantasies and emotions) may be safely repressed for long stretches of a person's life, they are liable to generate a trail of symptoms and substitutes which shape an individual's mental personality and emotional life. Potentially, the Oedipus complex is the 'nucleus of neuroses' in later life, elements of it re-surfacing at different points and forcing the individual to carry out fresh repressions. Relations with authority figures or carers, for example, may revive Oedipal *desires* and *fantasies*, as can relations with one's spouse or one's children. Within organizations, relations of power, rivalry and dependence are rarely devoid of Oedipal dimensions. These are liable to unleash powerful emotions of love, hate, anxiety, fear and contempt which are transferred from their unconscious associations on to new figures in an organizational context.

Kleinian theorists have given greater prominence to pre-Oedipal experiences as highly formative for each individual's later emotional life. In particular, they have drawn attention to the child's earliest relationship to the mother and the breast, the splitting, projection and introjection that occur in the earliest months of life, which have a capital influence on subsequent developments, including on the course taken by the Oedipus complex.

The myth of Oedipus and the Oedipus complex are foundational ideas in psychoanalysis. Beyond the dynamics of the family triangle, the Oedipus complex represents a major episode in the child's entrance into human culture with all the sacrifices, frustrations and promises which this entails. In the narrow sense, the Oedipus complex forces every child to accept the incest taboo, the prohibition on the consummation of his or her relationship with the person closest to them. In a broader sense, the Oedipus complex marks the internalization by each child of culture, an entity greater than itself, one that involves both constraints and rewards.

oral character
The character of an individual fixated in or regressing to the *oral stage*. The main characteristics of oral characters are impulsiveness, moodiness, generosity and excessive optimism and/or pessimism. Love and pleasure may retain their association with eating and being eaten. Oral characteristics often involve residues of primary *narcissism*, notably a disregard of external constraints and conditions, an over-valuation of independence, creativity and freedom and a preoccupation with consumption of objects and/or persons as a means of embellishing the *ego* and bringing it closer to the *ego-ideal*.

oral stage
The earliest stage of infantile sexuality in which the mouth is a major source of nourishment, interest and pleasure. During this stage, the child acquires a sense of a separate external reality, the breast, the mother, which is not directly under its control. Abraham subdivided the oral stage into an early sucking part and a later biting (oral-sadistic) part. Klein rejected Abraham's subdivision, arguing that from the moment that the infant recognizes the breast as a separate object, the breast, and subsequently the mother, is split into a good and a bad object. Love is aimed at the good object and hate at the bad.

paranoid-schizoid position
A pre-Oedipal position reached by the child at the oral stage, when, according to Klein, the breast is split into a good and a bad breast. Subsequently, the *ego* too is split into good and bad parts. The bad part, which includes aggressive impulses, is projected on to the object, which is experienced as persecuting and threatening. The good part of the object is introjected into the ego. The paranoid-schizoid position is associated with a view that divides up the world into extreme good and extreme evil and is characterized by persecutory *anxiety*. In normal development, the paranoid-schizoid position is overcome after a few months of life by the *depressive position*.

phallic stage
The stage of infantile sexuality which follows the *anal stage* and is rooted in the experience of pleasure deriving from the genital organs, the penis and the clitoris. This stage culminates in the

onset of the *Oedipus complex*, during which the development of boys and girls takes a different course.

phantasy   see fantasy

phobia
A neurotic condition characterized by overwhelming and often incapacitating fear of an object or a condition and an *anxiety* lest this object or condition be encountered. Particular phobias include claustrophobia (fear of closed spaces), agoraphobia (fear of open spaces), zoophobia (fear of particular animals) and so on. Such phobias are often found to be symptoms of unsuccessful or incomplete *repressions*, as in particular repressions of sexual *desires*. The object of phobia, in other words, stands for some other object, whose threatening quality cannot be acknowledged. Individuals suffering from phobias tend to avoid threatening objects and situations and become inhibited in their personal and social lives.

pleasure principle
A principle of mental functioning which describes the tendencies of unconscious impulses and *desires* towards instant gratification, prior to the mediation of the *ego* and the coming into effect of the *reality principle*. In most of his works, Freud viewed the pleasure principle as a tendency of the mental apparatus to reduce the unpleasant excitation which is generated by an unsatisfied desire. The fulfilment of desire leads to a reduction of such unpleasant excitation. In this sense, pleasure and pain are associated with quantities of excitation. In some of his later works, however, Freud acknowledged that not all increases of excitation are experienced as unpleasant; pleasure cannot, therefore, be equated with the sudden reduction of excitation, but involves a qualitative factor inherent in the nature of certain types of excitation. Thus, it is possible to enhance pleasure by a controlled build-up of excitation, on condition that at some point in time it will be discharged. Thus pleasure and pain themselves are not seen purely as bodily experiences, but are symbolically constructed.

preconscious
A part of the mind, which is descriptively unconscious (i.e. its content is not conscious) but dynamically conscious (it can be accessed by *consciousness*). Ideas belonging to the preconscious are not conscious at a particular moment in time, but may be easily invited into consciousness. Memories and encyclopaedic knowledge are generally preconscious. Preconscious material undergoes almost continuous transformation and may be influenced by *unconscious* processes. For example, a preconscious idea, like the name of a person, may be temporarily or permanently forgotten or mistaken (lapsus); nostalgia is a process whereby memories become coloured in a glowing and affectionate light. Hence, preconscious material can generally be seen as material which may become unconscious or may be altered in the course of a person's development by subsequent accretions and experiences.

primary processes
The processes which govern the behaviour of unconscious ideas and desires in the id. There ideas and desires enjoy great freedom and demand instant gratification. There is no contradiction between opposites, no logical inconsistency, no constraints of time and space. Primary processes include *condensation* and *displacement*.

psychoanalysis
The branch of *depth psychology* founded by Freud. Psychoanalysis is both a clinical practice for mental disorders, involving the use of a particular set of techniques, and also a theoretical body of knowledge about the *unconscious* and its effects. For a wide variety of personal, clinical and scientific reasons, Freud was keen to maintain the distinctions between his own doctrine and clinical practice and other traditions within depth psychology, most notably those founded by his early disciples, Alfred Adler and Carl Gustav Jung, who moved in their own directions. Adler founded a school of psychology known as individual psychology, while Jung developed his own

doctrine of *analytical psychology*. Both of these schools of thought rejected Freud's emphasis on *sexuality* and qualified his views on the *unconscious*. Following Freud's death, psychoanalysis re-absorbed various insights from these and other theorists who broke with Freud, notably Sandor Ferenczi and Otto Rank.

Within psychoanalysis itself, a number of different schools of thought have emerged, including Kleinian, Lacanian, object-relations, ego psychology, humanistic psychology and culturalist psychology. Each of these schools of thought has introduced novel features to the study of the unconscious and has qualified or revised some of Freud's theories. They have also modified clinical practice, offering different types of therapy and treatment. The orthodox Freudian school is generally identified by its continuing commitment to the *instincts* (including their quantitative aspects), its emphasis on Oedipal processes as formative in subsequent developments and its continuing use of the free-association technique in clinical practice. Orthodox Freudians tend to take a pessimistic view of the scope of therapy, seeing *neurosis* as a widespread condition which is inextricably linked to social and cultural processes.

Relations among the schools are very complex, having been coloured by interpersonal feuds and claims and counter-claims as to who represents the true legacy of psychoanalysis. Many of the disagreements among the schools have focused on clinical practice. In recent decades, some of the dogmatism and intolerance characteristic of earlier debates have abated, and constructive discussions across different schools are not uncommon. Needless to say, some of the most perceptive psychoanalytic writers have written from positions outside the established schools. These include many of the non-clinical writers, such as Rieff, Marcuse, Brown, Lasch and Sennett.

psychosis
A serious mental disorder, accompanied by grave *delusions* and serious difficulties in establishing meaningful relations with others. The scope of psychoanalysis in the treatment of psychoses (unlike the treatment of *neuroses*) is limited, due to the patient's general inability to form a *transference* towards the clinician. Jung saw psychosis (in particular, schizophrenia) as an invasion of the patient's ego by *unconscious* elements, which overwhelm the ego and undermine its links to reality, and argued that the mental life of neurotics can help us understand the more general nature of psychic reality. Most contemporary psychiatry has moved to the view that the origin of most psychoses is organic rather than psychic.

reaction-formation
A defence mechanism whereby a threatening impulse is *repressed*, leaving in its place one diametrically opposite; for instance, puritanism in place of sexual fascination or bashfulness in place of exhibitionism. It is also one of the two mechanisms (the other being *sublimation*) whereby various character traits which are not of a sexual nature are formed during a particular stage of a child's sexual development, e.g. cleanliness as a reaction-formation to the fascination with faeces during the *anal stage*.

reality principle
A principle of mental functioning which qualifies the operation of the *pleasure principle*, by postponing or altering the fulfilment of an impulse or *desire*, according to the requirements of external reality. Unlike the pleasure principle, which is innate, the reality principle derives from the development of the *ego* in its role as mediator between inner and outer reality.

regression
A tendency to revert to an earlier mode of mental functioning or an earlier character structure, notably under conditions of *anxiety*. Regression is generally viewed as a *defence mechanism*, through which an individual overcomes anxiety caused by a threatening situation by reverting to a mode of mental functioning which denies or disregards the sources of the anxiety. For example, regression to infantile dependency denies the need to make difficult and threatening decisions, taking responsibility for one's own actions. Alternatively, regression to an oral (narcissistic)

character structure denies the existence of a world which is largely indifferent to an individual's predicament and frustrates his or her sense of importance.

repetition compulsion
A strong tendency to repeat particular forms of behaviour or go through a specific type of experience, no matter how unpleasant or distressing it may be. It can be observed in numerous mental phenomena, including recurring children's games, nightmares, revisiting the site of distressing experiences or re-living traumatic events. The origins of this compulsion are *unconscious*, and, in as much as it brings about pain and distress, it goes 'beyond the pleasure principle'. In his later works, Freud came to view the compulsion to repeat as a manifestation of the conservative character of *instincts* which he used to support his postulation of the *death instinct*. The compulsion to repeat is of great interest in the analysis of personal, social and organizational life. At the personal level, it is manifest in individual habits and routines. It is also a vital element of cultural rituals, traditions and story-telling; in organizations, it can be observed in the mechanical adherence to organizational processes and routines displayed by functionaries and officials.

repression
The fundamental *defence mechanism*, through which painful or threatening *desires*, ideas and emotions are prevented from reaching *consciousness*, being restricted to the *unconscious*. Repression is only one of several mechanisms of defence, yet it is a fundamental concept of psychoanalysis, in as much as it defines the unconscious in a relatively unambiguous way. 'The theory of repression is the cornerstone on which the whole structure of psycho-analysis rests', wrote Freud (1914b). While much of the repressed unconscious contains ideas and desires repressed in early childhood, repressions continue throughout life, whenever something too painful threatens to reach consciousness. Repressed ideas and desires do not generally decay with the passage of time; they may surface in different guises, such as neurotic *symptoms*, *dreams*, *fantasies* and works of art. A distinction can be made between primary repression and secondary repression; the latter attempts to repress the symptoms which result from the former. Effective repressions tend to silence repressed ideas totally or allow them socially permissible ways to reach consciousness; unsuccessful repressions lie at the heart of the causation of *neurosis* – they either fail to suppress an idea totally, or the symptoms which result are themselves debilitating or anxiety-provoking. The relationship between repression and *anxiety* is a complex one. Anxiety is usually a trigger for repression; however, unsuccessful repressions may cause anxiety.

resistance
Initially a *defensive* process whereby patients refuse to allow their analysts access to their *unconscious*. In particular, patients may reject out of hand the interpretations offered by their analysts. In some instances, patients' resistance to recovery may be the product of the gain which patients derive from their condition; for example, the pity of others or the alleviation of a sense of guilt. More generally, resistance is taken to indicate an adverse attitude to an idea, an interpretation or a theory which stems not from rational considerations but from emotional hostility whose origin is unconscious.

secondary processes
In contrast to *primary processes*, secondary processes govern the association of ideas and *desires* in the *ego*. Here, impulses cannot demand instant gratification but are modified according to the demands of reality, ideas are subject to the laws of logical consistency and contradiction and ethical demands exercise control over expression and action. *Thinking* is governed by secondary process.

self
A concept referring to the subject as an active, aware and self-aware agent. The meaning of self varies widely across different philosophical traditions, which variously emphasize the reasoning,

cognitive, meaning-creating, willing, emotional, existential and transcendental qualities of the human subject. It is a concept which overlaps extensively with *identity*, *ego* and subjectivity. Psychoanalysis refuses to recognize a 'self' as a sovereign agency; instead, it approaches the self as a fragmented entity, often in conflict within its own boundaries and invariably containing a part of which it is not aware or conscious. Bettelheim (1983) offers some convincing arguments that the self, as an object of experience, is very close to what Freud referred to as *das Ich*, criticizing his English translators for rendering this as the *ego*. In many respects, the psychoanalytic idea of self prefigures the postmodern concepts of decentred or fragmented self. What, however, gives the psychoanalytic account extra interest is the view that the self is itself an *illusion* in the technical sense, i.e. a *wish-fulfilling fantasy* through which the ego seeks to console itself, as though it were unified and in control. In this respect, the self, far from being a sovereign agency, is itself a mental artefact, part of the content of the *ego-ideal*. Some psychoanalytic writers, influenced by existentialist and humanist ideas, have nevertheless sought to defend the self as a sovereign entity. At the same time, it must be recognized that in most composite forms (e.g. oneself, self-awareness, self-importance etc.) psychoanalytic writers use the 'self' in a conventional way.

sexuality

A complex motivational force, an *instinct*, which is the source of a wide range of *desires*, activities and experiences associated with pleasure and which go beyond the sating of physiological needs. One of the contributions of psychoanalysis was to uncouple sexuality from genital sex and discover a wide range of manifestations and vicissitudes. The expressions of sexuality may be physical, emotional, verbal or, even, artistic, but in a direct or indirect way these desires aim at *pleasure*.

While the sexuality of most individuals may seem consistent and stable (most desires, for example, directed towards pleasure through heterosexual intercourse), psychoanalytic, psychological and sociological research indicates that sexuality is highly complex and variable. In contrast to animal sexuality which is mechanically linked to instinctual behaviour, human sexuality is mediated by desires, a large part of which are either learned or symbolically constituted. Sociologists and anthropologists have observed wide variations of sexual behaviour across different cultures and societies. Malinowski, for example, studied the highly promiscuous sexual behaviour of the Trobrianders which contrasted sharply with the rigidly controlled behaviour of some of their neighbours. Western cultures, it has been argued, spotlight one feature of sexuality, *fantasy*, as it is uniquely suited to the demands of both consumer society and modern organization; they also create an obsessive preoccupation with penetrative sex and orgasm as the aim of all sexual activity, at the expense of other forms of pleasurable behaviour.

Psychoanalysis has made two important contributions regarding human sexuality: (a) it is dynamic, i.e. it develops through early childhood, going through a number of important stages, where different complications may arise; (b) it is complex, involving numerous desires, many of which may conflict, and most of which are *unconscious*. No line between 'normal' and 'perverse' behaviour can be drawn, since the sexuality of 'normal' people invariably contains *repressed* desires that could be classified as perverse. The study of sexuality as part of organizational life is a growing area. Current research has started to explore overt and covert types of sexual behaviour at the workplace. These include sexual harassment, office romances, sexual jokes and innuendoes, as well as the overt and covert sexualization of work environments in sectors like retailing, air transport and the media. The prevalence of sexual images in advertising has also received extensive research interest. The psychoanalytic study of organizations has also addressed some of the indirect manifestations of sexuality, notably in processes involving *narcissism*, *idealization* and *identification*.

splitting

A *defence mechanism* through which a mental structure or image is split into two, usually antithetical, elements. Klein viewed splitting as the earliest and most fundamental form of defence against *anxiety* and explored both the splitting of the object and the splitting of the *ego* into good and bad components (see *paranoid-schizoid position*). Splitting is of considerable interest in the study of organizations, where it usually takes a collective form: a group of individuals or even the majority of organizational members may collectively split the organization or its leadership into highly idealized good parts and highly vilified bad parts. Invariably, good parts are invested with love and introjected, while bad parts become legitimate targets of hate and are scapegoated.

sublimation
A term which has two related but distinct meanings. Sublimation represents a particular vicissitude of *sexuality*, whereby *libido* is desexualized and directed towards non-sexual but socially important ends. These may include creative, intellectual or artistic pursuits or the formation of desexualized social ties. In all of these ways, sublimation can function as an alternative to *repression*, one which generally does not involve the same risk of *neurosis*, as it involves a creative rather than a strictly defensive resolution of psychic *conflict*. Thus, the ego, instead of dealing with a threatening idea or *desire* by seeking to neutralize it or deny it, manages to re-orient the libido inherent in this idea or desire towards a higher and finer end. This meaning of sublimation is akin to the use of the term made by Nietzsche, who saw sublimation as the ability to replace a desire to destroy an opponent with a desire to excel him or her in spiritual contest. The second meaning of sublimation is related to the psychoanalytic theory of *character*, and represents the opposite process to *reaction-formation*. Through sublimation, various character traits which are not of a sexual nature emerge during a particular stage of a child's sexual development through the desexualization of a relevant *desire*; for example, parsimony results from the sublimation of the desire to withhold the faeces, nail-biting from the desire to bite the breast.

super-ego
An *agency* of the mental apparatus which assumed its clearer expression in the second topography (see *topographic point of view*), in its opposition to the *id* and the *ego*. The super-ego is the agency responsible for self-observation, self-criticism and the maintenance of the *ego-ideal*. The super-ego is formed during the *Oedipus complex* phase, as the child internalizes parental authority as a source of *repression* and identifies with the parent of the same sex. Subsequently, the super-ego is modified through further identifications with models of authority. While the super-ego is often equated with *conscience*, it must be noted that its contents and operations are predominantly *unconscious*. The super-ego is presented by Freud as the third of the *ego*'s harsh masters (the other two being the id and external reality), and imposes severe restrictions on the gratification of impulses and desires. To this end, it makes use of aggressive energy which it turns against the ego, in the form of an excessive sense of *guilt*. The super-ego is fundamental to the psychoanalytic study of social and organizational phenomena, representing culture's fifth column within the individual, an unrelenting force of submission to social morality.

Klein saw the super-ego as the outcome of a much longer development, which starts in the *oral stage*. On the basis of her analysis of very young children, she argued that the super-ego begins to function from the earliest months of life, through introjection of good objects (a forerunner for later *identifications*) and a projection on to bad ones. The severity of such a pre-Oedipal super-ego is said to derive from the infant's hate for and rage towards bad objects. Cultural and social commentators, such as Marcuse, Lasch and Sennett, on the other hand, have stayed closer to the Freudian view of the post-Oedipal super-ego. Since the 1970s, many social theorists, following Lasch, have argued that the importance of the super-ego has declined throughout the twentieth century, being virtually eclipsed by the *ego-ideal* in a culture of *narcissism*. This replaces the super-ego's stress on conformity and achievement with an emphasis on individuality, difference and being the centre of unqualified love.

symbols and symbolism
Psychoanalysis distinguishes between two types of symbol: in the first place there are symbols such as flags, words and badges whose referent is conscious, generally established by

convention. In addition to these symbols, psychoanalysis identifies those symbols which are the visible tips of wholly *unconscious* processes. This type of psychoanalytic or 'true' symbolism, argued Jones (1916: 158), 'arises as the result of intra-psychic conflict between the repressing tendencies and them'. In this type of symbolism 'only what is repressed is symbolized; only what is repressed needs to be symbolized'. The repressed wishes expressed in psychoanalytic symbols can be contradictory, for the unconscious can hold contradictory ideas or desires together. A person may, for example, be invested with both saint-like and devil-like qualities or love and hate may co-exist for the same object. In *interpreting* a symbol, one should not be surprised if one discovers a diversity of sometimes contradictory meanings. A potent symbol is one which often fulfils a diversity of unconscious wishes, evades a multiplicity of mental censors or is the simultaneous resultant of different mental conflicts. In this sense, *dreams*, *symptoms* and other symbolic phenomena are over-determined, the result of multiple processes converging in the same direction. Analytic interpretations are, therefore, rarely content with establishing a single link between a symbol and what it stands for.

symptom
A visible manifestation of an underlying condition or process. While in medicine symptoms may refer to the manifest consequences of a physical disorder, in psychoanalytic terms symptoms are visible manifestations of unconscious processes. A symptom is often a compromise formation between an instinctual impulse and the forces of *repression* which seek to silence it. A symptom is then a distorted form through which repressed material is allowed to reach *consciousness*. In this sense, a symptom is a phenomenon akin to a *dream*, a *fantasy*, a joke or a slip, i.e. material containing meaning, whose *interpretation* may lead to unconscious material. Symptoms can be relatively easily assimilated in a person's functioning or may have incapacitating consequences, when they are referred to as clinical symptoms (e.g. neurotic symptoms). Symptoms may be bodily as in hysteria (paralysis of a limb), or mental (compulsive idea) and behavioural (nail-biting) as in obsessional neurosis and phobia. In most instances, symptoms afford an individual with a substitute gratification. It is one of the fundamental tenets of psychoanalysis as clinical practice not to address the symptom directly but to seek to establish the underlying pathogenic processes. The patient's realization that the symptom is an outcome of an unsuccessful repression or an unfulfilled *desire* may be enough to bring about the dissolution of the symptom.

thinking
A mental process in which ideas are generated and tested in a logical manner. Freud observed that thinking can be considered a form of experimental mental activity, whereby one tests the implications of one idea for a whole range of others. In this sense, logical consistency takes primacy over *wish-fulfilment* without, however, completely eliminating the latter. Thinking, especially creative thinking, can be a pleasure-yielding activity and can be considered the product of *sublimation*, whereby small amounts of energy can yield rather significant conclusions. More routine thinking is entailed by the *reality principle* and seeks to establish the conditions under which an instinctual impulse may be fulfilled. Free-association is a form of thinking, liberated from the need to be consistent or logical. *Fantasy* represents a form of mental activity in which wish-fulfilment takes precedence over logical consistence. Thinking is generally regarded as a secondary process, in contrast to *unconscious* mental activity which is a primary process. Psychoanalysis has generally had much more to say about primary processes and emotional life than about cognition and secondary processes.

topographic point of view
One of the three types of analysis which combine to offer a metapsychological account of mental phenomena (the others being the *dynamic* and the *economic*). The topographic point of view deals with the different regions of the mind, the properties of ideas and processes which take place in these regions and the conditions under which they cross from one region to another. Two different mental topographies are presented by Freud's work. The early or first topography concentrates primarily on whether a particular idea or *desire* is accessible to *consciousness* and

distinguishes between the *unconscious*, the *preconscious* and the conscious. The later or second topography focuses on the dynamic of mental *conflict* and distinguishes between three mental *agencies*, the *ego*, the *id* and the *super-ego*. According to this topography, the id is entirely unconscious, but so too are large sections of the ego and the super-ego. The second topography is generally assumed to have subsumed the earlier one, though the relationship between the two has not been systematically analysed.

transference

A process whereby a patient transfers on to the analyst feelings and images associated with significant figures from his or her past. More generally, the propensity individuals have to relate to important figures in their lives (including leaders, doctors, spouses and friends) in ways which repeat earlier relations to parental figures. Transference is an important feature of the analyst–patient relationship, one that generally gives the analyst direct insight into the patient's past relationships. It generally involves both negative and positive feelings, i.e. it is *ambivalent*. Transference is of considerable importance in the study of organizational phenomena, as it is liable to affect relations between subordinates and superiors. Subordinates may experience their leaders as reincarnations of figures of parental authority from their past and experience acute feelings of love, envy, dependence, trust and so on towards them. Counter-transference represents the analyst's response to the patient's transference. It must be noted that both transference and counter-transference are *unconscious* processes and are not liable to rational controls. Thus, when a person says that they took a sudden like or dislike to someone they just met, it can be deduced that this is the result of transference.

unconscious

The fundamental concept of psychoanalysis, which, as part of *depth psychology*, is crucially concerned with the study of the unconscious and its effects. Although sometimes the unconscious is seen as a mysterious entity, reminiscent of the Platonic depths where the world of pure forms seeks expression through language, the Freudian unconscious is normal, structured and substantially knowable.

It is useful to distinguish between 'unconscious' as an adjective and a noun. As an adjective, unconscious describes the quality of an idea, a desire or a mental process which is not accessible to *consciousness*. In the first instance, unconscious *desires* are desires which have undergone *repression*. Unlike *preconscious* elements, unconscious elements cannot be brought into consciousness at will, and may only be studied through their conscious manifestations, which include *symptoms*, *symbols*, *dreams*, *fantasies*, slips, jokes, emotional outbursts, cultural artefacts and so on. Unconscious ideas and processes behave in a different way from conscious ideas, being governed by *primary processes*, notably *condensation* and *displacement*.

As a noun, the unconscious refers to the area of the mind which contains the unconscious ideas, desires and processes. In addition to the repressed material, the unconscious also contains *archetypal* images and primal phantasies, which can be thought of as mental structures inscribed in the genetic make-up of human beings over millennia of evolution. Freud referred to this material as the phylogenetic heritage of mankind. In the early *topography*, the unconscious featured as a mental system (sometimes referred to as system Ucs.) which included the representatives of the *instincts* (desires, wishes, phantasies) whose main purpose is to gain access to consciousness. In the second topography, the unconscious is no longer an *agency* – its agency-like properties are assimilated in the *id*. However, the second topography, the other two agencies, the ego and the super-ego, also contain unconscious elements and pursue many of their functions in ways which preclude access to consciousness. So, when the ego represses an idea, the process of repression itself is *unconscious*, i.e. the person is not aware of doing so. Most of the *defence mechanisms* operate unconsciously. In spite of surrendering its systemic qualities to the id, the quality of mental contents to be unconscious remained in Freud's view, 'our one beacon-light in the darkness of depth psychology' (1923: 368). This is the point where psychoanalysis gains access to those contents of the mental apparatus and those functions of mental life which mankind has traditionally concealed from itself.

While the unconscious is the central object of study of psychoanalysis, it is also a virtually indispensable assumption for most human sciences, including sociology, cultural studies, linguistics, art and literary criticism. It is at once the psychic layer in which culture becomes embedded within the individual and also the source of fundamental needs and desires which cultural institutions seek alternately to express, modify, frustrate, tame or gratify. It is for this reason that Foucault observed that 'the problem of the unconscious – its possibility, status, mode of existence, the means of knowing it and bringing it to light – is not simply a problem within the human sciences which they can be thought of as encountering by chance in their steps; it is a problem that is ultimately coextensive with their very existence . . . an unveiling of the non-conscious is constitutive of all the sciences of man' (1970: 364).

The unconscious has, throughout the twentieth century, pervaded our thinking about what makes us behave the way we do: it has virtually become common-sense to contend that people act for reasons of which they are unconscious. The idea that people have 'subconscious' motives, that they deny their desires, that they are gripped by powerful desires whose sources are hidden, that painful memories are obliterated from consciousness are now commonplace. Yet, as Mitchell (1974) has sharply observed, virtually all criticisms of psychoanalysis derive from an inability to accept the unconscious and its implications. It is all too easy for individuals (both in common and in academic discourses) to lapse into an assumption that others have unconscious minds, suffering from self-delusions, mysterious motives and neurotic symptoms, whereas they themselves are entirely transparent, consistent and rational. As Freud realized long ago, the existence of an unconscious part of our mind, a part of our mind which is beyond our direct knowledge and control, is a highly threatening and disturbing one. The view that our *ego* (what we refer to as 'I') is not the master even in its own house may suggest that we all harbour a stranger within ourselves – a highly disconcerting thought, when we consider that this stranger has unpredictable, destructive and self-destructive appetites.

wish

Another term for *desire*, the mental representative of *instincts*.

wish-fulfilment

In psychoanalytic terms, wish-fulfilment is not the actual fulfilment of a desire (for example, marrying the person one loves). Instead, it is the realization of a wish or *desire* in *fantasy*, *symptoms*, *dreams*, *illusions*, jokes or other mental and cultural phenomena which afford a substitute or *symbolic* gratification. Thus, the belief in a Christian God can be interpreted as a fulfilment of the desire for paternal protection, for justice and for parental love. Wish-fulfilments are compromise formations between the impulse or desire demanding satisfaction and the forces of censorship and repression which seek to deny or silence it.

REFERENCES

Abraham, Karl (1973) *Selected Papers of Karl Abraham*, trans. Douglas Bryan and Alix Strachey. London: Hogarth Press.
Adams, G. B. and Balfour, D. L. (1998) 'An Historical Analysis of a Destructive Organizational Culture: the Von Braun Team, the Marshall Space Flight Center and the Space Shuttle Challenger Disaster', *Administrative Theory and Praxis*, 20 (3): 300–13.
Adorno, T. W., Frenkel-Brunswik, E., Levinson, D. and Sanford, N. (1950) *The Authoritarian Personality*. New York: Harper.
Albrow, Martin (1992) '*Sine Ira et Studio* – or Do Organizations Have Feelings?', *Organization Studies*, 13 (3): 313–29.
Alford, C. (1988) *Narcissism: Socrates, the Frankfurt School, and Psychoanalytic Theory*. New Haven, CT: Yale University Press.
Allcorn, Seth (1997) 'The Search for the Organizational Solution to the Industrial Revolution', paper presented at the fall colloquium, Center for the Study of Organizational Change, University of Missouri, 19–21 September.
Allcorn, Seth and Diamond, Michael A. (1997) *Managing People during Stressful Times: the Psychologically Defensive Workplace*. London: Quorum.
Argyris, C. (1960) *Understanding Organizational Behavior*. London: Tavistock.
Argyris, C. (1993) *Knowledge for Action*. San Francisco: Jossey-Bass.
Argyris, C. and Schön, D. A. (1978) *Organizational Learning: a Theory in Action Perspective*. Reading, MA: Addison-Wesley.
Asch, Solomon (1956) 'Studies of Independence and Conformity. 1: A Minority of One against a Unanimous Majority', *Psychological Monographs*, 70: 1–70.
Badcock, C. (1988) *Essential Freud*. Oxford: Blackwell.
Bate, Paul (1994) *Strategies for Cultural Change*. Oxford: Butterworth-Heinemann.
Baudrillard, Jean (1968/1988) 'The System of Objects', in Mark Poster (ed.), *Jean Baudrillard: Selected Writings*. Cambridge: Polity Press.
Baudrillard, Jean (1988) *Selected Writings*, ed. Mark Poster. Cambridge: Polity Press.
Baum, H. S. (1987) *The Invisible Bureaucracy*. Oxford: Oxford University Press.
Baum, H. S. (1989) 'Organizational Politics against Organizational Culture: a Psychoanalytic Perspective', *Human Resource Management*, 28 (2): 191–207.
Bauman, Zygmunt (1988) *Freedom*. Milton Keynes: Open University Press.
Bauman, Zygmunt (1992) *Intimations of Postmodernity*. London: Routledge.
Bemporad, Jules and Herzog, David (1989) *Psychoanalysis and Eating Disorders*. London: Guildford Press.
Benjamin, Walter (1968) *Illuminations*. London: Jonathan Cape.
Bennis, W. (1989) *Why Leaders Can't Lead: the Unconscious Conspiracy Continues*. San Francisco: Jossey-Bass.
Berg, D. and Smith, K. (eds) (1985) *Exploring Clinical Methods for Social Research*. Beverly Hills, CA: Sage.
Berger, P. and Luckman, T. (1967) *The Social Construction of Reality*. Garden City, NY: Anchor.
Bergquist, W. (1993) *The Postmodern Organization: Mastering the Art of Irreversible Change*. San Francisco: Jossey-Bass.
Bettelheim, Bruno (1976) *The Uses of Enchantment*. London: Thames and Hudson.
Bettelheim, Bruno (1983) *Freud and Man's Soul*. London: Chatto and Windus.

Bettelheim, Bruno (1990) *Recollections and Reflections*. London: Thames and Hudson.
Biggart, N. W. (1988) *Charismatic Capitalism*. London: University of Chicago Press.
Billig, Michael (1989) *Arguing and Thinking: a Rhetorical Approach to Social Psychology*. Cambridge: Cambridge University Press.
Bion, W. R. (1961) *Experiences in Groups*. London: Tavistock.
Bion, W. R. (1970) *Attention and Interpretation*. London: Tavistock.
Biran, H. (1998) 'Relationship and Relatedness between the Elementary School as a System and its Violent Parts', *Symposium of the International Society for the Psychoanalytic Study of Organizations*, Jerusalem, 1–3 July.
Bly, Robert (1990) *Iron John: A Book About Men*. New York: Addison-Wesley.
Boje, D. M. (1991) 'The Storytelling Organization: a Study of Story Performance in an Office-supply Firm', *Administrative Science Quarterly*, 36: 106–26.
Boje, D. M. and Dennehy, R. F. (1993) *Managing in the Postmodern World: America's Revolution against Exploitation*. Dubuque, IA: Kendall-Hunt.
Bowles, M. L. (1989) 'Myth, Meaning and Work Organization', *Organization Studies*, 10 (3): 405–21.
Bowles, M. L. (1990) 'Recognizing Deep Structures in Organizations', *Organization Studies*, 11 (3): 395–412.
Bowles, M. L. (1991) 'The Organizational Shadow', *Organization Studies*, 12: 387–404.
Bowles, M. L. (1993) 'The Gods and Goddesses: Personifying Social Life in the Age of Organization', *Organization Studies*, 14: 394–418.
Boyce, Mary E. (1996) 'Organizational Story and Storytelling: a Critical Review', *Journal of Organizational Change Management*, 9 (5): 5–26.
Brill, A. A. (1938) *The Basic Writings of Sigmund Freud*. New York: Random House.
Brown, Norman O. (1959) *Life against Death*. Middletown, CT: Wesleyan University Press.
Brown, Norman O. (1966) *Love's Body*. New York: Random House.
Bruch, Hilde (1973) *Eating Disorders: Obesity, Anorexia Nervosa and the Person Within*. New York: Basic Books.
Bruch, Hilde (1978) *The Golden Cage: the Enigma of Anorexia*. London: Open Books.
Brumberg, Joan Jacobs (1988) *Fasting Girls: the Emergence of Anorexia Nervosa as a Modern Disease*. Cambridge, MA.: Harvard University Press.
Burns, J. M. (1978) *Leadership*. New York: Harper and Row.
Burrell, Gibson and Morgan, Gareth (1979) *Sociological Paradigms and Organizational Analysis*. London: Heinemann.
Campbell, Colin (1989) *The Romantic Ethic and the Spirit of Modern Consumerism*. Oxford: Macmillan.
Carlzon, J. (1989) *Moments of Truth*. New York: Harper and Row.
Carr, A. (1993) 'The Psychostructure of Work: Bend Me, Shape Me, Anyway You Want Me, as Long as You Love Me it's Alright', *Journal of Managerial Psychology*, 8 (6): 2–6.
Carr, A. (1997) 'Putative Problematic Agency in a Postmodern World', in H. Miller and C. Fox (eds), *Postmodernism, 'Reality', and Public Administration*, pp. 3–18. Virginia: Chatelaine.
Carr, A. (1998) 'Identity, Compliance and Dissent in Organizations: a Psychoanalytic Perspective', *Organization*, 5 (1): 81–99.
Casey, Catherine (1996) 'Corporate Transformations: Designer Culture, Designer Employees and "Post-occupational" Solidarity', *Organization*, 3 (3): 317–39.
Chasseguet-Smirgel, Janine (1976) 'Some Thoughts on the Ego-Ideal: a Contribution to the Study of the "Illness of Ideality" ', *Psychoanalytic Quarterly*, 45: 345–73.
Chasseguet-Smirgel, Janine (1984) *Creativity and Perversion*. New York, Norton.
Chasseguet-Smirgel, Janine (1985) *The Ego Ideal: a Psychoanalytic Essay on the Malady of the Ideal*. New York: Norton.
Chasseguet-Smirgel, Janine (1986a) *Sexuality and Mind: the Role of the Father and the Mother in the Psyche*. New York: New York University Press.
Chasseguet-Smirgel, Janine (1986b) *Freud or Reich? Psychoanalysis and Illusion*. New Haven, CT: Yale University Press.
Chia, R. (1994) 'The Concept of Decision', *Journal of Management Studies*, 31 (6): 781–806.
Chodorow, Nancy (1978) *The Reproduction of Mothering: Psychoanalysis and the Sociology of Gender*. Berkeley, CA: University of California Press.
Chodorow, Nancy (1989) *Feminism and Psychoanalytic Theory*. New Haven, CT.: Yale University Press.

Cleverley, G. (1971) *Managers and Magic*. London: Longman.
Cohen, Eliot A. and Gooch, John (1990) *Military Misfortunes: the Anatomy of Failure at War*. New York: Free Press.
Cohen, M. D., March, J. G. and Olsen, J. P. (1972) 'A Garbage Can Model of Organizational Choice', *Administrative Science Quarterly*, 17: 1–25.
Colman, A. D. and Geller, M. H. (1985) *Group Relations Reader 2*. Washington, DC: A. K. Rice Institute.
Connerton, P. (1976) *Critical Sociology: Selected Readings*. Harmondsworth: Penguin.
Cooper, R. and Burrell, G. (1988) 'Modernism, Postmodernism and Organizational Analysis: an Introduction', *Organization Studies*, 9 (1): 91–112.
Cousins, Mark and Hussain, Athar (1984) *Michel Foucault*. London: Macmillan.
Cravens, D. W., Piercy, N. F. and Shipp, S. H. (1996) 'New Organizational Forms for Competing in Highly Dynamic Environments: the Network Paradigm', *British Journal of Management*, 7: 203–18.
Crews, Frederick (1993/1995) *The Memory Wars: Freud's Legacy in Dispute*. New York: New York Review of Books.
Culler, Jonathan (1976) *Saussure*. London: Fontana.
Cummings, L. and Schmidt, S. (1972) 'Managerial Attitudes of Greeks: the Role of Culture and Industrialization', *Administrative Science Quarterly*, 17: 265–78.
Curtiss, Susan (1977) *Genie: a Psycholinguistic Study of a Modern-day 'Wild Child'*. New York: Academic Press.
Czander, William M. (1993) *The Psychodynamics of Work Organizations: Theory and Applications*. London: Guildford Press.
Czarniawska-Joerges, B. (1992) *Exploring Complex Organizations*. Newbury Park, CA: Sage.
Davies, C. (1988) 'Stupidity and Rationality: Jokes from the Iron Cage', in C. Powell and G. E. C. Paton (eds), *Humour in Society*, pp. 1–32. London: Macmillan.
Deal, T. E. and Kennedy, A. A. (1982) *Corporate Cultures*. Reading, MA: Addison-Wesley.
De Certeau, Michel (1984) *The Practice of Everyday Life*. Berkeley, CA: University of California Press.
Denison, D. (1990) *Corporate Culture and Organizational Effectiveness*. New York: John Wiley.
Derrida, J. (1976) *Of Grammatology*. Baltimore, MD: Johns Hopkins University Press.
Diamond, Michael A. (1985) 'The Social Character of Bureaucracy: Anxiety and Ritualistic Defense', *Political Psychology*, 6 (4): 663–79.
Diamond, Michael A. (1991) 'Stresses of Group Membership: Balancing the Needs for Independence and Belonging', in M. F. R. Kets de Vries (ed.) *Organizations on the Couch*. San Francisco: Jossey-Bass.
Diamond, Michael A. (1993) *The Unconscious Life of Organizations: Interpreting Organizational Identity*. London: Quorum.
Diamond, Michael A. and Allcorn, Seth (1987) 'The Psychodynamics of Regression in Groups', *Human Relations*, 40 (8): 525–43.
Dicks, H. (1972) *Licenced Mass Murder: a Socio-psychological Study of Some SS Killers*. London: University of Sussex Press.
Dixon, Norman F. (1976) *On the Psychology of Military Incompetence*. London: Futura.
Douglas, M. (1975) 'Jokes', in M. Douglas (ed.), *Implicit Meanings: Essays in Anthropology*. London: Routledge. pp. 90–114.
Drucker, P. F. (1980) *Managing in Turbulent Times*. Oxford: Butterworth–Heinemann.
Drucker, P. F. (1995) *Managing in a Time of Great Change*. Oxford: Butterworth–Heinemann.
Durkheim, E. (1915/1961) *The Elementary Forms of Religious Life*. New York: Free Press.
Durkheim E. (1951) *Suicide*. New York: Free Press.
Edelman, M. (1964) *The Symbolic Uses of Power*. Illinois: University of Illinois Press.
Edmondson, Ricca (1984) *Rhetoric in Sociology*. London: Macmillan.
Edwards, R. (1979) *Contested Terrain*. New York: Basic Books.
Elden, M. and Chisholm, R. (1993) 'Emerging Varieties of Action Research', *Human Relations*, 46 (2): 121–42.
Elgmork, K. (1988) *Aper – mennesker, slektskap og utvikling*. Oslo: Universitetsforlaget.
Emery, F. E. and Trist, E. L. (1969) 'Socio-technical Systems', reprinted in F. E. Emery (ed.), *Systems Thinking*. Harmondsworth: Penguin.
Erikson, E. (1950) *Childhood and Society*. New York: Norton.
Erikson, E. (1968) *Identity, Youth and Crisis*. New York: Norton.

REFERENCES

Erikson, E. (1982) *The Life Cycle Completed: a Review*. New York: Norton.
Esterson, Allen (1993) *Seductive Mind: an Exploration of the Work of Sigmund Freud*. Chicago, IL: Open Court.
Farrell, Em. (1995) *Lost for Words: the Psychoanalysis of Anorexia and Bulimia*. London: Process Press.
Ferguson, K. (1984) *The Feminist Case against Bureaucracy*. Philadelphia, PA: Temple University Press.
Feyerabend, Paul (1975) *Against Method*. London: New Left Books.
Feyerabend, Paul (1978) *Science in a Free Society*. London: New Left Books.
Feyerabend, Paul (1987) *Farewell to Reason*. London: Verso Press.
Fineman, Stephen (ed.) (1993) *Emotion in Organizations*. London: Sage.
Fineman, Stephen (1996) 'Emotion and Organizing', in S. Clegg, C. Hardy and W. R. Nord (eds), *Handbook of Organization Studies*. London: Sage. pp. 543–64.
Fineman, Stephen (1997) 'Constructing the Green Manager', *British Journal of Management*, 8: 31–8.
Fineman, Stephen and Gabriel, Yiannis (1996) *Experiencing Organizations*. London: Sage.
Fischer, Seymour and Greenberg, Roger P. (1996) *Freud Scientifically Reappraised: Testing the Theories and Therapy*. New York: John Wiley.
Fitzgerald, T. H. (1988) 'Can Change in Organizational Culture Really be Managed?', *Organizational Dynamics*, Autumn, pp. 5–15.
Flam, H. (1990a) 'Emotional "Man" I. The Emotional "Man" and the Problem of Collective Action', *International Sociology*, 5 (1): 39–56.
Flam, H. (1990b) 'Emotional "Man" II. Corporate Actors as Emotion-motivated Emotion Managers', *International Sociology*, 5 (2): 225–34.
Forrester, John (1991) 'Psychoanalysis: Telepathy, Gossip and/or Science', in J. Donald (ed.), *Psychoanalysis and Cultural Theory: Thresholds*. Basingstoke: Macmillan.
Forrester, John (1997) *Dispatches from the Freud Wars*. Cambridge, MA: Harvard University Press.
Foucault, Michel (1965) *Madness and Civilization*. New York: Random House.
Foucault, Michel (1970) *The Order of Things*. London: Tavistock.
Foucault, Michel (1971) *The Birth of the Clinic*. London: Tavistock.
Foucault, Michel (1977) *Discipline and Punish*. London: Allen Unwin.
Freud, Anna (1936) *The Ego and the Mechanisms of Defense*. New York: International Universities Press.
Freud, Sigmund (with J. Breuer) (1895) *Studies in Hysteria*. vol. 3. Harmondsworth: Penguin.
Freud, Sigmund (1900) *The Interpretation of Dreams*, vol. 4. Harmondsworth: Penguin.
Freud, Sigmund (1901/1986) 'On Dreams', *The Essentials of Psycho-analysis*. Harmondsworth: Penguin.
Freud, Sigmund (1904) 'Freud's Psychoanalytic Procedure', *Standard Edition*, vol. 7. London: Hogarth Press.
Freud, Sigmund (1905a) *Jokes and their Relation to the Unconscious*, vol. 6. Harmondsworth: Penguin.
Freud, Sigmund (1905b) 'Three Essays on the Theory of Sexuality', in *Freud: On Sexuality*, vol. 7. Harmondsworth: Penguin.
Freud, Sigmund (1907a) 'Totem and Taboo', in *Freud: The Origins of Religion*, vol. 13. Harmondsworth: Penguin.
Freud, Sigmund (1907b) 'Obsessive Actions and Religious Practices', in *Freud: the Origins of Religion*, vol. 13. Harmondsworth: Penguin.
Freud, Sigmund (1908) 'Character and Anal Erotism', in *Freud: On Sexuality*, vol. 7. Harmondsworth: Penguin.
Freud, Sigmund (1910) 'Five Lectures on Psycho-Analysis', *Standard Edition*, vol. 11. London: Hogarth Press.
Freud, Sigmund (1913) 'The Claims of Psychoanalysis to Scientific Interest', in *Freud: Historical and Expository Works*, vol. 15. Harmondsworth: Penguin.
Freud, Sigmund (1914a) 'On Narcissism: An Introduction', in *Freud: On Metapsychology*, vol. 11. Harmondsworth: Penguin.
Freud, Sigmund (1914b) 'On the History of the Psychoanalytic Movement', *Standard Edition*, vol. 14. London: Hogarth Press.

Freud, Sigmund (1915a) 'Observations on Transference Love – Further Recommendations', *Standard Edition*, vol. 14. London: Hogarth Press.
Freud, Sigmund (1915b) 'The Unconscious', in *Freud: On Metapsychology*, vol. 11. Harmondsworth: Penguin.
Freud, Sigmund (1917) 'A Difficulty in the Path of Psycho-Analysis', *Standard Edition*, vol. 17. London: Hogarth Press.
Freud, Sigmund (1920) *Beyond the Pleasure Principle*, in *Freud: On Metapsychology*, vol. 11. Harmondsworth: Penguin.
Freud, Sigmund (1921) 'Group Psychology and the Analysis of the Ego', in *Freud: Civilization, Society and Religion*, vol. 12. Harmondsworth: Penguin.
Freud, Sigmund (1923) *The Ego and the Id*, in *Freud: On Metapsychology*, vol. 11. Harmondsworth: Penguin.
Freud, Sigmund (1924) 'The Dissolution of the Oedipus Complex', in *Freud: On Sexuality*, vol. 7. Harmondsworth: Penguin.
Freud, Sigmund (1925a) 'An Autobiographical Study', in *Freud: Historical and Expository Works*, vol. 15. Harmondsworth: Penguin.
Freud, Sigmund (1925b) 'Negation', in *Freud: On Metapsychology*, vol. 11. Harmondsworth: Penguin.
Freud, Sigmund (1926) *Inhibitions, Symptoms and Anxiety*, in *Freud: On Psychopathology*, vol. 10. Harmondsworth: Penguin.
Freud, Sigmund (1927) *The Future of an Illusion*, in *Freud: Civilization, Society and Religion*, vol. 12. Harmondsworth: Penguin.
Freud, Sigmund (1930) *Civilization and its Discontents*, in *Freud: Civilization, Society and Religion*, vol. 12. Harmondsworth: Penguin.
Freud, Sigmund (1933) *New Introductory Lectures on Psycho-analysis*, vol. 2. Harmondsworth: Penguin.
Freud, Sigmund (1937) 'Analysis Terminable and Interminable', *Standard Edition*, vol. 23. London: Hogarth Press.
Freud, Sigmund (1939) *Moses and Monotheism*, in *Freud: The Origins of Religion*, vol. 13. Harmondsworth: Penguin.
Freud, Sigmund (1940) *An Outline of Psycho-Analysis*, in *Freud: Historical and Expository Works*, vol. 15. Harmondsworth: Penguin.
Freud, Sigmund (1954) *The Origins of Psychoanalysis: Letters to Wilhelm Fliess, Drafts and Notes, 1887–1902*, ed. Marie Bonaparte, Anna Freud and Ernst Kris. New York: Basic Books.
Friedan, Betty (1965) *The Feminine Mystique*. Harmondsworth: Penguin.
Friedman, M. (1970) 'The Social Responsibility of Business is to Increase Profits', *New York Times Magazine*, 13 September: 122–6.
Fromm, Erich (1941/1966) *Escape from Freedom*. New York: Avon Library.
Frosh, S. (1987) *The Politics of Psychoanalysis*. Basingstoke: Macmillan.
Frosh, S. (1991) 'Psychoanalysis, Psychosis and Postmodernism', *Human Relations*, 44 (1): 93–104.
Frosh, S. (1997) *For and Against Psychoanalysis*. London: Routledge.
Frost, P. J., Moore, L. F., Louis, M. R., Lundberg, C. C. and Martin, J. (1991) *Reframing Organizational Culture*. London: Sage.
Gabriel, Yiannis (1982) 'Freud, Rieff and the Critique of American Culture', *Psychoanalytic Review*, 69 (3): 341–66.
Gabriel, Yiannis (1983) *Freud and Society*. London: Routledge.
Gabriel, Yiannis (1984) 'A Psychoanalytic Contribution to the Sociology of Suffering', *International Review of Psychoanalysis*, 11: 467–80.
Gabriel, Yiannis (1988) *Working Lives in Catering*. London: Routledge.
Gabriel, Yiannis (1991a) 'Turning Facts into Stories and Stories into Facts: a Hermeneutic Exploration of Organizational Folklore', *Human Relations*, 44 (8): 857–75.
Gabriel, Yiannis (1991b) 'On Organizational Stories and Myths: Why it is Easier to Slay a Dragon than to Kill a Myth', *International Sociology*, 6 (4): 427–42.
Gabriel, Yiannis (1991c) 'Organizations and their Discontents: a Psychoanalytic Contribution to the Study of Corporate Culture', *Journal of Applied Behavioral Science*, 27: 318–36.
Gabriel, Yiannis (1992) 'Heroes, Villains, Fools and Magic Wands: Computers in Organizational Folklore', *International Journal of Information Resource Management*, 3 (1): 3–12.

Gabriel, Yiannis (1993) 'Organizational Nostalgia: Reflections on "The Golden Age" ', in Stephen Fineman (ed.), *Emotion in Organizations*. London: Sage. pp. 118–41.
Gabriel, Yiannis (1995) 'The Unmanaged Organization: Stories, Fantasies and Subjectivity', *Organization Studies*, 16 (3): 477–501.
Gabriel, Yiannis (1997) 'Meeting God: When Organizational Members Come Face to Face with the Supreme Leader', *Human Relations*, 50 (4): 315–42.
Gabriel, Yiannis (1998a) 'The Use of Stories', in G. Symon and C. Cassell. (eds), *Qualitative Research Methods and Analysis in Organizational Research*. London: Sage.
Gabriel, Yiannis (1998b) 'The Same Old Story or Changing Stories? Folkloric, Modern and Postmodern Mutations', in D. Grant, T. Keenoy and C. Oswick (eds), *Discourse and Organization*. London: Sage.
Gabriel, Yiannis (1998c) 'The Hubris of Management', *Administrative Theory and Praxis*, 20 (3): 257–73.
Gabriel, Yiannis (1998d) 'An Introduction to the Social Psychology of Insults in Organizations', *Human Relations*, 51 (11): 1329–54.
Gabriel, Yiannis and Lang, Tim (1995) *The Unmanageable Consumer: Contemporary Consumption and its Fragmentation*. London: Sage.
Gay, P. (1988) *Freud: a Life for our Time*. London: Macmillan.
Gerth, H. H. and Mills, C. W. (1946) *From Max Weber: Essays in Sociology*. Oxford: Oxford University Press.
Gherardi, Silvia (1995) *Gender, Symbolism and Organizational Cultures*. Thousand Oaks, CA: Sage.
Gillette, J. and McCollom, M. (1990) *Groups in Context Reading*. Massachusetts: Addison Wesley.
Ginzburg, C. (1980) 'Morelli, Freud and Sherlock Holmes: Clues and Scientific Method', *History Workshop*, 9: 5–36.
Gleick, James (1987) *Chaos*. Harmondsworth: Penguin.
Goffman, E. (1959) *The Presentation of Self in Everyday Life*. Garden City, NJ: Anchor.
Goldizen, A.W. (1987) 'Tamarins and Marmosets: Communal Care of Offspring', in B. B. Smuts et al. (eds), *Primate Societies*. Chicago: University of Chicago Press pp. 34–43.
Gordon, T. and Greenspan, D. (1994) 'The Management of Chaotic Systems', *Technological Forecasting and Social Change*, 47 (1): 49–62.
Gould, Laurence J. (1991) 'Using Psychoanalytic Frameworks for Organizational Analysis', in M. F. R. Kets de Vries (ed.), *Organizations on the Couch*. San Francisco: Jossey-Bass.
Gould, Laurence J. (1993) 'Contemporary Perspectives on Personal and Organizational Authority: the Self in a System of Work Relationships', in Larry Hirschhorn and Carole K. Barnett (eds), *The Psychodynamics of Organizations*. Philadelphia, PA: Temple University Press.
Gould, Laurence J. (1997) 'Correspondences between Bion's Basic Assumption and Klein's Developmental Positions: an Outline', *Free Associations*, 7 (1): 15–30.
Gouldner, Alvin W. (1954) *Patterns of Industrial Bureaucracy*. Glencoe, IL: Free Press.
Grant, David and Oswick, Cliff (eds) (1996) *Metaphor and Organizations*. London: Sage.
Greenwood, D. J., Whyte, W. F. and Harkavy, I. (1994) 'Participatory Action Research as a Process and a Goal', *Human Relations*, 46 (2): 175–92.
Gregersen, H. B. and Sailer, L. (1993) 'Chaos Theory and its Implications for Social Research', *Human Relations*, 46 (7): 777–802.
Grey, C. (1994) 'Career as a Project of the Self and Labour Process Discipline', *Sociology*, 28 (2): 479–97.
Grey, C. and Mitev, N. (1995) 'Management Education: a Polemic', *Management Learning*, 26 (1): 73–90.
Grünbaum, A. (1984) *The Foundations of Psychoanalysis: a Philosophical Critique*. Berkeley, CA: University of California Press.
Grünbaum, A. (1988) 'Are Hidden Motives in Psychoanalysis Reasons but not Causes of Human Conduct?', in S. Messer, L. Sass and R. Woolfolk (eds), *Hermeneutics and Psychological Theory*. New Brunswick, NJ: Rutgers University Press. pp. 149–67.
Guntrip, Harry (1971) *Psychoanalytic Theory, Therapy, and the Self*. New York: Basic Books.
Habermas, J. (1970/1976) 'Systematically Distorted Communication', in P. Connerton (ed.), *Critical Sociology*. Harmondsworth: Penguin. pp. 348–62.
Hacking, Ian (1990) *The Taming of Chance*. Cambridge: Cambridge University Press.

Hall, Richard H. (1987) *Organizations: Structures, Processes and Outcomes*, 3rd edn. Englewood Cliffs, NJ: Prentice-Hall.
Handy, C. (1986) *Understanding Organizations*. Harmondsworth: Penguin.
Handy, C. (1988) *Understanding Voluntary Organizations*. Harmondsworth: Penguin.
Hansen, C. D. and Kahnweiler, W. M. (1993) 'Storytelling: an Instrument for Understanding the Dynamics of Corporate Relationships', *Human Relations*, 46 (12): 1391–409.
Harrison, R. (1972) 'How to Describe your Organization', *Harvard Business Review*, Sept.–Oct.
Harrison, R. (1987) *Organization Culture and Quality of Service: A Strategy for Releasing Love in the Workplace*. London: Association of Management Education & Development Publications.
Hartmann, Heinz (1960) *Psychoanalysis and Moral Values*. New York: International Universities Press.
Hartmann, Heinz (1964) *Essays on Ego Psychology*. New York: International Universities Press.
Harvey-Jones, J. (1988) *Making it Happen*. Glasgow: Fontana.
Hassard, J. and Parker, M. (eds) (1993) *Postmodernism and Organizations*. London: Sage.
Hatch, Mary Jo (1997) *Organization Theory: Modern, Symbolic and Postmodern Perspectives*. Oxford: Oxford University Press.
Heller, Agnes (1979) *A Theory of Feelings*. The Netherlands: Van Gorkum Assen.
Helmers, S. (1993) 'The Occurrence of Exoticism in Organizational Literature', EGOS Conference, Paris, 6–8 July.
Hicks, David and Gwynne, Margaret A. (1994) *Cultural Anthropology*. New York: HarperCollins.
Hinschelwood, R. D. (1989) *A Dictionary of Kleinian Thought*. London: Free Association Books.
Hirsch, P. M. (1986) 'From Ambushes to Golden Parachutes: Corporate Takeovers as an Instance of Cultural Framing and Institutional Integration', *American Journal of Sociology*, 91 (4): 800–37.
Hirschhorn, L. (1985) 'The Psychodynamics of Taking the Role in Group Relations', in Arthur D. Colmann and Marvin H. Geller (eds), *Reader 2*. Washington, DC: A. K. Rice Institute.
Hirschhorn, L. (1988) *The Workplace Within*. Cambridge, MA: MIT Press.
Hirschhorn, L. (1993) 'Professionals, Authority, and Group Life: a Case Study of a Law Firm', in L. Hirschhorn and C. K. Barnett (eds), *The Psychodynamics of Organizations*. Philadelphia, PA: Temple University Press.
Hirschhorn, L. (1997) *Reworking Authority: Leading and Following in the Post-Modern Organization*. Cambridge, MA: MIT Press.
Hirschhorn, L. and Gilmore, T. N. (1993) 'The Psychodynamics of a Cultural Change: Learning from a Factory', in L. Hirschhorn and C. K. Barnett (eds) *The Psychodynamics of Organizations*. Philadelphia, PA: Temple University Press.
Hirschhorn, L. and Young, D. R. (1993) 'The Psychodynamics of Safety: a Case Study of an Oil Refinery', in L. Hirschhorn and C. K. Barnett (eds), *The Psychodynamics of Organizations*. Philadelphia, PA: Temple University Press.
Hochschild, A. (1983) *The Managed Heart*. Berkeley, CA: University of California Press.
Hochschild, A. (1989) *The Second Shift*. New York: Viking.
Hofstede, G. (1991) *Cultures and Organizations: Software of the Mind*. London: McGraw-Hill.
Hoggett, P. (1992) *Partisans in an Uncertain World: the Psychoanalysis of Engagement*. London: Free Association Books.
Hopfl, H. (1992) 'The Making of the Corporate Acolyte', *Journal of Management Studies*, 29 (1): 23–34.
Hopfl, H. and Linstead, S. (1997) 'Learning to Feel and Feeling to Learn: Emotion and Learning in Organizations', *Management Learning*, 28 (1): 5–12.
Horwitz, Leonard (1996) 'Narcissistic Leadership in Psychotherapy Groups', presentation at the Los Angeles Group Psychotherapy Society.
Huczynski, Andrej and Buchanan, David (1991) *Organizational Behaviour*, 2nd edn. London: Prentice-Hall.
Humphrey, G. and Humphrey, M. (1932) *The Wild Boy of Aveyron*. New York: Appleton-Century-Crofts.
Iaccoca, L. (1984) *An Autobiography*. New York: Bantam.
Isaacs, Susan (1948) 'The Nature and Function of Phantasy', *International Journal of Psycho-analysis*, 29: 73–97.
Jackall, R. (1988) *Moral Mazes: the World of Corporate Managers*. Oxford: Oxford University Press.
Jahoda, M. (1977) *Freud and the Dilemmas of Psychology*. London: Hogarth Press.

Janis, I. L. (1972) *Victims of Groupthink*. Boston, MA.: Houghton Mifflin.
Jaques, E. (1952) *The Changing Culture of the Factory*. London: Tavistock.
Jaques, E. (1955) 'Social Systems as a Defence against Persecutory and Depressive Anxiety', in M. Klein, P. Heimann and R. E. Money-Kyrle (eds), *New Directions in Psychoanalysis*. London: Tavistock.
Jaques, E. (1995) 'Why the Psychoanalytical Approach to Understanding Organizations is Dysfunctional', *Human Relations*, 48: 343–65.
Jay, Martin (1973) *The Dialectical Imagination*. London: Heinemann.
Jermier, J. M., Knights, D. and Nord, W. R. (eds) (1994) *Resistance and Power in Organizations*. London: Routledge.
Johnson, Craig (ed.) (1991) *Psychodynamic Treatment of Anorexia Nervosa*. London: Guildford Press.
Jones, E. (1916) 'The Theory of Symbolism' *Papers on Psycho-analysis* (1948). London: Tindall and Cox.
Jones, E. (1953–7) *Sigmund Freud: Life and Work*, 3 vols. London: Hogarth Press.
Jung, C. G. (1964) *Man and his Symbols*. London: Aldus Books.
Jung, C. G. (1968) *The Archetypes and the Collective Unconscious*, vol. 9. London: Routledge.
Jung, C. G. (1971) *Psychological Types*, vol. 6, *Collected Works*, 2nd edn. London: Routledge.
Kanter, R. M. (1983) *The Change Masters*. New York: Simon and Shuster.
Kaplan, Harvey Al (1997) 'Moral Outrage: Virtue as a Defense', *Psychoanalytic Review*, 84: 55–71.
Kaplan, Louise (1986) *Adolescence*. Northvale, NJ: Jason Aronson.
Kapuscinski, Ryszard (1983) *The Emperor*. London: Picador.
Kaufmann, Walter (1980) *Discovering the Mind, vol. 3: Freud, Adler and Jung*. New Brunswick, NJ: Transaction Publishers.
Kauffmann, S.A. (1993) *Origins of Order: Self-Organization and Selection in Evolution*. Oxford: Oxford University Press.
Kauffmann, S.A. (1995) *At Home in the Universe*. Oxford: Oxford University Press.
Keen, S. (1992) *Fire in the Belly: On Being a Man*. London: Piatkus.
Kenney, M. and Florida, A. (1993) *Beyond Mass Production*. Oxford: Oxford University Press.
Kernberg, Otto F. (1979) 'Regression in Organizational Leadership', *Psychiatry*, 42: 24–39.
Kernberg, Otto F. (1991) 'The Moral Dimensions of Leadership', in Saul Tuttman (ed.), *Psychoanalytic Group Theory and Therapy: Essays in Honor of Saul Scheidlinger*. Madison, CT: International Universities Press.
Kernberg, Otto F. (1993) 'Paranoiagenesis in Organizations', in Harold Kaplan and Benjamin Sadock (eds), *Comprehensive Group Psychotherapy*, 3rd edn. Baltimore, MD: Williams and Wilkins. pp. 47–57.
Kernberg, Otto F. (1994a) 'Mass Psychology through the Analytic Lens', in Arlene K. Richards and Arnold D. Richards (eds), *The Spectrum of Psychoanalysis: Essays in Honor of Martin S. Bergmann*. Madison, CT: International Universities Press.
Kernberg, Otto F. (1994b) 'Leadership Styles and Organizational Paranoiagenesis', in J. Oldham and S. Bone (eds), *Paranoia: New Psychoanalytic Perspectives*. Madison, CT: International Universities Press.
Kernberg, Otto F. (1998) *Ideology, Conflict, and Leadership in Groups and Organizations*. New Haven, CT: Yale University Press.
Kets de Vries, M. F. R. (1990) 'The Organizational Fool: Balancing a Leader's Hubris', *Human Relations*, 43 (8): 751–70.
Kets de Vries, M. F. R. and Miller, Danny (1984) *The Neurotic Organization*. San Francisco: Jossey-Bass.
Kets de Vries, M. F. R. and Miller, D. (1991) 'Leadership Styles and Organizational Cultures: the Shaping of Neurotic Organizations', in M. F. R. Kets de Vries (ed.), *Organizations on the Couch*. San Francisco: Jossey-Bass. pp. 243–63.
Kilduff, M. (1993) 'Deconstructing Organizations', *Academy of Management Review*, 18: 13–31.
Klein, Melanie (1935/1986) 'A Contribution to the Psychogenesis of Manic-Depressive States', in Juliet Mitchell (ed.), *The Selected Writings of Melanie Klein*. New York: Free Press.
Klein, Melanie (1940/1986) 'Mourning and its Relation to Manic-depressive States', in Juliet Mitchell (ed.), *The Selected Writings of Melanie Klein*. New York: Free Press.
Klein, Melanie (1946/1986) 'Notes on Some Schizoid Mechanisms', in Juliet Mitchell (ed.), *The Selected Writings of Melanie Klein*. New York: Free Press.

Klein, Melanie (1956/1986) 'A Study of Envy and Gratitude', in Juliet Mitchell (ed.), *The Selected Writings of Melanie Klein*. New York: Free Press.
Klein, Melanie, and Riviere, Joan (1964) *Love, Hate and Reparation*. New York: Norton.
Kohut, Heinz (1971) *The Analysis of the Self: a Systematic Approach to the Psychoanalytic Treatment of Narcissistic Personality Disorders*. New York: International Universities Press.
Kohut, Heinz (1985) *Self Psychology and the Humanities: Reflections on a New Psychoanalytic Approach*, ed. Charles B. Strozier. New York: Norton.
Krantz, J. (1989) 'The Managerial Couple: Superior– Subordinate Relationships as a Unit of Analysis', *Human Resource Management*, 28 (2): 161–76.
Krantz, J. (1990) 'Lessons from the Field: an Essay on the Crisis of Leadership in Contemporary Organizations', *Journal of Applied Behavioral Science*, 26 (1): 49–64.
Krober, A. L. and Kluckholn, C. (1952) *Culture: A Critical Review of Concepts and Definitions*. New York: Vintage.
Kunda, Gideon (1992) *Engineering Culture: Control and Commitment in a High-Tech Corporation*. Philadelphia, PA: Temple University Press.
Kvale, S. (1992) 'Postmodern Psychology: a Contradiction in Terms?' in S. Kvale (ed.), *Psychology and Postmodernism*. London: Sage. pp. 31–57.
La Barre, Weston (1979) 'Species-specific Biology, Magic and Religion', in R. H. Hook (ed.), *Fantasy and Symbol*. London: Academic Press.
La Bier, D. (1986) *Modern Madness: the Emotional Fallout of Success*. Reading, MA: Addison-Wesley.
Lacan, J. (1968) *Speech and Language in Psychoanalysis*, trans. A. Wilden. Baltimore, MD: Johns Hopkins University Press.
Lacan, J. (1977) *Ecrits: a Selection*. London: Tavistock.
Lacan, J. (1978) *The Four Fundamental Concepts of Psychoanalysis*. New York: Norton.
Lapierre, Laurent (1989) 'Mourning, Potency, and Power in Management', *Human Resource Management*, 28 (2): 177–89.
Lapierre, L. (1991) 'Exploring the Dynamics of Leadership', in M.F. R. Kets de Vries (ed.), *Organizations on the Couch*. San Francisco: Jossey-Bass. pp. 69–93.
Laplanche, J. and Pontalis, J. (1988) *The Language of Psychoanalysis*, trans. D. Nicholson-Smith. London: Karnac.
Lasch, Christopher (1980) *The Culture of Narcissism*. London: Abacus.
Lasch, Christopher (1984) *The Minimal Self: Psychic Survival in Troubled Times*. London: Pan.
Lasch, Christopher (1991) *The True and Only Heaven: Progress and its Critics*. New York: Norton.
Lawrence, J. (1991) 'Action Learning – a Questioning Approach', in A. Mumford (ed.), *Gower Handbook of Management Development*, 3rd edn. London: Gower.
Lawrence, W. G. (1977/1985) 'Management Development: Some Ideals, Images and Realities', in A. D. Colman and M. H. Geller (eds), *Group Relations Reader*. Washington, DC: A. K. Rice Institute.
Lawrence, W. G. (1979) 'A Concept for Today: the Management of Oneself in Role', in W. G. Lawrence (ed.), *Exploring Individual and Organizational Boundaries: a Tavistock Open Systems Approach*. Chichester: Wiley.
Lawrence, W. G. (1991) 'Won from the Void and Formless Infinite: Experiences of Social Dreaming', *Free Associations*, 2 (2): 259–94.
Lawrence, W. G., Bain, A. and Gould, L. J. (1996) 'The Fifth Basic Assumption', *Free Associations*, 6 (1): 28–55.
Lear, Jonathan (1995) 'The Shrink is In', *The New Republic*, 25 December.
Le Bon, Gustave (1895/1960) *The Crowd: a Study of the Popular Mind*. New York: Viking Press.
Levinson, Harry (1959/1980) *Identity and the Life Cycle: a Reissue*. New York: Norton.
Levinson, Harry (1968/1981) *Executive*. Cambridge, MA: Harvard University Press.
Levinson, Harry (1972) *Organizational Diagnosis*. Cambridge, MA: Harvard University Press.
Levinson, Harry (1976) *Psychological Man*. Cambridge, MA: Levinson Institute.
Levinson, Harry (1984) 'Management by Guilt', in M. Kets de Vries (ed.), *The Irrational Executive: Psychoanalytic Exploration in Management*. New York: International Universities Press.
Levinson, Harry (1991) 'Diagnosing Organizations Systematically', in M. Kets de Vries (ed.), *Organizations on the Couch*. San Francisco: Jossey-Bass. pp. 243–63.
Levi-Strauss, Claude (1963/1968) 'The Structural Study of Myth', in Levi-Strauss, Claude (ed.), *Structural Anthropology*, vol. 1. Harmondsworth: Penguin.

Lindholm, Charles (1988) 'Lovers and Leaders: a Comparison of Social and Psychological Models of Romance and Charisma', *Social Science Information*, 27 (1): 3–45.
Loevinger, Jane (1976) *Ego Development: Conceptions and Theories*. San Francisco: Jossey-Bass.
Lorenzer, A. (1970) *Symbol und Verstehen in Psychoanalytischen Prozess*. Frankfurt: Suhrkamp Verlag.
Løvlie, L. (1992) 'Postmodernism and Subjectivity', in S. Kvale (ed.), *Psychology and Postmodernism*. London: Sage. pp. 119–34.
McConnell, M. (1987) *Challenger: a Major Malfunction*. New York: Doubleday.
McCracken, Grant (1990) *Culture and Consumption: New Approaches to the Symbolic Character of Consumer Goods and Activities*. Bloomington, IN: Indiana University Press.
McCurdy, H. E. (1993) *Inside NASA: High Technology and Organizational Change in the US Space Program*. Baltimore, MD: Johns Hopkins University Press.
Maccoby, M. (1976) *The Gamesman*. New York: Simon and Schuster.
Machiavelli, N. (1961) *The Prince*. Harmondsworth: Penguin.
Machiavelli, N. (1983) *The Discourses*. Harmondsworth: Penguin.
MacIntyre, Alasdair (1981/1985) *After Virtue*. London: Duckworth.
Mahler, Julianne (1988) 'The Quest for Organizational Meaning: Identifying and Interpreting the Symbolism in Organizational Stories', *Administration and Society*, 20: 344–68.
Malinowski, B. (1922/1961) *Argonauts of the Western Pacific*. London: Routledge.
Malinowski, B. (1927) *Sex and Repression in Savage Society*. London: Routledge.
Mandelbrot, B. (1982) *The Fractal Geometry of Nature*. San Francisco: Freeman.
Mangham, I. L. (1986) *Power and Performance in Organizations: an Exploration of Executive Process*. Oxford: Blackwell.
Mangham, I. L. (1995) 'MacIntyre and the Manager', *Organization*, 2 (2): 181–204.
Mangham, I. L. and Overington, M. A. (1987) *Organizations as Theatre: a Social Psychology of Dramatic Appearances*. Chichester: John Wiley.
Mangham, I. L. and Pye, A. J. (1991) *The Doing of Managing*. Oxford: Blackwell.
Mannoni, O. (1971) *Freud*. New York: Random House.
Mant, A. (1977) *The Rise and Fall of the British Manager*. London: Macmillan.
March, J. G. and Olsen, J. P. (1976) *Ambiguity and Choice in Organizations*. Bergen: Universitetsforlaget.
Marcuse, Herbert (1955) *Eros and Civilization*. New York: Vintage Books.
Marcuse, Herbert (1964) *One Dimensional Man*. Boston: Beacon Press
Mayer, J. P. (1956) *Max Weber and German Politics*. London: Faber.
Menzies, Isabel (1960) 'A Case Study in Functioning of Social Systems as a Defence against Anxiety', *Human Relations*, 13: 95–121.
Menzies Lyth, Isabel (1988) *Containing Anxiety in Institutions: Selected Essays*. London: Free Association Books.
Menzies Lyth, Isabel (1989) *The Dynamics of the Social: Selected Essays*, vol. 2. London: Free Association Books.
Menzies Lyth, Isabel (1991) 'Changing Organizations and Individuals: Psychoanalytic Insights for Improving Organizational Health', in M. F. R. Kets de Vries (ed.), *Organizations on the Couch*. San Francisco: Jossey-Bass.
Meyer, J. W. and Rowan, B. (1977) 'Institutionalized Organizations: Formal Structure as Myth and Ceremony', *American Journal of Sociology*, 83: 340–63.
Milgram, S. (1974) *Obedience to Authority*. New York: Harper and Row.
Miller, E. J. (1993) *From Dependence to Autonomy: Studies in Organization and Change*. London: Free Association Books.
Miller, E. J. and Rice, A. K. (1967) *Systems of Organization*. London: John Wiley.
Miller, N. and Morgan, D. (1993) 'Called to Account: the CV as Autobiographical Practice', *Sociology*, 27: 133–43.
Minsky, Rosalind (ed.) (1996) *Psychoanalysis and Gender: an Introductory Reader*. London: Routledge.
Mitchell, Juliet (1974) *Feminism and Psychoanalysis*. Harmondsworth: Penguin.
Mitchell, Stephen A. and Black, Margaret J. (1995) *Freud and Beyond: a History of Modern Psychoanalytic Thought*. New York: Basic Books.
Mitroff, I. I. (1984) *Stakeholders of the Mind*. San Francisco: Jossey-Bass.
Mitroff, I. I. and Kilmann, Ralph H. (1976) 'On Organization Stories: an Approach to the Design and Analysis of Organizations through Myths and Stories', in Ralph H. Kilmann,

Louis R. Pondy and Dennis Slevin (eds), *The Management of Organization Design*. New York: New Holland.
Morgan, Gareth (1986) *Images of Organization*. Beverly Hills, CA: Sage.
Morita, A. (1987) *Made in Japan*. London: Fontana.
Mumby, Dennis K. and Putnam, Linda L. (1992) 'The Politics of Emotion', *Academy of Management Review*, 17: 465–86.
Nonaka, I. (1991) 'The Knowledge Creating Company', *Harvard Business Review*, Nov.–Dec.
Nonaka, I. and Takeuchi, H. (1995) *The Knowledge Creating Company: How Japanese Companies Create the Dynamics of Innovation*. Oxford: Oxford University Press.
Norris, C. (1987) *Derrida*. London: Fontana.
Nunberg, H. (1955) *Principles of Psychoanalysis*. New York: International Universities Press.
Nystrom, P. C. and Starbuck, W. H. (1984) 'To Avoid Organizational Crises, Unlearn', *Organizational Dynamics*, 12 (4): 53–65.
Obholzer, Anton (1994) 'Managing Social Anxieties in Public Sector Organizations', in A. Obholzer and V. Z. Roberts (eds), *The Unconscious at Work: Individual and Organizational Stress in the Human Services*. London: Routledge.
Obholzer, Anton and Roberts, Vega Zagier (1994) *The Unconscious at Work: Individual and Organizational Stress in the Human Services*. London: Routledge.
O'Connor, M. (1994) 'Complexity and Coevolution: Methodology for a Positive Treatment of Indeterminacy', *Futures*, 26 (6): 610–15.
Oglensky, Bonnie D. (1995) 'Socio-Psychoanalytic Perspectives on the Subordinate', *Human Relations*, 48 (9): 1029–54.
Orbach, S. (1978) *Fat is a Feminist Issue*. London: Hamlyn.
Orbach, S. (1986) *Hunger Strike: the Anorectic's Struggle as a Metaphor for our Age*. London: Faber and Faber.
Orbach, S. (1997) 'The Thin End of the Wedge', *Guardian*, G2: 4–5, 23 October.
Ottmann, H. (1982) 'Cognitive Interests and Self-reflection', in J. Thompson and D. Held (eds), *Habermas: Critical Debates*. Cambridge, MA: MIT Press. pp. 79–97.
Ouchi, W. A. (1981) *Theory Z: How American Business Can Meet the Japanese Challenge*. Reading, MA: Addison-Wesley.
Parker, M. (1982) 'Post-modern Organizations or Postmodern Theory?', *Organization Studies*, 13 (1): 1–17.
Pascale, R. and Athos, A. (1981) *The Art of Japanese Management*. Harmondsworth: Penguin.
Pastin, Mark (1986) *The Hard Problems of Management: Gaining the Ethics Edge*. San Francisco: Jossey-Bass.
Pedler, M. (1981) 'The Diffusion of Action Learning', Sheffield City Polytechnic, occasional paper no. 2.
Perry, T. S. (1995) 'Managed Chaos Allows More Creativity', *Research-Technology Management*, 38 (5): 14–17.
Peters, Tom (1987) *Thriving on Chaos: Handbook for a Management Revolution*. Basingstoke: Macmillan.
Peters, T. J. and Waterman, R. H. (1982) *In Search of Excellence*. New York: Harper and Row.
Pines, M. (ed.) (1985) *Bion and Group Psychotherapy*. London: Routledge and Kegan Paul.
Popper, Karl R. (1965) *Conjectures and Refutations: the Growth of Scientific Knowledge*, 2nd edn. New York: Basic Books.
Portelli, Alessandro (1990) 'Uchronic Dreams: Working Class Memory and Possible Worlds', in Raphael Samuel and Paul Thompson (eds), *The Myths We Live By*. London: Routledge.
Pusey, A.E. and Packer, C. (1987) 'Dispersal and Philopatry', in B. B. Smuts et al. (eds), *Primate Societies*. Chicago: University of Chicago Press. pp. 250–66.
Putnam, Linda L. and Mumby, Dennis K. (1993) 'Organizations, Emotion and the Myth of Rationality', in S. Fineman (ed.), *Emotion in Organizations*. London: Sage.
Quine, C. and Hutton, J. M. (1992) 'Finding, Making and Taking the Role of Head', presentation to the East Midlands Nine Consortium of LEAs Initial Seminar on Headteacher Mentoring, 16 January.
Racker, Heinrich (1968) *Transference and Countertransference*. New York: International Universities Press.
Rangell, Leo (1974) 'A Psychoanalytic Perspective Leading Currently to the Syndrome of the Compromise of Integrity', *International Journal of Psychoanalysis*, 55: 3–12.

Reed, B. D. (1976) 'Organizational Role Analysis', in C. L. Cooper (ed.), *Developing Social Skills in Managers: Advances in Group Training*. London: Macmillan.
Reich, W. (1970) *The Mass Psychology of Fascism*. New York: Farrar, Strauss and Giroux.
Renshon, S.A. (1996) *High Hopes: The Clinton Presidency and the Politics of Ambition*. Boulder, CO: Westview Press.
Renshon, Stanley A. (1998) quoted in Todd S. Purdum, 'Strong as Politics, Weakened by Lapses', *The New York Times*, 18 August
Revans, R. (1983) *The ABC of Action Learning*. London: Chartwell-Bratt.
Rice, A. K. (1963) *The Enterprise and its Environment*. London: Tavistock.
Rice, A .K. (1965) 'Individual, Group and Intergroup Processes', *Human Relations*, 22: 565–584.
Ricoeur, P. (1965 (1976) 'Hermeneutics: Restoration of Meaning or Reduction of Illusion?', reprinted in P. Connerton (ed.), *Critical Sociology*. Harmondsworth: Penguin. pp. 194–203.
Ricoeur, P. (1970) *Freud and Philosophy: an Essay on Interpretation*. New Haven, CT: Yale University Press.
Rieff, Philip (1959) *Freud: the Mind of a Moralist*. New York: Doubleday.
Rieff, Philip (1966) *The Triumph of the Therapeutic*. New York: Harper and Row.
Robbins, S. R. (1998) *Organizational Behavior: Concepts, Controversies, Applications*, 8th edn. Upper Saddle River, NJ: Prentice-Hall.
Roberts, Vega Zagier (1994) 'The Organization of Work', in A. Obholzer and V. Z. Roberts (eds), *The Unconscious at Work: Individual and Organizational Stress in the Human Services*. London: Routledge.
Robinson, P. (1993) *Freud and his Critics*. Berkeley, CA: University of California Press.
Roddick, A. (1991) *Body and Soul*. London: Edbury Press.
Rogers, W. P. (1986) Report of the Presidential Commission on the Space Shuttle Challenger Accident. Washington, DC: US Government Printing Office.
Rose, N. (1989) *Governing the Soul: the Shaping of the Private Self*. London: Routledge.
Ruelle, D. (1988) 'Can Nonlinear Dynamics Help Economists?', in P. W. Anderson, K. J. Arrow and D. Pines (eds), *The Economy as an Evolving Complex System*, vol. 5. Santa Fe Institute, Studies in the Science of Complexity. Redwood City, CA: Addison-Wesley.
Ruelle, D. (1991) *Chance and Chaos*. Princeton, NJ: Princeton University Press.
Rycroft, Charles (1968) *A Critical Dictionary of Psychoanalysis*. London: Nelson.
Saas, L. (1992) 'The Epic of Disbelief: the Postmodernist Turn in Contemporary Psychoanalysis', in S. Kvale (ed.), *Psychology and Postmodernism*. London: Sage. pp. 166–81.
Sandler, Joseph and Sandler, Anne-Marie (1994) 'Phantasy and its Transformations: a Contemporary Freudian View', *International Journal of Psycho-analysis*, 75: 387–94.
Scheff, Thomas J. (1990) *Microsociology: Discourse, Emotion, and Social Structure*. Chicago: University of Chicago Press.
Schein, E. H. (1968/1988) 'Organizational Socialization and the Profession of Management', *Sloan Management Review*, reprinted in Fall 1988, pp. 53–65 (originally pub. 1968).
Schein, E. H. (1985) *Organizational Culture and Leadership*. San Francisco: Jossey-Bass.
Schneider, Susan C. (1991) 'Managing Boundaries in Organizations', in M. F. R. Kets de Vries (ed.), *Organizations on the Couch*. San Francisco: Jossey-Bass.
Schorske, Carl E. (1961) *Fin-de-Siècle Vienna: Politics and Culture*. New York: Random House.
Schumacher, E. F. (1973) *Small is Beautiful*. London: Abacus.
Schwartz, H. S. (1983) 'Maslow and the Hierarchical Enactment of Organizational Reality', *Human Relations*, 36 (10): 933–56.
Schwartz, H. S. (1985) 'The Usefulness of Myth and the Myth of Usefulness: a Dilemma for the Applied Organizational Scientist', *Journal of Management*, 11 (1): 31–42.
Schwartz, H. S. (1987) 'Anti-social Actions of Committed Organizational Participants: an Existential Psychoanalytic Perspective', *Organization Studies*, 8: 327–40.
Schwartz, H. S. (1990) *Narcissistic Process and Corporate Decay*. New York: University of New York Press.
Schwartz, H. S. (1995) 'Review of D. M. Boje and R. F. Dennehy "Managing in the Postmodern World" (1993)' *Academy of Management Review*, 20 (1): 215–21.
Segal, Hanna (1964) *An Introduction to the Work of Melanie Klein*. London: Heinemann.
Segal, Hanna (1979) *Klein*. London: Fontana.
Selznick, P. (1957) *Leadership in Administration*. New York: Harper and Row.
Senge, P. (1990) *The Fifth Discipline: the Art and Practice of the Learning Organization*. New York: Doubleday.

Sennett, Richard (1977) *The Fall of Public Man*. New York: Alfred A. Knopf.
Sennett, Richard (1980) *Authority*. New York: Alfred A. Knopf.
Shepherd, Michael (1985) *Sherlock Holmes and the Case of Dr Freud*. London: Tavistock.
Showalter, Elaine (1997) *Hystories: Hysterical Epidemics in Modern Culture*. New York: Columbia University Press.
Sievers, B. (1986) 'Beyond the Surrogate of Motivation', *Organization Studies*, 7 (4): 335–51.
Sievers, B. (1990) 'Thoughts on the Relatedness of Work, Death and Life Itself', *European Journal of Management*, 8 (3): 321–4.
Sievers, B. (1994) *Work, Death, and Life Itself*. Berlin: Walter de Gruyter.
Sievers, B. (1998) 'Psychotic Organization as a Metaphoric Frame for the Study of Organizational and Interorganizational Dynamics', *Symposium of the International Society for the Psychoanalytic Study of Organizations*, Jerusalem, 1–3 July.
Simmel, Georg (1971) *Georg Simmel: On Individuality and Social Form*. Chicago: Chicago University Press.
Simons, H. W. (1989) *Rhetoric in the Human Sciences*. London: Sage.
Sims, D., Fineman, S. and Gabriel, Y. (1993) *Organizing and Organizations*. London: Sage.
Singh, J. A. L. and Zingg, R. M. (1942) *Wolf-children and Feral Man*. London: Archon Books.
Skogemann, P. (1987) *Kvinnlighet i utveckling*. Stockholm: Forum.
Slater, Philip E. (1966) *Microcosm: Structural, Psychological and Religious Evolution in Groups*. New York: John Wiley.
Smith, A. (1776/1970) *The Wealth of Nations*. Harmondsworth: Penguin.
Smith, V. (1990) *Managing in Corporate Interest: Control and Resistance in an American Bank*. Berkeley, CA: University of California Press.
Sokal, Alan and Bricmont, Jean (1998) *Intellectual Impostures*. London: Profile Books.
Spence, Donald P. (1987) *The Freudian Metaphor: Toward Paradigm Change in Psychoanalysis*. New York: Norton.
Stacey, Ralph D. (1992) *Managing Chaos: Dynamic Business Strategies in an Unpredictable World*. London: Kogan Page.
Stacey, Ralph D. (1995) 'The Science of Complexity: an Alternative Perspective for Strategic Change Processes', *Strategic Management Journal*, 16: 477–95.
Stacey, Ralph D. (1996) *Strategic Management and Organizational Dynamics*, 2nd edn. London: Pitman.
States, B. (1988) *The Rhetoric of Dreams*. Ithaca, NY: Cornell University Press.
Staub, Hugo and Alexander, Franz (1929, 1962) *The Criminal, the Judge, and the Public*. New York: Collier Books.
Steele, R. (1979) 'Psychoanalysis and Hermeneutics', *International Review of Psychoanalysis*, 6: 389–411.
Stein, Howard F. (1994) 'Workplace Organizations and Culture Theory: a Psychoanalytic Approach', *Symposium of the International Society for the Psychoanalytic Study of Organizations*, Chicago, 2–4 June.
Stein, Ruth (1991) *Psychoanalytic Theories of Affect*. London: Praeger.
Stewart, I. and Cohen, J. (1994) 'Why are There Simple Rules in a Complicated Universe?', *Futures*, 26 (6): 648–64.
Stokes, Jon (1994) 'Institutional and Personal Stress', in A. Obholzer and V. Z. Roberts (eds), *The Unconscious at Work: Individual and Organizational Stress in the Human Services*. London: Routledge.
Sulloway, F. J. (1996) *Born to Rebel: Birth Order, Family Dynamics and Creative Lives*. New York: Pantheon.
Swogger, Glenn, Jr (1993) 'Group Self-esteem and Group Performance', in L. Hirschhorn and C. K. Barnett (eds), *The Psychodynamics of Organizations*. Philadelphia, PA: Temple University Press.
Swogger, Glenn, Jr (1994) 'The Open Society and its Discontents: Psychoanalytic Perspectives on Environmental Concerns', *Technology: Journal of the Franklin Institute*, 331A: 67–75.
Swogger, Glenn, Jr, Johnson, E. and Post, J. (1988) 'Issues of Retirement from Leadership in a Family Business', *Bulletin of the Menninger Clinic*, 52: 150–7.
Thietart, R. A. and Forgues, B. (1995) 'Chaos Theory and Organization', *Organization Science*, 6 (1): 19–31.
Thietart, R. A. and Forgues, B. (1997) 'Action, Structure, and Chaos Theory', *Organization Studies*, 18 (1): 119–43.

Thomas, Alan B. (1993) *Controversies in Management*. London: Routledge.
Thomas, D. A. (1993) 'Mentoring and Irrationality: the Role of Racial Taboos', in L. Hirschhorn and C. K. Barnett (eds) *The Psychodynamics of Organizations*. Philadelphia, PA: Temple University Press.
Tolstoy, Leo (1869/1982) *War and Peace*, trans. Rosemary Edmonds. Harmondsworth: Penguin.
Torbert, W. R. (1991) *The Power of Balance: Transforming Self, Society and Scientific Inquiry*. San Francisco: Sage.
Townley, Barbara (1993) 'Foucault, Power/Knowledge and its Relevance for Human Resource Management', *Academy of Management Review*, 18 (3): 518–45.
Trento, Joseph J. (1987) *Prescription for Disaster: from the Glory of Apollo to the Betrayal of the Shuttle*. New York: Crown.
Trilling, Lionel (1955) *Freud and the Crisis of our Culture*. Boston: Beacon Press.
Trist, E. L. and Murray, H. (eds) (1990) *The Social Engagement of Social Science*, vol. 1. London: Free Association Press.
Trist, E. L. and Sofer, C. (1959) *Exploration in Group Relations*. Leicester: Leicester University Press.
Tse, N. S. F. and Robb, F. F. (1994) 'Dynamical-systems Theory Applied to Management Accounting: Chaos in Cost Behavior in a Standard Costing System Setting', *Transactions of the Institute of Measurement and Control*, 16 (5): 269–79.
Turner, B. A. (1971) *Exploring the Industrial Sub-culture*. London: Macmillan.
Turner, B. A. (1978) *Man-made Disasters*. London: Wykeham.
Turner, B. A. (1983) 'The Use of Grounded Theory for the Qualitative Analysis of Organizational Behaviour', *Journal of Management Studies*, 20 (3): 333–48.
Turner, B. A. (1986) 'Sociological Aspects of Organizational Symbolism', *Organization Studies*, 7 (2): 101–15.
Turner, V. (1974) *Dramas, Fields, and Metaphors*. Ithaca, NY: Cornell University Press.
Turner, V. (1980) 'Social Dramas and Stories Told about Them', *Critical Inquiry*, 7: 141–68.
Turquet, P. M. (1974) *Leadership: the Individual and the Group*, in G. S. Gibbard, J. J. Hartman and R. Mann (eds) *Analysis of Groups*. San Francisco: Jossey-Bass.
Vaillant, George E. (1977) *Adaptation to Life*. Boston, MA: Little, Brown.
Vaillant, George E. (ed.) (1986) *Empirical Studies of Mechanisms of Defense*. Washington, DC: American Psychiatric Press.
Van Maanen, J. (1988) *Tales of the Field*. Chicago, IL: University of Chicago Press.
Van Maanen, J. and Kunda, G. (1989) '"Real Feelings": Emotional Expression and Organizational Culture', in L. L. Cummings and B. M. Staw (eds), *Research in Organizational Behavior*, vol. 11, pp. 43–104. Greenwich, CT: JAI Press.
Vaughan, D. (1996) *The Challenger Launch Decision: Risky Technology, Culture, and Deviance at NASA*. Chicago: University of Chicago Press.
Vickers, G. (1967) *Towards a Sociology of Management*. New York: Basic Books.
Volkan, Vamik D. (1988) *The Need to Have Enemies and Allies: from Clinical Practice to International Relations*. Northvale, NJ: Jason Aronson.
Von Krogh, George and Roos, Johan (1995) *Organizational Epistemology*. London: St Martin's Press.
Wälder, Robert (1936) 'The Principal of Multiple Function: Observations on Over-Determination', *Psychoanalytic Quarterly*, 5: 45–62.
Watson, Tony J. (1994) *In Search of Management: Culture, Chaos and Control in Managerial Work*. London: Routledge.
Weber, Max (1913/1947) *The Theory of Social and Economic Organization*, (ed.) Talcott Parsons. New York: Oxford University Press.
Weber, Max (1946) *From Max Weber: Essays in Sociology*, (ed.) H. H. Gerth and C. Wright Mills. London: Routledge.
Weick, K. E. (1979) *The Social Psychology of Organizing*. Reading, MA.: Addison-Wesley.
Whitten, P. L. (1987) 'Infants and Adult Males', in B.B. Smuts et al. (eds), *Primate Societies*. Chicago: University of Chicago Press. pp. 343–57.
Whyte, Lancelot L. (1962) *The Unconscious before Freud*. London: Tavistock.
Wilkins, A. L. (1983) 'Organizational Stories as Symbols which Control the Organization', in L. R. Pondy, P. J. Frost, G. Morgan and T.C. Dandridge (eds), *Organizational Symbolism*. Greenwich, CT: JAI Press.

Wilkinson, B. (1996) 'Culture, Institutions and Business in East Asia', *Organization Studies*, 17 (3): 422–47.
Wilkinson, B., Morris, J. and Mundy, M. (1995) 'The Iron Fist in the Velvet Glove', *Journal of Management Studies*, 32 (6): 819–30.
Williams, T. A. (1982) *Learning to Manage our Futures: the Participative Redesign of Societies in Turbulent Transition*. New York: John Wiley.
Willis, Paul (1990) *Common Culture: Symbolic Work at play in the Everyday Cultures of the Young*. Milton Keynes: Open University Press.
Winnicott, D.W. (1958) *Through Paediatrics to Psychoanalysis*. London: Hogarth.
Winnicott, D.W. (1965) *The Maturational Process and the Facilitating Environment*. New York: International Universities Press.
Winter, R. (1989) *Learning from Experience: Principles and Practice in Action-Research*. London. Falmer Press.
Wolfe, T. (1979) *The Right Stuff*. New York: Farrar, Strauss and Giroux.
Womack, J. P., Jones, D. T. and Roos, D. (1990) *The Machine that Changed the World*. London: Macmillan.
Worsley, P. (1970) *Introducing Sociology*. Harmondsworth: Penguin.
Zaleznik, A. (1977) 'Managers and Leaders: Are They Different?', *Harvard Business Review*, May–June: 47–60.
Zaleznik, A. (1984) 'Charismatic and Consensus Leadership: a Psychological Comparison', and 'Power and Politics in Organizational Life', in Manfred Kets de Vries (ed.), *The Irrational Executive: Psychoanalytic Exploration in Management*. New York: International Universities Press.
Zaleznik, A. (1989) *The Managerial Mystique*. New York: Harper and Row.
Zaleznik, A. (1989/1997) 'Real Work', *Harvard Business Review*, January; reprinted in June 1997, (6): 53–61.
Zaleznik, A. (1991) 'Leading and Managing: Understanding the Difference', in M. F. R. Kets de Vries (ed.), *Organizations on the Couch*. San Francisco: Jossey-Bass.
Zaleznik, A. (1993) 'The Mythological Structure of Organizations and its Impact', in L. Hirschhorn and C. K. Barnett (eds), *The Psychodynamics of Organizations*. Philadelphia, PA: Temple University Press.

INDEX

Words in **bold** have entries in the Glossary (pp. 289–311)

Abraham, K. 22, 24, 60, 303
access (for research purposes) 258, 267f, 277
accessibility 150
achievement 31, 69ff, 72ff, 76, 79, 167, 171, 187, 196, 199
action 1, 17, 50, 51, 52, 85f, 124, 141, 182, 185, 216, 220, 232, 250, 259, 262, 265, 296
  anti-social 90, 243
action research 262–66
adaptation 18, 234
adaptive mechanisms 234f
adjustment 46ff, 56
Adler, A. 290, 293, 305
administration (and leadership) 213
adolescence 42f
Adorno, T. W. 180ff, 184, 266
affect 216, 234
  isolation of 219
aggression 21, 22, 23, 28, 45, 54, 56f, 74, 76, 102, 163, 177, 207f, 235, 236, 248, 250, 289, 292
alcoholism 143
Alexander, F. 234
alienation 54, 185.
Allcorn, S. 126f, 160–64, 256, 282
ambition 10, 66
ambivalence 23, 27, 38, 105, 156, 198, 221, 271, 290, 293, 310
  and groups 118
anal character and **anal stage** 60f, 64f, 92, 181, 290, 305
'anal personality' 24
anal-sadistic stage 24, 33, 61, 63ff
'analysed man' 76
analyst 38, 220, 258
analytical psychology 290, 293, 305
anatomical distinction of sexes 29
anorexia nervosa 42

anxiety 17, 22, 23, 27, 30, 37, 40, 43, 45, 61, 63ff, 84, 86ff, 91f, 98, 121, 128, 129, 156, 178, 187, 218, 223f 231 243, 244, 245, 249, 262, 266, 278, 283, 284, 287, 290, 293, 301, 303, 304, 305, 306, 308
  depressive 224
  guilt anxiety 226
  loss of love 31
  moral 93
  organizational causes of 226f
  persecutory 162, 220, 224
  shame 226
  signal of 17, 226, 228
archetypes 115, 131, 290, 296, 310
architecture, symbolism of 202ff
army (as group) 117, 125
art and artist 107, 172
artefacts (cultural) 11, 173, 190
Asch, S. 69
Askew-Renaut, B. 157
Auden, W. H. 51
authoritarian personality 180ff, 183, 187, 266
authoritarianism 180ff, 186, 228, 248f
authority 27, 62, 67f, 85ff, 94, 120, 137, 151ff, 165, 180, 184, 203, 236, 242, 252, 283, 302,
  rational-legal 74, 110
  template 156
avoidant culture 209

Badcock, C. 93
basic assumption 91, 101, 119, 124ff, 222f, 290
  baD 119, 124ff, 130
  baF 119, 121, 124ff, 128, 130
  baP 119, 124ff, 128, 130
  me-ness 125
  one-ness 125
  as solutions 129
  sophisticated use of 124f
Baudrillard, J. 111, 186
Baum, H. S. 77, 86, 153, 226, 256

Bauman, Z. 111
Bennis, W. W. 156
Bergson, H. 299
Bettelheim, B. 47, 56, 173, 289
Bingham, H. 120–23
Bion, W. R. 91, 101, 117, 119, 124ff, 130, 136, 141, 222f, 225, 284, 291
Biran, H. 275f
Black, M. J. 234f
blame 94f, 146, 219, 226f, 228, 231, 234, 282ff
boundaries (*see also* organization boundaries) 22, 90, 116, 141, 225, 249, 261
   defence of 98
   internal 98, 223
Bowles, M. L. 271
bravado 144, 247
breast 22ff, 30, 61f
Bridger, H. 223
Brown N. O. 41, 55, 159, 174, 295, 305
Bruch, H. 42ff
bulimia 42ff
bureaucracy 65, 78, 84, 99f, 103, 110, 184, 191f, 205, 211, 227, 284
   culture of 205
   'invisible bureaucracy' 86
   mixed with brutality 181, 184
   as social defence against anxiety 224f
bureaucratic culture (as organizational pathology) 208
Burns, J. M., 140, 213
Burrell, G. 78

Campbell, C. 218
career, 87, 170
caring (as attribute of leaders) 150, 153
Carlzon, J. 213
Carr, A. 78, 93–6, 254–56, 275, 283, 288
case studies (in research) 266ff
Casey, C. 105
castration 25ff, 29f, 32, 178, 291, 300, 302
castration anxiety 25ff, 30, 31
cathexis 14, 19, 28, 291, 301
censorship 271, 311
   political 6, 9
   psychological 6, 7, 10, 93, 173, 198
Challenger (space shuttle) 2–5
change, 69, 244, 263f, 281ff
   cultural 209
   management of 99, 262
   resistance to 65
   roles associated with 134f
chaos (*see also* complexity) 265, 280ff, 288ff
   inner and outer 284

character (psychological) 60–80, 291, 306, 308
   and organization 62ff, 74f
charisma 63, 73, 142, 154f
   distinguished from messianic 151, 155
charismatic/dramatic culture 208
Chasseguet-Smirgel, J. 23f, 89, 150, 187, 244, 295
child 21ff, 39
   to adult dependency 85, 88, 105, 117, 119
childhood 21ff
Chodorow, N. 32, 297, 302
church 117, 182
citizen 72, 74, 79, 121ff, 160f, 288
civic individualism, *see* individualism civic
civilization (*see also* culture) 16, 18, 66, 166f, 285
   as potentially neurotic 41, 230
classes 91, 107, 164, 175, 175
clinical material as research material 48ff
clinical practice 35ff
   and research 257
Cohen, E. A. 250
collectivism 66ff, 182
collectivities 81f, 191
collegiate cultures 208f
commodities 184, 187, 189
   feelings as 213
common sense 51
commonwealth 74
communication 3f, 44
community, normative 79, 105, 182, 194
complexity, 225, 248, 280
   moral 245f, 250
compromise formation 10, 141, 173f, 170, 311
compulsion 42
condensation 8, 10, 291, 294, 304, 310
conflict (*see also* politics)
   of allegiance 88
   between individual and culture 15, 28, 31, 176f, 221
   between morality and organization 249
   in groups 113ff, 121ff, 146
   of interests 74
   of love and hate 221
   mental or psychic 14ff, 18, 23, 42ff, 45, 46, 56, 141, 218, 238f, 291, 297, 308, 310
   organizational 165, 281ff
   with parents 236
   social 243
   truce 225
conformity 4, 67, 69, 138, 171, 195
conscience 20f, 27, 123, 176, 236, 292, 308
conscious and **consciousness** 6, 7, 8, 10, 14,

15, 17, 52, 53, 54, 57, 71, 79, 107, 147, 233, 254, 292, 304, 306, 309, 310
consolation 41, 45, 54, 175, 177f, 189f, 196, 209, 228, 271
consultants and consultation 209f, 218, 219, 222, 224, 238, 251, 256ff, 259ff
consumer 72, 111, 185, 186, 246
consumer society 42ff, 189f
contagion (of emotion) 116, 222
container (for anxiety) (*see also* protection) 123, 131, 223, 226, 265, 292
  and leaders 145
  of learning 265f
  for phantasies 135
'contamination' of data 48ff, 51
contempt (and leadership) 143, 144, 146, 158
control 27, 34, 64ff, 73, 76, 78, 103–106, 110, 146, 153, 186, 209, 280ff, 287
  of boundaries 97ff
  over bowel movement 24, 64
  over emotion 213f, 218
  as illusion 283ff
  over irrationality 77
  need for 244
  over own body 42ff
  precarious 282
  social 28, 171, 186
Copernicus, N. 53, 284
'corporation man' 73, 284
corruption 242f, 249
counter-transference 276f, 310
covert coalitions 225
creative individualism 195
creativity 30, 33, 62f, 65, 95, 107, 115, 282
Crews, F. 47, 48
crisis 219, 249, 273, 281f, 286
  in groups 122
  in organizations 209
critical incident analysis 273
crowds 81f, 89, 91, 110, 115
cruelty 181f
culture (*see also* organizational culture) 4, 8, 15, 28, 31, 34, 40, 41, 45f, 49, 51, 55, 56, 76, 166–91, 250, 254, 283
  characteristics of 167
  collegiate 207f
  as consolation 175, 177f, 189
  corporate 78
  functions of 171f
  material 202ff
  of narcissism 156, 175f, 186ff
  and nature 166f, 172

  and repression 174
  'strong culture' 192
cure 38
curiosity 33
cynicism 76, 87, 97, 156, 161, 207, 246f
Czander, W. M. 107

Darwin, C. 54, 284, 297
data collection 267ff
Deal, T. E. 203
death instinct 15, 28, 104, 175ff, 221, 289, 292, 296, 297, 299, 300
decision making 129f, 193
defence (psychological) 6, 33, 56, 118, 129, 207, 220, 228, 284, 290, 293, 295, 298, 299, 305f
defence mechanisms 16ff, 40, 218, 234, 234, 293, 306, 307f, 310
  social defences 224ff, 234, 243, 264
  used against the super-ego 239
dehumanization 211
delusion 44, 119, 138, 141, 187, 291, 293, 296, 298, 305
denial 17, 224, 253, 277, 293
dependence 62, 88, 97, 105, 117, 119, 137, 163, 181, 208, 219, 245, 249, 258, 284
depression 186
depressive position 23, 107, 124, 221, 225, 250, 293, 303
depth psychology (*see also* psychoanalysis) 5, 290, 293, 310
Derrida, J. 254
desexualization 18
desire (*see also* wish) 5, 6, 7, 11, 14, 16, 22, 23, 27, 30, 31, 32, 33, 34, 37, 39, 42, 54, 55, 60f, 67, 80, 92, 124, 141, 165, 173, 177, 210, 252, 255, 291, 293, 294, 296, 297, 299, 300, 303, 304, 305, 306, 307, 308, 309, 310, 311
  for baby 30
deskilling 185
destructiveness (*see also* aggression) 22, 56, 64
determinism (psychic) 233f
diagnosis 209, 260f
Diamond, M. A. 77, 126f, 225, 256, 261, 274, 302
discontent (*see also* suffering) 41, 107, 109, 175, 177, 189f
discourse 254
discrimination 10
disorder 281, 285, 287
displacement 6, 10, 216, 235, 254, 294, 304, 310

Dixon, N. 181
domination 40
dreaming matrix 275f
dreams 6–11, 44, 46, 141, 255, 275f, 284, 290, 291, 294, 306, 309, 310, 311
   and reality 141, 146
drives *see* instinct
Durkheim, É. 175, 214
dynamic point of view 14f, 21f, 294, 309

economic factors (*see also* energy, libido) 19, 76
economic point of view 14, 21, 294, 295, 309
economy as moral value 92, 96f
Edwards, R. 103
efficiency 65, 91ff, 110, 193, 239, 249
ego 16ff, 19ff, 28, 54, 62, 70, 72, 76, 91, 98, 103, 144, 156, 174, 187f, 218, 232f, 262, 284f, 289, 292, 295, 297, 298, 300, 301, 303, 304, 305, 306, 307, 308, 310, 311
ego psychology (school of thought) 18, 60, 295
ego-ideal 19ff, 24, 28, 34, 70ff, 73, 89f, 92, 105, 126, 149, 175, 187f, 189, 196ff, 222, 238, 243, 292, 295, 297, 298, 301, 303, 307, 308
   and groups 117
   and super-ego 187
embarrassment 170f
emotion (*see also* affect and feeling) 10, 11, 14, 53, 62, 76f, 80, 84ff, 90, 91f, 103, 112, 119, 124, 131, 137f, 156, 177, 183, 200, 209f, 211–31, 250, 273
   chain reactions 221
   colonized by rationality 213
   conscious and unconscious 218
   control of 213f, 218
   display 212, 229
   distinct from feelings 228
   emotional labour 212ff
   fantasy and desire 221
   in groups 222ff
   learned 214
   meaning of 214
   mobility of 216
   and morality 246f
   psychoanalytic theories of 215–30
   and rationality 211f, 230ff
   as social constructions 214f
   'switch off' 229
   transformation of 216ff
emotivism 246
energy (mental) (*see also* libido) 14, 15, 294, 295, 297, 298, 299

environment 97, 263
envy 29, 30, 38, 53, 137, 302
epic 66, 139, 199, 284
Erikson, E. 241, 243, 249, 298, 302
Eros 176, 177, 221, 292, 296, 299, 300
Esterson, A. 53
ethics 232–50
   imperativistic and goal 238
   research 268
'excellence' 192
experience 252
external reality (*see also* ego and reality) 98

facts as experience 199, 271
facts as information 199, 271
failure 145, 227, 282
faith 151ff, 237
falsifiability 48, 51, 271
family and family life 45, 132, 180, 225
   family romance 154
   organizations as families 193, 197
fantasy (*see also* phantasy) 8, 44, 48, 50, 66, 76, 85, 90, 92, 105, 122, 141, 146, 150, 156, 177, 187, 189, 196ff, 200, 210, 226, 228, 235, 236, 255, 262, 270f, 276f, 290, 292, 294, 296, 298, 301f, 303, 306, 307, 309, 310
   corporate fantasy 197
   distinguished from 'phantasy' 147
   followers' core fantasies 155
   in research 262, 269ff, 273f
   'run riot' 143
fascism 179ff
fate 28, 45, 46, 178, 285ff
father 20, 27ff, 32, 66f, 72, 86f, 89, 132, 155, 165
   father substitute, leader as 150ff, 155
   father substitute, researcher as 276f
   primal 117, 150ff, 244
fear 4, 89, 151, 181, 216, 245
   of failure 10
feedback, as part of research 263f, 277f
feelings (*see also* emotion) 5, 65, 67, 94, 112, 121, 128, 135, 199ff, 207, 211–31, 271, 274, 277, 288
   distinct from emotion 228
feminine 25
femininity 28ff, 296f, 300
feminist critics of Freud 29f, 179
Ferenczi, S. 220, 305
Feyerabend, P. 48, 283
Fineman, S. 77, 211, 215, 227, 228
firing an employee (*see also* redundancies) 245f

Fischer, S. 61
fixation 33, 61, 77
Fliess, W. 26
folklore 8, 55, 71, 271
followers (*see also* leaders) 139–65
    bonds with leaders 117, 119, 125f, 146–59
    collusion with leaders' fantasies 144, 242, 284
    fantasies about leaders 147–59
    seduced by leaders 144
Forrester, J., 51ff
Fortuna 286f
Foucault, M. 55, 103, 311
free association 8, 37, 38, 269ff, 274
French, R. 99–102
'Freud Wars' 35ff
Freud, A. 17, 219, 234, 295
Freud, S. (*see also* psychoanalysis) 5ff, 13–34
    ambitiousness 9,
    clinical practice 37ff
    criticism of religion 76, 237f
    critics of, 35ff, 47ff, 54, 178f
    cultural theories 40f, 172ff
    on emotion 215ff
    on groups 116ff
    heroic vision of work 107f
    on jokes 198f
    Jewish identity 8, 164
    and modernity 284
    as moral philosopher 237f
    not a therapeutic enthusiast 47
    political theory 159, 164f
    prisoner of his own culture 179
    propagandist for his theories 49
    and the Oedipus myth 26
    on the standing of psychoanalysis 49ff, 253
    on work 107ff
Friedan, B. 179
Friedman, M. 246f
Fromm, E. 55
frustration 23
fusion 22, 23, 27, 34, 62, 86, 90
    in groups 118
future 140

Gabriel, Y. 105, 187, 227, 257, 271
generosity 24
genital stage 297
Gilmore, T. 225, 228, 256
Goffman, E. 153ff, 214
Gooch, J. 250
good/bad dualism 23, 198, 220, 250
gossip 52, 259

Gould L. J. 124, 126, 223, 225, 256, 257, 282, 302
Gouldner, A. W. 104
Greenberg, R. P. 61
Grey, C. 284
group 20, 23, 67ff, 78, 81f, 91f, 110, 112–38, 187, 193, 220, 244, 263, 275
    developmental approaches 125ff
    dynamics 114ff
    as embodiment of perfection 68f
    emotions in 222ff
    Freud's definition of primary group 117
    great power of 89f, 126f
    ideals 92
    identity 96
    leaderless 126f
    as matriarchal entities 244
    and mother 118
    and organization 112
    politics 160–64
    relations 113
    'without too much organization' 215
    work group 91, 112–38, 222
group psychology 67, 91, 112–38
groupthink 67, 129f
Grünbaum, A. 48, 51, 255
guilt 20f, 27, 28, 40, 45, 72, 84, 86, 109, 176, 186, 187, 189, 219, 221, 224, 236f, 248, 250, 289, 292, 297, 308
    as cost of civilization 177f
Guntrip, H. 235

Habermas, J. 254
Handy, C. 205
happiness 27, 34, 46, 47, 53, 96, 238
Harrison, R. 205
Hartmann, H. 236, 238ff, 245, 248
hate 23, 39, 53, 61f, 211, 216
helper (deep role) 133
hermeneutics 254ff, 297, 299
heroism (*see also* individualism, heroic) 73, 183, 187, 199, 213, 271, 283
hierarchy 73, 85–8, 102, 110, 154, 156, 181, 183, 193, 205, 226
Hirschhorn, L. 77, 98, 107f, 126, 138, 139–65, 207f, 225, 226, 228, 234, 239, 243, 250, 256, 261, 302
Hochschild, A. R. 212f
Hoggett, P. 257
Hopfl, H. 214
Horkheimer, M. 180
Horwitz, L. 242
hubris of management 286f, 288

humanistic traditions 45, 46, 252
humour 235
hypnosis 38, 40, 215
hysteria 42, 297, 301

Iacocca, L. 73
id 15ff, 18, 20, 21, 70, 77, 98, 232, 289, 295, 298, 308, 310
idealization (*see also* ego-ideal) 28, 46, 67, 69, 79, 124, 138, 149, 157, 163, 182, 208, 224, 242, 298, 307
ideals (*see also* illusion) 41, 76, 92, 177, 187, 239, 274
   moral 238
identification 17, 28, 31, 62, 67, 69f, 93, 138, 149ff, 157f, 187, 196f, 208, 222, 236, 244, 249, 298, 301, 302, 307, 308
   with leader 117, 125, 149ff
identity 34, 43, 64, 81, 90, 93–6, 127, 172, 175, 183, 187, 189, 193, 298, 307
   formation 243
   group 96
   organizational 93f, 203
ideology 54, 55
illusion 39, 41, 55, 76f, 129, 175, 177f, 189, 215, 237, 244, 285, 287f, 293, 296, 298, 307, 311
   control as 283ff
   political 177
   religious 177
image 186, 189, 197, 207, 228
imago 299
immortality 88, 90, 187, 197
impersonality 65, 82–7, 110, 204, 226
impostor 121, 154f, 156
incest and incest taboo 31, 132
incommensurability 78
individualism 69ff
   civic 70, 72ff, 182, 208
   creative 195f
   heroic 70ff, 92
injustice 108, 125, 227
instincts 15, 16, 18, 23, 175, 233, 238f, 291, 292, 293, 295, 297, 299, 305, 306, 307, 310
institution 81, 182f, 190, 191, 244
interaction 112
interpretation 6–11, 13, 14, 32, 37, 38f, 44f, 48, 50, 52, 56, 185, 203, 251ff, 254–56, 258, 263, 291, 294, 297, 299, 301, 309
   as art 272
   of cultural phenomena 172ff, 190
   distinction between valid and spurious 11, 49, 272

   dream interpretation 7, 175
   of a building 203
   of Sophocles' Oedipus Rex 173f
   of stories 199ff, 271f
interviews (research) 260, 267ff
introjection 17, 220, 223
intuition 92
irrationality 10, 50, 65, 90, 112, 193, 211, 229
   combined with 'reasonableness' 123
Isaacs, S. 147
isolation 17
Itard, J.-M.-G. 166

Janis, I. 129
Japan 191ff
Jaques, E. 215, 223f, 256, 257, 284, 302
jealousy 29
jokes 8, 92, 105, 198f, 209, 271
Jones, E. 26, 179, 309
Jung, C. G. 114, 115, 131, 290, 291, 293, 296, 299, 305
juries as psychological groups 120–23

Kanter R. M. 102
Kaplan, H. A. 244
Kapuscinski, R. 87
Kaufmann, W. 233, 238, 245
Kennedy, A. A. 203
Kernberg, O. 126, 187, 241f, 248f
Kets de Vries, M. 77, 96, 197, 208, 256, 261
Klein, M. 22f, 30, 61, 107f, 118f, 124, 126, 132, 220ff, 226, 250, 301, 303, 308
Kohut, H. 151, 155, 157f, 187, 241
Krantz, J. 149, 225, 256, 284, 302
Kuhn, T. S. 48
Kvale, S. 254

La Bier, D. 257
Lacan, J. 62, 72, 254
Lang, T. 105, 187
language 55, 72, 78, 93–6, 103, 228, 254–56
   political language (*see also* political rhetoric) 94f
Lapierre, L. 144, 225, 228, 284, 287
Lasch, C. 186f, 189, 257, 305, 308
latency 32ff, 66
Lawrence, W. G. 92, 125, 265, 275
lay-off *see* redundancies
Le Bon, G. 89, 115, 117, 138, 214, 222
leaders and leadership 23, 24, 71, 77, 85ff, 136ff, 139–65, 287f
   accessible 150, 155
   caring 150, 155

leaders and leadership continued
  charismatic 63, 73, 142, 154f, 241, 243
  consensus 243
  and control 282
  and culture 194, 208ff
  and emotion 213f
  and fascism183
  fight leader 128, 136
  and followers 87, 139–65, 242
  'good enough' 145f
  and groups 114, 117, 119ff
  heroic 73, 142, 183
  leaderless groups 126f
  legitimacy 154f, 283
  and managers 139f, 213
  meeting the 147ff
  messianic 96, 151, 154f
  and morality 240ff, 247, 248ff
  mystery 53, 148
  narcissistic 142ff, 157ff, 241
  omnipotence fantasy 144, 153, 155, 228, 284
  and organizational pathologies 207ff, 222
  and transference 220, 220
  visions and dreams 139ff, 213, 296
  and Virtu 287, 288
Lear, J. 47, 50, 52, 53, 56
learning 276f, 283
  action 265f
  and culture 166
  of emotions 214, 230
  from experience 91
  organizational 209, 226, 228, 262–66, 282f
  and organizational socialization 195
Levinson H. 60, 71, 77, 85, 86, 87, 108, 197, 209, 215, 248, 256, 257, 258, 259f, 277
Lévi-Strauss, C. 173f
libido 16, 18, 19, 20, 33, 34, 42, 60, 62, 70, 76, 96, 107ff, 117, 149ff, 238, 295, 298, 299, 300, 301, 308
lies 52
Linstead, S. 214
Loevinger, J. 61, 67
Long, S. 262–66
Lorenzer, A. 254
love 19, 22, 23, 27, 32, 61f, 74, 137, 150, 158, 187, 211, 289, 300, 301
  of analyst 38
  as basis of group bonding 117
  as basis of social cohesion 67
  falling in love 19, 39, 144, 147, 215
  and hate as basic polarity 221, 250
  of leader 144
  of organization 109

  of truth 38, 232, 238, 258
  withdrawal of 181
loyalty 65, 69, 86ff, 129, 183, 198, 205
  work as display of 109

Machiavelli, N. 287f
MacIntyre, A. 226, 246f, 283
magic 92, 152
male fighting band 182
Malinowski, B. 178f, 307
managerial couple 149, 157–59
managers (*see also* leaders) 224, 250
  as cultural archetypes 246f
managers and management (*see also* leaders) 77, 194, 280–88
  and cultural 283f
  hubris of management 286
  lionization of 283
  meaning of 'to manage' 285, 287
  as moral art 288
Mangham, I. 214
Mant, A. 223
Marcuse, H. 40f, 55, 173, 179, 257, 295, 305, 308
Marx, K. 107, 175, 194, 237
masculinity 25, 296, 300
Mason, S. 93–6
mass organizing 182f
mature genitality 34
mature individual 77
McCollom Hampton, M. 112–38
McCracken, G. 187
McDougall, W. 222
meaning 1, 11, 12, 22, 33, 47, 49, 50, 51, 57, 76, 79, 94, 104, 171, 193, 195, 199, 210, 230, 251, 252, 255, 287
  of emotion 214
  of stories 271
  of work 106–10, 184f, 186ff
meaninglessness 184ff, 189
mental **agencies** 13ff, 22, 33, 289f, 310
mentor 133
Menzies Lyth, I. 215, 223f, 256, 284, 302
messiah and false messiah, 96, 151, 153ff, 198
metaphors (in research) 274
metapsychology 12ff, 300
Miller, A. 69
Miller, D. 96, 208
Miller, E. 223
mission 90, 113f, 127ff, 193
Mitchell, J. 30, 31, 179, 296, 311
Mitchell, S. A. 234f
Mitev, N. 284

modernism 78
modernity 81, 284
money 8, 64f, 107, 140, 215
moral ambiguity 245f
moral choices 239ff
moral courage 247f
moral illiteracy 246
moral responsibility 113, 233ff
morality (*see also* ethics and super-ego) 232ff, 235ff
  bourgeois 237f
  internalization of 236
  and leadership 241ff
  in research 268
  and self-interest 246f
morality 16, 27, 56, 90, 197
Morgan, G. 78
Morita, A. 193, 213
mother 21, 22, 23, 25, 27ff, 32, 34, 66ff, 86, 90, 118, 132, 155, 197, 235
  mother substitute, leader as 150
  mother substitute, researcher as 276f
  primal 148ff, 155, 207
motivation 51, 52, 53, 184f, 239
  and emotion 215
  and morality 233ff
motive 1, 50, 122, 140, 145, 221, 231, 251
mourning 89, 97, 300
Moxnes, P. 131–36
Mumby, D. K. 213
myths and mythology 8, 55, 66, 71ff, 79, 169, 171ff, 190

narcissism 19ff, 23, 53f, 71, 77, 84f, 105, 126, 141f, 151, 165, 202, 220, 236, 242, 250, 284, 289, 295, 300f, 303, 307, 308
  associated with different characters 71
  consolation 176, 186, 190
  and culture 156, 175f, 186ff
  malignant 243
  new narcissism 187f
  as organizational pathology 109
  primary narcissism 61, 89f, 149ff, 187
  secondary narcissism 62
  of small differences 176
narcissistic character 61–80, 92
narcissistic culture 156, 175f, 186ff, 206f
narcissistic process, detecting 144ff, 162
NASA 2–5, 6, 10f, 12, 39, 109, 206f
nation 91, 175, 182, 197, 220
nature 166f, 172, 178, 285
negation 293, 301

neurosis 35ff, 45ff, 56, 98, 237, 257, 291, 292, 294, 301, 305, 306, 308
  and normality 41ff
  potentially beneficial to bureaucracy 230, 257
  and religion 172ff
  as socially caused 40
neurotic symptoms 8, 33, 39, 42ff, 172ff, 216
Nietzsche, F. 18, 86, 237, 308
'normal' and 'normality' (*see also* pathology) 40ff, 46, 61, 208, 229f
norms 55, 104, 169ff, 191ff, 244
Norris, C, 254
nostalgia 22, 87, 204, 304

Obholzer, A. 92, 126, 137
object 19, 22, 23, 28, 30, 61f, 108, 118, 135, 149, 187, 189, 190, 220, 223, 289, 290, 298, 301f
object choice (*see also* cathexis) 19
object relations 23, 118, 128, 226, 295, 297, 300, 301f
observation 49, 51, 56f, 259
  participant 274f
  as research methods 262, 267, 269
obsessional neurosis 172, 301, 302
obsessive character 64–80, 184
obstinacy 24, 64
oceanic feeling 22, 90, 125, 149
Odysseus 133, 206
Oedipus 25ff
Oedipus complex 20, 25ff, 66ff, 69ff, 85, 187, 291, 296, 297, 302f, 304, 308
  and the girl 28ff
Oglensky, B. 156
oral character 61, 303
oral stage 22f, 24, 33, 61, 303, 308
oral-sadistic 23
Orbach, S. 42
order 281ff, 286ff
orderliness 24, 64f
organization ideal 90, 96, 157f, 176, 196
organizations 10, 20, 23, 58–80, 296
  as anti-cultures 191
  boundaries 59, 83, 97–103, 106, 110, 225
  and character (Table 3.1) 75
  charismatic 63, 154
  conflict 165
  as constructions 60, 79
  control 59, 73, 78, 101, 103–6, 280ff
  and counter-cultures 192, 199f, 203
  culture 100, 168, 191–210, 225, 243
  definition of 58–59, 81

organizations continued
  demands made on the individual 81–111
  discontents 109
  and environment 97, 263
  goals 59, 90ff, 110, 145, 183, 213, 239, 245, 246, 249
  and group 91, 112, 138
  as impersonal orders 65
  Japanese 193
  long-term 88ff, 110
  mission 90, 193
  morality 239–50
  non-profit and government 240f
  and other collectivities 81–111
  political 182f
  politics 93–6, 198ff
  relation between individual and 81–111, 194ff
  self-organization 281, 282
  size 88–90, 91, 110
  theories and academic traditions 78, 97, 253, 256, 288
  unmanaged 105
overdetermination 233f, 271
Overington, M. 214

pain (*see also* discontent and suffering) 218, 219, 250, 257, 262, 265
paradigms 78
paranoia 248, 255
paranoid culture 208f
paranoid-schizoid position 23, 61, 124, 198, 221, 303, 307
parsimoniousness 24, 64
participant observation 274
participative action research 262–66
pathologies, individual 37
  organizational 95f, 206ff, 229f
  relation between individual and organizational 230, 257
  and unethical behaviour 240, 242f, 250
patriarchy 31, 237
pecking orders 85
penis envy 29f, 178f
perception 4, 5, 44, 101, 135, 276
  and emotion 218
performance (emotional) 214
phallic stage 27ff, 33, 61, 66ff, 302, 304
phallus 30
phantasy (*see also* fantasy) 26, 32, 34, 68, 74, 76f, 80, 118, 131–36, 252, 310
  distinguished from 'fantasy' 147
  and group 117ff

primal 115
phobia 42, 301, 304
pleasure 21ff, 25ff, 32, 34, 64, 90, 105, 218, 271, 307
pleasure principle 16, 90, 216, 293, 295, 296, 298, 304, 305, 306
pluralism 79, 171
political experiences 156
political rhetoric 245
politics 159–65, 182–83, 185, 186, 212, 278, 283
  and authoritarianism 180–184
  as illusion 159
  in Oedipus myth 173
  organizational 93–6, 198ff
Popper, K. 48
popular culture 52
postmodernist theory 11, 78, 252f, 254–56
power 28, 30, 40, 66ff, 71, 86–90, 92, 103–6, 133, 154f, 159, 161ff, 181, 183, 185, 196, 215, 226, 248f, 276ff, 299
  accorded to parents 89, 117
  culture (*see also* organizations, political) 205
practical joke 195
preconscious 292, 304, 310
prejudice 245
primary processes 10, 298, 304, 306, 310
projection 17, 118, 128, 131, 135f, 137, 153, 155, 163, 220, 223f, 234, 235, 243, 248, 262f
projective identification 118, 131
promise 28, 31, 67, 70, 145, 150
promotion 73, 87
protection 87f, 89, 128, 132, 141, 143, 145, 153ff, 242
Protestant ethic 78, 92, 107, 184
psychoanalysis
  as archaeology 7
  as causal theory 255
  clinical practice and treatment 35ff, 232, 257, 304
  as detective work 7, 251
  as a discipline 5, 50ff, 293, 304f
  as hermeneutics 254–56
  as interpretive discipline 51
  limited effectiveness as psychotherapy 45
  main theories and concepts 13ff
  as management 184
  and morality 232–50
  multiplicity of perspectives 234f
  and politics 179ff
  as popular culture 51

psychoanalysis continued
    schools 235, 305
    technique 8
    theory and therapy 36ff
psychological contract 68, 76, 194, 196f, 258, 276
psychological man 238
psychosis 291, 294, 301, 305
    and group 119
psychostructure 93–6
Putnam, L. L. 213

race and racism 180, 228
Rangell, L. 241
Rank, O. 305
rationality 1, 10, 53, 77, 90, 119, 140, 193, 211, 228, 229, 238, 282, 284
    colonizes emotion 213
    instrumental 231
rationalization (as defence) 17, 231, 235, 248, 255
reaction-formation 17, 33, 60f, 64, 235, 293, 305, 308
reality (*see also* external reality) 5, 38, 45, 63, 72, 76, 90, 119, 199, 234, 244, 254, 270
    acceptance of 239
    denial of 143
    loss of 159
    symbolic/magical reality 131
    testing 17, 18, 163, 187
    and visions 139ff
reality principle 16, 20, 90, 293, 295, 304, 305, 309
reason (*see also* rationality) 76f, 80, 116
rebellion 42f, 125, 182, 195, 198
redundancies 69, 83, 94, 226, 231
regression 17, 33, 38ff, 61, 77, 142, 291, 293, 305, 306
    in group phenomena 117, 126, 138
Reich, W. R. 55, 180, 182
religion 22, 40, 46, 76, 150, 167, 171, 174ff, 186, 302, 311
    and neurosis as substitutes 174
Renshon, S. A. 241
reparation 107, 221, 250
repetition, compulsive 46, 64, 104, 285, 292, 306
repression 5, 6, 11, 14, 18, 22, 26, 27, 32, 33, 34, 37f, 45, 66ff, 76, 124, 210, 218, 232, 235, 254, 290, 291, 293, 297, 298, 299, 301, 302, 304, 307, 308, 309, 310
    of affects and emotions 218ff

and culture 174, 177, 178
and the social factor 40
research into organizations (*see also* interviews and observations) 251–79
    action 262–66
    as art and craft 258ff, 266, 278
    case studies 266ff
    ethics 268, 278
    exploratory 261
    listening skills 269f
    problem-driven 259ff, 277
    as social practice 259
    theory-driven 259f, 261ff, 277
    theory-testing 261
    and theory 259ff
    as wasteful activity 258
researcher and researched 262–66, 271ff, 276ff
resistance
    individual against culture 172, 177
    organizational and political 63, 103ff, 196, 198ff, 203, 209, 278, 286
    psychological 8, 37, 38, 45, 54, 56, 209, 252f, 258, 271, 277f, 294, 306
    symbolic 198ff
Revans, R. 265
revolution, sexual and political 180
revolutionaries 159
rhetoric 254
Rice, A. K. 91, 239
Ricoeur, P. 10, 11, 28, 52, 56, 251, 254
Rieff, P. 14, 40, 56, 76f, 80, 159, 237f, 284f, 305
risk 140, 145, 203, 268, 277, 287
ritual (religious) 169, 171, 174, 190, 191f, 209, 302
    organizational 225f
Roberts, V. Z. 98
Roddick, A. 213
role 84ff, 99–102, 114, 130, 136, 160, 168, 262, 276
    confusion 101
    deep roles 131–36
    and emotion 212f
    of manager 246
    symbolic roles 136
    task/process 130
    traditional social roles 182
Rosenthal, L. 182–83
routine 104
rules 63ff, 73ff, 79f, 83, 82ff, 88, 91, 103ff, 120, 141, 183, 196, 205f
Rycroft, C. 295

sacrifice 73, 91, 96f, 141
sadism, 22, 24, 184, 227, 243
saintlihood syndrome 176
Sandler, A.-M. 220
Sandler, J. 220
scapegoating 67, 97, 128, 130, 133, 216, 218, 220, 225ff, 234, 243, 245, 248, 261, 284
Schneider, S. 98
Schorske, C. A. 10, 164
Schumacher, F. 88
Schwartz, H. S. 1–12, 24, 58–80, 89, 105, 109f, 157f, 176, 196, 206f, 302
science 6, 11, 48, 56, 171
   and emotion 53
   human sciences, 36, 49ff, 253, 259
   natural sciences 49, 51, 52, 259, 288
   of man 55
   of meaning 52
secondary gain (from neurosis) 45
secondary process 306
self 14f, 17, 45, 54, 62, 68, 118, 187, 189, 194, 221, 254, 262, 307,
   fragmented 54, 103, 284
   grandiose 158
self-control 27, 108
self-deception 5, 9, 43, 45, 51, 55, 56, 209, 232
self-esteem 19, 34, 43, 54, 68, 72, 113, 143f, 146, 151, 157, 236, 241f
self-image 145
self-interest and morality 246f
selfishness 187
self-knowledge 38, 232
self-love (*see* narcissism)
Sennett, R. 187
separation 22
sexual development (stages of) 21ff
sexual frustration 189
   as cost of civilization 177f
sexuality (*see also* desire and libido)15, 16, 21ff, 175f, 296, 297, 299, 300, 307, 308
   mature 33
   shame over 181
shame 67, 86, 107, 250
Showalter, E. 42
Sievers, B. 90, 105, 185f, 197, 256, 257
Simmel, G. 214
Simpson, P. R. 99–102
Slater, P. 125f
Smith, A. 246
social bonds 176, 177
social constructionism 214f, 252
social defences 224ff, 234, 243, 264
socialization 166f, 192f, 194ff, 225

somatization 235
Sophocles 25f, 172f
soul 47, 54, 284
splitting 17, 23, 61, 118, 122, 126f, 128, 130, 131, 163, 198, 220, 224, 234, 235, 248, 250, 262f, 293, 298, 307f
Stacey, R. 226, 284
stakeholder 72, 79, 239, 247
Staub, H. 234
Stein, H. F. 271
Stein, R. 216, 218, 221
stereotypical thinking 181
Stokes, J. 124f, 223
stories and story-telling 7, 49, 79, 105, 147, 174, 190, 192, 199ff, 209, 227, 252
   and emotions 217
   in research 270ff, 274, 276
   types of 199f
sublimation 18, 33, 66f, 150, 175, 235, 292, 299, 305, 308, 309
   character as product of 60
   and work 107ff
substitute gratification 76, 175, 177, 309
success and failure 143ff, 165, 213, 227, 282ff, 287f
suffering 28, 45, 56, 57, 175ff, 179, 232, 237, 250, 285, 287
suggestion 38f, 44f, 47, 56, 258
   in groups 116ff
super-ego 20f, 27ff, 67ff, 72, 85, 93, 107, 109, 176f, 186, 187, 198, 233, 235f, 237, 238f, 243, 248, 250, 289, 295, 297, 300, 302, 308, 310
   and ego-ideal 187
   and the girl 31
Swogger, G. 113, 232–50
symbolic order 72
symbols and symbolism 7, 24, 51, 55, 76, 135, 169, 189, 190, 192, 202, 255, 275, 290, 293, 309, 310, 311
symptoms (*see also* neurotic symptoms) 172, 174, 216, 251, 292, 297, 301, 306, 309, 310
synergy 129
systems theory 97, 262ff, 281f

task 91, 102, 113, 117, 119, 126ff, 137, 146, 161, 206, 222f, 231, 242
   culture 206, 207
   primary 91, 92, 120ff, 124, 239ff, 249
   task/process 130f
Tavistock Institute 223f, 256
Taylor, F. W. 78

team and teamwork 78, 114, 126ff, 146, 184, 206
therapeutic 40, 237f
therapist 232, 238, 257
   narcissism 242
therapy and therapeutic 37ff, 42ff, 56
thinking and thought 17, 18, 306, 309
Thomas, A. B. 283
Tolstoy, L. 147
topographic point of view 14, 294, 308, 309, 310
tragic fate of humanity 45, 55, 56, 57, 173f
transference 37ff, 77, 126, 128, 163, 220ff, 254, 264, 276ff, 278, 290, 305, 310
   idealized 158,
   and power 159
tribes 69
trickster 200
Trilling, L. 250
Trist, E. 223
truth 52, 215, 238, 252f, 254, 258
   aversion to 144
   in lies 252
   in stories 271
Turquet, P. 125, 127

uncertainty 225, 248, 266, 279, 280, 282
'Uncle Josef' dream 7–10
unconscious, 5, 6, 7, 10f, 13, 14, 15, 18, 20, 27, 37f, 47ff, 53ff, 71, 74, 79, 93ff, 107, 109, 125ff, 138, 140, 145, 147, 172, 225, 232, 239, 252, 254, 256, 261, 269f, 271, 293, 294, 297, 299, 302, 304, 306, 307, 308, 309, 310
   collective 114f, 131, 291, 296
   and creativity 115
   emotion 218–22
   and moral responsibility 234f, 237
   stories and the 271
unit of analysis (in research) 261, , 266f
unlearning 195, 228
unmanageability 282f

USA Today 142ff
utopia 55f, 57

Vaillant, G. E. 234
valence 136
values (moral) 92, 104, 169ff, 186, 191ff, 205, 236ff, 239, 244, 246
   of researcher 264
   spiritual 193f
victim 134, 218, 271
vision 90f, 128, 139ff, 165, 213, 283
   and reality 141f
Volkan, V. D. 243

Wälder, R. 233, 238
wars 159, 182f, 218
Weber, M. 50, 68, 73, 74, 78, 84, 103, 110, 111, 156, 157, 169, 175, 191, 194, 211f, 213, 231
well-being (*see also* happiness) 238
wild children 166f
Wilkinson, B. 192
will 141
winners/losers (deep roles) 134, 164, 227
Winnicott, D. W. 301
wish (*see also* desire) 9, 11, 26, 38, 50, 74, 114, 210, 284, 311
wish-fulfilment (*see also* fantasy) 9, 74, 189, 209, 252, 271, 287, 293, 294, 298, 307, 309, 311
word association 279
work 106–10, 215, 243
   devaluation of 109
   emotion at 212ff
   psychological 15, 98
   psychological meaning of 106–10, 184f, 186ff
   'real work' 145

xenophobia 202

Zaleznik, A. 77, 113, 145, 213, 215, 243, 248